RENEWALS 4.

Between History and Literature

Between History
and Literature

LIONEL GOSSMAN

HARVARD UNIVERSITY PRESS
Cambridge, Massachusetts, and London, England   1990

Copyright © 1990 by the President and Fellows of Harvard College
All rights reserved
Printed in the United States of America
10 9 8 7 6 5 4 3 2 1

This book is printed on acid-free paper, and its binding materials
have been chosen for strength and durability.

Library of Congress Cataloging-in-Publication Data

Gossman, Lionel.
    Between history and literature / Lionel Gossman.
        p.   cm.
    Includes index.
    ISBN 0-674-06815-7 (alk. paper)
    1. Literature and history.   2. History in literature.
    3. Historiography.   I. Title.
PN50.G67   1990   89-15431
801—dc20   CIP

Contents

Introduction   1

PART ONE   HISTORY OF LITERATURE
1 *Literary Education and Democracy*   9
2 *Literature and Education*   30
3 *The Figaros of Literature*   55

PART TWO   LITERATURE OF HISTORY
4 *Augustin Thierry and Liberal Historiography*   83
5 *Jules Michelet and Romantic Historiography*   152
6 *Michelet's Gospel of Revolution*   201

PART THREE   HISTORY AND LITERATURE
7 *History and Literature: Reproduction or Signification*   227
8 *History as Decipherment: Romantic Historiography*
   and the Discovery of the Other   257
9 *The Rationality of History*   285

   Notes   327

   Acknowledgments   401

   Index   403

Between History and Literature

Introduction

THE YOUNG generation of teachers of literature in our colleges and universities has been raised on a rich diet of de Man, Derrida, Bloom, and Hartman. Along with most people in my generation, I received a Cold War starvation diet when I went up to Glasgow University in 1946 to study Modern Languages. The freshest item in it was some warmed-over New Criticism. Nevertheless, I enjoyed literature and foreign languages because I could look through them to a world of possibilities in which everything did not have to be the way it was, and we were then—the young men and women fresh from school as well as the returning ex-servicemen and women—of a mind to change the world we had known. History, in contrast, as it was then taught in schools and colleges, seemed dry and constricting, completely unrelated to the momentous events we had just lived through. A course I took in modern European history turned out to be a dismal recital of political rivalries, diplomatic maneuvers, wars, and battles. I memorized as much of it as I needed to pass the examination and never took another history course in my life.

But if I was not interested in that kind of history, I was interested in history. How could I not have been? All during the War we had been told repeatedly that the great struggle had a meaning, that it was the prelude to a new and better order. We wanted to understand the historical process of which the War and the new order to come were a part, and our imaginations worked hard to figure out what the new order should be. Naively, but with great intensity, I wanted to think about how justice and beauty had been lost from daily life and how they might be restored to it. The literary criticism that my teachers were adapting from English studies to the then backward and impoverished field of foreign language studies left me unmoved; it addressed none of the questions that concerned me.[1] On the other hand, Schiller's *Über naive und sentimentale Dichtung* and the speculations about the epic and the dramatic, the classical and the modern that I read in a volume of extracts from the Goethe-Schiller correspondence, which one of my German teachers—the only liberal in a department of arch-conservatives—had had the inspiration to put on the syllabus, carried me away. Then, sometime in 1947, I chanced on Georgy Lukács's study of the historical novel, which had made its way, no doubt through an oversight, into the library of the German Department. For the first time I discovered a way of thinking about literature that made sense to me. I read every book by Lukács that I could lay my hands on—without any discrimination whatever, I fear—and I applied his approach to everything. I even imitated his jargon-ridden German writing style. And so it was that in a remote Scottish university, in that bleak time of suspicion and blasted hopes that followed so quickly after the great expectations of 1945, I was largely formed by a Hungarian Marxist critic steeped in German idealist philosophy and social thought.

As a result, the relation between literature and history has been of central importance to me from the very beginning of my career. I have taken my distance from Lukács since—though I have found recently that he is a critic who can be returned to with profit. In the 1950s Sartre and Raymond Williams reinforced the orientation toward a kind of ethical and political concern with literature already fostered in me by Lukács. Subsequently, like everyone else, I have been more or less affected by the phenomenological criticism of the Geneva school, by the rediscovery of Russian formalism, by the French structuralists, by the Frankfurt School, by Derrida and Foucault. I have also had the great good fortune to have been at one time or another in day-to-day contact with many of the scholars and critics who have led these movements. I owe a great deal to René Girard, who was my colleague at Johns Hopkins for many years, as well as to Lucien Goldmann, Roland Barthes, Jacques Derrida, and François Lyotard, who were regular visitors to Hopkins in the 1960s and 1970s. The kinds of concerns that underlie the work of Lukács have remained with me, however, and it is always, in the end, against them that new ideas, as well as the historical experience of almost half a century, have had to be measured.

It is thus second nature for me to take a historical view of everything and anything and to regard texts, aesthetic and rhetorical codes, and theories themselves, old or new, as moves in a political, social, and cultural struggle which it is my job as a critic to identify and elucidate—thereby no doubt participating myself (in a modest way, to be sure) in the conflicts of my own time. I make no apology for that. But I do have occasional perverse impulses. I am sometimes carried away or overwhelmed by the experience of a literary work to the point where I am oblivious of or indifferent to its historicity. Naturally, I sometimes ask myself whether literature might not be deeply inimical to the historical categories in which, as a scholar and professor of literature, I try to capture and contain it.

The essays collected here represent moments in what has been a virtually continuous reflection on the relation of "history" and "literature," and on my own role as a teacher of literature who has always been vitally interested in history. Their topics are the literary dimension of historiographical texts, the historical dimension of literary texts and of the institution of literature itself, the role of education and of educational institutions in the formation of our notions and expectations of literature and history, and the role of literature and history in education. Underlying them all is the belief, which each exploration of a particular problem has tended to reinforce, that neither history nor literature offers a terra firma from which the other can be securely surveyed. Until recently at least, history has been a narrative in words, and for that reason it has been subject to literary and rhetorical analysis. Like everything else, moreover, it is itself a historical phenomenon and thus also subject to analysis in terms of its own categories. On their side, literature and even language are also historical phenomena. No essence of literature has ever been discovered, and the search for a defining characteristic ("literariness" or "literarity") in all probability reveals more about a particular cultural moment and its ideologies than it will ever reveal about the "nature" of literature.

As late as the eighteenth century, and probably beyond, history was still a literary genre. Voltaire and Gibbon had no doubt that they were "writers" in a genre with a pedigree as noble and almost as long as epic or tragedy. In the last century, Michelet and Burckhardt also thought of themselves as writers. History, in Walpole's witty formula, was "a species of romance that is believed," while romance was "a species of history that is not believed." That is not to say that history might not be now, in our time, finally pulling away from literature, as "natural philosophy" (a term still in current use in the Scottish universities) pulled away from philosophy to constitute the discipline we now refer to as physics. Whether it can or not, whether it ought to or not, is in fact one of the questions raised by the last essay in this book. But the literature of which history was considered a genre in the age of Gibbon was itself determined by culture and history. If awareness of the literary character of history dissolves for us the necessity and objectivity of historical categories, awareness of the historical character of literature forces us to recognize that literary categories are no more universal or necessary.

No doubt literature always has an element of negativity, even when it is most securely integrated into the general life of society. On this critics of the most diverse persuasions appear to be in agreement. According to Jan Mukařovský, even the highly structured or "normative" aesthetics of folk literature and classical literature cannot completely exclude the unstructured element.[2] Sartre makes a similar point when he argues that the deeply complicitous relation of writer and reader in the age of French classicism could not altogether eliminate negativity.

> Even though everything has been done to offer readers only a flattering and complying image, more subjective than objective and more internal than external, this image remains nonetheless a work of art, that is, it has its basis in the freedom of the author and is an appeal to the freedom of the reader. Since it is beautiful, it is made of glass; esthetic distance puts it out of reach . . . Even though it is made up of the commonplaces of the age and that smug complacency which unites contemporaries like an umbilical cord, it is supported by a freedom and thereby another kind of objectivity . . . It is, to be sure, a world of courtesy and ceremony which is offered to the reader, but he is already emerging from this world since he is invited to know it and to recognize himself in it . . . To paint passion is already to go beyond it, to shed it . . . The writer, though completely assimilated by the oppressing class, is by no means its accomplice; his work is unquestionably a liberator since its effort, within this class, is to free man from himself.[3]

So too Adorno: "Art—and so-called classical art no less than its more anarchical expressions—always was, and is, a force of protest of the humane against the pressure of domineering institutions, religious and others, even while at the same time it reflects their objective substance."[4] And Althusser: "I do not rank real art among the ideologies, although art does have a quite particular and specific relationship with ideology . . . Art (I mean authentic art, not just works of an average or mediocre level) does not give us *knowledge* in the strict sense . . . but what it gives us does nevertheless maintain a certain specific relationship with knowledge. This relationship is not one of identity, but one of difference." Art, according to Althusser, makes us *see* or *perceive* (which is different from knowing) "the *ideology* from which it is born, in which it bathes, from which it detaches itself as art, and to which it *alludes*." Its ability to "give us a 'view' of ideology . . . presupposes a *retreat*, an *internal distantiation*" from this ideology. Works of art, even works of realist art, "make us 'perceive' (but not know) in some sense *from the inside,* by an *internal distance,* the very ideology in which they are held."[5]

For reasons—historical reasons—that many scholars in a variety of fields, from Tim Clark to Peter Hohendahl, have explored and that I myself touch upon in the essay "Literature and Education" in this volume, it is the unstructured pole, in Mukařovský's terms, that has come to be emphasized in our time, the negativity of literature. In Roland Barthes's distinction between *textes de plaisir* and *textes de jouissance* (texts of pleasure and texts of bliss), as well as in many of his later essays, the negativity of literature becomes its supreme value. Because of "the assault on the subject, on the consistency and integrity of the subject, that results from writing," Barthes compares literature to drugs and other forms of "perversion": "For me, literature—and naturally I am speaking of a literature that is in some sense exemplary, exemplarily subversive, which is why I would prefer to call it *writing*—is always a perversion, that is, a practice that aims at unsettling the subject, dissolving it, dispersing it across the surface of the page."[6] The "perversity" of literature is explicitly acknowledged to be a response both to its alienation in the modern world and to the immense power of the agencies that are constantly recuperating it for their own ends. "Writing is a perversion. Perversion is intransitive. The simplest and most elementary figure of perversion is love-making without procreation. Writing is intransitive in that sense; it doesn't procreate. It does not deliver a product."[7]

There seems not much doubt that many modern practices of criticism attribute the highest value to the negativity of art, its power of corrosion and—in an age dominated by ideology, stereotypes, and the cynical manipulation of language—its irrecuperability. Thanks to its negativity, art remains pure in a world where almost nothing else is. Tim Clark's summing up of the current situation with respect to art and art criticism is valid for literature also: "First, negation is inscribed in the very practice of modernism, as the form in which art appears to itself as a value. Second, that negativity does not appear as a practice which guarantees meaning or opens out a space for free play and fantasy . . . but, rather, negation appears as an absolute and all-encompassing fact, something which once begun is cumulative and uncontrollable; a fact which swallows meaning altogether."[8]

In contrast to the pervasive negativity of literature and art, history may well appear as ideology, busily classifying, categorizing, explaining and thus in a way stereotyping and domesticating whatever it touches. History in this sense is inevitably seen as being in league with the conservative forces of "order" in our world.[9] That was already Nietzsche's view of history in the celebrated *Unzeitgemässe* on "The Advantages and Disadvantages of History for Life." The danger of history, as Matthew Arnold also noted, though from a quite different standpoint, was that of turning texts into objects.[10]

Such an opposition of literature and history, literature-as-negativity and history-as-ideology, seems to me too crude to be allowed to stand. Even negativity can be recuperated and made part of a historical scheme, as it risks being, in my view, in "reception aesthetics" criticism, where "modernity"—the breaking of established codes and expectations, the discovery of the new in the old, rather than the reasssuring discovery of the old in the new—becomes the criterion by which, in a historical perspective, past works of art are classified and evaluated.[11] Conversely, if history often lends support to ideology, it is also—as "genealogy"—a great corroder of ideology. By revealing how things came to be, it removes the ground of their necessity. The historical impulse and historical learning have also worked consistently to interrupt and undermine the continuities of tradition: from Luther to Winckelmann and to Nietzsche, the demand to recover past things in their pastness, other things in their otherness, rather than in the modernizing interpretations by which we accommodate them to our world, has always been a force of disruption and negativity. One of the objects on which this disruptive power of history can most usefully be exercised is the concept of literature itself and the aesthetic categories in which we think about it and which, for the most part, we take for granted, as if they were natural and necessary. Literature can look to history to save it from its own institutionalizations.

Yet it would be disingenuous of me not to acknowledge that I find it hard to accept negativity as an absolute value. I am tempted neither by political terrorism nor by cultural nihilism. My own ideal is a condition similar to that for which Sartre and Barthes, each in his own way, expressed a certain nostalgia: a condition such as was fugitively experienced by the men and women of the age of Enlightenment, that is to say, a condition in which there is no absolute break between literary language and public language and in which the negativity of literature is turned not against "culture" as such, but only against its inhuman aspects, a condition in which literature is part of a genuine public sphere. In the age of the mass media and the marketplace, no doubt that is something of a pipe dream. Even in the eighteenth century such a condition seems never to have been more than a normative ideal. And it appears most unlikely that a historical situation in which authentic literature can only be a negative force can be changed by the action of literature alone. Until it is, literature, if it is to retain its honesty and its purity, must no doubt remain negative. History, however, enables us at least to envisage an alternative literature.

PART ONE

History of Literature

1

Literary Education and Democracy

> Individual perfection is impossible so long as the rest of mankind are not perfected along with us.
>
> —Matthew Arnold, *Culture and Anarchy*

> Literature, strictly consider'd, has never recognized the People, and, whatever may be said, does not today . . . It seems as if, so far, there were some natural repugnance between a literary and professional life, and the rude rank spirit of the democracies.
>
> —Walt Whitman, *Democratic Vistas*

IN A CLASSIC article, published in Holland in 1929, Pyotr Bogatyrev and Roman Jakobson undertook an important reconsideration of the relation between written and oral literature.[1] Rejecting both the Romantic reverence for folklore as communal creation and the opposing view that all folk literature is *gesunkenes Kulturgut* (degraded high culture),[2] they found in the linguistics of Ferdinand de Saussure a model on which a more adequate theory of folklore creation and tradition might be built. Against the positivist and neo-grammarian view that only individual speech acts are real, while everything else is philosophical abstraction, a view that is easily compatible with the theory of *gesunkenes Kulturgut* in folkloristics, they set Saussure's view of language as a unity of *langue* and *parole,* of the system of language and of individual realizations of it, the former being as "real" as—because the condition of—the latter. When specific, individual exploitations of the speech code are sanctioned by the community, they become part of the general linguistic resources of the community, and thus, in a way, part of *langue.* Language, in short, is a constant interchange, of varying intensity, between the speech acts of individuals and the linguistic system, which alone makes these acts possible and through which alone they have any chance of survival. In folklore, according to Jakobson and Bogatyrev, a similar relation obtains between individual performances of folk works and the works themselves.

Individual performers of folklore works may well give an individual rendering of their models.[3] However, only those variations which the community finds acceptable, Bogatyrev and Jakobson claimed, are integrated into the work and taken up by subsequent poet-performers. In contrast, the written work, even though it may meet with indifference or misunderstanding on its first appearance, survives as a potentiality which may be and, as some celebrated cases in literary history testify, often is realized at a later date by subsequent generations of readers.

Bogatyrev and Jakobson did not deny that individuals contribute to folklore works, but they questioned our tendency to consider the latter in the same way that we consider products of written literature. For us, they argued, a work is born at the moment its author writes it down on paper; correspondingly, the moment at which the oral work is objectified—"performed," in other words—is taken by us to mark its birth, whereas in reality it becomes part of folklore only by being admitted into the tradition by the community. At the birth of folklore, in short, there is not an anonymous author but a collective one. Though this position seems close to that of the Romantics, it differs from it in that the Romantics merely applied an individual notion of authorship to the collectivity, whereas Bogatyrev and Jakobson are arguing that folklore creation requires a different and more comprehensive notion of authorship itself.

Above all, the folklore work, according to Bogatyrev and Jakobson, should not be seen as an individual objectification. Saussure's categories of *langue* and *parole* help us to understand the real nature of the folklore work, for, like *langue*, the folklore work has an impersonal existence as a complex of norms, a kind of scenario which individual performer-artists bring to life in their own particular versions. In contrast, the written work perpetuates a particular *parole,* and successive readers can go to it directly. In other words, previous "performances" or "readings" are only one ingredient in the reception of literary works, whereas they constitute the very being of folklore works, which exist and are known only through them.

Not the least important aspect of the argument developed by Bogatyrev and Jakobson is their conception of folklore and written literature as two distinct, albeit communicating, systems, which determine the character of individual works within the systems. Thus they admit that much folk material is indeed *gesunkenes Kulturgut,* the product, originally, of individual artists in the written tradition—though it could be shown that the original material is not always of notable artistic merit and may even be itself a degraded version of a folk work, as with certain broadsides of the seventeenth and eighteenth centuries[4]—but the question of origins, they held, is irrelevant. What counts is not the origin of the materials but the function of the borrowing, and the processes of selection and transformation of the materials borrowed. And here the folk is as creative in adapting "art" materials to its system as the cultivated artist is when he adapts folk materials. Both transformations—say, Beethoven adapting Scottish and Irish folksongs, and the people as it *zersingt* ("sings down"), in the contemptuous phrase, an art song—are acts of creation. Most important, the theory expounded by Bogatyrev and Jakobson implies that the "same" work outside of folklore and inside it constitutes two different artistic phenomena. They illustrate this point by a discussion of Pushkin's poem "Gusar" ("The Hussar"). Here the folk motifs taken over by the cultivated writer impart a flavor of naiveté to his poem, but this very naiveté is a sophisticated artistic phenomenon.[5] When Pushkin's poem went back into folklore in the Russian popular play *Tsar Maximilian*— similar in some respects to the traditional English pantomime—its subtle ironies were lost. Assimilated to the aesthetics of the popular play, it became virtually a different work.[6]

AMONG the many suggestive points made by Bogatyrev and Jakobson in their article, I should like to single out two which seem to me of considerable importance for literary culture in general: first, that oral "literature," unlike written, is synchronic, and second, that while literary texts enjoy a degree of autonomy and fixity unknown to oral works, they must still be actualized by successive individual readers. I should make clear from the outset that since the focus of my interest here is literary education, I shall be more concerned with some aspects of the literary culture than with others, with the relation of poets and poetic works to the community or public rather than with modes of composition or the structural characteristics of written and oral works.

It could be argued, I think, that it is here that the crucial difference between the oral and the written is to be found. Albert Lord and others have pointed out, of course, that the structure of individual written and oral works is significantly determined by the mode of composition imposed on the poet by his medium and by his relation to his audience.[7] It is also likely that it is rare—perhaps impossible—for a great artist in the oral tradition to be a great writer. By all accounts the abbé Galiani was a brilliant raconteur, but it was Diderot who wrote his anecdotes. Nevertheless, it is possible to exaggerate the difference between oral and written compositions, and in order to focus on the points that seem most important for my present topic, it may be appropriate to recall, as Lord himself did in a note to the *Singer of Tales,* that from certain points of view literature—verbal art would be a more accurate expression, but it is also a clumsy one—can be regarded as a continuous field accommodating a variety of different practices and different aesthetic values not finally reducible to a simple oral/written dichotomy.

Jakobson himself has defined poetic language in general as that in which the principle of equivalence (relations of similarity and dissimilarity, of synonymity and antonymity) is "promoted to the constitutive device of the sequence," and this definition may be taken as valid for both written and oral composition.[8] In the numerous studies that have been made of the working of repetition and metaphor—the principal devices which, in a variety of forms, establish relations of identity and difference in poetic discourse—no significant distinction is made between oral or traditional materials and written ones.

Repetition and refrain, for instance, which characterize folk works and oral compositions, are also found in more sophisticated verse. In her book *Poetic Closure,* Barbara H. Smith observes that Wyatt obtains some of his effects by "allowing a refrain to remain constant but altering its significance in succeeding stanzas through the material that precedes it."[9] This is the same principle that operates in a popular song such as *Corn Rigs are bonie* or in ballads such as *Lord Randal* or *Fine Flowers in the Valley.* The forms of repetition are, of course, varied, ranging from very simple ones, as in the examples referred to, to complex ones which are only half-consciously perceived by the reader and which occur not as refrains or even as repetitions of words or phrases but at the phonemic level only. The principle of operation is always the same, however: repetition establishes links and equivalences; it draws together and, at the same time, because it is never absolute—the context has always changed—it subtly separates and establishes difference. The greater the approximation to identity, indeed, the more sharply whatever elements of difference remain will be thrown into relief. Paratactic structure, it is true, remains more characteristic of folk and oral poetry—and Kernodle suggests that it is characteristic of popular theater too—allowing as it does infinite interpolation and substitution of similarly structured verses and requiring no complex back-and-forth scanning for the perception of the pattern, but whether the poem's structure is paratactic, sequential, or associative, to borrow some of the terminology used by Barbara Smith, does not substantially alter the poetic function of repetition.

From the point of view of aesthetics, as from that of poetics, the distinction between oral and written as such does not seem to be fundamental. Aesthetic categories cut across the oral-written boundary, to which they correspond only in part. Jan Mukařovský, for instance, distinguishes between two terms of the aesthetic—the "normative" or "structured," in which poetic diction is strictly codified and the category of the aesthetic in general is clearly defined and delimited, and the "functional" or "unstructured," which is more free and adventurous, and which aims to blur the boundaries between art and life, artistic language and everyday language. The former is socially supported and relatively stable, it aims at order, harmony, and euphony, and, because of its strict codification, it carefully controls the energy of its individual components; the latter is bound to smaller units of expression, it privileges the word—that "Pandora's box from which all the potentialities of language fly out," as Barthes was to put it[10]—over all grammatical relationships, subverts established aesthetic and linguistic categories, and opens the literary discourse to new and unpredictable possibilities of meaning. In some periods, according to Mukařovský, the structured aesthetic may predominate, in others the unstructured, but there cannot be one without the other, since literature requires the presence, in some measure, of both.[11]

In a similar vein Roland Barthes defines literature as a world which is full of meaningful signs but which resists any conclusive statement of its meaning—which constantly invites and encourages interpretation, in other words, but which can never be definitively interpreted ("emphatiquement signifiant, mais finalement jamais signifié").[12] This general "anthropological" character of literature, he holds, can accommodate quite widely varying kinds of literary practice. The literary devices or *signifiants* can be strictly codified, as in classical literature, or left to seek their fortunes, as in modern poetics.[13] They can be brought close to denotation or impelled to the outermost limits of meaningfulness, where they initiate "a discourse full of gaps and full of lights, filled with absences and over-nourishing signs, without foresight or stability of intention." But literature can never become a purely denotative system, nor a completely open one. It must always be suspended somewhere between the two poles of specific meaning and meaninglessness. "The play of signifiers can be infinite, but the literary sign itself remains fixed: from Homer to the tales of Polynesia no one has ever transgressed the simultaneously signifying and deceiving nature of this intransitive language which 'doubles' the real (without ever reaching it) and which we call 'literature.' "

Barthes adds that in certain periods great value may be placed on literary techniques that openly display the "deception" of literature, its artfulness, while in others the emphasis may be on clarity, simplicity, and the concealment of art. It does, indeed, seem likely that where the community is experienced as essential and the individual appears secondary, the emphasis in poetic theory may be on clarity, the observation of established conventions, and the revelation of the fundamental likeness or universality of things, and that where the individual is experienced as concrete, while the community appears abstract, the emphasis will be on openness of meaning, on poetic invention, and on the creation of new and unexpected relations of likeness whose purpose is to subvert the old ones.[14] Significantly, however, Mukařovský argues that a "normative" aesthetic was characteristic not only of folk literature but of classical literature as well. On his side, Barthes points out that in periods when audience and artist form part of a single, relatively homogeneous group, sharing the same values and the same language, the writer will be less aware than he is in periods when the public and its language are divided, of literature as an object, of his writing as something distinct from its instrumental function. In this respect, classical literature in France had, according to Barthes, some of the characteristics of a folk culture in that it "postulates the possibility of dialogue, it establishes a universe where men are not alone, where words never have the terrible weight of things, where speech is always a meeting with others." "Classical literary language," he goes on, "is a bringer of euphoria, because it is immediately social. There is no genre, no written work of classicism which does not suppose a collective consumption, akin to speech; classical literary art is an object which circulates among several persons brought together on a class basis; it is a product conceived for oral transmission, for a consumption regulated by the contingencies of society."[15]

Like Mukařovský, the Soviet scholar Iurii Lotman explicitly relates the aesthetics of folk literature and the aesthetics of classicism. Lotman distinguishes between an aesthetics of "identity," which constantly reaffirms identity against difference, the permanence of order against the vagaries of change, and an aesthetics of "opposition," which aims to frustrate the reader's expectations and to force him to consider in the work of art a different model of reality from the one he set out with. An aesthetics of identity is common, in Lotman's view, to folk culture, medieval culture, and the culture of classicism, while most modern movements—baroque, romanticism, and realism—are characterized by an aesthetics of opposition.[16] At no point in Lotman's discussion does the oral-written distinction assume any importance at all.

It might be supposed that, on the one hand, the autonomy and individuality of the writer (as opposed to the rhapsodist or performer) and, on the other, the autonomy and fixity of the written text (as opposed to what one might term the oral "program") radically distinguish the written and oral poetic traditions. On inspection, however, these two criteria appear less stable than one might have thought.

The solidity of the "author" has been dissolving for some time in the crucible of psychology, sociology, and literary history itself. The boundaries between the "writer" and all those, dead and alive, with whom he is in communion, for instance, are less clearly defined than they once seemed to be. Many texts themselves appear to be elaborations and combinations of other texts. Among the author's various manuscripts, representing different stages in the creation of the final text that passes for the work, and among the various editions of printed texts themselves, where should we look for the "true" embodiment of the author, the version that best fulfills "his" intention? The thing we call the work may be one crystallization of a scenario or program, of which there were other crystallizations, some preserved, though not easily visible, others erased, accidentally or deliberately.[17] Besides, the mere graphic recording of a *parole* does not commit us to a belief in a substantial and autonomous self behind it or incorporated in it. It remains arguable at least that there is no original individual essence supporting the *parole* and embodying itself in it. This position is fully assumed and made explicit, in fact, by some modern writers, such as the German poet, quoted by Hans Blumenberg, who prefaced a collection of his poems with the comment: "If some lucky lines on the pages of this book are successful, may the reader please forgive me the discourtesy of having usurped them. Our playing—yours and mine—is not very different: the circumstance that you are the reader and I the composer of these exercises is trivial and accidental."[18] The point of the comment is surely that the work is no closer to—or more alien from—the subjectivity of the author than that of the reader.

The autonomy and individuality of post-Renaissance writers, in other words, may well be a matter of ideology. Even as an idea, moreover, it has not been consistently at the center of all aesthetic systems since the Renaissance. Older models and ideas of literary practice survived well into the age of print and private property.[19] Classical aesthetics in particular was not favorable to the notion of auctorial originality and individuality. "We nourish ourselves on the ancients and ingenious moderns," La Bruyère observed of the *Modernes* in the famous *Querelle:* "We squeeze, we draw from them as much as we can, we rifle their works, and when at last we become authors, and think we can walk alone and without help, we oppose our benefactors, and treat them like those children, who, grown pert and strong with the milk they have sucked, turn themselves against their nurses."[20] On the fringes of high literature many writers were still willing to cooperate openly not only with the dead, but with the living too. The *Contes* attributed to Perrault, for instance, are an amazing conflation of folk materials and successive literary improvisations by various hands from the same coterie.[21] At the beginning of the eighteenth century Lesage, d'Orneval, and Fuzelier collaborated on a large number of plays in the commedia tradition for the Théâtre de la Foire. Diderot's contribution, half a century later, to the *Encylopédie,* to the *Correspondance littéraire* of Grimm, and to Raynal's *Histoire des Indes* is hard to ascertain, and Diderot himself was not concerned to distinguish it.[22]

By the eighteenth century, to be sure, a different conception of literary property, of the literary product, and of literary creation itself was already well established. But some writers who still remained close to older communal ways and ideas were acutely conscious of their passing. The conflict of two aesthetics is reflected in Diderot's work, for instance, in the contrast between Rameau's nephew, the brilliant medium and improviser, and his rather colorless conversation partner Moi, who is nevertheless, as narrator of the tale in which they both figure as characters, the creator and writer of the enduring—and inexhaustibly signifying—text we still read today. A similar conflict runs through the celebrated correspondence with the sculptor Falconet. Diderot was himself troubled by the fear that he was "dissipating" his talents in cooperative works, in advice to friends, in talk. In a well-known passage from his correspondence with Sophie Volland he likens his fellow-townsmen of Langres to weathercocks and adds somewhat ruefully: "As for me, I am a man of my home town; only residence in the capital and assiduous application have corrected me a little."[23] It is probably not indifferent that Diderot began his career with a translation. "I read and reread him," he wrote at the beginning of his translation of Shaftesbury's *Inquiry concerning Virtue and Merit.* I filled myself with his spirit; and I closed his book, so to speak, at the moment that I took up my pen."[24] To some extent, it could be argued, Diderot thought of all creation as translation. As late as 1828 we can still set the words of Goethe to Eckermann against Rousseau's ambition to cleanse his work of all otherness and make it a pure embodiment of his own unique self: "The Germans cannot cease to be Philistines. They are now squabbling about some verses which are printed both in Schiller's work and in mine, and fancy it is important to ascertain which really belong to Schiller and which to me; as if anything could be gained by such an investigation, as if the existence of such things were not enough. . . . What matters the mine and the thine? One must be a thorough Philistine, indeed, to attach the slightest importance to the solution of such questions."[25]

Autonomy, originality, and self-expression were thus fairly slow to establish themselves either as a description of, or as a prescription for, literary activity, and throughout the seventeenth and eighteenth centuries, it seems fairly safe to assume, many writers might have thought of themselves as artists in a way not too remotely unlike that in which the best singers of Russian *bylini* or the Serbian epic singers studied by Lord were great artists in their tradition. "In a game of tennis," Pascal remarked in a *pensée* concerning style, "both partners play with the same ball, but one of them returns it better."[26] In our own time Charles Dullin once compared the classical playwrights to performers or producers, interpreters like himself. "After all, what did Molière and Corneille do all their lives but adapt?"[27]

It is worth recalling, moreover, that on their side the folklorists, especially the Russian school, have come to emphasize the peculiar talents and styles of individual artists among the folk.[28] It is true that in most oral cultures gifted artists who have been heard to recount the same tale in different ways will deny ever changing a word or a line of the canon.[29] But they do so only because they do not think of the work as existing in their particular utterance of it. Fidelity to them means working within a given scheme and preserving both the scheme and the thematics, rather than repeating something word for word. The very notion "word for word"—which is surely closely linked to the written text—seems not to be meaningful to them. In all probability, it was only gradually, and in combination with a variety of historical circumstances, that the identification of works with individual graphically recorded utterances led to a conception of literary creation as absolutely original production, arising out of and in some way embodying a unique, substantial, and autonomous self.

It seems, in short, that although there are real differences in literary practice between oral and literate poets, the conventions and values of his society, as well as the nature of oral composition itself, make the oral poet blind to whatever contribution he himself makes to the tradition, while different conventions and values and a different mode of existence of the written, and particularly of the printed, literary product, encourage the literate poet—within a certain period of history at least—to deny that there is anything in his work that is *not* his own. Conceiving of himself not as a vessel, through which the tradition passes to be actualized for the community, but as an isolated individual objectifying an individual discourse, he tries, by establishing that it is his "property," to reappropriate that part of him which he feels is objectified in his discourse and to which he owes both an intense feeling of individual identity and a sinking sense of alienation of that identity.

Even the fixity of the written work, which is usually contrasted with the unstable oral tradition, cannot be simply taken for granted. I have already alluded to the material instability of a "text" which may exist in various manuscript and printed versions. But the text itself—the permanent graphic imprint—is not identical with the work. Let us imagine a text which exists, apparently, in fragmentary or somehow unfinished form. (Pascal's *Pensées* might serve as an example of such a text.) Whether we consider its fragmentariness to be the result of some mechanical defect or accident, or part of the author's design, will make all the difference to our idea of the work represented by this text. In order to form a conception of the work, therefore, we have to go beyond the text itself to the context— what we know of the author's intentions, for instance, or of the aesthetics of the period.

In general, the relative material stability of the written or printed text is complemented by an extremely mobile element which is as indispensable to the realization of the literary work as the graphic inscription itself. It is characteristic of all literary works, written or oral—that is, of all works which we decide to consider as literature—that unlike mere reporting, say, they are intended—or we judge them worthy—to be heard or read more than once.[30] Successive readings (or performances) of the same text, like successive performances of the same oral program, will, however, be different. This is easily accepted in the case of performances of oral works, but it is also true of written or printed texts. Indeed, it is well known that against a background of identity—the same musical score, for instance, performed on different occasions or by different performers—differences are the more acutely perceived. Theatrical performances of dramatic texts provide another illustration of this principle. Erwin Piscator has commented interestingly on two productions of Schiller's *Die Räuber* which he directed, the first in Berlin in 1926, and the second in Mannheim in 1957. In 1926, he recounts, the political situation was revolutionary, and Schiller's play was presented as a call to sustain revolutionary activity. The play's dramatic elements were therefore foregrounded in the early production, while the cynical reflective monologues of Franz were allowed to retreat into the background. The 1957 production took place in the totally different political and social conditions of what Piscator calls a successful Restoration. Deeply grounded doubts that any revolutionary might harbor had risen to the surface, and Piscator therefore highlighted the monologues.[31] As Lotman put it, increasing the element of identity in two "readings" to the point of complete coincidence of the textual parts throws into relief the parts that do not coincide.[32]

One might imagine that such difficulties are overcome and complete identity achieved in cases where variation is reduced to zero by the absence of a live interpreter or executant, as in works of figurative art, movies, music on records or tape, and productions of literary art which are meant to be read silently, with the eyes. It is doubtful that this is so, however. The work of art is not exhausted in the text (the score in music, the material part of a figurative work) but resides rather in "a relation of textual and extra- or con-textual systems," to quote Lotman again.[33] Without taking into account the contextual situation—the absent text, for instance, to which a given text is opposed and which thus constitutes its context, the tradition of which it is part and which may be incorporated in it as a complex pattern of quotations, allusions, and parodies, and in general the framework of beliefs and expectations in which it is or once was perceived—it is not even possible to determine what the structurally active and significant elements in the text are, or once were. The writer himself may point to the context he intends for his work. Lotman observes that even as he broke down the old rhythmic system of Russian poetry, Mayakovski was careful to keep the memory of it alive in the reader's awareness.[34] In time, however, we may lose sight of the author's context, and one of the most important tasks of literary history, probably, is to reconstruct it. Unless we view Wordsworth's prosody, for instance, against the background of eighteenth-century verse, we shall not know what to contemporaries was artistically effective in it. Moreover, as Wordsworth's prosody came to constitute, in its turn, the context of readers' expectations, the aesthetic norm, his poetry was perceived by a new generation of readers in a quite different light from that in which it was perceived by his contemporaries. It may not be entirely fanciful to speak of two different bodies of poetry. Similarly, a change in the contextual system may alter the relation of the various language functions in a work (expressive, communicative or denotative, poetic, conative), so that a work of history, for instance, or an autobiography, or a political pamphlet, in which the communicative or the conative function was once prominent, may in course of time come to be perceived in such a way that the poetic function dominates the others.

Changes in the contextual system, in short, produce changes in the degree of structural activity of the various elements making up the complex ensemble of the work. And such changes in the contextual system occur both in the course of history and in the normal life of the individual consciousness. Not everything that is present in a work is revealed to every reader at a single moment in his life. The self-identity of the written text is thus an abstraction, which is arrived at only by amputating from the work the contextual system without which it can have no meaning. The point was made simply by T. S. Eliot in his well-known essay *Tradition and Individual Talent:* "No poet, no artist of any kind has complete meaning alone. His significance, his appreciation is the appreciation of his relation to the dead poets and artists. You cannot value him alone; you must set him, for contrast and comparison, among the dead. I mean this as a principle of esthetic, not merely historical criticism. . . . What happens when a new work of art is created is something that happens simultaneously to all the works of art which preceded it. The existing monuments form an ideal order among themselves, which is modified by the introduction of the new (the really new) work of art among them." It is not preposterous, Eliot concludes, "that the past should be altered by the present as much as the present is guided by the past."

The written work of literature—"that strange spinning top," as Sartre calls it, "which exists only in movement"[35]—is thus, despite the (only relative) material stability of the text, no less dependent on performance of a kind than the oral one. It is always subject to variation according to the light that is projected upon it and the background against which it is viewed. The *Phèdre* that I hold in my hands in 1970 is not the work that was known to its first readers or even to the author himself. Nor can I hope to resuscitate exactly the contextual structure of Racine's time, in relation to which the text was then perceived. It is not simply that to resuscitate it I should have to know everything that Racine and his contemporaries knew (as a literary historian I may and must approach such a goal, even though I cannot reach it) but that I should have to unknow many things which enter into the perceptual context of our own time and of which Racine was necessarily ignorant. There is, in sum, a sort of feedback effect from the user of literary texts to the texts themselves, and this effect, which makes for the polyvalence of the text—what Plato condemned as its uncertainty—also guarantees its longevity and its capacity, within limits prescribed by its objective structure, to impart different information to different users at different times, and even to the same users at different times, or to different users at the same time. Texts, in short, are a little like those medals which, according to the author of a "Discours sur les Maximes" appended to the 1665 edition of La Rochefoucauld's work, "represent the figure of a Saint and that of a Demon on the same face and by the same marks. Only the different positions of those looking at the medal change the object that they see. One sees the Saint, the other the Demon."[36] More dryly, Lotman observes that "in art . . . the sign, or the element discriminating its meaning, may be projected against many backgrounds, becoming in each case a bearer of different meanings."[37] It was this characteristic of works of art, perhaps, that Schiller tried to define when he argued in the *Letters on the Aesthetic Education of Man* that the work of art combines freedom with law or limitation, its indeterminacy being not an empty infinity (*leere Unendlichkeit*) but rather a filled infinity or all-inclusiveness (*erfüllte Unendlichkeit*).

Performance thus appears essential to both written and oral literature—but in different ways. The number of different performances in an oral culture is obviously infinite, but the range of difference is fairly limited. All individuals do change, of course, if only as they age, and one can imagine that a Russian recruiting song, for example, might have a different significance for a woman who had seen a son or a husband drafted into the army and for one who had no immediate experience of this tragedy. (In Czarist Russia the period of service was something like twenty years!) Likewise, many works of ritual and liturgical art change their meanings or acquire new meanings in the course of the experience of a lifetime. Nevertheless, even the scope of personal development is probably restricted in oral cultures by the limited range of available experience. The homogeneity imposed by a relatively narrow range of possible activities and experiences is consolidated, moreover, by the strong mutual identification with one another of which the members of oral communities seem unusually capable. Most important, oral literature is in large measure synchronic, like the spoken language itself.[38] The entire tradition is immediately present and only immediately present. Nothing can be retrieved that has slipped from memory; almost all the elements in the tradition are thus fully intelligible in the light of present experience. There can be few problems of interpretation, since the process of preservation is at the same time a process of interpretation. Written literature, on the other hand, is asynchronic, since texts from various periods, crystallizations of various moments in the literary tradition, are preserved graphically and are available to subsequent generations of readers and writers as well as to totally nonindigenous groups. Code and performance are separated, and interpretation becomes a central concern. The history of religion would doubtless offer telling illustrations of this passage from the synchronic to the asynchronic. I shall use a simpler example.

Where proverbs are alive in an oral tradition, their meaning is never in doubt, even though it may vary with the context in which the proverb is used. "Every mickle maks a muckle," for instance, could be used positively as an encouragement to save or negatively as a warning against the cumulative effect of slight misdemeanors. But neither the user nor the listener will be in any doubt as to the appropriate meaning, and neither will distinguish between the form of the statement and its meaning. There will be no sense of *contradiction* between different usages. It is the collector of proverbs who becomes aware of them as structures distinct from their meanings and capable of generating meanings. Thus in England and France, "rolling stones gather no moss" ("pierres qui roulent n'amassent pas mousse") is universally taken to mean that if you wander about too much you will never settle down anywhere and build yourself a comfortable and enduring home. When I was a boy in Calvinist Scotland, however, I had no doubt, nor did any of my school-fellows or teachers, among whom it was popular, that it meant the opposite: if you don't keep moving and striving, you'll never amount to anything. You might have difficulty getting a user of proverbs to explicate the meaning of a particular proverb, but he will almost invariably be able to distinguish proper and improper usage. To someone who is not a user of proverbs, on the other hand—and I suspect the use of proverbs has been in decline since the last century—any proverb is problematic. I have asked several of my students what they understand by "rolling stones gather no moss," and I find that many hesitate and will subsequently entertain both the meanings I proffer. Their hesitation, I am convinced, has nothing to do with inability to explicate, but stems rather from lack of practice in using the proverb. To them, in short, it has become a *text,* like a passage from the Bible or from Shakespeare. Conversely, I would suspect, certain texts which have entered the popular culture to some extent—*Pilgrim's Progress* (until recently) or, in France, Hugo's *Les Misérables*—are not perceived as *texts,* but come, like oral materials, already fully clad in an interpretation that is part of a tradition.

The asynchronic character of written literature radically alters the range of possible relations between artists and public and between both and the tradition. An oral culture need not, of course, be uniform. It may be made up of an infinite number of particular local, professional, or even family traditions, but the point is that it is fully familiar to all those who are part of it and unknown to those who are not. It does not even offer itself to the outsider. The written tradition, on the other hand, is in principle open and universal. (It is surely no accident that universal religions are religions of scripture.)[39] Yet it is this very quality that makes it problematic. For though the texts are in principle universally available, the keys by which they can be deciphered are not. The very ability to read written characters was long the privilege of a few, and far from being a unifying force, writing was a divisive one. In a complex literate society the tradition may come to resemble a vast museum, filled with the discrete or only mysteriously interrelated relics and monuments of the past, to which a multiplicity of social classes and groups have widely varying access.

For the writer such a cultural environment may mean that the range of materials which he can draw upon in the creation of his own work is vastly enlarged and that his powers of selection and arrangement, as well as his personal responsibility, are enhanced. As Bogatyrev and Jakobson pointed out in their article, there is little or no variety of styles in individual folklore traditions, corresponding to different aesthetic models or intentions. Variety is determined solely by the different folklore "genres" (saga, legend, anecdote, song, riddle, charm, and so forth). Written literature, on the other hand, may embrace in a single period a number of schools of writers with independent or rival styles. Similarly, oral literature knows nothing of the revivals and renaissances which characterize written literature and which are due both to the physical preservation or recovery of past materials and to variations in the contexts of aesthetic perception.

For the reader—and the artist is also a reader in so far as he too must be a reader of others' works in order to produce his own—the passage from an oral to a written culture may mean an immense expansion of the scope of literature. Innumerable individual literary acts, performed at various moments in the course of the literary culture and graphically preserved as texts, are constantly available to be projected against a wide range of contexts, no single one of which, perhaps, need be considered the sole appropriate one. The feedback from user to work, to which I alluded earlier, has the potential to release the text from bondage to any particular context. The possibility that thus arises both of historically reconstructing the successive contexts in which a work has come alive and, in general, of multiplying the contexts in which we can view it by projecting onto it the light of our modern awareness and our modern disciplines—sociology, psychology, philosophy, and so on—enhances both the power of the text and the scope of our imaginative response to it. For each context will activate the potentialities of the text in a different way, by making different elements in it emerge as structurally significant. The effect I have in mind is similar to what is achieved in the theater by the now-familiar technique of shunting a text from one historical setting to another (for example, performing Shakespeare in Victorian setting and dress). The historicity which characterizes the written work of literature is thus the condition of the active and creative relation in which the reader stands to it. Indeed, it seems that, far from fixing or controlling a work and its meanings, the written text allows them to be released and engendered. "To write," Barthes observes, "is to offer your word (*parole*) to others, that they may complete it."[40] As it becomes unmoored from its original source and context and floats out into history, the written text lays itself open, like that "most ambiguous object imaginable" which Valéry's Socrates found on the beach, to varied and fruitful encounters.[41] The oral work, on the other hand, although it undergoes change, remains always, on any given occasion, undivided and fully present in its performance.

The reader's freedom, however, places on him the responsibility for selecting a context in which to situate the text and finding a key to decipher it with. In oral cultures, as I suggested, the tradition is internalized by all the members of the oral community, and the same knowledge and culture may be said to be shared *mutatis mutandis* by all of them alike. It is thus easy to see why all the members of an oral community perceive a work in more or less the same way, and are also, on the whole, widely *capable* of perceiving it, even if there are differences of sensibility among them, as there are among human beings in any culture. As Paul Radin put it, summing up the views of many folklorists and anthropologists, "An audience in an aboriginal tribe is far better prepared to understand the implications of their literature than we are of our own. Every person there—parts of Africa and Polynesia-Micronesia excepted—has an all-embracing knowledge of his culture and participates in every aspect of it; every person has a complete knowledge of his language. There are no 'illiterate' or ignorant individuals."[42] In literate cultures, on the other hand, the tradition is not homogeneous or immediately present, and although this widens the range of possible contexts and thus of possible meanings of a text, it may also, in the case of the poorly prepared or inadequately educated reader, make the context completely problematic and the text, in consequence, opaque, inert, and meaningless. "The works exist," in Sartre's phrase, "only at the level of the reader's capacity."[43]

This is all the more likely to happen as works in the written tradition are characterized by a richness of implicit and explicit quotation from and reference to other texts, by a textual volume or density which makes great demands even on the cultivated reader. The text, in other words, may be not only hard to separate from, but well-nigh unintelligible outside of, a complex pattern of intertextual references. Where the cultural development of the various groups and classes making up a society is seriously uneven or discontinuous, where there is no common language, and where literature, in consequence, has become a highly specialized activity, related to the language of a restricted and exclusive class, the freedom which the written tradition can introduce into the reader's relation to works of literature will thus be at the same time a cause of bewilderment and estrangement to the many.

It may be that historically, writing first divided the community only into those who had access to written culture and those who remained enclosed within the immediacy of oral culture. Both cultures, however, may have been relatively homogeneous at first. Though the revival of classical literature during the Renaissance implied the possibility of further revivals, the classical tradition was for a long time the only model for the modern literate writer; the canons and criteria of classical literature were experienced as in a sense present because they were atemporal, eternally true. On its side, the public too remained relatively homogeneous; it recognized immediately both the models to which the works of its writers referred and the models—often in the folk culture—to which they were opposed. Even in the seventeenth and eighteenth centuries the interplay of various rhetorical styles—Ciceronian eloquence and *style coupé*, the style of the Ancients and the style of the Moderns—occurred within a single, generally accepted tradition; they were thought of as constituting the unchanging repertory of ornamental options available to the civilized writer as he set out to clothe his thought. The very idea of revivals and renaissances is probably linked to some such notion of a fixed repertory. Even the *Querelle des Anciens et des Modernes* had a model in Roman times, and those who took up the fight again in the late seventeenth and early eighteenth centuries might well have thought of themselves as reenacting an eternal scenario. That was, after all, the way in which the early Enlighteners and champions of *philosophie* thought of themselves. The illusion of universality, the absence of a sense of history, in our meaning of the term, from the literary consciousness of the classical period, from the Renaissance down to the eighteenth century, reflects both the relative homogeneity of the culture of this period and the relative slowness of objective social change. The range of contexts against which a text could be projected in order to be realized or concretized remained limited and fairly familiar to all citizens of the Republic of Letters.

In the course of the late eighteenth and early nineteenth centuries, however, a new aesthetic situation seems to have arisen, doubtless as a consequence of altered historical conditions. The educated bourgeoisie of the ancien régime had occupied commanding positions of power and influence, but birth, even without letters, still remained a tangible value, and in a totally different and relatively autonomous sector of society, the old folk culture survived richly. In the nineteenth century the culture of the bourgeoisie, the symbolic counterpart of its economic and political power, virtually ousted all other values. Acquisition of this culture, literacy and education, came to seem like stages on the road to power and prestige in a society that proclaimed itself "open to the talents." At the same time, commerce, industry, and rapid urbanization broke up and transformed the rural communities, the erstwhile members of which, if they were ambitious, tried both to satisfy their own cultural needs and to improve their lot by the acquisition of the culture of the dominant class. In the end, the very success of the bourgeoisie in imposing its order and values was at least one of the factors that contributed to overturn the long-established and relatively stable division of society into an illiterate folk reared in its traditional folkways, and a literate upper class trained in the classical and contemporary languages and literatures, and attuned to the texts which were the constant point of reference of its own writers. A multiplicity of publics of extremely uneven cultural backgrounds came into being, and these finally undermined the political and, to some extent, the cultural hegemony of the old European *grande bourgeoisie,* that "great confederation," in Matthew Arnold's words, "whose members have, for their proper outfit, a knowledge of Greek, Roman and Eastern antiquities, and of one another."[44]

Released from direct relation to a collectivity, writers and artists achieved greater freedom than had probably ever been known, and this freedom with its attendant variety of traditions and styles emancipated literary language from any "natural" context and brought its specifically literary nature into view. The space between the language of ordinary use and literary language became a gulf, and literary language must have appeared to many as something *sui generis,* narcissistic and mysterious. Thus at the very moment when literate culture became a universally desirable commodity, both as the only feasible answer to genuine cultural needs and as a symbol of power and position in society, the possibility of acquiring it seems, for the vast majority, to have receded ever further out of reach. Although a small number of unusually well prepared readers came to enjoy a freer, and yet narrower and more specialized, relation to works of literature than listeners in an oral culture could possibly enjoy, the vast majority found themselves virtually debarred from literary culture altogether, incapable of arriving at any adequate perception of literary works at all.[45] I. A. Richards's evidence in *Practical Criticism* indicates that a school-sized dose of literary education does not necessarily cure this ill.

It is to the difficulties and injustices of life in modern open societies that we should probably attribute the remarkable survival, from the Renaissance to the present day, of the topos of the lost closed community. In the history of literature and in literary criticism this topos appears in the form of nostalgia for a lost oral culture.[46] Nostalgia for the oral—as for the "organic community"—is understandable at several levels, but its implications should be recognized. Frequently, as Raymond Williams demonstrated, it signifies ambiguously both rejection of the cultural and ultimately social inequality that has impoverished the lives of large numbers of mankind and compartmentalized the faculties and activities of the privileged themselves, and at the same time flight from the reality of cultural and social problems—and choices—into a realm of fanciful and subjectively satisfying solutions.[47] In the end, longing for a lost community is an idle and regressive, if poignant, indulgence; and as long as we continue to store our cultural products, it is hard to see what other solution there can be to the problem of estrangement, than education. It may well be, as Sartre says, that works of the mind, like bananas, should be consumed on the spot; it is not likely, however, that Sartre would have us jettison all our stored rations—though, of course, this solution has been proposed. And most of us do not know how to eat these naturally; we have to learn. Neither access to nor utilization of the literary tradition can be regarded as automatic.

To argue for literary education, however, is not necessarily to argue for its present practice and values. As things are at present, literary education, though it appears to mark a recognition of the importance of teaching the codes by which artistic productions can be deciphered, perpetuates and in a way consecrates the cultural inequalities which in our society correspond to social divisions and inequalities. There seems little doubt that where the early foundations of a cultural education have not been provided by the home, the family, the total social environment of the individual, the school will at best, in most cases, turn out persons of timid and routinized culture, whereas the highest ideal of our present culture is to be free—free, that is, precisely from school origins and school patterns. This free culture is in fact accessible, for the most part, only to those who have had the benefit of a large cultural formation outside of the school. What mass literary education does, therefore, is make a cultural distinction, which itself rests on social inequality, appear natural, grounded in inequalities of natural endowment and merit. "By symbolically shifting the essential of what sets them apart from other classes from the economic field to that of culture, or rather, by adding to strictly economic differences, namely those created by the simple possession of material wealth, differences created by the possession of symbolic wealth, such as works of art, or by the pursuit of symbolic distinctions in the manner of using such wealth (economic or symbolic), . . . the privileged members of middle-class society replace the difference between two cultures, historic products of social conditions, by the essential difference between two natures, a naturally cultivated nature and a naturally natural nature."[48] Almost all Pierre Bourdieu's work, from which the preceding sentence was quoted, has tended to show how literary and artistic "education" plays its part in the consecration of the social order, enabling educated men to believe in barbarism and persuading the barbarians of their barbarity. The mere existence of public museums, cheap books, schools, and teachers, in short, does not guarantee that literary education will be democratic.

It is also possible that a thoroughly democratic society will alter both the present emphases of literary culture and the present position of literature in relation to other expressions of culture. As Raymond Williams has pointed out, it has been characteristic of generations of reformers and public educators concerned with culture from within the bourgeoisie, the English one at least, that they have tried to affect and improve the culture of society without having to alter it in a larger and more fundamental sense. The aim has almost invariably been to entrust education to a clerisy, in one form or another. Probably this has something to do with a Romantic notion of the receiver or reader of genius, corresponding to the author of genius, and as distinct as he from the mass, in whose talents as readers no confidence could ever, in the very nature of things, be placed. It has been assumed, corrrespondingly, that what should be taught and transmitted is what, traditionally, in the existing society, has been "culture." Since possession of this culture serves as a justification for the privileges of the privileged, the culture itself was not open to question. Works in the literary canon were not only judged universal and eternal, they were conceived uniquely in terms of classification and appropriation (or appreciation). They had not to be criticized but to be acquired. The reader's task was to discover the universal validity of the texts in the canon or, more recently, to bring them "up to date" and make them "relevant." There was rarely any attempt to reveal their rootedness in a historical commitment, conscious or unconscious, which the present-day reader might wish to criticize and reject. Insofar as literary education, like much modern literature itself, refuses to be the servant of the present social conditions, I am not sure that it can be content with a combination of historical criticism and creative criticism—what Michael Hancher calls the science of interpretation (explaining the works of the past in the light of their own context, trying to recover their "essence") and the art of interpretation (reviving and interpreting them in the light of our present culture, making them usable, so to speak, by reactivating selected elements in them).[49] What makes me uneasy, from my present point of view, about such an easygoing combination is not only that it leaves deliberately unresolved the philosophical question of the essence of the literary work, but that it proposes no challenge to the existing culture, which is, indeed, characterized by its power of accommodation. As Umberto Eco has suggested, the dynamics of rediscovery and revitalization of past cultural products, which during the

Renaissance was accompanied by a global restructuring of rhetorics and ideologies, occurs in our time at the surface of culture and leaves its basis relatively little affected.[50]

It is not clear, as matters stand, how literary education can stop serving as a conservative ideological force. Perhaps a first step might be the adoption of a radically critical and alienating stance, from which the intimate relation of ideology and rhetoric could be explored and revealed, so that nothing in the literary tradition could any more seem innocent. In a moving passage at the end of *Writing Degree Zero,* Barthes summarizes the dilemma of modern literature, that is, of literature which is acutely aware of its own literariness. "Literary writing," he says, "carries at the same time the alienation of History and the dream of History: as a Necessity, it testifies to the division of language which is inseparable from the division of classes; as Freedom, it is the consciousness of this division and the very effort which seeks to surmount it." Perhaps it should be a part of literary education to show the rootedness of all writing in a condition of language and ultimately of social and class relations. But it would be foolish, I think, to imagine that techniques of demystification will in themselves produce the conditions for democratic culture or democratic literary education; they may easily become only another cultural commodity to be appropriated and used as a sign and confirmation of privilege. It would be idle to speculate on the form literary culture will take in a possible democratic society or on the relation which such a society will entertain to the literary heritage as we envisage it in our society. As teachers of literature at the present time, we cannot much affect the place literature occupies in the social system of which we are ourselves, often unconsciously, the instruments. Indeed, that place may be already be changing, as other symbolic values usurp the predominant place of literature, and to the extent that it is, so, we may be sure, is ours. As citizens, however, we may wish to work toward a society in which neither literature nor any other cultural product will function as a means of social and political exclusion and domination.

[1971]

2

Literature and Education

When we see the many different institutions for teaching and learning and the vast throng of pupils and masters, we might imagine
that the human race was very much bent on insight and truth; but
here appearances are deceptive. The masters teach in order to earn
money and aspire not to wisdom, but to the semblance and reputation thereof; the pupils learn not to acquire knowledge and
insight, but to be able to talk and chat and to give themselves airs.
Thus every thirty years a new generation appears in the world . . . It
now wants to devour, summarily and in all haste, the results of all
human knowledge that has been accumulated in thousands of years,
and then to be cleverer than all the past. For this purpose, the
youngster goes off to the University and picks up books, indeed
the newest and latest, as the companions of his time and age . . . He
then begins to judge and criticize for all he is worth.

—Arthur Schopenhauer, "On Learning and the Learned,"
in *Parerga and Paralipomena*

We are in a shadowy corridor, groping in the dark . . . We all lack
a basis—literati and scribblers as we are. What is the good of all
this? Is our chatter the answer to any need? Between the crowd
and ourselves no bond exists. Alas for the crowd; alas, especially,
for us.

—Gustave Flaubert, letter to Louise Colet, 24 April 1852

IN THE MID-1960s an Anglo-Indian film, directed by James Ivory, had
a brief showing in a few major cities. *Shakespeare Wallah* portrayed the
dwindling fortunes of an itinerant troupe of English Shakespearean actors
doing the circuit of the Indian hill towns in the years following independence. In the last scene of the movie, a class of Indian schoolboys
emerges from a performance of *Othello* and eagerly waits to catch a glimpse
of a sexy Indian screen actress who is scheduled to pass by.

The teaching of literature, until very recently at least, seemed as well established as the British Raj once was in India. Even now, in our time of austerities and cutbacks, departments of language and literature, graduate and undergraduate, still dot the academic landscape more thickly than Indian Army barracks were once scattered over the landscape of the subcontinent. The Modern Language Association now has so many thousands of members that only two or three cities in the country have enough hotel rooms to accommodate those who attend its annual conventions

It was not always so. Both the teaching of literature in colleges and universities and the category of literature itself, as we now know them, are of fairly recent date, not much more than a century old. Before that, English, and modern literature in general, were not regular subjects of instruction in most colleges and universities, and to the extent that they were taught, no special expertise was deemed necessary to teach them. The first experimental class in English literature at Princeton, for instance, was taught in 1846–1847 by a professor who usually gave the course in Christian evidences.[1] In 1877 William Stubbs, the great Oxford historian, testified before a Royal Commission that he opposed having "dilettante teaching, such as the teaching of English literature," connected in any way with the historical school at Oxford. Another witness would concede only that English literature might be a suitable subject for "women . . . and the second- and third-rate men who [will] become schoolmasters."[2]

In the remarks that follow I have tried to arrive at some understanding of the changing place of literature in education over the period extending approximately from the Enlightenment to the present time. I am aware that to attempt such a venture in the scope of an essay requires great naïveté, great foolhardiness, or a willingness to be satisfied with rapid generalizations that no true historian, perhaps, would entertain in himself or countenance in others. All the more reason for me to claim the customary privilege of an *excusatio propter infirmitatem*. I do not have a historical training, nor am I an expert in the history of education. It is as a teacher of literature that I have become interested in the history of the teaching of literature, and it is the uncertainty surrounding the teaching of literature at the present time as well as the perplexities that I myself often experience as a teacher that have led me to take a retrospective view of the activity I am engaged in.

NEITHER of the two terms—*literature* and *education*—whose relations I propose to explore is unproblematic, though there appears to be an intimate connection between them. (I am reminded of the late Roland Barthes's pithy definition of literature: "Literature is what gets taught.

Period.")[3] In the common usage of the seventeenth, eighteenth, and early nineteenth centuries, the term *literature* meant something different from what it means, except in rather special usages (for example, the "literature" *on* a subject), to us today. "Literature," Matthew Arnold wrote, "is a large word; it may mean anything written with letters, or printed in a book. Euclid's *Elements* and Newton's *Principia* are literature. All knowledge that reaches us through books is literature."[4] Such a comprehensive notion of literature may already have been an anachronism in Arnold's time,[5] but it corresponds to the idea people had of literature in the seventeenth and eighteenth centuries at least. It would be tedious to quote dictionary definitions from this period or to give examples of usage. I hope the reader will take my word that they bear Arnold out. The "Catalogue des écrivains français" at the end of Voltaire's *Siècle de Louis XIV* included, besides many entries that the twentieth-century reader would expect to find—Bossuet, Corneille, Molière, Racine, minor poets like Benserade and Chaulieu, novelists like La Calprenède and Scudéry—a considerable number that he would not have expected to find: the philosophers Descartes and Gassendi; Mabillon, the founder of diplomatics; Charas, "the first man to have written well on pharmacy"; Ozanam, "compiler of the first dictionary of mathematics." Even in the early nineteenth century, in a popular work such as Eichhorn's *History of Literature from the Origins to Most Recent Times* (Göttingen, 1805–1812), or in the still more popular and frequently reprinted *Introduction to the Literature of Europe in the Fifteenth, Sixteenth and Seventeenth Centuries* (1837–1839) of Henry Hallam, the term *literature* covers every conceivable branch of learning. We can now think of these only as autonomous disciplines: philosophy, history, mathematics, philology, anthropology, physics, chemistry, medicine, jurisprudence, and so on, but to Eichhorn or Hallam they are all part of literature, and in Eichhorn's preface no distinction is made, in fact, between literature and *Wissenschaft* or learning in general. In militant Napoleonic France, the author of a *Cours analytique de littérature générale,* given at the Paris Athénée (a private lycée) in 1810–1811 on the eve of the invasion of Russia, pronounced the empire of literature "sans bornes"—limitless—and specified that the literature of imagination (poetry and fiction) is only part of literature, the part in which writers "explore the domain of the possible."[6] In America, the handbooks for the College of New Jersey in the eighteenth and early nineteenth centuries proposed to describe "all the branches of literature taught here,"[7] and these, it turns out, included—besides Greek, Latin, and rhetoric—logic, mathematics, moral philosophy, natural philosophy, metaphysics, chronology, and geography.

There is nothing surprising about the range of the term *literature* in this early period. As the principal and virtually the sole means by which the accumulated culture of the highest strata of society was preserved and transmitted from generation to generation, literature was defined not, as among us, by its opposition to science—in the preindustrial age, the aesthetic and the instrumental, or utilitarian, had not yet been isolated as mutually exclusive terms—but by its opposition to traditional oral and rural culture. To enter the world of literature was to break out of the blinkered confines of local lore, to acquire a universal—a classical—viewpoint, embracing all times and all places. The great texts of Greek and Roman antiquity in particular provided a repertory of topoi and models for thinking in general terms about politics, ethics, metaphysics, language itself; they even offered a language for expressing ideas and communicating them to a universal audience unbounded by local limitations of time and place. No wonder that Greek and Latin literature dominated the freshman and sophomore years at the College of New Jersey, or for that matter at Yale or Harvard, or William and Mary, or at Edinburgh or Glasgow, to say nothing of many of the French colleges, where there was virtually nothing else.[8]

To judge by one of the most popular manuals for teachers—the *Method for Studying the Belles-Lettres* of Charles Rollin, a moderately progressive Rector of the University of Paris, first published in 1726 and reprinted in innumerable editions and in German, Italian, Russian, and countless English translations throughout the eighteenth century and into the nineteenth (it was still being quoted unconsciously by Herder at the end of the eighteenth century and by Henry N. Hudson, the so-called American Carlyle, as late as the 1880s)[9]—the study of literature at any fairly modern institution in the eighteenth century was partly a grammatical exercise, partly rhetorical (identifying tropes and "beauties" that the student might wish to imitate either in Latin compositions or in compositions in his own language), and partly an occasion for considering moral or metaphysical questions, or questions of government, history, and geography. Even Herder, who had ideas of his own about education and culture, gave primary importance in education to the learning of standard literary language and the study of literature. "To speak well and effectively, and to write skillfully and coherently—these are things that everyone must now be able to do. This is a speaking and writing age."[10]

Underpinning the central place of language and literature in the eighteenth-century college curriculum were certain ideas about the nature of man and of culture. One of these was that, as Herder put it, following Descartes more than a century earlier, it is language—the ability to manipulate symbolic systems—that distinguishes man from the beasts (and not science or technology as we might tend to think). To learn to speak and write well was to be humanized. Protestants, especially, valued literacy and—more cautiously—literature as the instrument by which man might enter into the immediate presence of the Word of God in Holy Scripture and thus be freed from narrow, traditional, and—as they saw it—corrupt doctrines and practices. "It being one chief project of that old deluder, Satan, to keep men from a knowledge of the Scriptures," as the Massachusetts School Ordinance of 1647 has it,[11] literacy was highly prized, indeed mandatory, in places like Scotland, Switzerland, Prussia, and New England. Whether Latin and Greek, and to some extent Hebrew, remained privileged or whether the vernacular was judged capable of substituting for them, the acquisition and use of correct literary models of expression was seen by Christians and *philosophes* alike as a defense against the constant threat of regression into the bestiality of our original condition. Rector Rollin recalled that "ever since the Fall . . . we come into the world surrounded with a cloud of ignorance which is increased by the false prejudices of a bad education. By study the former is dispersed and the latter corrected."[12]

Though he was critical of many aspects of the culture of his time, Herder was close enough to Rector Rollin when he advocated the teaching of language and literature as a means of weaning young men from their natural beastliness. "When we are born," he wrote, "we can only cry or yell, and many peoples and persons stay with such animal utterances throughout their entire lives. Whether they come from cities, or from the countryside, young men who still cleave to this disagreeable dialect of near animal sounds, must take all pains to acquire in high school a human, natural language, expressive of character and soul, and lose the habit of their uncouth peasant or alley dialects. They must give up their bellowing and braying, their spitting and spluttering, their swallowing and slurring of words and syllables, and speak human instead of animal language."[13]

Seventeenth- and eighteenth-century teachers thus saw in polished language and literature an essential instrument for removing their pupils from natural origins, releasing them from the narrowness of an oral, largely peasant culture, presumed to be shut in on itself and enslaved to routine and superstition—from rural idiocy, in Marx's later, pungent phrase—and for introducing them to the larger view of a universal, human culture, spanning the ages and the nations.

One can discern three principal ends which a literary education based on the great writers of Greece and Rome, with some admixture of neoclassical writings in the vernacular,[14] was expected to serve. First, it seems to have been a principle of order in that it enacted a distinction between the human and the animal, the urban and the rural, the self-conscious and the unconscious, law and custom, paternal and maternal, the governors and the governed. Literary taste, in short, was a way of inculcating a certain manner of conceiving the social and historical order, of acting within it, and of perpetuating it. According to Rector Rollin, literary good taste is the foundation of discernment and the love of order in every domain, including "public customs and the manner of living."[15] Second, to know and be able to use certain models of expression and of public and private conduct was a condition of communication and exchange with other civilized people in all places where public affairs were transacted: courts, clubs, salons, parliamentary assemblies, courts of law, government offices, and learned, polite, or diplomatic correspondences. Literary language was the language not only of the learned, but of all who would participate in worldly and public affairs.[16] Finally, literary education provided a repertory of universal models that could be used for interpreting the immense variety of particular moral, social, and cultural phenomena.

Literature in the neoclassical age was thus primarily associated with the public life and "manly" activities, as Gibbon liked to say, with government, politics, law, oratory; and literary culture stood apart from and opposed to the domestic, maternal world of oral culture, the world of women, children, and the people, of "false prejudices" and "bad education."

In certain novels and even, more modestly, in certain historical writings of the eighteenth century, there are significant signs of a revalorization both of the private, domestic sphere and of maternal origins, as opposed to paternal culture and law. It is as though a stratum of the bourgeoisie, conscious of its links to those origins—to the people and their material life—wished to rehabilitate them and to find a place for them in culture rather than to exclude and repress them as the other of culture. The hero of Marivaux's greatest novel, *La Vie de Marianne,* for instance, is a woman, and her quest is for her maternal origins. The world of women and feeling and private life is constantly opposed in this work to the world of men and law and public life. There seems to have been little question, however, that the idea of culture would remain linked to that of law and public life. The interest of some French revolutionaries in the dialects or mother speech of the various regions of France, for example, was inspired by the desire and the need to integrate the rural communities into the nation, to transform ignorant peasants into citizens. Dialects or patois were studied so that the laws and decrees of the new republic could be translated into them and made intelligible to the people, but only until such time as provincials and peasants could be transformed into proper Frenchmen by being educated away from their patois and imbued with "new sentiments, new customs and habits."[17] The patois, or mother tongues, of the people remained, in the words of a recent writer, an adulterating proximity, fascinating to the scholar and *philosophe,* but also dangerous.[18] One respondent to a questionnaire on patois issued in 1790 expressed his ambivalent feelings in the form of a cyclical view of language and history: the original language, he hypothesized, is always a patois undifferentiated by refined or complex syntax—this was true of Latin itself—and language always reverts to patois, as Latin did in the Middle Ages. "It is no further from the Latin patois of our scholastics to the harmonious language of Virgil and Cicero, than it is from the patois of our rural communities, our towns, and even of Paris itself, to the language of Racine, Buffon or Bossuet. To anyone who would desire to know to what language we shall return in the end, it seems as though the answer must be to the language of the people, since it requires neither combination, nor effort, nor labor."[19] As for Rector Rollin, culture remained, even for those who in the eighteenth century were curious about their mother tongue—or about folk poetry or local antiquities—a precious and precarious achievement of labor and effort, constantly threatened by the danger of regression into the supposedly undifferentiated world of nature, the mothers, and the people, and defended primarily by literary education.

Though elements of this attitude persisted in important ways throughout the nineteenth century, the rediscovery and rehabilitation of the primitive world of origins—of the feminine, the maternal, the popular, the infantile—and the creation of a unified and total culture without ruptures or exclusions was a major enterprise of Romantic poetry, historiography, and philology. Every historian, in Michelet's words, is an Oedipus, undertaking on behalf of humanity a perilous journey back to the mothers. Resolving the riddles of the past, giving a voice to its oppressive silences, deciphering its secret, forgotten, or suppressed languages, is the historian's sacred mission.[20] Augustin Thierry was hailed by contemporaries as the bard of the vanquished and the violated.[21] Bachofen, delving into the prehistory of Italy and Greece and arguing for a continuity between the maternal world of the Orient and the paternal culture of the Occident, between maternal custom and paternal law, took as his motto a phrase from Virgil: *Antiquam exquirite matrem* ("Seek out the ancient mother").[22] Jacob Grimm, embarking on his great dictionary in the late 1830s, conceived it not as a normative, legislative work in the manner of the seventeenth-century French *Dictionnaire de l'Académie,* separating the educated from the uneducated, but as an enterprise of unification: "Since the Wars of Liberation," he wrote in the preface, "a deep and abiding longing has arisen in all the best circles of the nation for the treasures that unite Germany instead of dividing her."[23] Grimm's *Deutsches Wörterbuch* was planned and executed as an immense, loving reconstitution of the maternal body of the German language. Though no one member of this linguistic body was privileged over any other, to Grimm a special aura attached to the earlier forms of the language, those that were closest to the beginnings, the original mother tongue. The intimate relation between nostalgia for an earlier and more glorious language of humanity and the desire to penetrate deeper and deeper into the dark underworld of maternal culture was the theme of Max von Schenkendorf's poem *Muttersprache:*

> Will noch tiefer mich vertiefen
> In das Reichtum, in die Pracht.[24]

> Ever deeper would I sink
> Into the treasure, into the glory.

Perhaps the emblematic figure of early nineteenth-century literary scholarship is the great Egyptologist Champollion, still in so many respects a man of the Enlightenment yet already, like Napoleon himself, a deeply Romantic figure, fascinated by the tomb and the archive—always figures of the womb and the origin, of birth and resurrection as well as of death—fascinated by Egypt and her enigmatic languages, pleading passionately against classicizing colleagues at the Imperial Institute of France for the beauty and dignity of the art and culture of the ancient land of Isis and for their right to equivalent status with those of Greece and Rome, protesting against the way history has invariably sided with the victors against the vanquished.[25]

Increasingly in the biographies and autobiographies of great writers from the end of the eighteenth century, it is from the mother, or a mother figure, rather than from the father, as in traditional culture, that the son is said to have inherited his artistic temperament; increasingly, it is the female—particularly the mother—who appears as the carrier of culture and who is said to have nourished and encouraged the child's nascent sensibility. Art and literature, in short, are no longer conceived of as an acquired skill to which some are initiated by their fathers or by male perceptors, but as the result of privileged access to a subterranean culture from which the majority of men have been cut off. The topos became so common that it was adopted by almost all autobiographers claiming a special destiny. In the *Autobiography of a Working Man,* first published in

1848, Alexander Somerville, the son of a poor farmer from the Lothians, tells of his first encounter with what he calls a "book subject." It occurred one evening when his father had to be away from home and his mother told him and his sisters the biblical story of Joseph. "To this day I remember the very manner of myself and my sisters, sitting around her on our creepie stools on the hearthstone. To this day, I can see the fire of logs and coals as it burned behind the bars of the grate . . . it was the first time that I felt an intellectual ecstasy. It came from my mother, as did many pleasing, good, and holy feelings."[26] In Michelet's lapidary phrase, "Every man of superior gifts is his mother's son."[27]

In this context, literature ceased to stand for what distinguishes town and country, paternal and maternal, rulers and ruled, and came to stand rather for what must unite them; and literary education was correspondingly conceived by the Romantics not as an instrument of division and discrimination but as a means of healing wounds, dissolving differences, and restoring lost totalities. "In spite of things silently gone out of mind and things violently destroyed," Wordsworth wrote, "the poet brings together by Passion and knowledge the vast empire of human society as it is spread over the whole earth and over all time."[28] The reading of books, according to Emerson, "is the desire to do away this wild, savage, and preposterous There and Then, and introduce in its place the Here and Now. Belzoni digs and measures in the mummy-pits and pyramids of Thebes, until he can see the end of the difference between the monstrous work and himself."[29] Lamartine claimed that literature is the foundation of human unity, the bond between the living and the dead generations: "It is literature that performs the work of transmitting spirit not simply from one man to another, but from one age to a hundred other ages."[30]

The divisions and discontinuities that literature was called upon to heal in the first half of the nineteenth century were conceived in various ways. There was the division created by historical time itself—the "Caesarean scar," as Michelet used to say[31]—and, above all, by the great rupture of the French Revolution. "The old Europe," wrote Ballanche, "which has traditions, memories, ancestors, wants to regenerate itself without renouncing its traditions, without trampling on its memories, without denying its ancestors."[32] Regeneration without repudiation: how to go forward while remaining faithful to everything on which the present and the future rest—and that was seen often to include not only the Christian Middle Ages and the ancien régime but the disruptive force of the Revolution itself, not only the maternal matrix but the separation from it—

how to reconcile the women's work of religiously remembering the dead and preserving the great community of which the dead are as much a part as the living with "manly" acceptance of a new scientific regime, in which the abstract, autonomous individual confronts the abstract, monolithic state, and the dead, together with the insane, the indigent, the infirm, and the Indians, are banished to special reservations—that was the problem literature was to help solve. It was, after all, the central ideological problem of a bourgeoisie that claimed to be not the oppressor of the people, as the old nobility had been, but itself part of it, its offspring as well as its new husband and master. "It is necessary to comprehend the past and to love it," Claude Fauriel, the editor and translator of Greek and Serbian folksongs and the historian of the defeated Provençal civilization of southern France, wrote to a friend, "but not at the expense of either the present or the future."[33] To one of his enthusiastic Collège de France audiences Michelet, in 1839, announced: "We must simultaneously feel regret and refuse regret, honor the past by legitimately, graciously, and piously preserving the memory of it, and at the same time never forget that we have to go forward to do other things."[34]

The division of present and past was often perceived as separating modern, rational, legal, and scientific civilization—the State—from what was generally thought of as the old, poetic, and symbolic culture, the culture of orality and of the mothers. Without what we might call the "feminine" moment or aspect of life, no human order can be satisfactory, according to Bachofen. Love, he wrote in one essay, summing up much German Romantic criticism of natural-law theory, has been exiled to the sphere of private life in modern times and is now thought to have nothing to do with civil, public life. But this is a disastrous error, a sign of personal and social corruption and decadence. "In the ages when the life of the State is healthy and young, much rests on love and inclination; in the ages of its decline, almost everything rests on the cutting edge of right and law. But right and law separate men and love binds them together." In the closing years of the preceding century, Wilhelm von Humboldt had already warned that a culture which suppresses sensuality (*Sinnlichkeit*) and fails to bring it into creative tension with reason can never realize its highest possibilities, for while reason "gives direction" to energy, "sensuality is the source of all vital energy."[35]

The division separating the learned and the untutored, the literate and the oral, was also, ideally, to be bridged by a new literature and a new literary education of the people. In his *History of France,* Michelet celebrated Rabelais, "who borrowed from none but the people," and castigated Ronsard, the joyless, fastidious "Orphée gentilhomme" of an exclusively literate culture, who "hit out like a man without hearing at the poor French language"—one is reminded of Leavis on Milton—and whose success as poet of kings and courts had condemned French literature to a life term of ceremoniousness and sublimity.[36] It was Michelet's unfulfilled dream that in his own work, both as a writer and as a popular educator, he would reunite the old oral culture of the people and the literate, learned culture of modern times. "If my heart is opened upon my death," he wrote, "you will find inscribed in it the idea that has always pursued me: 'How shall the books of the people be made?' " The consciousness that he had failed to produce the ardently desired "livres populaires" was a source of deep disappointment and bitterness to Michelet in later life. "I was born into the people, I had the people in my heart. The monuments of its past were my delight. . . . But its language, ah, its language remained inaccessible to me. I was never able to make it speak."[37]

The division of modern, rational civilization and the old culture of myth and symbol, literacy and orality, was repeated, for that age of speculative philosophy, in the human psyche itself. I shall let Emerson speak again: "The primeval world, the foreworld, as the Germans say, I can dive to it in myself as well as grope for it with researching fingers in catacombs, libraries, and the broken reliefs and torsos of ruined villas." Before Emerson, Humboldt had written in his now celebrated essay "On the Task of the Historian" that historical understanding is predicated upon "an original antecedent congruity between subject and object," so that "everything which is active in world history is also moving within the human heart."[38] Bachofen presented the study and contemplation of antiquity as at once a balm and a stimulant which would reintegrate the scattered or repressed parts of a divided self: "There is something about the walls of Rome that moves the inner depths of a man. When a metal plate is struck, the iron resounds and the echoing can be stopped only by placing one's finger on it. In the same way, Rome moves the spirit that is in communication with antiquity, one stroke following another until every side of a man has been shaken and aroused, and he finally comes to consciousness of all that was slumbering within him."[39]

The crucial role assigned to the teaching of Greek literature in the curriculum of the new German Gymnasien, or classical high schools, bears witness to the high expectation placed on literary education by the German neohumanists of the period following the Wars of Liberation. Greek culture, in the view of Schiller or Wilhelm von Humboldt, of August Böckh or Carl Otfried Müller, had realized in an exemplary way the integrated and complete development of all the faculties of the human being. Though the naive harmony and unity reflected in ancient Greek literature might be lost forever, men could still be reminded, by studying it, of what they once had been and what they could and should at least strive to be again. The highest goal of German neohumanist education in the early decades of the nineteenth century was a kind of secular redemption—the reintegration of intellect and feeling, prose and poetry, the masculine and the feminine sides of our nature, "Form" and "Life," to borrow the terms used by Schiller in his *Letters on the Aesthetic Education of Man.*

Finally, literary education, it was piously hoped, might lessen the social division of rich and poor, of the educated men of property and the propertyless toilers of the field or factory. This note was struck often, but nowhere more urgently than in England. Shelley boldly discerned a connection between the growing prestige of instrumental (as opposed to speculative) reason—"the calculating faculty," as he called it—and the exploitation of men by men, the instrumentalization of the human person;[40] and fear of that division of the two Englands or of the two Frances, which was denounced by Disraeli, Mrs. Gaskell, Michelet, and others, led many to look to literature to soften the hard edge of class hostility in the age of industrial capitalism.[41] Macaulay put it bluntly: The ignorance of the common people—and by that he appears to have meant above all those who, since 1832, were participating in the suffrage—was a menace to property. It was necessary to educate this class so that it would be immune to the blandishments of "demagogues" and "though naturally hostile to oppression . . . not likely to carry its zeal for reform to lengths inconsistent with the security of property and the maintenance of social order."[42]

In the utilitarian tradition, the reform and extension of education and, within certain limits, of literary education were advocated in a hardheaded way as a means of social control. The inspiration for literary education also came, however—perhaps more often—in a religious guise, as a means of promoting community. F. D. Maurice, a pioneer in the teaching of English literature in England both at King's College, London, and at the new workingmen's colleges in the industrial towns, believed that through literary texts a voice is audible "which can make the deepest mind of a great age of history be intelligible to our age; a voice which can teach us how all ages are united in Him, who is, and was, and is to come."[43] A decade after the Year of Revolutions, reminiscing about the experience of that "awful year" in an address to the Manchester, Ancoats, and Salford Working Men's College, Maurice denied that his concern for popular education had been motivated by class interest or fear. "It did cause us to fear, I own; but it was not fear for our property and position; it was the fear that we were not discharging the responsibilities, greater than those which rank or property imposes, that our education laid upon us. . . . We believed and felt that unless the classes in this country, which have received any degree of knowledge more than their fellows, were willing to share it with their fellows, to regard it as precious because it bound them to their fellows, England would fall first under anarchy, and then under despotism."[44] Wealth and property, in other words, were not the principal barrier to community that the lower classes might mistakenly have perceived them to be, and social reform was to be achieved not by altering the economic order but by a redistribution and sharing of literary culture.

If it was a coincidence, it was a striking one, that the teaching of English literature was first institutionalized, not at the traditional universities attended by the upper classes, but, as part of middle-class education, at Benthamite or evangelical foundations such as University College and King's College, London (1826 and 1831, respectively), at the urban Scottish universities (Edinburgh and Glasgow), and at workingmen's colleges up and down industrial Britain, as well as at the new northern universities that subsequently grew out of them. In North America, likewise, English and American literature first became a subject of lectures and instruction at the workingmen's and mechanics' institutes and libraries that sprang up in all the northern and midwestern states in the late twenties and thirties.[45]

It was, of course, Matthew Arnold who articulated most effectively the concerns of teachers and reformers such as F. D. Maurice and Charles Kingsley. To literature, and more particularly to the study of literature, to literary criticism and literary education, Arnold, as is well known, attributed a major social role. They were to resolve the antagonisms of the social classes by raising the members of these classes—or at least their leaders—above class interests and bringing them to awareness of their essential, unifying humanity. Arnold's consciously chosen masters were the German neohumanists—Schiller, Goethe, and above all Wilhelm von Humboldt—but the social situation of England in the 1860s, to which he applied their cultural idealism, was unlike anything they could have experienced or imagined in the still predominantly rural Germany of the early 1800s. Even Friedrich Engels, who was familiar with the beginnings of modern industry in Germany, was as astounded and horrified by what he found when he came to England in 1844 as Michelet had been ten years earlier.[46] Arnold himself was taken aback by the "miserable regions" of London's immense East End, with their swarms of children "eaten up with disease, half-sized, half-fed, half-clothed, neglected by their parents, without health, without home, without hope," which he had to pass through in the course of his duties as H. M. Inspector of Schools, and which inspired some of his finest rhetoric.[47] The poets and philosophers of early nineteenth-century Germany could not have envisaged the depth of the mutual fear and distrust that divided the social classes in mid-nineteenth-century industrial England.

Something of that fear and distrust surfaces in Arnold's own writing—in his account, for instance, of the growing ranks of class-conscious laborers organizing themselves "through trade unions" into "a great working class power" which will finally, "by dint of numbers, give the law" to all the other ranks of society and "itself reign absolutely," or of "that vast portion . . . of the working class which, raw and half developed, has long been half hidden amidst poverty and squalor and is now issuing from its hiding place to assert an Englishman's heaven-born privilege of doing as he likes, and is beginning to perplex us [the euphemism is typically Arnoldian] by marching where it likes, meeting where it likes, bawling what it likes, breaking what it likes."[48] Arnold's descriptions of what he terms the "Populace,"[49] except where the latter is presented as an object of noble compassion, reveal an unsuspected harshness in the advocate of sweetness and light; and his very attempt to mute conflict receives a curious illumination from an earlier remark by Engels. "Workers who are treated like beasts . . . retain their humanity," Engels wrote, "only so long as they cherish a burning fury against the property-owning classes. They become animals as soon as they submit patiently to their yoke and try to drag out a bearable existence under it."[50]

Arnold seems to have known that he was setting an unrealistic goal for literary education in mid-nineteenth-century England. He argued that study of a unified culture, such as he believed ancient Athens or Shakespearean England to have been, would "enable a man to construct a kind of semblance of it in his own mind," but it is not clear that he expected this would ever be more than a fragile personal and individual solution to the discordances of life in capitalist, industrial England. "The epochs of Aeschylus and Shakespeare make us feel their pre-eminence. In an epoch like these is, no doubt, the true life of literature; there is the promised land toward which criticism can only beckon. That promised land it will not be ours to enter and we shall die in the wilderness."[51] The Romantic ideal of totality and presence, the goal of a restored and unified national culture, must remain an ideal: in the real world, all are now condemned to live in alienation and fragmentation, far from the warm center and source of life, along "the vast edges drear and naked shingles of the world."

*   *   *

THE ROMANTICS had transformed the very meaning of the term *litera-ture*. In one sense they had vastly expanded its scope: it had come to include works in the vernacular that had hitherto had no place in the canon, or had not even been known outside the circles of oral culture; it embraced the ancient poetry of India and Persia as well as the literature of the European Middle Ages and the folk poetry of many lands and peoples.[52]

In another sense, however, Romanticism narrowed the range of liter-ature. Distinguishing between the enduring world of culture, wisdom, and feeling, on the one hand, and the changing world of practical knowl-edge and understanding, on the other, the Romantics tended to reserve the title of "literature" for those works that were usually held to reflect the former. In addition, they altered the reader's relation to literary texts. "The true poem," in Emerson's words, "is the poet's mind."[53] The emphasis was thus shifted from the text itself to the experience behind it, from rhetoric to history. "Formerly," President Noah Porter of Yale wrote, a year after the publication of *Culture and Anarchy,* "criticism confined itself exclusively to the proportion of parts, the order of development, the ef-fectiveness of the introduction, the argument, and the peroration . . . [but] now, . . . it thinks more of the matter, i.e., the weightiness and truth of the thoughts, the energy and nobleness of the sentiments."[54] Increasingly, literature assumed the character of a body of sacred texts, the Holy Scrip-tures of a secular religion, the refuge to which values and sentiments seemingly incompatible with practical life in the new industrial society had been evacuated.

In his history of English studies in England, D. J. Palmer noted a significant change that occurred in the teaching of literature sometime between the eighteenth and the nineteenth century. "The main emphasis in this moral, evangelical approach to literature," he wrote, referring to the activity of men like Maurice and Kingsley, "is upon reading, upon the value of making contact with the great imaginations of the past; the old rhetorical connection of reading with writing had almost disappeared by the middle of the century."[55] On the American side of the Atlantic, what study of English literature there was at Princeton University had tradi-tionally been linked to writing and to public speaking. Elocution was a part of English instruction in both the academic and the scientific de-partments until the late 1870s. After that point, however, English became, as in England itself, more and more exclusively a cultivation of the feelings and the imagination, an activity of appreciation and not primarily a way of learning how to produce fine speeches and essays oneself. Literature became, in the words of the popular lecturer Henry Hudson, "a holy sacrament of the mind." The study of literature, according to Hudson, has as its goal "drinking in the author's soul-power."[56] The reader's relation to books was thus no longer in the first instance that of a potential writer, a producer, an equal; it was that, at best, of an adept or worshiper, at worst, of a consumer.

As great literature—literature with a capital *L,* as Barthes used to designate it—was nothing less for the Romantics than a revelation of the hidden and forgotten world of origins, so the early teachers of Literature saw themselves as the priests of a new religion and the guardians and interpreters of its sacred texts. To August Böckh, who, as professor of classic philology at the University of Berlin in the 1820s and 1830s, played a role in philological studies analogous to that of his colleague Ranke in history, the special merit of classical literature was that of being close to the beginnings, to "the spiritual principle, the *arché,* which is often subsequently obscured unless one returns again and again to the origins." The task of the teacher of literature was to show the way back to those origins and to interpret them to his contemporaries.[57] The priestly role of the scholar and teacher as the guardian and interpreter of the great texts of the past was not confined to classical scholars. "The office of the teacher of German language and literature," Philipp Wackernagel claimed in his *Deutsches Lesebuch* of 1843, "is a royal, a high-priestly one."[58]

The prophetic and institutional aspects of literary education did not sit well together, however, and there was soon increasing tension between the disruptive, potentially revolutionary teaching of the charismatic prophet on the one hand, and the routinizing, ordering, adapting activity of the priest or bureaucratic servant of official culture on the other. Emerson addressed the problem early in his essay on education:

> Happy the natural college . . . self instituted around every natural teacher; the young men of Athens around Socrates; of Alexandria around Plotinus; of Paris around Abelard; of Germany around Fichte or Niebuhr. . . . But the moment this is organized, difficulties begin. The college was to be the nurse and home of genius; but though every young man is born with some determination in his nature, and is a potential genius . . . it is, in the most, obstructed and delayed. . . . They come in numbers to the College: few geniuses; and the teaching comes to be arranged for these many and not for those few. Hence the instruction seems to require skillful tutors, of accurate, systematic mind, rather than

ardent and inventive masters. Besides, the youth of genius are eccentric, won't drill, are irritable, uncertain, explosive, solitary . . . not good for everyday association. You have to work for large classes instead of individuals; you grow departmental, routinary, military almost with your discipline and college police.[59]

Early in his career Wilhelm von Humboldt had argued in favor of strictly limiting the power of the state, but as Prussian Minister of Education he found himself exploiting the very instrument he wished to hold in check in order to realize on a significant social scale his goal of regeneration through literary culture. It was Humboldt who set up the system of state-run classical Gymnasien, which was to institutionalize and routinize the ideas of the neohumanists in Germany and to transform them ultimately from a liberating force into a repressive instrument of class domination.[60] The involvement of the state in education and of education in the state in Prussia—and the Prussian system was the object of emulation and of countless fact-finding missions by officials from all the major Western countries—totally altered the character and goals of literary education originally argued for by the neohumanists. Students from the Gymnasien (as of 1834, *only* students from the Gymnasien) were admitted to the university, where they prepared State examinations for posts in the various branches of the government and administration. University professors themselves were salaried civil servants with rankings equivalent to those of counselors of state. The Gymnasien and the universities founded or remodeled in the enthusiasm of post-Revolutionary neohumanism were thus gradually integrated into the fabric of the German state, and their original function, the formation of free and harmonious personalities (in opposition to the specializing and fragmenting trend of modern times), was made over into something more like its opposite: the production of competent and disciplined bureaucrats and managers. *Eine Beamtendrillmaschine* was Theodor Fontane's word for Prussian education in 1897.[61]

The Prussian state, as is well known, was the model that Arnold constantly held up to his benighted countrymen and that he tried to persuade the English middle classes to forsake their liberal principles for. With his usual insight, Arnold recognized that the enlightened and active Prussian form of the state was the best bulwark against popular democracy and against the danger, as he put it picturesquely, of "becoming Americanized."[62] If they wish to retain their power, Arnold argued, the middle classes must allow themselves to be guided by the state, that is, by a bureaucracy of specialized experts—experts in industry, experts in commerce, experts in politics, experts in culture itself.

The course taken in the next fifty years by the middle classes of this nation, will probably give a decisive turn to its history. If they will not seek the alliance of the State for their own elevation, if they go on exaggerating their spirit of individualism, if they persist in their jealousy of all governmental action, if they cannot learn that the antipathies and shibboleths of a past age are now an anachronism for them—that will not prevent them probably from getting the rule of their country for a season, but they will certainly *americanize* it. They will rule it by their energy, but they will deteriorate it by their low ideals and want of culture. . . . In the decline of the aristocratic element, which in some sort supplied an ideal to ennoble the spirit of the nation and to keep it together, there will be no other element present to perform this service. . . . The middle classes, remaining as they are now, with their narrow, harsh, unintelligent, and unattractive spirit and culture, will almost certainly fail to hold or assimilate the masses below. . . . They arrive, these masses, eager to enter into possession of the world, to gain a more vivid sense of their own life and activity. In this, their irrepressible development, their natural educators and initiators are those immediately above them, the middle classes. If these classes cannot win their sympathy or give them their direction, society is in danger of falling into anarchy. Therefore, with all the force I can, I wish to urge upon the middle classes of this country, both that they might be very greatly profited by the action of the State, and also that they are continuing opposition to such action out of an unfounded fear. But at the same time I say that the middle classes have the right, in admitting the action of government, to make the condition that this government shall be one of their own adoption, one they can trust.[63]

What Arnold argues for is recognizably, I think, what we now have virtually everywhere, in the West at least.

To the technocratic, bureaucratic state—more supple, more open, and more adaptable than the rigid Prussian version of it known to Arnold—corresponds that professionalization of culture, or that "culture of professionalism," which is so characteristic of our time, and whose function, it has been argued, is to reconcile democratic principles, especially the principle of open access and the promise of social advancement for all, with the maintenance of rigid structures of authority.[64] Within this context, as is well known, the study of literature has become a specialism like any other, and to the degree that it has done so successfully and thus met the criterion of professional expertise that our society requires in order to acknowledge the validity of any branch of study, it has also—and this is perhaps, as I shall suggest again later, the dilemma of literary education today—gone a long way toward forfeiting its title or its original claim to a privileged position as the unifier and restorer of culture.

Criticism of the new bureaucratic culture, of which Arnold himself seems paradoxically to have been one of the early advocates, has come from a strange coalition of old prophets faithful to the early Romantic ideals, patrician and aristocratic aesthetes hostile to mass education and the threat it represents to their idea of culture as a sign of distinction or an object of refined consumption, and radical critics—not easily situated on the traditional Left-to-Right political spectrum—who see in the modern state the instrument of a social and economic order indifferent or even, in its nature, inimical to their own idea of what an authentic human culture should be.

The old prophets were quick to raise the alarm as they saw their ideas banalized and routinized by the clerks. In a journal entry for 1852, Michelet recorded a warning he had given himself: "What I had to fear most, was the sterility of mere routine, the stultifying uniformity of bureaucratic ways"; and in a moving text of 1855 he anticipated the dismay of Burckhardt and Nietzsche at the academic routinization of historical research and writing and the alienation of the historical writer from contemporary life: "The industry we created yesterday seems already to have become our burden, our evil destiny. We were to have been quickened by history, which is nothing less than the understanding of life, and instead we are being made old and cold by it. We called up history and now we find it everywhere; we are besieged by it, suffocated by it; we are weighed down by this baggage. We can no longer breathe. . . . The past is killing the future."[65] Ironically, Michelet's friend and pious biographer, Gabriel Monod, was one of those who worked hardest to professionalize the study of history in France, and in the preface to the first issue of the *Revue Historique,* the professional journal of which he was the editor, he announced with satisfaction that French history no longer had need of geniuses, since it was now organized on a sound methodological and scientific footing.

A more conservative and religious note was sounded by Woodrow Wilson in his famous essay of 1896, "Princeton in the Nation's Service." President Wilson complained of the excessive influence of scientific methods, and of humanists "imitating their ways of thought, ogling their results," and he noted with regret that "in our study of the classics nowadays [we look] more at the phenomenon of language than at the movement of spirit; we suppose the world which is invisible to be unreal, we doubt the efficacy of feeling and exaggerate the efficacy of knowledge."[66] Consciously or unconsciously, Wilson was echoing Humboldtian motifs—Humboldt had defined knowledge as "the recognition of the invisible in the visible"[67]—but in the context of the university over which he presided and the age in which he lived, Wilson's spiritualism had a different and possibly less liberal meaning than Humboldt's had had.

In England, as one might expect, criticism of popular literary education sometimes assumed a more blatantly antidemocratic and elitist tone than was acceptable in democratic America. In 1889 Walter Raleigh, a refined product of King's College, Cambridge, deputizing for the professor of English at Owens College in Manchester, the nucleus of the future Victoria University of Manchester, wrote scathingly of the students he had to teach there—poorly prepared, uncultured, and eager for self-improvement as a means of advancement: "They do not understand it all. They blink at it. I made some remarks on Poetry in general which cost me more than fifteen matter-of-fact lectures, and they laid down their pens and smiled from an infinite height."[68] In 1886 the Oxford Magazine reported condescendingly of the teaching of the ordinary man's classics that "English litera-ture . . . was found to be, of all subjects, the most convenient to the cram-mers, the most useless as a test of ability and of knowledge."[69] Literary education, it must be acknowledged, does seem to have been very routine. One need only look at the examination questions in English literature at Scottish or English provincial universities or, in the United States, at Princeton to see how uninspired it apparently was in the second half of the nineteenth century.[70] There was good reason for J. C. Collins, a cham-pion of English studies, to complain that, as it was being taught, English literature "fails to fertilize; it fails to inform; it fails even to awake curi-osity."[71]

Finally, the routinization of literary and humanistic education has been opposed by those who, fearful of the behemoth of the modern technocratic state, have come to see in a genuine literary and philosophical education the last redoubt of a beleaguered humanity, the place from which the monster can be observed and its movements charted and denounced. This critical function is what the old Romantic ideal of literature as a unifying and totalizing power seems to have been reduced to in the work of the Frankfurt school of philosophers, sociologists, and critics, who were active from the 1920s through the 1950s first in Germany and then in the United States. In opposition to the monolithic tendencies of the time, the Frank-furt school everywhere emphasized and valorized nonidentity. Though they claimed to be Marxists, they often turned out to be among the most ardent defenders of values usually associated with liberalism—but not very well defended by it—such as the active individual subject, or the historical consciousness, which alone makes possible, in their view, the type of integrated experience (*Erfahrung* as distinct from *Erlebnis*) necessary for the existence of such a subject.[72] Theodor Adorno, for instance, in one of his many essays on music, deplored the ousting of the piano—the "private," middle-class instrument, as he described it—which requires the active participation of the user of the musical text, as a personality in his own right, in the production of the music, by the phonograph and radio, which in his view degrade the musical amateur to a passive consumer and make possible the reduction of all responses to a calculable and predictable uniformity.[73] In the scope for mass manipulation that this development and similar ones in other areas provide, Adorno discerned one of the chief dangers to free and democratic societies.

There are some surprising similarities between the Leavis school in England and the Frankfurt school in Germany, despite the Leavisites' more exclusively literary orientation, their correspondingly weaker philosophical underpinnings and narrower focus, and their emphasis on positive values rather than on negativity and nonidentity. The editor of *Scrutiny* and his associates, while critical of the belletristic subjectivism and aetheticism of the academic literary establishment in England, also opposed the scientism and specialism that was displacing the belletristic tradition: not only the positivism of the Old English schools but also the formalism and the emphasis on technique of the New Criticism, in which they denounced "a new academic spirit no less potent than the old, with seemingly infinite possibilities of a strangling proliferation as time goes on."[74] Though it was critical of privilege, the Leavis school was as deeply opposed as the Frankfurt school to modern mass society, and like the Frankfurt philosophers it quickly assumed the appearance and role of an elite. It would have liked this role to be a leading one, corresponding to its revival of the Arnoldian claim that literary study, and in English-speaking countries the study of English literature in particular, should be the cornerstone of a humane education. "Leavis's goal," in the words of a recent historian of the movement, "was the formation of a new estate; a compact, 'disinterested' intelligentsia, united in commitment to 'human values,' whose function would be to watch over and guide the progress of society-at-large."[75] In fact, however, the Leavisites seem always to have been an embattled elite, swimming against the tide, a kind of latter-day Jansenists, bravely bearing witness in an ungodly age.

Close to Marxism, yet critical of it to the extent that socialism of itself, as it was understood by contemporaries, seemed to them to offer only the fulfillment of the capitalist promise and the perfection of the rationalist-industrialist dream, the Leavisites appear to have opposed not so much capitalism itself as industrial and technological civilization and what they perceived as the reduction of persons to mere functions in the machinery of production and consumption, the elimination of the moral and historical consciousness of individuals and communities alike. With them, as with the Frankfurt school, the constructive, unifying, and harmonizing role attributed by the Romantics to literary education—the role reclaimed for it by the Leavisites themselves—was reduced in the end to a critical one. The purpose of education, as Denys Thompson, Leavis's lifelong associate, saw it, "should be to turn out 'misfits,' not spare parts."[76] On the other side of the Atlantic another disciple of Arnold, who also attacked and was attacked by the technicians of the New Criticism, expressed a similar view. "The unargued assumption of most curriculums," Lionel Trilling observed in a poignant essay written about thirty years ago,

> . . . is that the real subject of all study is the modern world; that the justification of all study is its immediate and presumably practical relevance to modernity; that the true purpose of all study is to lead the young person to be at home in, and in control of, the modern world. . . . It might be asked why anyone should *want* to quarrel with this assumption. To that question I can only return a defensive, eccentric, self-depreciatory answer. It is this: that to some of us, as we go on teaching, if we insist on thinking of our students as the creators of the individual life of the future, there comes a kind of despair. It does not come because our students fail to respond to ideas, rather because they respond to ideas with a happy vagueness, a delighted glibness, a joyous sense of power in the use of received or receivable generalizations, a grateful wonder at how easy it is to formulate and judge, as how little resistance language offers to their intentions. When that despair strikes us, we are tempted to give up the usual and accredited ways of evaluating education, and instead of prizing responsiveness and aptitude, we set store by some sign of personal character in our students, some token of individual will. We think of this as taking the form of resistance and imperviousness, of personal density or gravity, of some power of supposing that ideas are real, a power which will lead a young man to say, "but is this really true, is it true for me?" and to say this not in the modern way, not following the pro-

gressive educational prescription to "think for yourself," which means to think in the progressive pieties, rather than in the conservative pieties (if any of the latter do still exist), but to say it from his sense of himself as a person rather than as a bundle of attitudes and responses which are all alert to please the teacher and the progressive community.[77]

There is renewed talk these days—most recently at the 1980 MLA meetings in Houston—about a crisis of literary education. To some extent, what is being referred to appears to be a temporary disorder of an essentially economic and demographic nature—supply outstripping demand. To some extent, however, the feeling of crisis reflects an unresolved tension not only between the dominant direction of our culture and the elitist character of literature (only that is admitted to the canon which can be demonstrated to be in some way "superior" or "unique"), but also between the residual yet tenacious claim of literature to offer some sort of humane culture and the ever-increasing fragmentation and specialization of knowledge—and of knowledge necessary for survival—in the modern world.

Literary education itself bears the marks of this tension. A good deal of what goes by the name of literary education today is "technical," as the Leavisites might say. It involves isolating a limited set of objects and problems which can be defined as specifically "literary" and proceeding to deal with these professionally, according to rationally justified and agreed procedures, as an administrator solves administrative problems or a technician technical problems, without necessarily inquiring into the value and meaning of the particular activity in relation to a larger whole. The bureaucratization of our entire culture and of our universities along with everything else has made this approach seem normal rather than aberrant, as it would have appeared to the Romantics.[78] Yet such specialization is probably inevitable, and may even be desirable, for it may well be that what is universal in literature is embedded in its very particularity.

In his moving essay entitled "Scholarship as Vocation," Max Weber defended technical scholarship on the ground that renunciation of ultimate, "unanswerable" questions involving totality and universality is the peculiar ascesis of the modern intellectual, the very mark of his integrity, and an essential defense of freedom under law against demagoguery and totalitarian pseudo-mysticisms. One can feel the force of Weber's argument, its moral intensity, and the deep concern for human freedom behind it—though one may doubt the efficacy of Weber's protective barrier of purely formal laws and procedures. Yet there seems no denying that the value of literary study, as distinct, say, from the study of chemistry or psychology or sociology, is harder to defend if one gives up not only the quick, facile, simplifying generalizations that it is sometimes required to yield but also the very belief in an elusive universal, of which any specific literary work can admittedly carry only tantalizing traces, which it can admittedly only adumbrate and never incarnate, since for it to do so would mean its own self-annihilation as a literary work. In short, the literary work, I am suggesting, is no longer for us, as it was for the Romantics, the locus of an achieved synthesis of the universal and the particular—reason and feeling, the State and the individual, paternal law and maternal nature—but itself the field of their unending and life-sustaining tension. The continued existence of literary education today, it seems to me—and I find myself very close in feeling to the Frankfurt critics, or what I understand of them—is part of a vital struggle against the deadening force of bureaucracy and manipulation, part of a desperate effort to keep alive questions of ends and meanings. It is a paradox, and also a constant danger, that this struggle must go on largely within the framework of bureaucratic and routinizing educational systems and institutions.

We cannot, it seems to me, speak in general or universal terms of the place of literature in education. We can only address this question concretely, responding more or less adequately, as people did in the past, to specific historical conditions. At the same time our response must, I think, reflect not only the particular problems of our times but also a general political ideal or commitment, a larger conception of the good life, as people used to say. At the present moment a case might be made for the educational value of the study of literature precisely because, despite everything, it continues to resist routinization (the multitude of warring methodologies, theories, and practices is striking illustration of this); precisely because it fails to provide positive doctrines and lessons but, on the contrary, continually opens up abysses before us and confronts us with uncertainty; precisely because, in short, it is the place where we encounter not presence, as the Romantics hoped, but absence, not security, but insecurity. I can think of no more fitting conclusion to these inconclusive reflections than a warning passage from a short essay by Theodor Adorno: "Art—and so-called classical art no less than its more anarchical expressions—always was, and is, a force of protest of the humane against the pressure of domineering institutions, religious and others, even while at the same time it reflects their objective substance. Hence there is reason for the suspicion that wherever the battle cry is raised that art should go back to its religious sources there also prevails the wish that art should exercise a disciplinary, repressive function."[79] In the doubtless well-intentioned efforts of those who would justify literature and the humanities in general as a kind of surrogate religion, Adorno goes on, the actual contents of both religion and literature become "identical, or at least reconcilable with each other, as 'cultural goods,' which are no longer taken quite seriously by anybody. The apparently humanistic emphasis on [the identity of art, religion, and philosophy] has turned into a mere ideology. Art that wants to fulfill its humane destination should not peep at the humane, nor proclaim humanistic phrases."[80]

[1982]

3

The Figaros of Literature

> The logical English train a scholar as they train an engineer. Oxford
> is a Greek factory, as Wilton mills weave carpet and Sheffield grinds
> steel . . . The effect of this drill is . . . the solidity and taste of En-
> glish criticism . . . The Great silent crowd of thoroughbred Gre-
> cians always known to be around him, the English writer cannot
> ignore. They prune his orations and point his pen. Hence the style
> and tone of English journalism.
>
> —Ralph Waldo Emerson, *English Traits*

> The realm of art is perhaps a realm of diabolical grandeur . . . in
> its core, hostile to god and, in its innermost and aristocratic spirit,
> hostile to the brotherhood of man.
>
> —Max Weber, *Science as Vocation*

ROBERT FROST once defined a liberal as someone who can't take his own
side in an argument. In more than thirty years of teaching and writing
about literature, I have not succeeded in developing a single, consistent
theoretical position of my own or, for that matter, in embracing anybody
else's. Competing arguments only too often strike me as equally compelling, and whereas an ideological or ethical preference can sometimes tip
the scales when reason alone cannot, that has rarely worked for me. My
loyalties are also divided. The following reflections bear the mark of my
indecisiveness, but I hope they are at least an honest account of uncer-
tainties, which may well be shared by others, about the professing of
literature.

Brought up in the 1940s and 1950s on Lukács, Sartre, and Raymond
Williams, I find it *natural* to take a historical view of everything. But I
do have occasional unnatural impulses, and there are moments when I
wonder whether I haven't built a fortress around myself and imprisoned
myself in it. Reading Franz Overbeck's *Christentum und Kultur* (*Christianity and Culture*) a few years ago brought on a fit of uncertainty that

has lasted longer than usual. So I should like to start with Overbeck, who is chiefly remembered—to the degree that he is known at all in this country—as Nietzsche's colleague, housemate, and loyal friend when he was teaching at the University of Basle in the early seventies of the last century, in order to consider the stance of the historically oriented critic, such as I take myself to be.

From his chair of Theology, Overbeck took the paradoxical position, worthy of a close associate of Nietzsche, of denouncing the very discipline he had been brought to Basle to teach, as "the Satan of religion."[1] According to Overbeck, the faith of the early followers of Christ, being exclusively oriented toward the imminent end of the world, was utterly indifferent to the world and to history. Theology, however, arose out of the effort to "save" Christianity for a world that did *not* end, by institutionalizing it and ensuring its accommodation to changing historical circumstances. "That theology has always been modern and for that reason has always been the betrayer of Christianity," Overbeck declared, was "one of the key arguments" of *The Christianity of our Present-Day Theology,* a polemical tract which he published in the same year and with the same publisher as Nietzsche's harsh second *Unzeitgemässe* against David Strauss (the two friends always referred to these two works as "the twins," and each had a copy of his own bound together with a copy of the other's), and in which he pilloried the leading Protestant theologians of the day for their efforts to adapt Christianity to the Second Empire Germany of railways, factories, banks, insurance companies, and mass circulation newspapers. For theologians in general Overbeck had no high regard. They are, he said, "traitors to the cause they are supposed to defend"; "panderers coupling Christianity and the world"; "the Figaros of Christianity"; "old washerwomen drowning religion for us in the endlessly flowing stream of their chatter."[2]

I think it was that last phrase in particular that induced a feeling of discomfort in me and made me wonder, first, how much of Overbeck's attack on theology was applicable also, *mutatis mutandis,* to my own discipline of literary criticism, and to those who, like me, profess to teach literature, which I suppose means explain it, elucidate it, and adapt it to changing times by constantly reinterpreting it; and second, what assumptions, what hidden agenda, as they say, might underlie Overbeck's own critique of theology.

The context in which I first began to reflect on the relevance of Overbeck's critique of theology to my own activity as a teacher of literature was neither fortuitous nor, probably, inappropriate. Not long ago, I was discussing Racine's *Phèdre* in an undergraduate class. On the one hand, I was trying—as I think quite a few of us do—to historicize the work: in this case by locating it both in a theatrical tradition whose conventions have become unfamiliar to us and in a social, cultural, and ideological context (essentially the Quarrel of the Ancients and the Moderns and the struggle between the Jansenists, opposed to all forms of compromise with the world, and the Jesuits, committed to the historical survival and expansion of Christianity in a universe radically different from that of the early Christians). On the other hand, I also wanted to make the play intelligible in terms of modern experience by referring the students to several recent readings of it—in particular to Lucien Goldmann's in *The Hidden God*. The unresolvable, tragic conflict of *Phèdre,* according to Goldmann, results from the heroine's attempt to realize totality, to overcome the separation of the sacred and the profane by remaining faithful to the past and at the same time living fully in the present. That reading, which Goldmann rooted in the political dilemma of the French *noblesse de robe* in the seventeenth century, might well have been informed, I suggested to the students, not only by the critic's historical research and learning but by his own historical experience, and by his discovery of himself in Racine's play—the very thing, let me note in anticipation, that Roland Barthes, then in his Brechtian phase, was to warn against several years later when he wrote that the task of the critic and the director "c'est de renoncer à nous chercher nous-mêmes dans ce théâtre" ("is to give up trying to find our own selves in those plays").[3] As a Marxist in the heyday of Stalinism, Goldmann could easily have felt that, like Phèdre (in his interpretation of the role), he also was confronted with two irreconcilable demands: that of remaining faithful to the principles of socialism, as he understood them, and that of adapting them to the world. In the conditions of the 1950s, the first course might well have seemed to condemn whoever followed it to historical impotence and irrelevancy, the second to require an accommodation of principles to historical realities that would "save" socialism for the world only at the cost of betraying it and turning it into a travesty of itself. Were *we* not ourselves confronted in the classroom with a similar dilemma, I asked the students—trying to bring the issue home—in our very effort to read and understand Racine's play. We might, out of reverence, refuse to "interpret" it, that is, to translate it into terms meaningful to ourselves, to find our own dilemmas in it, but then there was a risk that it might be lost to us altogether; if we did intepret it, however, we would save it only at a cost.

What role, the question seemed to be, should historical understanding and historical imagination play in literary criticism: Should they bring the past closer or help us to distance ourselves from our own present? And if they bring the past closer and make it "intelligible," do they not tend toward "modernization" or betrayal, an appropriation and trivialization of difference, as a result of which the modern reader ultimately loses the capacity to be challenged by the past as other and provoked into a truly intense reflection on or revaluation of his or her own ideas?

To illustrate the persistence of this question at all levels of experience, I should like to refer parenthetically to a recent Op-Ed page essay by Peter Bien, Professor of English at Dartmouth, on Martin Scorsese's controversial film of Kazantzakis's novel *The Last Temptation of Christ* (*New York Times,* 11 August 1988). Though several religious groups have called for the banning of this film, Christian fundamentalists have been in the forefront of the attack against it. Bien's defense of the film (or at least of the book, since at the time of writing the essay he had not seen the film) rested on the claim that it "does not undermine Christianity but rather makes Jesus's ministry more meaningful to modern man." "Of course [Kazantzakis] takes liberties," Bien explained. "But his aim, as so many readers have discovered, is to make Jesus accessible to the 20th century." The opposition of the fundamentalists, according to Bien, derives from their "pharisaical literalism . . . They are horrified by interpretation. Yet the major purpose of Jesus's ministry was to prod the descendants of Abraham to seek the spirit rather than the letter of traditional doctrine, *thereby making that doctrine relevant to their own condition*" (italics added). Not being well versed in matters of religion, I hesitate to make any comment on Bien's position. I cannot help observing, however, that it seems to reflect a vision of Christianity in which the original eschatological dimension is very weak. The chief concern appears to be not the end of the world but ensuring the continued relevance of Christianity in constantly changing historical circumstances.

Any critique of this relatively liberal view is going to raise the question of the nature and practice of interpretation. In the past—historians of the topic tell us—interpreters employed two methods to reduce the distance between readers and texts.[4] The *grammatical* or philological method aimed at a kind of literal translation, substituting for words and phrases that had become unintelligible because of linguistic change, corresponding words and phrases belonging to the readers' language. It tried to reconstruct the meaning a word had in the past and then to preserve that past meaning by substituting a new word or by explaining the old one in a note. Its goal (impossible, some would say) was the recovery of the past in the present. The *allegorical* method sought a new meaning, a *sensus spiritualis,* which, while not excluding the original meaning, completed or transcended it. It started out from the sign or word which had become strange in order to attribute a new meaning to it, a meaning engendered by the intellectual world of the reader and commentator, not by that of the text. Though often used together (as Tony Grafton has shown for the Renaissance),[5] these two methods are fundamentally opposed. While the allegorical method was common during the Middle Ages, the grammatical method was revived with the Reformation. Basing their view on the new philological learning of the Renaissance, the Reformers rejected allegorical interpretation and insisted that the original meaning as inscribed in Scripture was the only legitimate one; that the Christian must strain every fiber to reach out to the ancient text instead of relying on tradition; that he must seek God's meaning, not man's, not his own or that of the Church. Luther's claim that Scripture is self-evident and needs no interpreting agency (such as the Church claimed to be)—*sacra scriptura sui ipsius interpres*—is founded on the principle of the exclusive legitimacy of the original, past meaning. Rejection of allegorical interpretation thus seems closely related to a critical stance toward the social and cultural institutions which claim the authority to regulate it and which use it to provide the present with the legitimation that is supposed to derive from continuity with the past, the founding and authorizing moment.

Translation theory is marked by the same perennial ambivalences as interpretation. The old saying *traduttore, traditore* expresses forcefully the literalist position, underlining the danger of betrayal in any translation or modernization; the word *traditore* itself brings together in a shocking way two notions not *prima facie* connected: that of the go-between, the negotiator, the transmitter of tradition, and that of the traitor, as though history itself were a mark of sin and imperfection and there were something inherently untrustworthy and evil about any telling or retelling, about lacking a single, undivided identity. Although the dominant theory and practice of translation in the Counter-Reformation period of the seventeenth and eighteenth centuries might be described as allegorical—nearly all translations, especially those of noncanonical, vernacular works, were in fact what we might rather call adaptations—there was a persistent current of resistance to those "belles infidèles" which represent in the practice of translation the "Jesuitism," the modernizing, compromising, accommodating spirit that Overbeck denounced in his Protestant colleagues when he declared that "all theologians are Jesuits," and that Phèdre seems likewise to denounce as a fateful error when she turns in anger on Oenone, her worldy-wise nurse and confidant, for urging her, after receiving the news (false, as it turns out) of the death of Theseus, to adapt her behavior to the changed circumstances. The learned Mme Dacier, for instance, a respected Greek scholar and translator from the Greek (and, as one is not surprised to discover, a daughter of the Reformation who converted to Catholicism only at a relatively advanced age) came down strongly on the side of historical difference and fidelity to the originals of antiquity in her polemic with Houdar de La Motte over the latter's modernizing version of Homer. Later, at the beginning of the nineteenth century, Goethe renewed that strand of translation theory when he defended literal translation or, better still, a form of translation that would stretch and expand the resources of the target language as it reaches out to the alien source language, against what he called "parodistic translation in the fullest sense of the word," that is to say, the kind of translation "preferred as a rule by intelligent people," such as the French (Goethe's own example!), and "in which the translator supposedly wants to enter into the spirit of the foreign land, but in fact only tries to appropriate that spirit and reconstruct it in his national one."[6]

The liberal, modernizing view of interpretation is thus by no means self-evident, and the opposite view has had some eminent supporters. In fact the argument against hermeneutic put forward recently by Steven Knapp and Walter Benn Michaels in the pages of *Critical Inquiry* looks very much like a modern version of the critique of allegorical interpretation.[7] There is, moreover, another problematical aspect of the modernizing method of interpretation that Bien, in his defense of Scorsese's film, did not consider. Is it desirable, one might want to ask, to look at present-day problems through a glass provided by what Bien calls "traditional doctrine" without also examining that glass? It was Overbeck's view at least that whoever tries to distill out of Christianity what is "relevant" in it to the modern world does no service to either Christianity or the world, but simply exploits and distorts Christianity while helping us to avoid facing up to our own worldliness and modernity.

The issues I am evoking were also raised in a most poignant form in a recent series of Gauss seminars on the historiography of the Holocaust—or Final Solution, as the speaker preferred to say—given at Princeton in October of 1988 by Saul Friedländer of the University of Jerusalem. Friedländer's central questions—How do you interpret these events, without in some way banalizing or profaning them and depriving them of the absolute uniqueness and irreducibility, the almost sacral quality they seem to have to those who either still remember them or respond as intensely to them as they would if they had experienced them themselves? How do you translate memory into history? Should you? And what happens to memory when you do?—are very close to those that troubled Overbeck and that continue to trouble me.

At the very least, then, thinking about Overbeck's critique of theology in the practical context of my own teaching of a literary text had raised—not, I'm afraid, for the first time, but in an unusually direct way—the problem of my own activity as a teacher. Is my aim (or should it be) to defamiliarize texts and try to restore their potentially challenging and disturbing otherness, to make them as hard as possible, maybe even impossible, to "understand," or is it to appropriate them to my own and my students' time by discovering "meaning" in them (and how can meaning not be modern meaning?) and so ensuring their continued "relevance"? Are we, as teachers, the Figaros of literature, the middlemen, the procurers and even the corrupters of literature, in the way that theologians, in Overbeck's view, are the "Figaros of religion"? Is interpretation a form of accommodation, a way of making sure that literature, including past literature, will be placed in the service of the present—most often in such a way that the present is spared an excessively disturbing encounter with its own presentness? In Overbeck's eyes, such a practice of interpretation did not deal honestly with either the past or the present; it only perpetuated the half-hearted, hypocritical, and alienated culture that had emerged, according to him, from centuries of adapting the legacies of Christianity and antiquity to each other and to a world remote from both, and inhibited the development of a truly *modern* culture that would be as spontaneous and "natural" as he and Nietzsche believed the authentic culture of the ancient Greeks had been. For as much as he despised the modern in the "jesuitical" sense of the term, that is, in the sense of being always adapted to circumstances, brought up to date, Overbeck admired the modern in the sense of being absolutely at one with one's own time, without any falsely pious relation to the past.

At the same time, I do not think Overbeck's own ideas, powerfully as they may have affected me, should go unchallenged. In the rest of this essay I should like to look at a few episodes in the history of the study and teaching of literature, particularly vernacular texts from the past, as expressions of the human spirit, repositories of a wisdom that can be prized out of them by interpretative reading, and at the more recent critique of that kind of study and teaching of literature. I should like to suggest—there is nothing novel about this—that both have been a response to a particular development of the writer's and the critic's relation to the reading public and a consequence of their uneasy participation in and disaffection from the culture that emerged out of Enlightenment, political and social revolution, and the rapid development of industry and a market economy in the nineteenth century.[8] The interpretative critic occupies a particularly ambiguous position as a go-between purporting to connect the world of literature with the allegedly degraded world of everyday life. Interpretation, however, has a place in a liberal, pluralistic, free-market culture that prides itself on its tolerance and even encouragement of competition and diversity of views, on its ability to reconcile continuity and change, tradition and criticism. The rejection of interpretation, on the other hand, seems to be a far more extreme strategy of resistance, a refusal of the very codes and channels of communication on which culture depends for its survival.

The two positions appear to have been sketched out at an early stage in the argument over the relative merits of "symbol" and "allegory" in early nineteenth-century German aesthetics. Rejecting the dualism of the ideal and the real, the general and the particular, characteristic of eighteenth-century rationalism, Goethe, Hegel, and Schelling construed the sign above all as a symbol embodying the continuity of the ideal and the real, the general and the particular, the whole and the part. The symbol, for them, does not merely point to what it signifies; it is itself what it signifies. Novalis and Schlegel, on the other hand, rediscovered the allegorical nature of the sign, though in an altogether different sense from that of European classicism. For them, the sign is a fragment, a mere trace of something which is gone from the world and to which there is no longer easy access. What it signifies is not present in it, as in the symbol. On the contrary, it points to an absence, and the interpreter who hopes to read it must be willing to leave the world of the familiar and make a daring leap into the unknown: "sich in die Luft hinausstellen," as Overbeck himself liked to say.

In the Age of Enlightenment, when literary criticism in something like its present form was institutionalized, the relation between the critic and the public, we are told, was extremely close. The critic spoke for the public, and his aim was to propose judgments of literary works according to criteria accepted by the public, which always remained the supreme judge. Authors themselves did not want to be distinguished from the general public. In Paris, Marivaux declared that he wanted to write as a man, not as an "Author," and in far-off Edinburgh, Adam Ferguson agreed: "An author writes from observations he has made on his subject, not from the suggestion of books."[9] In Johnson's words, it is "the publick, which . . . never corrupted, nor often deceived, [will] pass the last sentence on literary claims."[10] The public itself—Johnson's "common reader"—was conceived as made up of intelligent and thoughtful laymen from all walks of life.[11] Criticism was essentially an agency of that public, clarifying and ordering its judgment—improving "opinion into knowledge," to quote

Johnson again—and engaged with it in the struggle for an enlightened, open social and cultural order.[12]

By the end of the eighteenth century, however, as a host of scholars have argued from Queenie Leavis in 1932 to my colleague Alvin Kernan, in our time, it was becoming clear that the Enlightenment public, conceived of as a society of equal, educated laymen, either always had been or had palpably become an idealization of reality.[13] This disillusioning experience, incidentally, appears to have occurred earlier in the literary public sphere than in the political one, which met its crisis during the industrial revolution and in the sobering aftermath of the 1848 revolutions. The very spread of education and literacy and the intense commercialization of literature, both of which had been promoted directly and indirectly by the Enlightenment itself, resulted in a disruption of the relation between writers, on the one hand, and the reading public, on the other. A discrepancy arose—or became visible—between the artistic intentions of writers and the taste of the general public, whose judgments the former, unlike Johnson or Voltaire, were less and less inclined to accept. This appears to have been especially the case in Germany, where the *opinion publique* of Enlightenment France and England had always been poorly formed and had never succeeded in imposing itself. Schiller noted in 1791 that "there is now a great distance between the masses of a nation and its select elements." In these conditions, the critic became unsure who his partner in dialogue was: was it the broad public—increasingly definable as the literary market—or an educated minority? On whose behalf was he to speak; which segment of the public was he to reflect and stimulate? Was his allegiance to the public or to the literary work? Schiller argued that aesthetic judgments must be sharply distinguished from audience reception and that the qualities that give a poem validity as an art work are "in no way dependent on the comprehension of readers."[14] Public approbation is simply an added asset for a work of literature that has already passed the test of autonomous aesthetic criticism. Schiller now saw the task of the critic as that of preserving the level of literary discussion which was threatened by new uncritical groups of readers. That function separated him, in a way Johnson probably would not have recognized, from the general reading public. But, as Peter Hohendahl has observed, "When the general public is considered to have an inadequate esthetic sense and only the minority is viewed as a deserving partner for discourse, the general validity of literary criticism can no longer be legitimated by the public sphere."[15] Criticism, which was institutionalized in the conditions of an open public sphere, is forced to seek support from a small literary elite, and the critic begins to appeal to values that are largely independent of social connotation. Schiller is blunt on this score. The division of labor in modern society creates conditions unfavorable to criticism, he writes in *Über naive und sentimentale Dichtung*. Only a class of people freed from the necessity of labor can come to an adequate judgment of poetry and "through its feelings provide laws for the common judgment in all matters of pure humanity"; for "the effects of any lasting exertion . . . hinder the aesthetic powers of judgment to such an extent that among the laboring classes [and that term must be understood to include merchants, shopkeepers, and business people] there will be very few individuals who, in matters of taste, will be able to judge with certainty . . . and consistency."[16]

The historical emphasis of Romantic criticism carried the questioning of the Enlightenment critic's and public's competence to legislate about art even further than Schiller did. In Germany especially, where Enlightenment values did not have a broad public base and were often associated, in addition, with foreign (that is, French) influence and with the culture and politics of courtly aristocratic regimes, historical criticism was a deliberate challenge to the hegemony and self-confidence of Enlightenment taste. For the idea of an aesthetic norm is clearly not essential to historically grounded criticism and represents only—as in Schleiermacher's hermeneutics—a factor to be taken into account in the process of interpretation. Aesthetic norms, in other words, are relativized; they are important to the interpreter only inasmuch as they contribute to determine the form and meaning of works produced in contexts where such norms prevail. The ideal criticism, for the Romantics, is one that empathizes with its object and adheres to it, and it is directed not to the public at large, but to the like-minded reader, the "happy few." The critic's task is not therefore to represent the public sphere or to mediate productively between the public and the writer.[17] It is to unveil the immanent nature of the work, to *understand* it out of itself, and to judge it not in terms of heteronomous aesthetic norms, but in terms of the idea of art itself, of which any particular work in its finitude must be an imperfect and incomplete realization. As Walter Benjamin later put it, "The critic does not judge the work of art; art itself is the judge."[18]

As a teacher, I am most concerned with literary criticism and interpretation as part of education, that is, as they are practiced in academic institutions. Not surprisingly perhaps, education turns out to have been caught in the same problematical relation to the public sphere as criticism. In a study of French education in the ancien régime, the historian Georges Snyders pointed out that in the old Church-run education system there were two dominant concerns: one was that education should protect the student from the world and its corruptions in order to ensure that he acquire the means to resist them later of his own accord; the other was to prepare him for an active life in the world by teaching him skills and moral precepts appropriate to the world and to his station and social rank in it.[19] ("His" is here, regrettably, the correct pronoun.) The emphasis in schools run by the Jansenists and the Oratorian fathers fell, on the whole, on the first of these concerns; the emphasis in Jesuit schools fell more on the second. The Enlightenment, as one might expect, came down strongly on the side of worldly education. "Society itself is the school, and its lessons are delivered in the practice of real affairs," if I may quote Ferguson again. That meant that refined social intercourse would improve judgment and taste, while the study of practical subjects like the natural sciences, foreign languages, and technology would gradually replace the traditional curriculum of the religious colleges, and that natural morality, social responsibility, and civic virtue, learned in the school of life, would replace a moral education learned by rote and designed to produce obedient Christian subjects. (Only in the narrow interpretation put on Enlightenment pedagogy by Napoleon and the so-called enlightened despots was education to be purely practical, a mere machine for producing engineers, artisans, and merchants.) At first, a potential contradiction in the Enlightenment pedagogical program between worldliness and virtue—one recalls Rameau's quip about the philosopher's education of his daughter: "What's the good of a Spartan education to a girl who will be living in Athens?"— could be put down to the decadent and corrupt condition of ancien régime society, which the reforms championed by the *philosophes* would put right. But it became apparent after the Revolution that there was a persistent tension between a pedagogy oriented toward the practical and utilitarian goals of a commercial society and one oriented toward wisdom, humane values, and civic virtue. Education, like criticism, lost the optimistic and harmonious relation it had seemed to have with the contemporary world at the time of the Enlightenment.

In the program for the reform of education that the Prussian neohumanists tried to put through in the early years of the nineteenth century, the study of literature and culture came to be not a dialogue with the contemporary world and contemporary values but rather a challenge to them. When Humboldt, Süvern, and other educators proposed both a considerable enhancement of the study of Greek in relation to Latin and a reform of the study of the classical languages and literatures generally, they were inspired by Enlightenment ideas of reform and at the same time critical of them. Essentially, their aim was similar to what Winckelmann's had been in his studies of the art of antiquity in the 1760s: to promote a

movement backward, behind the endless accommodations of an aristocratic and predominantly Roman neoclassical tradition, toward a younger,
fresher, more authentic, and less familiar classicism, which Winckelmann
associated with the free city-states of Greece, and which, in the minds of
Humboldt and Süvern, stood in direct opposition to the contemporary
heirs of imperial Rome—the Roman Church, the absolutist courts of the
ancien régime, and the imperialistic France of Louis XIV and Napoleon.
In addition, Greek was not to be studied as a grammatical and rhetorical
exercise in the traditional manner; instead, the student was to journey
backward in time and to grasp and appropriate the innermost way of
thinking and imagining of the Greeks by entering into the spirit of their
language, which the neohumanists viewed not as a mechanical system for
communicating meaning but as the very shaping power or *energeia* of the
Greek spirit, the core of the culture of an entire people, a collective vitality
that animated and manifested itself in the works of individual poets.
Through his immersion in the language of the Greeks, the student's present
thinking and imagining, which were in danger of being corrupted by the
derivative and imitative culture of the seventeenth and eighteenth centuries, were to be transformed and restored to that immediate relation to
nature that Humboldt and his friends considered characteristic of the
youthful age of Greek language and culture. The young German's study
of the Greeks was no longer to be rhetorical, his understanding of them
mediated by modern ideas and methods; classical philology now embraced
the totality of ancient culture, and its object was to accomplish a kind of
identification, even a conversion or rebirth—very much, one is tempted
to say, in the Lutheran mode. The neohumanist study of the past was thus
by no means the kind of easy—or, as Overbeck might have said, "Jesuitical"—adaptation and appropriation of it that was characteristic of the
era of the *belles infidèles*. It was directed, over an intervening time of
misunderstanding and misrepresentation, to a remote, unfamiliar, and
pristine origin, and it aimed not to read the past, and the other in general,
in the light of present ideas and understandings, but to transform the
present through embracing the past, as Goethe thought translating foreign
texts should do to the target language.

The neohumanists appear to have believed that the Germans were more
capable of carrying out this return to the original and unfamiliar culture
of the ancient Greeks—considered closer than any other people to the
pure humanity of the origins of the race—because they were themselves
supposedly less spoiled and corrupted by the derivative and second-hand
culture of Rome than were the Latin, predominantly Roman Catholic,

peoples—the French, in particular—who had inherited the mantle of Roman imperialism.

Early neohumanism thus had none of the languid passivity which Nietzsche later attributed to those he described as "historical virtuosos." It arose, in a revolutionary age, out of an ardent longing for rebirth and renewal. History here played the kind of active role, at once critical or destructive and inspirational or constructive, that Nietzsche could have approved. At the same time, the neohumanist program stood in direct opposition to the alleged materialism and mechanism of the French Enlightenment and its Revolutionary heirs. In effect, it proposed a non-revolutionary (not to say counterrevolutionary) way of regenerating Prussia and Germany as an alternative to the socially disruptive ideologies and politics of the Revolutionaries. In principle, it offered a revolutionary challenge to the ancien régime of Germany's many courts and principalities; but it did so while refusing the materialism and worldliness of the French Enlightenment.

This curious mixture of Enlightenment and religion, critical and deeply conservative impulses emerges clearly, it seems to me, from Friedrich Ast's *Grundlinien der Grammatik, Hermeneutik und Kritik* (Fundamentals of Grammar, Hermeneutic, and Criticism) of 1808. "The goal of philological criticism," according to Ast, "is to cleanse the spirit of everything time-bound, accidental, and subjective, and so to impart to it that originality and universality, which is necessary to higher and purer human beings, that is to say: humanity." That has a strong Enlightenment ring. But for Ast it meant, ultimately, recovering consciously and in freedom that unity of paganism and Christianity, pantheism and theism, which had existed, in his view, in the Oriental world, prior to History, that is to say, before the successive unfolding and development in history of all the different possibilities contained in original humanity. "The two poles of history are the Greeks and the Christian world; both emerged, however, from a single middlepoint in the Oriental world, and thanks to that original unity both are straining, in our world, to be rejoined with each other. The triumph of *our* education will be the freely and consciously produced harmony of the poetic (Greek and plastic) and the religious (Christian and musical) life."[20] The goal of the revolutionary neohumanist philology was thus, in the end, progressive reconciliation of the ancient and the modern, the East and the West, Christianity and classical culture.

At the level of practice, the neohumanist program quickly lost its early critical edge. From the beginning the neohumanists had had nothing but contempt for *Brotstudenten*—young men whose studies were intended to provide them with a career and a livelihood. Not everyone, it seems, was called to be reborn through contact with ancient Greece. The merchant class and the peasants in particular (Schiller's "laboring class") were too caught up in practical and utilitarian pursuits, it was believed, to be able to benefit from a humanist education. The chosen, in other words, were few in number, and their education was in large measure an act of resistance to the pragmatic and utilitarian culture of the modern world. Like the critic, the neohumanist educator had his back turned to the public and was dedicated to the service of values that the modern world appeared to spurn.

As the German school system expanded in response to the needs of the new commercial and industrial age, however, the study of classical language, literature, and culture soon came to serve as an alibi, a pseudo-culture protecting students both from the challenge of antiquity and from full acknowledgment of their own modernity. The neohumanists' cult of classical Greece was made over into a legitimation of the modern military-industrial state that Germany was on the way to becoming. History served not to challenge the present but to neuter the past and justify the present. In his reminiscences of the German Gymnasium around the middle of the nineteenth century, the sociologist Wilhelm Riehl reveals how the radical character of the original neohumanist impulse had been transformed into the very kind of smug, modernizing reading of ancient culture that disgusted Overbeck and Nietzsche.

> We regarded Greece as our second homeland; for it was the seat of all nobility of thought and feeling, the home of harmonious humanity. Yes, we even thought that ancient Greece belonged to Germany, because of all the modern peoples the Germans had developed the deepest understanding of the Hellenic spirit, of Hellenic art, and of the harmonious Hellenic way of life. We thought this in the exuberance of a national pride in virtue of which we proclaimed the German people the leading culture of the modern world, and the Germans the modern Hellenes. We announced that Hellenic art and nature had been reborn more completely in German poetry and music than in the poetry and music of any other people of the contemporary world . . . Our enthusiasm for Greece was inseparable from our enthusiasm for our fatherland [and] with all that we remained good Christians.[21]

THE CONNECTION between the Hellenism of Victorian England—itself the subject of two important recent studies, R. Jenkyns' *The Victorians and Ancient Greece* (1980) and F. M. Turner's *The Greek Heritage and Victorian Britain* (1981)—and German neohumanism is embodied in the person of Matthew Arnold, who was an assiduous reader and lifelong admirer of Humboldt and Schiller. Arnold's work exhibits a tension similiar to that already noted in neohumanism between the desire to retain a critical dimension for the study of literature as the repository of "the best that is known and thought in the world" ("The Function of Criticism") and a "criticism of life" ("The Study of Poetry"),[22] on the one hand, and, on the other, the desire to accommodate it to and make it serve the interests of the contemporary world. Literature could serve us, according to Arnold, in two ways, one indirect and one direct. Indirectly, it could "interpret life for us, console us, sustain us" ("The Study of Poetry")—that is to say, it could provide a harsh, exploitative, commercial and industrial society with an ersatz totality and an ersatz humanistic religion to smooth over its conflicts and divisions. Directly, Arnold believed, it could help to prepare the English middle classes for an increasingly competitive economic and geopolitical environment in which, in his view, education would be the key to success.

As is well known, Arnold believed that "in literature we have present and waiting ready to form us, the best which has been thought and said in the world" ("A Guide to English Literature").[23] It is remarkable how explicit this most distinguished of all Her Majesty's Inspectors of Schools was about the social function of the education he advocated. Though he was charitable enough to envisage distributing some of the accumulated literary treasure of the world to the children of even the humblest social classes (without, of course, questioning that it remained the prerogative of their betters to decide what that treasure was and how much of it they should receive),[24] Arnold made no bones about the essential purpose he had in mind for it in a state-administered national school system. It was to have the effect, he claimed, "of fusing all the upper and middle classes into one powerful whole."[25] Its chief beneficiary would be "that immense business class, which is becoming so important a power in all countries, on which the future so much depends, and which in the great public schools of other countries fills so large a place," but "is in England brought up on the second plane, cut off from the aristocracy and the professions, and without governing qualities."[26] Arnold was a great admirer of France and in particular of the French bourgeoisie. That class has in France, he claimed, "a homogeneity, an extent, and an importance, which it has nowhere else," and it owes these qualities to the superior education imparted in the state-run or state-supervised lycées and colleges.[27] It was that kind of self-consciousness, power, and influence that Arnold, who was a shrewd analyst of contemporary social, political, and economic trends, believed the English commercial classes needed to acquire and would acquire only through the educational reforms he advocated with passion and persistency.

On the one hand, therefore, Arnold had a fairly clear plan to make literary study and literary criticism relevant to the needs of the present, and that meant, in the conditions of mid-century England, to the needs of a deeply divided society in which it was no longer easy, or even honest, to believe in anything like Johnson's "public." On the other hand, on the part of this infinitely cultivated man who had read his Goethe and his Schiller attentively,[28] there was a certain resistance to modernizing interpretations, an insistence that the reading of the texts of the past not be influenced by present ideas and fashions, that it be, as he said, "disinterested."[29] In the midst of the social divisions of industrial England, the educated member of the middle and upper classes was to be able to claim and to be himself convinced that by virtue of his familiarity with the best that had been thought and said in the world, he represented not a particular interest but the universal-human, the permanent and enduring values of human culture. "Modern sentiment," Arnold declared in the essay "On Translating Homer," "tries to make the ancient not less than the modern world its own, but against modern sentiment in its application to Homer, the translator . . . cannot be too much on his guard," and he goes on to fault Ruskin for the "tender pantheism" the latter infused into his translation of a couple of lines of the Iliad. "It is not true . . . that this kind of sentimentality, eminently modern, inspires Homer at all."[30] More than once, moreover, Arnold expressed skepticism about the scholarly historical approach to literary texts that was already common in academic circles in Germany and France. The danger of historical inquiry into the author and the times, he observed, was that instead of preparing the reader for a richer experience, it often *took the place* of literary experience and transformed the literary work into a dead document, an object, the necessary product of historical conditions and forces ("The Study of Poetry").[31] What Arnold wanted, in contrast, was a usable past, which meant for him a past in which the present could find itself in a noble and ideal form, by which it might therefore be provoked, but never rudely or radically, since what was found in the past was never fundamentally strange to the present. There was no place in Arnold's canon for anything that struck him as— in his own words—"wholly obsolete and unfamiliar to us."[32]

The same expectations of the past determined Arnold's fondness for social institutions that allowed for continuity and uninterrupted adaptation, that is to say that were both faithful to what he thought essential and universal in the past and also modern and up-to-date—for instance, the Church of England, deemed preferable to the nonconformist sects because of its "power for development," as we are told in *St. Paul and Protestantism.*[33] In religion, his goal was to reconcile "Aryan" metaphysics and sophistication with "Semitic" faith, that is, modernizing theology and ancient or popular belief, or, as he also put it in larger cultural terms, Hellenism and Hebraism. There seems to be a real affinity on this point between Arnold and some of the German neohumanists, such as Ast. The contrast is striking, on the other hand, with Overbeck, who insisted instead that Western interpretation had drastically distorted both Greek culture and Christianity, producing a Christianized Hellenism and a Hellenized Christianity.[34] It is because Christianity, for Arnold, is part of "the higher culture of Europe"—the chief object of his veneration and the glue that held everything together for him—that it deserves to be preserved and must remain "ever . . . able to adapt itself to new conditions, and, in connexion with intellectual ideas changed or developed, . . . enter upon successive stages of progress." It must accommodate itself, in short, to what Arnold himself referred to as the *Zeit-Geist.*[35] In Overbeck's eyes, Arnold would be a perfect "Jesuit."

I SHOULD like now to look briefly at how the teaching and interpretation of literature were viewed and practiced by another, less widely known figure concerned with literary education in the nineteenth century—but one who has the special interest for me of having been among the earliest and most successful professors of French as a modern foreign language. From 1813 until 1837 Alexandre Vinet—to whom Arnold himself paid tribute as "one of the most salutary influences a man in our time can have experienced"[36]—taught French at the Pädagogium (a kind of super-Gymnasium) and at the University in Basle, where a half century later Overbeck was to settle. In 1835 he became the first occupant of a regular chair of French at the University. Vinet's appointment in 1813 had been part of a complete overhaul and modernization of education in the old commercial city-state immediately after the end of the period of Napoleonic control. A unified system from elementary school to university was established and placed under the supervision of the State rather than the Church; modern subjects such as foreign languages, science and technology, and economics were introduced or promised as part of a commitment to provide the citizens of what was essentially a merchant community with an education "appropriate to the times," as the administrators liked to say; and at the same time the teaching of traditional subjects like the classical languages was brought into conformity with the ideals of neohumanism. The context of Vinet's teaching was thus a commercial city-state, with no aristocracy or gentry to speak of, whose practical-minded but conservative leadership was set to embrace modernity while avoiding revolutionary change. The merchants of Basle understood that adapting quickly to new conditions of trade was essential to their survival and that education had a key role to play in that process. At the same time, having been returned to power as part of the Restoration, they wanted no more social upheavals.

Vinet's teaching reflects this *juste milieu* position. The tension between the "materialist" or "utilitarian" goal of instructing the children of the middle class in a foreign language that was indispensable for the conduct of their businesses and the "higher" goal of spiritual education through contact with the great works of the past was the theme of several addresses he gave to the parents of his students at the Pädagogium. Vinet scolded students and parents alike for being blind to all but the "immediate practical utility" of the study of foreign languages and for "cutting out of the discipline everything that does not seem indispensable to the conduct of everyday life." The study of French, he declared, ought to be seen as an inquiry into the "genius of the language," an investigation of "ideas through the medium of words," and of "the history of a people through that of its language." Above all, French should be thought of as the "organ of that entire universe of ideas and creations known as French literature."[37] At the time, the view that modern language instruction might be comparable with instruction in the classical languages was by no means common. Even where the student's native language is concerned, Vinet himself explained, "in most schools there is no middle ground . . . between the rudiments of grammar and the history of literature. The analytic reading of great masterpieces" is virtually unknown. "The idea that . . . it is possible to read a tragedy of Racine as one reads a tragedy of Euripides would strike most people as original and unheard of."[38]

Vinet's attempt to fulfill both the practical goal of language instruction (preparing the student for the contemporary world) and the higher goal of education through abstraction from the contemporary world gave rise to one of the earliest and most popular textbooks for the study of French. His *Chrestomathie,* a graded, three-volume selection of readings from French literature with introductions and commentary, was first published in Basle in 1827, went through hundreds of editions and was used not only in Switzerland but in Protestant schools in France, as well as in Belgium, the United States, Russia, and many other countries of the world until quite recently.[39] The aim of the *Chrestomathie* was not simply the practical and rhetorical one of illustrating grammatical points and presenting models of style; it also had the "higher" goal of raising the student above immediate practical concerns by placing him in contact with "the best which has been thought and said in the world."

For Vinet, as for Arnold or Ast, that involved abstracting the student from the context of the contemporary world. Vinet made a portentious distinction, one that had previously been relatively strange to the modern vernaculars, between contemporary writing (now the territory of the journalistic critic or the feuilletonist) and "literature"—that is to say, texts that can be regarded as classics (the domain of the academic critic). To the author of the *Chrestomathie,* texts become "literature"—and thus available for the edification of later generations—only after they have been released from their embeddedness in a concrete contemporary situation and become part of "history." "There are two ingredients in contemporary literature," he wrote in the introductory letter to the third volume of his texbook: "Literature, to be sure, but also time, above all time; that is, the desires, feelings, sufferings, and hopes that are all around us, our own desires, feelings, sufferings, and hopes . . . a life too real and too intensely engaging to be literature."[40] "Literary emotions," he explained, "are of another sort. Human, certainly; how could they not be, since literature is nothing less than man? Human, then, but not contemporary, actual, individual; the impressions of literature are received less by the individual in us than by the man . . . An emotion that touches us too keenly, throws our soul into turmoil and disorder, responds too immediately to life, is not a purely literary emotion." Inevitably, "literature is never pure at the moment when it first appears." It becomes literature only gradually, as it recedes; when, "having lost its first intense heat, it can be handled without danger; or rather when, having shed everything that kept it too closely and actively bound to the time in which it arose, it ceases to be topical and is only human. It had to be topical no doubt. An abstract literature is inconceivable. Literature is true and human only if it is not abstract, and the character which the passage of time alone causes it later to lose was necessary to it at the beginning. Otherwise it was not viable at its birth. Our literature too will one day be literary; and then it too will be an instrument of culture, but only for our grandchildren."[41]

As envisaged by both Vinet and Arnold, literary education was intended to develop the student's critical skills. It also developed his capacity to recognize and feel the essentially human in all works of literature and so allowed him to enter a paradise of culture, the true home of all people of taste, sensitivity, and discrimination. As Roland Barthes observed about modern interpretations of tragedy, in his book on Racine, "Eternity substitutes for the Polis."[42] We are not perhaps very far from Nietzsche's "historical virtuoso" who has "developed in himself such a delicacy and sensitiveness that 'nothing human is alien to him.' Times and persons most widely separated come together in the concords of his lyre. He has become a passive instrument whose tones find an echo in similar instruments, until the whole atmosphere of a time is filled with such echoes, all buzzing in one soft chord."[43]

Against the historical virtuoso, Nietzsche argued in terms similar to Overbeck's. "One hears only the overtones of the original historical note; its rough, powerful quality can no longer be guessed from these thin and shrill vibrations. The original note sang of action, need, and terror; the overtone lulls us into a soft dilettante sleep." The virtuoso's tolerant, benign, catholic historicity, in other words, always "leaves aside what cannot be explained away." It does not focus on what is different and truly challenging but smoothes everything over into something recognizable, reassuring, and in the end easily accommodated. "The power of gradually losing all feelings of strangeness or astonishment, and finally being pleased at anything, is called the historical sense or historical culture," Nietzsche observes sarcastically.[44]

What I have been trying to suggest so far is that any contextualizing is a way not only of making literary texts accessible and intelligible but of domesticating them. It could even be that from this point of view the difference between a historicizing and a classicizing approach is not significant. In both cases the educated reader finds himself—as Noel and Laplace put it in the Preface of the seventeenth edition (1829) of their *Leçons françaises de littérature et de morale*[45]—in "a kind of museum," free to commune at leisure, like a man of property, with "the best which has been thought and said."

It seems then that if we lose our sense of the strangeness of texts, we will also find that our habits of thought and feeling and our certainties are not challenged by them. On the other hand, the attempt to break down a routinized familiarity or an idealizing humanism and to restore originality and strangeness by using history (or some other method) as a means of defamiliarization may place the texts of the past out of history altogether, accessible to us either not at all or only by some extraordinary leap of the imagination which transcends history, and of which a select number of individuals are perhaps alone capable. In this way the literature of the past may well be saved from appropriation by the present, but it is also placed beyond common discourse and public function. If anything, in fact, it seems that the public function of literature and the common discourse about it are the chief targets of strategies of defamiliarization, and of those modern forms of literary criticism that are—to quote Susan Sontag—"against interpretation." A common feature of most of these anti-interpretation positions is their horror of the seemingly infinite capacity of (historical) culture to order, absorb, appropriate, and exploit everything, their anti-humanist and sometimes nihilistic thrust.

I BEGAN with Overbeck's criticism of theology, and I will return to that point of departure for some concluding reflections on one of the most brilliant and original of recent literary critics. On the face of it, Overbeck's hostility to theology continues a radical strand in the Lutheran tradition: by that I mean emphasis on justification by faith and suspicion of everything that comes between the Christian and direct religious experience. From this perspective theology may itself appear, as it apparently did to Overbeck, as a symptom of the alienation of religion from life, its absorption into "culture." Though he never placed any particular emphasis on his Protestant origins and upbringing,[46] it is striking that Roland Barthes was always intensely concerned about the alienation of literature in our culture, and that he expressed almost as strong reservations about the scholarly study and teaching of literature and its institutionalization as an academic discipline as Overbeck expressed about theology. Barthes liked to distinguish between the writer and the professor of literature. The latter, he once wrote, "est du côté de la parole" (that is, he is involved in the world of communication, persuasion, history, culture, ideology); he is "someone who completes his sentences" (in other words, someone bound to order, hierarchy, rationality).[47] The writer, on the other hand, "est du côté de l'écriture" (that is, a nontransitive, noncommunicative, nonutilitarian use of language). The professor is also involved in a complex institutional relationship with his or her students, a contractual, worldly relationship of exchange, which, in the case of professors and students of literature, happens to take place via literature.[48]

For Barthes, in contrast, the reading of literature seems to have an almost religious character, which is hardly effaced by the erotic or Freudian language he uses to describe it. Since he was himself associated with various teaching and research institutions, notably the old École Pratique des Hautes Études, the Centre National de la Recherche Scientifique, and toward the end of his career the prestigious Collège de France, his relation to his own professional activity may well have been as troubled and full of tension as that of Overbeck, the professor of theology who came to scorn the subject he was supposed to profess. Asked whether his relation to the CNRS required of him that he adopt the role of a scholar, Barthes replied by acknowledging the ambiguousness—"bad faith," as he said himself—of his position.

> If you agree to play that role, you're going to opt for a type of activity which is labeled scientific, a type of scientific discourse I call *écrivance*. And you're going to miss the text, because you won't be in a transferential relationship of self-analysis with the text. You simply won't be reading the text. You'll treat it as a semiological or historical document, for example; . . . you'll try to construct narrative models, narrative syntaxes, or poetics in the Jakobsonian sense. But you'll remain outside reading. You will not be part of an activity which displaces the reading subject through contact with the text, and so you will not displace the writing subject: you will be condemned to consider the subject who wrote the text under study as an *author* in the traditional sense of the word, *a subjectivity which expressed itself in a work*.[49]

The distinction between *texte de plaisir* and *texte de jouissance* develops the same religious (or erotic) idea of what the relation between literary works and readers should be. The act of reading texts of bliss (*textes de jouissance*), as Barthes describes it, seems far removed from any historical or interpretative criticism, indeed from any criticism, from any "theology." "You cannot speak *about* such a text," he says.[50] The pleasure of the text is "linked to a consistence of the self, of the subject," and the pleasurable text "satisfies, fills, brings euphoria, . . . comes out of the culture and does not break with it, is linked to a *comfortable* practice of reading."[51] The text of bliss or *jouissance,* in contrast, is at the extreme edge of negativity; it is that "system of reading and utterance, through which the subject, instead of establishing itself, is lost, experiencing that expenditure which is, properly speaking, bliss." Texts of bliss "are texts which may displease you, provoke you, but which, at least temporarily, in the flash of an instant, change and transmute you, effecting that expenditure of the self in loss."[52]

The utopianism of the *texte de jouissance* was not new. Barthes's acute sensitivity to the alienation of literature in the modern world had already produced some of the most moving passages of *Writing Degree Zero*, which appeared as early as 1948.[53] A quarter of a century later, in *The Pleasure of the Text,* his utopianism has assumed—or so, at least, it strikes me—an extreme radical and romantic form. Two languages confront each other in the modern world, he claims:

The language produced and propagated under the aegis of power is a language of repetition, and all the official institutions of language are machines for churning out the same old story: school, sports, advertising, products distributed by the mass media, popular songs, news and information constantly repeat the same structure, the same meaning, often the same words. The stereotype is a political phenomenon, the principal rhetorical figure of ideology. Over against all that, there is bliss—*jouissance.* Whence the present configuration of forces; on one side, a massive flattening (linked to the repetition of language)—a flattening that is outside of any bliss but not necessarily of any pleasure— and on the other, a reaching out (marginal and eccentric) toward the New, a reaching out that is quite wild and could result in the destruction of all discourse: an attempt to revive . . . the bliss repressed by the stereotype. The opposition . . . is not necessarily between established and identifiable extremes (materialism and idealism, reformism and revolution, etc.); but it is *always and everywhere* between the *exception and the rule.* The rule is abuse; the exception is bliss. For instance, at certain times it is possible to support the *exception* of Mystics. Anything, rather than the rule (the generality, the stereotype, the ideolect, the language of consistency).[54]

Barthes's utopianism of reading, if I understand it correctly, strikes me as intriguingly close to Overbeck's emphasis on the eschatological dimension of the original Christian faith. Overbeck highlights the difference between a kind of ecstatic primary experience and the ordering, intellectualizing, and institutionalizing which supervene later as the experience enters history. Barthes tries to define a practice of reading which is not guided by or translatable into any of the instutitionalized codes of criticism and interpretation, neither the platitudes of the majority nor the austere theoretical discourses of small groups of intellectuals[55]—a practice of reading which is at once impersonal (that is, unrelated to our so-called personal identities) and, as he put it himself, "asocial."[56] Holding the positions they held, however, both men had to find themselves in conflict with the institutionalized roles they were called upon and agreed to play—Overbeck as a professor of theology, Barthes as a professor of literature.

And I too, as I approach the end of these reflections and enter my fourth decade of teaching, am no nearer a satisfactory understanding of my job as a critic and teacher of literature. Most of my career has been devoted either to interpretation of the kind Overbeck's critique of theology makes me uneasy about (my own first book, on Molière, is a particularly blatant case of it, and characteristically it has been more successful than anything else I have done) or to studies that are basically historical, including the study of literature as a social institution and a cultural system. On the whole, as a student and admirer of the Enlightenment, I resist the sacralization of literary texts, and I prefer to think that both interpretation and historical inquiry, together with the exchange of views and the openness to criticism that these entail, are valid social activities that promote human culture and communication, as well as responsible thinking, acting, and writing, even if it is impossible to overlook that in a society characterized as ours is by disgraceful social divisions and inequalities, by a discouraging degree of apparently necessary specialization, and by the enormous power of agencies of mental manipulation, there can be no question of literature's belonging to a genuine public sphere but only of its action in relatively small and privileged groups.[57]

In many respects, therefore, theology and interpretative criticism, including historically informed interpretative criticism, are for me acceptable ways of ordering and socializing experiences that would otherwise be incomprehensible, incommunicable, and of course immune to criticism and correction. At the same time, however, I have to admit that I occasionally wonder what our critical and interpretative activities have to do with the extraordinary, exhilarating, overwhelming experience that reading a work of literature sometimes *can* be. Are they in some way a necessary, if not sufficient, propaedeutic, like learning a code in order to gain access to texts written in it? Or are they completely independent of the experience, in fact sustained and promoted by—and in turn sustaining and promoting—their distance from experience? Do they perhaps work to defend us against the negativity, the challenge to our pieties and assurances, that literature has come to represent for many of the most concerned and thoughtful critics of our time? I have to confess that I am often troubled by that thought. At the same time, I still entertain the ideal of a culture, such as the Enlightenment at least adumbrated, in which all will be participants and in which the negative power of literature will function not as a criticism of "culture" in general but of the inhuman aspects of culture. I would rather conclude, therefore, on a briskly witty affirmation, from the century of Figaro, of the social character of art and the necessity of interpretation and communication. In a fable written in the manner of La Fontaine and entitled *Le Conte du violon*, Frederick the Great tells of a virtuoso violinist, aptly named Vacarmini, who after a particularly successful concert is asked by a member of the audience to perform on three

strings, then two, then one—at which point the poor musician can produce
only "a common tune"—and finally on none at all, with the predictable
result. The moral of the little tale is summarized as follows by Frederick:

> Par ce conte, s'il peut vous plaire,
> Apprenez, chers concitoyens,
> Que, malgré tout le savoir faire,
> L'art reste court sans les moyens.

Loosely translated:

> Fellow citizens dear, from this tale
> You will, if it please you, conclude
> That talent's of little avail.
> Without instruments, art remains rude.

[1988]

PART TWO

Literature of History

4

Augustin Thierry and Liberal Historiography

The ways of providence are strange: God cannot have denied any
of his peoples the happiness of the Golden Age; yet no grateful
memory of these happy times survives among subsequent generations. Only the terrors of defeat and disaster force themselves
eternally on the memory. Italy's oldest memories represent the
death agonies of two once mighty nations, one of which subjugated
the other, only to go under itself, along with its victim, to a third,
established on the ruins of both, which it buried beneath it, as the
surface of our globe today rests on earlier creations.

> —J. J. Bachofen,
> *Die ältesten Völkerbewegungen*

Each paragraph of the Constitution contains in itself its own antithesis, its own Upper and Lower House, namely liberty in the
text, the suspension of liberty in the marginal gloss.

> —Karl Marx,
> *Eighteenth Brumaire of Louis Napoleon*

THE TRADITION of academic historiography has been well entrenched
since Ranke, but it has often been questioned, and it was not always dominant.
Ranke's own pupil Sybel declared that he was "four sevenths politician
and three sevenths professor." The Romantic school of French historians,
who renewed the writing of history in the early nineteenth century, were
thoroughly committed politically and openly active in contemporary politics.[1] After the achievement of the school's political goals in 1830, Augustin
Thierry repudiated his earlier use of history as a weapon in political struggles; but he still believed, in common with friends and fellow-historians
such as Carrel and Mignet, that it was impossible to write history except
from contemporary experience and concerns, since the historian's insights
into the past rested on his experience, and since it was his present concerns
that told him what questions to ask the past. The more conservative Thierry
of the years after 1830 wanted to distinguish between use and abuse, but

there was no question that history might be a disinterested search for truth, a purely academic matter. As a search for truth, it was itself, for Thierry, as for the great historians of the Enlightenment, a commitment. The outstanding French Romantic historian was in his day a noted political liberal, and an energetic and combative polemicist in the liberal cause. He was one of the founding contributors to the *Censeur européen,* a leading organ of the liberal opposition during the Bourbon Restoration, and to the *Courrier français,* with which the *Censeur* subsequently merged; and he was associated, from its founding in 1824, with the *Globe,* which the moderate opposition of his friends Royer-Collard, Barante, and Guizot found too advanced.[2] Much of his historical writing appeared in the form of articles and reviews in the *Censeur* or the *Courrier,* notably the essays subsequently collected and published as *Lettres sur l'histoire de France* and *Dix Ans d'études historiques.* Many of these pieces were polemical in intent and were so understood by those in authority.

All of Thierry's colleagues and collaborators, moreover—Mignet, Guizot, Thiers, Barante, and his own younger brother Amédée—were, like him, both writers of history and political activists.[3] Guizot and Thiers, indeed, are remembered primarily as statesmen: Barante and Amédée Thierry also had successful political careers. Though less successful than they, Augustin Thierry was always politically engaged. He started out as the secretary and collaborator of Saint-Simon, and in the mid-1820s he in turn took on as his own secretary Armand Carrel, who was to be a hero of the Republican liberals of 1830 and a future editor of the *National.*[4] In the elections of 1817 he campaigned for prominent liberal candidates—La Fayette, Chaptal, Lasteyrie, the bankers Lafitte, Casimir-Périer, and Delessert. "Here is the principle that should guide us in the forthcoming elections," he declared: "at the present time, when our primary interest is the activity of industry, it is vital for us that we be represented by men of industry."[5] He gave his full support to the Revolution of 1830 and to the July Monarchy, and he expected and finally received both recognition and recompense from it.[6] In France and abroad he was generally regarded as one of the leading figures of political liberalism. In Moscow, in the 1830s, he was being read avidly by the young Alexander Herzen, along with Michelet, Jean-Baptiste Say, and Guizot; and Herzen later translated the first of the *Récits des temps mérovingiens* into Russian for the *Otechestvennye zapiski (Annals of the Fatherland),* a journal of liberal leanings to which he had been introduced by Belinski. In Italy, Thierry's work was studied and admired by Manzoni; and in 1844, after the death of his wife and of his closest friend, the *idéologue* Fauriel, he went to live for a while with another old friend, the romantic Italian patriot, publicist, historian, and revolutionary Cristina Trivulzio, Princess Belgiojoso, the patroness of all the champions of freedom and all the exiled patriots of Europe—Bellini, Rossini, Chopin, Liszt, Heine, Michelet, Mignet, Musset, George Sand.

I propose to argue that the premises and ideals—and contradictions—of liberalism in early nineteenth-century France inform every aspect of Thierry's work: his philosophy of history, his idea of the function of historiography, the dominant themes of his work, and, most directly, the problems of composition he encountered as a writer of history.

Liberal Politics and The Reform of Historiography

Thierry never ceased to proclaim the political impulse behind his historical activity. Present political experience, he held, is the indispensable condition of any coherent view of the past, of anything that is to go beyond a mere counting out of years and events; and conversely, historical culture, the creation by the historian of a people's self-awareness, is one of the most effective of political acts. In the 1834 Preface to *Dix Ans d'études* he tells that when he began contributing in 1817 to the *Censeur européen*, "the most serious and at the same time the most theoretically adventurous of the liberal publications of the period," his historical writings "bore the imprint . . . of the political opinions that I then professed with passionate conviction: dislike of military regimes coupled with hatred of aristocratic pretentions, but without any specifically revolutionary tendency. I was full of enthusiastic aspirations toward a future—I knew not quite which—toward a freedom which, if I could find a formula to define it, might be described as: *any kind of government that would offer the greatest possible number of guarantees for the individual with the least possible amount of administrative action.*" The essays of 1817–1819 are indeed full of specific contemporary parallels. The one on the English Revolution of 1688, for instance, with a clear reference to Napoleon, warns against false revolutions that are manipulated from above, and ends on an oratorical exhortation to the reader to combat "every tyranny, in old or new guise, in ancient or modern times."[7] Later, in 1836, after the triumph of liberalism, and in the midst of threats from the left as well as from the right, Thierry became critical of what he called "my passion for politics and my inexperience in history"; and he compared his earlier writings with those of the eighteenth-century philosophical historians, who wrote "with the aim of abstracting from the historical account of events a body of proofs and systematic arguments, of providing a summary demonstration, and not a detailed narrative."[8] But if he repudiated the crudeness with which he had treated history as "an arsenal of new weapons to be used in the polemic I was engaged in against the revolutionary tendencies of the government," he did not repudiate his political involvement or question its significance for his work as a historian. When he had already begun to reflect on his method of writing history, he was caught up, he tells, in the violent agitation of the years 1821 and 1822—"from which I neither could nor wished to stand aside . . . The coup d'état of the double vote, the prelude to the great coup d'état against the Charter that was attempted ten years later, had provoked the least fanatical to extra-legal resistance."[9] Articles appeared in the *Censeur* proclaiming that any modification of the electoral law would justify revolutionary resistance.[10] The full flowering of the historical school, according to Thierry, was the direct outcome of the diversion of this revolutionary fervor from direct action into thinking and writing. It inspired his own work as well as that of his friends Barante, Guizot, Thiers, and Mignet. "We soon realized the futility of our efforts to bring about events that were not yet ripe; but, remarkably enough, that revolutionary effervescence was followed almost immediately by an outstanding movement in serious historical studies."[11] "Ecrivez, Messieurs, faites des livres," Royer-Collard is supposed to have said after the fall of the Decazes ministry; "il n'y a pas autre chose à faire en ce moment" ("Write, gentlemen, publish books; there is nothing else we can do at this point").[12]

The political activity of the liberals of 1820 was thus displaced and invested in the writing of history. The liberals were in any case intensely concerned with the question of national education and recognized that it was intimately linked to the question of liberty and political power.[13] As early as 1817, in the long essay he wrote for the first volume of Saint-Simon's *L'Industrie,* Thierry had described himself as addressing the nation, public opinion, which was now, he contended, an active force. The task of the writer who wanted to be useful was no longer, as it had been in the past, "to advise the leaders of the peoples how they should lead the peoples but to advise the peoples themselves what their conduct should be."[14] In the same text Thierry argued that those who sought to consolidate or to create a new society must hold up new models for men to follow. Denouncing ancient heroism, he pointed to Venice and England, which paid mercenaries to fight their wars for them.[15] Military glory and adventurism were thus rejected, but the liberal bourgeoisie still needed heroism on the home front in its struggle with the remnants of the old privileged classes. An important task of the politically committed historian was therefore to provide appropriate "domestic examples" of heroism. "Despite their quarrels, the noblemen of all lands held themselves to be brothers, and the gentleman was, above all, of the nation of gentlemen," Thierry wrote in the *Censeur* in 1820.

> We, on our part, as a man of freedom, are likewise, above all, of the nation of free men; and those who, far from our land, are engaged in the struggle for independence, as well as those who, far from our land, have already died for it, are our brothers and our heroes. The life of Colonel Hutchinson, the English patriot of 1640, belongs therefore to us as well as to England. . . . His Memoirs, which have lain long unknown, must have the same value in our eyes that the discovery of some legend recounting the virtues and courage of a martyr in far-off lands might have had for the early Christians.[16]

Subsequently, in the *Histoire de la conquête de l' Angleterre* (1825), his most popular work, Thierry celebrated the heroes of the Saxon resistance to the Norman overlords:[17] "I wanted the memories of popular courage, of bourgeois energy and liberty, to be collected with care and respect. In short, with the help of science joined to patriotism, I wanted our old chronicles to yield up stories capable of touching the vital fibres of the people."[18] Thierry's stories of "outlaws" in the *Conquête* and of rebels in the later *Essai sur l'histoire de la formation et des progrès du tiers-état* were thus intended as models of feeling and of action, and were written in the same spirit as Michelet subsequently wrote his accounts of the heroes and heroines of his *Légendes démocratiques du Nord*. History, Michelet would insist, is not only the record of the past; it makes the future. Thierry would not have argued with this: "We are constantly being told to model ourselves on our forefathers. Why don't we follow this advice! Our forefathers were the artisans who established the communes of the Middle Ages and who first conceived freedom as we understand it today."[19] Because he believed in the power of history, Thierry was concerned with the teaching of history in schools, and he proposed that history textbooks be reviewed carefully, "for if this kind of work is less original than other kinds, it exercises wider influence."[20] Eighteenth-century *philosophie,* he contended in another article, was now reaping the harvest of its exclusiveness, for the noblemen who had been the disciples of the *philosophes* had turned against their teachers and become the most vehement enemies of Enlightenment. Eighteenth-century *philosophie* "would have been immeasurably greater if it had been popular." The philosophy Thierry wanted for the young men of his own day was to be popular and was to appeal to the heart as well as the mind.[21]

Thierry's celebration of the heroes of old sometimes assumed an almost religious aspect. The second of the three letters on the *Commune* of Laon in the *Lettres sur l'histoire de France* of 1827 closes with the persona of the narrator addressing the persona of the reader on the significance of the tale that has just been told.

> I wonder whether you share my feelings as I transcribe here the obscure names of those outlaws of the twelfth century. I cannot help rereading them and saying them over out loud, as if they might disclose to me the secret of what, seven hundred years ago, was felt and longed for by those who bore them. A burning passion for justice, and the conviction that they were worth more than fate had granted them had dragged these men from their trades and their crafts, from the quiet life—but without dignity— that obedient serfs could lead under the protection of their lords.[22]

Repeating the names of the heroes of old, Thierry's narrator seems to want to appropriate for himself and his reader something of their spirit or *mana*.

History writing for Thierry was thus inseparable from political action. The ideological struggle, the struggle for the minds of men, was an essential part of politics, and it had always been so. All history, as Thierry saw it, was ideology, whether consciously so written or not, and had always been politically significant. The memory of popular virtues, he never ceased to complain, "shines but dimly in the minds of Frenchmen, because history, which should have transmitted them, was in the hands of the enemies of our fathers."[23] The reform of historiography was not, therefore, an academic matter but a political one, which Thierry saw as his contribution to the revolutions of his own day. The rhetoric he uses in describing his work is that of political activism:

> The vocation I embraced . . . with all the ardor of youth was not that of casting a solitary light on some little-known corner of the Middle Ages but of planting for nineteenth-century France the standard of historiographical reform. Reform of the study of history, reform of the way history is written, war on the writers without learning who failed to see, and on the writers without imagination who failed to depict; war on Mézeray, on Velly, on their continuators and disciples; war on the most acclaimed writ-

ers of the philosophical school, because of their calculated dryness and their disdainful ignorance of our national origins.[24]

Thierry's view of the ideological function of historiography led him to see the history of historiography as itself a significant part of history, and he explored the topic more vigorously than had any French historian before him. Taken together, the extensive historiographical essays in the *Lettres sur l'histoire de France* (1827), in *Dix Ans d'études historiques* (1834), and in the *Considérations sur l'histoire de France* (1840) constitute an original critical history of historiography in France. Again, Thierry's intent in writing these works was not academic. He wanted to unmask the ideological significance of the concepts and categories, of the very language that the leading historians of France had used, as if they were "natural" and could be taken for granted. Even the form history is written in is determined, he claimed, by the ideology it serves.[25]

History, according to Thierry, has not, in the past, been a direct reflection of past reality, but a construction of the historian: "We must beware of history. Only too often, instead of recounting naïvely what he sees before his eyes, the historian presents what he imagines, substitutes ideas for facts, or distorts the facts. . . . It is possible to prove anything with facts, with systems and allusions; often history is a continuous lie."[26]

The task of the new history is to unmask these systems of lies, to reveal the true motives and political ambitions behind laws and acts that are usually discussed from the point of view of pure constitutional history. "The new school that has just begun to regenerate historical studies in France has set out, in the first place, to counter abstraction in historical matters. This school has struck a mortal blow at the monarchical version of the History of France. We believe it is destined to carry out an equally vigorous assault on the constitutional version of the history of England."[27] Thierry praised his friend Abel Villemain, one of the most celebrated and influential liberal teachers and writers of the Restoration, for having seen through the ideological curtains that had been draped over the Levellers. "We are indebted to him for having been the first to observe that the odious epithets . . . which the most philosophical historians have applied to the party of the Levellers are products of the mind of Cromwell. . . . It is from his mouth that these words have passed into history. Mr. Villemain has also discovered that the terms 'madmen' and 'fanatics' with which Hume and Voltaire unhesitatingly tarnish the most venerable of patriots are the invention of General Monk, who was the first to apply them and who made them fashionable in the service of the Stuart Restoration."[28]

Thierry himself argued that the figure of Cromwell projected by French historians is a creation of the ancien régime, which supported myths of power wherever they were found.

> At the very time that the Englishman Sidney, each day of his life, was calling Cromwell a tyrant . . . the French minister Mazarin was hailing him as the genius of the age and the French King Louis XIV bared his head when he spoke to his ambassadors. Theirs, no doubt, are the estimable opinions on which our own have been based. The judgment of Sidney has been ousted by that of these great authorities. What indeed does a 'factious rebel' count for against two 'statesmen'! . . . The prestige that attaches to the name of Cromwell in the minds of people who know little of him but his name is in large measure the work of men of power and of those writers who serve power.[29]

The whole of written history reflects the power that commanded it. It is a history of great men, and the people are presented in it as mere material for the accomplishment of their designs. "With what singular obstinacy historians refuse to attribute any spontaneity, any power of conception to the mass of men. If an entire people emigrates and makes a new home for itself, the poets and annalists would have us believe that it did so because some hero, in order to illustrate his name, took it into his head to found an empire."[30] In the same way, many cases of popular resistance to an invader or oppressor have been attributed by historians to the designs of individuals.[31] Thierry never wearies of debunking the "notables" of history. Charles Martel appears in his writing as a brigand;[32] Charlemagne is presented as a barbarian chief named Karl, an adventurer, whose passage through history is as violent and as transitory as that of all similar adventurers down to Bonaparte.[33] In place of the heroes of power and repression, Thierry discovers the heroes of freedom. The last remnants of the Saxon resistance to William the Conqueror "are called brigands by the historians who favor the conquest, and these historians treat them as arming themselves maliciously and without provocation against a legitimate social order." In the songs of the people, however, the brigands are heroes.[34]

The form of history, as well as its heroes, is marked by the ideology of power. According to Thierry, the humanist manner of writing history is more appropriate than that of the old chronicles to celebrate the notable exploits and the government of princes. Du Haillan, for instance, considered the old chronicles "insufficient, silly, and confused," and he substituted for them the model of "ancient history touched up by the Italians and enriched by them with a wealth of politico-diplomatic reflections.

Holding that history must deal exclusively with affairs of State, he always places in the forefront of these affairs diplomatic negotiations, treaties and alliances. . . . The local color and the picturesque details, in which [Ville-hardouin, Joinville, and Froissart] are so rich and which appeal so strongly to us today, are seen by Du Haillan as a frippery unworthy of history, which, as he himself puts it, *should deal only with affairs of state.*"[35]

As much as the form of history writing, the periodization of the past, the very temporal categories used by the historian, have been ideologically determined and have served the myth of the continuous possession of power by the authorities that possessed it at the time of writing. The history of France is divided and marked by successive reigns; but, whereas the monks who first gave it this form in deference to their benefactors did not attempt to present it as more than a simple succession of different Frankish rulers, the moderns have made it over into the continuous, unbroken line of succession of a single family, or, at most, of two or three families. "The most scrupulous of our historians distinguishes three royal dynasties; but that is the ultimate limit, the pillars of Hercules beyond which no one dares go." In place of the questionable genealogies of the first two races of kings, Thierry called for the genealogy of the nation and claimed that, if historians were to establish such a genealogy, the traditional periodization of French history would be fundamentally modified.[36]

Above all, the political categories used by historians have often been mystifications in the service of established power. Terms that evoke contemporary political institutions or power relations are applied without warning by the historian to earlier and quite different situations, so that the reader imagines that these institutions and relations are natural and eternal. The words *rex* and *dux,* for instance, translated as *roi* and *duc,* acquire the modern meaning of those terms. "A king of the Franks is a chief of the Franks. But when one calls him King of France, what comes to mind is a different idea, that of a more modern and incomparably more complex political situation."[37]

The French "monarchy" did not enjoy fourteen centuries of history down to 1789. What the monarchy was varied constantly.[38] In England, the term "parliament" has had a similar fortune, according to Thierry.[39] The very names of countries can lead to confusions. It is not possible to talk of France at the time of Clovis, since what we now understand by France did not then exist.[40] Likewise, when Hume writes of a "king" of "England" at the end of the twelfth century, he ought to tell the reader what a king was at that time and what he is to understand by England. "By studying the reality of the mass of the population and revealing conflicting interests, two peoples locked in conflict, Sir Walter Scott," says

Thierry, "is the truer historian."[41] Though he later modified his views,[42] the young Thierry denounced the notion that nations are defined by "natural frontiers." A nation, according to the briskly realistic *fils adoptif de Henri de Saint-Simon,* is a society with a common goal and common interests. Geographic determinations—the boundaries of oceans, rivers, and mountain ranges—are superficial. Even language is irrelevant.[43] The use of the term *nation* to designate a society that is fundamentally divided in its interests is always a mystification. Thus the English nation developed through the consciousness of their common interests that the conquest produced in the conquered. "For it should not be imagined that before that time there was an English nation. There was a nation encamped on the land of England, a nation of foreigners [that is, a group united by their common interest as plunderers]; the natives, however, had nothing in common with each other but their misery."[44] Charles I's justification of the stamp tax on the ground that it was necessary to defend the honor and security of the nation is judged derisible: "The honor of the nation! the security of the nation! What did these terms mean when they were addressed to *subjects?* That it was to their advantage that naval forces should prevent the occupier from being chased out of his possessions and should help him, on the contrary, to win further possessions overseas? The King's *subjects* had no need of ponderous reflection to sense that this interest could well concern the nation of the conquerors, but that it had nothing to do with them. Their national security was to see that they were no longer exploited."[45]

The political significance Thierry gave to the new school of historiography indicates that his celebrated orthographic reform of proper names was more than a search for picturesque effect, a taste for *couleur locale* and exoticism. In the sixth of the *Lettres sur l'histoire de France* (1827), he proposed that Chilperic be written Hilpe-rik—"helpful or strong," he explained in a note—and Dagobert be written Daghe-berht—"a shining warrior." (Subsequent editions of the *Lettres* contained an appendix, in which Thierry listed, after "le savant Grimm," the meanings of the principal Frankish names.) The context of these proposals is an attempt to demonstrate that the early kings were conquering foreign chiefs on the soil of France and were in no way comparable to the seventeenth- or eighteenth-century kings of France. Orthographic reform was thus intended first and foremost as a defamiliarizing device. Replying in the 1840s to an article in the *Revue de Paris* in which Charles Nodier took him to task for his orthographic innovations, Thierry recalled that in varying degrees Fauchet, du Tillet, Belleforest, Scipion Dupleix, and even Mézeray had all attempted to restore a Germanic orthography to the names of the early Frankish leaders. "After Mézeray, unfortunately, these scruples of transcription and interpretation ceased to be felt by French historians. Daniel, Velly and Anquetil made no effort to warn the reader against the illusion produced by the fact that the names commonly given to persons having lived under the first or second race of kings are formally indistinguishable from those of modern French."[46] And against Nodier's accusations of barbarism and affectation in the terminology of modern science, philology, and history, the former secretary of Saint-Simon defended the absolute propriety both of scientific nomenclatures ("it is possible to speak in very good French of centimeters, liters or decaliters no less than of yards, pints, halfpints and bushels") and of his own orthographies: "The nomenclature usually employed for the early period of French history introduces something suspect into the mind which it is well to expel by a change of name or of orthography."[47] Voltaire himself, the greatest French neoclassical historian, had supported the principle of orthographic reform and had "extended [it] to everything that is alien to us because of difference of language or remoteness in space or time." *Kenterbury which we call Cantorbéry,* Thierry quotes Voltaire as having written in the *Essai sur les Moeurs.*[48] Thierry himself went further: "The monks betook themselves to the capital city, which was called the city of the men of Kent; in Saxon: Kent-ware-byrig."[49] Likewise Alfred appears in his work as Elfred. The Norman conquerors on their side get their Norman names back in place of the English spellings which disguise the clash of races. The aim is always to restore "to each of the periods covered by my narrative its own particular appearance, its original characteristics and, if I may say so, its full reality."[50]

Thierry's new history was thus intended to explode all the stereotypes of the old "history of France as we have all read and learned it."[51] It demanded that the historian no longer repeat the old stories in a new guise, like the retelling of a folktale,[52] but that he do his own research, that he seek out and study new sources and that he ask new questions. "The history of France as modern writers have given it to us is not the true history of our country, its national history, its popular history. . . . The whole system of our national history revolves around no more than a small number of princely families. . . . Accustomed from childhood to this historical pattern, we not only are not shocked by it, we do not even imagine that another could be devised. We ask of our writers only that they add as many good maxims and ornaments of style as they can." But "a true history of France should relate the destinies of the entire French nation: its hero would be the whole nation."[53]

About this history the historiographical sources, traditionally in the service of power, are most often silent. Trying to tell the story of Saxon resistance to the Conqueror, Thierry notes, he had no sources other than the occasional malevolent comments of the Norman chroniclers.[54] Nevertheless, it is what Michelet was later, in a famous passage, to call "les silences de l'histoire" that already interested Thierry. "The plan of this essay," he says of his *Formation et progrès du tiers état,* "is to pass quickly over the points where history speaks and to tarry over those where she is silent."[55] As the explorer of an uncharted territory, the historian must himself constitute the object of his knowledge. He cannot accept what has been handed down to him as inevitable or even appropriate, and the new questions he has to ask require an altered conception of his activity.

THE VALUE of history for the historian of the Enlightenment had lain not so much in the historical record itself as in the comments and reflections of the historian.[56] History writing had been a communication of one detached observer of the historical record with another. Both had discovered harmony and coherence not in the historical record itself but in the aesthetic order that the writer had succeeded in imparting to the record and in the rational order implied by his commentary, by the principles and maxims that explained and were at the same time confirmed by the spectacle of history.

Since his aim was to rewrite history, to write not a new or better commentary on the traditional historical account but a different history, the liberal historian of the Restoration could not afford to separate the literary and scholarly aspects of historiography, as the neoclassical historian had nearly always done. To probe the silences of history, he had to address himself directly to the sources, to discover new ones, and to force new meanings out of old ones. He could no longer leave historical scholarship to laborious Benedictines. To constitute his object, he had to do his own digging in the bedrock of history.

From the point of view of subsequent scholarship, Thierry's use of sources can, of course, be faulted. Both in principle and in practice, however, he accepted that historical scholarship and historical thought and writing are interdependent.[57] The *Tiers Etat,* for instance, was conceived as an introduction to the *Recueil des monuments inédits de l'histoire du tiers état,* on which he was appointed to work by Guizot in 1836, and which was to form part of a projected *Collection de documents inédits sur l'histoire de France.* This collection went far beyond the chronicle sources that Thierry had largely relied on in his early writings.[58]

In addition to erudition and critical judgment, the historian needed imagination, according to Thierry, for he had to recover the meanings of old documents, to discern what had been veiled to his predecessors. Describing in the *Conquête* the effort of imagination he required of the reader, he gave an account of what he asked of himself—to discover a reality "beneath titles and formulae which, if they are considered abstractly, have only a vague and indefinite meaning. The task is to find a way across the distance of centuries to men, to represent them before us alive, and acting upon the country in which even the dust of their bones could not be found today. . . . These men have been dead for fully seven hundred years, their hearts stopped beating with pride or anguish seven hundred years ago; but what is that to the imagination? For the imagination there is no past, and the future itself is of the present."[59] In the preface to *Dix Ans* he describes how he himself studied innumerable folio pages from which he might extract "a phrase, sometimes a mere word, out of a thousand." "My eyes acquired a surprising faculty that I cannot account for—that of reading, in some sort, by intuition, and of lighting almost immediately on the passage that was to interest me." It was, he declared, "a sort of ecstasy that absorbed me internally."[60] The power of effacing oneself totally before the object of study, of opening oneself to it and yet never being so absorbed by it that understanding is abandoned, is seen by Thierry as the hallmark of the great historian. Thus Sir Walter Scott appeared to him as "the greatest master of historical *divination* there has ever been." Scott, he had already observed in an earlier text, "seems to have for the past that *second sight* which in the ages of ignorance certain men attributed to themselves with respect to the future." "There is more true history in his novels of England and Scotland than in many compilations that still go by the name of histories."[61] Thierry's own physical blindness later provided an effective foil for his theory of the imagination. When he went on a journey to the south of France with Fauriel in 1825, he tells in the preface to the 1834 edition of *Dix Ans,* he had barely enough sight left to get about, but "before buildings or ruins whose date and style we wanted to establish, a mysterious internal sense came to the help of my eyes. Animated by what I would willingly call the passion of history, I saw further and more clearly."[62]

The faculty of imagination, which Thierry considers so important to the historian, is rooted in the historian's experience. It is because he himself was "born a commoner" that he sympathizes with and understands the commoners of old, his "forefathers," as well as those of other lands. His historical vision is grounded in this personal experience—"the love of men as men, irrespective of their renown or social condition."[63] Without it, according to Thierry, a historian cannot discern the internal coherence of history.[64] More specifically, the experience of the Revolution has made it possible to understand the great struggles by which the medieval communes tried to free themselves from their secular and ecclesiastical overlords. "The events of the last fifty years have taught us to understand the revolutions of the Middle Ages; to discern the fundamental character of things beneath the letter of the chronicles; to extract from the writings of the Benedictines what those erudite men never saw."[65] Likewise, to those who have lived through the collapse of the Napoleonic empire the dismemberment of Charlemagne's is entirely understandable, whereas during the ancien régime no one had been able to understand it.[66] The historian's participation in the political struggles of his own time is itself an experience that provides him with valuable insights. "If [political passion] closes off our understanding in some respects, it opens and stimulates it in others; it suggests insights, divinations, sometimes even leaps of genius to which disinterested scholarship and a pure zealous love of truth would not have led."[67] At times the conception of the historian as himself a participant in the action he is describing and of his own historical nature as both the condition and the limit of his understanding of the past—a conception reminiscent of Vico—seems to lead to historical relativism. "Whatever intellectual superiority one may have, one cannot go beyond the horizon of one's own century, and each new age provides history with new points of view and a particular form."[68] As we shall see, however, it is most likely that for Thierry, as for the eighteenth-century *philosophes* before him, relativism applied only to the past. His own age, he believed, was on the threshold of achieving a truly rational society from which all marks of oppression, conquest, and division would be removed. The vision of the historian in such an age would no longer be partial, but absolutely true and universal.

The Value of Continuity:
The Mediating Role of the Bourgeoisie

The Enlightenment historian's aim had been to establish or confirm an ideal community of like-minded, detached observers of the historical scene, united in their allegiance to reason and their contempt for all mere positive fact. The Restoration historian, however, aimed to win the practical support of a community that had tasted political power and that still had access to it in some measure. He could not, therefore, use the distancing techniques of his Enlightenment predecessor. His writing had to achieve the involvement of the reader in the story that was being recounted and his assent to the political values of the narrator. The narrator no longer presented himself, consequently, as a detached commentator, but as the active champion and apologist of his hero. Similarly, reason and order were no longer located in the mind, coolly observing and judging the welter of events, but were discovered in the events themselves by a mind that was in profound sympathy with them and had a privileged insight into them. The narrator no longer carefully preserved the reader's detachment and freedom—the condition of the kind of community the Enlightenment historian proposed to create—by distinguishing narrative from description and commentary, but tried to convey the image of the whole in the account of each part, so that the reader would be enveloped, as it were, in the seamless fabric of the past. "I believe history should no more paint a picture of the different ages by means of dissertations distinct from the main body of the narrative than it should represent characters by means of portraits distinct from the main body of the narrative," Thierry writes.

> Historical personages and even historical ages should come on stage, as it were, in the narrative. They should appear, so to speak, fully alive in it, and the reader should not have to leaf through a hundred or more pages to find out what their true character was. The method of writing history that tends to isolate facts from that which gives them their color and their individual physiognomy is a false art, and it is not possible for an historian first to narrate well without depicting, then to depict well without narrating. Those who have adopted this method have almost invariably subordinated historical narrative, which is the essential part of history, to commentaries that follow up and are supposed to provide the key to the narrative.

In the reader's mind, according to Thierry, the commentary remains distinct from the narrative and so the entire work is marked by a fatal discontinuity, being a conglomerate of two distinct works, one of history, the other of philosophy. "The former is ordinarily a mere repetition of the least defective of already existing narratives," and the historian reserves all his talent for the latter. Thus Hume's *History of England* is basically that of Rapin-Thoyras, to which have been added original and complete treatises of politics, archaeology, and economics, together with various maxims and reflections.[69] Thierry makes clear here that renewal of the rhetoric of history requires a reevaluation of the roles of erudition and imagination. The historian must acquaint himself directly with the sources, so that with the help of his imagination he can distinguish and select the details—events, gestures, objects—that will be most "characteristic" of the whole and produce an image of it in the reader's mind.

Eighteenth-century historiography, as Thierry sees it, maintains a separation between the syntagmatic ordering of events—the narrative chain in which A follows upon B, the world of individual happenings—and the paradigmatic ordering that establishes relations among elements widely separated on the syntagmatic chain—the world of reason. It accepts the former from tradition and expends all its ingenuity on the latter, arranging the material, for the most part, in terms of universal laws and the particular events that confirm and exemplify them. The immense space between laws and events reflects that between the mind of the narrator or reader and the "chaos," as Voltaire called it, of the particular incidents he finds himself faced with, between thought and world, reason and history. The historiography Thierry called for was one in which the syntagmatic ordering of events and the paradigmatic ordering that establishes relations among items distant from each other on the syntagmatic chain would be functions of one and the same operation. Incidents are selected, in this historiography, not only because they can be related syntagmatically to a preceding and a succeeding incident, but because they can be related paradigmatically, in the sense that each can be thought of as "characteristic" of the whole and hence related—"organically" related—to all the others as parts of the larger whole whose pattern is inscribed in miniature in each of them. Thierry describes going on long walks with Fauriel at the time when he was working on the *Conquête* and telling him "in inexhaustible abundance the minutest detail of chronicles and legends, everything that brought my victors and vanquished of the eleventh century to life for me. . . . Now it was a Saxon bishop expelled from his see because he knew no French; now a group of monks whose charters were torn up, as invalid, because they were in the Saxon tongue; now it was an accused person condemned by his Norman judges, who had refused him a hearing because he spoke only English; now a family dispossessed by the Conquerors and receiving as charity from them a tiny piece of its own heritage—incidents that are of slight significance in themselves, but from which I could derive the vivid tincture of reality which, if my powers of writing did not fail me, was to color the ensemble of the picture."[70]

CONTINUITY, for Thierry, is always privileged, a source of justification. If history according to kings and dynasties is shown to be discontinuous, then writing the "true history" of France, "the national history, the popular history,"[71] meant revealing a continuity that traditional historians had shrouded in silence. Thierry had read Voltaire carefully, and he must have noted with approval the passage in the *Essai sur les Moeurs* (chap. 81) where Voltaire describes the artisans and merchants of the Middle Ages as "des fourmis qui se creusent des habitations en silence, tandis que les aigles et les vautours se dévorent" ("ants that silently dig living quarters for themselves, while the eagles and the vultures overhead devour each other"). It was this silent story that Thierry wanted to tell and that he presented as the deep and continuous undercurrent of French history, in comparison with which the stories of royal dynasties and princely families—the stories historians have traditionally told—appear as ripples and eddies on the surface. Since the periodization of history that is based on the genealogies of rulers was thereby rejected as inessential, the founding of a royal dynasty could no longer be taken as a beginning point of historical narrative. French history could not be made to begin with the legendary Pharamond. For Thierry the history of France was continuous with that of ancient Gaul: "We are slaves whose freedom dates from yesterday and our memory has long recalled to us only the families and actions of our masters. It is hardly thirty years since we came to the realization that our fathers were the nation. We have admired everything, learned everything, except who they were and what they did. We are patriots, and we still leave in undisturbed oblivion those who, for fourteen centuries, cultivated the soil of our country through all the ravages to which it has been subject at the hands of others: before France, there was Gaul."[72] National history, as Thierry sees it, implies the restoration or preservation of a continuity that some outside force, some invader, some conqueror has tried to conceal or to deny by stifling the memory of it in the minds of the conquered. Thus the national history of France has to be discovered underneath the history which the Frankish conquerors have superimposed on it. The function of Irish national poetry and of the widespread national cult of the past is to preserve a continuity of manners and traditions against the efforts of the conqueror to destroy it. To this end "the bards and minstrels of Erin have become the archivists of their land." Similarly, Cedric in Scott's *Ivanhoe* "constantly gazes backward, beyond that fatal day at Hastings, on which England was laid open to the Norman invaders and to slavery." In contrast with Scott, Robertson is chided for having given the impression that "there is no history of Scotland, or even a Scottish nation, before the fourteenth century"[73]—that is, before the establishment of the Stuarts on the throne. The history of kingdoms, in short, is indeed discontinuous, but the people has everywhere a continuous history.

By demonstrating a continued existence of the nation, the historian identifies it, brings it to consciousness of itself, and thus, in some respects, invents it or delivers it. Discontinuities keep popping up, however, confounding the historian's best efforts, and presenting him with difficult and embarrassing problems. In a candid passage of the Preface to his study of the *Tiers Etat* (1853), Thierry recounts how "the catastrophe of February, 1848, burst suddenly upon us." "I have felt the result of it in two ways," he explains, "as a citizen and also as an historian. By this new revolution, filled with the same spirit and marked by the same threatening appearances as the worst times of the first, the history of France seemed to be thrust into as much disorder as France herself. I suspended my work from a feeling of despondency that is easily understandable."[74]

What the Revolution of 1848 appeared to confirm was what, in the very same Preface, Thierry vehemently denied—the disunity of the *tiers* or third estate. The unity of the *tiers,* as well as its continuous history as a unity, was the cornerstone both of Thierry's political ideology and of his history. The history of the nation, he declared, is the history of the *tiers,* and he quoted with approval the famous definition of Siéyès: "What is the *tiers état?* Everything." "The whole nation with the exception of the nobility and the clergy," he added himself.[75] Thierry's task was to account for the reality of division and violence in French history while maintaining the principle of the essential unity of the French nation. This he tried to do by arguing that the single united nation, which the historian discovers in the subterranean depths of history, had been plagued and tormented during almost all its existence by alien elements which introduced division and violence and with which historians have hitherto been almost exclusively concerned.

The theory of racial conflict as the key to the history of all the modern European nations is what is best remembered of Thierry's work. In fact, it was held in one form or another by nearly all the historians of the Restoration, and although Thierry mentions specifically his indebtedness to Hume and to Scott,[76] it is likely that he owed the best part of the theory to the "industrialist" philosophy of Jean-Baptiste Say and the editors of the *Censeur européen,* with their division of mankind into two races or classes, the industrious class that labors to be its own master and the conquerors who labor to be the masters of others,[77] and, above all, to the influential essay *De l'Esprit de conquête et de l'usurpation* (1814) by Benjamin Constant, whose name appears several times in the notes to Thierry's Saint-Simonian work *Des Nations.* Since violence, in the past, was the principal means of acquiring wealth, according to Constant, all past history is marked by conquest; and since production and exchange are recognized as the most effective means of acquiring wealth in modern societies, all future history will be marked by peace and harmony.

Thierry's racial history is quite remote, for the most part, from the "scientific" racism of later decades. There are a few passages where the concept of race is given a biological content, but there is no suggestion anywhere that biological factors might be historically determinant. The early writings show a tendency to center all conflict in racial difference itself, as, for instance, when "all the great revolutions either attempted or carried out in Scotland"—the dynastic wars, the wars of the nobles against the kings, the wars of religion, and the resistance to the Union with England—appear as rooted in an original "native hostility of Highlanders and Lowlanders";[78] or when the Civil War in England is represented as a reenactment of the old conflict of Saxons and Normans.[79] But even here racial conflict is not founded in biological difference; it is derived from the conquest theory and is always presented as a consequence of invasion, conquest, or harassment.[80] Social and economic conflict is the essential opposition that remains, Thierry believes, even after the original two racial groups—the autochthons and the aliens—have grown together and adopted the same language. And Thierry did recognize, quite early in his career, that the races fused, both in Gaul and in England.[81] By 1820 he was emphasizing the essentially political and social character of the conflict in France. As a liberal propagandist, he accepted the aristocratic challenge—notably from Montlosier—to play it out as a racial one, but he was fully conscious of the element of illusion and ideology in such a dramatization of contemporary conflicts.

> The physical mingling of the two original races may well have been accomplished, but the perpetual opposition of their spirit lives on to this day in two distinct portions of our fused population. . . . The present-day nobility is linked by its pretensions to the privileged men of the sixteenth century, and the latter claimed to be descended from the masters and owners of men of the thirteenth century, who in turn associated themselves with the Franks of Karl the Great, who can be traced back to the Sicambri of Chlodowig. *Only the natural filiation here can be contested.* The political descent is obvious . . . Let us claim the opposite descent. We are the sons of the men of the third estate.

What the liberal historian claims, in short, is not a racial identity between the ancient Gauls and the medieval serfs and burghers or the modern *tiers,* but a social and political one. In the Preface to the *Histoire de la conquête,* Thierry argues that the class struggles of his own day often continue earlier struggles of victorious and defeated peoples, but in the text he makes clear that "other revolutions, a great patriotic struggle entered upon in a completely new form, have substituted new political passions for these old resentments."[82] In France the old racial conflict devolved into an opposition of two ways of life. The conquerors became the nobility, the conquered native population became the bourgeois, the *classe industrieuse* of Saint-Simon, Constant, and Say. By the end of the eleventh century,

> the original distinction of races had disappeared, but it had been replaced in some sense by a difference of manners. The powers of the time bore the imprint of Germanic ways: disregard for the life and property of the weak, love of domination and of war, formed the distinctive character of the lords and the members of the higher clergy, while among the industrious inhabitants of the towns a predilection for work and a confused feeling of social equality survived, as it were, as the debris of the old civilization. It was in the national movement against the empire of the Frankish *Keisars* that the bourgeois or romance class ("classe bourgeoise ou romane")—for in the ninth century these two words were synonymous—drew forth the seeds of that energy which animated it two centuries later in a new revolution destined to drive all military and feudal power from the towns.[83]

Thus Thierry insisted increasingly on the political and economic content of the internal conflict that, for him, was characteristic of every historical society. Indeed, he came in the end to be critical of the theory of racial conflict that was based on the conquest theory. In the *Considérations* he writes that, as young men, he and Guizot had allowed themselves to be unduly influenced by this theory, which he now associates exclusively with Boulainviller and Montlosier. Montlosier had borrowed from his eighteenth-century predecessor, he said, "an eccentric phraseology, in which the idea of class and rank is replaced by the idea of different nations, and the vocabulary of the history of the migrations of peoples, of territorial invasions, and of conquests, is applied to the struggle of enemy or rival classes."[84] In such passages Thierry fully justifies Marx's subsequent description of him as "der père des 'Klassenkampfes' in der französischen Geschichtschreibung" ("the father of the 'class struggle' in French historiography").[85]

Yet it is by no means inconsequential that Thierry was attracted by the doctrine of racial conflict or that his theory of class conflict rested on the idea of a conquest, a foreign invasion. Division, for Thierry, is not original or essential. "Toute division est contre nature," the mother will protest in Michelet's Journal. For Thierry too, unity, the One, is natural and original; and division is always the result of an act of violence. History, however, is precisely the record of these acts of violence, the narrative of these "unnatural" divisions, without which, as Thierry recognizes, there would be nothing for the historian to tell. The One has no story. Thus the historian is always "le généalogiste du malheur," as Sismondi said of Thierry himself, and every historical narrative is the tale of an attack, a conquest, or an internal conflict that is the living trace of a conquest.[86] There is no history of the autochthons. Their time, their society, their consciousness are undifferentiated until invaders introduce differentiation and history into them.

It is not difficult to recognize in Thierry's thinking the same dominant pattern that shaped the thinking of Rousseau and that can doubtless be found throughout the intellectual tradition of which he was the heir. For Rousseau, man in the state of nature is whole and undivided, and the emergence of division—the result of an external calamity—is what marks the end of nature and the beginning of history. This state of division and conflict is finally to be transcended in turn by the realization of a rational (as opposed to a natural) unity, both within man and among men, in the community. Analogously, for Thierry, there appears to be an original state in which "natural" (that is, homogeneous or undifferentiated) peoples exist independently of each other and without contact.[87] Conquest and internal division mark the beginning of the period of historical development. This period is destined in turn, however, to be transcended by the new "industrialist" age, in which internally divided societies made up of mutually hostile natural peoples, one conquered and one conquering, one exploited and one exploiting, will be replaced by a concert of fully integrated, harmonious nations.

As Rousseau's state of nature was nowhere to be found on this earth, so Thierry's natural, homogeneous people constantly eluded the historian. The historian's glance inevitably revealed its objects as not natural but historical, for the very possibility of telling a people's story implies division. Thus every unity turns out to be division, every nature is in the end revealed as history. In the times before the Conquest, among the Anglo-Saxon kings, Thierry argues, there were none of the fluctuations of royal authority that are so characteristic of the descendants of the Conqueror. "All was simple, because the population was one."[88] On closer inspection, however—that is to say, as soon as it has to be described—Anglo-Saxon England turns out to have been itself, in turn, divided. After the Conquest, we read, the Anglo-Saxon race, "having lost its lands, also lost the franchises that, in the Dark Ages, were exclusively attached to them, and were degraded to that class of farmers and tributaries who are referred to in the old laws of the land as *keorls* and on whom these same laws, prior to the Conquest, had been extremely hard."[89] The Saxons themselves, in short, had once been invaders, and so, doubtless, had those whom they had conquered. The ancient Kelts claimed to have settled an uninhabited territory which they occupied without war or violence, Thierry relates, but "this honorable claim cannot be supported historically: in all probability the Cambrian immigrants discovered men on the island of Britain."[90] In his *Histoire des Gaules* (1828), Augustin Thierry's brother Amédée had to divide the Kelts themselves into two large families. The first, nomadic and pastoral, was followed by the second, the more advanced Armorike, Belgi, or Kimerii, who came over the North Sea, invaded the south and east of Ireland and of Britain, as well as the north and west of France, and pushed their predecessors back to western and northern Ireland and Britain. Likewise the soil of France has felt for twenty centuries, according to Augustin, the feet of successive conquerors.[91] The series of conquests and invasions is finally lost sight of in the mists of antiquity. "From the most remote times, several populations of different race inhabited the territory of Gaul: when they invaded this country, the Romans found three peoples and three languages. Who were these peoples? . . . Was there an indigenous race, and in what order had the other races which had immigrated from elsewhere, come and pressed upon the first?"[92] In the *Formation et progrès du tiers état* divisions are shown to have been well established both among the early Frankish invaders and among the Gauls themselves. "All that was elevated in the Gallo-Roman population" lived in the cities "surrounded by their domestic slaves," while the countryside was populated by "half-servile *coloni* and agricultural slaves."[93] Fratricidal conflicts mark not only the race of the conquerors in Thierry's writing, but that of the conquered too. To the quarrels between William and his son—repeated throughout the succession of the Conqueror—corresponds, on the Saxon side, the mortal rivalry of Harold and his brother Tostig.[94]

If no "natural" people escapes, on examination, the inevitable historical fate of division, the historian's investigation is equally damaging to the unity of the nation, which has supposedly, in very recent times, replaced the divisions of the age of conquest. Though Thierry himself affirmed and reaffirmed the unity of the *tiers état,* he was in fact himself the first, as Marx was quick to observe, to point up its multiple divisions. In Thierry's own narrative this unity is continually collapsing into conflicting elements. The bourgeoisie—"the middle class of the nation, the upper class of the *tiers état* . . . composed of the most well-to-do merchants and the lawyers of the sovereign courts"—had to be distinguished, according to Thierry, from the "intermediate class" of the *tiers,* "consisting of the wealthier among those who exercised manual trades, a class less enlightened and less refined in manners" and the ready instrument of every demagoguery, as well as from the urban "multitude," the breeding ground of irrational fanaticism and unchecked impulses, and the peasantry, a "savage force," whose blind revolts were incapable of achieving any permanent order.[95] In the fifteenth, as in the sixteenth, and again in the seventeenth century, there is disagreement and conflict between the two principal parts of the *tiers,* and it is Thierry himself who, describing the Ligue, anticipates the divisions and excesses of the Revolution. It was, he writes, among the inferior classes "that the dark enthusiasms and the energy of the earlier days of struggle were prolonged; it was they who imposed upon Paris, by a system of compulsion and terror, the exercise of the amazing patience with which this great city endured the fatigue and calamities of a seige that lasted four full years."[96] In the history of England and Holland, likewise, the *populace* is indifferent to higher public goods such as liberty, easily manipulated by despots, and dangerous to true patriots such as the de Witts.[97]

Yet in the preface to the *Tiers Etat* Thierry "waxes wrathful," as Marx put it, "over the 'moderns' who claim to discern a further antagonism, between bourgeoisie and proletariat, and who try to discover traces of this conflict in the history of the *tiers état* before 1789."[98] According to Thierry, the nation, having realized itself through the Revolution, "is today one and always the same," and the analysis of it into mutually opposed classes, which was relevant to the old régime, is so no longer.[99] Even less appropriate is the attempt of some writers "to suppose that the third order then answered to what is now called the bourgeoisie, and that it was a superior class among those classes which were beyond the pale of the nobility and the clergy, and, in differing degrees, inferior to them." This opinion, says Thierry, is not only false, it "has the evil effect of making an antagonism that is in reality an invention of yesterday, and that is destructive of all public security, appear to have its foundation in history."[100] Thus Thierry insists on unity even where his own historicizing gaze kept discovering division. This inconsistency points to an essential aspect of Thierry's work as a historian. The conquest theory transformed the logical priority of unity over division into a historical anteriority, and thereby defined division as a stage or phase, as something that had happened to an original unity, and not as an essential condition. If it was not an essential condition, it could presumably be healed, and unity was therefore in principle recuperable. Unity was also, consequently, defined as the telos of history, the final goal which it was fast approaching and which would be realized by the establishment of nation-states. The instrument of the weaving together of the divided parts into a single continuous whole was, for Thierry, the *tiers*. As the foundation of Thierry's historiography and of his political philosophy, the unity of the *tiers* had to be reaffirmed against the apparent divisions within it.

The strategy by which Thierry argued for the reality of unity despite the persistence of division altered slightly in the course of his career. During the period of his closest association with Saint-Simon and with the *idéologues*, Thierry's thinking was firmly rationalist. His goal in the essay that he and Saint-Simon wrote together, *De la Réorganisation de la société européenne* (1814), was "to inquire whether there is not a form of government, by its very nature good, founded on absolute, universal, and undeniable principles that are independent of time and place." In such an intellectual framework all disagreement is mere misunderstanding. Every controversy, every social conflict, Thierry declared in his 1817 essay on the English revolutions, in terms strikingly reminiscent of the Enlightenment, is due to the "hostility of words" and to our failure to create "an exact language, capable of expressing our particular desires in a manner intelligible to all. In their diverse expressions our wills seem to be in contradiction with each other, when they are in fact most in accord. . . . We believe we are enemies when we are all brothers." Disagreement, in short, is only apparent; it affects the surface covering, not the inner substance, the forms and not the content; ultimately it is unreal. In the same year Thierry could write optimistically that the end of all disagreement was at hand: "It is remarkable how we all immediately reach agreement today on each new point of discussion that arises concerning our civil interests, and how each controversy vanishes almost as soon as it springs up; politics is finally becoming a science."[101]

In this context, the division of bourgeoisie and people appears as a failure of cognition. The bourgeoisie is presented, indeed, as having embraced "the honorable part of distinterestedness and dignity."[102] It pursues no factional interests, and knows only the general and universal, never the particular.[103] Bourgeois liberty and bourgeois law are always contrasted with feudal liberty and feudal law as the universal on the one hand, the particular or local on the other. The law of the bourgeoisie, says Thierry, is distinguished from the beginning from the feudal law "by its very essence," since "it had as its foundation natural equity." Property, for instance, was equally divided among all the children of the property-holder. And whereas "the liberty of the noble . . . was entirely a matter of privilege," the bourgeoisie developed "the idea of another kind of liberty . . . within the reach of all, equal for all," and it pursued political freedom only in the context of political equality.[104] Freedom was not conceived of as privilege and could not therefore be the fruit of a struggle for privileges among different self-seeking factions, but had to be established by and for the whole nation. Thierry rejected the model of the English Revolutionary Settlement of 1688, since it resulted, in his view, from a struggle for privileges in which the "nation" itself did not participate.[105]

The people, on the other hand, is incapable of recognizing, let alone pursuing, the rational, universal goals of the bourgeoisie.[106] Its partiality, its inability to conceive the universal is in fact what defines it as the people and places it in opposition to the bourgeoisie. "The people counts for a great deal in the population," Thierry wrote in 1817, "but does it count for a great deal in the nation? Is not the nation made up of those who can think, who can judge, who can feel in harmony with the public interest? The people forms a separate society as long as it remains merely popular; its voice is null as long as it speaks against reason." The nation, in short, is defined as "those who think, those who think for themselves, those whose reason is not stifled by ignorance or distorted by contact with the image of power."[107]

For the young liberal secretary of Saint-Simon, then, the bourgeoisie is identified with totality, the universal, reason, spirit, truth, reality; the people with partiality, particularity, lack, appetite, the body, error, mere appearance. The conflict between them will quite simply disappear through an act of recognition on the part of the people, an act by which it will cease to be the people.

Thierry's more mature strategy was not simply to remove conflict by denying the reality or rational validity of one term, but to resolve it, as he believed, by integrating the two opposing terms into a third. Thus the typically Enlightenment oppositions and discontinuities—past / present, history / reason, evil / good, conquest / exchange, nobility / bourgeoisie, or people / bourgeoisie, to which could be added, at the level of the writer's practice, narrative / commentary—are resolved in a continuous whole that includes both terms. Like the historian-artist who records its history and who is presented by Thierry as blind yet insightful, passive yet penetrating, male and female in one, the *tiers* reconciles bourgeoisie and people and weaves them into a single continuous whole, making the specific functions of each subordinate to the whole that embraces both, resolving their mutual hostility. Thus the characteristics of the bourgeoisie—enterprise, willingness to take calculated risks, sacrifice of immediate satisfaction for future profit, the effort to penetrate history with reason and law—are directed not to the good of the bourgeoisie alone but to the good of the whole, and the bourgeoisie governs not for itself but for the sake of and in the name of the whole nation, which includes the people. Similarly, the characteristics of the people—passion, spontaneity, appetite, a visceral loyalty to tradition and to the past—must be harnessed, domesticated, and made subservient to the good of the nation as a whole. Energies that are destructive, like a disease, when they function autonomously, without regard to the good of the whole, become an indispensable and inexhaustible source of new life when they are properly integrated into the whole. The *tiers* or third term is thus no longer identifiable, in this later strategy of Thierry's, with the bourgeoisie, but includes in itself the two opposites—the bourgeoisie and the people, law and nature, the future and the past, male and female. Above all, the historical evolution of the *tiers* reveals it as a sedimentation of successive conquerors who have been identified with those they conquered by experiencing themselves, in turn, the humiliation of the vanquished, as an imbrication of opposites—of victors and victims, rulers and ruled—a constantly expanding totality.

There is no question, however, that the bourgeoisie plays the guiding role in the *tiers,* that it is, in Thierry's words, "the soul of the *tiers état*."[108] The one-sided development of any characteristic, insofar as it is partial and not oriented toward the good of the whole, should, in principle, be considered unhealthy by Thierry, in the way that the autonomous development of part of an organism would be considered detrimental to the organism as a whole. But it is apparently impossible for the characteristics of the bourgeoisie to be developed in any manner that would be detrimental to the whole. There is no excess of law, or of reason, or of prudence; and Thierry's vocabulary knows no pejorative terms for them. Of the excesses of the people, on the other hand, much is heard, and here the vocabulary of pejorative terms is rich. Passion easily becomes "fanaticism," spontaneity quickly turns into "orgies," "debauches," "drunkenness," and so on.[109] The bourgeoisie, in sum, does not appear as dangerous or potentially destructive, but its ground or source, the womb from which it emerges, *is* dangerous and potentially destructive, and must therefore be held in check. The *tiers* reconciles bourgeoisie and people; but there is no question for Thierry that the body should be ruled by the soul.

As the synthesizing or third term, the *tiers* not only weaves bourgeoisie and people into a single fabric, it is destined also to absorb the nobility. For if the *tiers* is a totalizing unity (conquered plus conquerors), the nobility (conquerors) is, like the people (conquered), partiality. In his essay on *L'Esprit de conquête* Constant divided history into two great ages, one dominated by the spirit of conquest and characterized by wars among the various peoples of the world and by oppression within each people, and another, just dawning, which would be marked by the spirit of "industry," that is, by peaceful exchange and "emulation" among individuals and nations. A version of the historical pattern outlined in Constant's essay, with its obvious relation to the historical thinking of the Enlightenment, was proposed by Thierry himself in *Des Nations* (1817). The spirit of conquest is here said to characterize the whole of antiquity. "The great industry was war. The means of production was the sword, the wealth of the State as well as that of individuals was enhanced by the sword."[110] Into this system of stark oppositions, however, Thierry introduces, even in the 1817 essay, an element of integration and conciliation, which resolves discontinuities in continuity. The hardworking ordinary people—the vanquished of an infinitely regressing series of conquests—are presented as standing to some extent outside the system that pits their masters against those of other lands and other peoples. Once defeated, in other words, a people is swept from the center of the historical stage to the obscure regions on its periphery, where it joins all the other vanquished populations, the debris of "history," in performing the silent, humdrum, endlessly repeated, unnoticed tasks that sustain human existence. Between the twelfth and the fourteenth centuries, however, according to Thierry, these humble laboring people ceased to suffer silently. Organizing themselves into the communes of the late Middle Ages, they drove a wedge into the system of conquest, and from then on the idea of a society founded on peace, tolerance, and mutual exchange began to emerge as a genuine alternative to violence and conquest. The Saint-Simonian essay "Des Nations" thus anticipates the theme of the much later work on the *Formation et progrès du tiers état*: the progressive development of the nation, under the leadership of the bourgeoisie, as a single united community of industrious individuals, each of whom respects and requires the freedom, productivity, and prosperity of all the others, whom he regards as identical to himself.

Thierry's identification of the bourgeoisie with the universal and, to a considerable extent, with reason raises problems for him as the historian of the bourgeoisie, notably in the *Formation et progrès du tiers état*. In the other major histories, the heroes are conquerors and aggressors; good or peace-loving characters are defined either as passive victims or, at best, as resisting aggression. Like the original nations of Thierry's historical imagination, the good heroes are outside history and are dragged into it only by the violent acts of the wicked. The source of action is thus not the good, but evil; not the rational, but the irrational; not plenitude and sufficiency, but lack and desire. Thierry's problem in the *Tiers Etat* is how to write a history of which the bourgeoisie—rational, peace-loving, universal—is the hero.

Thierry was aware of the problem. "Truth is simple and transparent," he had written in "Des Nations," "error is obscure, turned in upon itself, complicated." Every intrigue, every story or history, in short, is at bottom a history of evil, of erring. (Indeed, the word *intrigue* retains for us to this day the connotation of evil.) Two years later, in an article in the *Censeur,* Thierry contrasted true government—that is, rational government, government that conforms to rational principles, "the product of reason and the goal of science"—with despotism, which has "a thousand characters, a thousand modes, a thousand shapes, a thousand degrees." As the product not of reason but of fortune, despotism falls within the province of the historian; it is a phenomenon "whose existence cannot be qualified but only narrated."[111] There is, in other words, no history of the true, the rational, since it is simple, invariable, and one.[112] There can only be histories of what is divided, of that which, lacking completeness, is moved by its inadequacy to desire and to attempt to appropriate what it lacks—the other. At best there can be histories of the process by which evil and error are overcome—not in the sense of being vanquished by the good and the true (for that would be to continue violence and repression, and would reveal the good and the true as not genuinely universal, as exclusive of something), but in the sense of being subdued and adapted, just as in an organic development the various parts are integrated into and made subordinate to the needs of the organism as a whole. In either case, the stage will be occupied, for the most part, by evil and error. On the whole, the *Conquête de l'Angleterre* and the *Récits des temps mérovingiens* follow the first pattern, and their subject matter is largely tales of violent acts perpetrated upon innocent victims, although the Conclusion of the *Conquête* and the utopian community in the *Récits* adumbrate, at least, the possibility of a plotting in terms of romance, or of the final salvation of the hero. The *Tiers État,* on the other hand, because its hero is the bourgeoisie, presented a compositional problem. "I attempted to write a history which, strictly speaking, was without definite shape and connection among its parts," Thierry explains in the Preface. "My task was to supply the want . . . and to give the movement and interest of a narrative to a succession of rapid views and general facts."[113] The story of reason, in sum, is embedded in but distinguishable from the webs of cause and effect, of act and consequence, the plots and intrigues that for Thierry are the material of historical narrative. When it is disengaged from this material, it becomes difficult for the historian to present it historically—that is, for Thierry, in the form of a narrative. Nothing, in sum, is properly historical about reason and liberty; it is only through the obstacles they encounter, through evil, that they acquire a history.

The difficulty of writing a narrative of which the hero is without particularity and without desire may account for the frequency with which Thierry resorts to antithesis in the *Tiers Etat*. It is as though he expects antithesis to impart something of the interest of narrative to the history of the bourgeoisie. In particular, antithesis appears to mediate rhetorically between the welter of singular facts, the "thousand characters, thousand modes, thousand shapes, thousand degrees" of historical phenomena, and the monotonous, undifferentiated sameness of reason and truth, allowing the former to be organized into distinct and relatively stable units or classes and making it possible for the latter to be made manifest through the resistance it encounters. Throughout the text, the contrast of reason and passion, duty and desire, peaceful industry and the restless urge to plunder, informs both narrative and character. The portrait of Louis XIV is built up from the contrast between his character and role as national monarch and his character and role as chief of a nobility: "His determination to act in everything according to the rule of his duty, and to have no object but the public good, was profound and sincere . . . but he had not the strength always to follow the moral law which he imposed upon himself. . . . He too frequently mistook the voice of his passions for that of his duties, and the general interest—that which he boasted he loved the most—was sacrificed by him to his family interest, to an ambition that knew no limits and to an unregulated love of applause and glory."[114] The antitheses of desire and duty, appearance and reality, impulse and rational calculation, the accidental and the essential, the transitory and the eternally true, dissipation of wealth and accumulation of capital, again inform the parallel of the king and his great bourgeois minister, generating the series of characteristics by which each is defined against the other. The king is "young and brilliant, ostentatious, lavish, carried away by pleasure"; the minister, on the other hand, incarnates "the spirit of order, calculation and economy, the tone and manners of a bourgeois grown old before his time in subordinate duties and continual labors." Colbert, moreover, is "awkward" and "ungraceful" in external manifestations of speech and dress, "his features severe, even to harshness . . . This rude covering, however, enclosed within it a spirit zealous for the public weal, eager for action and power, but still more dedicated than ambitious"—above all, an impartial spirit, moved only by the rational and universal considerations of "the happiness of the people and glory of France," never by considerations of "private interest."[115] But if history continues to be recountable as a succession of different events, it is because Colbert did not succeed in making it rational. History, the narratable account of the myriad effects of desire and passion, wins out over reason, one and universal. "Reduced . . . to the ungrateful task of opposing the voice of reason to a party hurried onward by pride, violence, and foreign encroachments, of defending the exhausted treasury from continually increasing demands for fêtes, pleasure houses, and military government in the midst of peace, Colbert slowly went down, worn out by the fruitless and hopeless struggle."[116] The form of succession itself, the inmost form of history, is inseparable, for Thierry, from the contrasting manifestations of conflicting (and therefore, by his own definition, irrational) desires; at the very least, it requires the contrast of rationality and its opposite. The same antithesis that generates the portrait of Louis XIV and the parallel of Louis and Colbert, when turned on its side, as it were, distinguishes the successive periods of Louis's reign—"that of the successful years in which all is made prosperous by a powerful will directed by a sound reason; and that in which the decline commences, due to passion's assuming the empire at the expense of reason."[117]

The elementary conditions of narrative order—and for Thierry narrative order and the objective order of history are one and the same—are, on the one hand, the distinctiveness or discontinuity of individual actors and individual events, and, on the other, the possibility of classifying the particulars under larger contrasting categories. But if the contrasting categories were ever to dissolve, if evil and passion were finally to be subdued and reason to emerge supreme, there would be no more story to tell. The realization of reason, "simple and transparent," will mark the end of history.[118]

The Value of Continuity: The Mediating Role of History

In the obituary address he read to the Académie des Sciences Morales et Politiques on the death of Sismondi, Thierry's lifelong friend and associate François Mignet expressed the view that in all nations history writing is a latecomer among the activities of the human intellect. "It is the work of their intelligence arrived at maturity, as the epic is the triumph of their imagination in the first spring of their youth. To excel in it, it is necessary to be in a position to know well, in a condition fully to comprehend, with a right to pass judgment on every thing. Thus history has never truly existed except in enlightened ages."[119] History is a retrospective, in short; it is written not from a position within it (like the medieval chronicles), nor from a position absolutely exterior to it and discontinuous with it (like Enlightenment history), but from a privileged vantage point close to the end of it. Thierry's own view was, in all probability, similar to Mignet's. It is tempting to interpret certain expressions of it, like that, for instance, in the Preface to the *Conquête*—"it is impossible to transcend the history of one's own time, and each new age provides history with fresh points of view and a particular form"—as signifying that the rootedness of the historian himself in history is at once the condition and the limitation of all historiography. The interpretation that is most consonant with the rest of Thierry's writing, however, is a less radically relativist one. Until now, Thierry seems to be saying, until the present age, the form and content of historical narration was limited by the particular historical situation of the writer, his class associations, his political affiliations and interests. From now on, however, identifying himself with the emergent whole, the nation, rather than with any part of it, untrammeled by ties to any particular period, or province, or party, the historian is in a position to recount the past as it actually was. Bourgeois historiography is truth, not ideology, and it is so because the triumph of the bourgeoisie is the fulfillment of reason, of the universal, in history.[120] Writing the history of the *tiers état* during the July monarchy, Thierry relates, he believed he had before his eyes "the providential termination of the labor of all the centuries since the twelfth."[121] The "catastrophe" of 1848 threw the history of France, as Thierry and his friends understood it, into disorder, precisely because it indicated that history was *not ended*.

Both Constant's *De l'Esprit de conquête* and Thierry's "Des Nations" are constructed on the antithesis of before and now. All the *past* is given over to war and the economy of conquest; *from now on,* however, with the overthrow of the ancien régime, the world is dedicated to peace and the economy of exchange.[122] Even in Thierry's more organic conception of the historical process, in which reason does not replace history but rather espouses it, invests it, orients and controls it, the triumph of the *tiers* marks the end of history as it has been hitherto and its total penetration by reason. Reason and history are counterposed throughout Thierry's work, and the destiny of man is to pass from the dominance of history to the freedom of reason. "Simple freedom and history were like two different sources from which the regenerative principle drank from its birth," he notes in the *Tiers Etat* of the struggle for a society founded upon principles of civil right, "but . . . it drank more and more from the first and less and less from the second. . . . Ancient rights were nothing else but ancient privileges, the restoration of them in a body under the name of liberty could not be an object of serious desire except to the first two orders; with the exception of some old municipal liberties, which no longer interested anybody, the *tiers état* had nothing to regret in the past, and everything to expect from the future."[123] History is thus the record of the diminishing role of "history" in human affairs and of its gradual permeation by reason; its chiasmic structure is at the same time that of the historian's own discourse, as the opening paragraph of Michelet's *Introduction à l'histoire universelle* of 1831 makes vividly clear: "With the world a war began that is destined to end with the world, and not before; that of man against nature, of spirit against matter, of freedom against fate. History is nothing but the tale of this interminable struggle."

Later in his life Thierry criticized Michelet for turning history into a *psychomachie,* but for Thierry himself, in the end, history is the domain of evil. The good and the true are synonymous with reason, and history stands for the accidental, the discontinuous, the irrational, the inessential. "Government is the product of reason and the goal of science; despotism, the product of fate, is abandoned to history."[124] History is that which escapes man's control. Like nature, it is a devouring monster that must be domesticated. Always, both as *fatum* and as the *story* of man's deeds, it has stood in the way of human freedom, self-control, and rational social organization. "Men forgot their real interests, their concrete interests," Thierry wrote in 1817, of the Revolution. "But it would have been futile to try to point out to us the vanity of the objects we were pursuing; unfortunately, history was there, and we could have it speak for us and confound reason."[125] And like Michelet, Thierry conceives the triumph of reason over history, of mind over matter, of good over evil, as a destiny, or rather a providence. Since most men in history act blindly, irrationally, the order and direction of history, the movement toward reason and liberty, cannot be the consequence of rational choice. Thierry thus comes to emplot history as a romance, or a divine comedy, ending in the salvation, almost despite himself, of the sinner who has obstinately persisted in stumbling blindly in the forests of ignorance and error. "The continuous elevation of the *tiers état* is the predominant fact and the law of our history. This law of Providence has been accomplished more than once without the knowledge of those who were the agents of it, without the knowledge and even to the regret of those who would naturally reap its fruit."[126] The July monarchy is the appointed, the "providential termination" of six centuries of French history.[127] Thierry's language emphasizes the providential character of history as he sees it. Metaphors of nature—"ripeness," "readiness," "stages"—are everywhere. The relation of the *tiers* and the Crown is "natural"; there is a "natural extension" of her boundaries which France was destined to attain; Louis XIV deviated in the second part of his reign from the "true French policy, at once national and liberal" conceived by Henri IV and pursued by Richelieu, Mazarin, and Colbert.[128] Etienne Marcel "prematurely won" for the *tiers* a position it was destined to achieve only by "patient industry, less pretentious ambition, and slow but uninterrupted progress."[129] "Nothing was ripe in 1615 for the results that were achieved by the *tiers état* in 1789."[130] In a rather rare simile, the progress of the *tiers état* "resembles that of the rising tide, which seems to advance and recede without interruption, but which still gains ground and reaches its destined point."[131]

With the fulfillment of the destiny of the *tiers* and the triumph of reason, division ends and all conflict is resolved in unity. In 1814 Saint-Simon and Thierry had envisaged an Anglo-French parliament that was to lead to a single set of institutions—a single King, a single House of Lords, and a single House of Commons—for all Europe.[132] National rivalries, according to Saint-Simon himself at this point, were the result of old feudal rivalries and had nothing to do with the new industrial age—a view shared by Constant and other liberals at the time.[133] In the essay "Des Nations" Thierry had outlined three stages in the European political system: in the first, the *système catholique,* which corresponded approximately to the medieval period, an essentially transitory unity was imposed forcibly from the center (Rome) on isolated individual units that constantly tended to break loose and fall back into "personality," in Thierry's own picturesque phrase; in the second, the *système de l'équilibre religieux,* which obtained after the Reformation and which had its internal political counterpart in the class struggles between rival interest groups within particular countries, individual units were united in opposition to other groups of united individual units, so that unity remained subordinate to division; in the third, the *système politique,* the confederation of the "industrial" nations, that is, those in which commerce and the political system of liberalism had triumphed (France, England, and Holland), was to promote industrial activity and political freedom in all other nations, notably Germany, Italy, and Spain, until they too would be included in a vast confederation of all the free nations of Europe. The end of the regime of conquest in each country and the realization of nationhood would inevitably be followed, according to the young Thierry, by the association of all nations in a single universal confederation. "On the day the whole human race is convinced that the only aim of social union, the only object of the banding together of men, is the greatest happiness of each one of them, on that day there will be only one nation, and that nation will be the whole human race."[134]

The unity conceived by Thierry is thus one in which particularity is subsumed, not suppressed, as in the *système catholique.* Thierry's reason is presented as accommodating and tolerant, not exclusive or repressive. There is much sympathy, especially in his early writings—and in this he is again close to Benjamin Constant—with the ideals of federalism. In the creation of the modern French nation all the particular nationalities that constituted it—"la nation bretonne, la nation normande, la nation béarnaise, les nations de Bourgogne, d'Aquitaine, de Languedoc, de Franche Comté, d'Alsace"—preserved their distinctive characteristics but did not separate their individual existence from the great common existence. "Absolute centralization, the regime of a conquest, not a society, was not even fully realized by the power against which the Revolution was carried out and was certainly not the object of that Revolution." Thierry himself envisaged a complex system of representative institutions soliciting and reflecting the views of all members of society and culminating in the National Assembly. In the constant interchange of views and experiences between national and local assemblies, each, Thierry believed, would be enriched by the contribution of the other.[135]

The State, as Thierry imagined it, even in his later, more conservative period, was not intended to crush individuality or nationality, but to domesticate and fulfill it by orienting it toward the good of all. The State, in other words, was not, in principle, opposed to nature (or the "natural" desires of either individuals or individual communities) but, on the contrary, was continuous with it, a natural development from it. "The absolute unity of the State," says Thierry, is not an alien force, but "the spontaneous product of our social instincts."[136] Thus the model of the relation of the nation and the State, as Thierry presents it, is not that of discontinuous opposites, such as female and male, each of which seeks to appropriate the other, but rather that of mother and son—distinct, yet continuous, a relation of container to contained, whole to part. Duty thus appears to be in harmony with desire, the State with the communities or "nations" and individuals that compose it, reason with nature. This means that all the elements that are included in the State are harmonized in and through the State, which serves them all and which they all serve. There can therefore be no class struggle in the State which the *tiers,* led by the bourgeoisie, has created. As we saw, Thierry considers every attempt to theorize the struggle of bourgeoisie and proletariat as "destructive of all public security." "All classes," wrote Guizot, "all social forces amalgamate, combine, and live in peace within the great moral unity of French society."[137]

To Thierry, it seems, as to Constant or Guizot, social differences do not imply conflict but a variety of perspectives; and far from aiming to impose an external order on the various groups and individuals composing it, the State mediates among them and is the means by which all are fulfilled. "Variety," Constant proclaimed, "is organization; uniformity is mechanism. Variety is life; uniformity is death."[138]

* * *

FOR GENERATIONS, according to Thierry, the kings of France had tried to forge a single nation out of the two peoples over whom they ruled and to impose unity upon a divided country. What the kings could only hope to achieve from above by violence—which in turn created new divisions—the bourgeoisie achieved organically from within, realizing the unity of the nation without sacrificing the existence and value of individuals, securing the rights and liberties of individuals without sacrificing national unity. This reconciliation of the one and the many, unity and diversity, reason and history, order and freedom, which Thierry considered the achievement of the "middling class" in history, he also saw as his own task in the *writing* of history.

All the historians of the new school rejected the tendentiousness of "philosophical" historiography, its impatience with particulars, its eagerness to impose its own order on the past and to gather up the life of the past in its classifications. "I am so sick of writers with intentions, as almost all those of the eighteenth century were," Constant wrote to Prosper de Barante, "that I think I should prefer a fool telling a tale without purpose to an intelligent man in every one of whose stories I could discern some purpose."[139] Barante may have recalled Constant's words later when he wrote in the Preface to his *Histoire des Ducs de Bourgogne* (Paris, 1824) that years of demystifying widely held convictions, of public airing of opinions, of efforts to persuade and convince, had made people suspicious of arguments in general and intolerant of them in history books in particular. "People are tired of seeing history lend itself, like a paid and docile sophist, to providing whatever evidence anybody wants to extract from it."[140] Barante's Preface is a particularly lucid treatment of some of the main philosophical and rhetorical problems encountered by the new school of historians. Its dominant theme is one that Barante had discussed earlier in the *Life of Schiller*, with which he prefaced his translation of Schiller's dramatic works. It may seem presumptuous, he had said then, for an outsider, a casual student of German literature, to write such a biographical notice, but the writer can answer that the outsider often sees his subject better than the insider who lives with it. At the same time, Barante added, the advantage of being on the outside does not devalue the knowledge acquired from within. On the contrary, only the contemporary, the intimate friend, can offer insights which have the charm and the interest of life itself. The historian's aim must be to achieve a total, all-encompassing view, by combining both perspectives. Barante himself tried to do this by weaving his own text out of contemporary testimonies. It was through the reverent contemplation of these, he held, through "amour et estime," as he put it in the *Tableau de la littérature française au XVIIIe siècle* (1808), even more than through reflection and analysis, that the historian could expect to achieve insight into the past. The problem of reconciling the richness of immediacy and the intelligible order of distance and analysis preoccupied Barante throughout his career as a historian; and the same solution—a collage of contemporary testimonies—was adopted by him again and again, from the immensely popular *Ducs de Bourgogne* to his last work, a biography of his friend, the philosopher and statesman Royer-Collard.[141]

In the Preface to the *Ducs de Bourgogne* Barante praises the Old French chroniclers for the benevolent impartiality with which they report the events of their age. They do not sift, judge, and order, he says, but naively relate whatever immediately strikes them. They are masters of narrative. "Whether the facts unfold before them simply as a spectacle, or whether they try to probe them and to draw from them an understanding of men and of peoples, they always know how to make us see them exactly as they appeared before their own eyes." Narrative—at its most rudimentary, a simple succession of events, one after the other—is thus intimately associated with the fresh, immediate, uncomposed, often uncoordinated vision of the unreflective reporter. And it is contrasted favorably with reflection, which often imposes false patterns on events, distorts them, and deprives the past not only of its color and life, but of its complexity and its contradictions. "The very form in which the results of historical research are expressed imparts to everything an air of system and regularity. What in reality was only a kind of general spirit . . . is presented as a legal system, a set of well-ordered institutions. . . . Deceived by present-day habits of thought, the reader sees a social institution in a chaos that had only begun to ravel out; what was transitory seems to him to be fixed, and he takes what was accidental to be customary."[142]

Barante's criticism is addressed primarily to demonstrative history, to the use of history as a weapon in political argument. He objects strongly, for instance, to the notion of a feudal "system," since it suggests "a regime which bears the sanction of the ages and of the memories of our society, and which would be sufficient for the well-being, the morality and the dignity of present-day generations"—that is to say, an alternative constitution to the Restoration Charter. He is far less critical of efforts to discern patterns in history, an overall design or plan. Contemporary narratives are limited, he admits; the immediate vision is at the same time a restricted one. "The soldier who tells the story of a battle is in an excellent position to recount what happened before his eyes. He can tell us about this or that episode on the battlefield, his impressions and his language will be a sign of the spirit and the composition of the army, of the manners of the age, of the nature of war; but he does not know and cannot tell us the general plan of the battle. . . . Victory or defeat is within his ken; their causes and circumstances are beyond him." Moreover, the category of the important or significant is not the same for the contemporary witness and for the later historian. The contemporary is not struck by the everyday, by those general characteristics of an age that, rather than the singular or exceptional, interest posterity. For this reason, Barante has to confess, "one must be outside the picture in order to discern its salient and characteristic points."[143]

History "should narrate and not demonstrate," therefore, but this does not mean that the narrative itself should not contain "une instruction solide."[144] Barante's ideal is that the meaning and pattern of history will emerge from the narrative itself. Instead of the narrator's imposing them on the reader, or actively seeking to persuade him, they will be freely perceived by the reader as *objective,* in history itself.[145] "The author can . . . refrain from showing himself; he can count on the truth if he has succeeded in telling it naively. History, when it is sincere, imparts its lessons loudly and clearly."[146] Despite his emphasis on narrative, therefore, history is not a "divertissement" for Barante, and it does not leave the intellect idle.[147] But what Barante's reader is to find in history is not moral and political indoctrination, not a stimulus to criticism or action, but the passive contemplation of an objective and inevitable process. In recounting simple relations of cause and effect, Barante explained, "I did not believe that events followed one another in succession . . . without being destined by Providence to accomplish some great end." Seen from within, the events of history constitute a tale in which violence, deceit, and corruption are justified by success. Seen from without or from above, however—that is, from the vantage point of the "industrialist" age, from the threshold of the bourgeois monarchy—history "always reveals the presence of a Providence, which, having placed the need and the capacity for improvement in the heart of man, has never allowed the succession of events to throw doubt, even for an instant, on the gifts it brought."[148]

Barante's view of history thus requires that history be both a narrative of successive, singular events, linked by simple cause-and-effect relations,[149] and the revelation in those very events of lawfulness and order, of a teleology rather than a mere succession. Moreover, order is not to be either asserted or demanded by the historian, in the manner of the eighteenth-century historians, but the reader is to discover it embedded in singularity, just as, for the liberal political thinker—and Barante was one—the general welfare is implied in the desires and ambitions of the individual citizen, even though he himself does not know it. Barante always insisted on the impropriety of narratorial interventions. His own aim, he said, was "to make all trace of my own work vanish completely, to show nothing of the writer of the present day. I have therefore refrained from interspersing reflections and judgments among the events I relate."[150] For the same reason he accompanied his text with no critical apparatus and no notes.[151] Even the divisions of the book were made as noncommittal as possible. Rather than introduce a categorization that would point to the presence of the organizing historian, Barante was content to adopt a conventional ordering of the parts of the narrative according to successive ducal reigns. Every sign of narratorial presence, in short, was to be eliminated or concealed; and reading Barante's book, the reader was to have the impression that he was reading an eyewitness account contemporary or near contemporary with the events. As though to underline the absence of narratorial mediation and the absolute simplicity and transparency of Barante's account, a vignette was inserted after the Preface in later editions of the *Ducs de Bourgogne,* in which the rhetorial situation was made very clear. A young page in fifteenth-century costume—the image of the author—was portrayed reading from a book, which the reader was no doubt intended to identify with the one he, or she, was reading, to a lady of the court, in whom Barante's own, often feminine reader could be expected to recognize with pleasure her own image.[152]

In his apology for the late medieval chroniclers, Barante had contrasted "the spontaneous productions of nature"—the work of the chroniclers—with "the combinations of the artist"—the work of self-conscious, reflective historians. By keeping himself out of his work, as he thought, and making it, as far as he could, a collage of materials borrowed from the chroniclers, he hoped to impart to it something of this "natural" quality and to avoid the artifices of the "reflective" historian, to make it appear, in short, like history telling itself. "No doubt I could not completely make my work into a tissue of textual quotations. I had to give it order and an overall shape. . . . But at least nothing had been made unnatural or perverted from its true meaning."[153]

To the degree that the reader recognizes an order in history, then, this order will appear to him to be natural, inscribed in the very nature of things, rather than artificial, invented by the historian who comes to the monuments of the past with his own categories. It is hard not to see some political significance in the device of the absent narrator. Barante pointed out several times that the rage for discussion and debate during the eighteenth century and the period of the Revolution had made people skeptical and weary of arguments, since they knew that any argument could be countered by another equally plausible one. Justification by argument and reason was a fragile basis for any social order. The bourgeois state was not, therefore, to be argued for, as it had been by the philosophical historians of the eighteenth century; it was not to be defended rationally; nor was it to be thought of as having been imposed; it was to be presented as a natural fact, the culmination of an objective, inevitable, and "natural" process. The task of the historian was to instruct men to accept it and adapt themselves to it, not to stir up futile arguments or propose chimerical alternatives.

The absent narrator and the "natural" narrative are themselves, in short, artifices of rhetoric and ideology, by means of which the historian's order is made to appear objective, "real." It has been pointed out, for instance, that Barante found all the documents he quotes in his text in already published works and that he did no archival research. Obviously he did no research, because he did not work from documents. Documents were introduced into his text for rhetorical reasons only, to enhance the "effet de réel" that was his primary goal. In fact, Barante does intervene in his narrative, though always surreptitiously. Quite apart from the selection and arrangement of materials taken from disparate sources, a narrative voice intrudes from time to time to account for events by invoking familiar *sententiae,* to pronounce judgments, to orient the reader's attitude to what is being reported, and to anticipate what is to come later in the narrative.[154]

Far from eliminating ideology from his history, Barante's attempt to disguise his own role as writer made his history, if anything, more ideologically loaded. The work of collage, as he performed it, was not intended to function provocatively, to reveal discontinuities, suggest unexpected relations, or question expected ones. On the contrary, the activity of writing history was sedulously ignored. The writer, ostensibly, was a mere transcriber of the texts of the past. In fact, his principal activity was to use assumptions or rhetorical tricks to make discontinuous parts appear as a single, smooth-flowing relation.[155]

Barante was doubly timid as a writer: he tried both to mask his activity as producer of the text and to avoid giving the impression of submitting passively to the fascination of mere stories. In order to disguise his activity, he impressed himself only feebly on the texts he utilized to compose his own—the contrast with Michelet, who also made extensive use of other texts, is striking—claiming in justification that he did not wish to "denature" them.[156] He was thus, it seems, himself a victim of the naturalist ideology he propagated in the Preface. He had only to transcribe his chroniclers faithfully and the past would speak, as it were, out of its own mouth. The naturalist ideology was not with him, in other words, a respectable mask beneath which the artist's work might be pursued with undiminished energy; it clung fast to him and informed all his activity as a writer.[157] Inevitably, the *Ducs de Bourgogne,* after a period of immense popularity, fell from favor. The working over of the parts into a new text was not vigorous enough to hold them together. The cloth fell apart into its several pieces. Readers turned back to the texts Barante had borrowed and found them livelier than the later compilation. Anatole France, recalling that he had read the *Ducs de Bourgogne* with enthusiasm as a schoolboy, observed: "I have not reread it since. But I have read Froissart."[158]

Barante was also afraid of being carried away by his own delight in the singular, in the colorful detail of the narratives he was transcribing; and he seems to have sensed that this delight in the singular contained the seeds of a reprehensible exoticism, an evasion from the austere liberal-bourgeois world of truth, order, and reason. His justification of the singular rested, as we saw, on its ultimate subsumption into the category of the general. For him, as for Thierry, the interest of history and the very possibility of constructing it as narrative are associated with isolated, discrete, colorful events—for the most part, acts of violence, deceit, and corruption. Both history itself and historical narrative are possible only because the world is not simple like the good and the true, but full of the variety of evil and error. The good alone—whatever is orderly, rational, and lawful in history—cannot be the subject of a narrative; and the historian can only try to make it somehow shine through the opacity of particular events. Essences cannot be portrayed directly but may be, at best, adumbrated and anticipated in particular, imperfect existences. The historian's position thus turns out to be at least as ambiguous as the artist's. Evil—the infinite fecundity of existence—is the very condition of his work, the material he shapes in a gesture that is itself part of history, and insofar as he "amuses" or "pleases," it is because his readers, as creatures who themselves have "fallen" into history, are attracted—"distracted," in the words of Pascal, an author Barante read assiduously—by the inessential, by everything that bears the stamp of desire and singularity. As the historian rejects Aristotle's characterization of historiography as a mere collection of particulars, however, and claims that in modern times historiography, rather than the novel, has inherited from the old epic the task of disclosing the essential structures of the real, he must aim to "instruct" his reader by revealing the eternal rational order below the chaos of particulars, the essence of which each existent is the transient manifestation. The detail is justified to the degree that it is "characteristic." "I have not desired simply to excite a passing interest devoid of any moral character," Barante wrote; "all the dramatic qualities the reader discovers in my work should not make him forget that we are concerned with the fate of mankind and that all these characters, this entire entrancing spectacle lay such a strong hold on our imagination only because they are the signs of that great history from which proper names disappear, of that history which tells of the advance of human society." Every particular—and the proper name is the sign par excellence of the particular—is thus absorbed in the general; every individual act or event is to be understood as a synecdoche, or representative, of the entire character of a man, or a class, or a nation, or an age.[159]

But synecdoche serves not only as a justification; it serves also as a genuine artistic strategy. Reality—the Romantic historian's prize—cannot be grasped and contained in its fullness and freedom. To attempt to grasp it thus would simply result in the overwhelming of the narrative order that is the condition and the means of containment. By integrating selected "representative" features of men, of nations, or of ages into his narrative, however, the historian can give the impression, or have the illusion, of having embraced the whole of reality in it, while at the same time surrendering none of his control over it. His strategy recalls, in some respects, the effort of the liberal politician to embrace and at the same time control a vast, potentially engulfing society by including "representatives" of it in the political order. It also resembles that of the fetishist who renounces direct confrontation of the threatening sexual object and seeks to possess it instead in the more manageable form of a representative part. In all three cases, self and other, and their variants (the historian and reality, the politician and the people, the lover and the beloved), encounter each other in fear and hostility: terror of being overwhelmed and desire for absolute control feed upon each other, and a solution is sought in a strategy by which a relation of stark opposition and discontinuity is ostensibly transmuted into one of continuity, of container and contained.

THE OBJECTIVES and problems of composition encountered by Thierry are similar to those that faced Barante, and Thierry's solutions differ only slightly from Barante's. Like Barante, Thierry hopes to reconcile narrative and reflective history, though he gives relatively more weight to the latter.

> I desired to reproduce in my historical writing neither the manner of the philosophers of the last century, nor that of the chroniclers of the Middle Ages, nor even that of the narrative of antiquity, though I admired the last greatly. I proposed to combine, if I

could . . . the naive coloring of our legendary historians and the strict reason of the moderns with the broad epic movement of the Greek and Roman historians . . . In my effort to reconcile such diverse methods, I was tossed about unremittingly between two reefs: that of granting too much to classical regularity and thereby losing the power of local color and the truth of the vivid picture; and that, greater still, of encumbering my narrative with a multitude of petty facts, poetic perhaps, but incoherent and trivial, even meaningless to a nineteenth-century reader. One chapter suffered from the first vice, another succumbed to the second, depending on the nature of the material, which at times was scant, at times superabundant and not easily reduced, tamed, if I may be permitted the expression, and fitted into its appropriate frame.[160]

The terms of the problem are recognizably those outlined by Barante. On the one hand, a conception of knowledge as immediate knowledge of particulars, knowledge of existents; on the other, a conception of knowledge as mediated by the categories of the mind, knowledge of intelligible relations. On the one hand, an ideal of completeness made up of singular concrete persons and events, chaotic in its fullness; on the other, an ideal of completeness constituted by the power of a system to embrace, or "tame," in Thierry's own graphic term, past, present, and future phenomena. Correspondingly, Thierry envisages, again like Barante, two poles of history writing: at one, the historian is no more than the compiler or transcriber of "original" texts and documents, and history speaks out of its own mouth; and at the other, the historian takes an active part in selecting, arranging, and interpreting the materials from which he constructs an original work. On the whole, Thierry placed his ideal historian closer to the second pole than Barante did.

Like all the Romantic historians, Thierry emphasized the role of narrative in history writing. Through a well-conducted narrative account, he claimed, the reader will get the impression that he has discovered the character of a ruler, or the character of an age, in the facts themselves, without the mediation of the historian. Thierry's reputation rested, indeed, on his skill as a narrator. In the short introduction he wrote to his Russian translation of the first of the *Récits des temps mérovingiens,* Alexander Herzen pointed to the "purely narrative character of the historical work of Thierry," and claimed that it was the "secret of his extraordinary success." "Notwithstanding the general propensity of the young school for theoretical subtleties," he added, "Thierry wrote stories, and not philosophizings on the topic of history (like Michelet, for instance). . . . Although every line of his narrative is firmly supported by a great quantity of quotations and references, his stories have an autonomous existence independent of these. All the materials have been fused into some sort of living organic whole and no trace of the 'smell of the lamp' remains anywhere."[161]

Thierry sometimes defended the primacy of narrative on rhetorical grounds: a man's character, for instance, could be more effectively conveyed to the reader in the course of a narrative than through a formal portrait that the reader comes upon only after hundreds of pages.[162] But the rhetorical argument was not always the most important one. Frequently, the use of narrative was justified on epistemological grounds. "In matters historical, the method of exposition is always the surest, and the subtleties of logical argument are never introduced without imperilling the truth. . . . I wanted to reveal the democratic character of the founding of the medieval communes, and I believed I would best succeed by giving up the form of the dissertation in favor of a narrative, by making myself disappear from my story, and by letting the facts speak for themselves."[163] As with Barante, the assumption is that it is possible to relate the event "naively" and that through such a narrative, history itself will speak and not the narrator. The transparency of the historical text will be most firmly assured if it is itself part of the fabric of the past, or is woven from the fabric of the past. Thierry tells, in the 1834 Preface to *Dix Ans d'études historiques,* of a plan on which he and Mignet worked together to write "a history or rather a Great Chronicle (*grande chronique*) of France, that would bring together in the framework of a continuous narrative all the original documents of our history, from the seventh to the seventeenth century." The term *chronicle* was no doubt used advisedly to indicate a "naive" account, similar to the popular "Grandes Chroniques" of the Middle Ages. Thierry described the idea behind the work with customary clarity:

> I believed it would be possible to join together all the disconnected materials (in the recently published collections of chronicles and memoirs) by filling in the empty spaces between them and eliminating repetitions, while at the same time carefully preserving the expression contemporaries had given to their relation of events. It seems to me that from such a work, in which each century told its own story, as it were, by itself, and spoke out of its own mouth, the true history of France could be expected to

emerge, a history that would never be done over again, that would belong to no writer, and that would be consulted by all, as if it were the repertory of our national archives.

Barante himself never enunciated his ideal of the absolute, objective, authorless, historical narrative so clearly.

Thierry tells of this project, however, only to repudiate it. He had been, he says, "seduced and somewhat led astray" by the popularity of the published collection of chronicles; "fortunately," he and Mignet gave up their project when they realized that "a work in which art had no place" was unattractive to them.[164] A few years later, in the *Considérations sur l'histoire de France,* which were intended to serve as a preface to the *Récits des temps mérovingiens,* he expressed still stronger reservations. The ideal of a transparent historical account which, being absolutely true, would never be subject to rewriting or revision now seemed to him to be an illusion. "A completely pure testimony can only emerge from the historical documents taken all together and with no abbreviation of any; as soon as there is selection and editing, there is a man speaking, and a compilation of texts says, above all, what the compiler wanted to say."[165] In the weaving of the historical text, Thierry emphasized elsewhere, the weaver's role is by no means automatic. All writing is rewriting, and all rewriting is writing. Thus, in the *Récits des temps mérovingiens* (récit 5, the story of Radegonde), Thierry first establishes an apparent continuity between the events of Radegonde's childhood days, her recollection of them (which, we are told, even at the age of fifty "came back to her as fresh and as painful as at the very time she was taken into captivity"), the Latin text of Fortunatus (who "speaking in the name of the Queen tried to reproduce her melancholy memories as he received them from her lips"),[166] and the French version of it in the *Récits* (set off in quotation marks from the surrounding narrative text, as though to emphasize that it is "another voice," a faithful transcription into French of the Latin of Fortunatus, which itself is a pure transcription of the "voice" of Radegonde). There is apparently no interference between the events and their latest recital, no discontinuity between the heroine's voice and the final written text.[167] Yet, at the same time, and as if to undercut the claim to absolute reproduction of an original, Thierry signals the historian's role and the discontinuities of the process of transmission: Fortunatus's Latin text, quoted at length in a note, stands as a reminder both of the transformation that the poet must have imposed on the Queen's narrative when he rewrote it in Latin verse, and of the later transformation by which it appeared in the text of Thierry's *Récits* as modern French prose. In addition, the quotation marks, which thus ambiguously signal the fidelity of the passages borrowed from Fortunatus in the text, also signal the novelty of the rest of the text. What is not in quotation marks is, by implication, not the voice of the past; discontinuity is thereby introduced into Thierry's text. Barante, characteristically, did not use quotation marks, except to signal direct speech within a narrative that could always be supposed to be itself the voice of the chronicler.

Thierry describes his own writing as a constant process of altering, deleting, and "trying new combinations." "I made and unmade ceaselessly: it was the labor of Penelope."[168] A striking image in Michelet's *L'Oiseau* probably comes close to Thierry's conception of the historian's work, though it may carry the historian's part further than Thierry would happily have admitted. When it builds its nest, according to Michelet, the bird cannot choose ideal materials; it must work with what it finds, "in most cases, materials that are . . . quite coarse, not always what the artist would have preferred." But by pressing the pieces together and patiently shaping them with its body, it finally succeeds in transforming them, so much so, indeed, that it is its own form that now invests the materials: "The house is the person himself, his form and his unmediated energy."[169] It is not surprising that to an English reviewer of a work by Thierry's friend and disciple Armand Carrel, the French school of historians appeared distinguished above all else for "clearness and aptness at theory" and for the "ability to put history into order."[170]

Thierry's own text contains many explicit signs of the historian's presence and of his active role. Historical narratives are constructed on two axes— a horizontal or syntagmatic axis, constituted by the chain or sequence of events, and a vertical or systematic axis, constituted by the relation of each element in the narrative not to the preceding and the following elements but to the historical repertory, the "sources."[171] This character of the historical text is visible on the page itself, in the division between the upper text (narrative) and the lower text (sources and commentary). Since his aim was to "make the scaffolding disappear,"[172] to conceal the production of the text behind the product, Barante deliberately refrained from discussing or evaluating his sources critically.[173] There is virtually no lower text; a laconic footnote here and there refers the reader casually to "Froissart," "Monstrelet," "Les Religieux de Saint-Denis," "Histoire de Bourgogne," and so forth. Thierry's lower text, on the other hand, is substantial and quite richly developed, with frequent full quotations from original sources, as well as references to sources other than the one utilized or quoted, and to other modern historians. (The omission of the notes from a recent popular edition of the *Récits des temps mérovingiens* completely distorts Thierry's text, just as, in a strangely parallel way, Barante's text was distorted by the addition of lengthy scholarly notes in the 1839 Brussels edition.) By indicating his sources and often quoting them at length, the author places before the reader's eyes the problematic relation between the source texts and the final text—a relation of similarity, but also of difference. The upper text is obviously not the same as the lower one, and history is not speaking unambiguously out of its own mouth, since the text itself indicates a plurality of voices.[174]

In order to put into the foreground the syntagmatic aspect of his text and to give his narrative the appearance of history telling itself, Barante not only concealed the relation of his text to other texts; he minimized the paradigmatic relations that are an important part of most narratives, and an indispensable part no doubt (however much they may be reduced) of any narrative, since the intelligibility of a narrative is to some extent dependent on both relations of contiguity or succession and relations of similarity. Here too, Thierry's practice differed somewhat from that of his friend.

The very title of Barante's major work indicates a simple genealogical succession and refers obliquely to the predecessors and the successors of the Dukes of Burgundy. The Dukes of Burgundy constitute links in a chain that begins before them and continues after them. Indeed, the history of Burgundy, for Barante, simply becomes the history of France and is thus continued by that which is adjacent to it or contiguous with it. The internal divisions of the *Ducs de Bourgogne* are likewise as infrequent as Barante could make them and are determined largely by the successive reigns. Every effort is made, moreover, to maintain the flow of the narrative across the book divisions. Book II of *Philippe-le-Hardi* opens "Les Flandres *ainsi* pacifiées . . ." Book III opens "*Cependant* ce qui occupait le plus les esprits . . ." Each book thus begins by throwing a bridge over to the previous one.[175] Anything that might interrupt the syntagmatic chain is sedulously avoided. The dominant category of Barante's narrative is thus "metonymic" in the sense that Roman Jakobson gives to this traditional rhetorical figure. The title of Thierry's first major work, on the other hand, proposes a concept—that of conquest—and refers implicitly to other conquests, and to the elaboration of the concept itself in such theoretical works as Constant's *De L'Esprit de conquête*. In the Prospectus of his book, moreover, even though he vigorously defended the narrative mode of historiography against the reflective mode, Thierry made it clear that his history was not a mere linear unfolding, but a "construction."[176] What he addresses himself to, in the history of England, is not simply a period of time, but a problem.[177] Moreover, the conquest of England appears to Thierry and is presented by him to the reader as a metaphor or paradigm of all the great conflicts of European history: "This picture, which I shall retrace in all its detail and with the coloring proper to it, will be of a more general historical interest than the limits of time and place, within which it is contained, would seem to allow; for almost all the peoples of Europe have something, in their present-day existence, that derives from the conquests of the Middle Ages."[178] Some years later, in the Preface to *Dix Ans d'études historiques,* Thierry referred to the conquest and subjugation of Ireland by England as bringing before his eyes "in a . . . dramatic manner, what I confusedly perceived to be at the heart of the history of all the European monarchies."[179]

Whereas with Barante metonymic relations predominate in the text, with Thierry metaphoric relations are essential to the text's coherence and intelligibility. At the end of Book IV of the *Conquête,* for instance, after a detailed account of the way Hugues-le-Loup partitioned the area around Chester among his friends, the historian intervenes to observe: "These singular details are not very memorable in themselves but . . . all the settlements of interests, all the distributions of possessions and offices, that took place in the province of Chester among the Norman governor, the first lieutenant of the governor, and the five companions of the lieutenant, give a true and naive idea of similar transactions that were being carried out at the same time in all the provinces of England."[180]

Whether they set up relations among elements within the text or between elements in the text and elements outside it, in other texts, metaphors are frequent in Thierry's writing, leaping over chronological divisions and joining what time has separated. Cromwell and William III, and sometimes William I, the Conqueror, are commonly metaphors of Napoleon; Etienne Marcel is a metaphor of Robespierre or Danton; the Jacquerie of the "excesses" of the Revolution; the communal revolts of the Middle Ages and the alliance of upper bourgeoisie and people are metaphors of the liberal and constitutional revolutions of modern times; the rumor of a Popish plot in seventeenth-century England creates a climate that is a metaphor of the *grande Peur.*[181] Thierry's vocabulary itself is deliberately metaphorical: those Saxons who continued to resist the Norman invaders after the defeat of Harold at Hastings are described, in a pointed reference to the popular Spanish resistance to Napoleon, as *guerillas.*[182]

Many patterns interweave, in Thierry's work, with the narrative sequence. Barante, as we saw, reduces and trivializes the internal divisions of his book as much as possible, leaving the beginnings and ends of sections almost always unmarked. The conclusions of many of the main divisions of the *Conquête,* on the other hand, as well as the conclusions of most of the divisions of the *Récits des temps mérovingiens,* are marked and highlighted by a long narratorial comment on what has been recounted, a meditation on history itself and on the fate of its victims, or some other retrospective consideration designed to pull the material of the narrative together and to relate its elements otherwise than by mere links of succession. The strongly thematic organization of Thierry's narrative also highlights the historian's activity as weaver of his text. The themes of conquest and emancipation, victimization and justification, death and resurrection recur throughout his work, structuring and ordering it, and adding a different coherence from that of causal, or even chronological, sequence. The seven parts of the *Récits des temps mérovingiens,* for instance, are explicitly linked not so much syntagmatically as thematically. "I had a choice between two methods," Thierry explains in the Preface: "a continuous account, having as its guiding thread the succession of major political events, or an account made up of separate masses, each of which would have as its guiding thread the life or adventures of some personage of the time." He chose the second, since his aim was to establish the character of "social relations and of human destiny in the various spheres of political life, private life, and family life."[183] "Although they are filled with details and carry the stamp of essentially individual traits, each of these *Récits* has a general meaning, which can be expressed in each case without difficulty," he declared in the text itself.[184] He might have added that besides the general sense that unites the parts of each *récit,* there is a larger general pattern unifying all the *récits.* Every one of them, in fact, rests on an opposition, elaborated within it, of victim and executioner, civilization and barbarism, woman and man, people and warrior-aristocracy, law and violence, order and chaos, reason and brutal passion.[185]

The presence of the historian, indicated by these different patterns of organization of the text, is still more openly signaled in the *Conquête,* in the *Histoire du Tiers Etat,* and in the *Récits* by fairly frequent narratorial meditations on events or, even more explicitly, by metahistorical reflections on the process of writing history and on the production of the historical text.[186]

Yet Thierry's recognition of the historian's role in the creation of his text was never unequivocal. While the footnotes and quotation marks in the text are signs of discontinuity, he took care, as Herzen observed, to reserve for the upper or narrative text "an autonomous existence," independent of the lower one (the footnotes). Indeed, the compelling force of the narrative was such as to encourage the reader to disregard the footnotes. The discontinuity of the text as a whole thus left the narrative itself intact. Discontinuity was signaled and disavowed at the same time. Similarly, though narratorial interventions in Thierry's text are not as surreptitious as they are in Barante's, they are not as significant a part of the historical text as they were to be in the work of Michelet. The persona of the historian is relatively neutral with Thierry; he is not an important character in the narrative as he is with Michelet, and he does not attempt to engage the reader as directly and as intimately as Michelet does. Narrative continuity remains an essential artistic goal for Thierry, and prohibits the development of the narrator's role to the point where the narratorial voice becomes a prominent and autonomous voice in the text. In the *Récits,* indeed, Thierry found an original and characteristic solution to the problem of maintaining continuity and of reconciling narrative and commentary, the experience of the inside and the view from the outside. The historian appears here in the text itself, in the personae of Gregory of Tours and, to a lesser extent, Venantius Fortunatus, the two primary sources of Thierry's narrative, as an actor and even a hero of history.

Caught up himself in the cruel struggles and murderous passions of his age, striving to maintain what civilization he can in the midst of the wars, disorders, and devastations brought about by the invading barbarians, Gregory also stands, as priest and judge, aside from time and history. As the object of Frédégonde's fury he participates in the action and knows the history he relates from the inside, chronicling it event by event and thus constructing the syntagmatic chain; but, at the same time, as a reflective observer whose judgment is unshakably founded on eternal truth, his glance embraces eternity, and he understands and evaluates from the outside, thus establishing paradigmatic relations not perceptible to the immediate observer. Prudent, reflective, full of reason and moderation, he lives both in the moment, with its passions and illusions, and in the light of the eternal, unchanging truth. Similarly, Fortunatus, the facile versifier and improviser, whose guiding principle in life was to live in the moment, becomes, in the society of the elegant, melancholy Radegonde and her nuns at Poitiers, "the confidant of an intimate suffering" and its privileged recorder.[187]

The historian-hero of the *Récits* plays a role in that text similar to the role played in the *Tiers Etat* by the bourgeoisie. Both are implicated in history and both suffer from its violence and irrationality; but both, at the same time, as the representatives of order in the midst of chaos, truth in the midst of illusion, reason in the midst of passion, champion the cause of the often uncomprehending victims and, in the end, secure their salvation. The people recognizes Gregory as its leader, just as, in the *Tiers Etat,* it looks to the bourgeoisie.[188] And Gregory's work of establishing truth and justice in his chronicle of events is fulfilled by Thierry himself—"le chantre passionné des victimes," as Salvandy called him[189]—just as the bourgeoisie of 1789, according to Thierry, fulfilled the promise of the medieval communes.

The liberal, "industrial" dream of a new world, in which the parts and the whole, the individual and the State, spontaneity and reason, individual enterprise and general well-being will be harmonized, thus appears at the very center of the activity of the writer as producer of the historical text. The historian and the bourgeois are engaged in the same enterprise. The bourgeois produces civilization, which, because it is rational, is universal and suffers no exceptions, whether they be particular peoples, institutions, traditions, or even languages. As an authentic order, however, the order of civilization is not achieved by repressing whatever does not conform with it but by modifying it and integrating it. Likewise, the historian producing his text seeks to give it a general validity, and to achieve this he must "tame," as Thierry put it, all particulars, whatever exists simply in and for itself, in its mere facticity. But he too dreams not of a false order, an order imposed by the mind like that imposed by a conqueror on the vanquished, but of a true order, in which particulars will not have to be repressed but will somehow find an appropriate place. With the dream, however, appear the contradictions, and those of the liberal historian as writer of history are strikingly analogous to those of the liberal bourgeois as citizen and agent of history.

The Problem of Violence

The victory of reason in history is presented by Thierry as the achievement of their just rights by the oppressed. It is a victory without violence, since an order founded on reason and truth cannot be violent. Yet though it was won against history, the realm of violence, it was also won through history. The work of history is thus not rejected. European civilization, Thierry recognizes, grew strong on the ruin of the distinct individual cultures of the past, and while lamenting this harsh necessity, he accepts it. In the same way, the modern State was built on the violent reduction by the absolute monarchs of old liberties and old particularities—provinces, institutions, traditions, and languages—but Thierry justifies these acts of violence as necessary for the triumph of civilization, which thus appears at once opposed to history and to violence and dependent on them, interwoven with them. "The establishment of the great modern States," he declares in the Introduction to the *Conquête,* "has been mainly the work of force; the new societies have been formed out of the wrecks of old societies violently destroyed, and in this labor of recomposition, large masses of men have lost, amid heavy sufferings, their liberty, and even their name as a people, which has been replaced by a foreign name. Such a movement of destruction was, I am aware, inevitable. However violent and illegitimate it may have been in its origin, its result has been the civilization of Europe."[190] Thierry asks only that the historian be allowed to "regard with a certain tender regret the downfall of other civilizations that might one day have also grown and fructified for the world, had fortune favored them." "Regret for these changes," he emphasizes later in the text of the *Conquête,* "is futile: there are ruins made by time, which time will never repair."[191]

The historian should not, therefore, reject a victory that was based on violence; he should seek rather to neutralize violence, and to achieve, as far as possible, the reconciliation of the victors and the vanquished, the present and the past, the general and the particular. In a text that deals with the desperate efforts of the Irish to maintain their language and their traditions in the face of English aggression, Thierry praises Thomas Moore, the poet of *Irish Melodies,* for transcending the narrow local interests of the popular bards: "In place of their savage inspiration, he has all the grace of the cultivated talent; and his love of independence, enlarged by modern philosophy, is not limited to a longing for the liberation of *Erin* and a return to the *old green flag.* He celebrates liberty as the right of all men, and the charm of all the countries of the world. The English words he has composed to match the rhythms of the old airs of Ireland are filled with generous sentiments, while at the same time they are marked by local colors and forms."[192]

Earlier I drew a parallel between the role of the bourgeoisie and that of the historian himself in Thierry's writing. The problematic relation, for the liberal bourgeoisie of the Restoration, between violence and civilization, between the human desires and actions that effect changes in the social and political order and the objective (rational or providential) justification of the order thus produced, in turn confronts Thierry in his activity as a writer of history. The historians liked to consider the civilization of the European nations as an inevitable fact, at once natural and rational, even though they had to admit the agency of desiring, active human subjects; in the same way they liked to think of the historical account itself as natural, determined by the character of objective reality, even though they had to recognize that the historian's imagination and desire played some part in its production. Barante tried to moderate and disguise his own role as rewriter of the old texts by claiming to allow the sources to speak for themselves and by throwing a veil of modesty over the act of generation itself. Thierry aimed at a slightly different solution: the act of writing, his own generative activity, would be acknowledged, but it would be declared not an end in itself; it would be presented instead as subordinate to the revelation of truth, rather as the actions of the Revolutionaries were justified by the liberal historians in the name of the rational order they had brought to birth. Comparing Barthélemy's *Voyage du jeune Anacharsis* (1779) unfavorably with the work of the Romantic historians of Thierry's generation, Sainte-Beuve points at the same time to the ambiguity of imagination as an instrument of cognition:

> Barthélemy's ingenious exactness is not always true. It is in vain that we reproduce textually the note of the past, because the literal meaning is not the deep meaning. The deep meaning escapes unless it is discovered by genius, and often genius obtains it only by dragging it out of the texts. As they retreat from us and fall into immobility, earlier ages become sphinx-like; they have to be forced to yield up their secret. A Niebuhr or an Otfried Müller can prise out of the texts and the monuments what less bold and penetrating minds would never have seen. The only real memory is living memory. Memory, it has been said, requires a certain amount of imagination and even of creation.[193]

At every level of interpretation, Thierry's text is marked both by a preoccupation, even a fascination, with violence and desire, and by a disavowal of them, and an attempt to justify their results—the "final order"—as inherently rational, necessary, and true.[194] The final order, as Thierry would have the reader see it—the political order of the liberal politician, the narrative order of the omniscient narrator, the historical order of the modern historian—may be the consequence of violence, but it is not sustained by violence. It persists because it is the revelation of the timeless truths of reason, or of the divine plan, or of the objective structure of the real. These, not the ambition of an individual or a class, sustain it. In it are reconciled the individual will and the general good, the eyewitness report with its richness of detail and the philosopher-historian's treatise with its abstract general categories, the past itself and the present. Time, finally, without being denied, is transcended. "There is no past," as Thierry said, "and the future itself is of the present."[195]

Thierry's ideal of the transcendence of time accounts in part for the frequency with which, in common with other historians of the eighteenth and nineteenth centuries, he uses the metaphor of the theater and the tableau, transforming the movement of temporal succession in which history is produced into a spatial contiguity in which history is grasped and appropriated as product.[196] The theatrical metaphor is itself marked, however, by the problematic character of the reconciliation proposed by Thierry's text. The historian's insight into the past is presented as the privilege of the imaginative artist who dares to descend into himself and to recall the tumult and passion that characterize historical existence. It is also presented as impartial, because the historian stands, "all passion spent," beyond desire, beyond history, beyond time itself. The historian unites in himself, in other words, experience and reflection, the immediacy of the contemporary telling and the coherence of the retrospective telling. His work proposes, in sum, a representation of the real, in which his own activity is to be thought of as that merely of a mediator. The role of imagination and desire in the production of a new text out of encounters with existing ones is never recognized. To be sure, the content that is represented in Thierry's text is one that is hidden from most men, and accessible only to the artist-seer. Nevertheless, it is something objective or transcendent, to which, ostensibly, the writer is subservient, and which his text serves simply to make manifest or to re-present. Thierry's work, like that of nearly all the historians of the nineteenth century, comes to the reader bearing unequivocally the sign of the real.[197] The older texts that the author utilizes thus lose their right to independent existence and their power to continue to signify. They are saved, represented, but at the same time closely stitched in, and subordinated to the whole of which they now form part. A way of reading is imposed upon the reader, who is seduced into complicity with the narrator—in part, perhaps, by his own desire for domination and control—only to become the latter's puppet. There is no suggestion in Thierry's reflections upon his art, or in his practice of it, of a ludic relation between reader and narrator. In the name of the real, the former must submit completely to the latter. In the same way, the power to generate meaning and the openness to interpretation of the fragments sewn together to compose Thierry's unified and continuous narrative—both the source texts and the elements of the new text— are stifled and denied in the name of the real, which emerges as the alibi of the repressiveness of the text. Conflict is thus nowhere resolved, freedom nowhere upheld, and the violence by which the artist's order is sustained is simply concealed. Yet the images of the theater and the tableau give an indication of its continued sway. They suggest that for the historian, the infinite, unpredictable richness and overdetermination of reality, and of its signs, and the intricate processes of the production of history and of the texts that record it, have been "tamed," to use Thierry's own term, and constituted as a product, an object to be appropriated and manipulated by the historian. As process, history threatens the historian and confounds his claim to autonomy; as product, on the other hand, it becomes an object of possession and control.

The dream of domination has thus not, after all, been banished from liberal historiography; the historian's impartiality and the law of the real are simply alibis of unavowed desire and of the violence it must use to achieve its ends. In a similar way, reason is the alibi of violence in the liberal state, which officially denies the role of violence in it. During the disturbances of December 1830, Sainte-Beuve relates, Thierry's friend and former secretary, the liberal Armand Carrel—the man whom John Stuart Mill described as "the greatest political leader of his time"—declared that he would like to be prefect of police for twenty-four hours in order to "mettre tout ce monde à la raison."[198]

The masking of violence was no doubt often undertaken consciously and cynically. But where the liberal ideology was internalized and there was a strong desire that it should both be seen to be and *be* true, there could be no hypocrisy, there could only be bad faith.[199] Renounced and disavowed, the exercise of violence in such cases was displaced from the sphere of action to that of imagination.

To the artists and intellectuals who subscribed to it and supported it, the liberal ideology was not, usually, a convenient mask for private profit.[200] It seems rather to have been a means of reintegrating the life of instinct, feeling, and imagination—synonymous for many historians with what they called the life of the people[201]—into an increasingly rationalized society. If the ruptures and discontinuities in time, particularly the break between the past and the present, could be shown to be superficial, and if all history could be revealed as a progressive unfolding of the present order, if the particularity and individuality of the past could be rescued in the form of the "characteristic" detail or episode, then it might be possible to achieve an accommodation, on the same terms, between the rational society and the life of feeling and imagination that had had to be sacrificed to achieve it, between the bourgeoisie and the people, on whose sacrifice the triumph of the bourgeoisie rested. The cause of the past in its colorful singularity is identical, for the liberal historians, with the cause of poetry, of imagination, of feeling, of nature, and with the cause of the people, conceived of as the innocent victim on whose sacrifice the rational order, from which it is in danger of being excluded, rests.

It is to the imagination, however, that the violence and the desire which reason denies have also, in their turn, been exiled. What is saved with the imagination, therefore, is not only the sufferings of the victims, but the violence of the executioner; and what the civilized liberal reader of the 1820s found in a history such as Thierry's was the reflection in the past not only of the bourgeoisie as the victim finally vindicated and rescued from its persecutors both by history itself and by the historian, but also of the violence and ambition of the bourgeoisie, which it could not recognize in itself or exercise in good conscience but projected onto its enemy, the feudal lord. "It has to be admitted," Thierry had once written, "that the law, the brake imposed on our individual wills, is only too often an evil for us; if this evil is necessary, let us put up with it, but let us at the same time make it as slight as possible."[202]

The *Récits des temps mérovingiens* are particularly marked by tales and scenes of violence and cruelty. The opposition of the races often appears as a conflict between female victim and male aggressor. In the first *récit* Athanaghild, the king of the Goths, who are characterized as a people "more civilized than the Franks and more submissive to the discipline of the Gospel," is forced to give his daughter in marriage to Hilperik, king of the Franks. Galeswinthe, "naturally timid and of a gentle and melancholy disposition," is filled with terror at the idea of being separated from her mother and of belonging to "such a man." Hilperik, on his side, is harsh and cruel. "He loved her at first out of vanity . . . he loved her out of avarice. . . . He could not feel the charm of the moral beauty in her, of her humility, her charity to the poor; for he had sense and thought only for bodily beauty."[203] When he tires of her and takes a concubine, she "weeps silently"—a gesture that in Thierry's text marks her as the victim, the female, the speechless, tongueless one—and then asks to be repudiated, offering to give up all her wealth in exchange. But Hilperik, the man of greed and desire, cannot understand renunciation, and does not believe her. In the pathetic account of the efforts of Galeswinthe and her mother to delay their separation and the princess's final submission to her fate, Thierry recreates the structure of history as he envisaged it in the essay "Des Nations"—the violent sundering by an aggressor of an original closed natural unity (typically mother and child).

The story of Galeswinthe is reenacted in a variant form in the fifth *récit* by the gentle Radegonde, wife of Chlother I. Like Galeswinthe, Radegonde is unusually refined and delicate. Her education has not been that of the German women, "who hardly learn more than to spin and to gallop after the huntsmen, but the refined education of the rich women of Gaul. In addition to the elegant handiwork of a civilized lady, she studied Latin and Greek, and read the profane poets and the writers of the Church. The world with its violence and cruelty appeared repugnant to her and "she began to love books as if they might open the door to an ideal world better than the one that was all around her." Again like Galeswinthe, Radegonde has been promised to Chlother after the latter's defeat of her father, the king of the Thuringians, at the battle of Unstrudt. And like Galeswinthe, "turning her thoughts more and more from the things and the men of that age of violence and brutality, she awaited with terror the day when she would be pronounced of marriageable age and would have to belong, as a wife, to the king who held her captive." When the day came, moved by "an instinct of insuperable repugnance," Radegonde fled, but was brought back and forcibly wed at Soissons. Defeated and humiliated, she nevertheless continued an inner moral resistance to her brutal lord and husband. "Inexpressible disgust, which neither power nor wealth could overcome in a soul such as Radegonde's, immediately followed the forced union of the barbarian with this woman from whom he was separated, without any possibility of reconciliation, by the very moral perfection that so delighted him in her." She avoids her husband's company, will not eat with him, and at night leaves the conjugal bed to go and lie on a simple straw mat or a hairshirt, thus "associating in a strange way the mortifications of the Christian with the overwhelming aversion she felt for her husband." Her only solace was the society of "some pious and educated cleric, some man of peace and of sweet converse."[204] For such a "bruised" soul, the narrator explains, there was but one recourse, the life of the cloister, and indeed, after many efforts to escape from the clutches of her husband, Radegonde founds a convent at Poitiers where at long last she discovers with two other persons—a young woman of Gaul, whom she has befriended and raised to be abbess of the convent, and the poet Venantius Fortunatus—the companionship of the heart and mind that she has always craved. Together, the three are "united by ardent friendship, a common religion, love of the things of the mind, and a need for recreative conversation."[205] The terms "mother" and "sister" with which Fortunatus addresses Radegonde and Agnès are accompanied by expressions of the warmest tenderness, but "all that was, at bottom, no more than an exalted but chaste friendship, a kind of intellectual love."[206]

In the tale of Radegonde, political power relations and sexual relations are metaphors of each other, as they are in the tale of Galeswinthe and throughout Thierry's work. The essential mark of political violence is always, for Thierry, the victim's loss of his tongue. The defeated nation is thus represented as castrated, reduced by its humiliation to the role of silent sufferer, the role of the woman. The tongue of the peoples south of the Loire, for example, "the second Roman language, almost as refined as the first, has given place, in their own mouths, to a foreign tongue whose accentuation is repugnant to them, while their natural idiom, that of their freedom and their glory, that of the noblest poetry of the Middle Ages, has become the patois of day laborers and serving wenches."[207] Throughout the *Récits des temps mérovingiens,* in tale after tale of violence, mutilation, and murder, it is the very structure of the historical world, as

Thierry sees it, that is being laid bare. Order, law, reason, stability are constantly being overtaken by greed and desire.

There are ambiguities in this historical scheme. The male figures in the stories are associated both with reason, order, civilization, and with desire, violence, aggression. Correspondingly, the female figures are associated both with nature, humanity, civilization, and with blind, destructive passion. Both the effort to impose law on nature and the resistance of nature to law are seen as at once justified and unjustified. The absolutes of right and wrong, law and nature are thus placed in question: "law" and "nature" are equally inseparable from violence and desire, and the opposition between them becomes blurred. Civilization itself appears inextricably bound up with violence and oppression. But the ambivalence of male and female figures, of law and nature, is concealed in Thierry's text at the very same time that it is discovered. At no point do either the male or female figures in the narrative signify simultaneously civilization or law, and desire or nature. On the contrary, whenever desire appears, it is always carefully distinguished from and opposed to civilization, and the opposition between the two tends characteristically to be ontologized rather than presented dialectically. As carriers of civilization, the people and woman ("la femme, cet autre peuple," Alexander Herzen would say)[208] are represented as victims, castrated, without desire. As creatures of desire, their role is immediately reversed: they become objects of terror, furies, castrators, destroyers of civilization. Frédégonde, the wildly instinctual queen of the Franks, knows no limit, no law. She "has no fear of sacrilege."[209] Similarly, as carriers of civilization, the patriarchs are aged and satisfied beyond desire; as creatures of desire, fathers and sons alike are rapists, aggressors, destroyers of law and civilization. Passion or desire always appears, in short, as a transgression of the limits by which human culture defines itself against nature. Sometimes it takes the explicit form of incest;[210] almost always it sets father and son against each other in a life and death struggle for the possession of a woman, a struggle that is renewed with each generation, as each victorious son becomes in turn a father, a possessor.[211] The essential structure of Thierry's text thus remains a dichotomous one of contrast between evil and good; between desire and the absence of desire; between the castrators (male or female) and the castrated (male or female); between a world of transgressions and terrible retribution, and a world in which desire and violence have been renounced; between the cruel order of history itself, in the end, the senseless, endlessly repeated devouring of successive generations of victims, and the invariable order of reason.

Over against the world of history, Thierry places, in the story of Radegonde, the timeless world of the convent and the cultivation of eternal values—beauty and knowledge, literature and philosophy. All sexuality and all desire have been banished from this world. Time itself, marked by the discontinuities and rivalries of the generations, is abolished. The community of Poitiers is created *ex nihilo*. It is not related historically or genetically to any antecedent, the only links with anything outside itself being certain features of the plan that are rationally selected from another model. Generation does not occur here through conflict; since there are no male begetters, there is no division, nor any rivalry of father and son. On the contrary, instead of an infinitely receding history marked by an always existing division, there is a beginning, and it is marked by unity: the mother alone, sole founder of the community. Variety comes to be because of her own willing division of herself, by parthenogenesis. Difference is not fundamental, but is always laid over an underlying and original identity. Radegonde abdicates as first abbess of the convent and has her protégée Agnès elected to replace her; the daughter is thus mother and the mother is daughter; the two women are aspects of the same.

In this world, then, the violence that Thierry associates with bisexual generation is eliminated. Radegonde's piety, her gentleness, her repugnance for physical love stand in sharp contrast to the unbridled passions of the murderous Frédégonde, devourer of men.[212] The *mère-marâtre*, the violent castrating mother, belongs to the world; in the convent, there is only the *mère-nourricière*, the mother as nurse. "Most [of the nuns] were of Gallic race, daughters of senators; these were the women who, by their habits of restraint and domestic tranquillity, were likely to respond best to the maternal care and the pious intentions of their directress; for the women of Frankish race brought with them even into the cloister something of the native vices of the barbarians. Their zeal was fiery but short-lived, and, incapable of observing rule or measure, they shifted abruptly from intractable strictness to the most complete forgetfulness of all duty and subordination."[213] To this world of the mother and the Eternal Father, the male is admitted only on condition that the radical difference between him and the women be mitigated, and that he renounce all claim to the father's role. Fortunatus defines himself as the son and brother of Radegonde-Agnès,[214] and in embracing the monastic life renounces for her sake the violence of desire. Difference is gathered up in identity, and time in eternity. The mother is at once genetrix and sibling; the anterior is contemporary.

The "exalted friendship" of Radegonde, Agnès, and Fortunatus represents an ideal political order in Thierry's work. But if violence and desire have been banished, along with history, from the utopia of the convent, they haunt the imagination of its inhabitants. Radegonde "liked to retrace in memory, in minute detail, the scenes of desolation, murder, and violence, of which she was once the witness and in part the victim. . . . . The image of her dead and banished relatives never left her, despite the new attachments she had established and the peace she had made for herself."[215] Tales of these old times occupied the leisure hours that the three friends spent together in the quiet of Poitiers, for with what were they to fill their conversations, if not with reminiscences of a more eventful existence than the peaceful one they presently enjoyed? The historical world with its irrationality, its particularity, and its violence had been excluded from the convent, but it alone could be talked of, and only through it could the inhabitants of the convent acquire particular existence. It was preserved, therefore, but disarmed; made sufficient to sustain historical definition, but not sufficient to overwhelm it. An oppressive historical reality from which the three friends had taken refuge in the convent was transformed, in other words, into a representation. The container was contained.

The imagination of Fortunatus was in turn fired by the tales told by the gentle Radegonde, and they became the topic of his verse. Likewise, the later poet, writing in the ideal liberal world of the Restoration, from which, as from Poitiers, all violence had supposedly been banished, found his imagination filled with the same stories of invasion and conquest, of bloody battles and murderous crimes. The tale of Radegonde and of Fortunatus reflects, inside Thierry's text, the conditions of production of that text. Like his heroine, Thierry also seeks to tame an oppressive historical reality by transforming it into a representation that is subject to his control.

Ostensibly, the historical world that is the subject of Thierry's writing is one long past. As an ardent liberal, dedicated to the July monarchy, in which he saw not an episode in a continuing and violent class struggle, as even some of his contemporaries saw it, but the culmination and at the same time the transcendence of history, the first rational political order known to man,[216] Thierry could not write, as Balzac set out to do, the chronicle of his own time. The bourgeois state, as he envisaged it, no longer knew the conflict of rulers and ruled, but only an internal dialectic, in which the bourgeois played both the role of the self and that of the other, both that of the ruler and that of the ruled.

But if the setting was of the past, the artist's imagination was of the present. The violence and irrationality that could not be recognized in a political order from which they had supposedly been banished came to dominate the one sphere to which they could be readily admitted, that of the recollection of the past. The constantly recurring relations which the historian's imagination discovers in or projects upon the past reveal desires and anxieties of the present. With particular vividness in the *Récits des temps mérovingiens,* but already quite clearly in the early writings and in the *Conquête,* a number of key roles and relations stand out in Thierry's work, constituting within it an intelligible structure different from the sequential chain of events: the aggressive, bloodstained conqueror or usurper (William of Normandy, Hilperik), the gentle victim (Saxon England, Erin, Acquitaine, Galeswinthe, Radegonde), the compassionate, mediating priest-historian in whom all desire has been abolished and who seeks, above all else, peace and reconciliation (Gregory of Tours, Fortunatus, the Welsh and Irish bards). On the one hand, there is an ideal of enclosedness, of original unity, maternal warmth, and paternal protection, always longed for, always receding before the historian's probing view; on the other, a nightmare world of action and exploration, of conquest and discovery. The Irish weep over Erin, which they have never known except as "une mère malheureuse" or "une maîtresse absente ou perdue pour jamais."[217] At the point at which they enter the historian's view, Galeswinthe and her mother are already separated by the knowledge of separation. Radegonde at fifty keeps recalling "the impressions of her earliest childhood and . . . the memory of days spent in her own country and among her own people."[218] The historian himself reenacts his heroine's recollection and telling of the past; for him, as for her, "after so many years of exile, and in spite of a complete change of tastes and habits, the memory of the paternal hearth was still . . . an object of worship and passionate longing."[219] In this lost world, which is always before history—history opens with the act that destroys it—the male is presented as a protector, a Father, never as an aggressor.

For the ideal world before history is a patriarchal world. Thierry's imagination apparently recoiled from the idea of a matriarchal universe or of a primitive communism; even the initial stage of unity and maternal warmth appears in his work under the aegis of a protective father figure. At times he seems to envisage the possibility of a struggle between men and women that is older and deeper even than the struggles between fathers and sons with which history, as he presents it, begins. To be sure, the act by which history is initiated and which sets son against father in an endlessly repeated conflict also sets man against woman. Thierry's heroines are victims, carried off by the menfolk as spoils of victory in the struggle of the sons against the fathers,[220] and they look upon their husbands with fear and repugnance, as violators. Yet Thierry suggests that the enmity of man and woman is more profound and ancient than that of father and son. Telling of the death of Henry II's son, Henry the Younger, in the *Conquête,* the narrator comments that this misfortune provisionally "reconciled not only the sons and the father"—that is, Henry with his two remaining sons—"but also the father and the mother, a far more difficult thing, from the nature of the enmity existing between them."[221] Thierry does not develop this point, however, and the image he evokes of the ideal community that is shattered at the outset of history remains a patriarchal one, in which all arrangements are sanctioned by the father-protector; nature, in its ideal form, is always governed by law. The community of Poitiers, though governed by a woman, is presided over by the Father.

History, in Thierry's narrative, begins, therefore, not with the defeat and humiliation of the woman at the hands of the man but with the defeat and humiliation of the patriarch at the hands of the rebellious sons who covet his possessions. Thereafter, throughout all history—for every historical father is inevitably revealed as a parricide, just as every people turns out to have conquered another—authority has no foundation and law commands no respect, since they rest on an initial act of violence, or breaking of the law. The history of England, as Thierry writes it, and as Michelet was to see it after him, is a history of sons rising up against their fathers. William the Conqueror's authority is questioned from the very beginning, for on the death of his father, Duke Robert, the Norman chiefs claim they owe no obedience to a bastard; and this early rejection of authority at the opening of Book III of the *Conquête* is repeated later in the conflict between William and his son Robert at the opening of Book IV, and again in the dramatic tale, in Book X, of Henry II, "who saw his own children serve his subjects as instruments against him, and who, whirled to and fro, up to his last hour, by domestic feuds, experienced on his death bed the bitterest feeling a man can carry with him to the tomb, that of dying by the hand of a parricide."

The harmony that is destroyed with the advent of history survives in Thierry's text as a utopian dream in which men and women of good will and fine sensibilities can find consolation throughout the centuries and which the historian believed was about to be realized in his own time. In this dream the impossible is achieved—*Das Unzulängliche, Hier wird's Ereignis; Das Unbeschreibliche, Hier ist's getan:* the son enters into *legitimate* possession of the woman under the protection of the father, the final authority, and with his full sanction. The rivalry of father and son is abolished. The father now exercises no violence, and his love is of the spirit. "Is there not something touching in the character of this old man," the narrator of the *Récits des temps mérovingiens* remarks about Bishop Praetextus, "who was killed for having loved too well the child he held over the baptismal font and who thus realized the ideal of spiritual paternity instituted by Christianity?"[222] An inevitable victim of the harsh world of history, Praetextus nevertheless foreshadows the ideal spiritual father who, far from being his son's rival for the woman, secures her for him, as Praetextus secured Brunehilde for Merowig in defiance of the prohibition of the historical father and his law.[223]

The dream of the harmonious family is also a political dream, in which bourgeois property-holding is freed from the taint of violence and appears legitimate, implying no transgression—unlike feudal possession, which is always the fruit of conquest or usurpation. In the context of national history, the bourgeois finds himself in legitimate possession of the motherland, of France, under the aegis and with the sanction of the *roi des Français,* and ultimately of God. The process of history for Thierry is thus a movement from patriarchy, through the chaos and disorder caused by the revolt of the sons or *famuli*, to a restoration of patriarchy in which the patriarch himself, exercising a purely spiritual authority, authorizes and legitimates the power and property of the sons. The dream of the harmonious family also represents the reconciliation of history and reason, as reason, under the aegis of divine providence and without violence or transgression, penetrates all history. For the historian himself, it represents the reconciliation, in the act of writing, of spontaneity and reflection, the immediate testimony and the organized, self-conscious narrative. At all levels of meaning, however—that of the family, that of the city, and that of historiography—the renunciation of desire appears as essential to the realization of harmony. The bourgeois is therefore presented as without desire, a pure lover of reason; the historian, likewise, is impartial, a simple servant of truth.

Throughout recorded history, according to Thierry, the dream of harmony has been engulfed in a nightmare of chaos and conflict. It would have been surprising, therefore, if Thierry had not been apprehensive lest the realization of reason and providential purpose in history, which he believed the July monarchy had brought to pass, might itself turn into a nightmare. It must have been difficult in the 1830s not to hear the hounds baying at the gates.[224] Moreover, as we saw earlier, Thierry was unable to demonstrate historically the existence of any original condition of unity. The lost paradise—of Radegonde, of Galeswinthe, of the Saxons, of the Irish, of the Welsh—always turns out, on inspection by the historian, to be flawed by the presence of an Other, by division and conflict. The possibility remained, therefore, that the liberal paradise itself might be revealed as founded not on genuine unity and identity but on the suppression of the other by violence. And the effect of the violence that is intended to impose unity is always, as Thierry argues everywhere, to confirm and multiply division. The preoccupation with violence throughout Thierry's writing points to considerable anxiety.

The dream, in sum, is that the bourgeois monarchy marks the end and the transcendence of history; the nightmare, that it is, inescapably, only one more historical regime, founded on violence and destined to disappear, like all the others that have preceded it, into the insatiable jaws of history. In the nightmare, the son's hidden desires are revealed, and he is punished for them by being persecuted and mutilated by a cruel father, his rival instead of his protector, and then handed over by him to the ferocious, castrating *marâtre*,[225] as Chlodowig is handed over by Hilperik to the vengeance of Frédégonde. Since the son, in the nightmare, is at once guilty and innocent, an agent of history and at the same time a victim of history, he is doubly represented in Thierry's text, both as male and as female, both as the son and as the old father, betrayed and attacked by his own sons—executioner and, in his turn, victim.

As the ideologist of the liberal state and the champion of its essential unity, Thierry denied that violence played a role in it, and carefully opposed violence to civilization. As an artist, however, he could not deny violence its place. Indeed, as I have tried to show, it haunts his writing, and it was here, in and through his writing, that he tried, not so much to deny it as to disarm it. If by assuming power and leadership in the state, the son or bourgeois identifies with the fathers, the transgressors and perpetrators of violence, the former conquerors or nobles, he also identifies imaginatively, in his recollection of the past, with the mothers, the victims of violence, the common people. The dangerous division and opposition of oppressors and oppressed is resolved in the identity which the son—the middle or mediating term—establishes both with the agent and with the object of violence. Violence no longer signals division and otherness since, through the historian's text, the bourgeois can identify both with the victim and with the tormentor, and, experiencing his own acts upon himself, can realize in imagination that closed, self-contained, unbroken world that Thierry everywhere points to as the ideal.

The gesture in which the son at the same time renounces and reclaims his own aggressiveness is similar to that in which the narrator renounces and reclaims his role in the narrative, and to that in which the historian submits to time and at the same time tries to conquer it and to represent it as a tableau that can be embraced in a single glance. In all three cases, the object is to resolve a paradox, to achieve possession without transgression or violence. The appropriation of the other, conceived of as a threat to the self, the integration of difference into identity, the establishment of continuity between self and world and among the parts of the self that have been alienated by the passage of time, must be realized without any manifestation of desire or violence, since desire and violence in themselves reveal and perpetuate the incompleteness which the self longs to convert to a plenitude.

The Liberal Imagination: Constant and Thierry

Throughout this essay I have suggested the relatedness of a particular philosophy of history, a particular conception and practice of historical narrative, a number of prevalent literary themes, and the ideals and contradictions of the liberal bourgeoisie of the Restoration.[226] While the validity of my reading of Thierry cannot be demonstrated by an accumulation of evidence from other writers associated with the liberal cause, it is remarkable how many features of Thierry's work are also prominent in that of Benjamin Constant, whom Thierry himself looked upon, as did most of his contemporaries, as one of the leaders, perhaps the most outstanding spokesman, of political and intellectual liberalism.

Like Thierry, Constant is haunted by time, the devourer.[227] In a text that appears to have had some importance for him, since it occurs again and again in scarcely altered form throughout his work, man is presented as trapped between a threatening father and a devouring mother, between the forbidden future, his own manhood, and the past—"seul sur une terre qui doit l'engloutir." "The generations follow, on this earth, one upon another, transitory, fortuitous, discontinuous; they arise, suffer, die; no bond unites them. No voice carries forward from the races of men that are no more to those that are presently living, and the voice of the living will inevitably be drowned within a short time in the same eternal silence. What shall man do without memory and without hope, caught between the past, which abandons him, and the future, which is closed before him?"[228]

Like Thierry again, Constant is obsessed by the problem of violence. It is a dominant theme of his political writings, of his Journal, and of his best-known work, the short novel *Adolphe,* which turns on the hero's inability to reveal his desire openly, or openly to do violence to the woman who holds him in a relation of filial dependence. The relation of victim and tormentor is crucial in Constant's work, as in Thierry's. One of the most powerful passages in the Journal tells of a young English girl judged, sentenced, and hanged for forgery. Throughout her trial, according to Constant, she made not a move, and she never opened her mouth either to speak or to eat, until at the very end, "crushed beneath the iron fist of an implacable society," she let out "a single long cry."[229] Here, as elsewhere,

Constant identifies with the victim, and in other texts he imagines the same response to violence as he attributes to the English girl—closing off the orifices of the body, the passages by which communication with others can occur, by which one can act and be acted upon. "Silence and immobility," he writes of himself, "are my natural state." And elsewhere: "Struggle wearies me. No more plans. Lie down in the barque and sleep in the midst of the storm."[230] In *Adolphe,* Ellenore in her final agony is seen "often pressing her handkerchief to her mouth, as though to prevent herself from speaking," and in her lover's voice the dying woman recognizes "the voice that wounded me."[231]

Against the threat to its imagined or desired integrity, the self seeks a defense of enclosedness, exclusion of all that is not itself, contraction of itself to a single point. Time is refused ("no more plans"), and the self protects itself, recuperates itself by retreating from historical existence and from interaction with the other. But this solution is untenable. Since for Constant the self realizes itself and acquires content only by asserting itself against the other, withdrawal from history and from relations with the other reduces it to a shadowy abstraction. The fortress of the self's integrity turns out to be its tomb. Like Thierry, therefore, Constant resorts to a ruse to resolve an insoluble problem. The self accepts the loss of its autonomy and wholeness as the price of its entering into relations with the other and acquiring historical existence or content. But it tries to cheat by substituting itself for the other, and so transforming the relation between self and other, self and world, into an internal dialectic. Béranger is said to have remarked once of Constant himself in his relations with Madame de Staël: "He listens avidly to every word he speaks to her."[232] Similarly, throughout *Adolphe* the hero represents his victim to himself, experiencing in himself the suffering he inflicts on her, doubling himself as object and agent, "la plaie et le couteau." Indeed, Adolphe represents his victim to himself so effectively that nothing Ellenore thinks or feels is unknown to him; he can always forecast with certainty the move of hers that would "inevitably" follow any given move of his.[233] Thus Adolphe-narrator invents out of himself the characters and the action of his story. His novel becomes, in the full sense of the word, a *roman d'analyse.*

The existence of the self is temporal, but just as the self restores the integrity that it imagines it loses through its desire for the other, by substituting itself for the other, it overcomes its own alienation in time by representing to itself—making present—its own past and future states. "I suffer in advance," Constant wrote, "from what I am yet to suffer."[234] He is like a peasant, he says elsewhere, who, seeing one of his friends drunk in a ditch, might cry out: "This is how I shall be on Sunday."[235]

He loves and longs to retrieve himself in persons who belong to the past, as though he wished to recover for himself the emotions of which they were the occasions. "The past is presently the only thing that speaks to my heart, and what moves and interests me in it is simply its pastness. I reread the letters of people I loved twenty years ago and of whom most are no longer alive. I retrace for myself my hopes, the feelings of strength I had then, all the things that gave my life warmth. . . . I think that if I saw Mme Trévor again, I would fall in love with her because of her date."[236]

The past, indeed, is privileged, since it has already been invested by the self and emptied of its otherness. In contrast, "something quite new, it seems to me, could never be united with my being."[237] The other, who is ideally no more than the necessary precipitant of a movement that is circular, from self to self, loses in the past the threatening reality he has in the present. Only the emotion he has occasioned remains. Offering little or no resistance, the past can thus be represented easily, without violence. Reappropriating it is simply coming into possession of what is already one's own. Threatened by blindness, Constant expresses relative unconcern: "I shall sit quite still and I shall ruminate my past life."[238] The image conveys strikingly the process of reappropriation of the self that I have been describing. Withdrawal from time (blindness, motionlessness, closing off of contact with the outside world) no longer implies the annihilation of the self. Ruminating, feeding on its own temporal existence in the past, the self is assured of content, yet protected from being overwhelmed by content, and in representing this content to itself it finally achieves its goal of unity, self-sufficiency, and integrity. "There are two persons in me," Constant noted, "one of whom observes the other and knows that these convulsive movements of grief will pass."[239] All exteriority is abolished. By the ruse of substituting the self for the other, possession can be achieved without transgression. "As timid as [my father] but more restless than he on account of my youth," Adolphe tells, "I adopted the habit of shutting all my feelings inside me, of forming only solitary projects, of counting on no one but myself to carry them out, of considering the opinions, the interest, the assistance and even the mere presence of others as an encumbrance and even as an obstacle."[240]

The similarity is striking between Constant's ideal of solitary rumination and the convent at Poitiers, in which Thierry's heroine constantly recollects the past, or, for that matter, Thierry's own repeated gathering up and reforming of his earlier essays in new collections, his constant reflection in historiographical articles and prefaces, not only on his activity as a historian but on his previous historiographical essays. In Constant's case, as in that of the gentle Radegonde, time, desire, the open world of history, all associated with violence and danger, have been disarmed, as it were, rather than abolished, and appropriated to the self as recollections, ideas of memory or imagination. The self can thus enjoy, in imagination at least, the autonomy and self-sufficiency it longs for, without having to cut itself off from the historical existence which is both the condition of its content and particular identity and the cause of its alienation from itself.

In its form as well as in its thematics, *Adolphe* bears witness to the value of self-sufficiency and control. Here too exteriority (the other) is disarmed by anticipating the judgment of the other and substituting the self for him. If Adolphe as narrator encompasses in his tale both himself and Ellenore, he is in turn observed and his behavior commented upon by a person "dans une ville d'Allemagne" who asks to see the manuscript and conveys his impressions of it in a letter to the "editor"; but this comment is in turn superseded by that of the editor himself, who includes the other reader's letter to him in the final text and ensures that he, in his *Réponse*, will have the final word. Here too the movement is circular, from the editor back to the editor, and the other is admitted only to be transformed into an aspect of the self.

The ironic structure of Constant's short novel reappears in his political ideas. Constant liked to contrast the desire for uniformity, the intolerance of difference, which he attributed to both the champions of the ancien régime and the partisans of democracy, with the liberal's ability to entertain two positions at once, to be his own opposition. "It seems almost as though our French minds had the capacity to contain only one idea," he wrote in a short essay on the Revolution and the Empire; "this idea becomes a kind of religion and the faithful treat those who claim to have two ideas instead of one as heretics and blasphemers."[241] Absolutism and pure democracy, in short, are contrasted, as manifestations of deadening unity, with the two-headed, two-chambered, two-party state which ensures both freedom and control.

Similarly, according to Thierry, any attempt to impose absolute unity on the state by the total elimination of opposition and difference (that is, of the conquered, the female, the other) is doomed to failure, and can result only in the perpetuation of blind conflict. As the conqueror needs the conquered to experience himself as conqueror, and the victimizer needs the victim to assure himself of his power, the conquered and the victim must be perpetually reinvented. Democracy and despotism, the two forms of government that aim to eliminate the other completely, can maintain themselves, Thierry argued as early as 1817, only by reinventing the other as soon as he has been eliminated, either inside the state, in the form of a caste of slaves to be held down, or outside the state, in the form of enemies to be conquered or held at bay. The infernal cycle of violence perpetuates itself, and the attempt to abolish conflict by annihilating the other simply reproduces it. The trick, for Thierry, is not to try to abolish conflict and difference, but to disarm them by displacing them from the world of action to the world of representation and of language, where they can be controlled, so that they are at once sufficient to ensure the experience of freedom and not sufficient to constitute a threat to the experience of freedom.[242] Where lord and laborer stand, mutually excluding, in irreconcilable opposition to each other, the bourgeois, or middling man, plays the two roles of protagonist and adversary, and unites in himself—at once representing and represented—self and other, agent and object. "Le tiers état naquit," in Thierry's striking formula, "et aussitôt il fut représenté" ("The Third Estate came into existence and was immediately represented").[243]

I HAVE tried to show that Thierry's political ideology, his interest in history and his ideas about it, his conception of man's basic relation to the world and to others, and his aesthetic theory and practice are all closely related, and I have suggested that the patterns and the dilemmas which characterize his work are not unique to him, but are shared by other writers in his time, especially by those who, like Thierry himself, were committed to the philosophy and the cause of liberalism. The world of representation in which Thierry and others hoped to capture the historical world, in order that, preempting all the roles in it, they might subject it completely to their manipulation, met its nemesis in 1848. According to two acute observers—Marx in the *The Eighteenth Brumaire* and Herzen in *From the Other Shore*—the revolutionary leaders of 1848 lived in a historical fantasy world. Attentive only to their roles and to the lines they had to speak, incapable of understanding the situation they had helped to create, responding rhetorically to every challenge, they found that the action did not follow the scenario they had written for it. While they continued to posture, the show got out of hand, until, at the end, they were driven in humiliation from the stage. The collapse of 1848 cast a shadow over continental liberalism and turned many to other philosophies and other political ideals. But liberalism was not destroyed by the events of 1848. It seems to me that the patterns and the dilemmas I have tried to elucidate in Thierry's writing are intimately connected with the liberal and rational tradition of which we are still, despite the debacle of 1848, the heirs, and with the prescriptions and proscriptions implicit in continuing liberal notions of the nature and preeminence of reason, the value of property, and the integrity and dignity of the individual self.

[1976]

5

Jules Michelet and Romantic Historiography

A fine book I would like to write: *An Appeal to my Contemporaries.*
The idea would be to show the ultras that there is something worth
while in the ideas of the liberals, and vice versa . . . If it were
written . . . in a spirit of charity toward both sides and were widely
distributed, such a book might well do some good . . . If I had the
talent I would like to write inexpensive books for the people.

—Jules Michelet, *Journal*, June 1820

In this Chair of Ethics and History . . . I had taken up *the* issue of
the times: social and moral unity; pacifying to the best of my ability
the class war that eats at us with dull persistence, removing the
barriers, more apparent than real, that divide and make enemies
of each other classes whose interests are not fundamentally opposed.

—Jules Michelet, letter to the director
of the Collège de France, January 1848

FROM THE late Middle Ages until the end of the eighteenth century,
history was a branch of rhetoric. Most historical narratives had a relatively
invariant structure, rather like folktales; they could be added to and
brought up to date stylistically, but not revised. The historian's aim in
narrating such histories, which were often dynastic histories, was to reconfirm the continuity of the present with the past and, by reciting the
links in the chain of that continuity, to attest the due transmission of
authority in language appropriate to each new generation. At times of
social and cultural ferment, however, as during the Renaissance and Reformation or the Enlightenment, history assumed a more investigative,
questioning character. Traditional narratives were scrutinized critically in
the light of new, more stringent criteria and new documentation. Scholarship, research, and even reflection on the epistemological foundations
and the literary form of historical narratives became part of historiograph-

ical practice among historians who tried either to subvert established narratives or to shore them up against well-prepared hostile critics.

Romantic historiography was intimately associated with the moderately liberal and nationalist aspirations of the period immediately following the French Revolution and the Napoleonic wars. The political goal of the liberal bourgeoisie was to reestablish the European polities on a new, broader basis, national rather than dynastic. Since the essential objectives of the bourgeoisie had been realized, violence was rejected; the aim was rather to heal the wounds inflicted by decades of social turmoil and achieve a reconciliation of all parties in support of the new national state. At the same time, the revolutionary rupture on which the new state rested had to be shown to have been necessary and justified. The role of history in the political programs of the first half of the nineteenth century was crucial. By discovering the hidden anonymous history of the nation beneath the outmoded histories of its rulers and its narrow ruling class, historians were expected to provide the legitimation of a new political order, a new state, and at the same time to impose the idea of this state on the consciousness of its citizens. Since history's objective was at once revolutionary (to furnish a basis for a new political order) and conservative (to found and authorize that order by revealing it to be the culmination of a continuous historical development, albeit a long-concealed, underground one), part of its aim was to achieve in itself a reconciliation of the investigative and disruptive practice of historical criticism and scholarship with the narrative art that establishes connections and asserts continuities.

Among Romantic historians, the French appear to have achieved this synthesis of scholarship and narrative art more successfully than any others. Germany produced great Romantic scholars (Creuzer, Niebuhr, C. O. Müller, the Grimms), great Romantic philosophers (Hegel and Schelling), the exemplary historian of the age (Ranke), and the greatest of Romantic theologians (Schleiermacher), but the French historians of the Restoration and the July Monarchy—Barante, the two Thierrys, Guizot, Michelet, Henri Martin—probably stand alone in their combination of scholarship and artistry, attention to the specificity of the past and concern with the issues of the present. If the Revolution and its aftermath had introduced many new ideas into France and opened men's minds to a variety of peoples and cultures, of whose richness the ancien régime, even in its Enlightened form, had barely an inkling, traditional neoclassical rhetoric remained a powerful influence in France for generations. It was no more overthrown by the Revolution than the idea of the strong, unified, and centralized state inherited from the absolute monarchs of the seventeenth and eighteenth centuries. Indeed, the rhetorical ideal and the political one may well be intimately connected in France. Even as this rhetoric came into question—in conjunction with growing skepticism about the possibility of realizing a genuine, popularly based national state—it continued to provide a framework for the prose and the narrative composition of the French historians. The historian had become the explorer of the hidden, and often forbidden, world of the tomb and the archive, an intrepid Oedipus, as Michelet called him, confronting monsters, deciphering enigmas, journeying on behalf of his fellow-citizens to the dangerous and chaotic realm of the Mothers, but he always aimed to translate the obscure, ill-formed, barely comprehensible things he discovered there into luminous, communicable, intelligible prose, capable of conveying the full weight of what he had found to his readers without crushing them under it—into French, as Michelet would have said.

The best work of Barante and the Thierrys was written consciously as part of the liberal campaign against the reactionary regimes of the 1820s. Augustin Thierry especially never concealed what to him was the essential link between history and politics. Writing history in that literate age was a way of practicing politics. The foundation of Michelet's work also lies in that period of combative optimism and confidence in the possibility of fulfilling the Revolution—as the bourgeois historians understood it—which culminated in the "Trois Glorieuses" and the establishment of the July Monarchy in 1830. The period that followed the accession of Louis Philippe to the throne, though marked by disillusionment and growing social conflict, was the heyday of Romantic historiography. Out of the tension between the yearnings of their youth, in which they still found a source of inspiration, and the harsh realities of present experience, which constantly led them to doubt their earlier beliefs, aspirations, and literary practices and to seek new, more appropriate ones, historians like Michelet wrote their greatest works.

After 1848, it became virtually impossible for many bourgeois historians to sustain their earlier idealism. In the new world ushered in by the Second Empire, every effort at synthesis and reconciliation, all hope of restoring a genuine totality was abandoned. The old Romantic ideals began to appear more and more exotic, unreal, "literary"—fictional refuges of the bruised spirit. Realism, concurrently, became synonymous with an increasingly disenchanted and even cynical acknowledgment of the prevalence of self-interest. As history came to be viewed as the arena of an interminable and meaningless jockeying for power and possessions among races, nations, classes, and individuals, historiography was more and more taken over by conscious mythmakers (nationalist, imperialist, and racist ideologists) or mere entertainers, on the one hand, and, on the other, by agnostic positivists. Not infrequently these two lines of development came together, with the positivism sustaining scholarly research, the institutional business of history, while myth was brought in, in the absence of any other instrument of totalization, to provide a means of ordering the "facts."

JULES MICHELET, the greatest of French Romantic historians and one of the great historians of all time, was born in Paris on August 21, 1798, the only child of humble parents. Like many inhabitants of the capital, Jean-François Furcy Michelet and Angélique Constance Millet were recent immigrants from the provinces—he from Laon in Picardy, she from the Ardennes. Michelet attached great importance to the provincial origins of his family, but he also liked to emphasize his own roots in the working population of France's greatest city. He entered the world, he recalled later, "like a blade of grass, without sun, between two cobblestones of Paris."[1] All his life Michelet identified with the city of his birth: he spent most of his life in it; all his triumphs were associated with it; and he invariably wrote about it with passionate affection. His inaugural lecture series at the Collège de France in 1838 was devoted to the role of Paris in the history of France.[2] "As one is born Spanish, another English, another German," he noted in his Journal, "I was born a citizen of the rue du faubourg Saint-Denis."[3]

Michelet's father, a printer by trade, was a good deal younger than his mother: he was twenty-five, she thirty-four when they married in 1795. Michelet remembered him as light-hearted, easygoing, and affectionate, perhaps a bit improvident. As none of his many attempts to establish himself in business was successful, the family was perpetually on the brink of disaster. Sometimes there was hardly enough to eat. "I was accustomed to such frugality," Michelet recalled, "that eating a few . . . green beans was at times a sensuous pleasure for me."[4] Inevitably, it was Michelet's mother who bore the brunt of her husband's failure, and there were apparently many angry scenes between the two. Michelet describes her as nagging and irascible, "exasperated by . . . sorrow and privation."[5] For some time before her death, in 1815, she was ailing and often confined to bed. Michelet, who admits he often gave her a hard time, appears to have felt guilty and in some way responsible for her suffering. In his Memoirs he recalls imagining on his way home from school one day that the house with his sick, bedridden mother in it was on fire.[6]

To a generation raised on Rousseau, the importance of childhood and family was axiomatic. Michelet constantly thought and wrote about his childhood, his parents, and his relation to them, even long after they were both dead. Some of the essential ideas and themes of his work are inextricable from this uninterrupted meditation on his own past. Of his mother, for instance, he observed movingly at the age of forty-seven: "I lost her thirty years ago . . . nevertheless, still living in me, she follows me from age to age. She knew only my bad times and was not there to profit from my better ones. When I was young I made her unhappy and it will never be my lot to console her. . . . I owe her much. . . . I feel myself profoundly the son of woman. At every instant, in my ideas, in my words, to say nothing of gestures and traits, I find my mother again in myself. The blood of woman is in the sympathy I feel for bygone ages and my tender remembrance of all who are now no more."[7]

Michelet thus recognized his preoccupation with the mother image and with woman in general long before his modern interpreters. Almost invariably he identified woman with the past itself and represented her alternately—in the way he also thought of his mother—as overwhelmingly strong, the ruler and provider of her entire family, and as sickly, the victim of the ingratitude of her menfolk. Resurrecting the wounded maternal body of the past—"la grande blessée," in his own words[8]—honoring it and easing its pain, in order that the present might be relieved of the burden of guilt, treating it with tender respect even as it is laid back in its grave and left behind, was Michelet's acknowledged aim as a writer of history.[9] No one knew better than he how much he continued to be haunted by his mother. The startling reflections on the erotic character of mother-son relations in his Journal and the obsession with incest that runs through all his writing are only the most obvious manifestations of the continued presence of Angélique Millet in the work of her famous son.

Michelet recounts that his parents adored him and would often take him into bed with them in the morning, setting him down between them and singing to him. Weary from the constant struggle to make ends meet and from their own frequent quarreling, they had placed all their hopes of success and happiness in him. "I was to save all, to redeem all."[10] The immense faith and sacrifice of Michelet's humble provincial parents, their willingness to die in themselves, as their son put it, in order to live in him, the child of the faubourg Saint-Denis, is not only a theme of the historian's personal memoirs, it is one that resonates throughout his work: Paris gathers up and transcends or fulfills the labors of all the individual provinces, and France gathers up and fulfills centuries of European and world history. Just as Michelet became the spokesman for his inarticulate parents, France speaks "le verbe de l'Europe," and the historian himself speaks for France, telling her her "forgotten dream of the night" and bringing her to full self-consciousness; or for the people, "deaf and dumb";

or for Germany, whose vast wisdom he communicates to the rest of the world in French, the language of prose and reason, in the same way that the marvelously fine analytical instrument of Aristotle once transmitted and interpreted "le Verbe du muet Orient" to posterity; or for the wordless creatures of nature (*The Bird, The Insect, The Mountain, The Sea*); or for "that other Ocean, woman," notably in the form of the long-neglected, willfully misunderstood "witch" of the Middle Ages and the Renaissance (*The Witch*); or for his young second wife, Athénaïs Mialaret, whose groping efforts as a writer of natural histories he both integrates and develops in his own enormously successful works of natural history.[11] Michelet would have subscribed wholeheartedly to his friend Edgar Quinet's definition of man as "neither the master nor the slave of nature, but her interpreter and the speaker of her living word." It is man, Quinet went on, who "completes the universe and gives voice to dumb creation, proclaiming down the centuries the secret hidden in the entrails of the earth."[12]

The role of mediating, as a child, between his mother and his father, which Michelet ascribed to himself retrospectively in his Journal, thus epitomizes the mediating roles he took upon himself in later life. As a historian, Michelet believed it was his task to act as a bridge not only between the ancient provinces and the modern, centralized national state (a role he also ascribed to the city he identified with), or between past and future, but between the different classes of French society; and he believed he was particularly suited to perform that task. Though he became a celebrated and successful writer, teacher, and public figure, a professor at the prestigious Collège de France, and tutor first to Princess Louise, the daughter of the Duchesse de Berry and the grandchild of Charles X, and then after the July Revolution to the daughters of King Louis Philippe, he was himself, as he constantly reiterated, a son of the people. While ardently defending property and the family as the foundation of all human culture and the condition of progress, he always reaffirmed his "sympathy with the propertyless." It was, he declared, "natural in one who had been so poor and had worked with his hands."[13]

By "the people," however, Michelet did not mean, on the whole, the modern urban proletariat, the development of which in his own lifetime he observed with apprehension and dismay, but the solid peasantry and above all the artisans of preindustrial France. Occasionally he used the term to refer rather generally to the masses of the poor and downtrodden— the preindustrial proletariat which was not conscious of itself as a class. Notwithstanding the hardships of his childhood and his father's repeated failures, however, his own background was by no means that of the bottom rungs of society. His mother's family were fairly well-to-do landholding peasants, and there were times, by his own account, when it was "money from Renwez"—that is, from his mother's three celibate maternal aunts in the Ardennes—that kept starvation from the Michelets' door.[14] As for his father, being not only a printer but his own master, he belonged to a literate élite among the "people."

Michelet's family background and his parents' dreams of improving their sorry lot through the success of their child led them, after a period of neglect, to make a concerted effort to provide their son with as good an education as could then be had. In 1810 he was sent to a private teacher to learn Latin. Five years later, he entered the Collège Charlemagne. Awkward, ill at ease, and obviously underprivileged, the butt of his classmates' jokes and pranks, he compensated for many humiliations by studying hard. After a shaky start, he came out at the top of his class in 1816. By 1819 he had successfully defended his doctoral dissertation at the Sorbonne—then a rather skimpy affair consisting of two short papers of fifteen to thirty pages each, one in Latin on a philosophical subject (Michelet wrote what he described a few years later as a "misérable compilation de quelques passages de Locke"),[15] the other in French on a literary subject (Michelet chose Plutarch's *Lives*). In 1821 he placed third in the Agrégation, and was immediately offered a position as professor of rhetoric at Toulouse. In order to be able to stay in Paris, however, he accepted instead a temporary post at the Collège Charlemagne. A year later he was able to get a permanent appointment in history at the very conservative and right-thinking Collège Sainte-Barbe.

Michelet's Journal indicates that he had already espoused many liberal views by this time, as well he might, since he had not been raised in a religious or right-wing atmosphere. He appears to have kept them to himself, however, and nothing in his teaching apparently gave his superiors cause for alarm. Rising in the world and promoting himself from the artisan class, in which he was born, to the professional class had not been easy, and Michelet clearly did not intend to jeopardize his incipient career by inconsiderate expressions of liberal opinion.[16]

In 1824 Michelet married Pauline Rousseau, a young woman who had been born out of wedlock and had taken the name of her mother's lover— a tenor at the Opera—at the time of her birth. Seven years previously Pauline had gone to work at the sanatorium at which Michelet's father had found employment in 1815, and a few years later, when the sanatorium closed, she and the Michelets, father and son, were both taken in by its administrator, Anne Fourcy, a devout and kindly woman, to help her run the boarding house she had set up. During this time Anne Fourcy became a surrogate mother for Michelet, possibly also providing him with his sexual initiation, and Pauline, with whom he was in constant contact since they all lived in the same house, seems to have become his mistress. Pauline was six years older than Michelet. The age relation of Michelet's parents was thus repeated in the first important encounter of their son with the opposite sex. "I have always loved women older than myself, in memory of my mother," Michelet noted years later in 1857. "My first attachment was of this kind. The young woman seemed lovable and desirable to me, though she was quite old, because she resembled my mother."[17]

Michelet claimed to see advantages in the marriage. His wife, he wrote to his aunts in Renwez, was "an excellent housekeeper," she was in good health, she would keep him in clean linen—for he was now a young professor—more economically than he could do on his own, and she would give him a status he needed if he were to advance in his career. "One must be either a priest or married in order to be considered for certain places in the University."[18] In fact, Pauline was in an advanced stage of pregnancy when Michelet married her, and gave birth to their daughter, Adèle, three months later. The following year the couple had a son, Charles.

Though he loved his children and worried a great deal about them, Michelet was never much of a family man. His life, as he himself often remarked, was in his writing and his teaching.[19] His daughter was the apple of his eye, but if she remained close to him it was partly because of her marriage to his favorite pupil, Alfred Dumesnil, whom he later called "my adopted son, my son-in-law, myself," and who was the son of a woman Michelet appears to have loved deeply.[20] His own son, on the other hand, despite Michelet's solicitude, never amounted to anything and gave his father little satisfaction. He died in 1862, at the age of 35. Moreover, Michelet's relationship with Adèle deteriorated rapidly after his second marriage to a woman twenty-eight years his junior. As for Pauline, as his career progressed and prospered, Michelet became increasingly neglectful of her. By the time she died, in 1839, she had grown fat and drank too much. For a while Michelet was filled with remorse. He consoled himself by reflecting that it had been a mistake to attach himself "to someone of inferior education" from whom he had always been "divided in spirit."[21]

Perhaps the trouble was that he did not and could not educate Pauline. The destiny of woman, in Michelet's view, was to be reborn as the creature of man, to be transformed from the original all-powerful mother, holding her menfolk in her dependence, into a dutiful and educated daughter, dependent in turn on her menfolk.[22] Indeed, the emancipation of the son from thralldom to his mother, of the male from the female, was nothing less, for Michelet, than the progress of civilization itself, and in Michelet's work it is usually presented as equivalent to man's advance from matter to spirit, from geography to history, from necessity to liberty. That is why, no doubt, it had to be completed by the son's emancipation of his mother from the world of the flesh and the fatal cycle of birth and death. Civilization, in short, as Michelet sees it, is the progressive penetration of nature by spirit.[23] Man owes the original gift of material life to woman, to nature, but woman and nature are dependent on man—and notably on men like Michelet, on teachers and thinkers—for rebirth to the life of the spirit. Woman's evolution is from mother to daughter, from mistress to ward. In the same way, the bourgeoisie, which is born of the people, must in its turn take the people under its tutelage in order to educate it, release the spiritual energy embedded in its materiality, and thus lead it to freedom. According to Quinet, "If the bourgeoisie had a mission in the world, it was without doubt to become the guide, the teacher, or rather the head of the people; that was the sacred mission for the sake of which it came into possession of the intelligence, the knowledge, and the experience of past ages."[24] An analogous role, in Michelet's view, falls to Paris in relation to France, and to France in relation to the indecisive, directionless *populations flottantes* that surround her.[25] Since the original emancipation of man from his mother, nature, or—by analogy—that of modern bourgeois France from the ancien régime, does not occur without violence, however, and is therefore accompanied by guilt, much of Michelet's writing can be read as an attempt to placate the mother—the defeated of history—and, by so doing, to ward off the danger of a "return of the repressed."[26] The ultimate purpose of remembering is to be able to forget, the ultimate object of historiography to clear the decks for the future by identifying, defining, and naming the past, "ce mauvais songe," and so making it possible to set it aside.[27]

In 1849, when he was fifty-one, Michelet married Athénaïs Mialaret, then a young woman of twenty-three. She had come to Paris from Vienna, where she had been employed as a governess, to meet the eminent writer whose literary productions she revered. The marriage lasted until Michelet's death in 1874, and this time, in contrast to the earlier marriage to Pauline, Michelet was totally absorbed in his wife. He observed and noted every detail, even the most intimate, of her physical and mental existence. She was truly his possession, his creature, an aspect of himself, a daughter-wife who fully accepted his leadership and aspired only to emulate him. Through her, Michelet appears to have experienced a moderation of the difference between past and present, female and male, the other and the self, victim and victor, which he judged dangerous and destructive and which was the central theme of his work. He often remarked admiringly of his young wife that she looked like a boy. And like Joan of Arc, one of his dearest heroes, Athénaïs—as he himself presented her in his Journal and in the biography he wrote of her—seemed by nature not fully a woman: she menstruated irregularly and with difficulty, sexual relations were often painful or impossible for her, and she appears to have had trouble conceiving and carrying a child. The son to whom she did give birth on July 2, 1850, and to whom Michelet with characteristically defiant optimism gave the name Yves-Jean-Lazare, survived less than two months. Athénaïs's Viennese employer, the Romanian Princess Cantacuzène, also noted how boyish she looked, according to Michelet, and used to call her playfully "mon petit Rousseau."[28] Michelet's career thus led from the ancien régime of a mother-wife to the new order of a daughter-wife; from the very feminine Pauline Rousseau, who apparently never aspired to be anything other than his mistress, his housekeeper, and the mother of his children, to a masculinized, invented Rousseau, who saw herself as her husband's pupil, helper, and creature, and whose primary aim was to learn to wield, like him, the pen.[29]

Michelet himself was at least as drawn to this kind of relationship as to that with older maternal women, since it approached most closely that condition of brotherhood and identity which he believed to be the ultimate, yet never to be realized, goal of the entire historical adventure—"l'idéal impossible de l'identification."[30] Indeed, it was preferable to the realization of the ideal, inasmuch as the residual difference in the relation between a man and a virginal, boylike woman postponed the stasis of perfect unity and identity while permitting a considerable degree of community. Time and difference, in other words, were at once preserved and overcome. The dialectic of life continued, but no longer required violence and conflict. The ideal woman was thus, for Michelet, almost a man, as conversely the ideal man included in himself an element of femininity.[31] It cannot be coincidental that Michelet entertained nostalgic memories of early friendships, notably of his passionate friendship with Paul Poinsot, who had died in 1821. In friendship, law and emotion, "justice" and "grace" (to use the theological terms Michelet himself favored), the bourgeoisie and the people, the masculine and the feminine aspects of human existence, culture and nature, seemed to him to be reconciled. Friendship is at once an incomparably sweet, private, individual emotion—"Ah jours regrettables, vrai paradis sur la terre, quand il n'y a pas encore inégalité, servilité, envie ni bassesse"—and at the same time the foundation of any genuine public political order, "le vrai noeud de la cité." In the original relation of male and female, difference is radical, unresolvable, and thus permits of no dialectic; but in friendship difference is underlaid by an essential identity, toward the realization of which the parties strive in a progressive upward movement. "The Greeks understood how friendship, much more than love, is an engine of progress. For in love there is no emulation, in the real sense. The less advanced, being separated by the difference of sex, would have to change her nature in order to resemble the more advanced."[32]

IN 1826 Michelet applied for a post at the Ecole Normale, which had just been cautiously reopened as the Ecole Préparatoire, after having been shut down for political reasons in 1822. Again, in his eagerness to advance his career, he took care to conceal from the Minister of Education, Monseigneur Freyssinous, whatever ideas he had that the latter might not have approved of. His opinions, he implied, were thoroughly orthodox and conservative. "I am presently seeing through the press a translation of the work of Vico," he wrote, "in which the study of history is illuminated by a philosophy that is in complete conformity with religion." The Minister could check on the soundness of his opinions, he added, by consulting the members of the Royal Council, "ecclesiastics as well as laymen."[33]

It is a sign of the relative lack of specialization that then obtained in teaching and scholarship that Michelet declared himself a candidate for any chair at the newly reopened school—in the classical languages, in philosophy, or in history. As it turned out, he was offered a chair in philosophy *and* history, the previously separate chairs in these two disciplines, which were considered dangerous and potentially subversive, having been consolidated in order to advertise their diminished importance in the new curriculum.

The combination of history and philosophy was one that suited Michelet well, however. Like nearly all historians of his time and generation, he had a keen interest in philosophical issues and in literature as well as in history. His Journal shows that in the early 1820s his reading ranged widely over ancient and modern European history, philosophy, and literature. It covered the Bible, Greek literature (Homer, Aeschylus, Sophocles, Euripides, Theocritus, Pindar), Latin literature (Terence, Cicero, Ovid, Seneca, Pliny, Statius, Virgil), ancient philosophy (Plato and Aristotle), ancient historians (Herodotus, Thucydides, Livy, Tacitus, Diodorus Siculus, Seutonius, Arrian), modern and contemporary philosophy and political thought (Locke, Shaftesbury, Montesquieu, Condillac, Rousseau, Ferguson, Constant, De Gérando, Destutt de Tracy, and the then popular Scottish philosophers Reid and Dugald Stewart), modern and contemporary historians (Bossuet, Hume, Gibbon, Robertson, Schiller, Millot,

Daru, Sismondi, Guizot, Thierry, Barante, Mitford, Hallam, Niebuhr), and above all the great classics of French literature (Rabelais, Molière, La Fontaine, Corneille, Racine, Boileau, Pascal, La Rochefoucauld, Madame de Sévigné, Vauvenargues, Prévost, Voltaire, Marmontel, Chénier, Parny, Chateaubriand, and always, over and over again, Rousseau) as well as English literature (Milton, Swift, Fielding, Goldsmith, Sterne, above all Scott and a little later Fenimore Cooper). By 1824, when he established contact with Victor Cousin, then the most influential philosopher in France, the range of Michelet's reading had expanded to include Shakespeare, Italian literature (Dante, Boccaccio, Tasso, Machiavelli, Guarini, Goldoni), German literature and philosophy (Luther, Lessing, Herder, Kant, Goethe, Hegel), political economy (Smith, Sismondi, Say, Comte, Saint-Simon), and the history and theory of law (Burlamaqui, Mittelmaier, Hüllmann). He had discovered Vico and the contemporary German mythologist Friedrich Creuzer, both of whom were to prove vitally important to his work; Friedrich Schlegel's *Uber die Sprache und Weisheit der Indier;* and also the collections of folksongs and folk poetry of Scott, Arnim and Brentano, and von der Hagen. And all the while he continued to read the classics, those of antiquity as well as those in his own language and in the modern European languages, innumerable works of history, old and new, and the accounts of travelers to all parts of the globe. In addition to this extensive literary culture, Michelet had a lively interest in painting and architecture. On his journeys to Belgium and Holland, to Germany and Italy, to Switzerland and England, as well as through the French provinces, he never failed to seek out and comment on buildings and works of art in both private and public collections. His work as a historian bears witness to this lifelong interest in the visual arts: interpretations of art and architecture are an essential part of Michelet's reconstructions of the culture and outlook of past ages. In addition, he relied extensively on painting for his portraits of historical figures.

Michelet's approach to history was not and could not be that of the modern professional. Not only did the institutional basis of the "discipline" of history, as we now know it—the multiplication of universities and faculties, the creation of countless specialized chairs, the innumerable professional journals, the large numbers of students to be taught—not yet exist, but the historian was still, as Michelet's reading and formation indicate, a man of letters in the old eighteenth-century sense of the term. The autonomization of the various branches of science and learning had hardly begun. Michelet lived in daily familiarity with the literature (in the narrower sense of "belles lettres") of classical antiquity and especially with that of his own country; he also had a considerable knowledge of other vernacular literatures, as well as of philosophical, political, legal, and economic literature. In addition, he was a knowledgeable amateur of art and was keenly interested in folklore and popular culture. His social circle was neither restricted to nor dominated by other historians, but included classical scholars, egyptologists, poets, novelists, natural scientists, doctors, economists, statesmen, and businessmen.[34]

In our own time, only a few unusually privileged historians enjoy a comparably varied and rich literary culture. In Michelet's day, however, it was still the norm. Indeed, few generations have been as widely curious or as diversely cultivated as the remarkable first generation of European Romantics and neohumanists. In those days it was not uncommon for a classical scholar like Böckh to quote Sterne.[35] Not surprisingly, Michelet was thoroughly unsympathetic to the idea of specialist histories. "Plus de classifications, plus d'histoires spéciales," he noted in his Journal in 1842.[36] He conceived of history in the same way that the German neohumanist and Romantic philologists conceived of philology: not as a specialized technique, not as textual criticism, but as *Altertumswissenschaft*—the study of ancient society and culture in its entirety. Michelet himself defined philology somewhat more narrowly as "observation of the real, the science of facts and of languages," but he saw it as completed and fulfilled in history.[37] It may even have been the early classical training of Michelet and many of his contemporaries that kept them from the narrower view of history that became common among their professionally oriented and trained successors. Michelet's contemporary, the German historian Droysen, believed that the school of Ranke lacked a broad historical vision because they had had little intercourse with the ancient world. "Without Isaiah and Aeschylus, Aristotle and Augustine," one does not get this wider vision, according to Droysen. "Ranke's students see in history only what concerns the State. Sybel does not pause to reflect that this is only part of history, that social and cultural relations are just as essential to it, that all these spheres are simply many expressions of the One (*des Einen*) that moves them, and that our scholarship has to be concentric with our deepest inner and ethical life. . . . I know how much I owe to my familiarity with Bacon, Dante, Homer, and even the Pentateuch."[38]

Unlike many later historians, Michelet had a keen sense of what Droysen called the One. History, for him, was always one; it was always total history; nothing could be torn out of its context and understood in isolation from the whole of which, in his view, it was a part. In this respect Michelet was a true Romantic. Everything to him was both itself and a symbol of something else; understanding always involved interpretation; and the supreme mode of interpretation was metaphoric. "Mechanical" explanation in the Enlightenment manner—that is, in terms of cause and effect, before and after—was never enough. Only the "organic" part-whole paradigm was capable of producing full insight into reality. Michelet was thus as opposed to the idea of a positivist history that would be purely factual and free of all philosophizing as his contemporary at the University of Berlin, August Böckh, was opposed to the idea of a philology that claimed to be able to do without philosophy.[39]

As early as the 1820s Michelet was noting that he proposed to study many areas of history, including religion, customs, law, language, style, taste, politics, industry and commerce, philosophy, and the sciences, as well as "the mutual relations of these different areas . . . their reciprocal influence on each other" and the "relations of the relations." The ultimate goal was a total synthetic history—"systematization of everything."[40] The historian who later claimed that a whole chapter of social history was inscribed in the evolution of the bed[41] was from the beginning thoroughly convinced that every product of human culture, humble or grand, is historically significant if the historian knows how to interpret it. Interpretation is thus from the outset, along with "facts," at the heart of the historian's activity. The latter's task is not merely to relate the facts of the past but to discover and interpret them for the future.[42] The historian, in short, is neither a pure antiquarian nor a pure rhetorician; his work cannot be limited either to discovering fragments of the past or to retelling a traditional story in updated form, or even to critically evaluating such stories (the various roles played by historians in the sixteenth, seventeenth, and eighteenth centuries). For Michelet, the historian is more than a scholar, more than a narrative artist, more than a *philosophe:* he is, in Friedrich Schlegel's words, a "backward-looking prophet."

Michelet was thus likely to have been pleased by his appointment to a chair of "history and philosophy," as later, in 1838, he was happy to have been invited to take up the chair of history and ethics ("histoire et morale") at the Collège de France. From 1827 till 1829 he successfully taught several philosophy courses at the Ecole Préparatoire, in which, after a fairly full discussion of Fichte and Schelling, he appears to have come down on the side of the moderate and conciliatory rationalism of the Scottish school, then at the zenith of its influence in France.[43] Indeed, when two separate chairs of philosophy and history were reinstituted in 1829—possibly in order that philosophy might be entrusted to a teacher more securely orthodox than Michelet—Michelet requested the chair of philosophy as "the more important and the higher of the two."[44] Later still, in January 1848, when the government of Louis Philippe, alarmed at the growing political agitation in the country, ordered an indefinite suspension of the course

Michelet was teaching at the Collège de France, Michelet vigorously defended his right to broach general questions of public morality and social policy in his classes. A similar dispute had already led to the resignation of his friend Edgar Quinet from the chair of Southern European Literature, to which he had been appointed in 1842. As was customary at that time, Quinet had interpreted the term "literature" very broadly as signifying the whole of culture, and he had taught courses on the revolutions in Italy in the Middle Ages, on the religious institutions of southern Europe, and on Christianity and the French Revolution. In 1845 he announced a course entitled "Comparative literature and institutions of Southern Europe." The Minister of Education, under pressure from powerful conservative groups, including the King, demanded that the term "Institutions" be dropped from the title and that Quinet confine his instruction to literature in the narrow sense. Quinet refused to comply and resigned.

Quinet's resignation, the canceling of Michelet's course in the last days of the July Monarchy, and finally, in March 1851, the formal suspension of Michelet from all teaching responsibilities and his expulsion, along with Quinet and the Polish poet and patriot Adam Mickiewicz, from the Collège de France are among the most visible episodes in an important process by which the teaching of history was transformed in the course of the nineteenth century. The great French historians of the first half of the century—Chateaubriand, Sismondi, the brilliant liberal school of which Barante, the two Thierry brothers and Guizot were the leading lights, later on Michelet himself, Henri Martin, Louis Blanc, Lamartine, Quinet, Thiers—were all deeply involved and active in public affairs, as statesmen, as polemicists, or as both. For all of them, writing history was an integral part of their total activity as concerned and informed citizens and public figures; it could not be separated either from the general philosophical, moral, and even religious understanding of the world and of man's destiny that they were seeking or from their immediate political ideals and programs. Moreover, for all of them, as for their counterparts in Germany, their own involvement in present history, far from being an obstacle to understanding the past, was a condition of genuine historical insight. When George Sand declared that "with cold impartiality the historian can divine nothing of the past," she was expressing a commonly held view.[45]

Just as history was part of their own world view and contributed to the formulation of their own political opinions, the Romantics wanted it to inspire the entire nation. Their words were therefore addressed to as large and general an audience as possible. The historian, as they conceived of him, was quite remote from the specialist scholar he subsequently became. He was in the fullest sense of the word a teacher, the educator of his people, and a passionate participant in the political debates of the day. Michelet's rival as a historian of the French Revolution, the early socialist leader Louis Blanc, insisted—in a notice to his readers that was intended as a criticism of Michelet's scholarly procedure—that the historian cite all his authorities and discuss and compare their testimonies before the reader, who must in the end judge them. It is not enough, he declared, just to add another narrative of events to those that already exist: sources must be noted and difficult points candidly discussed.[46] At the same time, Blanc emphasized that the historian's dedication to "the party that must outlive all other parties, the party of truth" need not and should not make him neutral. "I am not a man who hides his sentiments," he wrote to a friend. "Whoever peruses my book will find out who I am. Yes, I wrote with a definite goal in mind; yes, I took up the pen to exert as strong an influence as possible on the minds of my readers; . . . yes, the historian in me is a man with a cause; I not only avow it, I am proud of it. I consider the cold impartiality which leaves the reader undecided between glory and shame, between oppressor and oppressed, to be a violation of the eternal laws of justice and of the most sacred duties of the historian."[47] It is hard to think of any of Blanc's contemporaries who would have disavowed this profession of the historian's faith. Michelet was certainly not one.

On the contrary, Michelet, as we shall see, was haunted by the idea of the *livre populaire*—books for the people—and he understood his own mission as a prophetic one: that of bringing the French people to a full awareness of itself, articulating its unconscious thoughts, and teaching it what it indeed already knew but could not, without his help, know clearly and consciously. The people, in sum, was inarticulate: it needed leaders to interpret it to itself, to point it in the direction it unconsciously wanted to go, and to lead it on that way.[48] Those leaders, for Michelet, had to be themselves from the people—a requirement that was interpreted idealistically to mean that they must not have been artificially removed by social convention from the maternal totality to which all men in principle belong. In other words, the new leaders of the people were to be recruited from Michelet's overwhelmingly youthful audience at the Collège de France.[49] His students were to serve as the guides of the masses, as men were to serve as the leaders and teachers of women, raising them up to the humanity that is latent in them; as sons were to be the saviors of their mothers, redeeming the flesh that bore them by realizing the spiritual idea in it; as Paris, for all those committed to a certain Jacobin idea of the Revolution, was to be the teacher of France, and France to be the teacher of Europe. The historian, Michelet liked to point out, is himself, like his students, an innocent, a Parsifal-like figure, in whom the original connection to nature, the mothers, the people—to beginnings in general—has not been complicated and distorted by official education and social conventions.[50] It was thus an audience of younger brothers—children of the bourgeoisie who had been preserved by the natural idealism of youth from the corruption their teacher had also escaped, thanks to his humble background, his moral integrity, and his unflagging youthfulness of spirit—that Michelet addressed in his lectures at the Collège de France on the eve of the 1848 Revolution. "Are we not all part of the people?" he cried. Yet, "there is an abyss between you and the people. . . . I mean by this word the thirty millions . . . who know nothing of your books, your newspapers, your theatres, nothing even of the laws they have to obey. . . . Gentlemen, there are more than thirty millions whose way of thinking has almost nothing in common with yours. That must be our point of departure."[51]

In inviting his young "messieurs" to turn away from the usual objectives of their class and to dedicate themselves, with him, to "saving" the people, Michelet appealed to what he believed was the common humanity in them, the common origin they shared with the oppressed and downtrodden. The religious, charismatic character of this teaching is obvious. Michelet's aim was to shape his students into a new brotherhood of disciples prepared to go out and work for the redemption of society, and the reconciliation of its warring elements. "As the child is the mediator in the family, the young man should be the mediator in the City. In family quarrels, when mother and father are at opposite ends of the table, it is the child who takes the hand of one and places it in that of the other. . . . Likewise in the City. That," he told his auditors, "is . . . what you will do, for it is you [who must serve as the chief agent of an immense movement of all toward all]."[52]

Varying the Saint-Simonian theme of a new church of artists, technicians, moralists, and entrepreneurs leading humanity toward the millennium, Michelet envisaged his professorship as a prophetic mission and the Collège de France as the pulpit from which he could preach the new gospel of "association" and organize the missionary work of a new clerisy. The university, he declared (and that term in French means the entire secondary education system) "must be the ministry of the future."[53] Had not "the true France, that of the Revolution" proclaimed that "teaching was a holy office and that the schoolmaster was equal to the priest"?[54] The vehemence of Michelet's campaign, in the 1840s, against the Church, the Jesuits, and the nefarious influence exercised by Catholic priests on women and simple folk underscores the context of rivalry in which he saw himself placed in relation to the Church. His high idea of the Collège de France and his passionate devotion to it—he always considered it the apex of French intellectual culture and a beacon of the modern spirit[55]—are inseparable from his conception of it as a kind of modern secular cathedral. That, at least, was the role Michelet, together with his colleagues Edgar Quinet and Adam Mickiewicz, believed it should play if it was to live up to the ideals that had presided over its foundation. As the Collège had in reality a quite different complexion, and included, along with many accomplished but cautious and by no means revolutionary scholars, a number who were neither distinguished nor inspired, the efforts of Michelet and his friends to get it to conform to their idea of it led them into conflict with their colleagues and ultimately, as the political climate soured, to their own expulsion from the Collège. In the end, the positivist spirit that Michelet and his friends had hoped to overcome triumphed over them.

After 1848 historians gradually ceased to view themselves as Michelet, Thierry, Quinet, or Louis Blanc had seen themselves. More and more they emphasized not the visionary and public aspects of their work and their role, but the scientific and professional ones. The problems the historian addressed were no longer large social and human problems but technical problems, and they were defined not by what the historian saw as the key issues of the times but by the discipline itself. Correspondingly, the audience addressed by the historian was no longer a general one, but an audience of professionals like himself. As they turned away from the tribune, which they now thought of as dangerous and compromising, and occupied themselves with enlarging and deepening their knowledge of the past, the younger generation of historians also renounced not only the philosophical ambitions but the philosophical interests and background of their predecessors. Philosophy, ideas, and speculation, it seemed, produced only dangerous illusions—and Romantic revolutions. The new historians intended to be sober and factual scholars, to keep out of mischief themselves and refrain from leading others into it. For the Romantic idealism, the inspired insights, and the literary language of their predecessors, they substituted an astringent, skeptical, and sometimes narrow positivism, an austere dedication to "facts," and an ascetic refusal to write anything that was not patently demonstrable. This new strategy produced some remarkable and enduring achievements, and in the work of the best of those who adopted it there is a tension that preserves, if only as an absence, that which they chose to renounce. Gradually, however, as the new method was routinized, history became a busy but relatively peripheral activity, which had not only willingly forfeited its earlier claim to be of central moral, political, and philosophical importance, but in fact no longer deserved to be thought of in that way.

*   *   *

IN 1827, the year in which he took up his appointment at the Ecole Normale, Michelet published a translation of Giambattista Vico's *Scienza Nuova*. There is little doubt that Michelet himself saw this work as a contribution to the philosophy of history. If it should prove impossible to make a complete translation, he had told the philosopher Victor Cousin in 1824 when he began work on it, he would make a substantial résumé of it which he would then incorporate "into my treatise on the philosophy of history."[56] As it turned out, Michelet's translation provided a smooth and somewhat simplified version of Vico's often dense and difficult original, together with a lengthy introduction. It thus constituted, along with Quinet's translation of Herder's *Ideen,* which appeared the same year and which had also been encouraged by Cousin, a major contribution to the Romantic philosophy of history. The object of Vico's new science, Michelet explained, was "to separate regular phenomena from accidental ones and to determine the general laws governing the former; to trace the course of that eternal and universal history that is produced in each epoch in the form of particular histories; and to describe the ideal circle in which the real world turns." Thus the *New Science* is "at one and the same time the philosophy and the history of humanity."[57]

What Michelet retained from Vico was the idea that history is the record of man's self-creation. Man, as Michelet put it, is his own Prometheus,[58] and history unfolds in an orderly pattern from a world of gods, through one of heroes, to one of men; from theocracy, through aristocracy, to democracy; from divine, symbolic, and poetic language, in which the sign and the thing it signifies are virtually indistinguishable, so that meanings are fixed and permanent, to rational, analytic human prose, in which the original connection of sign and thing signified has been severed and the relation between them is recognized as artificial and conventional, so that meanings become uncertain, problematic, and open to interpretation; from an original, natural world of material necessity (geography) to a new, humanized world of liberty (history). Where Vico saw this movement as continually repeated—*corsi, ricorsi*—Michelet tried to combine his predecessor's cyclical idea of history with an optimistic and teleologically oriented progressivism. For Vico's circles he substituted the characteristically Romantic image of the spiral, in which repetition and innovation, the real presence of the past and the absolute distinctness of the present, "metaphor" and "metonymy" (in the now familiar sense that Roman Jakobson has given to these terms), are combined and reconciled.[59]

In the great 1869 Preface to the Lacroix edition of his *History of France,* Michelet declared that "Vico was my only master," and two years before his death: "Vico gave birth to me."[60] These remarks were not rhetorical flourishes; throughout his life Michelet's historical writing continued to be informed by the ideas and patterns he had discovered in Vico. The first work to show Vico's influence appeared in 1831, in the warm afterglow of the successful July Revolution. Indeed, Vico and July were often associated in Michelet's mind with this high point of his own life—a marvelous time out of time when he himself was coming into full possession of his powers as a writer and when France too seemed on the verge of rebirth. "I began to exist, that is to say, to write, at the end of 1830," he recalled in May 1871, three years before his death.[61] His *Introduction to Universal History,* which appeared in April 1831, was written, he declared later in the preface to the *History of the Revolution,* "on the burning cobblestones" of Paris in those heady days. It represented universal history as an "eternal July," a constantly renewed victory of freedom over necessity.[62] In the *Roman History,* which appeared almost simultaneously, Vico's system was projected onto the history of the Roman republic. As Michelet himself wrote later in a new preface he prepared for a second edition of this work in 1866, "Roman history appeared clearly to me between two half-lights: the primitive age of gross myths and the bastard age of contrived and calculated myths, which served the ends of caesarism"—between the dawn of origins and the dusk of decline.[63]

The *Introduction to Universal History* is a remarkable little work which can be read as a piece of forensic rhetoric aimed at rehabilitating France and showing how the future of humanity is in the hands of the Christ-nation that has been treated by the others as a pariah. It presents the movement of history as passing from totality to individuality, from sacred to profane, from the dominance of the female to that of the male, from East to West, from divine origins in India through the heroic worlds of the Persians and the Jews to the humane, civilized order of the Greeks and the Romans. The cycle begins again, in modern Europe, in Germany— "India in the midst of Europe." To this ill-defined, watery land, where no boundaries are sure and no river courses fixed, where all philosophy veers toward pantheism and men retain the childlike candor and openness of earlier times, Michelet opposes Italy, the land of innumerable city-states, of measurers and mathematicians, whose goal is to domesticate and civilize nature, and England, the land of egotistical Byronic heroes, whose goal is self-deification and dominance over everything that is not themselves. In this latest turn of the historical wheel, France is to play the role of Rome, as Italy has played that of Greece. France's task, in other words, is to harmonize, humanize, and universalize all that in Italy or England remains local, particular, and self-centered, to mediate between extreme generality (Germany) and extreme particularity (Italy, England), and to lead mankind forward to the fulfillment of the present historical cycle and the edge of the next. "France," Michelet had already declared in his course at the Ecole Normale in 1828-29, "is the true centre of Europe."[64] Correspondingly, Michelet, the disciple of Vico and of Creuzer, as later of Grimm, the son of Italy and of Germany, was the proper interpreter of both not only to his countrymen but to the world.

Though Michelet himself appears not to have played an active role in the July days, he welcomed the 1830 Revolution enthusiastically. On a practical and mundane level, it provided a golden opportunity for him and others like him to acquire or to enhance already acquired positions in the government or the educational establishment. The professionals of the bourgeoisie all sensed that their time had come and that the new regime was their own. Augustin Thierry expected to be rewarded with a good post for years of supporting the liberal cause. Michelet wrote to Quinet urging him to come quickly to Paris: "You must come immediately, my friend. New things are materializing. New positions are being grabbed quickly. You'll find one easily if you arrive soon. Your friends are in power."[65] In April 1830 Michelet himself was appointed head of the historical section of the Archives Nationales (then Archives du Royaume), a post he held for twenty-two years until he was forced out by Napoleon III in 1852, and in 1838 he achieved what he saw as the culmination of his professional career when he was appointed to the chair of History and Ethics at the Collège de France, in his own eyes the highest seat of learning in the land.

On a more exalted level, the July days raised expectations of a new social order, a complete revolution, not to say a transcendence of history, and a rebirth of the fraternal spirit that had already manifested itself as a promise and intimation of future fulfillment in the Fête de la Fédération of July 1790—always in Michelet a point of reference and a kind of secular Revelation. The image of a new July, a new Eden, in which each will stand naked and innocent in the eyes of all, and all differences, obscurities, and secrets will be abolished in the full, even light, without shadows, of the noonday sun—the image of complete unity and transparency, in sum, such as was ardently desired by Rousseau—recurs again and again in Michelet's writing and distinguishes history's high points from its low points, its heroes from its villains, its end and fulfillment from its murky travails. In his *History of France* and again in his *History of the Revolution* Michelet recounted a pivotal moment in history, a moment of revolution, as a dissipation of darkness and shadow, a revelation and illumination—

in one case the revelation of France as a nation to herself (the famous "Tableau de la France"), in the other, of the people to itself as a people. The "Trois Glorieuses" of the 1830 Revolution were likewise represented by him as a moment of revelation and illumination "beneath the brilliant July sun," and as the dawn of a new day, a "brilliant July morning."[66]

It quickly became apparent, however, that the July days were not yet the fulfillment of history, but only another prophetic revelation, another reminder of 1790 and intimation of things still to come. In his *Histoire de la Révolution de 1848* Louis Blanc depicts Louis Philippe, the "bourgeois" monarch of 1830, as a thoroughly prosaic character—"neither the impulsiveness of passion nor the sublime joy of dedication . . . [but] a combination and rare equilibrium of secondary qualities"—whose mediocre virtues degenerated after his accession to the throne, instead of being enhanced. The entire period of the July monarchy is presented by Blanc as unprincipled, governed by greed. "The morality of self-interest was preached publicly, in an . . . official manner, and the doctrine of industrialism was seen seated upon the throne. Everything could be bought and sold: reputation, fame, honor, virtue. *Doing business* was the only thing anybody cared about." In these conditions, according to Blanc, France ceased to be herself—the daughter of Rome—and began to resemble a sordid and brutal Carthage.[67] A more factual history would record the strikes, the revolts, the luddite riots among the workers—as early as August 1830—all of which were mercilessly put down; the difficulties of the peasants; the shortage of credit that drove many artisans and small businessmen to the wall; the epidemics; and, at all times, the hardship, the ill health, the poverty, and finally the hunger that were the lot of the least favored—that is to say, of the vast majority.

Michelet felt as keenly as anyone the "moral cholera that followed so soon after July, the disillusionment, the loss of high hopes."[68] His position as head of the historical section of the Archives required him to travel throughout France, and both his Journal and his published writings bear witness to the close attention he paid to the conditions of life—economic and social as well as cultural—in the cities and provinces he visited. He was especially moved by the plight of the silk workers of Lyons, whose massive uprising in 1831 had been ruthlessly suppressed and whose miserable living conditions he observed at first hand on a visit to the city in March and April of 1839.[69] In descriptions of other journeys he undertook in these years to Switzerland, Belgium, Germany, and England, there is the same intense curiosity about the present as well as the past, about contemporary conditions as well as about monuments, archives, and works of art, the same eagerness to establish contact with good informants—

businessmen and ordinary citizens as well as officials. Michelet's account of his journey to England, for instance, provides a fascinating glimpse of a country bursting with energy and industrial activity but already gravely scarred by the social consequences of rapid industrialization. Less detailed than the work of Engels or even the earlier observations of Sismondi, it is comparable in certain respects with Tocqueville's, and deserves to be better known among students of nineteenth-century England than it is.

In these years, moreover, no one could ignore the "social problem," as it was called. On the one hand, there were the pioneering empirical studies of Count Villeneuve-Bargemont, a Prefect under the Restoration (*Econ-omie politique chrétienne ou Recherches sur la nature et les causes du paupérisme en France et en Europe*, 1834), of Frégier (*Des Classes dangereuses de la population dans les grandes villes*, 1840), of Eugène Buret (*De la Misère des classes laborieuses en Angleterre et en France*, 1840), of Parent-Duchâtelet (*Hygiène publique*, 1836), and above all the massive inquiry into the conditions of the workers of Lille, Rouen, and other textile-manufacturing cities by Dr. Louis-René Villermé (*Tableau de l'état physique et moral des ouvriers dans les fabriques de coton, de laine et de soie*, 2 vols., 1840); on the other hand, there were the economic, political, and social analyses and the programs of reform put forward by the so-called utopian socialists— Etienne Cabet (*Voyage en Icarie*, 1840), Fourier and his disciple Victor Considérant (*Destinée sociale*, 3 vols., 1834–1844; *Principes du socialisme*, 1847), Proudhon (*Qu'est-ce que la propriété?*, 1840), and Constantin Pecqueur (*Economie sociale*, 1839; *Théorie nouvelle d'économie sociale et politique*, 1842). Michelet was familiar with most of these works. In addition, he was personally friendly with many Saint-Simonians and former Saint-Simonians (Gustave d'Eichtal, Arlès-Dufour, and Jean Raynaud, who showed him around Lyons in 1839), as well as with Proudhon. The latter attended Michelet's Collège de France lectures faithfully from 1838 until 1842 and was a regular recipient of complimentary copies of the historian's books. A long, laudatory letter he wrote about the *History of the Revolution* was proudly reproduced by Michelet as part of a new preface to that work in 1868.[70] Though he was certainly not a socialist himself, Michelet read the works of the socialists attentively and tried at various times to answer them.[71] He even planned to write a book on socialism, and believed he had gone some way toward doing so in the last volumes of his *History of the Revolution*. As late as May 1871, physically sick and morally disheartened by the debacle of the Franco-Prussian war, he noted that he was "tout occupé de l'Internationale."[72]

Quite quickly, then, Michelet became disenchanted with the regime that had been put in place by the glorious July Revolution. The prudent foreign policy of the government, its refusal to intervene on behalf of the Polish patriots or to defend French national interests in the Near East in 1840, aggravated the sense of disillusionment among the headstrong and ardent patriotic and nationalist leaders that intellectuals such as Michelet, Quinet, and Louis Blanc took themselves to be. France, Michelet announced, had fallen far from the heights of July: "There is no other case of such a rapid decline."[73] According to Quinet, the bourgeoisie had betrayed its mission. Instead of educating the people, "it had no sooner acquired authority than it became infatuated with it like all the regimes that had preceded it; . . . the bourgeoisie repeats in turn, through a thousand mouths: 'L'Etat, c'est moi.' "[74]

Michelet's vision of French history had been that of a movement toward identity and unity, a communion of all provinces, all local traditions, all individuals with one another—not physically or racially, at the level of blood, flesh, and soil (it was left to a later generation to dream that wild dream, which Michelet would have considered regressive), but morally and intellectually, through the spiritualized *mère patrie,* the mother reborn and redeemed by her sons. "I love [the provinces]," he wrote in 1842, "and I thank them for restoring to us the adored mother, such as she was to another age, when, younger, she was not yet herself. They are, for me, the steps, the stations, on the way to supreme maternal beauty."[75] But the barriers that July had seemed to throw down were rising again, higher than ever, less now as barriers between provinces or regions—though these continued to exist, as Michelet discovered on his travels through France, especially in the contrast between northern and southern France— than as barriers between the classes. In his role as teacher and spokesman of the people, which he believed to be the obligation of the historian and which he accepted fully for himself, Michelet felt called upon to react.

If public life, as Michelet saw it, was in decline, the historian's private life was also in disarray. Pauline had died in 1839; Madame Dumesnil, to whom he had formed a close attachment, died in 1842. In the fall of 1842 he came near to a breakdown. "The feeling of the harmony of the world diminishes in me with each passing day," he wrote to Alfred.[76] The fear, never far from the surface of Michelet's thought, that his optimism might be an illusion, that nature might be an unreconciled, unreformed enemy, a careless devouring *marâtre,* rather than a loving and nourishing *mère,* now overwhelmed him. Existence seemed still to be dominated by discontinuity, absurdity, incessant and meaningless change, with nothing lawful or rational about it. "My children gathered flowers, made them into posies, and then discarded them. I am afraid that is how nature is too. She entertains herself making vital compositions, arranging harmonies of existences. Then she discards them by the wayside. But first she snaps the stems and tears the blooms apart."[77] Meaning, order, intelligibility are not in the existent: men must invent them and impose them on an irrational and unjust nature. "We draw out from ourselves, from our will, the means of rebinding the bleeding strands."[78]

Michelet worked his way out of his private and public despair by adopting a more activist, critical, and interventionist attitude to the existing order. His strategy was no longer to celebrate it and seek in it an achieved reconciliation of opposites, of past and present, tradition and progress, Christianity and Revolution—that reconciliation he now considered illusory—but to point to its contradictions and combat its injustices. In the course of the 1840s Michelet renounced the dreams of harmony and reconciliation which Burckhardt referred to bitterly, around the same time, as the "illusions of the spirit of 1830,"[79] and prepared to do battle to ensure the future triumph of the principles incarnated in the great Revolution. "I once thought monarchy was possible," he noted in July 1847. "But it makes itself *im*possible by associating its fortunes with those who . . . thrust their hands into the pockets of the people. . . . The son swindled by his own father! One's ideas about paternalist government are wonderfully altered by that."[80]

Michelet now associated his sympathetic portrayal of the Middle Ages as "haute harmonie" in the first books of his *History* with the conciliatory optimism of the immediate post-July days, and he renounced it angrily. "What a dream the Middle Ages are, what a world of illusion, fantasy, indifference to the real!"[81] The only thing that can redeem his account of that time, he writes, is the sincerity of the mistaken idealism that inspired it: "My regret . . . is to have given an ideal picture of those terrible Middle Ages. The ideal is true, because of its poetry and its aspirations, but totally unrelated to the historical reality I projected it onto."[82] To some extent too, Michelet appears to have associated the pleasures of art and illusion with this time of optimistic fantasies, and he became increasingly severe on what he called "the artist" in himself, the spinner of gratifying but deluding fancies. In the same passage of his Journal in which he renounces his belief in the viability of the monarchy and in the possibility of reconciling Christianity and the new social and moral order born of the Revolution, he criticizes the artistic impulse in himself and his friend Quinet. Both of them, he notes, were "retardés par des courbes, des distractions d'artistes, ce que j'appellerais les sensualités de l'art"—that is, the facile harmonies and satisfactions the artist creates to compensate for the discordances of reality.[83] As he turned his back on the easy optimism of the 1830s, in sum, Michelet also repudiated a certain artistic practice. This break in his work, which critics have always noted,[84] and which is above all a break with a certain mellifluous, oratorical rhetoric and a certain repertoire of poetic images, deriving in some measure from Chateaubriand, was often emphasized by Michelet himself. "History," he declared in the Preface to the volume of his *History* dedicated to the Regency of Orleans, "is not a professor of rhetoric working to ensure smooth transitions. If a passage from one point to another is sudden and the movement convulsive and rocky, so much the better; that is only another characteristic of truth. But I have to pay the price. The more I am true (*vrai*) the less I am probable (*vraisemblable*). What a marvelous point for the critics to latch onto. . . . What can I do about it? And what can I do about the facts? . . . I am the serf of time. And I cannot do anything except follow after it through all the diverse forms these figures get from it."[85]

According to Michelet's own account, therefore, he broke in the 1840s at one and the same time with the conciliatory political position he had held until then, with the Restoration cult of the past and the dead, with a desire for and belief in enduring personal happiness—mostly through women—and with an artistic practice and writing style that had remained essentially idealist and neoclassical, oriented toward the *vraisemblable* rather than the *vrai*. His leave-taking itself was still somewhat rhetorical, but its significance is clear. "Farewell my past, farewell Church, farewell my mother and my daughter. . . . All that I have known and loved I now turn my back on in order to go out toward the infinite unknown, toward the obscure depths, whence I sense, though I do not yet know it, the coming of the new God of the future."[86]

The movement outlined here—advancing from Mother to Father, past to future, the affective to the intellectual, "grace" to "law," even as the past is laid piously and tenderly to rest, so that it will not obstruct the hero (Michelet, France, Humanity) in his forward path—is a familiar one in Michelet, to be sure. It arises out of Vico, and it informs his early works—the *Introduction to Universal History*, the *Roman History*, the *Life of Luther*—as well as his later ones. In the early writings, however, the emphasis is on the struggles of the *past*, and the narrative ends on a note of achievement and synthesis: in the *Introduction*, the July Days; in the *Roman History*, the coming of Caesar—"who brings the Republic to a close and inaugurates the Empire." Later, the movement is seen as one which is endlessly repeated in the life of the individual, in that of nations, and in that of humanity, and from which no release can be expected. There is no moment of achievement and reconciliation, and the law of life is unremitting heroic struggle.

In 1843 Michelet's break with the past was expressed concretely by a temporary interruption of work on the *History of France*. The final volume on the Middle Ages appeared in 1844, but the volume on the Renaissance did not appear until 1855, although Michelet had in fact lectured on the Renaissance at the Collège de France in 1839–40 and 1840–41. Instead, Michelet turned to the Revolution and began to write its history, as though to revive and reactivate the heroic and revolutionary spirit of the French people. Michelet expected his readers to read all his works, as he himself, as a young man, had once read Thomas à Kempis's *Imitation of Christ* or as a Christian reads the Gospels. To none of his works, however, was this expectation more central than to the *History of the Revolution,* which appeared in seven volumes between 1847 and 1853. If the goal of history was revolutionary transcendence of history—putting the past behind one— then the history of revolution was the most important history of all and the key to present action. As George Sand had written in a commentary on the rival *History of the French Revolution* of Louis Blanc, the French Revolution "is truly the Book of Destiny of modern times. In it one can study the law of man's life."[87]

At the same time, Michelet also began to address the issues of the day directly. Indeed, his publicistic and polemical works were far more widely read than his histories. The first of these—*The Jesuits*—was written in collaboration with Quinet and was composed of lectures that the two friends had given at the Collège de France in 1843. Both Michelet and Quinet had been responding to what they perceived as a concerted attempt by the Right, notably by the Church, to undermine the achievement of the Revolution, and in particular the monopoly of secondary education which the Revolution had given to the State and its professors. The elementary school reform introduced by Guizot in 1833 and the passing of another law in 1836 containing provision for "freedom of teaching" in secondary schools were the thin edge of the reactionary wedge in the eyes of Michelet and his fellow radicals. Behind this legislation they discerned an intensive campaign, mounted by the Jesuits, who had returned to Paris in 1833, in favor of a "pluralist" and "free" educational system, from which the Church alone stood to gain. By 1841 a major assault on the University's monopoly of secondary education was in fact being conducted in the Catholic press, notably in Louis Veuillot's *L'Univers* as well as in countless books and pamphlets. *Monopole universitaire,* a Jesuit production that appeared in 1843, denounced the subversive, immoral influence of many professors on the young, and singled out Michelet as a particularly "impure blasphemer." Michelet and Quinet counterattacked in two independently devised series of lectures at the Collège in the Spring of 1843. When *The Jesuits* was published later the same year it became an instant best-seller.

Five thousand copies were sold in ten days, and the book went through five printings averaging two thousand copies each before the end of the year. In addition, *The Jesuits* provoked a vast outpouring of books and articles both supportive and critical of Michelet and Quinet. At issue for Michelet was above all the moral and spiritual leadership—and in the end, the control—of the nation.

Despite his later indictment of Robespierre and the Jacobins in the *History of the Revolution,* Michelet always subscribed to the essentially Jacobin ideal of the nation one and undivided. The Girondins had made a mistake, he acknowledged, when they allowed themselves to be drawn into supporting federalism. The full realization of France as a nation, as he saw it, must necessarily lead to a highly centralized state in which there would be neither disaffection nor dissent nor even significant difference, and in which all Frenchmen would be united as brothers. (French women, as we saw, would realize their humanity by becoming more and more like French men.) Michelet's criticism of the Jacobins mostly concerned their exclusiveness, their secretiveness, and their attempt to *impose* identity of views instead of allowing it to unfold. In Michelet's eyes, such an attempt could only aggravate dissension, not resolve it. Genuine identity of views was always achieved through each individual's free discovery and realization of his true self, and the leader's task was to assist the individual to make this discovery, not to impose an alien personality on him.[88] Michelet thus diverged from the Jacobins not so much on the question of ends as on the question of means and on the relation between means and ends. A recent scholar has aptly observed that Michelet had little taste for politics because he found political activity in its very nature both symptomatic of division and itself divisive.[89] He was by no means a liberal in the classic English sense of the term.

Oddly enough, Michelet portrayed the Jacobins in a manner very similar to that in which he portrayed the Jesuits or, for that matter, the modern European Jews: all three groups appear in his work in the form of a secret army of parasites infiltrating and undermining the healthy body of the nation. This vision seems inseparable from the general conviction shared by many nineteenth-century idealists that difference and diversity are the consequences of a kind of fall from Being into History, so that the goal of man must be to work forward through the dialectical resolution of successive oppositions to a restoration of unity and identity. " 'Ah! if I were one,' says the world,"—according to Michelet—" 'if I could at long last reunite my dispersed members, bring all my nations together.' "[90]

The ways of error, according to the old adage, are many, while that of truth is one. Though the achievement of unity and identity, whether of the nation or of humanity itself, may never be fully realizable—its realization would mark the end of history—it must always be pursued as a goal. Anything that deliberately obstructs it is evil; any promoting or reanimating of old divisions that are destined to be historically overcome is Satan's work. Michelet's response to the reappearance of "outdated" singularities and defeated differences is typically paranoid: he can see them only as attempts to drag men back into the dark cave from which they have struggled to emerge, only as a plot by the forces of Night to cheat the forces of Light of their legitimate victory. Thus Michelet's Jesuits—like Jews or gypsies in many European folk traditions—lure children from their parents, wives from their husbands. It is not surprising that the anticlericalism of the Third French Republic, which had its roots in the polemics of the 1840s, went hand in hand with a uniform vision of France and, above all, of French education, which owed much to Michelet.

In 1845 Michelet fired a second salvo against the Church. *Priests, Women and Families* sold fourteen thousand copies in eight months and went through nine printings in English in a year. This time the government began to be concerned, and the Minister of the Interior, the Minister of Justice, and the prosecuting attorney for Paris entered into discussion of possible legal sanctions against Michelet. Meanwhile, in 1846, Michelet published *The People*, the third of his popular writings of this decade.

If the theme of *The Jesuits* and *Priests* had been the defense of French nationality against the divisive influence of the Church, *The People* warned of no less serious dangers and divisions stemming from the "social problem." The ideal unity of the French "people," which had been manifested for Michelet above all in the Fête de la Fédération of 1790, had been disastrously undermined not only by the struggles of political factions during the Revolution itself and then by the political order of the Restoration, but by the development of commerce and industry under the July Monarchy. By devoting itself to the selfish pursuit of wealth, the bourgeoisie had cut itself off from the rest of the people. Well-to-do bourgeois, petty bourgeois, artisans, proletarian workers, and peasants were now divided from and suspicious of one another. To Michelet this was an unmitigated disaster. Whereas for Marx, and even for a non-Marxist socialist such as Louis Blanc, class division and class conflict were a given reality and the point of departure of any serious reflection about society, Michelet the mediator reaffirmed desperately the "essential" underlying unity of the French people, even as he acknowledged present divisions. Louis Blanc and Balzac, he protested, wanted to aggravate the split between the "two nations." His own aim, on the other hand, was to heal it, restore the people to its true nature, and find the way back to the true popular tradition of the Revolution.[91]

In later years, Michelet's disputes with Louis Blanc over their respective histories of the French Revolution (Michelet's appeared in 1847–1853, Blanc's in 1847–1862) were only apparently of a technical nature. In reality, it was a question of determining which of the two had the right to speak in the name of the Revolutionary tradition, which of the two rival versions of that tradition, which of the two histories and thus which of the two historian-authors, was truly authorized. Full and clear references to sources, the quality of the original materials consulted, and similar seemingly technical points of scholarship were important because they served to legitimate the rival narratives in which each claimed that the authentic and authoritative revolutionary tradition had been embodied.

To Blanc, the Revolutionary tradition was one of class struggle; fidelity to the Revolution meant continuing that struggle, even if Blanc was relatively moderate and circumspect in the way he proposed going about this. To Michelet, the Revolutionary tradition was enshrined in the Fête de la Fédération of 1790, and fidelity to it meant restoring and securing for all time the unity of which that moment had been the revelation.[92] He refused to accept Blanc's proposition that the bourgeoisie, which Blanc defined in economic terms as the possessor of capital and of the instruments of labor, was outside the people, defined as "those citizens who, possessing no capital, depend completely on others" and "are free in name only."[93] The bourgeoisie, according to Michelet, was virtually undefinable, since it ranged from wealthy industrialists to quite modest, even poor people. Michelet appears to have thought of the bourgeoisie as a moral entity, identifiable by its values, its codes of conduct, its own self-perception and the perceptions of others, rather than as an economic one. For this reason, it could not, "thank God, . . . be opposed to the people, as some would have it."[94] In sum, Michelet argued that the Revolutionary tradition was not identical with socialism,[95] and that fidelity to that tradition meant not engaging in and exacerbating class conflict, but transcending it.

Michelet himself was a radical; he was never a socialist. He claimed to have "refuted" Proudhon's attack on property by showing how access to property had marked the emancipation of the peasant,[96] and during an 1844 visit to Lyons, where he was dismayed to find the workers inspired by the "Christian communism" of Cabet, he tried to counter the utopian socialist ideal of a "grande communauté" with proposals of his own for small-scale cooperative ventures in home heating and cooking. Not surprisingly, he discovered that the men who dreamed of "refontes totales" were not much impressed by his "petites idées d'amélioration." These little communist cells, he noted testily, "feraient obstacle à la grande réunion."[97] Like the Jacobins during the Revolution, the socialists of the 1840s, in other words, were a divisive force impeding the union of the nation.

Michelet never changed his position. He never accepted either the Left's critique of property or its critique of the family, and he never wanted radical revolution. His aim was to reestablish continuity with the tradition of the great Revolution, which to him was itself the fulfillment of the entire history of the French people, not to make a new, socialist revolution. "Desired two things," he wrote in his Journal on April 15, 1869: "(1) to re-establish the tradition of France, of the *Patrie,* rejected by our Utopian Socialists, who speak of an absolute difference, a new start. . . . (2) to strengthen the family and the home, and make them the keystone of the temple of the City, the firm support of the *Patrie,* and all this in opposition to the literature of the day. The Utopians—Saint-Simon, Fourier—on the one hand, the novelists—Sand, Balzac, etc., on the other, have this much in common: they both despise marriage."[98]

Michelet's reflection on social questions, in the end, is strongly marked by what Marxists would describe as a petty-bourgeois refusal of both reactionary restoration and revolutionary socialism. It is dominated by political idealism, fear of modern economic developments, rejection of the primacy of the economic, longing for peace and reconciliation, and dislike of violence and crude authoritarianism, which are seen as fatally divisive.

The social groups that Michelet most identified with and sought to promote were not the rural proletariat but the small property-holding peasantry, not the developing urban proletariat of factory workers but independent artisans possessing a skill and the tools of their trade. The progressive replacement of such artisans by mere factory hands in the textile industries of Reims and Elbeuf filled him with apprehension and dismay.[99] Whereas for Marx, social progress passed by way of the industrial organization of labor, for Michelet, at the same moment, the mill hand represented not an advance but an absolute regression from the laboriously acquired individuality and autonomy of the artisan to a more primitive, communal, and dependent condition. Michelet looked on the factory worker with compassion, but also with fear, for the monotony of his labor and his servitude to the machine, he argued, made it virtually impossible for him to learn responsibility and self-reliance. "Incapables de fixité, amis du changement," the proletarian masses, Michelet seems to have feared, offered easy material for manipulation by future tyrants.[100]

Nor was there much to inspire respect or confidence in the new class of shopkeepers. Michelet regarded them as a shifty, deceitful lot, "always waging a war on two fronts: a war of cheating and cunning against the . . . customer, and a war of vexations and outrageous demands against the manufacturer."[101] Unlike the peasant, the artisan, and even the manufacturer, the shopkeeper has no roots and does not produce anything. He is simply an agent of exchange, a parasite living off the labor of others.

Equally characteristic of Michelet's social thought is his consistent propensity to interpret social phenomena idealistically in political, moral, and even metaphysical terms, his avoidance of economic categories or retranslation of them into noneconomic ones. The primordial issue, he asserted, is Liberty. Economic questions are subordinate to it, consequences of it; they are never determining.[102] Social relations and social classes are not definable economically or even, in the end, only politically. Michelet's categories of analysis form part of a system that sucks their specific content into a whirlpool of metaphors in which all categorical hierarchies are destroyed. The economic is seen as a mirror image of the psychological, which may in turn reemerge as a mirror image of the metaphysical. This mobility of meanings is part of the great attraction and interest of Michelet's work to us today, for it suggests relations, which are indeed worth exploring, between aspects of reality that are kept strictly isolated from each other in positivist historiography and social science. Michelet avoids analyzing these relations, however. Indeed, the analogical structure of his historical texts foils every attempt at critical and positive analysis so effectively that it is, in the end, potentially as mystifying as any positivism.

Finally, Michelet ascribes a crucial role in all his historical writing to the mediator and conciliator. In the all-embracing philosophy of history which he shared with many other writers of the Romantic period (notably the German Romantic poets and philosophers whom he knew well and loved, as well as Quinet, Hugo, Renan, even Baudelaire), woman, the people, nature, the Orient, beginnings, the affective, poetic or symbolic discourse, primitive communism, promiscuity and "incest" (not the transgression of boundaries, taboos, and properties, but the condition supposedly preceding their institution), pantheism, and the complete submersion of the individual in the community, together with a battery of attributes such as humidity, heat, fecundity, vegetativeness, depth, and materiality, are all part of a single semantic field and are set in an undefined and unexplained relation to one another, as are the equivalent contrary terms: man, the nation, culture, the West, ends, the profane, the intellectual, the analytical discourse of prose, a social order based on property and the family, and the emancipation of the individual, together with attributes such as dryness, coldness, crystallinity, sterility, elevation, spirituality.

The dynamic element in Michelet's texts, as we have seen, is the movement from the first set of terms to the second. Since this passage requires a good captain to negotiate it, someone who knows both the sea and the land, both the beginning and the end, both the people and what it is destined to become (the nation), both the poetry of the past and the prose of the future, mediating figures play a privileged role in all Michelet's writing. The historian himself is one, especially the historian who, like Michelet, can claim to have been born of the people; so is the poet (Virgil above all); so is the great historical agent, such as Caesar, half-man, half-woman in Michelet's portrait of him, standing at the crossroads of the ancient, local world of city-states and the modern world of universal empires; and so, in their more humble station, are the pilots of the Gironde who negotiate the dangerous passage from the open sea to the domesticated river.[103]

The truly successful mediator, as Michelet presents him, always knows how to avoid exclusiveness and violence. Thus the writer who would write for the *nation,* rather than for a small group within it, must "follow the popular tendency, while at the same time cultivating what is best in it."[104] He must, in short, be passive and active at the same time, combining and reconciling both roles. Michelet is distrustful of every movement that is forced, always fearful that the new, instead of emerging from the old, as the son emerges from the womb of the mother, and leading the old forward with it, will attempt to dominate or even to destroy the old. Violence and tyranny, whether exercised by the overbearing nobleman, the great landlord or industrialist in the English manner, or a small band of moral fanatics such as the Jacobins, always produce rupture instead of continuity, forced conformity instead of unity, conflict and repression or opposition, followed inevitably by revolt or the "return of the repressed" instead of harmony. The difficulty, Michelet noted in 1847, is this: "1) If it is left as a matter of feeling . . . fraternity is not effective, or it is so only in the hour of enthusiasm (as at the time of the early Christians). 2) If it is formulated as law and made imperative, it is no longer fraternal. It is unfraternal fraternity. . . . An enforced community will have the barbarizing consequences of war—it will be big on destruction, but weak on production. 3) If you want fraternity to spread, it must be voluntary. . . . So instead of forcing men, train the children, give them a fraternal education that will make them want fraternity."[105]

Michelet's new, more aggressive and pugnacious attitude was thus significantly mitigated by its goal, which remained that of unity. Not any revolt was justifiable, only that which, like his own or like that of his heroine Joan of Arc, is sanctified by selfless dedication to the restoration of unity. And since violence may not be exercised against those within, against the other who has to be seen as a brother, an aspect of the self, the blame for division can be placed only on the foreigner or the parasite, the outsider or the alien within, the absolute and absolutely evil Other, who seeks to obstruct the reintegration of what in its essence is One and only by accident (of history) divided and separated. As fomentors of division, Englishmen, Jews, Jesuits, Jacobins, and socialist "priests" as well as Christian ones become legitimate objects of hatred in what emerges as a paranoid vision of history. War against the foreign enemy, the Other, is permitted—and Michelet's imagination is aroused by the idea of the young men of France going off to holy war in defense of the *patrie,* "les baionnettes frémissantes"—but war within, class war, civil war, is sacrilege.[106]

For Michelet, who, as he himself remarked, had lived with his father for forty-eight years and been separated from him only by death, who had considered his father more alive in him than he was in himself, and to whom his father had always represented "la vraie France de Voltaire et Rousseau," conflict between father and son is unthinkable.[107] Though in fact it happens all the time, it is always an aberration. To account for it, Michelet provides his good fathers and good sons with a dark double, an Other. His histories are filled with evil father-kings (often dominated by castrating, phallic mother-queens) and evil sons. Conflict always involves an evil father or an evil son; it is always Satanic, a deviation from the norm. Thus England, France's Other, riven by intractable social conflict, is from the very beginning the land of Cain, its king a "méchant fils qui bat son père." Though great, active, and powerful, it is destined to be forever an unhappy and divided land, an agglomeration of Byronic individual heroes stricken with spleen and incapable of "association," never a genuine society.[108] In France, on the other hand, law and love are reconciled and mutually enhanced in the figure of the good father-king, who combines in his person both male and female characteristics; both the analytic, boundary-setting, individualizing faculty and the faculty of synthesis, comprehension, and inclusion; both modern property, together with its counterpart the modern family (culture), and primitive communism, the original sharing of goods and women (nature). It is this capacity to achieve differentiation without conflict or loss of community which, according to Michelet, makes France exemplary, a light unto the nations and their guide into the future. For in France "la patrie" is or should be "like a woman (mother, wet-nurse, etc.)," and man feels or should feel that "the law is like a mother and that he lives in the warmth of her presence. That is the ideal, at least, that we must always pursue."[109]

As Michelet's aim—the resolution of all conflict—is predicated, like that of the Enlightenment *philosophes* he loved so well, on the free recognition by all men of their common humanity (and Michelet's *peuple,* far from being a genuine *social* category, is, in the end, nothing other than this common humanity, which explains why he can claim that the bourgeoisie is not outside it but part of it), education inevitably plays a crucial role in his social and political thinking.[110] In this important respect, the Romantic historian is truly the child and the loyal champion of Enlightenment. Indeed, as we saw earlier, the educator, and above all the historian, is for Michelet the supreme architect of the City, the true politician. Michelet not only tended to stand back from the specifically political arena, whether the Chamber or the street, his highly theatrical struggle with the authorities at the Collège de France in the mid to late 1840s indicates that, like many intellectuals since his day, he believed the great conflicts of his time could be and were being played out in university lecture rooms. His most recent biographer in English, Stephen Kippur, rightly draws attention to Michelet's unflagging belief in the power and centrality of words, and consequently in his own importance as a writer and orator.[111] There seems not much doubt that he experienced the pleasures of the exercise of power as he swayed and seduced the large audiences at his lectures, and he was disappointed if the electric charge failed to ignite, or if the number of his auditors dwindled, as it often did during the exciting early months of 1848, when "the people's heart," as he himself put it somewhat forlornly, was "elsewhere."[112]

Any shift of the locus of action from the classroom to the street and the Chamber threatened not only Michelet's personal status and public role, but also the kind of solution he proposed to bring to the social and political conflicts of the day. Real struggle, real violence, as distinct from verbal and ideological engagement, could not, as he saw it, resolve social conflicts; on the contrary, they exacerbated such conflicts. Like many of the men of 1848, it seems, Michelet preferred theater to reality and words to actions. Reflecting in 1847 on the fear that "communism" inspired in some and the equally immense hope it inspired in others, he wondered if the disagreement might not one day explode in armed conflict: "Ce pays sera-t-il le théâtre d'une vaine et terrible expérience?"[113] Against such futile, terrible, and irrevocable experiments Michelet advocated words, teaching, argument, and persuasion. Conflict, he held, had first to be removed from men's hearts and minds; the rest would follow. In the midst of the Revolution, on February 23, 1848, he noted in his Journal that, looking back over his lecture course for the year, he found in it much that reflected an era now on the verge of being overtaken, an era when history had advanced at a walking pace and had not yet taken wing. What he had to say remained valid, however. "I established the rational order in which, in normal times, things should occur. Events may invert that order; it is nevertheless the order of reason. That order requires that fraternity precede legislation and that improved laws be the result and expression of it."[114]

As one might expect, those who have to carry out the "oeuvre de la fraternité," those who must bring about the transformation of men's minds, are the teachers and their students, the sons of the bourgeoisie. They are the evangelists of the new revolutionary and nationalist faith, and they must write its gospels. "If my heart is opened up at my death," Michelet wrote later, "the question that has haunted me all my life will be found inscribed in it: How shall the books of the people be produced?"[115] The *livre populaire* was indeed an obsession of Michelet's. It is a typical Romantic oxymoron, a dream of reconciliation and reunion, similar to the idea of a *monarchie constitutionnelle,* or Michelet's description of Paris as the *centre excentrique* of France, or indeed the key concept of the *mère patrie,* in which love and law are yoked together. Through the *livre populaire* the two parts of the "people" (that is, of humanity), the illiterate or uneducated and the literate or educated, the mother and the son who has detached himself from her in order to become a father, were to be reunited.

Thus, in Michelet's thinking, the social antagonism which others defined in economic and class terms as that between bourgeoisie and people came increasingly to be redefined in less abrasive and more manageable cultural terms as a division between the learned part of the people and the unlearned part, between those who represented the mind or reason of the people and those who represented its body. Intelligent, informed, and reflective, the former was sterile and unproductive without the affective and instinctual energy of the latter, which was thought of as being still in communication with man's natural origins; conversely, without the leadership of the former, the latter was a blind, potentially destructive power, like nature herself. The harsh reality of economic relations in the early stages of industrial capitalism was thus softened and made more presentable by Michelet and other ideologists of the period, and the *livre populaire* was touted both as a means of resolving class conflicts and as a utopian image of achieved resolution. Michelet himself always hoped that his books would be popular, and it was with regret and some self-recrimination that he acknowledged they never reached the masses.[116] Likewise, he at first placed great faith in the new power of the press, only to confess later that the newspapers to which his liberal and radical friends contributed also did not reach the people. The latter thus remained vulnerable to the blandishments of rivals—the priests of the old religion in the first instance, but also a new tyrant, the "Napoléoncule," who was already waiting in the wings.[117]

Michelet, it should be emphasized, never doubted that the people had to be led or that its books had to be written *for* it. Like nature, or woman, or the past, in other words, the people was inarticulate, *infans*, and could attain self-awareness and self-expression only through the mediation of one who was both of it and beyond it, like Michelet himself. The successful poet Béranger mildly scolded Michelet for his lack of confidence in the people, but Michelet never shared his friend's optimism. "After the dark and terrible affair of June 24, 1848," he wrote in *Our Sons*, "bowed down and overwhelmed by pain and sorrow, I said to Béranger: 'Who will speak to the people? write its new gospel? Without that there is no life for us.' That strong, cool spirit replied: 'Patience! The people will write its own books.' Eighteen years have passed. And where are those books?"[118]

In the end, it is not easy to forgive the patronizing sentimentality, verging on hypocrisy, of Michelet's proposed solutions to the social problem. His compassion for the despised and humiliated, the hungry and the homeless of his society is not in doubt, nor is his commitment to a somewhat idealized peasantry and artisan class. But did he really believe that mutual affection, even if it could be instilled by education, would eliminate suffering and injustice? Or did he simply soothe his ruffled sensibility with pious hopes and pleasant dreams, while refusing to countenance the more radical measures that a fundamental restructuring of the social and economic order would have required? What is one to make of a passage like the following?

> If these two children who had sat on the benches of the same school could continue to see each other every evening after one had become an apprentice, the other a college student, they would achieve more between them than all the moral lessons and political doctrines in the world: they would preserve the true bond of the City. How keenly the rich man would feel the misery of the poor one and suffer because of his wealth; how unbearable he would find the burden of inequality. How eagerly the poor man would take part in the advancement of the rich one: *Be you great. That is sufficient for me!* The rich man would be poor in heart and voluntarily egalitarian. Does that mean he would cast away his goods and share them with others, as the Gospel would have it? No, he would keep them. Without wealth, there is no respite from manual labor, and without this respite, there is no

work of the spirit. The rich man is the repository of wealth; he owes, in return, the work of the spirit and the dispensation of spiritual riches.[119]

The impatience of Albert Mathiez, the great left-wing historian of the Revolution, is understandable. Michelet, he wrote, "was undoubtedly concerned about the miseries of the people, but his response was only a series of protests and pleas which sometimes bordered on the ridiculous. At the time Marx was writing the *Communist Manifesto,* he [Michelet] was bleating for the union of the classes. Far from having nourished the democratic opposition, he probably exhausted it and certainly led it astray. Because he had lived his first years in the midst of his father's printing business, he boasted of being from the people. An unbearable pretension . . . He was in reality one of those beautiful fruits of the classical education that the sons of the bourgeoisie received in the private schools: fruits of dazzling colors, but frequently hollow inside. I am struck by the incoherence and by the frequent banality of his thought."[120]

MICHELET continued "bleating" for the union of the classes and for better understanding between the sexes in a series of works that appeared in the 1850s and 1860s: *Love* (1858)—"immense succès . . . livre répugnant," Baudelaire wrote to his mother—*Woman* (1859), *Our Sons* (1870). In none of them did he challenge the existing social and economic order. His aim, one must conclude, was not to change it, but to "harmonize" it and make it humane. Neither the privileges of the bourgeoisie nor those of the male were threatened—any more than the preeminence of France and of the West in general in human history. The masters were simply urged to exercise their civilizing mission with compassion and bear the white man's burden nobly.

The ideal of the *mère patrie*—the State as benevolent parent of *all* its children—was the cornerstone of Michelet's social thought. "Let them love this house of France as much as and more than their father's house," he wrote. "If your mother cannot feed you, if your father treats you badly, if you are unclothed, if you are hungry, come, my son, the door is open wide and France is there on the threshold to embrace you and take you in."[121] Michelet was above all concerned that Frenchmen should think of their state in this way. Though they might in fact be quite unequally treated, he wanted all Frenchmen to feel that they shared in France the same loving and providing, just and equitable parent, at once mother and father. To construct and win acceptance for such an image of *la mère patrie,* by means not only of books and newspapers but of popular songs, popular theater, public concerts, and other means of publicity which were more likely to be effective with the masses, was the special task, in Michelet's view, of the writer and the artist.[122] If Michelet was later adopted by the Third Republic as one of its chief ideologists, he had in fact accepted that role in advance.

His solutions, however, have the fragility of all modern constructed myths. Since they are not truly popular but devised and imposed by a leader, their success cannot be fully assured. The cosmetic covering may at any time come unstuck or be peeled off in anger and resentment by those it was designed to manipulate. Michelet wanted to engrave in the hearts of his countrymen an image of the *mère patrie* as at once loving and just, organically connected to the entire past and tradition of the people and at the same time grounded in a timeless rational ideal that both fulfills and cancels tradition. Subjected to stress, however, that image could crack and revert to the shifting, uncertain, frightening image of the arbitrary "natural" mother it was designed to supplant, the mother who dispenses death as well as life, and passes capriciously from indulgence to deprivation. The unsettling alternation between the two aspects of the mother or of nature—the good mother (*la mère*), a dream of warmth, plenty, and community, and the bad mother (*la marâtre*), a nightmare vision of cruelty, alienation, and irrationality—which characterizes the life of man through all of history, as Michelet saw it, and which haunts his own work from the early *Introduction to Universal History* and the *Roman History* through the volumes of the *History of France* and the *History of the Revolution* to the natural history writings of the 1860s, thus recurs as a potential alternation between the austere synthesis of the *mère patrie* and the dualism it was supposed to overcome. The possibility of illusion—a persistent nightmare in all of Michelet's writing—has not after all been dispelled. On the contrary, the synthetic construct that was to have resolved the repetitive alternation of dream and disillusionment simply prolongs it in an altered form. Behind the image of the *mère patrie,* the lawful, orderly, rationalized mother, looms the primitive *mère-marâtre,* the "incestuous Circe," the Moloch-state, deceiving and devouring her children, indifferent to their fate; behind the ideal *peuple* is the *peuple-populace,* harboring murderous intentions beneath a kind and friendly exterior.[123]

"As the social war grows more bitter," Michelet noted shortly after the death of the infant son Athénaïs had borne him, "it becomes dangerous to entrust oneself to a wet-nurse. To do so is to entrust oneself to the enemy. Wet-nurses, like servants, have become impossible."[124] A decade later, in *La Mer,* he evoked the image of "a terrifying mob, a horrible populace," lacking any recognizable human traits and resembling "howling, wild, or rather mad dogs."[125] The harmonies and meanings attributed to history are swallowed up in a dreadful whirlpool of inescapable and cruel contradictions. The Other—nature, woman, the people, the past, our own past, our unconscious (the Other in us)—for a moment seemingly transparent, readable, identifiable with ourselves, suddenly becomes opaque again, irreconcilably different, illegible. In *La Mer* the historian describes how the watery medium, the origin of all life, in whose ample maternal interior her trusting offspring feel "heureux comme un poisson dans l'eau," suddenly becomes dark and menacing ("laide, d'affreuse mine"), a watery grave filled with victims ("ossements et . . . débris"). The sea now "loses its reassuring transparency, becomes opaque and heavy."[126]

Barely two years after the publication of *The People* and in the midst of his work on the *History of the Revolution,* which consistently argues for the unity of the French people in the 1789 Revolution, the events of May and June 1848 had already revealed the depths of the divisions in Michelet's *peuple.* The historian was shattered by the people's invasion of the Assembly in May, depressed and disillusioned by the brutal repression of June, in which thousands were massacred. These events "bled the heart of M. Michelet," according to his son-in-law Alfred Dumesnil, "and stopped all his work, which is something no public event has ever done to him before." Another young friend observed that "M. Michelet has been wounded in his love for France. . . . A frightful breath of reality has exploded his fantasy."[127]

Not surprisingly, in view of these disconcerting events, Michelet was haunted by the fear that he who claimed to speak for the people had never been able to understand or capture its language and had never truly communicated with it.[128] At such moments he was brought face to face with the imaginary, almost oneiric character of all his activity and was struck by the enormity of having devoted his entire existence to the writing of books, the spinning out of dreams. He had, he once confessed, been so obsessed by writing that he had omitted to live. Life, he insisted then, is not "a sheet of paper." The artist cannot create out of nothing; he must live in order to create. By removing himself from the people, losing touch with nature and experience, the artist or intellectual becomes sterile and impotent. "Need to be, rather than appear. To immerse oneself in being," he noted in 1847. "Absent for so long from the realities of life, exiled in a world of paper, return oh my soul, my child, return to your origins. . . . Place yourself next to the poor and beg for life. You will become a man, less of a book, less of a scribe, less of a legless cripple. . . . And perhaps you will be cured of that yielding softness of the artist to which Dante pointed with scorn. You will be less subject to dreams and to woman, the living dream."[129]

In the same way, the historian must have the courage to recognize and forgo the effects of rhetoric, to renounce the pleasing and harmonizing models of art, for these, according to Michelet, are only fanciful dreams that will inevitably be dissipated on contact with reality. Harmony, whether of the modern world or of the modern historical narrative, is no longer simply given, "natural"; it is a rational ideal which must be laboriously constructed out of the often disconcertingly disparate pieces and fragments discovered in empirical reality by historical or social analysis. The easy synthesizing, unifying, mollifying activity of the "artist," in Michelet's words, must yield to the hard labor of the "historian" (or the social engineer), who insists "on the differences, . . . the originality of each trait."[130] At the same time, the ideal of original harmony—the "natural" harmony of childhood and nature—is not to be disregarded or scornfully rejected. Even as he recognizes its inadequacy and works to achieve transcendence of it, the historian is guided, inspired, and sustained by it, and he must therefore try to preserve the memory of it in his writing. Michelet's Romantic view of history as at once paradigmatic (symbolic, legendary, figural, "metaphoric" in Roman Jakobson's terminology) and syntagmatic (causal, sequential, "metonymic" in Jakobson's terminology) was intended to resolve the oppositions of nature and reason, female and male, poetic or symbolic and prosaic or scientific, the still almost undifferentiated One and the highly differentiated Many, by placing the powers of the former at the service of the latter in a synthetic construction that transcended the one-sidedness of both.

Like the *mère patrie* of the historian's radical-nationalist ideology, however, this synthesis was always in danger of collapsing back into the elements composing it. Art and history, legend and fact, subjectivity and objectivity, illusion and disillusionment are as abstractly and monolithically conceived in Michelet's historical hermeneutics as self and other, male and female, culture and nature, writing and "life." At the limit, the specter that haunts all of Michelet's work, his nemesis both as a historian-artist and as a social thinker, is a vision of the Other not as *mère* but as *marâtre,* not as a dream of reason but as a *mauvais songe,* not as intelligible to and compatible with the self but as absolutely inhuman, impermeable to and destructive of the human languages men try to embrace it with, as madness and chaos.

The fragile synthesis that Michelet struggled to sustain fell apart among his successors into a popular novelistic practice of historiography on the one hand, and a more or less agnostic and academic positivism on the other. History after him was either lively narrative or scholarly disquisition. Though traces of both positions are found, for instance, in Renan, they are no longer joined, as they were for Michelet, in fruitful tension; they merely coexist. Renan's conflation of the aesthetically smooth and satisfying (the *vraisemblable,* as Michelet still called it) with the historically true—"every trait that clashes with the rules of classical narrative should be a warning to us to watch out . . . Suppose that we undertook to reconstitute the Minerva of Phidias according to the texts and produced a dry, uneven, contrived ensemble? What conclusion would we draw? Only one: that the texts must be interpreted with taste, that they must be solicited gently until they come together and furnish an ensemble in which the data are all harmoniously fused"[131]—contrasts sharply with Michelet's valiant efforts to resist the temptation of the well-rounded narrative and maintain a degree of openness to the shocks and discordances of reality.

On the other hand, Renan's agnosticism—Michelet himself declared that "Renan's vice is doubt"[132]—brought him close to the anti-aesthetic, "scientific" historiography that became entrenched in the Academy and presided over the founding of the great professional historical journals, such as the *Revue historique.* Dedicated to the empirically verifiable fragment, this positivist historiography was often concerned with minutiae or with the collecting and editing of documents, and at best subscribed to a pious hope that the fragments of knowledge it unearthed might one day be fitted together to form a total view. Since the positivist scholar had no rationale for fitting the pieces together, however, no way of conceiving totality except as an aggregate of parts, since indeed he had a considerable—and not wholly unhealthy—skepticism about totalities altogether, such a total view inevitably had for him something of the character of God for an agnostic. Positivist historical scholarship tended to eschew philosophical speculation as unprofitable and irrelevant to historical research and to history in general, considered as the science of facts. It thus refused to become aware of or to problematize its own philosophical assumptions or methodological principles. Totalities might be looked upon with disdainful skepticism, but there was dogmatic certainty about the fragments the historian investigated or discovered, about individual "facts," and unthinking acceptance of the narrative schemata according to which these were arranged. Scornful as they were of "art" and proud of being hard-headed "scientists," the positivist historians were often hardly aware of the principles guiding their own work.

The collapse of Michelet's historiographical synthesis, which coincided with the collapse of Romantic poetics and of Romantic politics, thus led to a resigned acceptance of the unknowableness of the historical world as a whole and a complacent dogmatism about the knowableness of individual facts and fragments of it. Almost all the elements of Michelet's world view can be found in Renan, but in a state of disintegration and extreme hypostatization. The educated and the simple, history and myth, science and art, the bourgeoisie and the people structure Renan's world as they did Michelet's, but the links Michelet tried desperately to forge between the elements in these pairs have been broken and the oppositions have become acute. Culture, education, and rationality are now perceived as radically sterile, while the underground world of popular belief and illusion is abundantly, indeed frighteningly, productive. The leadership depends dangerously on the led, but if it still occasionally presents its task as that of helping the people toward self-realization, it now more often acknowledges openly that its aim is to manipulate the people and control it by means of adroitly conceived fictions.

In Renan, Michelet's sentimental longing for synthesis and harmony and his anxiety at the prospect of failure have given way to resigned acceptance of a sclerotic dualism. The ideological solutions that Michelet still wanted desperately to believe in as true were now cynically adopted as useful and necessary fictions, even as those who saw them in this way remained blind to the ideological character of their own supposedly "scientific" conception of knowledge, history, and society. Science, according to Renan, will ultimately provide the leadership with the means of absolute moral and physical control of the masses. At that point, truth and power will coincide completely. In the speculations of his successor, Michelet's dream of the *mère patrie*—a social world permeated by reason—turns out to be indistinguishable from the absolute tyranny of a social and intellectual elite.

THE SUSPENSION of Michelet's course at the Collège de France in January 1848 was almost immediately lifted by the provisional government that assumed power and proclaimed the Republic on February 24. But as the Republic veered increasingly to the Right after the climactic June of 1848, Michelet again found himself in conflict with the administration of the Collège. The government of Louis Napoleon, who had been elected President in December 1848, considered Michelet's lectures dangerous and was afraid of the large throngs of students they attracted. Michelet was accused of encouraging disturbances and political protests. When he entered his classroom, he was greeted, it was said, with cries of "Long live the social and democratic republic!" His lectures, copied down by spies posted in the classroom, were allegedly full of atheist and revolutionary propaganda. Finally, on March 11, 1851, on the basis of a garbled transcript, the Director of the Collège was able to have Michelet's teaching censured by his colleagues. On March 13 he was formally suspended, and on April 12, 1852, by a special decree of Bonaparte, now Napoleon III, he was expelled, along with Quinet and Mickiewicz, from the Collège de France.[133] In June of the same year, having refused to take the oath of allegiance to the new imperial regime, he lost his position at the Archives, and that same month he left Paris with Athénaïs for Nantes and semi-exile.

The Michelets spent a dismal year in Nantes. Michelet was depressed by the political situation, by the turn of his own fortunes, by the narrowness and mediocrity of provincial life in what had once been a thriving commercial city.[134] "Every literary voice had been silenced," he wrote. "All life seemed to have been interrupted."[135] In addition, he was almost continuously in poor health. In 1853 the couple moved to Italy—"ma nourrice," as Michelet liked to say[136]—to spend a year at Nervi on the Ligurian coast, not far from Genoa. In July 1854 they returned to Paris and in August moved into the apartment at no. 44 rue de l'Ouest (now rue d'Assas) which remained their home for the rest of their lives.

Michelet lived to see the disastrous end of the second Empire, but he never again held an official position. His new situation as a private scholar had two consequences. He had always wanted to write popular books; now he had to, since he and Athénaïs were dependent financially on income from the sale of his works. In the years between 1852 and his death, the character of his literary production altered noticeably. To these years belong, in particular, the natural history writings: *The Bird* (1856), *The Insect* (1858), *The Sea* (1861), *The Mountain* (1868), and the popular books on women (*Woman*, 1859) and love (*Love*, 1858). The second consequence was that Michelet, as a private scholar, no longer had ready access to the archival materials that had immeasurably enriched his earlier histories, especially the *History of the Revolution*. According to most critics, the historical work undertaken by Michelet after 1852 was far less scholarly and more subjective, more affected by the historian's personal obsessions, than anything he had done before.

Both these changes in the character of Michelet's writing almost certainly owe a great deal as well to the shattering experience of May and June 1848. He himself declared that "the awful night of June 24 after the great light and hope of February struck me the most terrible blow I have ever received. I tried to write a popular book, but couldn't do it. I returned humiliated, sad, and somber to the impersonal work of my historical research." It was then that he found consolation in the generous self-sacrifice of the women of the Revolution and realized that "if I was going to find a solution, it would be found in woman, in love."[137] The program of the books on woman, on love, and on nature—always an analogue of woman for him—was thus announced by Michelet himself as early as February 1849. The fact that in the winter of 1848–49 he met and married Athénaïs, who appeared to him as a kind of savior, another virginal Joan of Arc, in a time of terrible need and despair, and that Athénaïs was deeply interested in natural history, gave a further impetus to a tendency that was already present.

Michelet's natural history books were an immense commercial success. *The Bird* went through seven printings in four years and by 1867 had sold 33,000 copies; the first printing of *The Sea* in 1861 called for 24,000 copies; there were seven printings of *The Mountain* in the year it first appeared. *Love,* written for the same public and in the same vein, though not strictly a natural history book, sold 30,000 copies in two months. These works were thus far more popular than any Michelet had written before, but not in the sense of the *livre populaire* that had haunted him in the 1840s. They were bought and read by the bourgeoisie and by the vast new petty-bourgeois reading public created by universal education and increasing prosperity, and they were in no way comparable with the polemical writings of the 1840s. The lessons they taught were on the whole compatible with current bourgeois views about progress, science, and the role of women.

There is a fairly strict correspondence, for Michelet, between history's relation to nature, man's relation to woman, and the relation of historiography to natural history. Just as the proper role of the past, in the view and the practice of the Romantic historian, is to nourish the present without dominating it, the goal of history is not to abolish nature but to permeate it and find an accommodation with it. Moreover, at times when history seems to stand still or even to retrogress, nature, Michelet now argues, will provide sustenance. Nature is not to be seen as the absolute enemy of history and progress. The most dangerous enemies are within history itself, in man. Likewise, woman is not to be seen as the chief threat to man; instead, she is his consolation in times of distress or flagging spirits. The love of woman is the "cordial" that refreshes the weary man of action, as the writing of natural history is the cordial that restores the strength of the historian worn out by delving into the secrets of the archives.[138] As Vergniaud and Danton "shut themselves up at home and took refuge" from the pressure of public affairs "at their fireside, in love and nature," Michelet himself withdraws from the strenuous labors of history and finds recreation in collaborating with Athénaïs on nature books.[139] Even within the natural history writings, two possible ways of doing natural history are represented. On the one hand, there is the passive, affective naturalist, still hardly disengaged from the object of his study, which he pursues more as a passionate and intimate observation than as a scientific inquiry (Michelet's model here is Alexander Wilson, the humble Scots weaver who, being poor, propertyless, and unmarried, has not yet broken out of the original community of nature and who still lives in peace with all her creatures, "ami des buffles et convive des ours, mangeant les fruits sauvages"); on the other hand, there is the modern race of intrepid explorers ("amants ardents"), penetrating and conquering untamed jungles and bringing back specimens to be analyzed, classified, and exhibited in the Museum of Natural History.[140]

The consistent lesson of the natural history writings is one that we have already seen in Michelet's historical and political writings: that nature and history, female and male, empirical observation of particulars and rational, scientific systematization of the data provided by observation, working class and bourgeoisie, provinces and centralized state, are not to be thought of as being in a relation of mutual antagonism. On the contrary, the latter (whose essential characteristics were well summarized in the category of "Form" in Schiller's *Aesthetic Education*) depends for support and sustenance on the former ("Life" in Schiller), while the former is dependent on the latter to develop its latent resources and bring it to self-consciousness and self-expression.

It is certainly true that natural history was both a rather lucrative activity and a relatively safe one, which the adverse political conditions of the Second Empire had made very popular. It is also true that Michelet himself admitted he had resorted to this kind of writing as a refuge or "alibi" from "the troubled history of humanity, so harsh in the past and still so harsh in the present."[141] It seems not quite correct, however, to present Michelet's natural history writings as proposing a world view diametrically opposed to that of his histories—"a timeless and historyless Utopia," as one critic has put it.[142] Not only had Michelet been interested in natural history all his life, there are many passages in his earlier works, even in the most polemical of them, that anticipate the natural history writings. Few readers of *The People,* for instance, can forget the fine poetic evocation of the bird at the end of Part I, chapter 3, or the astonishing sixth chapter of Part II. In fact, nature in Michelet turns out to be a mirror of history as well as an escape from it. The same themes, the same obsessions, the same fears that dominate Michelet's national history recur in his natural history: above all the overriding desire to find that the Other is transparent to the Self, that nature, like history, is amenable to reason and intelligible, even in her apparent cruelties, and that law, not caprice, and unity, not division, inform the universe; and the terrible fear, never completely exorcised, that it is not so, that order is a fiction and that the last word is chaos. "Le jour baisse de plus en plus, la nuit se fait en Europe," Michelet noted in 1853.[143] He turned to nature to restore his faith at a dark moment in history. But in nature he merely encountered once again the aspirations and anxieties that motivated him as a historian.

The subjectivism and the personal obsessions, especially with sex, that professional historians, beginning with contemporaries or near-contemporaries like Burckhardt, deplore in Michelet's later work, notably in the volumes of the *History of France* devoted to the seventeenth and eighteenth centuries, were also no doubt exaggerated by his enforced retirement from public life, his political disappointment, and his ever-increasing involvement with Athénaïs, which also estranged him from his son-in-law, Alfred Dumesnil, and from his old friend and companion-in-arms Edgar Quinet. It was not simply, it seems, that Michelet no longer had access to archival materials; it is alleged that he did not even trouble to read the printed works that were readily available to him and that he himself refers to, preferring instead to write history out of his own imagination.[144]

The criticism of Michelet's later works is by no means without foundation. Yet the vice, if it is one, was there from the beginning. A reviewer was already complaining in 1842 of Michelet's "abus de la synthèse . . . du symbole."[145] In the earlier works, however, the organizing patterns, images, and analogies were supplemented and richly filled out with the results of intense scholarly and, wherever possible, archival research. At the basis of Michelet's powerful historical imagination there is a Romantic world picture in which, as each part of the universe is held to be informed by and to mirror the structure of the whole, every thing is a metaphor of everything else. The system of correspondences links not only different "areas" of human and natural activity, but also different time periods. Successive ages are related to each other not only causally but figurally, with earlier series of events being repeated in a new guise by later ones, just as the higher coils on a spiral, to borrow Michelet's own image, repeat and at the same time continue the lower ones.

From the beginning, then, the life of nature, the life of society, and the life of the individual are analogically related for Michelet. To the struggles of the natural world (the jellyfish, for instance, striving to transcend its limited and closed existence) correspond those of the political world (the primitive community striving to become a complex, articulated society) and those of the individual (the son striving to detach himself from the mother). At all three levels there is also the same danger and the same allure of transgressing painfully instituted limits. As the higher forms of life long to emancipate themselves from constraints and conventions perceived as having become inimical to life, and seek renewal at life's eternal origins, they run the risk of self-destruction: higher forms of biological organization may undo themselves and be superseded by lower forms; higher forms of social organization may revert to the "primitive communism" of the earliest human groupings; in the struggle to transcend the boundaries of his own ego, the developed human individual (always conceived of, of course, as male) challenges the rules of civilized behavior and finds himself drawn into a violent and phantasmagoric world of unregulated sexuality, where distinctions between good and evil, true and false no longer hold. The same ambiguous trajectory—in which the movement of transcendence is always potentially a movement of regression—recurs at all levels of existence: biological, social, and individual.

Every term in Michelet's narratives thus evokes a corresponding term in another parallel series. The opposition of herdsman and crop-grower, of pastoral and arable, animal and vegetable, for instance, opens on to other oppositions: the rebel son and the dutiful son (Cain and Abel); power acquired by conquest or oppression and protective, paternalist authority; sexuality as aggression by the male against the female and sexuality consecrated by marriage; consumption and production; aristocrat and peasant; entrepreneur and artisan. Such analogies inform Michelet's writing from beginning to end. He had always characterized the English, the chief rivals of the French, the victors of Agincourt and Waterloo, as cruel, lawless transgressors, "red-faced" men, voracious meat-eaters; the French, in contrast, are seen as a race of vegetarians, living in harmony with nature and feeding modestly on milk and cereals. At the end of Michelet's life when, in the wake of the Franco-Prussian war, he began to see in the new Germany the greatest danger France had ever had to face and to place his hopes for the future on a rapprochement between France and England, he did not forget to find a confirming alimentary analogue for the political rapprochement he wanted. The English, he noted in his *History of the Nineteenth Century,* now have more cereal in their diet, while the French consume more meat than they did.[146]

Its pervasive metaphors are in the end the enormous attraction—and seduction—of Michelet's text, which itself enacts the very process it so often describes. The apparent synthesis or reconciliation of art and science, of synthesis and analysis, generality and particularity, metaphor and metonymy (in Jakobson's sense), which Michelet hoped to achieve in his work and which was the strict historiographical analogue of the *mère patrie* on the political level, may at any time be perceived by the reader as illusory, simply another disguise of the original, dangerous Circe-text. The reader is sucked into it as helplessly as the two hundred passengers on board the *Amphitrite,* evoked in Michelet's Journal, were swallowed up by the treacherous waters of the English Channel, which had yet seemed "so blue."[147]

It is this incurably literary quality of Michelet's work, its capacity to draw the reader into it and to stimulate the play of his imagination, which ensures not only its unity—it is the *oeuvre* of a powerful writer, and all the individual works in it are drawn centripetally toward each other far more than they are drawn centrifugally to other scholarly studies of the same topic—but its continued life. Michelet can still excite the ordinary reader, whereas Louis Blanc, for instance, cannot. As for the purely technical historian, his work never survives as a text; it is always taken up and absorbed in the general knowledge historians have of the past. In addition, it is this literary quality which has made Michelet one of the most productive and stimulating of modern *historians. The Witch,* published in 1862, enrolls and reorders once more the major themes and images of all his work and can easily be shown to be a mirror of his own erotic obsessions. Yet this highly imaginative and unorthodox text is still, without question, one of the most illuminating studies of the history of woman and of witches that has ever been written. Michelet's own obsessions and those of his age and his class are eminently present in all his work; his ideological thrust is insistent and unmistakable. Yet it is because he allowed his own imagination far more freedom than did almost any historian before or since— the real task of Michelet scholarship is not to continue praising the historian for his unbelievably candid exploration of sexuality, beginning with his own, but to discover what he succeeded in repressing!—because he was such a "bad" historian by certain standards, that he helped to transform historiography and continues to inspire the most innovative historians, from Lucien Febvre to Fernand Braudel.

It was the historian of the witch, the man obsessed and terrified by the opacity of the Other, by all that is hidden from view, by the material foundation that masculine pride and philosophical idealism try to deny— the secrets of nature, the secrets of woman, the secrets of the unconscious— who began to unveil the secrets of history and to give a voice, as he said, to its enforced silences. Thanks to him and to his wild imagination, we now know that alongside or beneath political history, diplomatic history, military history, the history of kings and states and assemblies, there is also an alimentary history and a demographic history, a history of sexual practices, a history of the family, a history of cultural representations or *mentalités.*

[1985]

6

Michelet's Gospel of Revolution

> I need a God for the heart and for the mind, for civic life, for
> sacrifice.
>
> —Jules Michelet, lectures at the Collège de France, 1849

> If we attempt to force and "invent" a monumental style in art, such
> miserable monstrosities are produced as the many monuments of
> the last twenty years. If one tries intellectually to construct new
> religions without a new and genuine prophecy, then, in an inner
> sense, something similar will result, but with still worse effects.
>
> —Max Weber, *Science as Vocation*

LIKE THE Revolution, as he recounted it, Michelet's *History of the French Revolution* was a brief interval of light in an otherwise dismal time. The preface was written in the declining years of the July Monarchy, the conclusion in the bleak aftermath of the Revolution of 1848. The book itself opens and closes on images of dereliction. The Revolution, we are told in the Preface, is embodied in no physical monument or institution; it has left nothing comparable to the cathedrals of the Middle Ages or the secular palaces of the ancien régime. It survives only as what it always was— according to Michelet, a pure spirit—and its sole monument, fittingly, is an empty space, the Champ de Mars, "that sandy piece of ground as flat as Arabia," site of the great Fête de la Fédération. But an unworthy and forgetful generation has allowed that temple of the Revolutionary spirit to be desecrated by the Revolution's enemies. English horses now "gallop insolently" across the Champ de Mars, which has been turned into a fashionable race-course (*HR*, I, 1).[1]

The dismal tone of the Conclusion is anticipated by a bitter anecdote, at the end of the last chapter of the last book, about a child of ten—a child of the Revolution—who, on being taken to the theater after the death of Robespierre, hears for the first time, as the audience leaves at the end of the performance, words till then completely foreign to his young ears—"Faut-il une voiture, *mon maître?*" ("Will you need a carriage, master?"). The central image of the Conclusion itself is a cemetery: Monceau, the burial place of Danton, Robespierre, Saint-Just. Again, the historian laments the desecration of a hallowed site; a common dancing spot draws crowds where once the Revolutionary heroes were laid to rest. "Gay and careless," the historian observes, "France dances on her dead" (*HR*, II, 993).

Whether we consider the book itself or the event it narrates, the *History of the Revolution* emerges from drabness and emptiness and peters out again in drabness and disillusionment. The Revolution, it seems, is always an interlude, a flash of illumination in the dreary round of indifference and routine, a momentary penetration of matter by spirit, in the terms Michelet himself liked to use. In both Preface and Conclusion, however, the gap between present nothingness and absent being is bridged by an ardent profession of faith. Despite the experience of absence and loss, despite the triumph of banality, a higher reality, a spiritual presence, we are assured, can still be felt by the faithful.

The Champ de Mars remains the dwelling place of a God ("ici réside un Dieu"), and a "mighty breath still blows across it, such as you will feel nowhere else, a soul, an all-powerful spirit." Appropriately, the historian's profession of faith is made in the form of a biblical parallelism: "And though that plain be arid, and though that grass be withered, it will be green again one day" (*HR*, I, 2). The end of the book reiterates this message of hope and confidence in the ultimate triumph of spirit. In the pages of his history, Michelet writes, the men of the Revolution "will be resuscitated and will retain through all future time the life that history owes them in return for the life they heroically gave up"(*HR*, II, 996).[2]

Though he was not raised as a Christian, Michelet had been converted in late adolescence by the *Imitatio Christi* of Thomas à Kempis. Later, as a young professor, he was drawn to philosophies of history deriving in some measure from Christianity. (His career would not have gotten off to such a good start had he not had the reputation of being moderately *bien pensant*.) Victor Cousin's watered-down version of Hegelianism left a considerable mark on him, and it was also through Cousin that he was led to study and translate Vico, whom he interpreted in a strongly liberal and progressivist but still spiritualist light. In the enthusiasm of the July Revolution of 1830 ("on the burning cobblestones of July"), he produced an intoxicating thirty-page *Introduction to Universal History*, in which the culmination of all human history was seen to have been reached in Paris in the year 1830. As an interpretation of history, this apparently secular work is every bit as figural as Christian exegesis traditionally had been in its interpretation of Old Testament history.

In the *Introduction to Universal History,* Greece, which—as Michelet puts it—translated and rationalized the instinctive, mute wisdom of the East, and Rome, which translated and universalized what would otherwise have remained the particular possession of a hundred petty Greek city-states, appear as figures of France, which in turn gathers up the cultures of the various European peoples—the negativity and skepticism of the English, the spirited concreteness of the Italians, and the enthusiastic, totalizing but all-confusing pantheism of the Germans—relieving each of its one-sidedness and translating them all together into a world doctrine. France speaks the *logos* or *verbe* of Europe, as Greece is said to have once spoken that of the Orient.[3] "France speaks what the world thinks," we read again later in the *History of the Revolution* (*HR,* I, 70). If Greece and Rome are figures of France, France itself is a figure of Paris, which gathers up, fuses, and raises to a "higher level" the experience, wisdom, and language of all the provinces of France, from the primitive, granite-like poetic symbolism of Celtic Brittany to the fulsome winy rhetoric of Burgundy and the sparkling flinty prose of Champagne.[4] As one might expect from a world view based on universal analogy, on the "harmonies," as Michelet put it (*HR,* I, 9), among all the fragments of a whole whose basic patterns are inscribed in each of its parts—and that world view is both the strength and the weakness of Michelet as a historian—these processes of historical life are also said to characterize the life of natural organisms[5] and the life of the individual mind. As France speaks for all of Europe, and Paris for all of France, Michelet himself, as a historian and as a son of Paris, claims to speak for "all those who have no history," that is to say, for all those whose voices were never heard by the writers of official history—women, the poor, the humble, the defeated.[6] It ought not, after all, to come as a surprise that for the future historian of the Revolution, in 1833, "Christ is still on the Cross . . . The Passion endures and will endure for all time. The world has its Passion, as does humanity in its long historical march, and each individual heart during the brief span in which it is given to beat. To each his cross and his stigmata."[7]

The man who wrote those words cannot be assumed to have chosen casually the terms of his famous definition of history: *résurrection de la vie intégrale* (resurrection of life in its totality). History was Michelet's religion, the Revolution was its Revelation, and his own *History of the Revolution* was intended as nothing less than the Gospel of a new religion of humanity, through which alienation would be overcome, the dead resurrected to eternal life, and man at last set free by the searing, liberating truth that the God he worships is himself.[8] The *History of the French Revolution* was from the beginning a *sacred* history—the story of the Passion of the Christ-people, through whose sacrifice humanity was to be redeemed—and it aimed to inspire its readers and promote an *imitatio*, an identification and dedication equivalent to those inspired by the Gospels. Michelet quotes with satisfaction a remark by the popular poet Béranger, who is supposed to have said of the *Histoire de la Révolution:* "For me it is a holy book"; and he invariably presents himself as the evangelist of a new faith (*HR*, I, 15).[9] "I am endeavoring to describe today," he wrote in the 1847 Preface, "that epoch of unanimity, that holy period, when a whole nation, free from all party distinction, as yet a comparative stranger to the opposition of classes, marched as one beneath the flag of brotherly love. Nobody can behold that marvelous unanimity, in which the selfsame heart beat together in the breasts of twenty millions of men, without returning thanks to God. These are the sacred days of the world" (*HR*, I, 8). If those days were to come again, however, the original spirit of the Revolution had to be revived; and to achieve that was the stated purpose of Michelet's history. "May the sublime vision we had [of the new God] . . . raise us all, author and readers alike, above the moral misery of the times and restore to us a spark of the heroic fire that consumed the hearts of our fathers" (*HR*, I, 608–609).

The sacred character of the Revolution is a constant theme of the *History*. The unanimity, generosity, and child-like faith of those who brought it about, we are told, are signs of its divine, providential nature (*HR*, I, 11). Michelet not only makes ample use of biblical language and imagery, he frequently suggests analogies to the Gospel story. The hundred thousand armed peasants of the Vivarais, who set out from their homes in the midst of winter in a spontaneous gesture of fraternity at the time of the first federations, recall those who almost two millennia earlier had heard the "bonne nouvelle" of the birth of Christ. "A new breath of life was in the air, which inspired them with a glow of enthusiasm; citizens for the first time, and summoned from their remote snowy regions by the unknown name of liberty, they set forth, like the kings and shepherds of the East at the birth of Christ, seeing clearly in the middle of the night, and following unerringly, through the wintry mists, the dawn of spring, and the star of France" (*HR*, I, 328). France herself, we are told, like Christ, brings to the nations not peace but a sword; by that sword, however, as by the message of Christ—"tellement Dieu était en la France"—they are not harmed but healed, not enslaved but liberated, reawakened to new life.[10] "La France," Michelet had proclaimed in his lectures at the Collège de

France in 1845, "La France est le sauveur" ("France is the redeemer").[11]

The words "miracle" and "miraculous," "prodigy" and "prodigious" are never absent for long from Michelet's text. The taking of the Bastille—"le grand coup de la Providence"—is of course a "miracle" and is fittingly recounted in deliberately biblical language: "A voice was heard in every heart: Go forth and ye shall take the Bastille" (*HR*, I, 146, 141, 145). The use of the past historic tense—the effect of which is difficult to render in English—underlines the miraculous immediacy of thought and action. On the morning of July 14, "one idea dawned upon Paris, . . . and all were suddenly illuminated with the same light" ("une idée se leva sur Paris . . . et tous virent la même lumière"). Despite the practical difficulties, "All immediately had faith" in the call to attack the Bastille ("Tous crurent"), "and it was done forthwith" ("et cela se fit"). The whole affair, in short, was "completely unreasonable. It was an act of faith." There was no preparation, no proposal, no plan: "No one proposed. But every one believed, and every one acted" (*HR*, I, 145).

Later, evoking the universal feeling of fraternity created by the Federations, Michelet asks the rhetorical question: "Is it a miracle?" to which the answer is of course a resounding affirmative: "Yes, the grandest and the most simple" (*HR*, I, 404). In particular, the twelve months from the taking of the Bastille to the Fête de la Fédération are a "miraculous year extending from July to July" (always, as we shall see, a magical month for Michelet, July 1789 announcing July 1790 and July 1830) (*HR*, I,˙396). Obstacles disappear as if by magic, whether it be the rain which abruptly lets up, allowing a momentary illumination of the sodden Champ de Mars on that famous July 14, 1790, or the obstacles to fraternity itself: "At length the shades of night disappear, the mist is dispelled, and France beholds distinctly what she had [obscurely] loved and followed, without ever having been able to grasp it—the unity of the native land . . . Every obstacle vanishes and all opposition is removed" (*HR*, I, 403). The unmediated nature of events is always the most effective marker of their miraculous and mythic character: "France," we are told, "was born and rose to her feet to the sound of the canon of the Bastille. In a single day, with no preparation" (*HR*, I, 397). Not surprisingly, the historian asserts that "it is impossible to assign a specific cause to those great spontaneous events" (*HR*, I, 326). "Those millions, who were serfs yesterday and who today are men and citizens, who have been summoned up suddenly in a single day from death to life, these newborn of the Revolution . . . what were they? A miracle. Born around April 1789, already men by the 14th July, they rose fully armed from the furrow" (*HR*, I, 428).

The contrast with Tocqueville, which underlies François Furet's argument in his recent but already classic *Penser la Révolution française* (1978), is nowhere more glaring than in this insistence of Michelet's on the abruptness of the change signified and accomplished by the Revolution. For Michelet represents the Revolution as nothing less than an irruption of a different temporality into the time of profane history. The Revolution does not belong to ordinary history; it occurs in a time out of time, the sacred time of origins. On the day of the Fête de la Fédération, we are advised, "Everything was possible. Every division had vanished. There was neither nobility nor bourgeoisie nor people. The future was present. That is to say: time was no more: a lightning flash and eternity" (*HR*, I, 430). "Time is abolished," the narrator had already pronounced several chapters earlier; "space is abolished: those two material conditions to which life is subject have ceased to be. A strange *vita nuova* is now beginning for France, an eminently spiritual one, which makes her entire Revolution into a kind of dream. That new life knows neither time nor space" (*HR*, I, 406).[12] The Revolution, in short, is more than a political, social, or economic change for Michelet. It is a veritable rebirth, the beginning of a *vita nuova*, as he so often liked to say, an intimation of universal redemption. It is not for nothing that the revolutionary people is described as fundamentally innocent, "bonne enfant" (*HR*, I, 142, 181–182, 225–226, 276, 400), the new France as a newborn child. A miracle occurred, Michelet tells us, at the Fête de la Fédération, that first celebration of the Fourteenth of July, which drew thousands from all over France to the Champ de Mars: "From that sublime moment, from so many pure and sincere desires, from so many mingled tears . . . a God was about to be born" (*HR*, I, 428)— France, the Christ-child of the nations, ready to sacrifice herself on the altar of history for the redemption of mankind ("La France est l'enfant sur l'autel," *HR*, I, 415–416).

The end of the ancien régime thus "by no means" signals "death, but on the contrary, birth, the coming renewal." "It sent a tremor through the whole world," we are told (*HR*, I, 9, 11). Kosciuszko in Poland, Tom Paine in England, Beethoven and old Klopstock in Germany wept for joy, and—a miracle in its own way—Kant in far-off Königsberg changed the direction of his daily walk. Images of renewal had often marked the traditional *entrées solennelles* of newly crowned kings into their capitals. But the renewal Michelet expects is not to be thought of as a late, pale copy of Christ's entry into Jerusalem. The Revolution is portrayed as a radically new beginning (*HR*, I, 77–79), a new and higher Revelation. "Did France exist before that time? It might be disputed" (*HR*, I, 200). "An entire people emerged at one blow from nonentity to existence (*HR*, I, 77, 78). If the day the Bastille fell was a day of deliverance—"o beau jour, premier jour de la délivrance" (*HR*, I, 203)—Michelet made sure to use a term that in French also signifies the bringing forth or delivery of a child. (The accepted translation, "first day of *liberty*," misses the point.) The opening of the Estates General was a time, if ever there was one, he tells us, to sing a prophetic hymn: "Thou wilt create peoples, and the face of the earth shall be renewed," for on that great day, "the first of an immense future," "a mighty thing began" (*HR*, I, 88). Like an infant pushing its way out of the womb, France emerged from the tomb of the ancien régime to a prodigious *vita nuova:* "The resurrection of the people which at long last breaks open its tomb" inaugurates a new era, accomplishing "the labor of ages in a single night." And that, writes Michelet, is "the first miracle—the divine and authentic miracle—of the new Gospel" (*HR*, I, 217).

As in many myths, and as one might expect from the historian of universal "harmonies," the rebirth of the hero marks a new season of fertility: "The earth, sterile and sad yesterday in the withered hands of the priest, passed into the strong, warm hands of this young ploughman . . . In the midst of the federations, there was a proliferation of the natural federation, marriage. In that glorious year of hope, the number of marriages increased by a fifth—something unheard of before" (*HR*, I, 428).[13] For the same reasons, no doubt, the philosopher Condorcet, at the age of forty-nine, "se retrouvait jeune . . . commençait une vie nouvelle" ("rediscovered his youthful vigor and began a new life"). The only child of his many years of marriage to the "noble et virginale" Madame Condorcet "was born nine months after the taking of the Bastille, in April 1790" (*HR*, I, 656). The miracle of nature—conception and creation through the self-transcendence of male and female—and the miracle of history—the French Revolution—are indistinguishable. "Rare instant in which a world can come to birth! . . . Who will undertake to explain the profound mystery of the birth of a new man, a new people, a new God. Who will explain conception! that unique, rapid and terrible instant!" (*HR*, I, 429).

As Michelet presents it, then, the French Revolution is not what it became in Tocqueville's ironic vision—a prosaic phenomenon, whose underlying causes and significance have to be understood by the detached scientific analyst and were never accessible to those who acted in it and who, in their blindness, actually promoted what they thought they were undoing. The truth of the Revolution, for Michelet, is no less hidden from view than it was for Tocqueville. But it lies precisely, as we shall see, in the consciousness of Tocqueville's ignorant actors, and it is to that consciousness, from which Tocqueville sought to emancipate himself and his reader, that the historian, according to Michelet, must find his way back. The deepest reality of the Revolution is a "spiritual" one; it is an experience, an idea, a project, a "prodigious dream"—not simply the working out of subterranean historical forces. It is not at all surprising, given their different points of view, that Tocqueville writes at length in *The Ancien Régime and the Revolution* of the gestation of modern France over two centuries of the ancien régime and tells nothing, virtually, of the Revolution itself, whereas Michelet's *History* deals with the revolutionary moment and devotes very few pages to the process of gestation that preceded it. Belonging to a special time, a sacred time, a time of renewal, the Revolution—for Michelet—is fundamentally different from and impervious to the profane history that preceded and followed it. As the living spirit of France, it is, as Michelet declares in the 1847 Preface, like the Kingdom of God for the Christian, "within us" (*HR*, I, 1).

It needs to be emphasized, however, that Michelet rejected every attempt to present the Revolution as simply the fulfillment of the teachings of Christianity. Many of his contemporaries "considered democracy a necessary outcome of Christian ideas," in the words of his friend Alphonse Esquiros, and saw the Revolution as a product of the Gospels, as "the Gospels embodied in historical fact."[14] A good deal of Michelet's polemic against Christianity, not only in his histories but in his popular writings on love, woman, the Jesuits, and so on, was without doubt directed at those so-called Christian socialists. But his enemy was not, I think, religion, or a religious understanding of history or the Revolution. On the contrary, it was the attempt to deny the religion of the Revolution by absorbing it back into Christianity. As the prophet of an up-to-date, modernized religion, the religion of France and of the Revolution, Michelet was as intolerant of the earlier, rival religion as Christians had often been of the religion of the Jews. Between the old, alienated religion of Jews and Christians alike, in which man worships a transcendent God, and the new immanent religion, in which Frenchmen worship themselves in the form of France, there could be no compromise, he maintained. Both vied for the same territory. "I . . . see only two great facts, two principles, two actors, two characters on the stage: Christianity and the Revolution" (*HR*, I, 21).

The *History of the Revolution* marks Michelet's farewell to his own optimistic belief, which had reached its zenith in the enthusiasm of the July Revolution of 1830 and the *Introduction to Universal History*, that the whole history of mankind, from the civilizations of the ancient world through the Christian Middle Ages down to the great monarchical states of the seventeenth century and the Revolution, was about to be gradually and, as it were, effortlessly fulfilled. The ferocious suppression of workers' protest movements in Paris and Lyons in the early 1830s quickly cooled the enthusiasm with which Michelet had at first greeted the regime of Louis Philippe, and in later years he recalled with bitterness the "loss of high hopes," the "moral cholera" that—like a spiritual reality of which the medical epidemic sweeping through Paris at the time was but the physical sign or figure—"followed so soon after July."[15]

By the mid-1840s Michelet's disenchantment with the bourgeois monarchy was so great that he decided to interrupt his *History of France,* which told the story of a gradual movement toward social and national union, and embark on the *History of the Revolution,* the message of which is that true union can be achieved only through a prior transgression, a sacred act of violence and rupture, such as the storming of the Bastille or the Revolution as a whole. The old must be repudiated, he now urged, the old idols expelled from the temple of the new faith. Christianity and monarchy were finished.[16] The Revolution was neither, as some had claimed, "the fulfillment of the Christian promise" (*HR,* I, 24), nor, as others would have it, its mere negation or reverse image. "The Revolution goes beyond Christianity and contradicts it. It is at once Christianity's heir and its adversary" (*HR,* I, 25). In other words, the religion of the Revolution was destined to supersede Christianity in the same way that Michelet and many of his contemporaries believed Christianity, as a young religion of faith and spontaneity, had once superseded its mother Judaism, allegedly grown old, sterile, and legalistic.

Echoing the opinions of contemporaries or near-contemporaries, like Constant and Feuerbach, Michelet held that Christianity was already a spent force by the end of the eighteenth century. The Jansenists, he claimed, had been the last authentic Christians. Like Nietzsche's friend Franz Overbeck some three decades later, Michelet deeply admired those obstinately faithful survivors of the old religion, who refused to compromise their faith even for the sake of its historical or worldly survival, but he had no doubt that their time had passed. "I . . . seek my faith elsewhere," he declared (*HR,* I, 384). The Revolution was the new faith, the new Church—"la grande Eglise" (*HR,* I, 20)—at long last the true Church universal. Judaism had been the religion of a single people; Christianity, though it promised universality, in fact left many, the majority, outside— all the graceless and damned of the earth. But "we who, by its monopoly, are deprived of temple and altar . . . we had a temple on that day [the day of the Fête de la Fédération]—such a temple as no one had ever had before" (*HR,* I, 412).[17] If Michelet completely rejected every attempt to represent the Revolution as the realization of Christianity, that was, in his own words, "because [the Revolution] was itself a Church"—and one that was truly superior to all those that had preceded it. "As agape and communion, nothing in this world was ever comparable to 1790, to the spontaneous impulse of the Federations" (*HR*, I, 609; I, 12). Michelet could even claim that the difference between the Revolution and the Counter-Revolution was that the latter, though posing as the champion of religion, was not a religion, whereas the Revolution was (*HR*, I, 394).

As a Church, a communion, the Revolution stands for unity, not only the breaking down of all barriers to communication and exchange but the transcendence of difference, the unanimity of wills in brotherly love: "no more classes, only Frenchmen; no more provinces, a single France" (*HR*, I, 217).[18] In the famous "Tableau de la France" at the beginning of Book III of his *History of France*, Michelet had described the gathering up of all the various provinces of France, beginning with the most primitive and "poetic," into a final unity to which all contributed but in which all were "fulfilled" and relieved of their exclusiveness and particularity. The movement—in space, in time, and in the historian's own narrative—had the characteristic Romantic form of a spiral, the figure of progress *toward* unity. For what chiefly attracted Michelet, it appears, was not the condition of unity, not a featureless identity, but the *experience* of union, the realization of continuity with others and with the universe as a whole. In other words, it is the transgressive act of overcoming separation that is Michelet's ideal, the "spasmodic" moment, in Georges Poulet's apt formulation.[19] Michelet's politics, one might say, is an erotic politics. His unflagging criticism of the Jacobins' efforts to impose permanent and absolute uniformity and of their willingness to sacrifice the living present to an ideal condition in the future[20]—in short, his rejection of their austere emphasis on abstract morality—is entirely consistent with his anarchist ideal of a spontaneous, creative union of wills, as, equally, is his rejection of a liberal parliamentarianism founded on the fundamentally pessimistic idea that division and disagreement are a permanent condition.

Innumerable passages from Michelet's work, nearly all of them colored by his characteristic erotic symbolism, could be brought forward to illustrate his longing for a miraculous synthesis of the particular and the universal, the individual and the communal, the moment and eternity. "One France, one faith, one oath," he demanded (*HR*, I, 395), and that seemed to him to be also the aspiration of all nature. The entire universe and every individual in it, according to Michelet, yearns to overcome division, to recover "unity," or rather continuity. " 'Ah! if I were *one*,' says the world; 'if I could at length unite my scattered members, and bring my nations together!' 'Ah! if I were *one*,' says Man; 'if I could cease to be the complex being that I am, rally my divided powers, and establish concord within myself!' In that fugitive hour a nation seemed to be realizing that ever unfulfilled desire both of the world and of the human soul, seemed to be playing the divine comedy of concord and union which we never behold but in our dreams" (*HR*, I, 416). The reader is reminded here of the curious comment some ten pages earlier that the Revolution was "une sorte de rêve"—"a kind of dream" (*HR*, I, 406).

Reality, in fact—historical reality—seems curiously destructive of this dream. Michelet's Julys, like all epiphanies, wither and fade in the winter of history. "How many centuries have passed since the Federation of July?" he exclaims (*HR*, I, 471). Time and again, he emphasizes the brevity of the Revolution's supreme moment of union and brotherhood—always the Fête de la Fédération, the pure and spontaneous expression of the national spirit, uncontaminated by any partisan "political" design. "Oh! who would not be touched by the remembrance of that incomparable moment, when we started into life? It was short-lived, but it remains for us the ideal we shall ever strive toward, the hope of the future! O sublime Concord, in which the nascent liberties of the classes, subsequently in opposition, embraced so tenderly like brothers in the cradle,—shall we never more see thee return upon our earth?" The participants themselves sensed this, Michelet notes. One of them closes his account of the unforgettable day with the comment: "Thus passed away the happiest moment of our lives" (*HR*, I, 409).

At various points, the historian wonders whether such a fall from grace might not be inevitable, whether the perfection of that moment of time could be sustained. "That day, everything was possible," he wrote triumphantly of July 14, 1790. "Nothing, it seems, prevented the realization of the social and religious age of the Revolution, which we see presently receding constantly before us" (*HR*, I, 430). A new day might have dawned, in other words, on which the light would never go out, an eternal July, that Joachimite "troisième âge du monde" of whose advent Michelet wrote with burning desire.[21] But it did not, and the historian asks himself the obvious question: "Can such a condition endure?"[22] Is not the moment of perfection always also the moment of decline? Is there not, in other words, a radical discontinuity between sacred and profane history, between the time of origins and ends and the time of maturation? "The time of waiting, striving, longing, during which all dreamed and strove to realize this day, is over! . . . It is here. . . . Whence these feelings of anxiety? Alas, experience teaches us the sad fact, strange to relate and yet true, that unity brings a diminution of union. In the will to unite there was already the union of hearts, perhaps the best kind of unity" (*HR*, I, 423). The essence of the Revolution, as Michelet presents it to us, turns out to be something that cannot be sustained in history. Not only could the initial unanimity of the Revolution not be sustained, the very effort to preserve it contributed to its undoing. To protect itself against its enemies, internal and external, the Revolution was forced to abandon its "credulous humanitarianism" (*HR*, I, 426). "If it is not to will its own destruction, the Revolution cannot linger in the age of innocence" (*HR*, I, 426).[23] Spontaneity ceases and the era of Jacobinism begins. The Revolution is destroyed, however, by the practical effort to save it: "Who slew the Republic? Its government. The form obliterated the content" (*HR*, II, 794),[24] rather as—according to a certain tradition of Christian thought—the Church and theology destroyed Christianity. One cannot help thinking of the young Nietzsche's comment in a letter to Carl von Gersdorff that "truth seldom dwells where people have built temples for it and have ordained priests."[25]

What is at issue here is Michelet's attitude to history and the historical; and, somewhat surprisingly, the Romantic historian's relation to history seems to be no less ambivalent than that of his Enlightenment predecessors. In a striking passage, curiously reminiscent of the eighteenth century, Michelet declares that history is mostly the description of error and evil— "the register of the crimes, follies and misfortunes of mankind," as Gibbon put it—except that in Michelet's more dynamic, Romantic view, "follies" become "obstacles" and the ideal is not a community of reasonable men, but a condition of brotherhood, a union of consciousnesses. Just as the obstacles that delay the accomplishment of a quest are the condition of narrative (without them there would be nothing to tell), the obstacles that prevent the full realization of human brotherhood—the end of history and the goal of the Revolution—are the condition of history for Michelet. Without them, time would collapse into a single instant and the final parousia would have come. As a historian, therefore, Michelet is bound to be chiefly concerned with the obstacles that prevented the Revolution from achieving its promise. At the same time, he constantly denounces this ordinary history, the indispensable material of his narrative, as a *néant*, a non-thing, while its transcendence is said to be "true history."

> I have related fully the resistance offered by the old principle,— the *parlements*, the nobility, and the clergy; I am now going to introduce, in a few words, the new principle, and to expound briefly the immense fact in which all those various movements of resistance were absorbed and annihilated, the admirably simple . . . fact of the spontaneous organization of France. That is history, the real, the positive, and the durable; and the rest is nothingness. It was, however, necessary to tell at great length

the story of that nothingness. Precisely because it is nothing but an exception, an irregularity, Evil requires a minute narration of particulars in order to be understood. The Good, in contrast, the natural, which flows forth evenly and of its own accord, is almost known to us beforehand in virtue of . . . the eternal image of the good which we carry within us. (*HR*, I, 395–396)[26]

As many readers of Michelet have remarked, from Georges Poulet to Roland Barthes, his history—be it the *History of France* or the *History of the Revolution*—is a long and weary road punctuated by moments of brilliant illumination, a "recréation spasmodique," in Poulet's words. "The narrative," Barthes observed, "is calvary; the vision is glory."[27] Michelet himself describes the task of realizing the Revolution as a "Sisyphean" task.[28]

One begins to see what it was that drew Michelet to the Jansenists—and made him hate and scorn the Jesuits. In a striking passage at the end of Book I, chapter 3, he describes how one of the "intrepid curés" who had voted for the clergy to go over to the Tiers, "long afterwards, when the Empire had so cruelly erased every trace of the Revolution, its mother, used often to go and visit the ruins of Port Royal not far from Versailles; one day . . . he entered the *Jeu de Paume*—the first in ruins, the second derelict. Tears flowed from the eyes of this steady and courageous man whose resolve had never weakened . . . To have to mourn two religions! It was too much for a strong man's heart." And the historian-narrator adds, speaking now in his own name: "We too revisited, in 1846, that cradle of Liberty, that place . . . which received and still preserves her memorable oath. But what could we say to it? What news could we give it of the world it had brought forth? Oh! time has not moved fast; generations have succeeded one another; but the work has not progressed. When we stepped on those venerable paving stones, a feeling of shame rose up in our heart at what we are, and at the little we have accomplished. We felt unworthy, and quickly left that sacred place" (*HR*, I, 110–111).

If the Revolution is a religion, like Christianity, if it is destined to replace Christianity as a truly universal religion, as Michelet everywhere suggests, does it then suffer from the same fatal defect that certain nineteenth-century historians and theologians attributed to Christianity, namely the inability to subsist in time, in history, in the world, without compromising itself beyond repair? "Can such a condition endure?" According to Nietzsche's friend Franz Overbeck, Christianity was a world-denying religion; its earliest adherents expected the imminent end of the world; worldly success, historical success, had no meaning for them, since as far as they were concerned there would be no worldly future. The time of revelation did not belong to historical time but was outside of time, a turning point opening onto eternity, "un éclair et l'éternité," in Michelet's words (*HR*, I, 430). The fact that the end of the world did not take place presented Christians with an acute problem. They could continue to live and to believe, as though the world were about to end, and to prepare themselves for that moment; but that meant doing nothing to preserve their faith against the ravages of time. Or they could become politicians, adroitly maneuvering among the forces of history so as to ensure their historical survival as a Church, and theologians, rationalizing the continued existence of the world and their own compromises with it—in other words, they could consent to the transformation of a world-denying eschatological belief into an institution that was itself a considerable worldly and historical power. Overbeck admired the Jansenists because, as he understood them, they refused those compromises with the world that the Jesuits eagerly embraced, refused to give up the purity of principle for the base brokerage of politics, and remained essentially indifferent to worldly success and historical survival, faithful to the original doctrine of Christ.[29]

Michelet admires the Jansenists for similar reasons. The proof that they are the true modern Christians, persecuted as they are by the Church, lies in their very refusal of modernity, their unworldliness, the way they bear witness not stridently and publicly in the manner of Molière's Alceste, whose criticism of the world only confirms his intense participation in it, but "in concealment and resignation, dying off noiselessly and without revolt" (*HR*, I, 384–385). Michelet is fascinated both by the Jansenists' stubborn, undeviating loyalty to what they construe as the pure and original Christian message and by their vigorous eschatology. "I have been unable to behold without the deepest emotion those men of another age silently becoming extinct," Michelet writes, yet never wavering in their faith that "the great and last day when both men and doctrines will be judged, cannot be far off; the day when the world will begin to live and cease to die" (*HR*, I, 384–385).

As an advocate of secularism and progress, Michelet had to believe that his own religion of brotherhood and equality would ultimately be vindicated by the realization of liberty, equality, and fraternity *in the world*—that is, by the redemption of the original totality of nature through the marriage, as he liked to say, of Heaven and Earth. Nevertheless, there is evidence that he was troubled more often than his reputation as the prophet of the Revolution would lead one to expect by the thought that it might be with the Revolution and with his entire view of history as it was with Christianity, that they too might be a "prodigious dream," to which no mundane reality could ever correspond. There were times of terrible doubt, when the possibility of regression and illusion—a persistent nightmare in all his writings from the *Introduction to Universal History* of 1830 to the natural history books of the 1850s and 1860s, but increasingly frequent after 1848—overwhelmed his faith in the order of nature and the meaning and direction of history, when the future spiritual transcendence and fulfillment of individuality in fraternal union appeared to him in the disturbingly similar form of what he conceived as its opposite: that is to say, a regressive retreat from individual identity—which Michelet saw as the painfully won, but still incomplete, achievement of history and civilization, and as essentially masculine—to the original (and, in his imagination, feminine), material continuity of nature. As early as the *Tableau de la France* (early 1830s) he had admitted to a feeling of uneasiness concerning the pantheistic tendencies of the German Romantic philosophies, to which he himself was strongly attracted: "There is an all-powerful lotus flower there that makes one forget one's fatherland."[30]

Michelet wavered all his life between confidence that a spiritual power informs the material substance of nature, rendering it orderly and intelligible despite its sometimes cruel or chaotic appearances and guaranteeing its progressive redemption from its own materiality, and a nightmarish fear that the reality of nature is nothing but the endless cycle of birth and death, and that nothing "makes sense." It is in the later natural history writings (*The Bird, The Insect, The Sea, The Mountain*)—because they are so patently at odds with modern scientific modes of thought and inquiry, so transparently projections of his own imagination—that this ambivalence strikes the reader most forcibly, but it is present in all of Michelet's historical work too, from the *Roman History* and the *Introduction to Universal History* on.

On the one hand, Michelet salutes the Promethean triumphs of nineteenth-century science. By discovering the laws of the winds and the ocean currents, he announces, science has tamed the tempests and mapped the mysterious ocean depths, the home of "the man-eaters, the monsters, the leviathan, the kraken, and the great sea-serpent."[31] (Michelet followed with at least equal intensity the efforts of medical and biological research to penetrate the secrets of what was for him the most mysterious ocean of all, the female body.) The investigations of Maury, Romme, Reid, and Piddington have demonstrated, he proclaims, that what had been thought of as caprice could be reduced to law.[32] On the other hand, however, Michelet's writing is punctuated by moments when the intelligible nature, seemingly obedient to law, discovered by the all-conquering man of science, suddenly reveals or reverts to its dreaded, undecipherable underside—the seductive, incestuous Circe, the unredeemed, lawless female beneath the loving, nursing mother. And as the *mère* (good nature) turns into a *marâtre* (chaotic and cruel nature), so the patently masculine *peuple*, the hero of the Revolution, takes on the terrifying aspect of a raging, shapeless, and patently female *populace*—no longer men, as Michelet puts it himself, but "howling dogs, a million, hundreds of millions of relentless, . . . raging hounds . . . But why call them dogs or hounds. . . . Not even that. Hideous and nameless apparitions, beasts without eyes or ears, nothing but foaming jaws."[33] In the same way, the pleasant green meadow becomes a treacherous marsh[34] or a pestilential swamp,[35] the tropical savannah turns out to be a heaving mass of living creatures all of which devour one another. Everywhere the investigator, as he probes, discovers forces that are destructive of order, design, definition, and identity, of thought, and of sanity itself—an irrational, violent, but at the same time dangerously alluring subterranean continuity. "If you were to set foot in [these calm green waters], you would discover with horror that they are solid . . . The moment a living creature appears, everything lifts up its head, everything begins to swarm; one sees the strange assembly rise up in all its terror . . . Those monsters that rule over the surface have their own tyrants down below. The piranha, the razor-fish, as fast as the cayman is heavy, before the latter can turn around, cuts off its tail with the fine saw of its teeth and carries it off."[36] In the virgin forest the precarious and hard-won identity of individual forms is threatened, literally, with disintegration. "If you were to yield to your weariness, a silent army of implacable anatomists would take possession of you, and with a million lancets would make of all your body tissue a fantastic piece of lace, a gauze, a vapor, a nothing."[37]

Meaninglessness and the danger of regression in nature are the mirror of meaninglessness and the danger of regression in history. In a few pages devoted to Sade and the survival of aristocratic libertinism, Michelet evokes the "terrible situation of a still fragile Republic, which in the chaos of a world in ruins, found itself surprised from below by frightful reptiles. Vipers and scorpions seethed in its foundations" (*HR*, II, 847–848). At the other end of the social spectrum, the dark face of the people is revealed in a figure like the Capuchin Chabot, "a hero of the populace, violent and licentious" (*HR*, I, 1063). Michelet's fear of the modern industrial proletariat—his concern at the displacement of the independent male artisan by the female factory worker—seems neither trivial nor incidental, for he saw the proletariat as a dangerous regression from his ideal *peuple*. For that reason, he was forced to defend his optimistic vision of the *peuple* as the subject of a progressive history by disputing what the pioneer social scientists of his time, such as Parent-Duchâtelet, Buret, and Villermé, had been reporting about the character and conditions of popular life in urban France. "They have all concerned themselves almost exclusively with an exceptional part of the people," he complained. But France is not England, "where the industrial population makes up two-thirds of the total."[38] Nevertheless, on many occasions he himself acknowledged his doubt and anxiety. Seeking a refuge in nature from the desolation of history, he writes in *L'Oiseau,* "I encountered for the first time the head of the viper." "Shattered, silenced to death" by this manifestation of "evil" in Eden, he is obliged to confess that "the great mother, nature, in whom I had sought refuge, terrified me."[39]

It is at this point, where the optimism and progressivism usually attributed to Michelet appear to falter, that we can begin to measure the importance of his presentation of the history of the Revolution as the Gospel of a new religion and, in general, the importance of the mythical dimension of his narrative. At the high points of that narrative, the indication of times that are repeated—mythic times, such as time of day and season or month of the year—becomes at least as important as chronology.[40] July, in particular, has a significance that appears to have little to do with chronology. It always designates a moment of unity, transparency, and plenitude, the burning light of the high summer sun—in Michelet's own words: "Universal history as the struggle of liberty, its victory over the world of fatality, constantly renewed, brief as an eternal July."[41] The July of the taking of the Bastille is repeated in the July of the Federations and in the July of the 1830 Revolution, and it is identified in Michelet's mind with the climaxes, the moments of illumination of his own spiritual (and no doubt sexual) itinerary. "O mon Vico! o mon juillet," he exclaimed once.

The intrusion of the time of myth into the chronological time of history in Michelet's narrative led Frank Bowman of the University of Pennsylvania to raise—quite properly, in my view—the question of Michelet's understanding of the Revolution as a historical event. "What is in fact the date of the Revolution?" Bowman asks. "Is it 1789, 1848, is it in the past or in the future? . . . The Revolution is at once event, goal, and continuity. Need one remark that . . . for Michelet the time of the Passion and the Imitation of Christ is the same as the time of the Revolution?"[42]

When the narrator of the *History of the Revolution* invokes the Revolution in his Introduction—"From the priest to the king, from the Inquisition to the Bastille, the road is straight, but long. Holy, holy Revolution, how slowly dost thou come!—I, who have been waiting for thee for a thousand years in the furrows of the middle ages,—what! must I wait still longer?

Oh! how slowly time passes! Oh! how I have counted the hours!—Wilt thou ever arrive?" (*HR*, I, 75)—it is left unclear whether the historian is speaking for France or for himself, whether the temporal perspective is that of the narrative (that is, the eve of the Revolution of 1789) or that of the act of narration (that is, the eve of the Revolution of 1848). It is as though the "Revolution" belongs to a different order of things from ordinary history, into which it erupts from time to time, like an ever-renewed promise of redemption. The longing for holy Revolution, it appears, is without end, and may belong to any time.

CLAIMING to have discovered an affinity between Michelet and Nietzsche in their common condemnation of their own century as "lifeless" ("en quelque sorte éteint"), Roland Barthes argued that what Michelet shares with Nietzsche is the "apocalyptic" idea that "we are in the time of the End of history."[43] No doubt one of the best ways at present to dust off any old writer and bring him up to date is to find anticipations of Nietzsche in him. But if Barthes's suggestion has any validity—and there may be something Nietzschean about Michelet's impatience with history and his rejection of "imitation" in favor of new creation—it seems to me that it underscores the ambivalence of the fashionable modern idea of a post-historical time.

The religion of Revolution—with its longing for union and redemption, its expectation of a miraculous transcendence of the humdrum world of practical politics and class struggle ("n'importe où hors de ce monde"), and its rejection of the prosaic and often painful compromises that practical politics entail—can lurch unpredictably from passionate idealism to pessimism and despair; moreover, it seems capable of attaching itself to a wide variety of policies and programs, provided these promise immediate deliverance from the world as it is, that is to say, from a world characterized by division and conflict—between the classes and between the sexes. Though Michelet thought of himself as a champion of democracy (and there is no doubt, in my view, of the authenticity and intensity of his hatred of every tyranny and oppression)[44] one is bound to ask how compatible both his Gospel of Revolution and his historical writing are with the actual practice of democracy, or at least of the liberal democracy we are most familiar with.

In the original, pure faith of the Revolution—obscured, misunderstood, or simply forgotten in the half-century since 1789 (*HR*, I, 2), but buried deep, he claimed, in the heart of every French man and woman—Michelet hoped to find the ground of a still unrealized national union which would put an end to the bitterly divisive social and political struggles of his own time. "In moments of weakness, when we seem to have forgotten who we are, it is there that we must seek ourselves," he declared (*HR*, I, 2). The aim of the *History of the French Revolution* was to promote union and resolve class conflict by resurrecting the original faith. Michelet's task as historian of the Revolution was not, therefore, primarily critical. There is an essential connection between his practice of historiography—the way he *wrote* history—and his conception of his subject. His aim was not to "think" the French Revolution, as François Furet would have us do, to disengage himself from its continuing legends in order to study it as a remarkable though contingent historical phenomenon. It was the opposite: to recover what people believed, the power of the founding myth. What Michelet appears to have expected from the spirit of the Revolution was something similar to what he expected from sex—a reusable means of renewal or rejuvenation. ("Woman," he once said, is "the elixir of man.") In keeping with this objective, he not only presented his narrative as a founding history, but he explicitly rejected critical, conceptual, and "scientific" historiography in the form most familiar to him—that of the Enlightenment—as an arbitrary projection of mental constructs onto a reality that had in the end broken over them in an immense tidal wave and swept them away.

His own celebrated injunction to hearken to history's silences implies an operation different from that of the critical historian. Just as it was not for the relatively educated Jacobin or Girondist leader, in Michelet's view, to prescribe policies to "save" the people, it is not for the historian to impose his theories on the past. "We are doctors; the patient does not know what she is talking about"—that is the language of the Jacobins, he says, "clumsy surgeons who in [their] profound ignorance of medicine, think [they] can save everything by driving [their] knife arbitrarily here and there into the patient"(*HR,* I, 301). But all their science, Michelet charges, adopting an image common among Romantic critics of the analytical procedures of the Enlightenment, "consists of cutting, cutting, and cutting again" (*HR,* I, 301).[45] Since the past is not a lifeless cadaver, Michelet goes on, this method is inadequate and inappropriate. The proper model for the historian is not the surgeon but the physician—the hermeneut—"sounding" the patient with his stethoscope. His first task is to listen to what the people whose story he proposes to write has to tell him. His history will be no more or less than that story, only so interpreted that it gives the people a clearer understanding of itself. "Our confidence in a superior education and culture, in our specialized research, in the subtle discoveries we believe we have made must not be allowed to make us despise the national tradition. We must not lightly undertake to alter that tradition, to create or impose another." For in the end, "legend is another kind of history—the history of the people's heart and imagination" (*HR*, I, 282).

So it was clear from the outset that Michelet's history of the Revolution was going to follow the lines that those who made the Revolution had drawn for it and to reflect their understanding of it.[46] "Have I not lived with them, followed each one of them, like a faithful companion through his deepest thoughts and in all his changes," he wrote of the Revolution's actors. "In the end I was one of them, a denizen of that strange world. I had trained my eyes to see in that world of shadows, and I believe they knew me . . . I was not an 'author.' I was thousands of miles away from thinking of the public, of literary success; I was full of love, that's all. I went here and I went there, eager and hungry; I breathed in and I wrote the tragic spirit of the past" (*HR*, I, 14–15).

Michelet frequently asserts that he *is* France, that he *is* the Revolution. In several passages of his book he presents his own life at the time of writing as a reenactment or reliving of an episode in the history he is writing,[47] and he speaks of the heroes of the Revolution in the same terms he uses to speak of himself. For example, when he promised that through his book the men and women of the Revolution would be resurrected to eternal life in exchange for the earthly life they had given up for the sake of the Revolution, he was offering them exactly what he hoped he himself would obtain in exchange for the simple experience of living that he had given up for the sake of his *Revolution*. As he often noted, he had not really lived, but had always sacrificed living to the supreme law of his existence: writing. "Il faut vivre et mourir comme un livre, non comme un homme" ("I have to live and die as a book, not as a man"), he used to say.[48] Not surprisingly, Michelet held that it is by an intense effort of identification, a kind of magical transubstantiation or, as he put it himself, a "strange alchemy," not by detached scientific analysis, that the historian may hope to penetrate the secrets of the past.

For this method of doing history, however, the object of the historian's investigation must always in fact be a subject like himself. The historian does not start with a problem or a question—either a classic problem such as the causes of the military and political decline of states (taken up once again only recently by Paul Kennedy) or a more modern one such as the transformations of family structure and demographic patterns in Western Europe since the Middle Ages, or the conditions favoring the rise of different varieties of fascism. He starts with an active subject, and his aim is to get inside that subject and reconstitute its experience as a story so that all of its seemingly disparate parts come together to form a single, "meaningful" whole. It is entirely appropriate that Michelet's *History of the Revolution* is full of personalities and dramatic scenes and episodes— in stark contrast with the austere, dedramatized, and heroless histories of Tocqueville or Fustel only a few years later. Romantic history, as practiced by Michelet, is a close cousin of other forms of Romantic narrative, especially biography and autobiography. It is a search for—or an invention of—unity and identity.[49] Just as Romantic autobiography defined an identity for the modern *individual* that was no longer dependent on lineage, community, or traditional models, Romantic historiography set out to invent an identity for the modern *nation* that could replace the identity once provided by the representative figure of the King (to whom the old historians and playwrights used to refer as "England," "France," or "Spain").

On his side, the reader is not expected to stand back critically from the history he is reading, as he was from the texts of the Enlightenment historians. Michelet's *History* does not invite discussion or debate. It is not an argument, it is a revelation. Just as the author claims to have eschewed the rules of selection and composition that had governed classical narrative and to have grasped the inner form or spirit of reality by an act of love, an all-encompassing imaginative insight into reality and identification with it, the reader is expected to immerse himself in the narrative and to identify, as the author did, with its "spirit." Reading, in a word, no less than writing, is a kind of *imitatio*. Michelet's aim could not be to encourage criticism and reflection. Conversion, not inquiry, had to be the goal of his history. One might even say that his *History of the Revolution* is offered not as a work of historical analysis but as a kind of Eucharist.[50] Through the child of the historian's labor, the flesh of his flesh, the short-lived unity of the Revolution is to be restored, France is to become one, the nations are to be joined in fraternal communion, and all humanity is to be reunited with itself. If Michelet understood revolution in general and the French Revolution in particular in a quasi-religious light rather than as a mundane historical phenomenon occurring in certain conditions, which one might wish to investigate and try to understand better, that is also how he thought of his own work.[51]

Michelet's practice as its historian thus corresponds to the value he attributed to the Revolution. In both cases, the ideal was union and unanimity. Just as the *History of the Revolution* was not really a contribution to a collective and continuing critical investigation, a dialogue with other historians, but a revelation of the truth, the Revolution itself meant above all the immediate *experience* of revolutionary fervor, an erotic participation, rather than the inauguration of a sustained, difficult ethical and political practice. The "Trois Glorieuses" of 1830 had already inspired the young professor of history and philosophy to compose an enthusiastic hymn to the French people and its aptitude for revolutionary transcendence. "No people," he wrote in the *Introduction to Universal History,* "is more electrified in battle by the feeling of community . . . It is in the midst of danger, when a brilliant July sun illuminates the fête, when fire responds to fire, when bullets and death burst forth inexhaustibly, that stupidity becomes eloquent and cowardice courageous. At such moments the living dust of the people coheres and scintillates, stupendously beautiful. A burning poetry sparks forth from the mass."[52]

Where breaking through to such an intense experience of community is the ideal, political life itself must finally seem second-rate, banal, diminished by compromise and self-interest. "Toute la politique est un expédient" ("All politics is mere expediency"), Hugo wrote in *L'Année terrible.* But when revolution is hypostatized to the point where it far outweighs its specific objectives, one is bound to ask whether revolutionary politics does not have more to do with religion or aesthetics than with ethics, more to do with poetry than with history, for "ethics," as Constant observed, "needs time."[53] Is it not, in fact, by transforming it into literature that Michelet hopes to suspend the fragile epiphanic moment and make it eternal, indefinitely re-presentable and renewable? And could the actual events of 1789–1790—or any actual events, which must inevitably be hostage to time and fortune—ever match their representation in the *History* or realize as fully that *spirit* of the Revolution, which, as Michelet said, "is within us"? The best Revolution for Michelet, one feels, is the Revolution that has been remembered and represented by the historian in literature. The best of times is that "temps des cerises" that brings tears to the eyes of old revolutionaries and old lovers. It is well known that Michelet played almost no part in the 1848 Revolution, but spent most of his time worrying that he was finding it difficult to write and occasionally lamenting the sparse attendance at the once crowded classes where, in the years leading up to 1848, he had excited the young men of France with his oratory and his poetic evocations of history.[54]

What I have emphasized here does not, of course, exhaust Michelet's immensely rich, generous, and often dazzlingly insightful *History.* But it is a significant enough part of it to raise in my mind the question whether that *History* does not encourage, on the one hand, a vicarious participation in revolution as a literary experience that can be comfortably enjoyed in the drawing room, a kind of political pornography, which is equally compatible with political quietism and with radical negation or nihilism, and, on the other, a potentially dangerous inclination to play out personal, probably erotic fantasies on the stage of politics, using other people as props.

It has even been suggested that there may be an inner link between the Romantic, anarchist revolt against the philistinism of nineteenth-century bourgeois existence—Hedda Gabler playing with General Gabler's pistols and dreaming of a beautiful and authentic act—and certain features of fascist ideology. The experience of transcending the bounds of the everyday, as we now know, may be completely indifferent to ethical considerations, and glorification of the *moment*—the moment of crisis or illumination, Barthes's "End of history" or that "state of exception" when "the strength of real life breaks the hardened crust of mechanical repetition," to quote Carl Schmitt, a Nazi intellectual who is back in vogue again—at the expense of the banal bourgeois time of cause and effect, maturation and compromise, calculation and preparation, leads easily into a political Walpurgisnacht, in which all the cows are black.

"The difference between Left and Right," a young Italian scholar observed recently, "is, first and foremost, a product of temporality: of the weight and memories of the past, the open-ended conflicts of the present, the prospects and hopes of the future. . . . When a culture concentrates on the superstitious uniqueness of the moment of crisis . . . temporality will be contracted and abolished: past, present and future will all vanish, and with them all meaningful political determinations." Writing from the point of view of a chastened post-1968 Left, Franco Moretti insists that revolution "should be seen neither as a value in itself, nor as a mechanism to generate values: but [only] as the possible *consequence* of a given set of values in given circumstances." The Left, in other words, must rid itself of "the most equivocal of contemporary political phenomena, left-wing terrorism"; hence, "no tragic yearning for catastrophe as the well-spring of truth, . . . no metaphysical contempt for 'consequences,' no Baroque delight in 'exception.'" For an answer to those who would charge that the sobriety he recommends is at best an unprincipled pragmatism, at worst a capitulation to compromise and intrigue, Moretti looks, as I too am often inclined to do, to Max Weber, and quotes from a speech of Weber's from which, as he says, "there is still a lot to learn," and on which I shall end these reflections on the writing of revolution.

> From a human point of view I don't find anything inspiring in [those who feel unconcerned about the consequences of their actions and are simply intoxicated by their romantic sensations]. What does move me deeply, on the other hand, is . . . a *mature*

person—it doesn't matter whether young or old in years—who, feeling truly and wholly his personal responsibility for consequences, and acting according to the ethic of responsibility, still of a sudden says: 'I cannot do otherwise. I will not retreat from here.' That is behaviour that is truly moving and truly human; and such a situation must be possible at any moment for all of us who have not yet lost our inner life.[55]

[1989]

PART THREE

History and Literature

History and Literature:
Reproduction or Signification

> The basic question is whether the object is signified or reconstituted, or rather which of the two we aim for, since, as a matter of fact, the object is never reconstituted.
>
> —Claude Lévi-Strauss, in Georges Charbonnier,
> *Entretiens avec Claude Lévi-Strauss*

FOR A LONG TIME the relation of history to literature was not notably problematic. History was a branch of literature. It was not until the meaning of the world *literature,* or the institution of literature itself, began to change, toward the end of the eighteenth century, that history came to appear as something distinct from literature.

Quintilian treats history as a form of epic. Of all prose forms, it is the closest to poetry—a kind of prose poem: "Est enim proxima poetis et quodam modo carmen solutum est et scribitur ad narrandum non ad probandum."[1] Because his object is not to demonstrate or argue or persuade, but to narrate and to memorialize, according to Quintilian, the historian may properly employ unfamiliar expressions and bold figures that would be out of place and ineffective in forensic rhetoric. The brief discussion of particular historians in the *Institutio* deals almost exclusively with the stylistic features of their work. Cicero also distinguishes between the mere chronicling of events "sine ullis ornamentis," such as was practiced by the earliest Roman annalists, and the literary productions of the Greek historians. Like Quintilian, he emphasizes that the rhetoric of history is not part of forensic rhetoric—few of the Greek historians, he claims, had any experience of pleading in a court of law—and he complains that no rhetorician has yet formulated the principles of historical writing.[2]

Cicero's own tentative formulation of the basic principles of a future rhetoric of history—the historian may say nothing false, he must dare to say all that is true, he must avoid partiality—seems to remove the question of history from the province of rhetoric to that of epistemology. In fact, Cicero does not neglect matters of style and presentation; he merely questions the relevance of forensic rhetoric to the writing of history. And his conception of the historian as the impersonal mirror of reality is entirely consistent with traditional philosophy and aesthetics. It is repeated, moreover, by other classical writers who concerned themselves with history: Tacitus, Polybius, Plutarch, Lucian. "The ancients' theory of history," it has been said, "was limited largely to questions of technique and presentation."[3]

Renaissance reflection on historiography conformed, as one would expect, to the precepts of the ancients. History writing was viewed as an art of presentation and argument rather than a scientific inquiry, and its problems belonged therefore to rhetoric rather than to epistemology. Though seventeenth- and eighteenth-century theories of poetry usually left room for a neo-Platonic notion of divine inspiration inherited from the Renaissance, literature had, for the most part, the sense of a practice, a technique. A person "of considerable . . . literature" (Mary Edgeworth, 1802, quoted in the *Oxford English Dictionary,* s.v. "literature") was someone who had a considerable repertory of the models by which a good craftsman should be guided, not only in his judgments of the work of others but in his own activity. Speaking of France, Sartre observes that the gap between writer and reader in the seventeenth century was not great. Every reader was himself, in a lesser way, a writer.[4] "Literature" thus referred to the practice of writing. And history—along with sermons, eulogies, and letters—was one of the kinds of writing that could be practiced. The subjects varied and required different treatment, but the craft was the same.[5] History thus had its place in manuals of rhetoric throughout the eighteenth century. It was always distinguishable from "mere" scholarship and antiquarianism, and the ground of the distinction was in large measure that the historian was a writer, whereas the scholar and the antiquarian were not. Gibbon expressed a common view when he wrote that histories become of less and less interest to readers as the events of which they tell become more remote. They come, indeed, to lose "presque tout leur mérite, excepté celui que leur auteur a su leur donner par la manière dont il a traité son sujet."[6] Rudolf Unger's characterization of historiography in the classical period—"historiography was accounted to be, in the first instance, a *literary* genre"[7]—remains valid for the practice of history until nearly the end of the eighteenth century.

In the final phase of neoclassicism, however, the long association of rhetoric and literature began to break down. The term *literature* gradually became more closely associated with poetry, or at least with poetic and figurative writing, and, especially among the Romantics and their successors, took on the meaning of a corpus of privileged or sacred texts, a treasury in which value, truth, and beauty had been piously stored, and which could be opposed to the empirical world of historical reality and even, to some extent, to historiography as the faithful record of that reality. Indeed, it was at this point that historians began to look in the history of historiography itself for the origins of a divorce—which they felt their own time was about to consummate—between historical writing and poetic writing. In the article "History," which he wrote for the *Encyclopédie moderne,* Prosper de Barante located in ancient Greece, just before Herodotus, the fatal moment when "the real was separated from the ideal, poetry from prose, the pleasures men allow themselves in the domain of the spirit from the positive aspects of life."[8] The new conception of literature was more appropriate than the earlier, artisanal one to the condition of the writer in the age of the triumphant bourgeoisie and of industrial capitalism, marking both a criticism of these and a complicity with them. It allowed the products of art to appear as essentially different from all other products of labor in the degraded world of industry and the market, but in order to do so, it foregrounded, indeed fetishized, the product, concealing or mystifying the processes of its production. Literature thus ceased to be thought of as an art by which ideas could be conveyed effectively and elegantly, and which could be pursued with varying degrees of skill and success by all educated people. More and more it came to be regarded as a magical or religious mission, which only those endowed with the gift of prophecy or second sight could fulfill.

Most recently, throwing off in turn the mantle of prophecy, writers have sought to emancipate literature from the myth of Literature, and to turn it into a self-conscious tool for exploring language and extending its range—that is to say, the range of social perception and meaning. Instead of simply accepting language, together with the secondary categories of literary norms and genres, as given, and working within the conditions it provides, the modern writer is constantly crossing frontiers and extending outward the limits and possibilities of writing. The focus of the literary artist's activity, in short, has shifted from rhetoric to poetics. The writer is now not so much a revealer of truths, a speaker of divine language, as a maker of meanings and a restorer of human languages.

At the same time that literature began to detach itself from rhetoric, history was also altering the focus of its concern. For the first time, the epistemological basis of its ideal of impartially copying or representing the real was put in question. As early as 1752 the German theologian Johann Martin Chladenius, elaborating a position outlined by Leibniz and Bayle, made the concept of point of view fundamental to all historical narrative.

> We cannot avoid that each of us looks on the story according to his point of view and that therefore we also retell it according to that point of view. . . . A narration wholly abstracted from its own point of view is impossible, and hence an impartial narration cannot be called one that narrates without any point of view at all, for such simply is not possible. Likewise to be biased in the telling cannot be equated with narrating a subject or a story from one's point of view, for if that were the case all narrations would be biased.[9]

Though Chladenius himself resolved the difficulty too neatly, suggesting that a combination of points of view would allow the object to be located and perceived "objectively," subsequent reflection on historiography, particularly in Germany, was overwhelmingly preoccupied with discovering a more comprehensive theory of historical objectivity than naive realism, one that would include and subsume subjectivity. Despite their differences, Humboldt, Savigny, Ranke, Creuzer, Schleiermacher, Gervinus, and Hegel were all concerned with this problem. Their speculation led to a conception of historical knowledge that emphasized its peculiarity with respect to the knowledge provided by the natural sciences. Positivist theories of history, on the other hand, aimed to bring history as close as possible, epistemologically and methodologically, to the natural sciences. Reflection on historiography was thus more and more concerned with the problems of historical knowledge, and very rarely, or only incidentally, with the problems of historical writing. The separation of literature and historiography was institutionalized, moreover, by the breakup of what had once been the republic of letters—a society in which the historians, both of the Enlightenment and of the early Romantic period, especially in France, England, and Scotland, had mingled freely and shared common experiences and aspirations with novelists, poets, philosophers, political thinkers, economists, scientists, and statesmen. In the course of the nineteenth century historians withdrew more and more to the university, to be followed by historians of literature and by literary critics; and thus history, like literary scholarship, passed from the hands of the poet and man of letters into those of the professor. Finally, in our own times, the very idea that the historian's activity consists in discovering and reconstituting, by whatever means, a past reality conceived of as something objectively fixed has begun to be questioned. The old common ground of history and literature—the idea of mimesis, and the central importance of rhetoric—has thus been gradually vacated by both. The practicing historian is now rarely a practicing literary artist, and the long road traveled by Herodotus, Sallust, Livy, Plutarch, Voltaire, Gibbon, Macaulay, and Michelet appears finally to have been abandoned by all but a handful of stragglers.

OVER a long period of time, then, it seems that the terms whose relations we have to explore are not so much literature and history—since these were not exclusive—as fictional narrative ("fictional history," as Hugh Blair called it) and historical narrative, that is to say, the two terms whose relation has traditionally been of concern to rhetoricians. I would like to comment briefly on this relation, which was a productive one for both fiction and history, before broaching the question of the relation of history and literature in a more recent context.

The traditional outline of the relation was traced by Aristotle in two famous passages of the *Poetics*.

> A poetic imitation, then, ought to be unified in the same way as a single imitation in any other mimetic field, by having a single object: since the plot is an imitation of an action, the latter ought to be both unified and complete, and the component events ought to be so firmly compacted that if any one of them is shifted to another place, or removed, the whole is loosened up and dislocated; for an element whose addition or subtraction makes no perceptible extra difference is not really a part of the whole.
>
> From what has been said it is also clear that the poet's job is not to report what has happened but what is likely to happen: that is, what is capable of happening according to the rule of probability or necessity. Thus the difference between the historian and the poet is not in their utterances being in verse or prose (it would be quite possible for Herodotus' work to be translated into verse, and it would not be any the less a history with verse than it is without it); the difference lies in the fact that the historian speaks of what has happened, the poet of the kind of thing that *can* happen. Hence also poetry is a more philosophical and serious business than history; for poetry speaks more of universals, history of particulars. "Universal" in this case is what kind of person is likely to do or say certain kinds of things, according to probability or necessity; that is what poetry aims

at, although it gives its persons particular names afterward: while the "particular" is what Alcibiades did or what happened to him. (51a30–51b13)

It is clear that epic plots should be made dramatic, as in tragedies, dealing with a single action that is whole and complete and has beginning, middles, and end, so that like a single complete creature it may produce the appropriate pleasure. It is also clear that the plot-structure should not resemble a history, in which of necessity a report is presented not of a single action but of a single period, including everything that happened during that time to individuals or groups—of which events each has only chance relationships to the others. For just as the sea battle at Salamis and the battle against the Carthaginians in Sicily took place about the same time of year but in no way pointed toward the same goal, so also in successive periods spread over time it often happens that one event follows another without any single result coming from them. Yet, speaking by and large, most poets compose this way.

That is why, in addition to what has been said about him previously, one can hardly avoid feeling that Homer showed godlike genius in this case also, namely in the fact that although the Trojan War had a beginning and an end, he did not undertake to compose it as a whole either. For the plot would have been bound to turn out too long and not easy to encompass in a glance, or, if it held to some measurable length, to become entangled with the diversity of its events. Instead, he has singled out one part of the whole and used many of the others as episodes. (59a20–59a37)[10]

Aristotle thus defines history and poetry, in typically classical manner, antithetically: poetry is unified, intelligible, based on proper subordination of the part to the ends of the whole, whereas history knows only the paratactic organization of contiguity or succession. "Aristotle took a low view of history," D. W. Lucas writes in his recent edition of the *Poetics*. "It contains a mere congeries of events, either those of a short period, which will belong to numerous different *praxeis* [actions], or those of a longer period, which will again tend to no one *telos* [end]. As Aristotle nowhere censures the historian he must have thought that the complexity of events combined with deficiency of information made it impossible to disentangle the underlying relationships. . . . The point is that history, not being concerned with *praxeis,* is not intelligible in the same way as the

actions?

mythos [plot] of a play."[11] The distinction, in short, is in some measure, at least, formal, and the operative characteristic of the *mythos* is not apparently whether it is fact or fiction, as we would say, but its unity or unifying power.[12]

Traditionally, then, history and fictional storytelling confront and challenge each other at opposite poles of narrative practice. The actual development of each, however, reveals both great similarities and some significant tensions. Since each is realized in and through narrative, the shape of the narrative and the view of the world that particular narrative forms convey may well be common to both at any given time. In some periods both will be constructed according to a principle of accumulation, association, or addition—vividly described by Albert Thibaudet's term *lopinisme*—in others, such as the neoclassical period, both will strive to conform to ideals of order, coherency, and hierarchical structure. But the tension between the requirements of system and those of change, between order and adventure, will usually persist in all kinds of narrative practice (historical or fictional) and may at certain moments become acute enough to become itself the principal theme of narrative works. At such times history may come to be associated, as it was in the *Poetics,* with the singular, the unexpected, the uncontrollable, the unsystematic, and fiction, on the other hand, with the ordered, the coherent, the general or universal. We may then discover that while historians are striving to achieve maximum narrative coherency and to approximate to the forms of fiction, certain novelists are trying to undercut these very forms and conventions by an appeal to "history."

As ONE of the founding fathers of modern historiography, Voltaire was much concerned with matters of form, and his lifelong reflection on historiography began, characteristically, as reflection on epic. In the early *Essay on Epick Poetry* (1727) he emphasized, conventionally enough, the exemplary character of the epic action and its unity. At the same time he declared that he preferred the subject to be "true," and he criticized Le Bossu for advocating that the epic poet invent subjects out of his imagination. Virgil was said to have gathered together for the *Aeneid* "different materials which were scattered through several books and of which some can be found in Dionysius Halicarnassiensis."[13] Virgil's materials, in sum, were basically "true." The notion of "true" here, however, is one that has become strange to us. Essentially, Voltaire means "familiar," "legendary," or "held to be true." The idea is hard to convey now, since the legendary has come to be synonymous with false. The important thing for Voltaire,

in this context at any rate, was not objective truth, as distinct from subjective belief, but the fact that the material was part of a widely accepted
tradition. For this very reason, he held that the modern writer should
remove from traditional material all elements that might run counter to
what his own readers would consider true, anything they might find unacceptable or "improbable." In short, the material best suited to the epic
writer is that which has already been selected, filtered, and shaped by
literary tradition and popular imagination, and which the epic writer in
turn filters with his own audience in view; and preferably such material
should be regarded by the public as generally "true." Recent history, which
has not yet been worked over and given shape, is too raw to serve successfully. With much sympathy for Lucan, Voltaire attributes what he
considered the failure of the *Pharsalia* to the recalcitrance of the material,
and he makes a similar point somewhat later in a comment on his own
epic poem *La Henriade* (1728): "This poem is based on a known history,
the truth of which has been respected in the principal events. The others,
being less reliable, have been either omitted or rearranged according to
the requirements of verisimilitude (*vraisemblance*) in a poetic composition.
In this way, every effort has been made to avoid the weakness of Lucan,
whose poem is nothing but an overblown chronicle."[14] Lucan is compared
favorably with Tasso, however, because the latter invented his subject.

Voltaire's alternatives in this early essay are clearly those of the *Poetics*:
the pure succession of history and the formal unity of legend. The "truth"
he requires of the epic narrative is not yet defined against legend or myth.
Yet in his own first attempt at epic composition—roughly contemporary
with the *Essay*—Voltaire shows the influence of the demand for criticism
and verification which corresponded, in the scholarly circles of the seventeenth century, to the austere standards of the new philosophy and its
obsession with falsehood and error. The notion of the "true" in the *Henriade* is already close to that of modern historical "science." The *Henriade*
was always regarded by both the author and his readers as a work of
history; and both considered that, as such, it had to meet the standards
of the new historical criticism. It was not enough simply to work over
familiar material widely held to be true; the material had to be authenti-
cated, the subject shown to be true. Early editions of the text were accompanied by an "Histoire abrégée des événements historiques sur lesquels
est fondée la fable du poème de la Henriade." A "Dissertation sur la mort
de Henri IV" was added by Voltaire himself to the 1748 edition, and the
Kehl editors appended further documentary evidence, as well as a translation into French of the "Essay on the Civil Wars in France," which had
accompanied the first edition of the *Essay on Epick Poetry*. In the late

nineteenth century Louis Moland still gave serious consideration to the historical value of the work.

The demands of historical criticism affected content alone, however. They imposed new constraints and obligations on the historian in the selection of the material he proposed to work over, but did not alter the fundamental fact that his task was to *write,* to compose a coherent work of literature with data provided by history. The "Essay on the Civil Wars" and the "Histoire abrégée" are revealing in this respect. Doubtless they were to be understood as the unadorned version, the bare bones of the literary work. Each canto, moreover, opens with a brief prose summary of the events or the theme to be amplified in verse in it, a tactic that Voltaire continued in his later prose histories and that was traditionally followed by writers of romances and writers of histories alike. The difference between the historian and the epic poet, for Voltaire, thus lay in the nature of the material out of which each composed his work. In the conditions of modern critical thought the material of the one could no longer be identical with that of the other. Historical material and legendary material were now distinct. Nevertheless, the essential concerns of the epic poet and of the historian, not as scholar but as writer, were the same: careful selection of an appropriate subject matter and skillful narrative composition. Voltaire's discussions not only of the *Henriade* but of the *Histoire de Charles XII* and the *Siècle de Louis XIV* leave no doubt about this; the comments of his correspondents—especially of those who wrote to him about the *Histoire de Charles XII*—make it abundantly clear that readers, on their side, judged historical narrative according to the criteria applied to fictional narrative. "L'histoire," in Cideville's pithy phrase, "n'est qu'un plus long conte."[15] Voltaire, in short, preferred his epics to be true and his histories to be epic. Indeed, it is possible to view his historiographical career as the continuation of a career begun in the practice of epic. When he wrote to Hénault about the design of the *Siècle de Louis XIV* he probably still had Aristotle's observations on history and epic in mind:

My aim has been to make a great picture of events that are worthy of being painted, and to keep the reader's eyes trained on the leading characters. History, like tragedy, requires an exposition, a central action, and a denouement. Otherwise the historian is no more than a Reboulet, or a Limiers, or a La Hode. There is room, moreover, in this vast canvas for interesting anecdotes. I hate petty facts; plenty of others have laden their enormous compilations with them. . . . My secret is to force the reader to wonder: Will Philip V ascend the throne? Will he be chased out of Spain? Will Holland be destroyed? Will Louis XIV go under? In short, I have tried to move my reader, even in history.[16]

Voltaire was not alone in wishing to make history the modern successor of the epic. Gibbon's "Mr. Hurd's Commentary on Horace" (1757) shows how much thought he gave to questions of epic composition, and the narrator of the *Decline and Fall* accompanies his narrative with a continuous commentary on its composition.[17] As is well known, Gibbon considered a number of topics before finally selecting the decline and fall of the Roman Empire as the subject of his great history. His principal concern was the appropriateness of the subject matter to the kind of literary treatment he had in mind. In his *Lettre sur les occupations de l'Académie* (1716) Fénelon had already urged a reform of the manner of writing history that would have given to history the status and the form of epic. "A dry and dreary compiler of annals knows no other order than that of chronology. . . . But the historian of genius selects among twenty possible places in his narrative the one where a fact ought to be placed to throw light on all the others."[18] Aristotle notwithstanding, in other words, the historian ought to be concerned with "actions" and ought to organize his material accordingly. Instead of a pure succession, a genealogy, he should recount an action that has an exposition, a central intrigue, and a denouement, and that illustrates some important principle.

Later in the century, Hugh Blair's teaching in his rhetoric classes at the University of Edinburgh was similar. "Historical composition is understood to comprehend under it, Annals, Memoirs, Lives," Blair allowed. "But these," he added, "are its inferior subordinate species. In the conduct and management of his subject, the first attention requisite in an Historian is to give as much unity as possible; that is, his History should not consist of separate unconnected parts merely, but should be bound together by some connecting principle, which shall make the impression on the mind of something that is one, whole and entire." The reader is most pleased and instructed "when the mind has always before it the progress of some one great plan or system of actions; when there is some point or centre, to which we can refer the various facts related by the Historian."[19] Just as Montesquieu claimed that in the *Lettres persanes* he had joined philosophy, politics, and morals to a novel, and bound them into a unified composition by "une chaîne secrete," Blair argued that in history "we should be able to trace all the secret links of the chain, which binds together remote, and seemingly unconnected events," and Fénelon declared that "the main point is to place the reader at the heart of things and to reveal to him the links among them."[20]

The aesthetic character of the proposed reform of historiography is made particularly clear in the preface written by Jean-Jacques Garnier (1729–1805), Inspector of the Collège de France, for his revised edition and continuation (1770–1778) of the popular *Histoire de France* of the ex-Jesuit abbé Paul-François Velly (1709–1759). Velly's history, which was the basis of successive revised editions in the course of the eighteenth century, was itself essentially a revision of a traditional royalist history-of-France, the function of which was basically the legitimation of political authority, and the fundamental form of which goes back to the medieval *Grandes Chroniques*. "The history of France, from the fifteenth to the nineteenth century," Philippe Ariès remarks, "is not a series of episodes whose mutual relations and relative importance are subject to the scrutiny and revision of the scholar, the critic, the philosopher. . . . There is a history of France as there are subjects of tragedies and of operas, as there is an Orpheus or a Phèdre which each artist exploits in his own way. It is a subject: not History, but the History-of-France, which each generation rewrites in its own style and according to its own manner."[21] Garnier's proposal, which he himself did not carry out effectively, involved above all reshaping that history aesthetically, giving it the form of a literary narrative rather than of a folktale. He did propose, like Sorel, Mézeray, and others before him, that patently "legendary" material (that is, material unacceptable to a public for which *vraisemblance* had become a condition of acceptance) be scrapped, and that material on laws, customs, and the arts be introduced, but this implied no more fundamental a change in the historical account than the addition, today, of some mention of demography or nutrition in works whose form remains obstinately that prescribed by traditional political history.

The essence of Garnier's proposals was aesthetic. There is a clear echo of Aristotle in the statement that "a fact is any kind of event whatsoever; one may be completely ignorant of its causes and relations . . . An action, on the other hand, has necessarily a beginning, a middle, and an end." Garnier criticized the earliest historians of France for having simply gathered isolated facts and arranged them in chronological order, without any concern for possible internal relations among them. Those who came after them, he went on, simply followed the path that had been traced out for them and were satisfied if they could enrich the existing story with some new anecdote, or correct a date. "Every one has tried to add to the discoveries already made, to substitute a pure and sometimes decorative style for the gross and semibarbarous language of our old chroniclers, but nobody has thought of altering a fundamentally vicious plan." Garnier's own suggestion involved the same kind of reordering that Voltaire and Fénelon had demanded: the historian "should find a luminous point of view from which the reader could easily allow his gaze to embrace the entire sequence of facts, a pregnant principle of which each particular fact would be only a development or consequence." Isolated facts that cannot be related to the principal action should be treated in digressions if they are important in themselves, and simply abandoned if they are not. In this way, "a reader can traverse a long succession of centuries without weariness or boredom; he sees the facts follow one another in their natural order; in a way he knows them in advance, since with the help of the principles with which he has been provided and which are constantly in his mind, he can already divine what will be the outcome of such and such a combination of events. He puts himself in the place of the principal actors, and experiences, in part, the passions that agitated them."[22]

The recurrent comparison of historical narrative with *peinture d'histoire* and the allusions to the requirements of perspective that are so characteristic of eighteenth-century discussions of history, whether by obscure figures like Garnier or by eminent ones such as Voltaire and Marmontel (see especially the latter's article "Histoire," in his *Eléments de littérature*), point clearly to the nature of the goal neoclassical historiography set for itself: to recast the mere succession or juxtaposition of chronicle narrative in the same way that the masters of perspective had transformed painting. Instead of being placed in immediate relation to the object of narration, the reader, like the narrator, was to be placed at a distance from it, so that it appeared to him as if it were situated in a framed and closed space upon which he could look out, as through a window. As it was unfolded, the narrative would assume the characteristics of a painting or tableau which could be embraced in a simultaneous vision similar to that enjoyed by the eye as it moves over the canvas. While following the sequence of events, in other words, the reader was to anticipate the entire plot, so that each event as it was narrated would fit into its allotted place. Thus the *fortschreitende Handlung* (progressive action) of epic narrative, in Lessing's terms (*Laokoon*, XV), would be gathered up constantly in the *stehende Handlung* (stationary action) of the visual arts. At the same time, by occupying the proper point from which the narrative was intended to be "viewed," the reader, like the art lover looking at a *peinture d'histoire*, would perceive correctly the groupings of the figures and the relation of the details to the principal figures or action. The viewer standing close up against the canvas or the reader closely concerned with the events being narrated (the aristocratic reader, for instance, who knows the characters personally or has himself participated in the action) would see the details, and might well find pleasure in them, but the reader standing back from the canvas or the story (the bourgeois who does not make the political or military history that is the principal object of historical narratives, the philosopher, posterity, the universal reader) would alone dominate the entire work, discerning the order and hierarchy of its parts, and so be able truly to *read* the canvas before him. The ideal reader of the eighteenth century is the detached, philosophical observer, the bourgeois spectator, who masters history by reducing it to order or theory, not the actor on the stage or those too close to the action to be able to view it as a self-contained entity, complete in itself, an object removed from the continuity of reality.

In neoclassical historiography the part is thus subordinated to the whole, the particular to the general, the syntagmatic to the paradigmatic. What the reader of history observes is the unfolding of a distinct, autonomous action, which is already inscribed, from the beginning, in the elements that consitute it. "From his position at the origin of things," Fontenelle wrote of an ideal history, "the reader would entertain himself by contemplating the consequences that he had already foreseen; for once the general principles have been grasped, everything that can possibly come of them can be embraced in a universal view, and the details are only an entertaining diversion, which may even, on occasion, be dispensed with, being excessively facile and of no great utility."[23] History here is turned into destiny, and time made into the medium in which a timeless order unfolds.

Meanwhile, at the other end of the spectrum, the novel was giving itself an air of history and offering itself to the reader as reportage, the order of which is prescribed by events as they occur, not by art. In Diderot's *Jacques le fataliste* the narrator exposes the banality of the reader's expectations and takes delight in frustrating them in the name of the arbitrariness and unpredictability of a reality that supposedly accompanies its narration instead of preceding it. There is no *point de vue lumineux* here, and the grand perspective of the historian has become Jacques's *grand rouleau*. With his faith that events always follow familiar patterns, the reader in Diderot's text resembles Jacques's master, of whom it is said early in the novel: "He has eyes like you and me; but most of the time it is by no means certain that he looks." In other words, his ideas about the world he lives in derive from mental schemata, not from observation. To the master's belief that he can fully discern the essential and unchanging features of an order that happens to suit him very well, Jacques responds by pointing to the great scroll of destiny, which, being infinite, cannot ever be totalized, and so guarantees the unpredictability of the historical order.

In a similar way, the narrator opposes the richness and arbitrariness of "reality" to the orderly and ordering categories of the mind and of literary convention.

But Diderot's analysis of the relation of history and fiction, or arbitrariness and order, is not settled in favor of the former.[24] The text leaves no doubt that the writer is inventing even when he claims to be following reality, and that this claim is itself a fiction, a move in a rhetorical and artistic strategy, not a step outside the world of art and rhetoric. Writing always implies selection, organization, signification, or the making of meaning. In *Le Neveu de Rameau,* Rameau fills the slot that Jacques filled in the other work: he is receptive to experience, adaptable to circumstances as they present themselves, endlessly changeable. Moi, the philosopher, on the other hand, fills the slot of the master: he is a dreamer and a schemer, who imagines he controls his destiny but turns out to be completely cut off from the world—Diogenes masturbating in his barrel. And yet it is not Rameau but Moi who, as narrator, devises, emplots, and composes the entire dialogue in which Rameau is by far the livelier and more colorful participant.

Schiller, who knew his Diderot well, expresses in a striking formula the essential tension that runs through nearly all Diderot's reflection on science and art:

> The more multiform the cultivation of the sensibility is, the more variable it is, and the greater surface it offers to phenomena, the more world does Man *apprehend,* the more potentialities does he develop within himself; the greater the strength and depth that the personality achieves, and the more freedom the reason gains, the more world does Man *comprehend,* the more form does he create outside himself. Thus his culture will consist of two things: first providing the receptive faculty with the most multifarious contacts with the world, and as regards feeling, pushing passivity to its fullest extent; secondly, securing for the determining faculty the fullest independence from the receptive, and as regards reason, pushing activity to its fullest extent. Where both qualities are united, Man will combine the greatest fullness of existence with the utmost self-dependence and freedom, and instead of abandoning himself to the world he will rather draw it into himself with the whole infinity of its phenomena, and subject it to the unity of his reason.[25]

Not surprisingly, Schiller's view of history includes the same polarities that characterized fictional narrative for Diderot. In his inaugural lecture at Jena in May 1789, "What Is Universal History and Why Do We Study It?" Schiller distinguishes carefully between the course of the world ("der Gang der Welt") and the course of world history ("der Gang der Welt-geschichte"), between events and their history. Only some of the waves on the immense river of the past are visible to the historian, says Schiller, and, in addition, the historian's perception is determined by his own situation, so that events are often torn out of the dense and complex web of their contemporary relations in order to be set in a pattern constructed retrospectively by the historian. The order of history is not given; it is constructed by us as a kind of wager on the rationality and intelligibility of historical existence, and because—especially if we are eighteenth-century Deists—we can scarcely think of the universe except in terms of orderly design. "One after another phenomena begin to withdraw from the sphere of blind chance, or lawless liberty, and to find their places as concordant parts of a coherent whole (which to be sure, is present only as an idea in the historian's mind). . . . The historian thus draws that harmony forth from himself, and transplants it, outside himself, in the order of external things, that is to say, he brings a rational end to the course of the world, and a teleological principle to world history." He applies this harmonious model to every phenomenon presented by the great theater of the world, and finds that many confirm it and many contradict it. As long as he cannot establish all the links in the chain, the question of the order of history remains unresolved, but "that opinion carries the day for him, which offers the highest satisfaction to the understanding and to the heart the greatest felicity."[26]

The polarity of the receptive faculty and the determining faculty, of the world and of reason, or, we might also wish to say, of the syntagmatic and paradigmatic, is thus in no way identical, in the neoclassical period, with the polarity of history and fiction. It operates *within* both. Fictional writing is constantly questioning existing fictional conventions, and for centuries it did so by appealing to history. But historical writing operates in the same way: every attempt to devise an order different from that of pure chronicle involved an appeal to the order of art—of fictional narrative or of drama. And correspondingly, when the intention was to reject a highly structured model of historical narrative, emphasis was again placed on the syntagmatic, and on the historian's task as simple reporter or eye-witness. The little-known but extremely interesting work of Prosper de Barante, an outstanding member of the narrative school of historians during the French Restoration, is an illuminating case of a move in this direction. As we saw in Chapter 4, the very title of Barante's work, *Histoire des Ducs de Bourgogne de la maison de Valois* (1824–1826), signals the predominance of the syntagmatic: the unity of the elements of the narrative lies in genealogical relations, relations of pure succession. In contrast, Augustin Thierry's *Histoire de la conquête de l'Angleterre par les Normands,* which appeared in 1825, announces in its title the unifying role of the general concept of conquest, an important historical category at the time and one that had been the subject of an influential essay by Benjamin Constant. In his Introduction, Thierry explicitly drew attention to the paradigmatic aspect of his narrative. His history of the Norman Conquest, he said, was a model of all the histories of the European countries. Yet Thierry was in no way critical of narrative history; on the contrary, he is rightly considered one of the leaders of the narrative school. But he emphasized the paradigmatic aspect of the historical text as well as the syntagmatic one.

ALTHOUGH at times historical narrative and fictional narrative may seem to have been straining in opposite directions, they have both traditionally accepted the essential conditions of classical narrative and have operated within the framework these provide. The framing of narrative, the establishment of a special time of narrative discontinuous with the time of the narrator's own telling, is signaled, according to Emile Benveniste, by the use of a certain set of verb tenses, notably the simple past or aorist, assisted by the imperfect and pluperfect. These tenses constitute in this respect a system, and the present, the future, the perfect constitute another. The tenses of the second system all maintain a relation to the present and direct attention to the subject, to the act of speaking (*l'énonciation*), and to the present relation between narrator or speaker and reader or listener, rather than exclusively to the narrative of events (*l'énoncé*).[27] The use of the appropriate tense system is a condition of narrative, whether the latter is presented as true or as fictional, whether it is, in Voltaire's words "le récit des faits donnés pour vrais" or "le récit des faits donnés pour faux."[28] Despite his efforts to subvert the traditional form of narrative, in *Jacques le fataliste,* by foregrounding the narrator and the act of telling, and by presenting the act of telling as contemporary with what is being told, Diderot did not succeed in eliminating the past tense itself even from the narrative of his frame story. He could illuminate the processes of telling and reading or listening, but he could not actually fuse the two planes of enunciation which Benveniste characterizes as *histoire* and *discours*. These, with their respective verbal systems, remain clearly distinguishable throughout his text. *Jacques,* moreover, includes many traditionally told tales within the frame story, as though to emphasize that the construction of intelligible models of experience is both necessary and inevitable, and that the revelation of the role of the narrator in their production and of the reader in their interpretation can make us aware of what we are doing but cannot alter the actual form in which we do it.

By means of the "discourse" with which he is free to accompany his narrative of events, however, the historian and the novelist alike can comment on the action being related and orient the reader's attitude toward it. Not surprisingly, at any given time there tend to be many points of resemblance between the discourse of historians and that of novelists.

The characteristic feature of eighteenth-century fiction is the ironic distance most eighteenth-century novels establish between the narrator and the narrative, and the complicity they set up between the reader and the narrator over against the narrative—that is to say, the clear distinction they make between *discours* and *histoire,* and the privilege they accord to the former. This is also what characterizes Voltaire, Hume, and Gibbon as historians. The Enlightenment historian tells his tale under the same conditions as the eighteenth-century novelist, and, like him, engages the reader with him as ironic spectator of the historical scene or tableau. The ultimate unifying center of eighteenth-century historical writing, it has been said, is the narrator himself rather than the narrative of events:[29] the latter exists largely as a pretext for "philosophical" commentary, and for the sake of the community of *philosophes* that this commentary was expected to establish between narrator and reader, and among readers. History, in this important respect, was not essentially different from fiction, and d'Alembert's remark that the writings of Tacitus "would not lose much if we were to consider them only as the first and truest of philosophical novels"[30] probably did not seem as odd or shocking to the eighteenth-century reader as it does to us, or at least as it must have done to the serious nineteenth-century reader. Voltaire also distinguished between the value of an intelligible model—which fiction can presumably be as well as history—and merely factually true accounts. "We have to make distinctions among the errors of historians. A false date, a wrong name, are only material for a volume of *errata.* If the main body of the work is otherwise true, if the interests, the motives, the events have been faithfully unfolded, we have a well-made statue which can be faulted for some slight imperfection of a fold in the drapery."[31]

Voltaire himself never justified his constant correction and revision of his historical writings, and his tireless seeking out of new information, except on the grounds that a healthy respect for truth was generally a good mental hygiene. The overall pattern, in Voltaire's histories, was always being subverted by individual acts, the ideal universal truth by particular events, the general maxim by the exceptions to it; and the endless confrontation of the particular and the general led, in Voltaire's case, not to a solution at the level of the object, but to one at the level of the subject—to irony. It reinforced and justified the central position of the narrator, and privileged the act of thinking "en philosophe" about history and about the problematics of history over the matter of the objective truth or otherwise of the narrative. What was important was not the truth of the narrative so much as the activity of reflecting about the narrative, including that of reflecting about its truth. History, in the eighteenth century, raised questions and created conditions in which the individual subject, the critical reason, could exercise and assert its freedom. It did not present itself as an objectively true and therefore compelling discovery of reality itself. On the contrary, its truth and validity were always problematic, provoking the reader's reflection and thus renewing his freedom. In an important sense, therefore, historical narrative and fictional narrative were constructed in fundamentally similar ways in the eighteenth century.

It would not be too difficult to show that nineteenth-century historical narrative also shares important structural features with nineteenth-century fictional narrative, notably the explicit rejection of the clear Enlightenment separation of object and subject, past and present, narrative and commentary or discourse, and the attempt to make them continuous with each other. The dominant feature of both fictional and historical narrative in the nineteenth century is the replacement of the overt eighteenth-century persona of the narrator by a covert narrator, and the corresponding presentation of the narrative as unproblematic, absolutely binding. The nineteenth-century narrator appears as a privileged reporter recounting what happened. The historical text is not presented as a model to be discussed, criticized, accepted, or repudiated by the free and inquiring intellect, but as the inmost form of the real, binding, and inescapable. In the struggle to establish *philosophie,* in other words, the eighteenth-century historian accepted his ideological function proudly; in the nineteenth century the historian's ideological function and the rhetoric he deployed in its service were denied, in the deepest sense, since the historian himself did not recognize them.

In our own time, there appear to be correspondences between developments in historiography and certain developments in modern fiction—among them the repudiation of realism, the collapse of the subject or character as an integrated and integrating entity, and an increasingly acute awareness of the fundamental logic or syntax of narrative and of the constraints and opportunities it provides. In a wise and entertaining book published after his death, Siegfried Kracauer took malicious pleasure in showing how even an eminent historian like Henri Pirenne used time-worn rhetorical tricks to bring together relatively discontinuous persons and events in a single, continuous, and unified narrative.[32] The relations between different historical series (political actions, institutions, economics, nutrition, climate, population, regions, towns, language, literature, philosophy, and so on) now appear problematic at least, since time is no longer assumed to be a uniform medium in which historical events occur or historical phenomena have their existence, and which in itself establishes a continuity among these diverse phenomena, but seems rather to be multiform, constituted differently by the phenomena placed in series. The same is true of space.[33] Braudel's three-level distinction of *histoire événementielle, histoire conjoncturale,* and *histoire de longue durée* is now familiar to a wide public. Earlier, Lucien Febvre had called for a historiography which, instead of being located in a supposedly even and objective time-flow (and thereby in fact positing such a time-flow), would select moments of crisis, collision, and breakdown. Discontinuity, in short, rather than continuity was to be placed at the heart of history as it had been placed already at the heart of fiction.[34]

Above all, the attack on historical realism, begun in the early nineteenth century, has become more intense and more radical. Nineteenth-century philosophers challenged the naive realism of the classical historians and emphasized the place of subjectivity in historical knowledge. For many who reflected on the problems of historical knowledge, the fact that the knower is himself involved in the historical process as a maker of history and is thus unable to achieve the "objective" view aspired to by the natural scientist was the very condition of historical knowledge, as opposed to knowledge of the natural world. There was no question, however, that the historian's aim was to know and to reveal the reality of the past. Only that reality was now thought of as at once given and concealed, so that the historian's job, as Humboldt had said at the beginning of the century in his essay *Die Aufgabe des Geschichtschreibers,* was to divine (*ahnden*) it. The historian was to reach through to past reality by a process of divination or symbolic interpretation of the evidence. Recent reflection on history, like recent reflection on literature, in contrast, has tended increasingly to question the mimetic ideal itself.

In an article first published in 1943, Lucien Febvre recalled that in 1860, in the flush of the first successes of organic chemistry, Berthelot was already proclaiming that "chemistry makes its object." According to Febvre, Berthelot claimed that, unlike the natural and historical sciences, whose object is given in advance, independently of the scientist's will and action, chemistry, like art, has the power to create a multitude of artificial substances similar to natural ones. It is thereby released from bondage to the object. In Febvre's view, however,

> this distinction between chemistry and the other sciences is no longer valid. All scientists now define Science as creation, present it as "creating its object," and insist on the constant play of the scientist's will and activity. Such is the climate of Science today. A climate that has nothing in common with the Science of yesterday—the Science of the days when I was twenty. That Science and the postulates on which it was founded have been thoroughly shaken, criticized, left behind. Scientists gave them up years ago and replaced them with others. So I ask a question—one simple question: Are we historians alone going to continue to recognize them as valid? . . . Is it not time to stop, once and for all, looking to the "sciences" of fifty years ago to shore up and justify our theories—since the sciences of fifty years ago are no more than memories and ghosts.[35]

In a similiar vein, it has sometimes been argued by philosophers that the historian's objects are not unproblematically situated on the other side of the evidence, as it were, but are constructs, whose function is to account for the present evidence. "George Washington," one such argument runs, "enjoys at present the epistemological status of an electron: each is an entity postulated for the purpose of giving coherence to our present experience, and each is unobservable by us." According to the same argument, "the forthright empiricism which has generally prevailed in the historical trade" has laudable objectives,

> but its view of the process by which historical knowledge is attained is naive. In holding that external and internal criticism yield statements from which facts are determined, and that the function of interpretation is to account for all, or a preselected few, of these facts, it badly distorts the actual practice of historians. In fact, interpretation enters at every step along the way. External criticism is really a process of testing classificatory hypotheses about objects and so depends upon such interpretative hypotheses being made. Similarly, the attribution of meaning and reference to an inscription is an interpretative or hypothetical process. Historical facts are not established from pure data—they are postulated to explain characteristics of the data. Thus the sharp division between fact and interpretation upon which the

classical view insisted and which the revisionists have accepted, does not exist.[36]

The historian appears here as someone who attempts coolly to resolve problems that are absolutely external to him. But many writers have emphasized the important role played by the historian's imagination, his concerns as an individual and as a social being, and even by his unconscious, both in the determination of the problem to be studied and in the shaping of the historical narrative. Hayden White quotes H. I. Marrou, the historian, who, as "Henry Davenson," author of a valuable *Introduction à la chanson française* (1941), knows a great deal about poetry: "If the historian is a man and if he actually reaches the level of history (if he is not a mere academician, busy selecting materials for an eventual history), he will not pass his time in splitting hairs over questions which do not keep anyone from sleeping . . . He will pursue, in his dialogue with the past, the elaboration of *the* question which *does* keep *him* from sleeping, the central problem of his existence, the solution of which involves his life and entire person."[37] Without going so far as to claim with Unamuno that "the tyrants depicted by Tacitus were all himself,"[38] Alain Besançon argues that all historical research is in some measure "recherche de soi-même . . . introspection." According to Besançon, "the fundamental operation of the sciences of human behavior is not the observation of the subject by the observer. It is the analysis of their interaction in a situation in which both are at one and the same time subjects and observers." It follows that Besançon is skeptical of certain orientations of contemporary historiography, which he identifies as alibis for the genuinely fruitful but disturbing encounter of the historian with the texts of the past. "The piling up of factual references in card-index boxes, the complete count of the number of pairs of shoes exported from Livradois to Forez, utilizing higher mathematics and computers, become so many maneuvers whose aim is less the advancement of scientific knowledge than the removal of the specific anguish that attaches to the act of creation." In the end, what historical study produces, Besançon insists, is not unified or total knowledge of the past or of some fragment of it, but a *book*, a text. The unity of history lies in the books written by the great historians. "If we ponder over Fustel's *La Cité antique*, Bloch's *Société féodale*, whereas we only consult corresponding works, it is because between one group of writings and another, there is the same kind of difference as between the works of Dostoyevsky and those of Eugène Sue, which inspired them."[39]

One of the most effective and radical criticisms of historical realism has been made by highlighting the linguistic existence of historical narratives, by emphasizing that history constructs its objects, and that its objects are objects of language, rather than entities of which words are in some way copies. From this point of view, the *battle of Gettysburg,* for instance, does not designate unproblematically something solid in reality that is prior to any naming of it. The semiology of history, moreover, is more complex than that of language itself. In historical writing, the signs of language become signifiers in a secondary system elaborated by the historian. What already has meaning at the level of language becomes an empty form again until, being brought into relation with a historically definable *signifié,* or concept, it constitutes a new sign at a different level of meaning. Historical discourse thus has the character of a language constructed out of material that is itself already language. Roland Barthes has been especially critical of every failure to acknowledge the linguistic character of the historical text, and of a persistent tendency to see the text as the mere copy of another existence situated in an extrastructural field, namely "the real." "Like every discourse that claims to be 'realist,' " Barthes writes, "historical discourse believes it knows a semantic system constituted by only two terms—the signifier and the referent."[40] It thus dispenses with a term that is essential to language and fundamental to every imaginary structure— the *signifié.* Far from the world of things founding and supporting the world of signs, as classical historical discourse appears to suppose—Barthes objects—it seems rather that the world of signs constitutes and calls into existence the world of things. Reality, in sum, is human; it is always that which we make signify, never a mere given.

Those historians who have been most willing to recognize the role of imagination in the writing of history or the proximity of history and fiction have also, understandably, been most concerned to distinguish between the two, and to establish the specificity of history. Though there appears to be a certain longing to found the difference in the historical narrative's continued dependency on the real world, the specificity of history can probably be more easily defined in terms of its own rules, its own system, than in terms of a direct relation of dependency upon the real world. R. G. Collingwood, for instance, proposes three rules or conditions for history—that the historian, unlike the novelist, must localize his story in time and place; that all history must be consistent with itself, since there is only one historical world, whereas fictional universes, being autono- mous, need not agree, and cannot clash; and that the historical imagination is not completely free but is bound to work from "evidence."[41]

Of these rules, the first seems to be an aspect of the second. Space and time are not absolute but are themselves defined by the historian, so that the first rule really reads: the historian's space and time must be consistent with the space and time of other historians. Interestingly, many novelists, anxious to give an air of history to their fictions, accept the space and time of the historian and try to observe this rule wherever their narratives do impinge on those of the historian. Space and time, in other words, do not appear to be objective realities that found the historian's work and differentiate it from the imaginary writings of the novelists, but rather a particular space and time act as signals to the reader that a work is to be regarded as history. The specificity of the text, in short, is not established by something outside it but by its own system. The second rule—the historian must verify whether his story tallies with the stories of other historians and with the documentary record—rests on the premise that the historical world is one, and this may be seen as a regulative idea rather than a statement of fact. The consistency rule suggests that the goal and purpose of history may well be, at certain times anyway, to establish or affirm the unity and coherency of the historical world or of the part of it being related, but the rule itself does not seem to have any objective justification. Once again, the specificity of the text is not established by something outside it, but by its own system. The fact that a story is presented as consonant with other stories and verifiable in relation to them establishes it as history.[42] The rule founds the historical world; it is not derived from it. Moreover, it is still possible for the historian, without infringing the consistency rule, to emplot the "same" events in different stories, and to construct different events from the same evidence. The consistency rule, it seems, limits what the historian may do, rather as conventional ideas of probability limit what the novelist may do; but within these limits, the historian may propose a variety of configurations, and the rules according to which these are engendered may well be the same as the rules by which fictional narratives are engendered. The simplest of events, after all, is itself a story, the interpretation of which involves a larger story of which it is part, so that history could be envisaged as a complex pattern of stories each of which contains another complex pattern of stories, and so on without end. There seems to be no outside of stories, no point at which they stop being stories and abut on hard particles of "facts."

Collingwood's third rule, the rule of evidence, also limits the historian rather than determines him. Collingwood himself acknowledges that it is not easy to separate evidence from the explanation and interpretation that it supports: we can only recognize evidence as evidence, he explains, because we already have a system or hypothesis in terms of which it acquires significance.[43] Once more, therefore, the historian's constructive and imaginative activity is involved in the very foundations of his work. Evidence—texts, documents, artifacts—is by definition a sign, and it signifies within a system of signs. The historian's narrative is constructed not upon reality itself or upon transparent images of it, but on signifiers which the historian's own action transforms into signs. It is not historical reality itself but the present signs of the historian that limit and order the historical narrative (just as, conversely, the historical narrative limits and orders them). Almost all historians acknowledge this implicitly in the act of placing their notes—sources, evidence—at the foot of the page. The division of the historiographical page is a testimony to the discontinuity between past "reality" and the historical narrative; and those historians who have wished to create the greatest impression of continuity between their text and reality have in fact taken care to eliminate the telltale scar separating the two parts of the page.

If it was Collingwood's intention to establish the difference between fiction and history less on history's *claim* to be "true," its constant signifying that the events it relates really happened, than on some kind of effective determination of history by past reality, then it is not clear, in my view, that he has succeeded.[44] Nevertheless, despite decades of demonstrations by philosophers and by historians themselves that history is a construct, the belief that it is an immediate representation of reality, and the historian's own complicity with this belief, have remained remarkably vigorous. Indeed, the tenacity of the belief itself is something that requires explanation. Barthes's analysis of this phenomenon is extremely pertinent to the question of the present relation of history and literature. Barthes argues that the realism of historical discourse is part of a general cultural pattern manifested in the persistent popular predilection for genres such as the realist novel or the diary, in the vogue of exhibitions of antique objects of daily use, and, above all, in the enormous development of photography, the pertinent characteristic of which (in relation to drawing, for instance) is precisely that it signifies that the event or object represented *really* happened or existed.[45] For Barthes, this cultural pattern points to an alienating fetishism of the "real," by which men seek to escape from their freedom and their role as makers of meaning. The "real" appears to him as an *idol*.

The ideological burden of history is aggravated by its closeness to what Barthes calls contemporary myth.[46] Myth, in this sense, is a secondary system of signs which uses elements already invested with meaning within a prior semiological system (ordinary language): these elements become signifiers or forms in relation to the *signifiés*, or ideological concepts, with which the mythical discourse connects them. This is the source of the ambiguous, dissembling chracter of myth. If the reader were to read myth innocently—that is, if he were to take the elements that compose it for what they are and fail to recognize the concept to which they point—nothing would have been gained by proffering it to him; if, on the other hand, reading it thoughtfully, he were to see clearly that the elements are intended to signify the concept, it would be no more than a straightforward political proposition. What constitutes myth as myth, according to Barthes, is precisely its avoidance of this alternative: the relation between signifier and concept is presented as unmotivated, in some way natural. Although it summons the reader to read it in terms of the concepts to which the signifiers have been linked, mythical discourse never admits that it does, or that the signifiers are arbitrarily and not naturally linked to the *signifiés*. When challenged, it can always plead innocence, and take refuge behind the original meaning of the signifiers in the primary system. It is thus neither brazen nor innocent: it is, one is tempted to say, discourse *in bad faith,* founded on a shifty refusal to clarify the relation between the signifier and the *signifié,* or concept. "Myth," in Barthes's own words, "is read as a factual system, whereas it is a semiological system."

History appears to share a number of the features that Barthes considers characteristic of myth, in this modern sense. I have already suggested that historical narrative constitutes a secondary semiological system whose elements—events, actions, and so on—already have a meaning within the system of ordinary language, prior to being appropriated by the secondary system and adapted to its ends. While the language of classical historical narrative, as Barthes himself pointed out, presents itself as a two-term system in which the *signifié* is dispensed with and the signifier is directly linked to the referent, in the larger context of the historical work itself—that is, of the secondary semiotic system constructed upon the primary one of language—the supposedly direct verbal representations of events in the primary system become signifiers in relation to the *signifiés* of the secondary system. What is taken to be reality itself, or at least its immediate verbal representation—rather than a sign—thus acts as the signifier in the secondary system. As in myth, therefore, the signifier seems naturally to lead to the *signifié,* as if the latter emerged out of it and were continuous with it, in the way that photographs, being taken as direct visual representations of the real, appear to found their *signifié* naturally, without the intervention of any act of signifying.

Barthes is concerned to unmask the fundamental inauthenticity of myth, which he sees proliferating over the entire domain of culture, appropriating and turning to ideological ends every authentic expression of human creativity. Insofar as history does not point to its signifying activity, it would seem to be subject to the same criticisms that Barthes makes of myth.

From our point of view, it is interesting, therefore, that Barthes finds the strongest center of resistance to myth in poetic language. Whereas myth fills our universe with meanings that masquerade as natural, produced by no one, poetic language seeks to escape from the inauthenticity of culture toward an authentic language that will somehow recover direct contact with things, from the pseudo-nature of a mystified and mystifying culture to a true nature.

> Whereas myth aims at ultra-signification, at the amplification of a primary system, poetry tries to recover an infra-signification, a pre-semiological state of language; . . . its ideal . . . would be to reach not so much the sense of words as the sense of things themselves. That is why it disturbs language, exaggerating to the maximum the abstract character of the concept and the arbitrariness of the sign and pushing to the limit of the possible the relation of signifier and signified . . . It is the full potential of the signified that the poetic sign tries to release and make present, in the hope of finally reaching a sort of transcendent quality of the thing, its natural (and not its human) meaning. Whence the essentialist aspirations of poetry, and the conviction that it alone can grasp the thing itself—to the degree, precisely, that it aims to be an anti-language. . . . That is why modern poetry is always affirmed as an assassination of language, a kind of spatial, sensible analogue of silence. Poetry is the reverse of myth: myth is a semiological system that claims to transcend itself in a factual system; poetry is a semiological system that claims to withdraw behind itself in an essential system.[47]

Even in the case of prose, as Barthes points out, modern literature seeks constantly to avoid being taken up in the myth of Literature. Every literary movement of modern times has been an attempt to reduce literary language to a simple semiological system (ordinary language), and to repudiate Literature as a mythical sign, the sign of Culture.

Barthes's essay on myth seems to me to shed a disquieting light on a great deal of the historical writing of the last century and a half. After the French Revolution, the dominant ambition of historians was to make history—rather than fiction—the successor of epic as the repository of society's values and of its understanding of the world. "Our age," Barante declared, "seeks in the past the reasons for confidence in the future, and intends that the historian shall assume the high mission of the prophet."[48] History, consequently, had to be cleared of the stigma attaching to the "merely" successive event, the isolated, individual episode. Historical discourse had to order individual events into episodes, individual episodes into stories, and individual stories into the single unifying and signifying history of humanity, of civilization, and of the modern bourgeois nation-states. Barante, who was himself most attracted by the singular, picturesque episode, the historical *fait divers,* as it were, explained that "the writer must show us the facts moving steadily toward a goal, he must make us understand every step along the way. Reason is as exacting as imagination, it demands unity, and desires that its drama and its epic, the hero of which is an idea, be also portrayed."[49] With the Romantic attempt to create the illusion that the relation between the individual event or episode reported by the historian and the concept or *signifié* with which he associates it is natural—in other words, that signification in historical writing is unmotivated, unproblematic, somehow rooted in the nature of things themselves—history comes perilously close to what Barthes describes as myth. And at the same time, in a corresponding and inverse movement, literature comes to repudiate the mythos with which Aristotle had associated it, and to strive toward the unelaborated, the "pre-semiological" (Barthes), the "unstructured" (Mukařovský).[50] Since about the middle of the nineteenth century, in Barthes's view, literature has been engaged in a tireless struggle to halt the appropriation of language by myth and to break down the parasitic secondary systems of meaning which threaten creative culture with strangulation. Thus the wheel has turned full circle and the relative positions of history and poetry, as Aristotle perceived them, have been reversed.[51]

MANY modern historians, as we have seen, have repudiated the goals and premises of historical realism, and certain aspects of the rhetoric of the old historical realism have in fact disappeared from modern historical texts. But there seems to have been no radical reform of the historian's mode of writing comparable with the changes that have affected literary writing and fiction in the last half-century. Historical texts continue to recount calmly events and situations located in the past as though the "age of suspicion" had never dawned. In the remarkable Preface to *La Méditerranée,* Fernand Braudel acknowledges that there is a subject of the enunciation of the historical account, but the signs of this subject are erased from the main body of Braudel's text. Of the historical writings I know, the one that comes closest to breaking the historical code is perhaps Michelet's *La Sorcière,* which appeared more than a hundred years ago. Yet the historians who have recuperated Michelet from the domain of literature, to which he had been banished by their positivist predecessors, have been attentive above all to the range of questions he asked of the past, to his acute sense of the richness of historical phenomena. They have hardly commented at all on the peculiar features of a text of unusual density and complexity, in which the account of events is so shot through with lyrical and confessional writing, and fiction is so intimately interwoven with traditional historical narrative, that the reader is disoriented and made uncertain as to what is history and what is dream or poetic effusion, what is a narrative of past events (*histoire*) and what belongs to the situation at the time of writing or enunciating and to the subject of the enunciation (*discours*).[52] It is as though Michelet were stretching to the limit the distinctions between subject and object, fact and fiction, present and past, *énonciation* and *énoncé*, *discours* and *histoire*. It is this disturbing feature—disturbing even today—of Michelet's writing that historians neither comment upon nor, apparently, wish to emulate.

In literature, on the other hand, attempts to push outward the limits of language have become the central focus of the writer's activity. In Barthes's words, "The writer [*écrivain*]—and in this respect he stands alone, apart from, and in opposition to all speakers and mere practitioners of writing [*écrivants*]—is he who refuses to let the obligations of his language speak for him, who knows and is acutely conscious of the deficiencies of his idiom, and who imagines, utopically, a total language in which *nothing* is obligatory."[53] Not surprisingly, several contemporary "novelists" are probing the very distinction of *histoire* and *discours* on which, as we saw, classical narrative (including, naturally, classical historical narrative) rests. In Sollers's novel *Drame,* Barthes writes,

> we are placed in the presence not of something narrated but of the labor of narration. This thin line separating the product from its creation, the narrative-as-object from the narrative-as-labor, is the historical divide that sets the classical tale, which emerges completely armed from a prior labor of preparation, over against the modern text, which has no desire to exist prior to its enunciation and which, presenting its own labor to be read, can only be read, in the end, as labor . . . The classical narrator *sets himself up* in front of us, as one says "to sit down to table" (even in the special sense in which this expression is used in the language of crime) [*se mettre à table* = to confess, to "come clean"] and exhibits his wares (his soul, his learning, his memories); to this position corresponds, in punctuation, the fatidical colon of the exordium that is poised, ready to top itself off with a fine tale.

The narrator of *Drame* has erased the colon and given up all idea of setting himself up.

Similarly, the time of this "novel" is no longer marked by the two axes of the time of the narrative and the time of the narration, the imagined time of the story (*axe de fiction*) and the very time of the succession of the words of the text (*axe de notation*).

> The axis of notation absorbs all temporality: there is no time outside the Book: the scenes that are related (and we can never tell, for good reason, if they are dreams, memories, or fantasies) do not imply any fictitious frame of reference which would be "other" than their situation on the page. The notational axis is absolutely the only one. A writer could indeed reject all narrative chronology and yet subordinate his notation to the flux of his impressions, memories, sensations, etc., but that would still be to maintain the two axes, making the notational one a copy of *another* temporality. That, however, is not the technique of *Drame*; there is literally no time here, other than that of the words. What we have is an undivided present, which is that of the subject only to the extent that the latter is entirely absorbed by his function as narrator, that is to say, spinner of words.[54]

In Voltaire's or Gibbon's time, as in that of Thierry or Macaulay, the work of the literary artist and that of the historian were intimately connected, even, as I have tried to argue, indistinguishable. Voltaire was at one and the same time a writer, as we say, and a historian, and Gibbon and Hume both considered themselves men of letters. Literature, by Hume's own account, was "the ruling passion of my life and the great source of my enjoyment." Thierry and his friends were closely attentive to the work of contemporary novelists, and the latter returned the compliment. It is not fortuitous that Scott was a key figure for both Thierry and Balzac, or that Thierry and Manzoni followed each other's work carefully. Modern history and modern literature have both rejected the ideal of representation that dominated them for so long. Both now conceive of their work as exploration, testing, creation of new meanings, rather than as disclosure or revelation of meanings already in some sense "there," but not immediately perceptible. In the course of this change of orientation, however, literature has come to be increasingly preoccupied with language as the instrument of meaning, whereas history may well dream of escaping from ordinary or natural language to the highly formal languages of the sciences. As a result, it is not easy for us today to see who is, as a *writer*, the Joyce or the Kafka of modern historiography in the way that Gibbon could be viewed as its Fielding, Thierry as its Balzac, Michelet as its Hugo.

Moreover, many historians cling to a notion of writing or of literary style that is remote from the modern writer's conception of his art. Stressing the value of clarity and elegance, a distinguished historian recently reaffirmed the ornamental and rhetorical function of literary style in the writing of history. The function of style, he says, is to capture and hold the reader's attention, to convey ideas as effectively as possible, and, in the end, to confirm the pact that unites writer and reader in a common universe of meanings. "Unless the substance is good, the appearance, painted even an inch thick, will not please." Since the aim of literary style is to ensure "readability," and the historian's primary concern as a writer is to secure his audience, "books should differ with the people to whom they are addressed." The historian writes for an audience that already accepts his terms and that shares his basic values and assumptions. "Regard your audience as intelligent though possibly uninstructed . . . No problem of historical study that I have come across, has seemed to me incapable of being explained with full clarity to any person of reasonable intelligence, and no person of insufficient intelligence will anyhow be in the way of reading or hearing historical analysis and description."[55] For the historian, in sum, rhetorical rather than poetic considerations remain paramount, and literature is still a craft or skill by which the *dulce* can be joined to the *utile* and the friendly reader delighted even as he is instructed. Literary artists and historians are apparently much further apart both in their conception and in their practice of literature than they have been in the past. Indeed, the historian who conceives of literature in this way—as "style" or as a means of adorning otherwise simple propositions—may bring history close to Literature (in Barthes's designation); but he will be further than ever from the concerns of the contemporary literary artist.

[1978]

8

History as Decipherment: Romantic Historiography and the Discovery of the Other

> Take pity on yourselves, you poor men of the West. Restore yourselves, think of the common salvation. The Earth begs you to live. . . . In losing you she would lose herself. For you are her genius, her spirit of invention. Her life depends on your life, and your death would be her death.
>
> —Michelet, *La Mer*

> Freedom consists in my having no absolute Other opposed to me, but in depending on a content which I am myself.
>
> —Hegel, *Enzyklopaedie*

IN THE EIGHTEENTH CENTURY history was a branch of eloquence, a mode of legal and constitutional argument, or a source of evidence for those laws of the social world that enlightened scholars such as Montesquieu or Malthus hoped to discover in emulation of Newton's laws of the physical world. By the beginning of the nineteenth century, however, it was already being thought of and practiced as a branch of philosophy, not to say theology, a means of restoring contact with origins and of reconstituting what was experienced as a fractured totality. The tumultuous decades of the Revolution and the Napoleonic conquests seemed to have demonstrated that neither reason nor existence offered an adequate foundation for political and social order. On the one hand, the revolutionary ideal had proved unable to impose itself on the world. Reason, one might say, had met its Waterloo. On the other hand, the established regimes had been shaken to the core by the revolutionary challenge. Restoration was thus an ideological as well as a political undertaking, and in the period between 1815 and 1848 the task of providing a convincing foundation for the postrevolutionary regimes was taken up by philosophers, lawyers, and historians alike. Hegel attempted to overcome the Kantian dichotomies of phenomenon and noumenon, reason and understanding; Savigny tried to get around the opposition of natural law and positive law by discovering the axioms of law in the legal tradition itself; and the young Ranke undertook to reveal the underlying continuities of history. Though God would always remain inaccessible and inscrutable, he wrote, He "dwells, lives, and can be known in all of history. Every deed attests to Him, every moment preaches His Name, but most of all . . . the connectedness of history in the large. [This connectedness] stands [before us] like a holy hieroglyph."[1] To decipher this hieroglyph, according to Ranke, is to serve God as priest and teacher. God, in short, is in historical continuity, and the study of history, for the scion of pastors who stands at the beginnings of nineteenth-century historiography, is no longer modeled, as it had been for the scholars of the Enlightenment, on the physical and mechanical sciences. It is a form of hermeneutic.

The role the Romantic historian attributed to himself was similar to that of the Romantic poet. If the poet, according to Baudelaire, was the interpreter of "le langage des fleurs et des choses muettes" ("the language of flowers and speechless things"),[2] the historian was to recover and read the lost languages of the mute past, and thus to unveil a history that both the rulers of the ancien régime and the new masters of the Europe created by Enlightenment and Revolution had allegedly tried to ignore or deny. By making the past speak and restoring communication with it, it was believed, the historian could ward off the potentially destructive conflicts produced by repression and exclusion; by revealing the continuity between remotest origins and the present, between the other and the self, he could ground the social and political order and demonstrate that the antagonisms and ruptures—notably the persistent social antagonisms—that seemed to threaten its legitimacy and stability were not absolute or beyond all mediation. Understandably, in these circumstances, the historical imagination of the nineteenth century was drawn to what was remote, hidden, or inaccessible: to beginnings and ends, to the archive, the tomb, the womb, the so-called mute peoples, such as the Egyptians and the Etruscans, whose language and history remained an enigma.[3]

The fascination with what is mysterious, original, or hidden in the past is probably the occulted sign of another, more pressing anxiety, that aroused by the equally mute popular mass from whose ancient womb, in the Romantic historian's own vision of history, both the modern bourgeoisie and the modern bourgeois historian have sprung. Toward this Other the historian entertained troubled feelings of guilt, fear, and tenderness. (Michelet, for instance, regularly attributes such feelings to the young man destined, in his view, to be the lord and protector of the female that bore him and once held him dependent and defenseless at her breast.) In Romantic historiography, nature, the Orient, woman, the people, and the hidden past itself are almost always metaphors of each other and of the oppressed and the repressed in general—figurations of the Other of reason and bourgeois order.[4] At the limit, the historian could claim to be reestablishing communication with a very ancien régime indeed—a remote realm prior to all separations, distinctions, and prohibitions, prior to law itself, an original condition of fusion in which, in Michelet's words, "beasts still had the power of speech and man was still wedded to his sister nature." At the same time, however, he was laying the ghosts of that past to rest, so that "honored, consoled . . . and blessed, they might return in peace to their tombs."[5] In this way the historian was both the faithful child of the "maternal" past and the architect of a "paternal" future. Through him, it was to become possible for modern man to contemplate his origins—everything he feels he has forgotten or repressed—without being destroyed by them.

The legitimation and consolidation of the new postrevolutionary social orders required that apparent discontinuity and rupture be shown as resolved in a "higher" continuity (usually called "Progress"). Hidden mediating links had to be disclosed between forces that were visibly in conflict: man and nature, man and his own nature, male and female, the West and the East, the postrevolutionary bourgeoisie and the people, the scholarly historian and the common people to whom he owed his existence and whose history was in many cases the preferred object of his study. This could only be done, however, by bringing to light, naming, and acknowledging what the historical record had so often tried to suppress—the injustices of the past, the acts of violence by which the distinctions and discriminations (such as property, the family, and the state) that the historian himself accepted as the condition of civilization and progress had been established, and which had been repeated at each successive stage in human development. In his *Life of Luther* (1835), Michelet saluted the great Reformer as an emancipator and hero of modern times. At the same time, however, he refused to repudiate the old Catholic church of the Middle Ages out of which modern Protestantism was born. He would rather wish, he writes, to lower her gently into the grave like a beloved and revered mother.[6] Earlier, in the *Roman History* of 1831, he had explained how the ancient historians of Rome had tried to conceal the violence of the colony's subjection of its "mother Alba," and had argued that to bring this covert operation—the condition of Rome's realization of its historical destiny—to light was one of the chief obligations of the modern historian of Rome.[7] Likewise, Edgar Quinet later excoriated contemporary historians who took official documents as reliable indices of the reality of the past. These "dupes de l'écriture scellée," as he put it (dupes of writing that bears an official stamp), had forgotten that the chief obligation of the historian is to save future generations from being deceived by "ce grimoire officiel."[8] Only by acknowledging what had not been admitted to public memory could the past (behind which it is not difficult to discern the still fresh outlines of the French Revolution, the execution of the King, and the Terror) be exorcised, the present (the postrevolutionary order of constitutional monarchies) firmly founded, and the forces of life released from guilt and repetition to evolve freely toward the future. Remembering, paradoxically, is the condition of forgetting, and it is probably not an accident that *oublier*—to forget—is a leitmotif of Michelet's journals, or that the ideal of a life relieved of the burden of the past is the persistent message of his friend Quinet.[9]

The practice of historical writing is itself evidence of the historian's belief in his mediating mission. In neoclassical narrative familiar rhetorical devices served to hold the two elements of narrative—the individual item ("life," as Schiller expressed it in his *Letters on the Aesthetic Education of Man*) and the organizing structure (Schiller's "form")—in equilibrium, thus reconciling discontinuity with continuity, the particular with the general. Writing history at a time when "life," in the guise of new individual and collective energies, had triumphantly asserted itself against prevailing social forms, the Romantic historian had to come to terms with an especially acute sense of the uniqueness and originality of historical phenomena, and therefore of rupture and discontinuity. The rhetorical conventions that eighteenth-century historians had accepted as the condition of any representation and any understanding no longer seemed sufficient; the Romantic historian was impelled to reach beyond them to the "real life" of the past, where both individual phenomena and the vital relations among them could be grasped in their immediacy and presence. The "realist" techniques of description, which Romantic historiography borrowed from the contemporary novel, were designed to make the reader feel that there was no barrier between him and the object, that what he beheld in his mind's eye was not a conventional representation, but the object resurrected "wie es eigentlich gewesen" (as it truly was), to quote a famous phrase—or, in different terms, that no signified intervened between signifier and referent.[10] In an extreme case, such as Prosper de Barante's immensely successful *History of the Dukes of Burgundy* (1824), this design gave rise to a historical text that was nothing less than a collage of contemporary testimonies. Barante's method was to transcribe freely and stitch together selected passages from the late medieval chroniclers (Froissart, Monstrelet, Commynes); in this way his text not only related the past but was itself part of it.[11] With Barante, history seemed literally to speak out of its own mouth, and there appeared to be no breach of continuity between past reality and present narrative.

The real in its concrete and vivid presence was also, moreover, a symbol, a hieroglyph, to recall Ranke's term. Thus individual events pointed beyond themselves to a meaning which was imparted to them by their place in a narrative order. Individual narratives, in turn, had a meaning in terms of the larger narrative of which they were part. Thus for Michelet each episode in the history of Rome acquired meaning from the fact of being part of the history of Rome. The history of Rome itself, however, acquired its meaning from its place in universal history. Conversely, it was one of the keys to the understanding of universal history; in particular, it prefigured and suggested the meaning of the history of France. "Rome," Michelet wrote in the heat of the July Revolution, "is the nodal point of the immense drama of which France presently directs the peripeteia."[12] The Romantics' concern to retain distinctions while at the same time affirming unity and continuity—in historiographical terms: to preserve the specificity of events and analyze the causal relations among them, and at the same time to discover their "meaning" through hermeneutical interpretation—imparts to their work a religious, even theological character that seems closer in spirit to speculations about the relation of the historical Jesus to the kerygmatic Christ than to the efforts of Enlightenment scholars to discover the "laws" of social and historical existence. Michelet's comment, in 1833, that "Christ is still on the Cross" and that "the passion endures and will always endure" need come as no surprise.[13]

It was almost universally agreed that in order to write the new history, the traditional skills of the neoclassical historian—erudition, critical judgment, and rhetorical facility—had to be supplemented by unusual powers of divination. On this point Humboldt, Niebuhr, and Michelet were at one. Aligning themselves consciously with the Orphic figure of the poet and prophet, the new historians thus resembled the heroes or "representative men" who were the principal actors in their histories. As these heroes participated in the energies of their time and simultaneously raised them to their highest degree of potency, thus bringing about "change" and making "history," the historian-genius—Michelet explained in *The People*—was part of the people and for that very reason could bring to light and articulate its deepest experience, thereby providing it with the eyes it needed to move forward and fulfill its historical destiny. The writer of Romantic histories, in short, understood his heroes from within; like Christ, Caesar, or Joan of Arc, he too was a resolver of riddles, a facilitator of new births who ensured by his own sacrifice the continuity between the old world and the new. His enterprise, as Michelet put it, was "démesurée"—excessive—and not anyone could carry it out, only the pure in heart, those whose candor had not been clouded by the false learning of schools and official culture.[14]

Romantic historiography could not survive the shocking experience of 1848. A chastened, prosaic generation of historians denounced the optimistic confidence of their Romantic forebears in the imminent reconciliation of myth and history, poetry and science, people and bourgeoisie, as an illusion. Among the heralds of the new hard-headed times were Tocqueville, who calmly undertook the task of desacralizing the most popular of cult objects, the French Revolution;[15] Fustel de Coulanges, who repudiated as a dangerous presumption his predecessors' habit of reading ancient history in the modernizing light of present ideas and concerns;[16] Taine and Renan, with their clinical and at times cynical scrutiny of the most venerable historical ages and events; and Gabriel Monod, Michelet's admirer and biographer, who announced in his introduction to the first issue of the *Revue Historique* (1876), the official organ of the new historical profession in France, that historiography, having now been placed on a sound scientific footing, no longer had need of inspired geniuses like those of the previous age. Turning their backs on a Romantic representation of the past which, in their view, had proved tragically incapable of grasping the real forces at work in history, and on the hermeneutical approach that had given rise to that representation, a new generation of historians repudiated the prophetic role in favor of an austere ideal of science. At the same time, they withdrew from the often turbulent public forum occupied by Michelet and Quinet to the stillness of the study and the quiet of the seminar room.

IN WHAT FOLLOWS I propose to consider more closely some aspects of the shift from neoclassical to Romantic historiography. I want to suggest, first, that the Enlightenment itself, and then the Revolution, disturbed a traditional conception of historical time and traditional methods of historical composition. Next, I shall argue that the Enlightenment attack on tradition, the attempt to cut the present adrift from the past, was by no means incompatible with the idea that being cured of what was perceived as an alienated and weary traditional culture might involve a journey back to origins, even if it is hard to imagine that any Enlightener would have represented that journey as Michelet did when he made taking the baths at Acqui—sinking ever deeper into the restorative mud of *terra mater*—or exploring the hidden depths of the sea, *La Mer,* and giving voice and definition to its unknown denizens, images of the poet-historian's descent into the past.[17] Nevertheless, between Rousseau, Diderot, and Winckelmann, on the one hand, and Michelet and Quinet, on the other, there are mediating figures, notably those sober scholars of the late Enlightenment who dedicated their lives to excavating the tombs and recovering the lost languages of Egypt, Assyria, and Etruria—"la muette Etrurie," "le muet Orient," as Michelet liked to say.[18] I shall briefly discuss two of these figures before taking up the theory of history as decipherment, as it was elaborated in German academic discourse in the early and middle decades of the nineteenth century, notably by Hegel's colleague in classical philology at Berlin, August Boeckh.

I shall conclude with a comment on the special historiographical mission attributed to France in the writings of the French Romantic historians. For if Germany was the "India of Europe," as Michelet called it, of all Western lands the one that had best preserved the innocence and simplicity of childhood origins and that therefore best represented in modern times the sacred wisdom and unity of the East[19] (we have here, incidentally, the basis of what we now refer to as the Aryan myth and of the idea of German, that is, "Aryan," superiority), the French—from Madame de Staël to Edgar Quinet—saw themselves as the interpreters of Germany to the world. Their task was literally to translate or hand over that country's precious, poetic, but dangerously obscure and pantheistic wisdom to the rationalist, individualist, and prosaic West in such a way that the recipient would not be overwhelmed or driven mad by the gift, but would be able, on the contrary, to appropriate it and to exploit its secrets to his advantage.[20] As Michelet put it in what seems to be an updated version of the old *translatio studii*, it is the role of modern France, as it had once been that of Greece and then that of imperial Rome, to "disseminate the new revelation and interpret it. Every social and intellectual solution is sterile for Europe until France interprets, translates, and popularizes it. . . . France speaks the logos of Europe, as Greece once spoke that of Asia."[21] France, in short, gathers up the world's wisdom, universalizes it, and brings it to self-consciousness, in the same way that the historian of France collects, unifies, and presents to his countrymen the scattered fragments of the national past. France, in Michelet's words, is both the object and the subject of history: "She makes history and recounts it."[22] And this rhetorical privilege is also, as we shall see, a political one.

II

Writing narrative history in the sixteenth, seventeenth, and even the eighteenth century was often a matter of retelling a well-known tale whose general contours were fixed and unchanging, bringing it up to date stylistically, and making it more or less compatible with the slowly changing ideas and values of an evolving audience, rather as oral storytellers or modern tellers of jokes adapt a fundamentally invariant structure to the expectations and clichés of varying publics. Successive histories of France, from the old *Chroniques de Saint-Denis* to the histories of Dupleix, Sorel, and Mézerai in the seventeenth century, or the popular eighteenth-century histories of the abbé Velly and his continuators, show a remarkable degree of structural consistency and continuity. One could say without too much exaggeration that the old chronicles simply devolved, by way of early printed versions, into the later humanist-influenced histories. In his *Deffence et Illustration de la langue françoyse* Du Bellay saw the task of the historian of France as primarily rhetorical: "to employ great eloquence in putting together fragments of old French chronicles, just as Livy did with the old annals and chronicles of Rome, making out of them the complete body of a harmonious history and interspersing it at the right moments with fine set pieces and harangues in imitation of Livy himself, or Thucydides or Sallust or some other well approved author."[23] Alternatively, the historian might write the history not of a dynasty—offering tradition as the legitimation of the reigning monarch—but of an individual prince, distinguished and legitimated by his charismatic power to rule and impose order and by his martial successes. This type of history, which was most common in the age of the baroque, also leaned heavily on earlier models such as Plutarch and Quintus Curtius. Historians vied explicity with their classical predecessors as painters of great men and recorders of memorable events. Whether traditionalist or heroic, historical writing so understood was often literally composition. As late as 1805 the author of a new history of France, avowedly based on a compilation of four well-known existing histories (Dupleix, Mézerai, Daniel, and Velly), explained that "when I had to treat any topic, I looked to see which of the four had best presented it, and took his narrative as the basis of my own; then I added what I thought was lacking in the preferred narrative."[24] The practice of the majority of historians of France is well illustrated by an anecdote from the first half of the eighteenth century. It tells of a visit paid to the Royal Library in Paris by the successful Jesuit historian Father Daniel. The Father was shown two voluminous collections of manuscripts containing ordinances, charters, and letters of the Kings of France by a well-meaning librarian. He spent a couple of hours perusing them, pronounced them very interesting, and never set foot in the library again for fear he might be shown them once more. He had, he is reported to have said to a friend, "no need of all those scraps of paper to write history."[25]

A radical revision of the canonical history of France was in all probability unlikely as long as the only politically meaningful principle of narrative order was the succession of monarchs in the royal line or the succession of heroic acts that constituted the career of the baroque prince. The purpose of recounting the succession of rulers and presenting it as an unbroken chain was, after all, to confirm the legitimacy of the current reign by showing it to be grounded on tradition, while on his side the author of heroic and princely histories grounded the ruler's authority on his manifest charisma. The Romantic remake of the history of France, the discovery and substitution of the people for the royal dynasty as the hero of the piece, and the transformation of the problematics of history as a whole seem inseparable from a larger ideological program designed to legitimate the postrevolutionary nation and—more particularly—the postrevolutionary bourgeoisie, and to justify the latter's claim to be at once the child, the liberator, the guardian, and the representative or spokesman of the popular mass on whose back it had risen to power, the agent of freedom and progress (the ends of history), and thus the culmination of centuries of historical development. Until the end of the ancien régime, in short, the history of France was virtually bound to remain what it had been, more or less, since the Middle Ages: a cycle or collection of stories, not unlike the legends of saints, and bearing little or no relation to other story cycles.

There was another historical tradition, running parallel to the one I have been describing but rarely intersecting it—a tradition closely associated with humanist philology and with the historical study of laws and institutions. This tradition has been thoroughly investigated for France by Donald Kelley in his *Foundations of Modern Historical Scholarship: Language, Law, and History in the French Renaissance*. It is an important tradition, not unrelated to my present theme. Guillaume Budé's description of philology, for instance, as the "means of revival and restoration" would not have been disavowed by any Romantic philologist.[26]

Nevertheless, the relation of Renaissance scholars both to the past and to historiography seems to have been significantly different from that of their Romantic successors. The road back to origins was apparently not so obstructed in the eyes of the Renaissance scholars that special divinatory powers were required by those who intended to pursue it, as the Romantics usually claimed. Nor did the object of study have about it the aura of desire and taboo that led even Ranke to describe the labor of seeking out and unveiling hidden sources in erotic terms. In addition, as Kelley repeatedly points out, the scholars of the sixteenth, seventeenth—and I would add eighteenth—centuries almost never adopted the form of large-scale historical narrative. Indeed, they were thoroughly suspicious of narrative histories and of "literature" in general.[27] Finally, though the scholars, who were most often magistrates and lawyers, did entertain a far broader view of history than the narrative historians of the period, who were usually rhetoricians in the service of royal or princely houses, they still left a great deal out of account. To François Baudouin, for example, "integral history" meant joining together "the history of our pontiffs, emperors and kings"[28]—a combination of legal, ecclesiastical, and political history that still seems quite thin gruel compared with what Michelet, writing in the age of democratic revolutions, had in mind to serve up.

According to Philippe Ariès, the past appeared to most moderately educated Europeans of the classical age in the form of a series of discrete traditional stories or story cycles—the story or stories of France (or England or Spain), the story or stories of classical antiquity, the biblical stories and the story of the Church, the story of the province or locality one was born in, and the story of one's own family.[29] Though Ariès himself questioned whether universal history still had the overarching significance it had had in the Middle Ages, the medieval Christian idea that the history of man and the history of nature are parts of a single all-encompassing history—the history of Creation—did continue, I think, to dominate men's conceptions of themselves and of the meaning of their lives and to provide a framework for the individual histories until well into the eighteenth century.

Gradually and deliberately, however, this conception of history, along with the practices of historiography associated with it, was undermined by the Enlightenment. Throwing doubt on the traditional stories and chronologies, subjecting all their elements to hostile scrutiny, opening up the scope of history to include China and America alongside the medieval, classical, and biblical worlds, challenging the assumption that yesterday's dispositions are relevant to the needs of today, the Enlightenment dug a trench between the present and the past of the historians, and between the "philosophical" reader and the traditional narratives on which he was now invited to exercise his critical reason. In addition, the speculations of naturalists and geologists created an uneasy sense that the past was not the mapped-out and limited landscape of historical tradition. A revolution comparable perhaps to that which had already upset the neo-Aristotelian view of the physical universe and prompted Pascal's anguish about "the silence of these infinite spaces" seems to have transformed time also, in its turn, into an immense, featureless, interminate medium—"No vestige of a beginning, no prospect of an end," in the words of James Hutton in his *Theory of the Earth* of 1795. Familiar historical sequences, drastically diminished and fragmented in the light of historical criticism, might now seem to float in this medium, but they no longer constituted and defined it. To some enlightened minds, it appeared that what was referred to as history was a relatively insignificant part of a much vaster temporal process of which man himself was no longer the subject or the center.

As he looked back upon the past, therefore, the late-eighteenth-century historian began to find himself confronted by something that no longer seemed immediately intelligible and representable, a preformed story waiting to be unraveled out of its first principles, like the baroque princely histories, or simply retold, like the traditional dynastic histories. His position was remarkably similar to what Rousseau's had been when he undertook to write his *Confessions*. Rousseau's sense of insignificance and marginality, of lack or loss of identity—as member of a family, a social group, a trade, a religious community—was most probably the original impetus behind the writing of his autobiographical narrative, the aim of which was precisely to invent or reinvent an identity. The historian felt similarly bereft, especially after the cataclysmic events of the Revolution and the Empire. Nothing now was familiar or secure. Events did not fall easily into place or illustrate a familiar story, a meaning already given. Where scholars had once written histories of particular states or events or persons, they now no longer wrote histories; they wrote History.[30] In Voltaire's *History of Charles XII,* the entire narrative seems to be an *amplificatio* of the initial data, a dramatic development, as Voltaire himself emphasized; but in the new world created by Enlightenment and Revolution, history, like the novel and the autobiography, had to look for its meaning, if it had one, to be discovered in its unfolding. Nothing could be known beforehand or determined in advance, as the servant in Diderot's *Jacques le fataliste* liked to remind his master, and nothing could be known fully until the whole scroll of destiny had been unwound. Diderot's witty novel suggests the social transformation that underlies the rejection of history as a story constructed on the model of a rhetorical figure—the development of a parallel or antithesis, for instance—or of classical tragedy and comedy, with their fixed and predictable roles and plots. It is Jacques, the servant, who delights in upsetting narrative conventions and who demonstrates that in history nothing can be known by simple deduction from an a priori given, and it is the master who imagines that events repeat themselves infinitely with different actors in the same roles and the same scenarios. The servant's repudiation of the traditional belief that the past is repeated in the present and the future is his declaration of independence.

But this new-won independence was not without its problems, especially after the radical surgery of the Revolution seemed to have separated the present irrevocably from the past. Individuals and communities, victors and vanquished alike, felt suddenly bereft of any secure identity or legitimacy. The problem was practical and legal as well as ideological. In France, for instance, it was necessary to settle the property of lands acquired by new owners from dispossessed noblemen who returned after the Revolution to reclaim them. But the very need for reasoning and argument only highlighted the uncertainty that now reigned where once there had been unquestioning conviction. "The historical ground has given way under nearly all the European peoples," Burckhardt wrote in 1842 to his friend Kinkel. "All attempts at restoration, however well intentioned, however much they may seem to be the only way out, cannot extinguish the fact that the nineteenth century has begun with a complete tabula rasa." A well-known passage from Benjamin Constant discovers the other side of Jacques's freedom:

> Victorious in the battles he has fought, man looks on a world depopulated of protective powers, and is astonished at his victory. . . . His imagination, idle now and solitary, turns upon itself. He finds himself alone on an earth which may swallow him up. On this earth the generations follow each other, transitory, fortuitous, isolated; they appear, they suffer, they die. . . . No voice of those that are no more is prolonged into the life of those still living, and the voice of the living generations must soon be engulfed by the same eternal silence. What shall man do, without memory, without hope, between the past which abandons him and the future which is closed before him? His invocations are no longer heard, his prayers receive no answer. He has spurned all the supports with which his predecessors had surrounded him; he is reduced to his own resources.

Constant's hero Adolphe was more terse. "I felt the last bond snap," he tells, as he witnesses the death of the woman he had struggled so hard to be free of. "How burdensome that liberty I had so longed to retrieve was to me now. How my heart yearned for the dependency I had found intolerable."[31]

The striking contrast between Constant's bleak vision of the human condition and the one presented by Michelet only eight years later in his opening lecture at the Sorbonne in 1834 conveys an idea of the ideological program Romantic historiography had taken upon itself. Where Constant gazed ruefully on a scene of rupture and alienation, Michelet, writing in the glow of the 1830 revolution, protests the continuity of past and present. The past, he insists, in a passage that could be duplicated from the writings of Emerson or Novalis or Grimm, is inscribed in ineffaceable letters in the very body of the present:

> This house is old; it may be painted white and in fine repair, but it has seen much; many centuries have lived in it, and all have left something of themselves. Whether you can discern it easily or not, have no doubt, the trace is there. So it is with the heart of man. Men and houses, we all bear the imprint of the ages that have passed. Young men though we may be, we have in us countless ancient ideas and feelings of which we are not even aware. These traces of former times lie confused and indistinct in our souls; at times they are disturbing to us. We find we have knowledge of what we never learned and memories of things we never witnessed; we feel the dull reverberation of the emotions of people we never knew.[32]

III

The writers of the Enlightenment had actively sought to produce the alienation from traditional history that Constant found both hard to bear and impossible to give up. It represented their freedom. That is a commonplace not worth belaboring. That their own analytical, reflective, self-conscious, and sophisticated culture was irremediably derivative and incapable of producing anything original or truly great was a topos on which many of them exercised their considerable eloquence, whether wittily and ironically, as in Voltaire's occasional verse, or gravely and sententiously, as in Rousseau's *Discourses*. In Protestant and often strongly Pietist Germany a similar impatience, a similar longing to break through the coils and constraints of a decadent culture, mark the writings of Winckelmann. To Winckelmann, however, this was not simply a rational or critical exercise; it was also a historical or archaeological one. What the thinkers of the Enlightenment often conceived of rationally as an essence or a timeless nature had, for Winckelmann, been uniquely embodied in a specific historical culture, and the task of the art critic or the art historian was to cut a way back from the corrupt neoclassicism of baroque and rococo—the culture of the petty German princes—across centuries of pedantry and misguided learning to an occulted ideal that had been historically incarnated in the civic republican culture of fourth-century Greece. In Winckelmann's radical neoclassical aesthetics, history and tradition were the sickness, but historical scholarship was the cure.

What Winckelmann looked for and found in classical Greece was the true, beautiful, and unspoiled image of the Self, our lost original; the contemplation of the pure form of that ideal was the highest goal and the richest source of inspiration for the conduct of life that he could conceive. On the other hand, to Winckelmann's successor and junior by a generation, Georg Zoega (1755–1809), the son of a pastor from the then Danish province of Schleswig, and a Christian deeply convinced of Man's fallen nature, the object of historical study lay beyond all visible and sensuously beautiful signs. That object was a world of which only worn, fragmented, and barely decipherable vestiges survived, a world far earlier than that of the classical art of Greece and the civic culture with which Winckelmann, anticipating Diderot and Hegel, had associated classical art. The origin, in short, or the true self—in the case of the Christian Zoega, one should perhaps say the Divine—was in fact an Other, infinitely remote, strange, and inaccessible, separated from contemporary humanity by an almost unbridgeable divide. It was not, therefore, easily perceptible as sensuous form on the surface, but needed to be painstakingly discovered, sometimes literally excavated or dredged up. The great philologist Friedrich Welcker, who, as tutor to the Humboldt children in Rome, had become a close friend of Zoega's and who wrote his biography, recounts how the earnest Dane would wander for hours among the tombs of the Eternal City, talking to him of the silent realm of Kore or Persephone. Zoega's principal work, *De origine et usu obeliscorum* (1797), is largely concerned with the funerary rites of the ancients. "Whereas Winckelmann admired above all the imagination of the artist in the works of sculpture and poetry he studied, and saw in them first and foremost the free form, the means by which the poetic imagination expresses itself," Welcker wrote—that is to say, a projection of man himself in the beauty of his original form—"Zoega read in both the deeply concealed idea which he then allowed to work on his spirit like the most profound energies of nature and life."[33] For Zoega, in short, the outward form was always a cipher pointing to a transcendent reality beyond the presently visible historical world. According to Welcker, Zoega believed that we totally misunderstand Greek culture if we cut it off from its subterranean religious roots. What we usually see and admire in classical Greece is thus for him a late achievement, based largely on the overcoming or even repression of a primitive, original wisdom that we must try to recover through its vestiges in the culture that replaced it.[34]

As one of the earliest and most original of the new breed of historian-decipherers, Zoega deserves to be better remembered than he is. But the more familiar, almost legendary figure of Champollion, the modern Oedipus who solved the age-old riddle of the hieroglyphs, is in many ways quite close to Zoega. In fact, Champollion knew and respected highly

Zoega's work on the hieroglyphs. Quite apart from his strangely Romantic personality, which would repay further study, Champollion shares with Zoega the same conviction that what is generally taken to be the culture of classical antiquity, even that pristine antiquity pointed to by Winckelmann, is a relative latecomer among cultures and in no way a privileged manifestation of the human, man's true original. To both the Christian Zoega and the staunchly democratic Champollion, who never wavered in his loyalty to the French Revolution, it was essential that the Other of classicism, everything that classicism seemed to have excluded or denied, should be reinstated in man's consciousness of the past.[35]

Champollion has written movingly of the mixture of awe and longing with which he stood before the precious papyri of the Royal Library in Turin and later penetrated the sacred tombs of ancient Egypt. And there is no doubt some affinity between the late Enlightenment scholar and his full-blown Romantic successors, one of whom relates that on first setting foot in the archives, he had the feeling of having at last entered the holy of holies, the sacred place to which he had been obscurely drawn all his life.[36] Yet a significant difference, I think, separates Champollion and Zoega on the one hand, and Michelet and Quinet on the other.

Champollion and Zoega would probably have subscribed to Michelet's famous formulation of the historian's task—"faire parler les silences de l'histoire"[37]—and might well have accepted it as a description of their own enterprise. But I am not sure they would have understood it in quite the sense in which Michelet and his friend Quinet understood it. To the latter, decipherment meant giving the past or the Other a power of articulation it never had, bringing it to a self-awareness it never had or could have, illuminating it and interpreting it to itself through the later and "higher" discourse of science and history. It was characteristic of both Champollion and Zoega, in contrast, that they did not see the unfamiliar Other they were trying to reach as formless, shapeless, or inarticulate, the inexhaustibly creative but terrifying Other of culture in general. To Zoega, the task of the scholar was to gather up the scattered and broken vestiges of an earlier language, the language of divine creation itself. The signs or hieroglyphs he studied pointed not to a world that lay buried, repressed, or inarticulate within the present world, to a past continuous with the present that has superseded it, but to a world totally different from the present world and even incompatible with it—a pristine, divinely ordered, prehistorical world that could be restored only by a revolutionary poetic act, the rediscovery or reinvention of an original poetic language. The language that was the key to that world was not, therefore, confused or chaotic. On the contrary, it was infinitely more beautiful and orderly than the vulgar, debased, and mutilated languages that had replaced it. Poetry, in sum, was not to rise to the clarity of prose; the past was not to be articulated by the present. It was rather the prose of rational and practical discourse that was inferior to the poetic language that had preceded it. Truth was to be found in poetry, not in prose, and the past was not only different from the present, it was better. "Only the look that is turned backwards can bring us forwards," Novalis would write later, "for the look that is turned forwards leads us backwards."[38]

To Champollion likewise, though for different reasons, there was no question of treating the past as *infans* (literally: speechless) and reading it with the superior knowledge of the present. From his tenaciously rationalist perspective, the pastness of a civilization did not make it any less articulate or intelligent than the present. Anteriority may not have been a privilege, as it was for Zoega, but it did not constitute a handicap either. Ancient Egypt, for him, was a great civilization, and his task was to convince his blinkered and prejudiced contemporaries that it could not be understood or its true history reconstructed, as many of them were satisfied it could be, from the publications of Napoleon's Commission d'Egypte, the travel descriptions of Vivant Denon, and scattered observations in the works of Greek and Roman writers. He had to keep arguing that the authentic history of Egypt could be learned only out of her own mouth, only through the hieroglyphs, and not, as in the past, through the words spoken *for* her or *about* her by her conquerors. At the same time he had to challenge the neoclassical aesthetic canon and to demonstrate that the art of the Egyptians was not only not inferior to that of the Greeks—as Winckelmann, for one, had claimed[39]—but in many respects more powerful and original.[40] The remote, preclassical past, the Other of the dominant classical culture, may have been reduced to silence, in short, but to Champollion and Zoega it was not dumb or inarticulate; and it was threatening and barbaric only to those who had not made the effort to understand it. Despite their sense of what we might call the transgressive aspect of their scholarship, Champollion and Zoega still considered the Other both intelligent and intelligible, Champollion because he still visibly shared in the rationalist optimism of the Enlightenment, Zoega because he believed that the closer we approach the original divine creation, the more harmony and order we can expect to find. In fact, it may well be misleading, in the case of Champollion at least, even to speak of "the Other." For to speak of the Other is to define the non-Self in relation to the Self, and from that perspective all differentiation within the object world fades into insignificance in comparison with the essential difference separating the object from the subject. That was not, I think, Champollion's perspective.

The concreteness and multiplicity of phenomena had not yet been extinguished for him in the blinding glare of their "meaning."

Michelet sometimes shares this view that the "primitive" is intelligent and intelligible. Early in his career, in the copious notes that run to more than twice the length of the text of his brief *Introduction to Universal History* of 1831—a highly schematic narrative describing the progress of civilization from Orient to Occident and the contribution of the major peoples and cultures to a world-historical process that the historian represents as having culminated in the July Revolution in Paris—Michelet quoted lovingly and at length, in literal translations, from the old German texts that were his delight. In one note he even asserted the impossibility of achieving an adequte translation, in any form, of the popular poems that had enchanted him in the famous collection of Arnim and Brentano, *Des Knaben Wunderhorn.* "These popular songs are still in my heart and in my ears," he wrote, "alongside the most beautiful cradle songs I ever heard on my mother's knee. I don't dare to translate a line of them."[41] The implication of this comment is that the Other, even when untranslatable, is not meaningless or unreadable. Many years later, in *The Bird,* Michelet again sounded this note in a eulogy of Alexander Wilson, the pioneer Scottish-American ornithologist. Wilson's knowledge, according to Michelet, was of particulars, not generals. "Wilson does not know the bird in general, but this or that individual bird, of this or that age, with this or that plumage, in these or those circumstances. He knows him, watches him, revisits him, and he will tell you what he does, what he eats, how he behaves, various adventures that befell him, various anecdotes about him." Wilson, a poor Scottish weaver, has not yet cut himself off from the wholeness of nature. "The friend of the buffalo and the guest of the bear, living off the fruits of the forest," he "has no home to return to, no wife or child waiting for him." His family is "the great family he observes and describes." Because he is still the child of nature, no doubt, because he has not yet carved out property and a family, her rich variety does not provoke anxiety in Wilson but love and respect. He does not attempt to reduce and master her; he does not translate, he transcribes.[42] Later still, in *Nos Fils,* Michelet confessed in a tone of mingled admiration and despair that though he had loved the people all his life, he had never succeeded in translating its language into his own.[43]

In many respects the tension between veneration of the Other—that is to say, not just the primitive or alien, but the historical particular, the discontinuous event or phenomenon in its irreducible uniqueness and untranslatableness, the very energy of "life" which no concept can encompass—and eagerness to translate it, represent it, define its meaning, and thus, in a sense, domesticate and appropriate it, can be seen as the very condition of the Romantic historian's enterprise. For the persistence of at least a residual gap between "original" and translation, between "Reality" or the Other and the representation of it, was what both generated and sustained the historian's activity, rather as the condition of history itself, in the Romantics' vision of it, was the infinite deferment of that final fulfillment of the entire process, that denouement of the story, which the Romantic historian so often evokes in his portrayal of history's epiphanies, and which he both longs for and dreads. The preservation of the Other seems to have been necessary, in sum, for the continued existence both of history, as the Romantics conceived it, and of Romantic historical narrative. That is no doubt why the Other survived in its uniqueness in Michelet's most schematic text, even if it was banished to the margins and notes of the narrative. It was in the historian's notes, one could say, that the Other was given sanctuary and protection from the appropriating energy of the historical narrative.

Michelet's work also presents, however—and just as frequently—an alternate vision of the Other, one that expresses both the urgency of the historian's desire to justify and sanctify the historical process and his fear that it may not be possible to do so, that there may be no way to subsume the discontinuous and incomparable individual manifestations of "life" in a continuous and intelligible pattern—in a word, that history does not make sense. The hidden object of curiosity and desire—the excluded, the alienated, the repressed, the feminine—is here identified with the chthonic, the unbounded, the unstructured, the lawless, that is to say, with all those "primitive," preindividual and almost prehuman forces, blindly productive and destructive at the same time, that the propertied, patriarchal culture of the modern West seems to have invented in order to define itself against them. The Other of the Romantics here assumes a threatening as well as an alluring aspect. If at times it seems ultimately reducible, by virtue of the historian's heroic efforts, to intelligible order, at other times it looms before him as the terrible, unreadable, unrepresentable image of the ultimate irrationality and meaninglessness of existence, his own dreaded Nemesis.

The Other thus evoked in its investigators a combination of terror and desire, reverence and an exacerbated need for mastery. The dialectic of Self and Other (form and life, culture and nature, male and female, the bourgeois and the people) was intensified to an unheard-of pitch as the historian struggled desperately to reintegrate and reappropriate an Other that seemed constantly to elude him and to be rediscovered (or reinvented) just as it appeared to have been finally overcome or brought to order.

When the Swiss philologist and legal historian J. J. Bachofen, for instance, tried to extend the realm of culture to include prehistory and forms of society that were quite different from those of the West—and in the strenuously patriarchal world of the mid-nineteenth century his idea of *Mutterrecht* or Mother Law applied to the remote past (that is, the idea that woman, not man, is the founder of culture) was an even more challenging oxymoron than Michelet's utopian *livre populaire*—he succeeded only in pushing the terrifying, chaotic, nameless and propertyless Other further back into what he called primitive promiscuity, hetaerism, or sometimes, quite simply, communism. As mother, educator, and founder of the earliest orderly communities, woman could be reintegrated into culture and perceived as lawful, but part of her—the female—still remained apparently irrecuperable, indistinguishable from a lawless nature, Salome dancing before an aged, shriveled, yet fascinated Herod, as in Gustave Moreau's popular painting of 1874.

In his book on the sea (*La Mer*), Michelet hailed the triumphs of the nineteenth-century Prometheuses—Romme, Reid, Peltier, Piddington—who had tamed the tempests by discovering their laws. "What we thought was caprice was seen to be subject to law," he wrote triumphantly.[44] But Michelet's work shows repeatedly that at any moment this intelligible nature, seemingly obedient to law, might suddenly uncover her dreaded, undecipherable underside—the untamable female ("Circe," "marâtre") beneath the gentle, suckling mother. France, in Louis Blanc's words, is "a country where the life of kings is full of torments, and where the multitude has its ebb and flow like the sea."[45] The Other, in short, as woman, as the remote past, as civilized man's own past, and as that living survival of it, the people—not, to be sure, in the constructive or heroic role assigned to it in the inspiring narratives of the new national historians, but in its unaccountable moments of terrifying fury—persistently resisted the historian's efforts to integrate it and subject it to his categories of language, description, and understanding.[46] In a strikingly prophetic passage in *Le Peuple,* written two years before the 1848 revolution, which shattered so many hopes and illusions, Michelet recalls a nightmare vision he claims he had while visiting Dublin. The appearance of the quays of the Liffey, the river itself, reminded him of Paris, he says, but Paris without its glories, its monuments, the Tuileries, the Louvre, the opulent shops. He then observed some poorly clad people coming over the bridge. They were not like French workers because they were not wearing workers' smocks ("blouses"), but old stained clothes. "They were arguing violently, in harsh, guttural, barbaric tones, with a frightful hunchback dressed in rags. . . . Others came by, all wretched and misshapen." Suddenly, he was seized with terror. "All these figures were French. . . . It *was* Paris, it *was* France, a France turned ugly, brutal, savage."[47]

But the historian never gives up the search for order. Romantic historiography is always "modernizing" historiography. Despite his much-touted sense of the uniqueness of individual historical phenomena and his sympathy for the dumb and unsung, the Romantic historian did not allow himself to doubt for long that the perspective of his own time and his own knowledge, because it was more advanced, closer to the denouement of the story, so to speak, was also superior. The bare facts of the past are always translatable into coherent narrative. "The events of the last fifty years," Augustin Thierry wrote in 1840, "have taught us to understand the revolutions of the Middle Ages; to discern the fundamental character of things beneath the letter of the chronicles; to extract from the writings of the Benedictines things those erudite men never saw."[48]

The supreme insight is thus that in which sympathy for the past is combined with knowledge and active promotion of the present. Every artist, Michelet once wrote about Rubens, is his mother's son,[49] and he might have added: and every historian too. It is through him, the historian-artist, the man who is his mother's son, nature's child, that the dumb and mute of history are permitted to accede to speech and made both available and innocuous to the living.[50] All life, Michelet declared in *The Bird,* salutes the sun "but one alone utters the praise, speaks it for all, sings it out. . . .The bird says the blessing of the day. The bird is its priest and augur."[51] In the same way, the witch speaks for ordinary women ("It's no good your trying to speak, little silent one. You won't be able to bring it off. I shall speak for you");[52] Paris speaks for France; France speaks for Europe and the modern world; the genius speaks for the masses; and Michelet speaks for the people and all the provinces of France, interpreting to them their "forgotten dreams of the night,"[53] and for his young wife, Athénaïs Mialaret, whose biography he wrote and whose groping efforts as a writer of natural history he gathered up and incorporated into his own texts.[54] In the 1869 Preface to the *History of France* the historian compared his own account of the fourteenth century with Prosper de Barante's popular *History of the Dukes of Burgundy* of the 1820s. "What would have become of me in that fourteenth century," he wrote, "if I had stuck to the method of my illustrious predecessor and turned myself into the docile interpreter, the servile translator of the narratives of the time. As it enters periods rich in official records and authentic documents, history comes of age and achieves mastery over the earlier chronicle form, dominating, purifying, and judging it. Armed with reliable records that the chronicles never knew of, history holds chronicle on its knee, so to speak, like a small child whose babbling it willingly attends to but whom it must often correct and contradict."[55]

Since Champollion appears not to have considered the past he studied either inarticulate or threatening, there was no reason why he should have experienced Michelet's intense need to dominate and control the voices he claimed to have liberated from the silence of the tomb. It is characteristic, in this connection, that the great Egyptologist did his best to put a stop to Western plundering of the ancient stones of Egypt—an activity that seems to have been motivated, when it was not just a matter of greed, by a desire not only to preserve the venerable body of the past but to imprison it in the temples and museums of Western science; and equally characteristic that of such immurements in the name of science the author of *The Witch*, otherwise so obsessed by the horror of the *in pace,* had little to say. On the contrary, his enthusiasm for the Museum was unbounded.[56]

IV

None of the French scholars and historians—not even Thierry, who wrote extensively on the history of historiography—theorized the practice of history. The French Romantic historians remained individualists, and they did not dream of professionalizing their craft. It was at the German universities, in lecture courses like those of Hegel and later Droysen, that the new philology and the new history were systematized, philosophically grounded, and transformed into an academic practice. In a series of lectures given over almost five decades, from 1818 to 1865, at the University of Berlin, and attended by generations of historians including Burckhardt and Droysen, August Boeckh, Professor of Classical Philology, provided a philosophical foundation for an optimistic Romantic philology and historiography, in which the Other turns out to be not radically discontinuous with the Self, but a temporarily alienated and ultimately recuperable aspect of it.

The scope of philology, for Boeckh, is immensely wide. It is "Erkenntnis des vom menschlichen Geist producierten, d.h. des Erkannten" ("knowledge of whatever the human spirit has produced, knowledge, that is, of what once was known to other minds"). In other words, it is reappropriation by the spirit of its own alienated products: "Wiedererkenntnis und Darstellung des ganzen vorhandenen menschlichen Wissens" ("recognition and re-presentation of the totality of human knowledge"). For Boeckh, as for his colleague Hegel, what is given to us in experience is not objects as such, but objects already known under a concept. Knowledge of phenomena (such as philology and history aspire to) and knowledge of ideas (philosophy) are not therefore completely distinct, but complementary and inseparable from each other. The only difference is that whereas philosophy goes directly to the object of its knowledge ("erkennt primitiv"), philology relearns or re-cognizes it ("erkennt wieder"). Boeckh rejects the view that philology should confine itself to textual criticism. For him it is above all a search for understanding of what lies behind the texts and produced them—that is, the "life" of the human spirit to which the texts bear witness. Philology is thus to be defined not by its methods but by its goal. It is not a technique of textual criticism, but a branch of learning with its own specific object.[57]

Moreover, though philology has as its aim knowledge of another, lost or alienated knowledge, that does not in any way mean that it does not seek or acquire a knowledge of its own. The knowledge of philology is not identical with the knowledge that it knows; the thought of the historian or philologist is not the thought that he aims to comprehend. The ideas of the Other, as long as they remain other, are not yet ideas for me. My task as philologist is to make them properly mine. The goal that Boeckh attributes to philology seems thoroughly Hegelian:

> First and foremost, it is the task of reproducing all that alien thought so that it becomes mine, so that nothing external or alien remains. . . . At the same time, however, the task of philology is to *dominate* what it has thus reproduced, in such a way that, though it has been made mine, appropriated to myself, I can still hold it before me like an object and in this way be said to have knowledge of that integrated knowledge of knowledge ["ein Erkennen dieser zu einem Ganzen formierten Erkenntnis des Erkannten habe"], to know my own knowledge of the knowledge of the past; for only then can I assign it a place in my own thought, which is an act of judgment.[58]

In other words, I become the master of the reappropriated Other that I have represented to my Self. The fragments and broken pieces of past life recover their wholeness and are reintegrated into present life by the philologist-historian, but at the same time they are wholly subordinated to the present. Continuity is restored between the present and the past, one might say, but with no sacrifice of the privileges of the former.

Boeckh's high idea of philology as a passing behind texts to the living ideas that produced them and that now lie buried deep within them, and as a means of overcoming alienation and restoring wholeness and harmony, is also, he claims, the true idea of history. For him, the historian and the philologist are engaged in a common hermeneutic pursuit: deciphering the various "signs and symbols," as he put it, in which "the human spirit has communicated itself," bridging the gulf between the present and the past, the Self and the Other.

In Boeckh's optimistic vision of philology, it is by reestablishing contact with classical antiquity that modern man can best hope to achieve renewal. His version of neohumanism, in which the spirit of Winckelmann is still very much alive, was a characteristic product of the political and intellectual climate of Berlin in the 1820s and 1830s. But many Christians had misgivings about attributing too much wisdom to a people who, as Guillaume Budé had put it in the early sixteenth century, lacked any knowledge of "sacred and incorruptible history,"[59] and throughout the seventeenth and eighteenth centuries there had been a persistent undercurrent of speculation— often relegated to the lunatic fringe by official culture—about civilizations prior to those of Greece and Rome. Among early nineteenth-century Christian scholars, objections were again raised to the neohumanist contrast, deriving from Winckelmann and strongly marked by the ideas of the Enlightenment, between the closed, calm, serene world of classical antiquity, represented as an Eden within history in which men lived in joyful harmony with nature and the Gods, and the tormented, unhappy world of modern—that is, Christian—man, who experiences life as division and exile.[60] Even the horror of death—the ultimate otherness— had been overcome by the Ancients, according to the neohumanist view of them. "The wind that blows from the graves of the Ancients smells sweetly," Goethe wrote, "as if it had passed over a hill covered with roses."[61]

To many Christian scholars it was inadmissable that a pagan people ignorant of Revelation could be thought of as living a serenely contented life. The Greeks had not escaped the Fall. The beautiful surface of Greek life and art, the harmonious forms admired by Winckelmann, could only be a covering drawn over intense and unresolved primitive terrors and confusions. It was these scholars who first sought—and found—what has been called the *Nachtseite,* the dark underside of ancient civilization, which they claimed was closely related to the oriental cultures classicism had tried to reject and disavow as barbarian. And it was they who issued the only significant challenge to the neohumanist version of classical antiquity that had established itself as an orthodoxy in the German universities.

The leading figure in this movement—at least the one with the greatest international reputation as a philologist and scholar—was Friedrich Creuzer, Professor of Classical Philology at Heidelberg. In his *Symbolik und Mythologie* (1810–1812) Creuzer presented the symbolism of the Ancients in the manner of Zoega, as the expression of a religious consciousness and a religious world view, rather than as the invention of a free poetic imagination.[62] The implication of Creuzer's work, which revived ideas mooted by Vossius (*De theologia gentili,* 1641) and Kircher (*Oedipus aegyptus,* 1652) a century and a half before, was that there had been an original religious consciousness, an original knowledge of the Divine, shared by all men and corresponding to the original adamitic language. This original religion had subsequently been corrupted and fragmented into a thousand "pagan" cults, just as the original language had broken up, after Babel, into a thousand alien tongues. But to the Christian mythologists it had been restored by Revelation. Christianity did not therefore abolish or reject the pagan cults of antiquity but—in a characteristically Hegelian movement—it gathered them up, interpreted them, fulfilled and transcended them at the same time. In Michelet's words, "The Christian world contains all the worlds that preceded it; the Christian temple contains all other temples."[63] Christian Rome thus appeared to Creuzer, as it appeared later in Michelet's *Roman History,* and later still in Fustel's *Ancient City,* as the point of contact and passage from the pagan and classical world of small city-states and local religions to Christianity, from a fragmented world and world view to a new imperialism and universalism.

These were not, it should be emphasized, the eccentric ideas of an obscure German professor.[64] Creuzer was read with attention by Hegel, who had been his friend and colleague for a time at Heidelberg.[65] He was made an associate of the Paris Académie des Inscriptions in 1825, and he was considered a sage in France. Michelet and Quinet both made pilgrimages to Heidelberg to sit at his feet. The translation of the *Symbolik* into French was the life's work of Joseph-Daniel Guigniaut, the Perpetual Secretary of the Académie des Inscriptions, a director of the Ecole Normale, and the teacher of Fustel de Coulanges.[66]

The same vision which represented historical Christianity as gathering up, interpreting, and renewing the fragmented cults of antiquity and producing an understanding of them that they had not had and could not have had of themselves made it possible to construe the activity of contemporary historians and philosophers as a reenactment or modernization of that of the early Christians. Christianity itself could thus be viewed as a kind of prefiguration of the Romantic philosophy of history. In this way, Hegelians like David Strauss interpreted the old myths and religions, including Christianity, as preconceptual modes of philosophizing, a kind of primitive, concrete thinking which philosophy does not negate but which it completes, purifies, clarifies, and explains. In France, many progressive historians emphasized the popular and revolutionary character of primitive Christianity and denounced its occultation by an institutionalized and repressive priesthood. The rewriting of history, the rediscovery of the authentic voice of the past thus had a quasi-religious and prophetic character for them in that it involved, as the original Christian revelation had done for Creuzer, a disclosure of meanings imperfectly understood or distorted by the passage of time and the ignorance or evil intentions of men. To Philippe Buchez—the author of a well-known *Histoire parlementaire de la Révolution française*—there were passages in the Gospels themselves which suggested that "revelation was not complete, that there was something beyond the Biblical dogma, and that . . . the teaching of the evangelists had stopped at the point at which the men of that time were capable of understanding it—a point men would be able to go beyond once their eyes had been opened more widely."[67] In Buchez's application of the traditional exegetical principle of accommodation—the assumption that revelation and other divine institutions are adjusted to the capacity of men at different times to perceive and receive them—the sense of the Gospels was explained and fulfilled by the revolutions of his own age, and in particular by the promised social democratic revolution.

It was indeed a new gospel that Michelet claimed to preach both in his writing and in his popular Collège de France lectures of the 1830s and 1840s. The *Bible de l'humanité,* integrating all the myths and religions of the past—especially, it is curious to note, those of the Aryans, who were already being claimed as the ancestors of the contemporary Europeans—was to supersede the holy scriptures of the Jews and Christians, and the historian was to replace the Christian priest as the interpreter of human existence. By giving words and a meaning to a past that was inscribed, he said, in the minds of his listeners and readers, but that they themselves could not decipher, Michelet claimed to be able to read their destiny to them.[68] (This, incidentally, proved to be nothing less than to soldier on toward the infinitely receding consummation of history, that "translation du ciel sur la terre," in which all the oppositions and contradictions of historical experience, and not least the tension between the individual phenomenon in time and the transtemporal totality that alone provides it with "meaning," would be finally resolved.)[69] The historian can perform this priestly function and successfully serve as a bridge builder (*pontifex*) between the dead and the living, the past and the present, the people and the bourgeoisie, the collective unconscious and the consciousness of the modern individual, because he maintains contact with those superseded worlds without being in thrall to them. The hieroglyphs he deciphers in the unconscious minds of his listeners and readers were first discovered in his own, Michelet writes, and it is in himself that the historian first encounters the past: "What is history made with, if not with me? What shall it be remade with [that is, retold with], if not with me?"[70]

The privilege of the historian is that he can maintain self or identity without denying the underlying continuity of the Self with the Other and the past. In the great 1869 Preface to his *Histoire de France,* Michelet explains that the vision of the Other, which is the object of the historian's journey to the nether world of the tomb and the archive, does not drive him mad or destroy his identity, as his friends fear it will. On the contrary, he alone remains himself, while preserving full consciousness of the Other in himself (as professor at the Collège de France, Michelet repeatedly recalled his humble origins as a "son of the people"); he alone can translate the confused and confusing messages of the Other into language intelligible to his educated contemporaries, and he alone, therefore, can be the instrument of an orderly reconstruction and harmonization of society. When he wanted to write the history of the simple people of the Middle Ages, Michelet explained, all he had to do was to dive down into himself and discover there the level at which all life—natural, animal, and human—is one. "I went down on all fours," he wrote, applying to himself the phrase he was to use later with reference to the Witch.[71] The scientific historian thereby declared his ability to embrace and rediscover in himself his origin and Other, the intimate, almost animal friend of nature, the female Seer, the popular Sorcière, and to recover and speak what no Inquisitorial court ever dared to record or even to hear.

V

For the predominantly Christian German Romantics, it was the coming of Christ that marked the beginning of a *vita nuova* for humanity. For Hegelians, it was the emergence of philosophy. For the bourgeois historians of early nineteenth-century France, it was the Revolution. The Revolution illuminated all previous history and made it possible to totalize and thus decipher it. "Even more than the lack of political freedom," Michelet's friend and contemporary Henri Martin wrote in the Preface to his *Histoire de France* (1837), "another obstacle made it impossible to write the history of France before 1789: the fact is, history could then have no plan, since it did not yet have a conclusion."[72] Only after the Revolution was it possible, in other words, to construct French history as a genuine narrative.

It could even be said, as I have suggested, that the past that had been illuminated and made intelligible by the Revolution included the earlier Christian Revelation itself; this could now be interpreted as a prefiguration of the Revelation of 1789. "The fifty years that had just passed," in Martin's words, "had provided the key to the riddle of twenty centuries."[73] If the task of the French historian was henceforward to spread and interpret the new gospel of the Revolution, that almost inevitably involved both some sympathy with the earlier, imperfect Gospel and, in general, with the ancient and predominantly feminine and popular world of myth that had now been superseded, and at the same time opposition to it, inasmuch as it had been distorted into an institutionalized instrument of repression—the Church—which blindly resisted the doctrine of its own transcendence by the new religion of the Revolution. The relation of Christians to Jews, of so-called New Testament to so-called Old Testament, of inspired, charismatic prophets to traditional, conservative priests (the essential theme of Renan's later *Life of Jesus*), was thus repeated in the mixture of respect and hostility with which Michelet, Quinet, and other progressive French historians regarded the Catholic Church and the traditional religious beliefs and practices of the French people.[74]

The Romantic historians' conception of France and her historiography as "le verbe de l'Europe," the interpreter of the nations to themselves and to one another, and the prophet of a new social order underlay both the humanitarian impulses of the early French Left and the ambitions of the Right. It served to legitimize not only social and political revolution but also the political rule and cultural hegemony of the bourgeoisie, the industrial conquest of nature, and the West's domination of the rest of the world. The *beau rôle* of spokesman for the Other apparently had its own hidden agenda. Handed down by Michelet and Henri Martin, the central doctrines of Romantic and revolutionary nationalist historiography were invoked not only by Fourierist socialists, such as Michelet's friend, the popular naturalist writer Alphonse Toussenel—in whom one already finds a characteristically paranoid brew of anticapitalism, anti-industrialism, anti-Semitism, antiliberalism, and anglophobia[75]—but also by apologists of late nineteenth-century French imperialism like Etienne Clementel and Paul d'Ivot, who argued in terms directly borrowed from Michelet and Quinet that, unlike other imperialist powers, notably England, republican France was interested not in profit or exploitation but in the "conquête morale des peuples."[76]

The Romantic idea of the Other, and of history as the discovery and decipherment of the Other's languages, thus underlies both an immense and generous expansion of the scope of historiography in the nineteenth century and the imperiousness with which that historiography defined the Other and claimed to integrate it into its discourse. The relation of history-as-decipherment to the world of past time seems to have been characterized by an ambiguity strikingly similar to that which marked the anthropological investigation of the world of space in the nineteenth century. The devoted, patronizing, and not always disinterested attention the Western anthropologist bestowed on those alien, "prehistorical" peoples who were widely believed to represent the original condition from which the "historical" peoples of Europe had raised themselves was by no means foreign to the Romantic historian. The development of modern anthropology, it has been claimed, was directly linked to European overseas expansion and colonial administration (in the United States to the problem of the indigenous Indian populations).[77] Romantic historiography seems to have been no less deeply implicated in the nineteenth-century ideology of progress and the white man's burden.

[1987]

9

The Rationality of History

Man's respect for knowledge is one of his most peculiar characteristics. . . . But what distinguishes knowledge from superstition,
ideology or pseudoscience? . . . The demarcation between science
and pseudoscience is not merely a problem of armchair philosophy:
it is of vital social and political relevance.

—Imre Lakatos, *The Methodology*
of Scientific Research Programmes

Some people believe that the poet and the historian practice the
same craft; but in this they are quite mistaken, for the poet and
the historian are different artificers who have nothing in common
with each other.

—Pierre Ronsard, *La Franciade*

THE VIEW of historiography that I try to develop in the following pages
is not one that I have espoused in the past. Implicitly, at least, I have been
close to the position with which I now take issue. Thus I do not write
without sympathy for the ideas I now find problematical.

My interest in historiography dates back to the doctoral dissertation
that I wrote at Oxford in the mid-1950s under the late Jean Seznec. Published a decade later, in 1968, as *Medievalism and the Ideologies of the Enlightenment,* that early work was concerned not so much with the
historiographical text as with the institutions and methods of historical
scholarship and literary history in the seventeenth and eighteenth centuries.
My aim was to "contextualize" the activity of scholarship and to establish
its relation to contemporary ideologies and to the social and institutional
conditions in which it was pursued. In the last chapter I touched on the
different ways in which history was understood and used in the Enlightenment and in the Romantic period, and it was to nineteenth-century
historiography that I turned shortly afterward, focusing now more on
narrative historical texts than on historical scholarship and attempting

something like a literary analysis of those texts. I had already published in 1963 a short article on Voltaire's *History of Charles XII* in which I tried to demonstrate that, although individual constituents of the narrative had been borrowed from oral and written testimonies and from other historical narratives, after being subjected to the careful scrutiny expected of a modern writer and a *philosophe*, the narrative itself was essentially literary and rhetorical. The *History of Charles XII* was not, I maintained, substantially different in design from Voltaire's better-known *contes,* and, as with the *contes,* its meaning was an effect of the narrative design rather than a rational deduction from the "facts" of the case. Crudely articulated as it was, this article did attempt to challenge the institutionalized boundary between "history" and "literature" by showing that historical discourse is subject to the same kind of analysis as any other discourse, and that historical narrative has much more in common with fictional narrative than historians are normally willing to allow—in short, that history is not a science in the naive sense in which that term might still have been understood by some historians two decades ago. To a large extent, this is what I have tried to do in subsequent studies of Michelet (1974), Augustin Thierry (1976; Chapter 4 of this volume), and Gibbon (1982).

The complement to the project of reading historical texts as literature has been a continued commitment to a historical approach to literature. For this reason, I have always wanted to reinsert into history the very historical texts that I had analyzed as literature. Just as historical narratives are not transparent representations of historical reality, however, the historical meaning and testimony of literary texts does not lie, as I see it at least, in their passively "reflecting" reality, but in their structuring of it, in the kind of relation they establish with their readers, and in the different ways in which literature itself has been defined and institutionalized. Besides attempting literary analyses of historical texts, therefore, I have also tried to argue that the categories of literature and history have a history; that literature as a social institution and, above all, as a subject of instruction in schools and an instrument of cultural formation and communication is part of history and subject to historical analysis; and, more specifically, that the idea of literature underwent a significant transformation in the early nineteenth century.[1]

The relation between literature and history remains a practical problem for me as a teacher of literature. If I juxtapose different types of text— say, Descartes's *Discourse of Method,* Corneille's *Cinna,* Richelieu's *Testament politique,* and the Preface to the *Dictionnaire de l'Académie française*— and try to show that all of them define a similar problem and promote a similar solution, I am at least dealing with comparable items. But how does one establish a relation between a rhetoric or an ideology and historical reality (not an account or representation of class conflict, for instance, but actual class conflict)? When literary scholars set a text in historical "context," as some of us are prone to do, what are we actually doing? What is the context? How do we know it? Is it ontologically prior to the text under review, and indeed to any text, as was once unreflectingly assumed? Is there, in short, "another side" of stories that is accessible to us? Or, in reaching out beyond stories, do we simply abut on other stories? And if that is so, what are our explanations and interpretations but new stories constructed out of bits and pieces of already existing ones? The issue—which no literary scholar interested in the political and historical dimension of literature can escape—was clearly stated by Hayden White:

> Within a long and distinguished critical tradition that has sought to determine what is "real" and what is "imagined" in the novel, history has served as a kind of archetype of the realistic pole of representation . . . Nor is it unusual for literary theorists, when they are speaking about the "context" of a literary work, to suppose that this context, the "historical milieu," has a concreteness and an accessibility that the work itself can never have, as if it were easier to perceive the reality of a past world put together from a thousand historical documents than it is to probe the depths of a single literary work that is present to the critic studying it. But the presumed concreteness and accessibility of historical milieux, these contexts of the texts that literary scholars study, are themselves products of the fictive capabilities of the historians who have studied those contexts.[2]

White's position is not popular among historians, as one can imagine. Most "practicing" historians profess to distrust him or try to ignore him. But a few have expressed views that are at least compatible with his. In the postscript of his *Reappraisals in History* (1961) and in *The History Primer* of a decade later, Jack Hexter, for one, adopts a surprisingly ironical view of his activity as a historian. In his own historical writing, Hexter declares, he is interested in presenting a model of experience, not just an account of the facts. While the story he tells is limited by the rules of the historical game, a code of behavior that all historians subscribe to, his ultimate goal is to tell a story similar to that of the fictional writer, to convey a sense of "triumph and tragedy."[3] Hexter's position could prove perilously close to that of Maurice Barrès, who once remarked impatiently to a friend: "My book on Persia is already done . . . The only trouble is that I have to go to the damn place—to satisfy a bunch of idiots" (that is, philistine bourgeois readers who expect a travel narrative to "reflect" a concrete experience of the place in question).[4] Such comments highlight the problem of the cognitive content of historical texts, the relation between the meaning of a historical narrative and the empirical facts it refers to. What is it, they provoke us into asking, that orders the historical text and governs its meaning? Is it the "reality" to which the individual statements in the text ostensibly refer? Or is it a principle of literary composition? How, in short, do the idea and order of history which we derive from historical texts, and to which, if we are literary scholars, we refer the texts (including the historical texts) that we study, relate to historical "reality"? Is "the past as history" no more, in Valéry's pithy phrase, than "a piece of imagination based on records"?[5]

In addition, the debate about literature and history seems deeply embedded in an institutional rivalry of which no literary scholar can remain long unaware. When the modern study of literature was institutionalized in the last century it was quite clearly associated with and subordinated to history, as part to whole. The "other" of literature was then, thanks to the Romantics, not history but rhetoric. The present organization of literary studies in the university (by national languages and historical periods) reflects that association and that subservience. The collapse of historical optimism and the concomitant decline of Hegelian historical philosophies in the aftermath of 1848 provoked a revival of eighteenth-century attempts to divide the sphere of knowledge into clearly demarcated territories subject to different criteria of validity. Literary texts were henceforth to be considered as aesthetic objects, literary history as distinct from social history.

More recently there appears to have been an *Umwertung* of established values and hierarchies as the languages of philosophy and history, which for so long have sat in judgment over all other forms of discourse, have themselves been put in question. Visibly, it is the renewed contemporary emphasis on language and rhetoric, not as mere vehicles of thought or ornaments of texts but as their deep structure—and, I would add, as institutions in which social meanings and cultural patterns are already inscribed—that has produced the discomfort presently felt both by historians who worry about the epistemological foundations of their discipline and by literary critics who have been accustomed to thinking of history as a solid ground supporting imagination.

To some extent this development can be seen as a long-term consequence of the shift from an eighteenth-century ideal of history as a system of explanation, on the model of Newtonian physics, to a Romantic vision of history as hermeneutic, on the model of biblical studies and neohumanist classical philology. From this Romantic perspective, reality itself came to be viewed as a "text" to be interpreted.[6] More immediately, however, the reexamination of historical discourse and of the validity of studying literature in historical context appears to have been provoked by two influences in particular. The first is that of the Anglo-American school of analytical philosophy of history (Danto, Gallie, Mink, Morton White). The implication of the analytical philosophers' view of narrative form as constitutive of meaning in history is that the meaning of the historical work, as of any text, is discovered not in its referentiality but in its textuality. The second influence is that of French and American deconstructionism, with its emphasis on the virtually uncontrollable signifying power of language, which overwhelms all attempts at "scientific" discourse. The deconstructionist perspective privileges literary discourse over all others as the only one that is not deluded, the only one that knows its true character is to be untrue. Not surprisingly, self-consciousness and irony are seen as the distinction and the defining characteristic of literature.

The combined influence of the analytical philosophy of history and deconstructionism, especially in the popular academic form taken by the latter in this country, has ensured that what was an avant-garde opinion when it was proposed by Hayden White—basically, that history is a linguistic and rhetorical artifact constrained by a genre rule specifying reference to conventionally agreed upon historical "facts," that "fiction," in other words, informs "history"—has become the orthodoxy of today, the common coin of popular journalism and undergraduate essays.[7]

I acknowledge that I have become increasingly irritated by the casual and irresponsible banalization of formerly avant-garde positions. My misgivings have been expressed more effectively than I could have stated them myself by Jörn Rüsen, a leading German historian, who argues that the present reexamination of historiography

coincides with a notable turn in the value system of cultural discourse. The Enlightenment tradition, with its dominant concepts of critical reason and emancipation, is losing its power to carry conviction and, in striking analogy to the culture criticism of the late nineteenth century, irrationalism and mythical thought are acquiring more and more literary, academic, and journalistic prestige. Nietzsche is the leading figure of a post-structuralist intellectual avant-garde that is fascinated by the destruction of reason . . . The weaker the conviction among historians that their intellectual activity is, or at least should be, rationally informed, the more easily historiography is made over into an instrument of ideology. The much celebrated revival of narrative in historiography erodes that conviction, as does the much discussed metahistorical thesis of the essentially rhetorical character of historiography. The new irrationalism finds allies in those historians to whom the task of interpreting the historical experience of what men have done to each other and to their world in the course of time in terms of rational criteria has come to seem too difficult. The rationality of historical thinking fades when historians give up on providing historical memory, through their work of interpretation, with a glimmering of discernible and intelligible coherency. In such conditions Clio, their muse, might well reach for the greasepaint of irrational meanings as a cover for meaninglessness. In this way, history get decked out as a poetic activity. (It is not an accident that Theodor Lessing's well known *Geschichte als Sinngebung des Sinnlosen* has been recently reissued) . . . History as a scholarly activity rests on rational principles that have been achieved and elaborated as a result of a long historical process. That process is called 'emancipation.' In our time, that notion of emancipation, together with the Enlightenment tradition on which it is supported, has a bad press. It is up-to-date and certain to win the applause of the post-modern intellectual avant-garde to unmask whatever is connected with emancipation and Enlightenment as illusion, and to celebrate the counterhistory to the history of modern emancipation as the one by which the contemporary situation is determined . . . History must resist the temptation to swim with the tide of the new longing to forget the horrors of the present in the arms of the past. Instead, it should constantly remind us of those historical experiences that are intimately connected with the currents of irrationalism, the effort to bring the civilizing culture of Modernity to an end, and the creation of myths that promise to release us from the burden of discursive thought.[8]

The Necessity of Narrative

Suspicion of narrative attended the beginnings of modern historiography in the late seventeenth century, and it has never altogether abated.[9] The great age of historical narrative, usually celebrated as the heyday of "history" in general, was preceded by an age of historical criticism. It is at least arguable that Bayle's influential *Historical and Critical Dictionary* is as exemplary as any of the Romantic narratives. And in this founding work, not only is the choice of the dictionary form with the conventional alphabetical arrangement of material a striking repudiation of narrative, but the challenge to narrative is repeated in each individual article. The thin narrative line of each entry (often a bare line or two at the top of the folio page) is invariably interrupted by innumerable note signs referring the reader to the copious scholarly discussions that fill up the space below, question the reliability of the narrative, and generate further distracting notes in the margins. It is virtually impossible to read Bayle for the narrative without feeling the ground give way under one's feet.[10] As he himself liked to say, "On ne sait où planter les pieds." In his preface, moreover, Bayle makes his distrust of narrative explicit by citing a perfectly coherent but factually "false" narrative sentence ("Coriolanus's mother obtained of him what he refused the sacred College of Cardinals and the Pope himself, who went to meet him"), in order to demonstrate that such a sentence may be as meaningful and as rhetorically effective as any "true" narrative.[11] Nevertheless, even Bayle, critical and antisystematic as he was, could not conceive of history except as a narrative against whose seductions the honest historian must be eternally vigilant. If history was possible at all, it could only be as a narrative—one that historians constantly weave, unravel, and weave back again.[12]

Later Enlightenment critics of traditional historical narrative—and I am thinking much more of Malthus or Playfair or Eden than of Voltaire or Macaulay, who never really did much to avoid it—were also unable to escape narrativity. Though they are intended to establish correlations, Eden's elaborate tables of incomes and prices both imply and support a narrative of the changing state of the laboring people of England and of the evolution of English society from Norman times to those of the historian himself at the end of the eighteenth century. Likewise, nonverbal, predominantly graphic representations of historical data—an invention of Enlightenment scholars who wanted to avoid rhetoric and natural language and, in Playfair's words, speak "a language that all the world understands," thus ensuring that the information, from which they hoped future generations would be able to derive the *laws* of historical development, "should go down in such a form and manner as that any person might, even though a native of another country, understand the nature of the business delineated"[13]—even such graphic representations, familiar to us from historical atlases and the tables accompanying modern historical texts, can only be interpreted by being translated into the form of a narrative. Minard's *carte figurative* of the gradual disintegration of the Grande Armée in the course of the Russian campaign of 1812–1813, first published in 1861 and celebrated on account of its clever representation of multivariate data, in fact "tells a rich coherent story," as one scholar has said, "far more enlightening than just a single number bounding along over time."[14]

More recently, the repeated attacks on narrative by members of the *Annales* school of historians, starting with the classic little book of Marc Bloch, have likewise not really been targeted at narrative as such. They turn out, on inspection, to be directed rather against a certain kind of narrative, one that has been abandoned by many writers of fiction and even by some writers of history: I mean what we usually refer to as "classical" narrative, with its well-defined characters, plot-line, and point of view—the "healthy" kind of narrative that Ortega y Gasset once contrasted with Proust's "sickly" descriptions of shifting psychological states, or that Voltaire had in mind when he criticized Montesquieu's *Considérations sur la grandeur et la décadence des Romains* for its provocative disdain of it.[15] What the critics of narrative reject is in fact the primacy of political history and the liberal assumption behind it—that men make their own destinies, ultimately that history is the story of liberty. Already in the mid-nineteenth century, historians disillusioned by or ill-disposed to the "march of history" were denouncing that kind of history in favor of a much slower-moving history, a history without events or heroes: cultural history (Burckhardt) or institutional history (Fustel). It is the narrative of traditional political history that the pioneers of the *Annales* school wanted to relegate to the dustbin of historiography, not narrative as such, about which most of them probably did not think very hard or at all.[16]

Some narrative framework seems to be implied in the very act of recognizing and identifying an individual historical fact. (Would a fact which was identified in terms of a nonnarrative system of relations be recognizable as a *historical* fact?) It is only by being recognized as part of a potential narrative, in other words, that historical material becomes meaningfully historical. For example, Collingwood's hypothesis (based on the deciphering of tombstone inscriptions) that parties of Scots had settled down peacefully in southern England at the time of the Roman occupation— which Leon Goldstein cites as an example of scholarly reconstituting of the historical record, in contrast to narrative art[17]—is itself not a single nugget of fact but a small narrative, which in addition implies a larger context or argument in which it takes its place and in light of which the "raw" data were themselves perceived.

It seems to me difficult to avoid the conclusion that narrative is an essential and not an accidental characteristic of historiography, despite the persistent—and probably necessary—suspicion of it among historians and their constantly renewed attempts to escape its constraints and routines. Jörn Rüsen and Hans Baumgartner have also argued that description and explanation in historiography turn out on examination to be not equivalents of or alternatives to narrative, but subordinate, in any historical account, to a basic narrative scheme, so that "narration is a structural concept of the historical object, of historical objectivity, and not merely one form of representation along with others."[18] Historical works which at first sight might appear deliberately to eschew narrative, such as Tocqueville's *The Ancien Régime and the Revolution,* Burckhardt's *Civilization of the Renaissance,* Fustel's *Ancient City,* or, in more recent times, Laslett's *The World We Have Lost,* do in fact turn out, on inspection, to have a strong, if deeply embedded, narrative structure. Similarly, the most elementary "facts" of history, from the fall of Constantinople or the modernization of Japan under the Meiji to the cult of the dead in the ancient city or the behavior of Louis XIV's courtiers, are always apprehended as narratives, composed of other, "smaller" facts, arranged in a particular yet variable way. And these in turn prove to be themselves more or less complex narratives, be it a single "event" or act of the French Revolution, or the demography of a single parish.

The Problem of Incommensurability

What disturbs many practicing historians, as well as some who, like myself, have argued for greater recognition of the literary and rhetorical aspects of historiography, is less the claim that historical explanation always assumes a narrative form than the argument for the incommensurability of historical narratives that often accompanies that claim. That historical narratives are incommensurable with one another appears to follow from a combination of two prior arguments. The first is that no narrative is a simple reflection or copy of past reality, since past reality is by definition no longer present. "No historian can go down into the past like a deep sea diver to describe what he sees," Chaim Perelman writes in one of his fine essays on historical and legal argumentation. "We can know the past only from the traces of it that remain."[19] It is impossible, therefore, to evaluate different narratives of the same occurrence or situation by comparing them with the occurrence or the situation they are supposed to represent. In fact, to the degree that the narratives actually construct the occurrence, it is probably not strictly correct to speak of the "same" occurrence. Peter Munz has described this position very effectively: "We can compare one clock to another clock, but we cannot compare any clock to time and it makes therefore no sense to ask which of the many clocks we have is *correct.* The same is true of any story, including historical narratives. We cannot glimpse at history. We can only compare one book with another book."[20] Munz still writes here of comparing different narratives, as did W. B. Gallie, one of the early narrativists: "The kind of explanation that I claim to be characteristic of histories cannot be confirmed, or even preferred against other possible explanations, except via the acceptability of the narrative which it enables the historian to reconstruct or resume. If the narrative has now been made consistent, plausible, and in accordance with all the evidence, it if is the best narrative that we can get, then the explanation that helped us to get to it is the best explanation as yet available."[21]

Although the criteria that Gallie advocates for comparing different narratives—internal consistency or "plausibility" and conformity "with all the evidence"—have not been universally accepted, the essential point remains that Gallie does not seek to deny either the possibility, in principle, of making comparisons or the fact that these comparisons have a bearing on the validity of historical narratives *as knowledge*.[22] The view that historical narratives cannot be measured against historical reality does not, for Gallie, make them incommensurable with one another. On the contrary, such narratives can only be evaluated by being compared with one another.

It is when the antirealism of the narrativists is complemented by a second claim—namely, that the shape of historical narratives is determined by rhetorical tropes—that historical narratives come to seem thoroughly incommensurable. Though few eighteenth-century historians or critics ever lost sight of the relation between rhetoric and history (Gibbon and Blair can both be usefully consulted on this point), and even certain nineteenth-century critics, like Sainte-Beuve, noted that historical narratives are much affected by literary and rhetorical patterns,[23] the systematic elaboration of a modern poetics of history has been principally the achievement of Hayden White. White's view is essentially that history is "ultimately determined by formal and rhetorical structures, most fundamentally the tropes of metaphor, metonymy, synecdoche, and irony, and that it can escape the impasse it now allegedly finds itself in only by ironic consciousness of its own formal nature, that is by accepting its similarity to fiction."[24] Distinguishing between different aspects of the narrative text of history ("chronicle," "story," "plot"), White argues that "the events reported in a novel [that is, the elements of what the Russian formalists refer to as "fable"] can be invented in a way that they cannot be (or are not supposed to be) in a history." Because of this, it is easier to distinguish "story" or "fable" from "plot" ("sjuzhet" or "subject" in the terminology of the formalists) in a work of history than in a literary fiction. For, "unlike the novelist, the historian confronts a veritable chaos of events already constituted, out of which he must choose the elements of the story he would tell. He makes his story by including some events and excluding others, by stressing some and subordinating others. This process of exclusion, stress, and subordination is carried out in the interest of constituting a story of a particular kind."[25]

Now if it is true that the historian simply *uses* materials haphazardly thrown together in a repository conventionally designated as history, in order to construct his narratives according to the same rules as the writer of fiction, then indeed different histories are incommensurable. To a narrativist like Gallie, historical narratives do propose an analysis of past reality based on historical materials, even if they cannot be held up and measured against that reality. From White's perspective, the historian is not even offering an analysis of past reality (even though the historian himself may not know this). The kind of understanding he provides is no different from that provided by the writer of fiction. Histories are thus incommensurable in the way that novels are. Two different accounts of what we conventionally designate as "the French Revolution" (but what is the French Revolution, the rhetorician would ask, except what it is figured as in the narratives that purport to "describe" or "analyze" it?)[26] are in fact simply two different stories, whose materials happen to have been selected from those usually placed in a bin marked "French Revolution." In a short essay written for George Iggers' and Harold Parker's *International Handbook of Historical Studies,* Louis Mink formulated the incommensurability argument with his customary force and clarity:

> If the cognitive content of written histories is in part exhibited in its form (over and above that part of its cognitive content which consists of the referential meaning of its factual statements), then it is difficult to see in what sense two different histories can be said to agree or to be incompatible with each other, since complex forms cannot be restated as propositional assertions, which alone can be comparable or incomparable. The response of what might be called the New Rhetorical Relativism in historiography to these considerations is that indeed narrative syntheses are cognitively incommensurable with each other.[27]

In a later essay Mink reaffirmed this assessment of the consequences of White's "poetics" of history. Though it contains relativism within the limits set by the four types of emplotment, Mink wrote, *Metahistory* "specifically rejects any possibility of a rational choice among them. Of course, something accounts for the historian's choice of one mode of emplotment rather than another, but what that choice expresses is both extra-historical and extra-philosophical; it represents an esthetic or political preference, as a matter of individual taste or commitment."[28]

Romantics and Positivists

The incommensurability argument has created few ripples among those who actually *do* history. In general, historians tend to go about their business casting only an occasional, indifferent glance in the direction of philosophers and literary critics. In this respect they are not very different from natural scientists. Many of them probably hold intuitively to some form of realism. I know of one brave effort to resurrect historical realism theoretically, but to the best of my knowledge it has found few takers.[29]

A more plausible defense of historical knowledge against the narrativist erosion of it has been attempted on the basis of the old distinction between historical writing and historical research. Leon Goldstein's *Historical Knowing* (1976) is interesting because it upholds the "scientific" character of historical research without being in any way committed to mimetic realism. On the contrary, Goldstein adopts a constructivist position: "As much as we may want to say that a true account of some past event is true in virtue of the fact that it accords with what actually took place when the past was present, we have no way to make that belief operative in historical research . . . What we know about the historical past we know only through its constitution in historical research, never by acquaintance."[30] The very choice of "knowing" rather than "knowledge" in the title of Goldstein's book suggests that history is more a way of knowing than a content of knowledge.

The relation of historical fact to historical evidence, Goldstein argues, is not one of inference: "Rather the historical occurrence is hypothesized in order to make sense of the evidence."[31] Goldstein is thus by no means a historical realist. "Historical knowing," he insists, "is a way of knowing not by acquaintance."[32] In conformity with this definition, Goldstein specifically excludes the material of memory from properly *historical* knowledge. Memories of lived experience, he maintains, including the testimonies and written narratives of historian-participants, must be treated as documents and evidence, not as authorities, and "they must be subject to the same sort of critical examination that a properly trained historian applies to all of his evidence."[33]

"Presence" is thus in no way an ideal for Goldstein. On the contrary: all knowledge, as he sees it, implies alienation. Goldstein's rejection of realism, which is no less radical than that of present-day narrativists, has nothing to do with narrativism, however. Indeed, if anything, it has been the partisans of narrative history, history *ad narrandum,* as advocated by the Romantics, in opposition to the intellectualist history *ad probandum* of the Enlightenment, who, in the past at least, have wanted to recreate the living reality of history in the reader's imagination, to *resurrect* it, in Michelet's phrase. According to many historians, the function of the story in history and the special gift of the great history teacher are precisely that—to reawaken the dead, make the past speak, and put the reader or listener in its living presence.[34] Admittedly, such a claim is not compatible with modern narrativist theories. The foundation of Romantic historiography was not a rhetoric but a metaphysics, a philosophy of universal analogy, according to which the mind can grasp the world, the self the other, because they are structured in the same way. To the Romantic historian, the imagination provided a true insight into the nature of historical reality, and it was this insight that made it possible to select, group, and interpret evidence. The modern narrativist espouses no such philosophy; no claim to provide true knowledge, in the sense of "corresponding to historical reality," is made for history as he describes it.

Nevertheless, it is worth noting the explicitly anticritical, anti-Enlightenment ideological stance of many of the former partisans of history *ad narrandum,* among whom one must count not only Ranke but his wayward pupil Burckhardt.[35] To the nineteenth-century historicists, the function of history was not to establish a critical and ironical distance between the present and the past, but to reconcile them and reestablish continuity between them. The famous phrase, not often quoted in full, in which Ranke disclaims any ambition to treat history in Enlightenment style as *magistra vitae*—"The task of judging the past and instructing the present for the benefit of the future has been ascribed to history: the present essay does not aspire to such high office: it aims only to show what actually happened"—may be slightly disingenuous in the way it presents narrative continuity, and thereby the continuity of history, as somehow self-evident, simple, and unreflected, in contrast to the artificial and contrived nature of the "lessons" that the Enlightenment historians sought to draw from the facts.[36] Different as they are from their Romantic predecessors, many modern versions of narrativism continue the Romantic opposition to the rationalist, "scientific," or nomothetic ideal of historical study that was common to Enlightenment scholars such as Malthus, Süssmilch, or John Millar, and extend it to the revised versions of that ideal that survive among Marxists as well as positivists.

At any rate, it is on the basis of a rejection of historical realism, which he shares with modern narrativists, that Goldstein proceeds to build a case for history as an investigative activity, a method of establishing what he likes to call "the historical record," rather than an imaginative or poetic activity, a way of arranging "materials" in a meaningful order. The essential task of history for him is research, not writing: it concerns the establishing of facts, not meanings. Goldstein would reject out of hand White's often repeated assertion that all history is philosophy of history.

Yet the two views of history, that defended by Goldstein and that defended by the narrativists, do not so much exclude each other as divide the territory of history between them. While the narrativists concern themselves with the way historical narratives shape the "raw materials" of history into configurations or stories and thus create and communicate meaning (in other words, with *Auffassung* and *Darstellung,* the third and fourth stages respectively in Ernst Bernheim's classic *Lehrbuch der historischen Methode* of 1889), those who emphasize historical scholarship concentrate on the "logic of discovery" (*Heuristik* and *Kritik*) and leave the writing of historical narratives out of account as a matter of aesthetics or ideology.

Thus, on the one hand, Hayden White concentrates on "historians and philosophers of distinctively classic achievement, those who still serve as recognized models of possible ways of conceiving history." The status of these writers as possible models of representation, he explains,

> does not depend upon the nature of the "data" they used to support their generalizations or the theories they invoked to explain them; it depends rather on the consistency, coherence, and illuminative power of their respective visions of the historical field. This is why they cannot be "refuted," or their generalizations "disconfirmed," either by appeal to new data that might be turned up in subsequent research or by the elaboration of a new theory for interpreting the sets of events that comprise their objects of representation and analysis. Their status as models of historical narration and conceptualization depends, ultimately, on the preconceptual and specifically poetic nature of their perspectives on history and its processes.[37]

On the other hand, Goldstein dismisses the narrative part of history disparagingly as mere superstructure, icing on the cake—"that part of the historical enterprise which is visible to nonhistorian consumers of what historians produce."[38] Strikingly, however, he seems not in disagreement with those who claim that historical narrative is subject to unchanging rhetorical categories, by which it is *prefigured:* "The superstructure has had comparatively little history . . .We find a greater similarity between the way historical accounts were constructed in antiquity and the way such things were done in the later periods than between, say, the science of the Greeks, that of the Renaissance, and that of our own times."[39] To the degree that history is a science that has developed its techniques and expanded its field of investigation, then, it is one at the level of what

Goldstein calls its infrastructure—"that range of intellectual activities whereby the historical past is constituted in historical research." It is at this infrastructural level that there has been an expansion and refinement comparable to that which has occurred in the natural sciences: "The very . . . domain of historical evidence has been expanded from the reports of eyewitnesses, to which the ancient historians were largely limited, to the wide variety of things from which present-day historians have learned to extract such a variety of historical truth."[40]

Certain features of Goldstein's point of view would no doubt have been approved by the pioneers of modern historiography. To Marc Bloch, it will be remembered, history had "grown old in embryo as mere narrative" and had only just emerged as a "newcomer in the field of rational knowledge." Bloch placed his hopes for history as "a science in its infancy" in the expansion both of the range of evidence available to the historian and of the techniques for "cross-questioning" it. For Bloch appears to have believed, like Goldstein, that the application of new evidence and of new techniques of analysis, themselves borrowed from burgeoning new human sciences such as economics and demography, would ensure the "progress" of historical science. "Our history need be no more like that of Hecataeus of Miletus than the physics of Lord Kelvin or Langevin is like that of Aristotle."[41] Until recently at least, the same optimism motivated many of the leading figures of the *Annales* school.[42]

Between these two distinct views of what constitutes the work of history, there is thus a surprising measure of agreement. Rejecting narrative as inessential to the historical enterprise, Goldstein contends that narrative autonomy, the cognitive incommensurability of different historical narratives, is inseparable from the narrativist position. Gallie's view that we prefer one historical explanation to another because the narrative it enables us to construct seems more "acceptable," more "consistent, plausible, and in accordance with the evidence" than competing narratives, is judged insufficient. Goldstein comments severely:

> That the narrative must be "in accordance with all the evidence" is something anyone who chooses to write about history is expected to say, but it is not easy to determine from the passage— or from the book from which it is taken—how the nature of historical evidence functions in Gallie's thinking about history. But this apart, the words that tell . . . in our present context are those which proclaim that no explanation in a work of history may "be preferred against any other possible explanations." The reason for so striking a position is that, in Gallie's view, what

determines or motivates any explanation is the role it plays in the narrative account in which it appears. Each narrative, having been produced in isolation from any other purporting to deal with the same theme, contains nothing that may be understood as in conflict with—or in any other way related to—narratives produced by other writers. Each work of history is to be judged only with reference to its own coherence and in isolation from everything else.[43]

According to Goldstein, the incommensurability thesis is exactly what makes at least the more radical forms of the narrativist thesis, however consistent, unacceptable as an account of what historians do and what history is about. Historians do agree, disagree, and debate, he maintains, and the working out of their differences is an essential moment in their constitution of the "historical record." The kind of agreement and disagreement he is interested in, however, is not that which "has to do with such matters as the significance of some course of events or the ways in which some historical occurrence is to be interpreted"; it is not the kind of disagreement that "takes place during that phase of [the historian's] work which follows the stage at which the historical past is being constituted." Such disagreements may well tell us "about the character of the intellectual climate within which debate among historians takes place, about the ideological conflicts of the time, and about unresolved issues of theoretical social science. But they do not tell us anything about history qua that practiced discipline of which the purpose is to constitute the historical past."[44]

The disagreements that interest Goldstein are those that occur not at the level of large-scale interpretations of the meaning of events, but at the lower level at which historians try to determine "what different parts of the past must be like given the evidence."[45] At this level—that of the "facts" of history, of what he himself refers to as "the historical record"—he insists both on the fact of disagreement and on the possibility of resolving it. The fact of disagreement underscores his contention that history is the product of research and discussion of evidence, not of a direct and incontrovertible vision of reality, and that "rather than confront [the *real* past], the historian constitutes the *historical* past." The disagreement of historians, in short, cannot be resolved by confronting their testimonies with the real past. On the contrary, "if the real past played any sort of role at all, then the sort of disagreement we are considering could not be possible."[46]

On the other hand, the possibility of reaching agreement, even if only provisionally, serves to confirm Goldstein's basic contention that much historical disagreement is of a scholarly or scientific, nonideological kind: it concerns the evaluation and working up of evidence, according to "methods and techniques generally agreed to." That is "what enables us to expect that, in the course of time, disagreements may be overcome and some tradition of scholarship established."[47] When we consider history as a professional discipline, the specter of skepticism is conjured. For Goldstein, disagreement in historical scholarship is similar to disagreement in the physical sciences: it has a dynamic rather than a static character, guaranteeing both the reality and meaningfulness of research, dialogue, and exchange, and the impossibility of ever finding a definitive answer that can be checked against "reality."

To a narrativist like Hayden White, in contrast, disagreement among historians is less the sign of a lively, ongoing process of communication and criticism in a common endeavor, as in the physical sciences, than an absolute condition. "The physical sciences," he writes, "appear to progress by virtue of the agreements reached from time to time among members of the established communities of scientists, regarding what will count as a scientific problem, the form that a scientific explanation must take, and the kinds of data that will be permitted to count as evidence in a properly scientific account of reality. Among historians, no such agreement exists, or ever has existed."[48]

One of Goldstein's illustrations of agreement having been reached and the historical record established tells a lot about the kind of problem he has in mind and the kind of solution he envisages. It concerns the deciphering of cuneiform by Sir Henry Rawlinson in the last century. Goldstein quotes from the memoir of Rawlinson written by his son:

> From the ruins of a temple at Kileh Shergat, where researches were still being pursued, was exhumed a clay cylinder which "turned out to be a most valuable relic." It contained the annals of the first Tiglath-Pileser, a document of great length, belonging to a monarch anterior to the time of David in Israel, and by far the oldest historical inscription which had, up to that time, been discovered in the country. The cylinder reached Colonel Rawlinson in a very bad state, broken into fragments and in some parts pulverized. Colonel Rawlinson, however, succeeded in uniting the fragments with a composition of gum-water and powdered chalk, and obtained a copy of the entire inscription

(with the exception of a few paragraphs), above 800 lines in length—a copy afterwards verified by duplicate cylinders, procured from the same mound, and in an almost perfect state of preservation. It was this inscription which afterwards played so important a part in the general verification of cuneiform interpretations, being simultaneously submitted for translation to the four chief experts, Sir Henry Rawlinson, Dr. E. Hincks, Dr. Jules Oppert, and Mr. Fox Talbot, who severally, without any communication, produced renderings which were substantially identical.

Goldstein makes two observations on this passage. First, it allows us to appreciate Rawlinson's formidable command of Akkadian. For the task he confronted was far harder than the already difficult one of fitting together the pieces of a jigsaw puzzle, when one has no antecedent idea of the picture they are supposed to form after they have been reassembled. Since many of the fragments were not clearly cut but worn, damaged, and incomplete, only his knowledge of the language enabled Rawlinson to bring off the reconstruction of the cylinder. Second, and more important, it was the coherence of the several translations that gave credibility both to the assumption that scratch-like marks on old baked clay were really human language and to the claim that some individuals had in fact learned to read that language.

What the Rawlinson case shows above all, for Goldstein, is both the inappropriateness of historical realism and the crucial importance of the commensurability of historical explanations. The realist would say that the cuneiform text is rendered accurately only if the scholar's present understanding of it accords with what the ancients who wrote it intended to express, just as the realist historian would claim that only an account of events that accords with the reality of the past is accurate. But such conformity cannot be realized either in the case of historical texts or in that of historical events. Goldstein maintains—and the point of the story and of the experiment it recounts is to have shown—

> that we are confident that we have arrived at a notable degree of historical truth when those members of the historical community engaged in research on the subject in question reach a level of agreement . . . The plausibility that accrues [to history] accrues to it, not because the results of its researches may be shown to satisfy the correspondence theory of truth . . . but rather . . . from the fact that many different scholars, by applying

the techniques of the discipline to the body of so-called historical evidence, which in no way resembles events or historical facts, are able to achieve as broad an agreement as they actually have.[49]

The truth we can expect to achieve in history is thus similar to the kind of truth we get from an autopsy or an investigation of an air crash.[50]

In the last few years, my work on the maverick nineteenth-century classical scholar J. J. Bachofen has made me increasingly aware of a disturbing kinship between many modern (or postmodern) orthodoxies and the ideologies of the revolutionary Right. I am now concerned that the current tendency to conflate "historical" and "fictional" narrative and the new emphasis on the "poetics" of history—which I once welcomed as a salutary release from the smug certainties of historical positivism—may be promoting a facile and irresponsible relativism which will leave many who espouse it defenseless before the most dangerous myths and ideologies, incapable of justifying any stand. Gradually, I have begun to feel more sympathy with the point of view represented by scholars like Goldstein, who—as I read them, at any rate—are trying to rehabilitate rationality and due process as essential moments of all our intellectual enterprises, without retreating to traditional metaphysical realism. Goldstein complains that "when philosophers discuss the problem of relativism in history . . . they are likely to talk about the ways in which the ideological orientations or commitment to values, from which there is no way to extricate the historian, lead to that state of affairs. But what we do not find are systematic discussions of the character of disagreement in history of the sort that would tend to illuminate the practice of history."[51] I find this remark well taken. I am uncomfortable, however, with Goldstein's sharp distinction between infrastructure and superstructure in history, and with his abandonment of the latter to ideology and aesthetic preference. I do not believe the problems of historical scholarship can or should be so neatly distinguished from those of historical narrative.

What gives me pause in Goldstein's position is that his dichotomy of historical narrative and historical scholarship reflects and reinforces the well-known division in philosophy between the existentialist emphasis on praxis and the positivist emphasis on reason. As Hans Albert observes, these two philosophical orientations rest on a shared view of the world; they "differ hardly at all on the dichotomy between knowledge and decision, but adopt radically different points of view in their evaluation of it." Whereas one underlines the freedom, indeterminacy, and irrationality of decision and dismisses scientific knowledge as uninteresting precisely because of its objectivity, the other emphasizes the foundability and rational character of knowledge and dismisses decision and commitment as subjective, arbitrary, philosophically uninteresting.

> One side seeks to eradicate objective knowledge because it allegedly fails to make contact with existence; the other seeks to avoid subjective decision because it appears to lie outside the sphere of rationality. However little they may have to say to one another, it is nevertheless clear that both movements start to some extent from common presuppositions. Both opt for a view in which rationality and existence part company, but one emphasizes the rational analysis of facts, while the other glorifies irrational existential decisions. Both are inclined toward a *facticist* conception of knowledge . . . Similarly both incline toward a *decisionist* treatment of value problems . . . Any discussion between these two trends seems not merely unnecessary—since they have no need to dispute about the presuppositions they share—but actually impossible, because each party, by virtue of this shared ground, is obliged to concede to the other a sphere of influence that its own methods render inaccessible—the sphere either of "pure" fact or of "pure" decision.[52]

The modern opposition was already foreshadowed in a division between the empirical fact-gatherer and the theoretical or speculative thinker, the *érudit* and the *philosophe,* that seems to be as old as modern historiography—or modern science—itself, though of course the terms and the context of that earlier division were different from those in which the positivist was later pitted against the existentialist. By the middle of the eighteenth century the division between "facts" and "reasonings" had led to skepticism about all historical knowledge based on traditional historical narratives, including those of the Ancients, and to the view, expressed on many occasions by Voltaire, d'Alembert, and Rousseau, that those traditional narratives are to be regarded as moral or political fables, whose value or "moral truth" is independent of their "factual truth." The truth of historical narratives which in the medieval period had been on the whole internally a figurative and religious one and externally a matter of authority (a true story was one that was founded on an authoritative text) was now perceived as largely intelligible and philosophical.[53] In this respect it was no different from the truth of fictional narratives. "History is only a longer *conte,*" as Voltaire's friend Cideville once declared.[54]

The work of Montesquieu and his disciples—among them nearly all the Scottish economic and social historians—marked an attempt to reunite scholarship and philosophy, empirical research and theoretical reflection. As Gibbon observed, Montesquieu had shown how the dross of erudition could be turned into history, and the study of facts reconciled with the activity of reason.[55] The Romantics, however, rejected Montesquieu's mechanistic model of historical explanation (and along with it the metaphors he liked to draw from mechanics and hydraulics) in favor of an organicist one. Individual facts were revealed as rational and intelligible not by demonstrating their *lawfulness* in terms of a system of causes and effects (that is, deriving the laws of history and society from facts, and, in turn, testing these laws against the facts) but by discovering their *meaningfulness* as parts of a larger whole, at once figures of the whole of human history and moments in the process of its unveiling or revelation.

But the Romantic vision of history as a kind of sacred text to be interpreted by the methods of hermeneutic has proved no better able to effect a lasting reconciliation of research with narrative and of the individual fact with its meaning than could the Enlightenment vision of history as a kind of machine to be understood by the methods of science. The danger for the Romantics, who always emphasized the quasi-divinatory powers needed by the historian in his work of decipherment, was that they would see too precipitously behind the fact to its meaning and that the meaning would overwhelm the fact. It was only to be expected that the rights of fact would be reasserted at some point, even at the expense of meaning, in a new positivism.[56]

One cannot but be struck by the survival power of the division of historiography into the production of solid bricks by those one might be tempted to term the respectable bourgeois of the profession and the deployment of those bricks by "inspired" artists to create beautiful and seductive palaces of interpretation. In one of the most recent defenses of narrativism the Dutch philosopher F. R. Ankersmit, referrring in particular to Huizinga, recalls that in German and Dutch philosophy of history,

a distinction is often made between "geschiedsvorsing" and "geschiedschrijving," i.e. between "historical research" and the "narrative writing of history." The term "historical research" refers to the historian's desire to establish the facts of the historical process with a maximum of exactitude. When the historian does his research well we can compare him with Collingwood's well-known detective who wishes to find the murderer of John Doe: he wants to know what actually happened, who did or wrote what, how texts should be interpreted and so on. A number of "auxiliary sciences" (of which modern socio-economic history is the most conspicuous) have been evolved to assist the historian in his attempt to establish the facts. But a historian is essentially more than a "fact-finder" or a detective. Getting to know the facts is only a preliminary phase in the task he sets himself. For his real problem is how to integrate these facts into a consistent historical narrative.[57]

While an excessively sharp line should not be drawn between the two aspects of history, Ankersmit explains, facts being "generally only looked for and described within a specific frame of narrative interpretation,"[58] historical practice itself argues against those who deny the distinction altogether. There are in fact historians who are predominantly research historians and others who are predominantly interpretative historians.[59] Ankersmit concludes that the two activities of research and interpretation or writing have distinct philosophies that account for what they do. To investigate how historical events come to be established is not the province of "narrativist philosophy." That, he says, is "the department of the philosophy of historical research," adding prudently that this "in no way commits narrative philosophy to the view that the historian is free to fabricate historical events."[60] Historical narratives are built up, in short, out of elements borrowed from a repertory of facts or events commonly recognized as historical thanks to the work of historical scholars.

Despite its obvious tenacity, the sharp division—essential to White's argument and to the incommensurability thesis—between historical research and the unstructured historical record on the one hand, and historical narrative on the other, between "facts" and "meaning," "science" and "interpretation," what is found and what is created by a poetic act, is not something simple or obvious. It is both historically located, as I have tried to suggest, and itself a philosophical position, as White's best and most astute critics have not failed to observe. The general thrust of their criticism, if I read them correctly, is that White's absorption of history into literature leaves intact, indeed depends on, a more fundamental and traditional distinction—which White himself never questions but which his critics wish to challenge—between literary or poetic language and "literal" or scientific language.[61] Because it is believed to be purely referential, the latter is not considered subject to the elaborate formal analyses that the critic makes of the former. "White's typology is only apparently formal," Suzanne Gearhart contends. "Underlying its fourfold categorization is an opposition between figurative and literal language, and any distinctions between the various forms are ultimately of secondary importance next to this master opposition between language that is essentially formal in nature and language that is essentially referential and, as a result, cannot be subjected to formal analysis." Moreover, Gearhart adds, in an extension of an argument that has often been applied to the literary genres, the tropes themselves were not laid up in heaven.[62] Wilda Anderson expresses the central objection of White's younger critics succinctly when she charges that White's metahistorical model depends on a nondiscursive and nonhistorical definition of knowledge.[63]

History as Product and as Process

History was perceived by the Romantics as a divine text of which the historian was to serve as the faithful interpreter.[64] Hayden White's view of criticism and interpretation is more modern: for him the interpreter is a creator, a poet in his own right, and he implicitly rejects—as do many contemporary literary critics—the rigid, ultimately theologically grounded distinction between poet and critic, the divine Author of history and the historian as His faithful interpreter. Nevertheless, his view of historiography remains firmly text-oriented, and his emphasis has always been, as he himself puts it, on "the great historical classics," on "historians and philosophers of distinctively classic achievement."[65] But to place the emphasis there is surely to prejudge the issue. History inevitably becomes subject to literary categories of analysis the moment the decision is taken to consider it in its classic texts, that is to say in a select body of timeless, finished verbal structures that can be and have been evacuated from the ongoing processes of which they were once part and kicked upstairs, as it were, to permanent seats in historiography's House of Lords.[66] From this classical perspective, historical narratives are of course incommensurate, and even in a sense beyond judgment. They are to be studied, admired, interpreted, and, if possible, imitated.

Compared with historical texts, the processes by which historical knowledge is produced, established, criticized, and transformed are not well understood and have not been much studied. Perhaps more attention needs to be paid to the preparation of articles and position papers and the way these are modified in response to the criticisms of colleagues and editors, to professional debate at colloquia and in the scholarly journals, to the vast literature of reviews and the exchanges they quite often provoke, to more or less formally concerted programs of research that have been stimulated by a challenging and innovative narrative.[67]

In several years of service on the editorial board of two university presses, I have been impressed by the effect that the process of review of a manuscript can have on the final published version. Arguments may be changed, chapters shifted around, entire segments dropped and others added, the organization of a work completely redesigned in response to the often surprisingly detailed criticisms of press readers. I am not talking about minor cosmetic changes, or changes intended to communicate the initial argument more effectively, though these are obviously the most frequent; I am talking about truly substantive changes which significantly alter the character of the original manuscript as first submitted. In response to what, I wonder, are such changes made? How is one brought to adopt a perspective one has hitherto rejected, to "see" a configuration that one did not see before, and to substitute this new configuration for an earlier one? Is it pressure, the fear of being isolated professionally, the desire to maintain or acquire professional standing? How, to put the matter in a nutshell, does one change one's mind? Are there *reasons* for doing so, or only causes and motives?

Let me advert for a moment to a humble case of mind-changing from my own experience. For several years I have been studying the society and culture of the Swiss city of Basle in the nineteenth century, having originally been intrigued by the fact that a small, oligarchic, and from most points of view anachronistic city-republic, wedged between France, Germany, and the other Swiss cantons, and governed for centuries by a politically conservative elite of some fifty merchant families, served as a sanctuary for intellectual dissidence and a focus of radical speculation in the second half of the nineteenth century. Largely under the influence of Goldmann's work on the seventeenth-century French Jansenists—and of Thomas Mann's *Buddenbrooks*—I had developed an elegiac narrative of a business class that was losing its grip and, because of that, found itself in tune with such critics of nineteenth-century progressivism as Burckhardt and Bachofen, Nietzsche and Franz Overbeck. This schema was, I now believe, full of flaws. But at the time I did not see them. On the contrary, for reasons I suspect were closely connected with my own personality and my own general feeling of political disillusionment, I was very attached to my schema and had invested it with a good deal of psychic energy. One day, Carl Schorske visited the seminar I was teaching on Basle and Berlin, in order to hear a paper by one of the students. In the course of the discussion that followed, Schorske, quite innocently, began to draw a picture of the Basle patriciate that was totally at odds with the one I had developed. Whereas I saw them clinging to old ways of doing business and falling behind economically and commercially, he presented them as feisty entrepreneurs with an eagle eye on the main chance. I still recall his referring to their respect for "smarts." I don't think a physical blow would have wounded me more. But soon, because of my respect for Schorske (we had taught the course together in a previous year), I began slowly and then with increasing momentum to look into the commercial habits and practices of the Basle businessmen. I read economic histories, company histories, histories of banking and of the silk and chemical industries, and I gradually came to the conclusion that Schorske was right, certainly more right than I had been. A new narrative gradually began to take shape in my mind. No doubt, if it is ever written, it will conform to one of the major tropes and will in that sense be subject to metahistory. But neither my ideology nor my aesthetic preferences, nor, I fear, my basic personality structure, changed much during the period I am talking about. So it does seem to me that it was the discovery of significant new evidence, provoked admittedly by an important psychic interaction with a senior scholar to whom I am very attached, that led me to revise my earlier pattern.

The way historians communicate with each other and criticize each other's work suggests that they do indeed expect their colleagues to be able to recognize the force of contrary arguments and narratives and to adjust their own accordingly—either by developing answers to these arguments or by revising their own. The remarkable study of slavery in the southern states by Robert Fogel and Stanley Engerman, *Time on the Cross*,[68] created a stir not only because it claimed to set a new standard in historical method through the use of quantitative data and analysis, but because it advanced, in addition, a striking thesis about slave society in the antebellum South—namely that, contrary to common opinion, the slave economy of the South on the eve of the Civil War was well-managed and profitable, that the slaves were anything but lazy, backward, and unteachable, and that the system as a whole provided the South (including the slaves themselves, in comparison with the European industrial proletariat) with a higher standard of living than was enjoyed in most European countries at the time. For both reasons—the originality of the method and the originality of the argument—*Time on the Cross* was carefully reviewed in a large number of professional journals: journals of history, southern history, black history, economic history, sociology, and so on. Anyone who takes the trouble to read even some of this critical literature cannot fail to be impressed by the very high standard of the discussion. But it is the character of the discussion that I want to emphasize here.

In keeping with their candidly acknowledged positivism,[69] Fogel and Engerman radicalize the common division of the historiographical text into the elegant continuous narrative above stairs and the nitty-gritty scholarship in the kitchen below by organizing their work in two separate volumes: one to present the thesis or narrative, the finished dish, and the other to display the evidence, the ingredients and processes, which went into producing it. The vigorous disapproval with which many historians reacted to this strategy suggests that the implications of such an extreme division between historical narrative or argument and historical scholarship were sensed and resisted by the profession.[70]

In fact, the criticisms of Fogel and Engerman address *all* aspects of their work, the narrative as well as the "findings." Both are obviously assumed to be subject to discussion, comparison, and evaluation on other than ideological or aesthetic grounds. The critics do duly point out both the polemical thrust of *Time on the Cross* and its ideological slant. The book seeks "to vindicate American blacks by defending them against three sorts of defamation"—to wit, that they are inferior racially; or were irreparably degraded and demoralized by the experience of slavery; or lack the kind of initiative and enterprise that other peoples have[71]—and to destroy "myths that turned diligent and efficient workers into lazy loafers and bunglers, that turned love of family into disregard for it, that turned those who struggled for self-improvement in the only way they could into 'Uncle Toms.' "[72] By trying to rehabilitate American blacks in this way, however, Fogel and Engerman are said to be expressing an ideological commitment to "the basic Smithian view that the search for profit via market exchange is a 'natural propensity' of humankind." Their revision of the traditional interpretation of slavery, which represented it as economically irrational behavior, can thus be read as an attempt to remove what was an anomaly from their point of view and thus to reconfirm their vision of the world.[73] As Gutman puts it, "Sambo, it turns out, was really a black Horatio Alger, made so by his owner, who was nothing more than a rational profit-maximizer." Thus both "the enslaved and their owners performed as actors and actresses in a drama written, directed, and produced by the 'free market.' "[74] Many of the reviewers—Paul David, Martin Duberman, Peter Temin, Herbert Gutman himself—make the point that Fogel and Engerman "save" the blacks only by integrating them into the mainstream of American culture.[75] Gutman reinforces this point when he proposes that *Time on the Cross* can be regarded as a belated contribution to the consensus historiography of the 1950s, in which the motif of conflict in American history was underplayed while greater emphasis was placed on the way political adversaries were often bound together by shared values. With Fogel and Engerman, Gutman argues, the synthesis is now stretched to include even the most recalcitrant element, the African-American.

The exposure of ideologically loaded assumptions and political and economic values is not, however, equivalent to a denunciation of such assumptions and values as totally irrational. On the contrary, it is an invitation to those who have them, in this case to Fogel and Engerman, to become cognizant of the fact that they do, and to justify them or reconsider them. It is only because assumptions are themselves in some measure at least discussable—that is, in the sense that a rational person ought to be accountable for his assumptions and values and to be able to defend them, if not to *demonstrate* them—that it is worth exposing them in public discussion of issues in the first place.

But the debate over *Time on the Cross* extended beyond basic ideological commitments. Reading the criticisms, one has the sense that a great deal of what historians do is in fact subject to fairly stringent criteria of evidence and reasoning, criteria acknowledged by the entire profession, whether it is being practiced in the West or in the East, by Marxists or conservatives, in rich countries or in poor ones. Gutman, for instance, proposes to ask "a variety of questions about the evidence and arguments in [*Time on the Cross*] . . . These questions," he claims,

> are appropriate to all historical works and to all sorts of historical evidence. Have the authors asked the right questions? Have the questions asked been answered properly? Have the right sources been used? Have the sources used been properly studied? Are there conceptual errors in the use of the sources? Are there errors in what quantitative historians call "executional computations"? Has the work of other historians on similar subjects been properly used? Have the arguments of other historians on similar subjects been properly summarized? How do the new findings measure against the published findings of other historians and against other sources not examined by the author? What is the relationship between "hard" empirical findings and speculative inferences and estimates?[76]

The criteria here are admittedly criteria of rightness and propriety, that is to say that they refer to the rules and codes established by a community, but that does not place them beyond rational discussion.

Gutman's debate with Fogel and Engerman ranges in fact from detailed questioning of their sources and their utilization of them to a much broader questioning of the model of socialization that they use in their study of the slave. I shall give only one example of innumerable detailed criticisms. It concerns the computation of the frequency of slave whippings, the basis of the claim by Fogel and Engerman that whipping was not a significant part of the slave system.[77] Using the diary kept by one plantation owner, well known for his belief that to spare the rod was to spoil the slave, they compute "an average of 0.7 whippings per hand per year." Gutman objects that "the wrong question has been asked." The average number of whippings per hand is not the essential figure; it does not measure the utility of the whip as an instrument of social and economic discipline. It is much more relevant to know how often the whip was used, and that "slave men and women were whipped frequently enough—whatever the size of the unit of ownership—to reveal to them (and to us) that whipping regularly served as a negative instrument of labor discipline."[78]

Gutman questions not only the way Fogel and Engerman used the material in Barrow's diary but their reading of it, and he argues plausibly that in fact the figure of 200 slaves on Barrow's plantation, the figure on which Fogel and Engerman based their computations, was arrived at by a series of erroneous assumptions and reasonings. It turns out that 129 is a more likely figure, so their averages are not only irrelevant, they are probably wrong. By throwing doubt on the data on which Fogel and Engerman constructed their narrative, Gutman threatens the validity of that narrative as history. No internal coherency or plausibility can save it. It may be a good story, and it may make a good point about life or human nature or whatever, but it will not pass as what it purports to be—a history of slavery in the antebellum South—unless Fogel and Engerman somehow reestablish the validity of the elements from which they have constructed it.

It is hard to tell, however, at what point the weakness of the component parts disqualifies a historical narrative irremediably. Some arguments or narratives can apparently stand a good deal of buffeting and erosion without collapsing. The various elements historical narratives are built up out of are obviously of varying structural importance. In his review of *Time on the Cross,* Gutman recognizes a distinction between technical flaws and structural weakness. Even "if the estimates were more accurate and the quantitative data examined more soundly, the model meant to explain slave beliefs and behavior would still be inadequate," he asserts.[79] For one thing, the narrow, exclusively economic explanations given by Fogel and Engerman may be necessary, but they are not sufficient.[80] But in addition, Gutman claims, in order to explain the beliefs and behavior of the slaves, Fogel and Engerman have used a flawed analytical model that goes back to the work of U. B. Phillips and Stanley Elkins, two scholars who are severely criticized in *Time on the Cross.* That model, in Gutman's words,

> views slave belief and behavior as little more than one or another response to planter-sponsored stimuli . . . More needs to be asked than the question Phillips posed. Simply changing the factors in the Phillips equation and, of course, rejecting his racial assumptions does not necessarily make for more truthful answers

or better social history. We need to know in close detail what enslavement did to Africans and then to their Afro-American descendants. But we shall never comprehend slave belief and behavior by just asking that question. We need also to ask what Africans and their Afro-American descendants did as slaves. That is a very different question and the answers to it are not the mirror-image of what owners did to slaves.[81]

Fogel and Engerman tell a very good story in my view. But Gutman's criticism of it is neither aesthetic nor by any means exclusively ideological: he believes that both the empirical scholarship and the explanatory model used are faulty, and that a *better story* could be told. This kind of criticism is such common practice among historians that it seems hardly necessary to have gone to such lengths to illustrate it. But if we want to understand what historians are doing, we must recognize the preponderant place such work occupies in their overall activity. Gutman's own book is also a work of history, although it is exclusively a rebuttal of Fogel and Engerman and is not itself a narrative. In this respect, it follows a model that was established at the very beginnings of modern historiography. The writing of Pierre Bayle, one of the founding fathers of modern historiography, was almost always critical, whether we think of his reviews in the *Nouvelles de la République des Lettres,* of the articles in the *Dictionnaire historique et critique,* or of more extended works like the *Critique de l'histoire de Maimbourg.* In this respect modern historiography may well stand closer, as has sometimes been observed, to the genre of literary criticism than to that of the epic or the novel.

Historians do apparently believe that there are procedures of verification and criteria for judging between different hypotheses and different narratives. They do constantly attend to the research of their colleagues to see whether it corroborates their own findings or not, and they build upon the results of the work of others both to modify hypotheses that they currently hold and to develop new hypotheses and new programs of research. Le Roy Ladurie, for instance, at one time used to take special pleasure in referring to theses and articles still unpublished that bore upon his own work and were in fact largely stimulated by it, as though to underscore the collective character of historical research. (That was in the days when the leading French historians were still optimistic about the scientific vocation of their discipline.) Fogel and Engerman also acknowledge receiving help in the writing of *Time on the Cross* from innumerable colleagues, including many whom they criticize (like Stampp) or were subsequently criticized by (like Gutman). The work of the modern historian is no solitary activity in which a person of imagination constructs a narrative to convey a certain vision and certain values, while paying a kind of ritual respect to the "conventions" of historiographical writing (such as checking on evidence and the like). That *might* have been the case in the eighteenth century—though even then pioneers like Malthus, Playfair, and Eden were outlining a different kind of historiography, one more indebted to Montesquieu and to Adam Smith than to Livy and Tacitus[82]—or in the early nineteenth century, especially in France, when history was not yet organized professionally and was still, as Monod remarked in the Preface to the first issue of the *Revue historique,* the product of individuals of genius. Clio and Calliope then still apparently retained something of that union with each other and with all their sister Muses which was supposedly their original condition, the division of labor among them and the attribution of specific and distinct functions to the individual Muses being a late invention, we are told, of rationalizing Hellenistic scholars and commentators.[83]

We do well to remember that our present disciplinary boundaries are neither necessary nor eternal. At the same time, there cannot really be any question of rejecting the differentiations and the specialized techniques and procedures of analysis that have been elaborated through the ages in order to make human knowledge and action in the world more effective. Such an ambition, as Stanley Fish pointed out in a recent defense of professionalism,[84] is comparable to the Romantic desire to leap back from language into some impossible immediacy of expression, untouched by collectively developed differentiations, definitions, and procedures. The differentiation of history from fiction, and of both from myth,[85] and, more recently, the professionalization of history have resulted in the elaboration of highly refined and carefully monitored methods of investigation. Every affirmation is now much more subject to scrutiny and control than in the age of traditional histories or the heady time of charismatic Romantic historiography. Fraud and shoddy application of research techniques are notions that are as real to historians as to physicists or chemists and are perceived by both groups as threats to the viability of their discipline. The writing (and rewriting) of histories is no longer, for the most part, a matter of adapting a fairly well established story line to a new language or rhetoric, or even of interpreting it in a new way, emplotting it differently, and thus expressing through it an ideology or a vision of the world. It is not just a matter of "decoding" and "recoding" a set of events that the historian simply comes upon as given and that have been established as a result of a totally autonomous operation,[86] even if such strategies are still followed in some branches of historiography.[87] It is also, perhaps primarily, a matter of discovering and responding to new professional and scientific exigencies, new kinds of questions, new evidence that either provokes new questions or has been turned up as a result of the invention of new questions, and it involves constant critical exchanges with colleagues.

In this respect history, it seems, is not radically different from other kinds of scientific inquiry. In *The Great Devonian Controversy* Martin Rudwick observes that historians of science have focused too much on the work of single individuals and have neglected the "complex web of social and cognitive interactions that bind even the most distinguished or reclusive scientist into his or her immediate network of colleagues, in collaboration, or rivalry, or both." The Devonian controversy in nineteenth-century geology "displays the processes of scientific knowledge making as ineluctably and intrinsically social in character, not (or not primarily) in the sense of the pressures of the wider social world, but in the sense of intense social interaction among a small group of participants. But it also shows," Rudwick adds, "that the knowledge produced through this interaction is not 'merely' a social construction, and that the concrete natural world does have an identifiable input, constraining though not determining the eventual outcome of the research." In the particular instance of scientific "knowledge making" that he studied, Rudwick claims that "while the 'Devonian' case was argued out in courtrooms such as the Geological Society by the persuasive advocacy of major participants [and Rudwick emphasizes the rhetorical element in *all* scientific reasoning], other competent geologists, who in effect constituted the jury in the case, were not swayed into a consensual verdict only by the rhetorical skills of those presenting one side of the case, still less by being bribed out of court by promises of advancement in their careers . . . What swayed them was the combination of rhetoric and evidence, persuasive argument and *pièces justificatives*. Like a court of law, and unlike, for example, a debating society, the geologists were concerned not with evaluating rhetorical performance but with reaching a justifiable conclusion about concrete past events in a real world." Rudwick adds this important comment: "Significantly, both sides were obliged to shift their position during the protracted hearing, in response to the other's arguments and evidence, and the final verdict was based on a case that neither side had anticipated when the hearing began."[88]

Modern historiography, like modern science, is a professionalized and regulated activity in which no individual can any longer imagine that he or she works alone or enjoys a special relation to the past. In this respect it differs from neoclassical or Romantic historiography. On the whole, I believe this state of affairs is a good one. Every historian is now answerable for his statements and his stories to well-informed, critical peers, like a citizen in some ideal democracy. Prophetic utterances and the manipulation of feelings and opinions are disapproved, and failure to observe established procedures results in loss of credibility.

It is sometimes said that professionalism resembles a democracy less than it resembles a bureaucracy, that it encourages routinized scholarship, fear of intellectual independence and risk-taking, and even the avoidance of criticism itself. A conservative desire to maintain the system replaces the adventurous spirit of the pioneers of the discipline. This is an important objection. The chief advantage of professionalism is that it ensures responsibility and accountability, opens everything up to critical inspection, and promotes continuity and commonality of research and knowledge, among specialists at least. That advantage would be dearly purchased if it involved the repression of initiative and imagination. A deadening uniformity might even lead to a recrudescence of prophetism, as the imagination, excluded from the channels of professional discourse, assumes an aggressively anticritical rather than simply noncritical or precritical stance. It is essential, therefore, that space be reserved within any professional system for speculation and experiment, even for ideas that challenge the most widely shared and well-established doctrines, and that a fair and genuine hearing be granted to even those views that put in question the efficacy of the very programs by which competing arguments are rationally sifted and compared—that the system, in short, allow and provide for its own renewal. It is probably not possible to ensure the preservation of such free spaces in a profession, or in a society, by legislation alone: much will depend on the good will, vigilance, and commitment to freedom of the members of the profession themselves. And just as civil liberty, in social life, permits the expression of ideas and opinions that the majority judges "outrageous" and that command only a limited audience, professional freedom should leave room for unorthodox or "crackpot" ideas that are not widely attended to. It might be objected that marginalization of the unorthodox is the preferred technique of an ostensibly liberal profession which cannot openly repress challenges to dominant beliefs. As long as liberty of expression is guaranteed, however, unorthodox ideas have as good a chance of getting a hearing as it is possible to provide. It is up to the proponents of such ideas to make a good case for them, and it is up to the practitioners of history to maintain an open mind in judging whether they are worth entertaining or pursuing. There is no reason to believe that the commitment of the professionals to the received opinion of the profession is greater than their commitment to the intellectual discipline they pursue. Challenges to received opinion have been made in the past, and many new and disturbing ideas have overcome the objections they provoked to become, in turn, widely accepted.

The question that the critics of professionalism are asking may be a more far-reaching one. They may be asking whether professionally regulated languages of communication are capable of change; whether the professionals can recognize the merit and interest of ideas, concepts, categories that challenge their institutionalized discourse and require a considerable, even a wholesale, revision of it; and whether such change can occur for "reasons," that is, according to the norms of the system or discipline itself. For if "reasons" can only be defined in terms of the system they ultimately sustain, how can they ever effectively challenge it? Such questions are by no means restricted to the historical profession; they directly concern any science, as we have learned from scholars like Popper and Kuhn, Lakatos and Feyerabend. The commensurability of historical narratives is a more restricted problem, however, which can probably be answered *within* the terms of a given intellectual practice. Comparing two narratives of the French Revolution is more like comparing two theories of matter than comparing the modern "scientific" understanding of nature with the knowledge of nature and the practices used to affect it in another culture. There may be, in other words—indeed there are—different conceptions of history and different practices of historiography from those that have established themselves in the modern West. The question is only whether, within our present professional framework, it makes sense to compare different historical narratives and whether there are rational grounds for preferring one to another.

The Rationality of Historical Argument

The problem we have now returned to is the one defined earlier as "changing one's mind" or, on a larger scale, changing a story or a professional paradigm within a context in which truth, in the sense of some correspondence between ideas and reality, or propositions and facts, can never be demonstrated. What are the processes by which that change occurs? Is there any rationality about them, or are they arbitrary, a matter of fashion or desire or ideology? As Ian Hacking put it not long ago in a review of some essays by Thomas Kuhn, if the structure of our science, whether physical or social, "is ultimately a human creation and we populate a world which is partly an artifact of human discourse, then it is less than clear what makes theory-choice 'objective.' "[89] If "objective" here means ontologically founded, then I am not sure how it can be demonstrated that theory-choice is objective. If, however, "objective" has a more modest meaning—something like rationally justifiable or defensible, not arbitrary, open to criticism—then there may be some hope for objectivity.

To find a middle ground between absolute truth (metaphysical and logical truth based on correspondence with "reality" or internal coherency and systematicity) and irrational arbitrariness or "decisionism," as the German philosophers say (truth as a product and instrument of will, desire, interest), to mark out, in other words, a territory appropriate to what human beings can realistically achieve in the matter of scientific objectivity, seems to be the principal aim of Stephen Toulmin's *Human Understanding*. The first volume of this work (the only one to appear so far) is an extended argument, largely directed against Collingwood and Kuhn, in favor of the continuity of the practice of science as a discipline and of the reality of communication among different theoretical positions.[90] Toulmin holds that we "can no longer afford to assume"—as both absolutists like Frege and relativists like Collingwood allegedly do—that our rational procedures, if they are to be impartial, must "find a guarantee in *unchanging principles* mandatory on all rational thinkers." We should reject, in his view, "the commitment to logical systematicity which makes absolutism and relativism appear the only alternatives available." Toulmin suggests that we redirect our attention instead from arguments or explanations considered as formal structures in themselves to "explanatory activities and procedures . . . other than those which involve appeal to formal, demonstrative arguments."

A scientific practice, as he proposes that we understand it, is "transmitted from one generation of scientists to the next by a process of *enculturation*, . . . an apprenticeship, by which certain explanatory skills are transferred, with or without modification, from the senior generation to the junior." The rationality of a science, consequently, is not embodied in the specific intellectual doctrines that are adopted at any given time by individual practitioners or by a professional group as a whole; it is related rather to *"the conditions on which, and the manner in which,* [an individual or a group] *is prepared to criticize and change those doctrines as time goes on,"* to the procedures that allow for discovery and conceptual change through time. The specific character of scientific doctrines, as opposed to ideologies or religious beliefs, for instance, is that they are "historically developing 'rational enterprises' . . . committed to their own self-transformation."[91] The ability to change one's mind for *good reasons* thus becomes for Toulmin the very criterion of rationality: "We judge the rationality of a man's conduct by considering, not how he habitually behaves, but rather how far he modifies his behavior in new and unfamiliar situations, and it is arguable that the rationality of intellectual performances should be judged, correspondingly, not by the internal consistency of a man's habitual concepts and beliefs, but rather by the manner in which he modifies this intellectual position in the face of new and unforeseen experiences."[92] The distinction between rationality and irrationality, in other words, is a methodical, not a foundational, distinction, and as such it must have reference to practice and find its proper place *within* the sphere of evaluation and decision.

Although history may still be only a "would-be discipline" in Toulmin's terms,[93] it does seem to be more organized both theoretically and institutionally than it was even a hundred years ago. Techniques of discovery and analysis are constantly being expanded and refined, and many of the changes win acceptance regardless of ideological allegiances. "Historical judgments," one contemporary historian has said, whether they take the form of narratives or typological constructs, "are *intersubjectively understandable*. [They] are also *intersubjectively verifiable*." Thus it is possible to formulate a number of questions that all historians will ask as part of the verification of a given hypothesis, such as "(a) to what extent relevant sources have been utilized and the present state of research has been taken into consideration, (b) how close these historical judgments have come to reaching an optimum plausible integration of all available historical data, and (c) how logically rigorous the explanatory models underlying them are, that is, how consistent those models are and whether they are free of self-contradictions." If these conditions are met—or come reasonably close to being met—the system of historical judgments in question will be considered not only "intersubjectively plausible but also 'correct,' though only in terms both of its presuppositions and its methodological appoach."

These standards of historical judgment, Wolfgang Mommsen claims, constitute a framework within which it is possible to speak of a "progress" of scholarly knowledge. To the degree that historians subscribe to the standards, they create the possibility of free exchange of information and sustained critical evaluation of historical judgments across social and ideological lines. In the course of time, a body of historical knowledge about certain subjects can be expected to arise that is well established and universally accepted.[94]

Mommsen does not answer the question: At what point does empirical counter-evidence refute a theory or invalidate a narrative? How much and what kind of evidence are required? I noted earlier that Hayden White considers the great historical narratives to be impervious to empirical data on the ground that their truth lies in their systematicity or internal coherency (which is not affected by the truth or otherwise of their individual referential statements) and in the vision of the world that—like great works of literature—they propose or stimulate in successive generations of readers. But even among those who, like myself, would wish to place historical narrative closer to scientific theories than White would allow, only a few diehards would want to contest nowadays that the relation of theory to "facts" or "observations" is by no means a simple one. A theory does not collapse simply because a number of "facts" have been discovered to be inconsistent with it. Indeed, Imre Lakatos argues the opposite. A good theory is one that is so designed that its core is virtually invulnerable to such observational refutation: "Purely negative, destructive criticism, like 'refutation' or demonstration of an 'inconsistency' does not eliminate a research programme. Criticism of a programme is a long and often frustrating process."[95] Falsification, in other words, is not the straightforward business some Popperians might have thought. Likewise, the fact that a hypothesis or program is discovered to rest on some questionable observations or data does not immediately disqualify it. The merits and fruitfulness of a hypothesis are not strictly dependent on the observations and data that may have given rise to it or been used initially to support it.

The same may perhaps be said, *mutatis mutandis,* of a historical hypothesis or argument. A case in point is David Abraham's book on the relation between the Nazi party and the German industrialists in the 1930s. The book was attacked by a distinguished professor at Yale on the grounds of inaccuracies and, as he charged, falsifications of evidence in the argument. (Something, incidentally, that is as threatening to scientists as to historians.) But Abraham's defenders, while acknowledging the shoddiness of his technical procedure in places and admitting the possibility of tendentiousness in certain allegedly inaccurate quotations from the archival materials, held that in the end the criticisms concerned relatively minor points and did not drastically affect the structure or validity of the book's argument. The criticisms thus damaged Abraham's authority and reputation as a historian far more seriously than his thesis itself.

To acknowledge that we do not well understand the relation between evidence and the theories or narratives it is used to sustain or refute does not require us to revert to the view that the facts are simply not relevant to the validity of the narrative, and that our grounds for preferring one narrative to another or for changing our minds are aesthetic preference or ideological commitment. It does require that we address the problem honestly and that we try to understand how and in what conditions a theory comes to seem more or less plausible. Is the significant factor the capacity or incapacity of a theory to account for accepted facts—in Popperian terms, to resolve conflict between accepted theories and accepted basic statements? Or does our decision involve, as Lakatos would have it, a judgment as to which of several competing theories seems most capable of stimulating further research and creating new knowledge?

If we adopt Hayden White's position—namely, that the validity of the historical text lies in the vision of the world it proposes rather than in any merely factual knowledge or understanding it provides—then we also commit ourselves to the view that the two realms of fact and value, knowledge and decision or will, are distinct and uncommunicating. If, on the other hand, we adopt the second position—that there are rational grounds for preferring one theory to another, however difficult it may be to describe precisely how the process of persuasion works—we are committed to no such assumption. On the contrary, no radical distinction, no breach of continuity is assumed between knowledge and decision. Thus, according to Hans Albert, the process of cognition in science is "shot through with regulations, valuations, and decisions . . .We choose our problems, evaluate solutions to them, and decide to prefer one of the available solutions to others." In this way, "ultimately decisions lie 'behind' all knowledge." Similarly, Lakatos acknowledges that in adopting a theory or research program, a scientist *decides* to accept its hard core—that part of it which Lakatos describes as the "negative heuristic" because it is the part that may not be modified or altered. But if "knowledge as a whole seems to slip" as a result of this insight into the role played by decision, and "its objectivity to become questionable," so, conversely, does "the hitherto unanalyzed and unexplained equation of decision and arbitrariness—the thesis of the fundamental irrationality of all decision."[96] It becomes possible to consider whether value judgments themselves need be located entirely outside the realm of rationality. "It is true that one cannot without more ado deduce a value statement from a factual statement," Hans Albert— whose argument I have been following closely here—concedes. "But particular value judgments can certainly turn out to be incompatible with previously held value convictions in the light of a revised factual conviction."[97]

Mommsen's idea of how historical knowledge "progresses" and one account supplants another may not, in sum, be entirely adequate. Nevertheless, I have cited it as symptomatic of the professional historian's general notion of the enterprise he considers himself engaged in. And it is not any more inadequate than the notions some natural scientists entertain about the way their knowledge changes. What is worth noting is that it is the rationality of the historian's activity—"the constant 'feedback' process that subjects to examination the underlying hypotheses, theorems, and explanatory models, and finally results in a reexamination of the ide-

ological or social premises underlying these concepts"[98]—that for Mommsen defines historical thought and gives it its social significance and value.
History as a discipline, he argues, subjects prevalent historical assumptions
to rational analysis, and thereby tests the validity of the understanding
that social groups have of themselves. It is significant that this testing process is not dependent on the historian's own ideology, by which
Mommsen presumably means that though ideology may in part determine
the choice of the question to be analyzed, it does not determine the process
or the outcome of the analysis. Mommsen emphasizes that this clarifying
function does not make professional historiography a neoconservative instrument for filtering out extreme positions. "Scientific neutrality," in other
words, does not reduce the whole range of possible views to some golden
mean corresponding to liberal-democratic politics. Its aim is simply to
"work toward a clearer rational understanding of the positions themselves"
and ultimately "to show opposing social and political groups the way
toward pragmatic compromises and peaceful resolutions of conflict." History does this, according to Mommsen, "by creating better conditions for
maximum communication across ideological lines or, indeed, by first creating conditions of communication as such."[99] In this connection it is
worth recalling that the idea of mediating conflict through argument and
discussion presided over the very beginnings of modern historiography.
I quote from a recent book on Bayle:

> In Bayle and his contemporaries we can observe the emergence
> of a project that is the exact opposite of the one motivating
> contemporary thought. Our aim is to expose the manifestation
> of power and the confrontation of competing forces behind the
> notions of law, meaning, and truth. At that time, the object was
> to disengage knowledge from power struggles and to disarm the
> violence of confrontation by establishing a truth of fact that
> would dissipate the aggressiveness of the pronouncements bran-
> dished by the parties in conflict. For as soon as truth ceases to
> impose itself as an atemporal absolute, but is made subject to a
> series of mediations, all of which have to be scrupulously ex-
> amined, there is a displacement of the point at which it intervenes.
> More precisely, two types of truth are opposed: a truth of faith
> that demands total spiritual consent and adherence and may
> therefore exercise physical constraint on the recalcitrant; and a
> truth of fact, which, by situating the truth of faith inside history
> [that is, for Bayle, inside a historical *body* of texts] and considering

it as a simple question of fact, deprives it of its relation to the absolute and thereby of all right to exercise constraint.[100]

As a modern professional discipline, history, it seems to me, is deeply engaged in that process of rationalization and "disenchantment" that Weber considered "the fate of our times." As such it follows rules and procedures which appear to be distinct from those of artistic creation. In many respects, it seems that history's deepest affinity is to the law. In a review of two recent historical films—Edgar Reitz's *Heimat* and Claude Lanzmann's *Shoah*—in the *New York Review of Books,* Timothy Garton Ash emphasized the selectiveness of the memory that presided over the making of both works. In Reitz's case, the selective memory of his characters is integrated into his film as its very subject. Lanzmann, on the other hand, presents his film more explicitly as a work of history and thus raises in a more acute form the question of the relation between history and art. He acknowledges, for instance, that he threw out some of the hundreds of interviews he taped because the interviewees were "weak" as characters; and on one occasion he described his film tantalizingly as a "fiction of reality . . . made out of my own obsessions." In both films, but especially in Lanzmann's therefore, Ash discovers that the relation between what he calls the "artistic truth" and the "historian's truth," between "artistic completeness" and "historical completeness," between history and memory, is the central problem. The importance, and the poignancy, of the distinction are well conveyed in the comment with which Ash closes his review. It expresses more effectively than I could myself the reason why I believe it is important to emphasize the rationality of the historical enterprise and the commensurability of historical narratives, their vulnerability to criticism and review.

> The one conclusion to which [both films] lead me is: Thank God for historians! Only the professional historians, with their tested methods of research, their explicit principles of selection and use of evidence, only they can give us the weapons with which we may begin to look the thing in the face. Only the historians give us the standards by which we can judge and "place" *Heimat* or *Shoah.* Not that any one historian is necessarily more impartial than any one film director. But (at least in a free society) the terms of the historians' trade make them responsible and open to mutual attack, like politicians in a democracy, whereas the film director is always, by the very nature of his medium, a great dictator. So the historians are our protectors. They protect us

against forgetting—that is a truism. But they also protect us against memory.[101]

I am aware that the position I seem to be moving toward may have political and ideological implications. I cannot be blind to the analogy between my idea of an intellectual system which includes mechanisms of adaptation and self-correction and a familiar liberal vision of society, politics, and economics. By choosing to consider historiography as an evolving system of argument, exchange, criticism, and self-criticism, rather than as a collection of colliding, uncommunicating, and incommensurable world views, I am no doubt signaling not only a belief in underlying continuities but an ethical preference for evolution and reform rather than revolution, for dialogue and compromise rather than violence. I must simply accept this, constantly examine and reexamine my motives, and consider with as open a mind as possible all objections and criticisms.[102]

[1988]

NOTES
INDEX

Notes

Introduction

1. I cannot forbear to pay tribute here, all the same, to my teachers in the Department of French Studies at Glasgow: Alan Boase, Sam Hackett, Francis Scarfe, and, in linguistics, Stephen Ullman. They were outstanding and imaginative scholars. I was not ready to benefit from their teaching because my concerns were more historical and ethical, less purely aesthetic than theirs, but they were invariably supportive and encouraging. Norman Cohn, who taught medieval French Literature, had interests that were far closer to mine, but I did not know this until much later.

2. Chapter 1 of this volume.

3. *What Is Literature?*, trans. B. Frechtman (New York, 1949), pp. 95–97.

4. Theodor Adorno, "Theses upon Art and Religion Today" (1945), in *Noten zur Literatur*, vol. XI of *Gesammelte Schriften* (Frankfurt am Main, 1974), p. 648. (Adorno's English text slightly modified for clarity.)

5. Louis Althusser, "A Letter on Art, in Reply to André Daspre," in *Lenin and Philosophy, and Other Essays* (London, 1971), pp. 202–203.

6. Roland Barthes and Maurice Nadeau, *Sur la Littérature* (Grenoble, 1980), pp. 16–17. Throughout the present volume, all translations, in the text and in the notes, are mine unless otherwise indicated.

7. Ibid., p. 41.

8. T. J. Clark, "Clement Greenberg's Theory of Art," *Critical Inquiry* 9 (1982): 154.

9. I myself have argued this point in a review of Thomas Schleich's *Aufklärung und Revolution* (Stuttgart, 1981), in *American Historical Review* 88 (1983): 402–404.

10. "The Study of Poetry," in *The Portable Arnold,* ed. Lionel Trilling (New York, 1949), pp. 302–306; see also "A French Critic on Milton" in *Mixed Essays* (New York, 1899), p. 191.

11. See the interesting discussion of Jauss in Manfred Naumann et al., *Gesellschaft, Literatur, Lesen: Literaturrezeption in theoretischer Sicht* (Berlin and Weimar, 1973), pp. 131–144.

1. Literary Education and Democracy

1. Pyotr Bogatyrev and Roman Jakobson, "Die Folklore als eine besondere Form des Schaffens," in *Donum Natalicium Schrijnen* (Nijmegen and Utrecht, 1929), pp. 900–913. The ideas set forth in this paper were adumbrated by Cecil Sharp (*English Folk Song: Some Conclusions* [London, 1907] and the Introduction to *English Folk-Songs from the Southern Appalachians* [New York, 1917]), and they have been confirmed, on the whole, by subsequent scholarship; see Albert B. Lord, *The Singer of Tales* (Cambridge, Mass., 1960) and Lord's contribution to *Four Symposia on Folklore*, ed. Stith Thompson (Bloomington, Ind., 1953), pp. 305–315. Bertrand Bronson has criticized Sharp's notion of tradition as a debate between individual creativity and the censoring control of the group. Tradition, he claims, is not opposed to but built into the creation of individuals, so that individual creation does not seriously transgress the framework prescribed by tradition ("The Morphology of the Ballad Tunes," *Journal of American Folklore* 67 [1954]: 1–14). This refinement of Sharp's position seems compatible with the views of Jakobson and Bogatyrev.

2. Summed up in the statement of Hoffmann-Krayer, "Das Volk produziert nicht, es reproduziert" (see Hans Naumann, *Primitive Gemeinschaftskultur* [Jena, 1921], p. 5). A version of this view is at least as old as Scott ("Introductory Remarks on Popular Poetry," in the 1830 edition of *Minstrelsy of the Scottish Border*, ed. T. F. Henderson [Edinburgh, 1902], I, 8–15). It is still widely accepted among nonspecialists of literature (Charles Lalo, *L'Art et la vie sociale* [Paris, 1921], pp. 142–145, puts it forward as a fact). Alan Dundes has made what he calls the "devolutionary premise in folklore theory" the subject of a general survey of the ideologies underlying folklore studies in *Journal of the Folklore Institute* 6 (1969): 5–19.

3. One should distinguish between free-form and fixed-form types of folklore—tales, for instance, on the one hand, and proverbs, on the other. Only the first category is subject to modification by individual performers. In addition, Bogatyrev distinguishes between "active-collective" and "passive-collective" works of oral poetry. The former category includes works which can be performed by all members of the community (cradle-songs, ceremonial songs, and so forth); the latter includes those works which are performed by specialized—often quite rare—members of the community, though the whole community considers them its spiritual heritage. The evolution of the tradition is different in the two cases, according to Bogatyrev, and should be studied separately; see "Über die Rolle von Sänger, Zuhörerschaft und Buch bei der Überlieferung and Veränderung epischer Lieder," in *Sowjetische Volkslied- und Volksmusikforschung: ausgewählte Studien*, ed. E. Stockmann et al. (Berlin, 1969), pp. 187–201.

4. See an interesting short study of *The Bold Soldier of Yarrow* by Norman Cazden in *Journal of American Folklore* 68 (1955): 201–209.

5. On the distinction between primitive and simple, see I. Lotman, *Lektsii po struktural'noi poetike* (Brown University Slavic Reprints, 5 [Providence, 1968]), pp. 52–55. Simplicity, according to Lotman, can be perceived only against a background of complexity or ornamentation: "Artistic simplicity is more complex than artistic complexity, for it appears as a simplification that occurs later than and against the background of complexity." In English poetry, the practice of Wordsworth and

the theory laid out in the Preface to the *Lyrical Ballads* illustrate Lotman's point well. Similarly, W. K. Wimsatt, comparing the Scots of Fergusson and that of Burns, clearly implies that Burns's "naive" language is in fact more complex in its artful simplicity than the "literary" English against which its readers read it ("Imitation as Freedom, 1717–1798," *New Literary History* 1 [1970]: 215–236). See also B. Hrushovski, "On Free Rhythms in Modern Poetry," in *Style in Language,* ed. T. A. Sebeok (New York, 1960), pp. 173–190: Hrushovski argues that free rhythms, though they may professedly aim at more "prosaic" or "speech-like" effects, often have a more "rhythmical" and less prosaic impact than many metrical texts. It has long been held—since Rousseau and Herder at least—that prose, apparently more simple, is a later development than poetry and a more complex one; cf. recently Northrop Frye, "The Critical Path," *Daedalus* 99 (1970): 317.

6. Bogatyrev returns to this problem in "Über die Rolle von Sänger, Zuhörerschaft und Buch."

7. On the possibility afforded by writing of an overview which spoken language does not permit, see, for instance, Richard Müller-Freienfels, "Zur Psychologie und Soziologie der Schrift," in *Beiträge zur Gesellungs- und Völkerwissenschaft, Prof. Dr. Richard Thurnwald zu seinem 80. Geburtstag gewidmet,* ed. Ilse Tönnies (Berlin, 1950), pp. 297–312.

8. Roman Jakobson, "Linguistics and Poetics," in Sebeok, *Style in Language,* p. 358. See also Roger Fowler, "Linguistic Theory and the Study of Literature," in *Essays on Style and Language,* ed. R. Fowler (London, 1966), pp. 1–28. Fowler is skeptical of the possibility of finding features that will distinguish "literature" from "non-literature," but he also rejects as irrelevant the distinction between oral and written. Whether language uses noises in the air or marks on paper as its substance, he argues, its form remains the same, and it is form that both the linguist and the literary critic are interested in, not the physical representation of form.

9. Barbara H. Smith, *Poetic Closure* (Chicago, 1968), pp. 62–63. See also the discussion of repetition in Lotman, *Lektsii po struktural'noi poetike.* Jeanroy considered that the earliest refrains were fragments of different works from those in which they were inserted, so that from the outset, in his view, the refrain introduced a kind of counterpoint into the song. (See G. Lote, *Histoire du vers français* [Paris, 1951], II, 186–189.)

10. Roland Barthes, *Writing Degree Zero,* trans. Annette Lavers and Colin Smith (London, 1967), p. 54.

11. Jan Mukařovský, "The Esthetics of Language," in *A Prague School Reader on Esthetics, Literary Structure and Style,* ed. Paul Garvin (Washington, D.C., 1964), pp. 31–69. In his *Letters on the Esthetic Education of Man,* notably letter 15, Schiller was already insisting on the dialectical unity, in the aesthetic, of what he called "form" and "life" (corresponding approximately to Mukařovský's categories of normative and functional). The tendency to absolutize the functional in modern aesthetics has been criticized by René Wellek (Sebeok, *Style in Language,* pp. 415–416), by Lotman, notably in his criticism of Shklovski (*Lektsii po struktural'noi poetike,* pp. 156–159) and by Michael Riffaterre ("Stylistic Context," in *Essays on the Language of Literature* [Boston, 1967], p. 431).

12. Roland Barthes, "Littérature et signification," *Tel Quel* 16 (1964): 9.

13. Cf. Auerbach's contrast in the first chapter of *Mimesis* (Bern, 1946; Princeton, 1953) between the Homeric style—"fully externalized description, uniform illumination, uninterrupted connection, free expression, all events in the foreground, displaying unmistakable meanings"—and that of Genesis—"certain parts brought into high relief, others left obscure, abruptness, suggestive influence of the unexpressed, 'background' quality, multiplicity of meanings and the need for interpretation."

14. The displacement of grammatically homologous rhymes and the increasing preference since the Renaissance for rhyming morphologically dissimilar words is a simple illustration of such a shift within the context of rhyming practice, rhyme itself being, of course, historically conditioned (see Jean Cohen, *Structure du langage poétique* [Paris, 1966], pp. 81–86). English critics have frequently observed that Pope is a virtuoso at varying the grammatical forms he reconciles in rhyme.

15. Barthes, *Writing Degree Zero,* p. 55. Cf. Jean-Paul Sartre, *Qu'est-ce que la littérature* (1948), chap. 3.

16. Lotman also distinguishes between aesthetic structures with predominantly intratextual relations, which are thus perceived as artistically complex (medieval literature, folklore, baroque literature, romanticism), and aesthetic structures with predominantly contextual relations, which are perceived as artistically simple (classicism and realism). The distinction cuts across and complicates that between the aesthetics of identity and the aesthetics of opposition, but it still ignores the boundary between oral and written; see Lotman, *Lektsii po struktural'noi poetike,* p. 179 et passim.

17. Illustrations of changes in the printed versions of poetry from one edition to another have been brought together by A. F. Scott, *The Poet's Craft* (Cambridge, 1957). Among novels, obvious examples of texts that evolved considerably are Flaubert's *Education sentimentale* and *Tentation de Saint Antoine.* Many nineteenth-century English novels also exist in several "texts," though this problem has not attracted much critical attention; see Royal Gettman, *A Victorian Publisher* (Cambridge, 1960), chap. 8. On the fluidity of the concept of "text," see Lotman, *Lektsii po struktural'noi poetike,* p. 154.

18. Hans Blumenberg, "Die essentielle Vieldeutigkeit des ästhetischen Gegenstandes," in *Actes du Ve Colloque International d'Esthétique* (The Hague, 1968), pp. 64–70.

19. On medieval conceptions of authorship, see E. P. Goldschmitt, *Medieval Texts and Their First Appearance in Print* (Oxford, 1943); see also John Livingston Lowes, *Convention and Revolt in Poetry* (Boston, 1922); Charles Lalo, *L'Art et la vie sociale* (Paris, 1921), pp. 52–54; and Marshall McLuhan, *The Gutenburg Galaxy* (Toronto, 1962).

20. Jean de la Bruyère, *Characters;* trans. Henri van Laun (London, 1963; orig. French ed., 1688), p. 3.

21. See Marc Soriano, *Les Contes de Perrault: culture savante et traditions populaires* (Paris, 1968).

22. See Michèle Duchet in *Revue d'Histoire Littéraire de la France* 60 (1960): 531–556.

23. Letter to Sophie Volland, 10 August 1759 (Denis Diderot, *Lettres à Sophie Volland,* ed. André Babelon [Paris, 1938], 2 vols., I, 45).

24. Denis Diderot, *Oeuvres,* ed. Jules Assezat (Paris, 1875–1877), I, 16.

25. *Conversations with Eckermann,* 16 December 1828. The erosion of individualism in recent times has led to several attempts to get away from the conception of literary property. In his autobiographical sketch, *I myself,* under the year 1920, Mayakovski notes: "Finished *150,000,000.* Published it without my name. Wanted anyone who wished to continue and improve it."

26. Blaise Pascal, *Pensées,* ed. Léon Brunschvicg (Paris, 1917), no. 22, p. 329.

27. Quoted in André Veinstein, *La Mise en scene théâtrale et sa condition esthétique* (Paris, 1955), p. 297.

28. As early as 1873 Hilferding had begun to classify Russian folk material by author or singer rather than genre, but the model for many folklorists has been Mark Azadowski's study of Vinokurova, the great Siberian *bylini* singer (*Eine sibirische Märchenerzählerin,* Folklore Fellows Communications, 68 [Helsinki, 1926]).

29. See Lord, *Singer of Tales;* Iurii Sokolov, *Russian Folklore,* trans. C. R. Smith (New York, 1950); J. H. Delargy, "The Gaelic Story-Teller," *Proceedings of the British Academy* 31 (1965): 177–221; Linda Dégh, *Märchen, Erzähler und Erzählgemeinschaft* (Berlin, 1962); Ruth Finnegan, *Limba Stories and Story-Telling* (Oxford, 1967); see also Cecil Sharp, Introduction to *English Folk-Songs from the Southern Appalachians;* Ruth Benedict, *Zuni Mythology* (New York, 1934); Geneviève Calame-Griaule, "Pour une étude ethnolinguistique des littératures orales africaines," *Langages* 18 (1970): 22–67. In certain cultures strict fidelity to tradition in more than fixed form types does, however, seem to obtain, according to some observers; see Mary M. Edel, "Stability in Tillamook Folklore," *Journal of American Folklore* 57 (1944): 116–127, and Nora K. Chadwick and Viktor Zhirmunsky, *Oral Epics of Central Asia* (Cambridge, 1969), pp. 224–225, on the Turkmens of Central Asia. Nevertheless, the Chadwicks considered that strict memorizing was to be regarded as exceptional (H. Munro Chadwick and Nora K. Chadwick, *The Growth of Literature* [Cambridge, 1940], III, 867–869).

30. This point is made vividly by C. S. Lewis, *An Experiment in Criticism* (Cambridge, 1962), p. 2.

31. *World Theatre* 17 (1968): 337–345. See also Gaston Baty's account of three versions of a scene from *Le Malade imaginaire* in *Théâtre,* ed. Paul Arnold (Paris, 1945), pp. 91–96.

32. Lotman, *Lektsii po struktural'noi poetike,* p. 84.

33. Ibid., p. 85.

34. Lotman, *Lektsii po struktural'noi poetike,* p. 113. See also W. K. Wimsatt ("Imitation as Freedom"): "The escape from models [in eighteenth-century poetry] *was* freedom, *was* expression, *was* fun, only so long as the models were present as fields of reference for the realization of new meanings" (p. 218).

35. *Qu'est-ce que la littérature?* (Paris, 1948; rpt. ed. 1964), p. 52. See also some pertinent observations by Northrop Frye, "The Critical Path," *Daedalus* 99 (1970): 322–325.

36. Edition of Paris, 1714, pp. 18–19.

37. Lotman, *Lektsii po struktural'noi poetike*, p. 42. Cf. Felix Vodička, "The History of the Echo of Literary Works," in *A Prague School Reader in Esthetics, Literary Structure and Style,* ed. Paul Garvin (Washington, D.C., 1964), pp. 71–78: "As soon as the work is perceived on the basis of the integration into another context (a changed linguistic state of affairs, other literary requirements, a changed social structure, a new set of spiritual and practical values), then precisely those qualities of the work can be perceived as esthetically effective which previously were not perceived as esthetically effective, so that a positive evaluation may be based on entirely opposite reasons" (p. 79).

38. Edward Stankiewicz contrasts poetry, which he considers asynchronic, with language, which is synchronic. "We return often to poetic traditions. Non-poetic, ordinary language knows no returns; it is a progressive development in time" (Sebeok, *Style in Language,* p. 430). Oral literature, however, *is* like language in this sense, as Bogatyrev and Jakobson affirmed. On the synchronic character of oral culture in general, see Jack Goody and Ian Watt, "The Consequences of Literacy," in *Literacy in Transitional Societies,* ed. J. Goody (Cambridge, 1968), pp. 27–68, especially pp. 30–31.

39. See on this Goody, *Literacy in Transitional Societies,* pp. 2–3 and passim.

40. Barthes, "Littérature et Signification," p. 17. In a similar vein, see Pierre Boulez, *Pensez la musique d'aujourd'hui* (1963), quoted in H. Osborne, *Aesthetics and Art Theory* (London, 1967), p. 188: "It remains fundamental in my view to safeguard unknown potential which lies enclosed within a masterpiece of art. I am convinced that the author, however perspicacious he may be, cannot conceive the consequences—immediate or distant—of what he has written." All these comments recall Roman Ingarden's discussion of the determinate qualities and the indeterminate areas of the work of art. The possible or legitimate concretions of a work of art are negatively determined, according to Ingarden, but never completely determinate (*Das literarische Kunstwerk* [Halle, 1931]).

41. See *Eupalinos ou l'architecte,* in Paul Valéry, *Oeuvres* (Paris, 1931), I, 133–142.

42. Paul Radin, "The Literature of Primitive People," *Diogenes* 12 (1955): 3.

43. Sartre, *Qu'est-ce que la littérature?,* p. 59.

44. *The Function of Criticism,* in Matthew Arnold, *Complete Works* (Ann Arbor, 1962), III, 284.

45. George Miller put the problem wittily at the Indiana University Conference on Style. Developing the theme of predictability/unpredictability, expectation/surprise, norm/variation, which ran through many of the discussions, he used the analogy of the relation of probability to surprise in a bridge hand to illuminate the importance, for the "surprise" concept, of *value* in the context of the game, and went on to ask what the rules of the literary game are. Perhaps great writers change them, he suggested, so that the critic's job is to discover the new rules. At any rate, in his view skillful people know them at some level, and they can be learned (Sebeok, *Style in Language,* pp. 394–395). The problem is precisely that (1) most people no longer intuitively know the rules, (2) in our own period they are constantly being changed or scrambled, and (3) they are not taught to most people.

46. Also, to some extent, in the persistent reluctance of many critics and amateurs of poetry to admit as proper to it what is not spoken or can only be perceived

by the eye. It is true that, even unspoken physically, the sound of the poem is still present for most readers as a background against which the printed text is perceived. But the latter may have its own conventions. "Any thorough formalistic analysis of the structure of poetry and of its relation to the language in which it is written," John Hollander writes, "must deal with the written language as a system in itself, as well as with the spoken one" (*The Untuning of the Sky* [Princeton, 1961], p. 7). From the camp of the linguists Angus McIntosh points out that written signs carry two information loads—linguistic meaning, a direct reference to the code, and phonic meaning, information on how to speak the message should this be desired (" 'Graphology' and Meaning," in A. McInstosh and M. A. K. Halliday, *Patterns of Language* [Bloomington, Ind., 1967], pp. 98–110). Clearly the two can function independently, and interplay between them enhances the possibilities of the poem. So too, in some recent writing, do typography and layout, which may also be made to convey their own load of information; in a poem, however, as distinct from a drawing, these visual messages are always in an intimate relation to the visual and spoken aspects of the linguistic message.

Suspicion of the written text probably goes back to suspicion of language in general. The view that "mere" words betray the living thoughts of which they are the images, and that written words, as images of images, are even less trustworthy, is a persistent one and pervades what has been called the folklinguistics of Western culture (see H. M. Hoenigswald, "A Proposal for the Study of Folk-Linguistics" in *Sociolinguistics*, ed. W. Bright [The Hague, 1966], pp. 16–21). Jack Goody (*Literacy in Transitional Societies*, Introduction) shows that the prejudice is by no means confined to the West. The prejudice in favor of the spoken has, in addition, an echo in an important debate in linguistics, with some linguists (for instance, Hjelmslev, Uldall, McIntosh) maintaining stoutly that the system of language is independent of the substance (the stream of air or the stream of ink) in which it is expressed, so that from a strictly linguistic point of view the privilege of the spoken is unwarranted; see B. Siertsema, *A Study of Glossematics* (The Hague, 1965), pp. 111–113, for some pertinent quotations; see also A. McIntosh, " 'Graphology' and Meaning," p. 99.

47. Raymond Williams, *Culture and Society, 1780–1950* (London, 1958). See also Richard Altick, *The English Common Reader* (Chicago, 1957), and various articles by Leo Lowenthal and his associates: "The Debate over Art and Popular Culture in Eighteenth Century England" (with Marjorie Fiske Lowenthal) in *Literature, Popular Culture and Society* (Englewood Cliffs, N.J., 1961); "The Debate on Cultural Standards in Nineteenth Century England" (with Ina Lawson), *Social Research* 30 (1963): 417–433; "Der menschliche Dialog" (Lowenthal's own independent critique of the mass media), *Kölner Zeitschrift für Soziologie und Sozialpsychologie* 21 (1969): 463–473.

48. Pierre Bourdieu, "Outline of a Sociological Theory of Art Perception," *International Social Science Journal* 20 (1968): 609–611. See also J. A. Bizet, "L'Action culturelle et les produits artistiques," *La Pensée* (March-April 1970), pp. 84–92.

49. Michael Hancher, "The Science of Interpretation and the Art of Interpretation," *MLN* 85 (1970): 791–802.

50. Umberto Eco, "Formes et communication," *Revue Internationale de Philosophie* 21 (1967): 231–251.

2. Literature and Education

1. Thomas Jefferson Wertenbaker, *Princeton 1746–1896* (Princeton, 1946), pp. 232, 235–236.

2. Quoted in D. J. Palmer, *The Rise of English Studies* (London, 1965), pp. 71, 111.

3. Roland Barthes, "Réflexions sur un manuel," in *L'Enseignement de la littérature,* ed. Serge Doubrovsky and Tzvetan Todorov (Paris, 1971), p. 170.

4. Matthew Arnold, "Literature and Science," in *The Portable Matthew Arnold,* ed. Lionel Trilling (New York, 1949), pp. 411–412.

5. Arnold was replying in part to Herbert Spencer's relegation of literature to the category of miscellaneous activities which make up the leisure part of life and are devoted to the cultivation of the taste and feelings, the last and least important of the five categories into which he divided human activities. See Herbert Spencer, *Education: Intellectual, Moral, and Physical* (New York and London, 1860), pp. 1–14.

6. N. L. Lemercier, *Cours analytique de littérature* (Paris, 1817), p. 14.

7. See, for instance, *An Account of the College of New Jersey, published by the Trustees* (Woodbridge, N.J., 1764), pp. 23, 29.

8. The course of study at Princeton was described in *An Account of the College of New Jersey* (1764) as follows: "The *Freshman* year is spent in the latin and greek languages, particularly in reading Horace, Cicero's *Orations,* the *Greek Testament,* Lucian's *Dialogues,* and Xenophon's *Cyropedia.* In the *Sophomore* year, they still prosecute the study of the languages, particularly Homer, Longinus, etc.; and enter upon the sciences, geography, rhetoric, logic, and the mathematics. They continue their mathematical studies throughout the *Junior* year; and also pass through a course of natural and moral philosophy, metaphysics, chronology, etc., and the greater number, especially such as are educating for the service of the church, are initiated into the hebrew. . . . The *Senior* year is entirely employed in reviews and composition. They now revise the most improving parts of the latin and greek classics" (p. 25). See likewise President Witherspoon's *An Address to the Inhabitants of Jamaica and other West-India Islands in Behalf of the College of New Jersey* (Philadelphia, 1772). As late as 1835 at Harvard, always more quick to change than Princeton, the freshman, sophomore, and junior years were spent in Greek, Latin, mathematics, and modern languages. In the junior year chemistry was introduced. Only in the senior year were the classics dropped in favor of Natural Philosophy (physics), Philosophy, Political Economy, Rhetoric, and other subjects (see the Harvard Catalogue for 1835). Frederick Rudolph characterizes this education succinctly: "In one sense the curriculum was a course in the learning and use of language" (*Curriculum: A History of the American Undergraduate Course of Study since 1636* [San Francisco, Washington, London, 1977], p. 36).

The provisions at Harvard and Princeton were similar to those at the Scottish universities, where, after the complete abandonment in the early eighteenth century of the "regenting" system (in which each student was guided throughout his college career, in all subjects, by a single regent or tutor), the course of study was approximately Humanity (Latin) in the first year, Greek in the second, Logic in the third, and Natural Philosophy or Physics in the fourth, along with Moral Philosophy and Mathematics (Sir A. Grant, *The Story of the University of Edinburgh* [London, 1884], I, 263–264).

In France, education in the collèges before the Revolution, as in the lycées after it, was primarily in the classical languages and literatures. Modern subjects, such as physics, were taught (F. de Dainville, "L'Enseignement scientifique dans les Collèges des Jésuites," and Pierre Costabel, "L'Oratoire de France et ses collèges," both in *Enseignement et diffusion des sciences en France au XVIIIᵉ siècle,* ed. René Taton [Paris, 1964], pp. 27–65, 67–100), but since physics classes were given only in the second year of "philosophie" (the last year of college), very few students stayed long enough to take them (Dainville, p. 61). The nineteenth-century curriculum marked only a slight modification. In Matthew Arnold's account of the lycée of Toulouse in 1859, classical languages and texts still dominate the curriculum (*A French Eton, or Middle Class Education and the State* [London and Cambridge, 1864]). In a detailed "Rapport au Roi sur l'instruction secondaire," published in the *Moniteur universel,* 8 March 1843 (pp. 385–391), Abel Villemain described the curriculum of the collèges royaux as "au fond, et sur le point principal, l'ancien système de Port-Royal et de l'université de Paris, le système qui, depuis deux siècles a fourni pour la magistrature et les affaires, tant d'hommes capables et d'esprits éclairés."

9. The purpose of education, according to Hudson, is "to educate the mind and the heart" (*English in Schools* [Boston, 1881], p. 5). The reference is to Rollin's "former l'esprit et le coeur," which had become a byword. (The phrase was frequently alluded to ironically by Voltaire.) Hudson was described as the American Carlyle by an admiring reviewer in the *Boston Sunday Herald,* 3 October 1880.

10. Herder, "Vom Fortschreiten einer Schule mit der Zeit" (1798), in *Herders Sämtliche Werke,* ed. B. Suphan (Berlin, 1889), XXX, 240.

11. Quoted in Carl Bode, *The American Lyceum: Town Meeting of the Mind* (New York, 1956), p. 29.

12. Charles Rollin, *Method of Teaching and Studying the Belles-Lettres,* 2nd ed. (London, 1737), I, 6.

13. "Von der Ausbildung der Rede und Sprache in Kindern und Jünglingen" (1796), in *Herders Sämtliche Werke,* XXX, 217.

14. Rollin, in France, used Bossuet as a model; the Princeton handbooks show that Addison served a similar purpose in the American colonies.

15. Rollin, *Method of Teaching,* p. 53. See also Sheldon Rothblatt, *Tradition and Change in English Liberal Education: An Essay in History and Culture* (London, 1976), pp. 44–49.

16. The *Account of the College of New Jersey* for 1764 promises practice at reciting "select pieces from Cicero, Demosthenes, Livy and other ancient authors,—as well as from Shakespeare, Milton, and Addison, and such illustrious moderns as are best suited to . . . exemplify the graces of utterance and gesture." The authors go on to explain that "a good address and agreeable elocution are accomplishments so ingratiating and so necessary to render a public speaker . . . popular; and consequently useful, that they are esteemed here as considerable parts of education, in the cultivation of which no little pains are employed" (p. 26).

17. Michel de Certeau, Dominique Julia, and Jacques Revel, *Une Politique de la langue. La Révolution française et les patois: L'Enquête de Grégoire* (Paris, 1975), p. 10.

18. Ibid., p. 155.

19. Quoted by de Certeau, ibid., p. 104.

20. See the celebrated passage on the historian as Oedipus in Michelet's *Journal*, ed. Paul Viallaneix (Paris, 1959–76), I, 377–379. Earlier, Champollion had insisted that ancient Egypt could be understood only by attending to her own voice, only through a decoding of the hieroglyphs, and not through the accounts of Greek and Roman historians and travelers. (See *Lettres de Champollion le jeune,* ed. H. Hartleben [Paris, 1909], I, 124 [editor's note].)

21. "Le chantre passionné des vaincus," in the words of Salvandy (quoted in Louis Trenard, *Salvandy en son temps 1795–1856* [Lille, 1968], p. 886).

22. J. J. Bachofen, "Das Naturrecht und das geschichtliche Recht" (inaugural address at University of Basel, 7 May 1841), in *Johann Jakob Bachofens Gesammelte Werke,* ed. Karl Meuli (Basel and Stuttgart, 1943–), I, 18.

23. Jacob Grimm, *Deutsches Wörterbuch von Jacob Grimm und Wilhelm Grimm* (Leipzig, 1854), I, vii.

24. Quoted in Horst Joachim Frank, *Geschichte des Deutschunterrichts von den Anfängen bis 1945* (Munich, 1973), p. 443. See also Frank on Grimm, p. 448.

25. See H. Hartleben, *Champollion: Sein Leben und sein Werk* (Berlin, 1906), I, 143, quoting the manuscript of Champollion's opening lecture at the *Lycée* in May 1810.

26. Alexander Somerville, *The Autobiography of a Working Man,* ed. John Carswell (London, 1951), p. 42.

27. Michelet, *Le Prêtre, la femme et la famille* (1845; rpt. Paris, 1861), p. 297. See also Michelet's notes on Rubens in *Journal,* I, 442.

28. "Of the Principles of Poetry and the 'Lyrical Ballads'" (1798–1802), in *The Prose Works of William Wordsworth,* ed. Alexander Grosart (London, 1876), II, 91.

29. Emerson, "History," in *The Portable Emerson,* ed. Mark van Doren (New York, 1946), p. 144.

30. Lamartine, *Cours familier de littérature* (Paris, 1856), I, 82.

31. Michelet, *Journal,* II, 321 (January 1857).

32. Pierre-Simon Ballanche, *Essais de palingénésie sociale,* in *Oeuvres de M. Ballanche* (1830), cited by Charles Rearick in *Beyond the Enlightenment: Historians and Folklore in Nineteenth Century France* (Bloomington and London, 1974), p. 42.

33. Letter from Fauriel to Mary Clarke, 15 August 1822, cited in Rearick, *Beyond the Enlightenment,* p. 75. The idea that the bourgeoisie is born of the people yet destined to be its guide and leader is vividly expressed in the destiny Michelet traces for woman, "cet autre peuple," as Herzen remarked later in his "Lettre à Garibaldi" (*Sobranie sochinenii* [Moscow, 1954], vol. XXX, bk. 2, p. 529). From being the all-powerful, alternately nourishing and devouring mother on whom her son is totally dependent, like a small bark on the vast ocean, woman must advance to the position of dutiful daughter and spouse; the reign of law, in short, originally dependent on nature, must be extended until it includes nature. In return for the protection of the male, Michelet's female continues freely and generously

to provide him with the sustenance he needs after his arduous labors on her behalf. Michelet extends this restorative function of the female to natural history—the "feminine" science—which he views as a "cordial" for the social and political historian fatigued by strenuous, manly laboring in the archives. (See in particular the early chapters of *L'Oiseau,* written in collaboration with his wife Athénaïs Mialaret.) To the role of the bourgeoisie in relation to the people and of the male in relation to the female corresponds, of course, that of the historian in relation to the past for which he speaks.

34. Quoted in Oscar Haac, *Les Principes inspirateurs de Michelet* (Paris and New Haven, 1951), p. 103.

35. Bachofen, *Politische Betrachtungen über das Staatsleben des römischen Volkes,* ed. Max Burckhardt et al., vol. I of *Gesammelte Werke* (Basle, 1943), p. 60. The Humboldt passages are from a 1791 letter to Gentz, cited in Paul R. Sweet, *Wilhelm von Humboldt: A Biography* (Columbus, Ohio, 1978–1981), I, 109–110.

36. *Guerres de religion* (1856), vol. XI of *Histoire de France* (Paris, 1898–1899), chap. 8, pp. 114–117.

37. Michelet, *Nos Fils* (Paris, n.d. [1902]), p. 300.

38. Emerson, "History," p. 153. Humboldt, "On the Task of the Historian," *History and Theory* 6 (1967): 65.

39. Bachofen, *Selbstbiographie und Antrittsrede über das Naturrecht,* ed. A. Baeumler (Halle/Saale, 1927), pp. 32–33.

40. Quoted in Raymond Williams, *Culture and Society 1780–1950* (Harmondsworth, 1961), p. 59.

41. According to the authors of a report on the teaching of English in England in 1921, "Fear of the danger to the state that an illiterate population might constitute became a powerful motive for [educational] reform after the Reform Bill of 1832" (*The Teaching of English in England: Report . . . of the . . . Committee . . . of Inquiry into the Teaching of English in the Educational System of England* [London, 1921], p. 41).

42. Quoted in John Clive, *Macaulay: The Shaping of the Historian* (1973; rpt. New York, 1975), p. 112.

43. Quoted in Palmer, *Rise of English Studies,* p. 37.

44. Quoted in Williams, *Culture and Society,* p. 122.

45. On the teaching of English literature at University College and King's College, London, see Palmer, *Rise of English Studies,* pp. 15–28; on the Scottish universities, see George Elder Davie, *The Democratic Intellect: Scotland and her Universities in the Nineteenth Century* (Edinburgh, 1961), pp. 206–211; on workingmen's libraries and institutions in the United States, see Bode, *The American Lyceum,* passim.

46. Michelet, *Journal,* I, 121–161; Friedrich Engels, *The Condition of the Working Class in England* [1845] (Moscow, 1973), passim.

47. Matthew Arnold, *Culture and Anarchy* (Cambridge, 1969), p. 195.

48. Ibid., p. 105.

49. The "Populace," like other social categories, is transformed by Arnold into a moral and psychological category—"the eternal spirit of the Populace"—and is identified with what is frequently referred to as "the animal" in all of us; see *Culture and Anarchy,* p. 107.

50. Quoted in A. E. Dyson and Julian Lovelock, *Education and Democracy* (London and Boston, 1975), p. 119.

51. "The Function of Criticism," in *The Portable Arnold*, p. 267. For a contrary view of Arnold as a progressive, see Maurice Mandelbaum, *History, Man, and Reason: A Study in Nineteenth-Century Thought* (Baltimore and London, 1971), pp. 200–201.

52. There is a world of difference between the exclusive and selective idea of a classical literature and the post-Revolutionary idea of *Weltliteratur*—a kind of ingathering of literatures separated by the boundaries of language, time, and culture, a totalization of hitherto autonomous and fragmentary traditions. The immense energy and seriousness with which the Coppet group around Mme de Staël took the task of translation is symptomatic of a new enthusiasm for a truly international, comprehensive world literature.

53. Emerson, "History," p. 149.

54. Quoted in Laurence Veysey, *The Emergence of the American University* (Chicago, 1965), p. 182n.

55. Palmer, *Rise of English Studies*, p. 39.

56. Henry Hudson, *English in Schools* (Boston, 1881), p. xviii.

57. Böckh, *Encyklopädie und Methodologie der philologischen Wissenschaften*, ed. Ernst Bratuschek (Leipzig, 1877), p. 32.

58. Wackernagel, *Deutsches Lesebuch* (Stuttgart, 1843).

59. *The Portable Emerson*, pp. 264–265.

60. Fritz Ringer, *The Decline of the German Mandarins: The German Academic Community, 1890–1933* (Cambridge, Mass., 1969), pp. 26–31.

61. Ibid., pp. 26, 32; see also Fritz Ringer, "Higher Education in Germany in the Nineteenth Century," in *Schule und Gesellschaft im 19. Jahrhundert*, ed. Ulrich Herrmann (Weinheim and Basel, 1977), pp. 332–347; R. H. Samuel and R. Hinton Thomas, *Education and Society in Modern Germany* (London, 1949), chap. 8. The Fontane quotation is taken from Kenneth Atwood, *Fontane und das Preussentum* (Berlin, 1970), p. 267.

62. "Democracy," in *The Portable Arnold*, p. 452.

63. Ibid., pp. 463–464.

64. See Burton J. Bledstein, *The Culture of Professionalism* (New York, 1976).

65. Michelet, Preface to *Histoire de France au seizième siècle: Renaissance et Réforme*, ed. Robert Casanova (Paris, 1978), *Oeuvres complètes*, VII, 50.

66. In *American Higher Education, a Documentary History*, ed. Richard Hofstedter and Wilson Smith (Chicago, 1961), II, 692–693.

67. Quoted by Jean-Jacques Anstett in his Introduction to Friedrich Schlegel's *Philosophie der Geschichte*, in *F. Schlegel: Kritische Ausgabe*, ed. Ernst Behler (Munich, 1971), XI, vi.

68. Quoted in Palmer, *Rise of English Studies*, pp. 59–60.

69. Ibid., p. 90.

70. See ibid., pp. 21–22, for examples of examination questions in English literature in English universities. See the original version of the present essay (*New Literary History* 13 [1982]: 341–371, n.70) for questions in the English literature classes at Princeton University and the University of Glasgow in the 1860s and 1870s.

At Glasgow in the 1860s the requirement for graduation from the Faculty of Arts included—besides two sessions of Humanity (Latin), Greek, and Mathematics and at least one session each of Logic, Moral Philosophy, and Natural Philosophy—one course in English literature. A chair of English Literature had been established following the recommendation of a Royal Commission in 1858 (see the *General Report of the Commissioners under the Universities [Scotland] Act, 1858* [Edinburgh, 1863], p. xvi), but there was no "major" as yet in English. According to the University Calendars for this period, degrees with "honors"—that is, degrees requiring supplementary study and examination—were obtainable in Classical Literature, Mental Philosophy (logic, metaphysics, and moral philosophy), Mathematics (including natural philosophy or physics), and Natural Science (botany, geology, zoology, and chemistry). The English course was thus only a relatively small element in the "ordinary" or non-honors degree curriculum. As described in the University Calendar for 1874–75, it consisted of "about 80 lectures," covering philology, rhetoric or composition, and history of literature. The examinations were devised accordingly to test students on the "facts" of the history of language and literature and on the rules of English composition as imparted to them in the lectures. It is clear that students were not expected to have reflected independently or critically on any of this.

71. Quoted in Palmer, *Rise of English Studies,* p. 65.

72. See Martin Jay, *The Dialectical Imagination: A History of the Frankurt School and the Institute of Social Research, 1923–1950* (Boston, 1973), pp. 178, 187, 215.

73. Ibid., p. 187.

74. Robin Mayhead, "American Criticism," *Scrutiny* 19, no. 1 (October 1952): 75.

75. Francis Mulhern, *The Moment of "Scrutiny"* (London, 1979), p. 33.

76. Thompson, "Advertising God," *Scrutiny* 1, no. 3 (December 1932): 246.

77. Trilling, "On the Modern Element in Modern Literature" (1961), reprinted in *The Idea of the Modern in Literature and the Arts,* ed. Irving Howe (New York, 1968), pp. 61–62.

78. The relation between the fashionable concept of "literarity" or "literariness" and the positivist orientation of modern scholarship—even when it rejects old-fashioned historical positivism—would be worth investigating. It was positivist literary scholarship that first formulated the need for a strict definition of what literature is; see P. Lacombe, *Introduction à l'histoire littéraire* (Paris, 1898), pp. 1–2: "How is it possible to bring even a minimum of scientific method to what is not a subject but a collection of subjects?"

79. Theodor Adorno, "Theses upon Art and Religion Today" (1945), in *Noten zur Literatur,* vol. XI of *Gesammelte Schriften* (Frankfurt am Main, 1974), p. 648. (Adorno's English text slightly modified for clarity.)

80. Ibid., p. 650.

3. The Figaros of Literature

1. Franz Overbeck, *Christentum und Kultur: Gedanken und Anmerkungen zur modernen Theologie,* edited from the "*Nachlass*" by C. A. Bernoulli (Basel, 1919), p. 13.

2. Ibid., pp. 273, 274, 253.

3. Roland Barthes, *Sur Racine* (Paris, 1963), p. 143. Lucien Goldmann's *Le Dieu caché: étude sur la vision tragique dans les Pensées de Pascal et dans le théâtre de Racine* appeared in Paris in 1955. The bulk of the book is devoted to the Jansenist movement in France in the seventeenth century and to Pascal; the section on Racine is quite short.

4. For a brief and lucid overview, see Peter Szondi, "L'Herméneutique de Schleiermacher," *Poétique* 2 (1970): 141–155.

5. "Renaissance Readers and Ancient Texts," *Renaissance Quarterly* 38 (1985): 615–649.

6. "Three Types of Translation," trans. Luna Wolf (from "Noten und Abhandlungen zu besserem Verständnis des westöstlichen Divans" [1819]), *Delos* 1 (1968): 188–190.

7. "Against Theory," *Critical Inquiry* 8 (1982): 713–742, and "Against Theory 2," *Critical Inquiry* 14 (1987): 49–68.

8. Even the Prince Consort had to observe at the time of the Great Exhibition in 1851 that "works of art, publicly exhibited and offered for sale, become commercial commodities and as such follow the irrational laws of the market and of fashion, which exercise a tyrannical influence on the patronage of the public and even on the taste of individuals" (*Le Prince Albert*, translated from the English by M[me?] Guizot [Paris, 1863], pp. 13–14.)

9. *An Essay on the History of Civil Society* [1767], pt. 3, sec. 8, 6th ed. (London, 1793), p. 294. Ferguson even wondered "whether the trouble of seeking for distant models, and of wading for instruction through dark allusions and languages unknown, might not [quench the writer's] fire and [render] him a writer of a very inferior class."

10. Quoted in Alvin Kernan, *Printing, Technology, Letters, and Samuel Johnson* (Princeton, 1987), p. 226.

11. A letter from Voltaire to Frederick the Great of 25 April 1739, in which he tells him he is dedicating his poem *La Henriade* to him, speaks eloquently of the passage from aristocratic patronage to the new Enlightenment idea of the public: "Deign to accept this testimony of my affection and respect. It cannot be suspected of flattery. And that is the only kind of homage that the public approves. I am but the interpreter of those who are acquainted with the outstanding qualities of your mind. They all know that I would say as much of you if you were not the heir to a great monarchy. I dedicated Zaire to a simple merchant [the Englishman Falkener]. I saw in him only the human being. He was my friend and I wished to honor his virtue. I dare to dedicate La Henriade to another superior spirit. Though he be a prince, I respect his mind more than I revere his rank," (*Complete Works of Voltaire*, ed. T. Besterman [Geneva: Institut et Musée Voltaire, 1968–1977], VI, 351).

12. According to Kernan, Johnson's idea of the common reader "dramatized the best that could be expected from such a democratic social group, both appealing to and calling into being their good sense, their fundamental humanity, their awareness of permanent social and experiential truths" (Kernan, *Printing, Technology, Letters*, p. 230).

13. Q. D. Leavis, *Fiction and the Reading Public* (London, 1968 [first publ. 1932]), pt. 2, chap. 3 ("Growth of the Reading Public") and chap. 4 ("Disintegration of the Reading Public"); Kernan, *Printing, Technology, Letters,* pp. 222–223, 284–285.

14. *Schillers Werke* (Berlin: Gustav Hempel, n.d. [1868–1870]), 16 vols., XIV, 523, 525–526 ("Über Bürgers Gedichte" [1791]).

15. Peter Uwe Hohendahl, *The Institution of Criticism* (Ithaca, N.Y., and London, 1982), p. 55.

16. *Schillers Werke,* XV, 542.

17. "The Romantic critic," in Hohendahl's words, "stands with his back to the literary public, whose preferences and opinions can exert no influence, whether positive or negative, on the evaluation of an art work" (*The Institution of Criticism,* p. 59).

18. *Schriften* (Frankfurt am Main, 1955), II, 486, quoted in Hohendahl, *The Institution of Criticism,* p. 59.

19. See Georges Snyders, *La Pédagogie en France aux XVII et XVIII siècles* (Paris, 1965).

20. Extracts from Ast are from Hans-Georg Gadamer and Gottfried Boehm, *Seminar: Philosophische Hermeneutik* (Frankfurt am Main, 1976), pp. 111–130. The passages cited here are on pp. 112–113.

21. *Kulturgeschichtliche Charakterköpfe* (1891), quoted in Fritz Blättner, *Das Gymnasium* (Heidelberg, 1960), pp. 161–162.

22. *The Portable Arnold,* ed. Lionel Trilling (New York, 1949), pp. 264, 301.

23. "A Guide to English Literature" (review of Stopford Brooke, *A Primer of English Literature*), in *Mixed Essays* (New York, 1899), p. 136.

24. Arnold favored an integrated, state-administered education system, in which the cultural well-being of the common people would also be attended to in elementary schools and it would be possible theoretically for a student, even of humble origins, to progress to higher and even to university education. He much admired the teaching of literature and foreign languages in German and Swiss elementary schools. Somewhat more ambiguously, he scoffed at the Anglo-American concern to keep religion out of schools so as to protect minorities from the majority, professed his admiration for the teaching of religion in German and Swiss schools and for a kind of "undogmatic religion" that was making its way in French elementary instruction, and reported with obvious satisfaction a conversation with Mommsen in Berlin, in the course of which Mommsen "quoted . . . the words of Goethe . . . : 'He who has art and science, has religion.' But . . . with an addition which I had forgotten: 'He who has not art and science, let him have religion.' The popular school is for those [Mommsen] said, who have not art or science; to leave religion out of its programme would therefore be a great mistake." Arnold comments weakly that he doubts "whether the religious feeling of England would not be as much shocked as the democratic feeling of America by the notion of teaching religion in the popular schools as a thing which uncultivated people require, though cultivated people do not" ("Common Schools Abroad," lecture at the University of Pennsylvania, 1886, in *Essays, Letters, and Reviews,* ed. Fraser Neiman [Cambridge, Mass., 1960], pp. 294–295). By his own account, however,

Arnold had often been "reproached with wishing to make free-thinking an aristocratic privilege, while a false religion is thrown to the multitude to keep it quiet" ("Dr. Stanley's Lectures on the Jewish Church," [1863], in *Essays, Letters, and Reviews*, p. 80). The charge is false only in that it is a massive simplification of the views of a writer who, as a matter of strategy and almost, it seems, of principle, sedulously avoided taking a simple position on any topic whatsoever.

25. Originally in a government blue-book, 1859, and quoted by Arnold himself in "Porro unum est necessarium," *Mixed Essays*, pp. 108–109.

26. Ibid., p. 111.

27. Ibid., p. 121.

28. What *Culture and Anarchy* owes to Schiller's *Letters on Aesthetic Education* has never, to the best of my knowledge, been fully acknowledged, and it is clear from the remarks on translating Homer that Arnold had not forgotten *On Naive and Sentimental Poetry* either.

29. "The Function of Criticism," in *The Portable Arnold*, p. 248.

30. *The Portable Arnold*, pp. 210–211. Arnold's enthusiasm for entering into community with the greatest spirits of all ages of history led him to place more emphasis on the classical, the universal, and the permanent than one might have expected in the golden age of historical scholarship. Dramatic poetry, for instance, has an edge for him over epic, because, he says, it is more generally human, whereas epic is more embedded in history, more other: "The dramatic form exhibits, above all, *the actions of man as strictly determined by his thoughts and feelings;* it exhibits, therefore, what may be always accessible, always intelligible, always interesting. But the epic form takes a wider range; it represents not only the thought and passion of man, that which is universal and eternal, but also the forms of outward life, the fashion of manners, . . . that which is local or transient . . . In the *reconstruction*, by learning and antiquarian ingenuity, of the local and transient features of a past age, . . . it is impossible to feel the liveliest kind of interest" ("On the Modern Element in Literature," in *Essays, Letters, and Reviews*, p. 16).

31. "The Study of Poetry," in *The Portable Arnold*, pp. 302–306; see also the reservations about the "method of historical criticism . . . the old story of 'the man and the milieu,'" judged by no means certain to lead to a "right understanding" of literary works, in "A French Critic on Milton," *Mixed Essays*, p. 191.

32. Said of Sir Walter Raleigh, in contrast to Thucydides, in "On the Modern Element in Literature," *Essays, Letters, and Reviews*, p. 11.

33. *St. Paul and Protestantism*, 3rd ed. (New York, 1875), p. 176.

34. On "Aryan" theology and "Semitic" faith, see *Literature and Dogma*, ed. James C. Livingstone (New York, 1970), chap. 9, pp. 120–122, 129–131, 140, 143, and Conclusion, p. 158. Among other things, Arnold realized fully that the eschatological problem was the crucial one for modern Christianity. Characteristically, however, unlike Overbeck, he tried to "save" and "modernize" Christianity by attributing the eschatological strain ("imagining that the world was to end within the lifetime of the first Christian generation") in the early Christians to "the turbid Jewish fancies about the 'grand consummation' which were then current" and to the early disciples' "having put their own eschatology into the mouth of Jesus when they had to report his discourse about the kingdom of God." Jesus, in short,

was not "a co-partner in their eschatology" but was "almost as much over the heads of his disciples and reporters then as he is over the heads of the mass of so-called Christians now" (ibid., chap. 4, pp. 92–93). This was the very kind of reasoning that Overbeck despised from his heart.

35. "Dr. Stanley's Lectures on the Jewish Church," in *Essays, Lectures, and Reviews*, pp. 78–79.

36. "A French Critic on Milton" (review of a book by Edmond Scherer), in *Mixed Essays*, p. 190.

37. Alexandre Vinet, *Quelques observations extraites d'un compte rendu de l'enseignement du français au Paedagogium, présenté en octobre 1836* (Basel, 1837), pp. 15–20.

38. "Lettre à M. Monnard," at the beginning of *Chrestomathie: Littérature de l'Enfance*, 5th ed. (Basel, 1849), p. vii.

39. Professor Lucien Dällenbach, a young professor of French literature at the University of Geneva, assures me it was still in use in Swiss schools when he was attending them, and Professor Charles Issawi of Princeton University recalls that it was assigned by the French teachers at the lycée in Alexandria where he went to school in the 1930s. A short bibliographical survey of the *Chrestomathie* can be found in Pierre Kohler's preface to his edition of Vinet's *Mélanges littéraires* (Lausanne, 1955), p. xi, n. 1.

40. "Lettre à Monsieur Andre Gindroz," at the beginning of *Chrestomathie*, vol. III, "Littérature de la Jeunesse et de l'Age Mûr," 3rd ed. (Basel, 1841), p. x. My thanks for picking out this and the following passages to Eric Rauth, who allowed me to inveigle him into the study of early school textbooks of literature.

41. Ibid., p. xii.

42. Barthes, *Sur Racine*, p. 143.

43. Friedrich Nietzsche, *The Use and Abuse of History*, trans. Adrian Collins (Indianapolis, 1957), p. 36.

44. Ibid., p. 45.

45. François-Joseph Noel and François de Laplace, *Leçons françaises de littérature et de morale* (Mons, 1829 [1st ed., 1804]), p. v.

46. See an interview in *Réforme*, 2 September 1978, in Roland Barthes, *The Grain of the Voice: Interviews 1962–1980*, trans. Linda Coverdale (New York, 1985 [orig. Fr. 1981]), p. 306.

47. Roland Barthes, *Le Plaisir du texte* (Paris, 1973), p. 81; see also pp. 79–81. In the notes and jottings posthumously published as *Incidents* (Paris, 1987), Barthes does not miss an opportunity to deride the academic study of literature as a bureaucratic, institutionalized occupation or career.

48. "Ecrivains, Intellectuels, Professeurs," *Tel Quel* 47 (1971): 71. See also *Le Plaisir du texte*, p. 95: "What relation can there be between the pleasure of the text and the institutions of the text? Only the slightest. The theory of the text postulates bliss, but it has little in the way of an institutional future: what it founds, its precise fulfillment, its assumption, is a practice (that of the writer), and in no way a science, a method, an activity of scholarly research, a pedagogy. By its very principles, such a theory can produce only theorists or practitioners (*scripteurs* [that is, writers]); it cannot produce specialists (critics, research scholars, professors, students)."

49. Barthes, *The Grain of the Voice*, p. 165; this chain of reading and writing seems to have a certain analogy with Gadamer's supra-personal "tradition of interpretation," in which it is the tradition that speaks through the interpreter rather than the interpreter who makes the tradition, in the way that "I do not speak language, language speaks me."

50. Barthes, *Le Plaisir du texte*, p. 37. See also Roland Barthes and Maurice Nadeau, *Sur la Littérature* (Grenoble, 1980), p. 31: "Artaud's writing is located at such a level of incandescence, of burning fire and transgression, that in the end there is nothing to say *on* Artaud. There is no book to be written on Artaud. There is no criticism to write on Artaud. The only solution would be to write like him, to engage in a plagiarism of Artaud."

51. Barthes, *Le Plaisir du texte*, p. 25.

52. Barthes, *The Grain of the Voice*, p. 206. See also *Le Plaisir du texte*, p. 25.

53. This utopianism is also expressed very forcefully in conversation with Maurice Nadeau; see Barthes and Nadeau, *Sur la Littérature*, pp. 42–44.

54. Barthes, *Le Plaisir du texte*, pp. 66–67; see also Barthes and Nadeau, *Sur la Littérature*, p. 41.

55. Barthes, *Le Plaisir du texte*, p. 75.

56. Ibid., p. 63.

57. The Norwegian critic Stein Olsen argued in a recent book for an understanding of literature as a social institution—that is to say, "as a practice whose existence depends both on a background of concepts and conventions which create the possibility of identifying literary works and provide a framework for appreciation, and on people actually applying these concepts and conventions in their approach to literary works." "The institutional approach to literature rests," he adds, "on an assumption of a fundamental agreement concerning what literature is and what literary judgments are. The task of literary aesthetics is to display the nature of this agreement" ("Literary Aesthetics and Literary Practice," in *The End of Literary Theory* [Cambridge, 1987] pp. 12–13). There is something reminiscent of Johnson in this highly social view both of literature and of literary criticism, but the audience Olsen is thinking of is more like an audience of professional readers than the broad—in principle universal—"public" imagined by Johnson.

4. Augustin Thierry

1. On academic historiography and the attack on it, see Hayden V. White, *Metahistory: The Historical Imagination in Nineteenth-Century Europe* (Baltimore, 1973), and the admirable essay of 1935 by Charles Beard, "That Noble Dream," reprinted in *The Varieties of History*, ed. Fritz Stern (Cleveland and New York, 1956), pp. 315–328. On Sybel, see Herbert Flaig, "The Historian as Pedagogue of the Nation," *History* 59 (1974): 18–32. On the politics of historiography during the Restoration, see Jacques Barzun, "Romantic Historiography as a Political Force in France," *Journal of the History of Ideas* 2 (1941): 318–329, and Stanley Mellon, *The Political Uses of History: A Study of Historians in the French Restoration* (Stanford, 1958).

On Augustin Thierry himself, the standard biography—largely anecdotal, but a mine of information—is A. Augustin Thierry, *Augustin Thierry, d'après sa correspondance et ses papiers de famille* (Paris, 1922). The principal studies of his work are by Ferdinand Brunetière in *Revue des Deux Mondes* 82 (1895): 469–480; K. J. Carroll, *Some Aspects of the Historical Work of A. Thierry* (Washington, D.C., 1951); Friedrich Engel-Janosi, *Four Studies in French Romantic Writing* (Baltimore, 1955), pp. 88–120; Camille Jullian in *Revue de Synthèse Historique* 13 (1906): 125–142; B. Reizov, *Frantsuskaja Romanticheskaja Istoriografija* (Leningrad, 1956), pp. 69–122. A recent book-length study by Rulon Smithson, *Augustin Thierry: Social and Political Consciousness in the Evolution of a Historical Method* (Geneva, 1973), contains a full bibliography of Thierry's writings and of writings on Thierry, and provides the most detailed chronological account available of Thierry's literary career. Thierry's increasingly moderate and conciliatory political and literary stance, even before the 1830 Revolution, is well documented here, notably in the chapters on the successive editions of the *Conquête de l'Angleterre* (pp. 157–170, 275–284; also 287–288, 296–297). In general, Thierry emerges from Smithson's biography as a rather unattractive, vain, querulous, and trying invalid. Thierry's work is treated throughout in immediate relation to the evolving political situation and to his interest in his career and his reputation.

2. On the *Censeur,* see two studies by Ephraim Harpaz, "Le *Censeur Européen*: Histoire d'un journal quotidien," *Revue des Sciences Humaines* 114 (1964): 137–259, and "Le *Censeur Européen:* Histoire d'un journal industrialiste," *Revue d'Histoire Economique et Sociale* 17 (1959): 185–218, 328–357, and a contemporary essay on Comte by François Mignet in his *Notices et portraits historiques et littéraires,* 3rd ed. (Paris, 1854), II, 83–114. On the *Globe* and its contributors, see A. G. Lehmann, *Sainte-Beuve* (Oxford, 1962), chap. 3; H. J. Hunt, *Le Socialisme et le romantisme en France: Etude de la presse socialiste de 1830 à 1848* (Oxford, 1935), pp. 37–81; and René Bray, *Chronologie du romantisme* (Paris, 1963), chap. 7.

3. On Amédée Thierry, see A. Augustin Thierry, "Histoire d'un historien: Amédée Thierry, 1797–1873," *Revue des Deux Mondes* 47 (1928): 900–930; 48 (1928): 157–185, 647–673.

4. On Carrel, see the essay by Sainte-Beuve, *Causeries du lundi* (Paris, 1857–1872), VI, 84–145, and the obituary tribute by John Stuart Mill in the *Westminster Review,* October 1837 (reprinted in John Stuart Mill, *Dissertations and Discussions, Political, Philosophical, and Historical,* 2nd ed. [London, 1867], I, 211–286).

5. See Augustin Thierry, review of two pre-election pamphlets, *Manuel électoral à l'usage de MM. les électeurs des départements de France, par un électeur éligible* and *Candidats présentés aux électeurs de Paris pour la session de 1817, par un électeur du département de la Seine,* in *Censeur Européen* 2 (1817): 107–168. The passage quoted is on p. 112. Subsequently, Thierry served for a while as speech writer to the banker Lafitte, after the latter's election.

6. In a letter to Villemain in 1836 he complained of the slowness with which favors came his way from former friends and associates who were now in power. Subsequently these friends were to come under attack for feathering the nests of their associates at the public expense (cf. Louis Trenard, *Salvandy en son temps, 1795–1856* [Lille, 1968], pp. 470, 829–830). In the end, Guizot did find an appointment for Thierry; he put him in charge of a government-sponsored project, con-

ceived on the model of the great Benedictine collections of the seventeenth and eighteenth centuries, to search out, edit, and publish historical documents relative to the history of the third estate.

7. Augustin Thierry, *Dix Ans d'études historiques* (1834; Paris, 1867), pp. 2–7; italics in text.

8. Ibid., pp. 127–128. "When he who was our William III reentered Paris preceded by cannon, lighted matches and bared sabers, were we in good faith when we believed in our power and our will, of which he declared he was the work?" (p. 127).

9. Ibid., pp. 6, 17–18.

10. Charles Ledré, *La Presse à l'assaut de la monarchie* (Paris, 1960), p. 41.

11. Thierry, *Dix Ans d'études*, p. 18.

12. Quoted in Prosper de Barante, *Souvenirs* (Paris, 1890–1891), III, 29.

13. See Douglas Johnson, *Guizot: Aspects of French History, 1787–1874* (London, 1963), chap. 3, "Education and Public Instruction."

14. *L'Industrie, ou discussions politiques, morales et philosophiques*, I, seconde partie: Politique. Par A. Thierry, fils adoptif de Henri de Saint-Simon. Mai 1817, "Des Nations et de leurs rapports mutuels." This text is found in *Oeuvres de Saint-Simon et d'Enfantin*, 47 vols. (Paris, 1865–78), XVIII. The passage quoted is on pp. 19–20n. (Another edition of "Des Nations" appeared in the *Censeur Européen* 2 [1817]: 112–246.) Cf. Charles Dunoyer, "Considérations sur l'état présent de l'Europe," *Censeur Européen* 2 (1817): 92: "Our aim should be not to overthrow governments but to become so enlightened ourselves and to propagate sound ideas so widely that it will be impossible for bad governments to do evil." Not revolution but the influencing of public opinion was the goal of the liberals of the Restoration. Dunoyer argued strongly that revolution was always destructive of liberty and prosperity and was generally counterproductive (pp. 78–92).

15. Thierry, "Des Nations," p. 96.

16. Thierry, *Dix Ans d'études*, p. 96.

17. Notably in book V.

18. Thierry, *Dix Ans d'études*, pp. 11–12.

19. *Censeur Européen* 4 (1817): 105, quoted in Thierry, *Dix Ans d'études*, Preface, p. 3.

20. Thierry, *Dix Ans d'études*, p. 292.

21. Ibid., p. 268.

22. Augustin Thierry, *Lettres sur l'histoire de France* (Paris, 1827), pp. 310–312. All references are to this edition unless otherwise specified. The order and numbering of the letters were changed in subsequent editions.

23. *Censeur Européen* 7 (1818): 250, quoted in Thierry, *Dix Ans d'études*, p. 5.

24. Thierry, *Dix Ans d'études*, pp. 10–11; see also p. 379.

25. Ibid., pp. 365–374.

26. Ibid., p. 38.

27. Ibid., p. 161.

28. Ibid., pp. 94–95.

29. Ibid., pp. 78–79.

30. Ibid., pp. 321–322.

31. Augustin Thierry, *Histoire de la conquête de l'Angleterre par les Normands*, 3 vols. (Paris, 1825), I. v. All references are to this edition unless otherwise specified.

32. Thierry, *Dix Ans d'études*, pp. 317–318.

33. Ibid., p. 319. There is an equally unflattering portrait of Charlemagne in *Conquête*, I, 152–153. This portrait was toned down by Thierry in later editions of the *Conquête*, no doubt in accordance with the author's increasing conservatism.

34. Thierry, *Conquête*, II, 4.

35. Thierry, *Dix Ans d'études*, pp. 365, 374; italics in text.

36. Ibid., pp. 308, 310.

37. Ibid., p. 296; see also p. 336 on *dux*.

38. Thierry, *Lettres sur l'histoire de France*, letter X.

39. Thierry, *Dix Ans d'études*, pp. 162, 199–200.

40. Thierry, *Lettres sur l'histoire de France*, letter IX, pp. 86–87; see also letter II, p. 15.

41. Thierry, *Dix Ans d'études*, pp. 139–140.

42. See, for instance, Augustin Thierry, *Formation and Progress of the Tiers Etat* (London, 1859), I, 282–283, 322. (The French text, *Essai sur l'histoire de la formation et des progrès du tiers état*, appeared between 1846 and 1850 in the form of articles in the *Revue des Deux Mondes* and as a single volume in 1853. The English translation first appeared in 1855. The text of the 1859 edition, quoted here, is identical with that of 1855.)

43. Thierry, "Des Nations," pp. 26–28.

44. Thierry, *Dix Ans d'études*, p. 57. See also *Lettres sur l'histoire de France*, letter II; and addition to the 6th ed. (1839), letter VI: "When I say nation, do not take this word literally; for the Franks were not a people but a confederation of tribes that in early times were quite distinct, even of different origin, although all belonged to the Germanic or Teuton race."

45. Thierry, *Dix Ans d'études*, p. 66

46. Ibid., p. 440. See also the long essay "On Fourteen Historians before Mézeray," in the same volume, pp. 358–423.

47. Ibid., pp. 425, 450–457.

48. Ibid., pp. 428–429.

49. Thierry, *Conquête*, I, 60. Likewise Celtic names are defamiliarized, even if only in a note. The "Clyde" of the text is given as "Ystrad-Clwyd" in a note; Dunbarton is revealed as "Autrefois Dun-briton, la forteresse des Bretons." Notes also reproduce the original Saxon or Latin of passages given in translation in the text.

50. Thierry, *Conquête*, I, xxvi–xxvii.

51. Thierry, *Dix Ans d'études*, p. 379

52. The comparison is made by Philippe Ariès in a study of seventeenth- and eighteenth-century historiography in his *Le Temps de l'histoire* (Monaco, 1954).

53. Thierry, *Dix Ans d'études*, pp. 302, 307–308. See also *Lettres sur l'histoire de France*, letter VIII.

54. Thierry, *Conquête*, I, 366.

55. Thierry, *Tiers Etat*, p. 285. Thierry's point was a commonplace of liberal historiography in the nineteenth century. Cf. Macaulay: "The circumstances which have most influence on the happiness of mankind, the changes of manners and morals, the transition of communities from poverty to wealth, from knowledge

to ignorance, from ferocity to humanity—these are, for the most part, noiseless revolutions. Their progress is rarely indicated by what historians are pleased to call important events. They are not achieved by armies or enacted by senates. They are sanctioned by no treaties, and recorded in no archives. They are carried on in every school, in every church, behind ten thousand counters, at ten thousand firesides. . . . [The historian] must not confine his observations to palaces and solemn days. He must see ordinary men as they appear in their ordinary business and in their ordinary pleasures. He must mingle in the crowds of the exchange and the coffee-houses. He must obtain admittance to the convivial table and the domestic hearth. . . . He must not shrink from exploring even the retreats of misery." ("History" [*Edinburgh Review*, 1828], reprinted in *Varieties of History*, ed. Stern, pp. 84–86.) Cf. similar statements in Carlyle ("On History" [1830], ibid., pp. 97–98).

56. There is an enormous critical literature on Enlightenment historiography. Two outstanding studies, written from different perspectives, develop the particular point made here: Leo Braudy, *Narrative Form in History and Fiction* (Princeton, N.J., 1970), and Boris Reizov, *Frantsuskaja Romanticheskaja Istoriografija* (Leningrad, 1956).

57. Cf. Guizot in the Preface to his *Histoire de la Révolution d'Angleterre* (Paris, 1826): "J'ai publié les mémoires originaux de la révolution d'Angleterre; j'en publie aujourd'hui l'histoire" (quoted from 1841 edition, I, vii).

58. Thierry provides a summary account of the documents he attempted to gather together in *Tiers Etat*, II, Appendix 1: "Documents Relative to the Personal Condition of the Plebeian Classes," "Documents Relative to the Condition of the Bourgeoisie Considered in Its Various Corporations," "Documents Relative to the Ancient Condition of Cities, Boroughs and Parishes of France," "Documents Relative to the Part Played by the *Tiers Etat* in the Assemblies of the General or Provincial Estates." The range of documents reviewed was fairly wide—charters, royal and municipal ordinances, petitions, title grants, *cahiers*, and proposals not included in the definitive *cahiers*.

59. Thierry. *Conquête*, I, 430 (end of Book IV).

60. Thierry, *Dix Ans d'études*, p. 14.

61. Ibid., pp. 10, 146. In a brief discussion of Thierry's idea of insight, Smithson argues that the historian was "uncomfortable" with it and was more drawn to a positivist view of knowledge as grounded in erudition and "facts" (Smithson, *Augustin Thierry*, pp. 297–300). He refers to a frequently quoted passage in the *Considérations* of 1840 in which Thierry claims that synthesis and historical intuition are best left to those who are irresistibly drawn to them "à leurs risques et périls." Thierry may have veered in the direction of positivism in his later, more conservative period, but he at no time held that "second sight" made scholarship unnecessary; it was always seen as a moment in the act of understanding. His later reservations were provoked in considerable measure by what he considered the abuse of imagination among some younger historians, notably those who, like Michelet, had been influenced by the theory of myth in Friedrich Creuzer's *Symbolik und Mythologie der alten Völker* (1810–1812), translated and adapted by J. D. Guigniaut as *Religion de l'antiquité* (Paris, 1825).

62. Thierry, *Dix Ans d'études*, p. 19.

63. Ibid., pp. 12, 304.

64. That is, "gather round a single interest the innumerable parts of the tableau." Failing this, he resorts to external principles of organization such as royal genealogies (ibid., p. 304).

65. Augustin Thierry, *Considérations sur l'histoire de France* (Paris, 1840), p. 193. The theme was common to nearly all the historians of the Restoration. According to Guizot, the French Revolution made it possible for the historian to shed new light on the English one and permitted Frenchmen, such as Villemain or himself, to understand the English Civil War better than Englishmen themselves could (*Histoire de la Révolution d'Angleterre* [1826; Paris, 1841], I, xxiv–xxviii). Guizot's claim has received support in our own time from Christopher Hill, *Science and Society* 12 (1948): 132.

66. Thierry, *Lettres sur l'histoire de France*, letter XIII.

67. Thierry, *Considérations*, p. 72.

68. Thierry, *Conquête*, I, viii.

69. Thierry, *Lettres sur l'histoire de France*, letter VI, pp. 56–57.

70. Thierry, *Dix Ans d'études*, p. 16.

71. Ibid., p. 302.

72. *Censeur Européen*, 7 (1818): 250, quoted by Thierry himself in *Dix Ans d'études*, p. 5. Similarly, Amédée Thierry wrote in the introduction to his *Histoire des Gaulois* (1828) that he had been inspired to write by "a sentiment of justice and almost of piety." As a Frenchman himself, he wanted to "know and make known a race from which nineteen out of every twenty of us Frenchmen are descended" (16th ed. [Paris, 1866], p. 1).

73. Thierry, *Dix Ans d'études*, pp. 132, 142, 155. See also pp. 128–129, and, on the Welsh, the end of book 1 of the *Conquête*.

74. Thierry, *Tiers Etat*, p. 7.

75. Ibid., pp. 2–3.

76. Thierry, *Dix Ans d'études*, pp. 2, 138–146.

77. Cf. Thierry himself on the two races of humanity, one of which labors to be its own master while the other labors to become the master of others, in "Vue des révolutions de l'Angleterre," *Censeur Européen* 5 (1817): 47.

78. Thierry, *Dix Ans d'études*, p. 158. This essay is one of the few places where Thierry tries to give his racial differences a permanent biological basis. See notably the passage on pp. 156–157: "Recent research in physiology has demonstrated that the physical and moral make-up of a people is far more dependent on the original race from which it is descended than on the influence of the climate in which it has been placed by mere accident." But even that passage may have to be read partly in terms of the liberal claim, forcefully articulated by Michelet, that in the course of human development history and culture replace geography and nature as the chief influences on the lives of men and societies. The idea of an internal, "organic" development is in general more congenial to Romantic ways of thinking than the external causation implied by the climate theory, which enjoyed great popularity during the Enlightenment.

79. Thus the king—"the general in command of the army" (*Dix Ans d'études*, p. 49), "the supreme guardian of the conquest" (ibid., p. 55)—is seen as planting "the standard of the Norman chieftain" near Nottingham, while his supporters

are described as all those "whose ancestors had signed up to join the invasion army" (ibid., p. 72; see also p. 176).

80. Cf. the description of the spoliation of England after the Conquest and the identification of royal power, violence, and spoliation. The invaders, according to Thierry, were not even "nobles" in their own lands, but a riffraff of adventurers bent on plunder (Thierry, *Conquête*, I, 275, 325–338). Likewise, the king appears as a robber chieftain (*Dix Ans d'études*, pp. 49, 50–51, 55, 58).

81. See notably Thierry, *Conquête*, Conclusion, sec. V; *Tiers Etat*, pp. 22–23, 36.

82. "Sur l'antipathie de race qui divise la nation française" (1820), quoted in Thierry, *Dix Ans d'études*, pp. 279–280 (italics added); *Conquête*, I, v–vi, 173.

83. Thierry, *Lettres sur l'histoire de France*, p. 233.

84. Thierry, *Considérations*, pp. 169–186. On the theories of Montlosier, Thierry, and Amédée Thierry, see M. Seliger, "Race Thinking during the Restoration," *Journal of the History of Ideas* 19 (1958): 273–282.

85. Letter from Marx to Engels, 27 July 1854, in *Marx-Engels Briefwechsel* (Berlin, 1949–50), II, 56–58.

86. Simonde de Sismondi, in *Revue Encyclopédique* 28 (October 1825): 77–91.

87. In Thierry's early writings, societies appear as provisional and transitory groupings of individuals banded together for some determinate end. When the end has been achieved, the "society" disbands ("Des Nations," pp. 20–21).

88. Thierry, *Dix Ans d'études*, pp. 166.

89. Ibid., p. 167.

90. Thierry, *Conquête*, I, 3.

91. Thierry, *Dix Ans d'études*, p. 291.

92. Ibid., p. 311.

93. Thierry, *Tiers Etat*, pp. 18, 19.

94. Thierry, *Conquête*, Books III, VI, VII. In *The Development of the Marxist View of History*, chap. 2 ("French Historians of the Restoration"), G. V. Plekhanov long ago pointed out that the conquest theory, by which the Restoration historians tried to explain social inequalities, could not in fact satisfactorily account for them (*Selected Philosophical Works* [Moscow and London, 1961], I, 558–571).

95. Thierry, *Tiers Etat*, pp. 79, 91, 73–75.

96. Ibid., pp. 91–96, 200, 297–298.

97. Thierry, *Dix Ans d'études*, pp. 101, 104, 123.

98. It is worth quoting Marx's comment in full: "A book that interested me greatly is Thierry's *Histoire de la formation et des progrès du tiers état*, 1853. Strange, how this gentleman, the père of the 'class struggle' in French historiography, waxes wrathful in the preface over the 'moderns,' who now see a further antagonism between bourgeois and proletariat, and who seek to discover traces of this conflict even in the history of the tiers état before 1789. Thierry goes to a lot of trouble to demonstrate that the tiers état includes all estates other than *noblesse* and *clergé* and that the bourgeoisie plays its role as the representative of all these elements . . . Had Herr Thierry read our pieces, he would know that the decisive opposition of the bourgeoisie to the people does not set in until the bourgeoisie ceases, as tiers état, to oppose the *clergé* and the *noblesse*. Concerning the 'roots in history' of an antagonism 'born only yesterday', however, Thierry's own book

offers the best evidence that these 'roots' arose at the very same time as the tiers état" (letter to Engels, 27 July 1854, in *Marx-Engels Briefwechsel*).

99. Thierry, *Tiers Etat*, p. 2.

100. Ibid. Similar views were held by Guizot: see Johnson, *Guizot*, pp. 76–77. Smithson (*Augustin Thierry*, pp. 247–258) outlines the ideological context of Thierry's insistence on the unity of the *tiers* in face of both right-wing and left-wing arguments to the contrary.

101. *De la Réorganisation de la société européenne . . . par M. le Comte de Saint-Simon et par A. Thierry, son élève* (1814), Introduction by Alfred Péreire, Preface by Henri de Jouvenel (Paris, n.d.), p. 28; *Dix ans d'études*, p. 29: *Censeur Européen* 2 (1817): 145–146.

102. Thierry, *Tiers Etat*, p. 232.

103. Thus the charters of the bourgeoisies of the Middle Ages are presented as if they were determined entirely by the "spirit of justice and reason" (Thierry, *Tiers Etat*, pp. 49–50), rather than by the specific interests of a social group.

104. Thierry, *Tiers Etat*, pp. 49, 32, 123; also pp. 120, 345.

105. Thierry, *Dix Ans d'études*, pp. 107–128. Thierry may have derived his view of the 1688 Revolution from the opening pages of Burke's *Reflections on the Revolution in France* (1790).

106. Thus Colbert, the incarnation of bourgeois rationality and impartiality in the *Tiers Etat*, is "unpopular even to being hated. . . . The people, especially the people of Paris, hated Colbert" (Thierry, *Tiers Etat*, p. 329).

107. Thierry, "Des Nations," p. 34.

108. Thierry, *Tiers Etat*, p. 213.

109. See, for instance, Thierry, *Dix Ans d'études*, pp. 101, 104, 123. The dual character of the "people" as *bourgeoisie* and *populace* is a common feature of liberal historiography; it can be found in Voltaire, and it occupies a significant place in the work of Barante, Sismondi, Guizot, and Michelet. Barante, for instance, refers frequently to the judgment of "men of good sense and good counsel"—that is, "that aristocratic bourgeoisie below which agitated the turbulent and barbarous masses, always ready for bloody seditions" (*Histoire des Ducs de Bourgogne* [ed. of Brussels, 1835], I, 39). On this aspect of Barante, see Engel-Janosi, *Four Studies*, pp. 75–82, and above all the valuable monograph of René Teuteberg, *Prosper de Barante (1782–1866): Ein romantischer Historiker des französischen Liberalismus* (Basel, 1945). Sismondi faces the problem of liberal distrust of the people candidly in his essay "On Universal Suffrage" (1834) in *Political Economy and the Philosophy of Government: Essays Selected from the Works of M. de Sismondi, with an Historical Notice of His Life and Writings by M. Mignet* (London, 1847), notably pp. 289–292, 294–295. One of the aims of Sismondi's *Economie politique* (Paris, 1837) was to "assurer la souveraineté à la volonté éclairée plutôt qu'au nombre." For an early and forthright expression of liberal distrust of the people, see the essay "Sur l'état présent de l'Europe" by Thierry's early associate Charles Dunoyer in *Censeur Européen* 2 (1817): 67–106. Dunoyer's stated aim was to "rappeler les hommes au travail et à l'industrie, les détourner de la recherche du pouvoir" (p. 105).

110. Thierry, "Des Nations," pp. 37–38. These ideas had been anticipated to some extent in *De la Réorganisation de la société européenne* (1814), written in collaboration with Saint-Simon; they were repeated in an essay of 1817 on the English

revolutions (see *Dix Ans d'études*, pp. 33–34). See also Charles Dunoyer's essay "De l'Organisation sociale dans ses rapports avec les moyens de subsistance des peuples," *Censeur Européen* 2 (1817): 1–66. Dunoyer argued that different forms of social organization are appropriate to different forms of economic organization, to the different ways in which a society tries to ensure its material subsistence. There are, he claims, basically three such ways: food-gathering, conquest or pillage, and industry. All three are followed to some degree in every society, but in every society one way is dominant. Thus, for instance, the Romans and the Franks are "peuples essentiellement pillards et guerriers." Dunoyer could have found this view of the Romans in Bossuet or Montesquieu.

The distinction between the feudal world, in which closed, mutually exclusive units confront each other in absolute hostility, and the modern bourgeois world of openness, free communication and exchange (orderly cities, safe roads, money and letters of credit) goes back, of course, to the historians of the Enlightenment. See for instance, Voltaire, *Siècle de Louis XIV*, chap. 1. There is a striking discontinuity in Voltaire's histories between the ages of barbarism and those of civilization. Voltaire's culture-heroes—Peter the Great or Louis XIV—mark a new beginning. Some of their predecessors may have anticipated their work, but Voltaire sees no continuity between these early abortive efforts to introduce civilization and the great achievements of Peter or Louis.

111. Thierry, "Des Nations," p. 58; *Dix Ans d'études*, p. 213.

112. Hence Thierry's youthful impatience with history, which he interprets as obstacle, opacity, entanglement. "In our old continent of Europe," he wrote on the subject of political representation, "where nothing proceeds straightforwardly, where each century is dragged backwards by the century preceding it, where the heritage of prejudices is transmitted along with the heritage of Enlightenment, and passes from one generation to the next, this system was born almost six hundred years ago, and it was corrupt from the moment of its birth. In America, where there are neither hovels nor memories, the institution was founded pure and has preserved itself pure" ("Manuel électoral," p. 129).

113. Thierry, *Tiers Etat*, p. 11.

114. Ibid., pp. 306–307.

115. Ibid., pp. 311–312.

116. Ibid., p. 326.

117. Ibid., p. 308.

118. Thierry almost everywhere uses antithesis to structure his narrative—Normans and Saxons in the *Conquête*, Franks and Gallo-Romans in the *Récits des temps mérovingiens*. Antithesis has the advantage not only of establishing differentiae but of defining them strictly in a logical relation to each other, and thus allowing the historian to steer a course between the twin perils of absolute uniformity or undifferentiatedness and absolute, chaotic particularity.

119. "Historical Notice of the Life and Work of M. de Sismondi," in *Political Economy and the Philosophy of Government*, p. 8. The idea of history as latecomer among the arts of civilization is characteristic of Enlightenment thought: see John Hill, "An Essay upon the Principles of Historical Composition," *Transactions of the Royal Society of Edinburgh*, I, ii (1788): 189–190.

120. In 1814, when Thierry believed that the English system of government

could be taken as a model by all bourgeois regimes, he admired it because it was "founded not on prejudices and customs, but on that which is of all times and all places, on that which ought to be the ground of every constitution, the freedom and happiness of the people" (*Réorganisation de la société européenne,* p. 9). Subsequently, the universality of the *tiers* and of the insights it provided rested less on abstract reason than on the role of the *tiers* as the *third* or mediating term in the process of history itself.

121. Thierry, *Tiers Etat,* p. 7.

122. Cf. notably Thierry, "Des Nations," pp. 38–43. A typical statement of this position can be found in the first number of the *Censeur Européen* 1 (1817): 50–51: "L'industrie, en détruisant la domination qu'exerçait une partie de l'espèce humaine sur l'autre, ou, pour mieux dire, en faisant disparaître les maîtres et les esclaves, a donc créé de nouveaux hommes, étrangers aux préjugés et aux habitudes des uns, à l'avilissement ou à la bassesse des autres" ("Considérations sur l'état moral de la nation française et sur les causes de l'instabilité de ses institutions").

123. Thierry, *Tiers Etat,* p. 345.

124. Thierry, *Dix Ans d'études,* p. 213.

125. Ibid., p. 32.

126. Thierry, *Tiers Etat,* pp. 214–215. Cf. ibid., p. 71, on the career of Etienne Marcel—"a premature attempt at the grand designs of Providence" which were "destined to advance to their accomplishment at another time." The providentialist view of history was particularly popular among the German Romantics. See, for instance, J. J. Görres in an article of 1804: "Wie ein ungeheurer, verworrener, wild in einander gezerrter Knäuel erscheint die Geschichte, ein Schwindel erregendes Gewühl von kämpfenden Menschen und schlagenden Armen, von geschwungenen Schwertern, wehenden Fahnen, wogenden Helmbüschen, geballten Fäusten, und schnaubenden Pferden . . . Wie die Sonne aber steht die Vorsehung am Himmel und schaut hinunter in den Sturm, und ihr Strahl wird die schwühle, trübe, aufgeregte Malerei klären" (*Aurora,* no. 133, reprinted in *Charakteristiken und Kritiken von Johann Joseph Görres aus den Jahren 1804 and 1805,* ed. F. Schalk [Cologne, 1900], p. 49).

127. Thierry, *Tiers Etat,* p. 7.

128. Ibid., pp. 6, 322–323.

129. Ibid., pp. 76–77; cf. pp. 340, 343.

130. Ibid., p. 269.

131. Ibid., p. 81.

132. *De la Réorganisation de la société européenne,* book II.

133. *L'Industrie,* in *Oeuvres de Saint-Simon et d'Enfantin,* XVIII, 62–63. Similar ideas were expressed by Charles Comte, "Considérations sur l'état moral de la nation française," *Censeur Européen* 1 (1817), and by Charles Dunoyer, "Considérations sur l'état présent de l'Europe," *Censeur Européen* 2 (1817): 67–106. The rationalist convictions of the early nineteenth-century liberals are still audible in a famous speech by Richard Cobden, the champion of Free Trade and repeal of the Corn Laws, given in Manchester on 15 January 1846: "I see in the Free Trade principle that which shall act on the moral world as the principle of gravitation in the universe—drawing men together, thrusting aside the antagonism of race, and creed, and language, and uniting us in the bonds of eternal peace. I believe

that the effect will be to change the face of the world, so as to introduce a system of government entirely distinct from that which now prevails. I believe that the desire and the motive for large and mighty empires; for gigantic armies and great navies—for those materials which are used for the destruction of life and the desolation of the rewards of labour—will die away; I believe that such things will cease to be necessary, or to be used, when man becomes one family, and freely exchanges the fruits of his labour with his brother man . . . I believe that the speculative philosopher of a thousand years hence will date the greatest revolution that ever happened in the world's history from the triumph of the principle which we have met here to advocate" (*Speeches by Richard Cobden, M.P.*, I, 362–363, in *The Liberal Tradition from Fox to Keynes*, ed. Alan Bullock and Maurice Shock [London, 1956], pp. 53–54). The *locus classicus* of liberal internationalism was book IV, chap. 3 of *The Wealth of Nations* (Modern Library edition [New York, 1937], pp. 460–465).

134. Thierry, "Des Nations," pp. 63–67, 25.

135. Thierry, *Dix Ans d'études*, pp. 255–257, 273–274. Cf. B. Constant, "De l'Esprit de conquête et de l'usurpation," in *Cours de politique constitutionnelle*, ed. Edouard de Laboulaye (Paris, 1861), II, 129–282, especially chaps. 12 and 13. To Constant, uniformity is "la suite immédiate et inséparable de l'esprit de conquête" (p. 171).

136. Thierry, *Tiers Etat*, p. 343. See also p. 254, on the monarchy as a symbol of the social unity toward which the people aspired. Thierry appears to be anxious to reconcile the rationalism of the natural-law theorists, for whom the individual is prior to society, and the organicism of conservatives like de Bonald, for whom society is prior to the individual—that is, to reconcile the revolutionary implications of natural-law theory and the conservative implications of organicist theory. This effort at reconciliation seems characteristic of much Restoration thinking.

137. Quoted in Johnson, *Guizot*, p. 74.

138. Constant, "De l'Esprit de conquête," pp. 173, 174.

139. Letter of 1807, published in *Revue des Deux Mondes* 34 (15 July 1906): 246–247.

140. Prosper de Barante, *Histoire des Ducs de Bourgogne de la maison de Valois, 1364–1477*, 12 vols. (Paris, 1824–26), I, xxxvi. All references are to this edition unless otherwise specified.

141. Royer-Collard, lamenting the fate of orators, had once remarked to Barante that "the speeches of political orators can be brought to life again only if they are framed in an historical narrative" (quoted in Teuteberg, *Prosper de Barante*, p. 75). Barante's biography of the statesman provided the frame in which his subject's own discourses could be inserted. The *Ducs de Bourgogne*, likewise, was composed from such contemporary chronicle sources as Froissart, Commynes, and the Grandes Chroniques, and some later ones such as Jakob Meyer's Latin History of Flanders and Dom Planchet's *Histoire de Bourgogne*. Barante's goals and methods were shared by many compilers of biographies and autobiographies in the nineteenth century. In the letter to N. P. Ogarëv with which Alexander Herzen opens his remarkable memoirs, for instance, the various stages of composition and publication of the parts composing the text are described in some detail: "*My Past and Thoughts*," Herzen sums up, "was not written consecutively: between some

chapters there lie whole years. Therefore the whole of it retains the colour of its own time and of varying moods—I should not care to rub this off" (*My Past and Thoughts,* trans. Constance Garnett, rev. Humphrey Higgens [London, 1968], p. xliii). Both the goal of authenticity and the incorporation of fragments from the past as the means of achieving it were clearly outlined by the father of modern autobiography. In chapter 37 of book II of the *Essays* ("De la ressemblance des enfans aux pères"), Montaigne writes: "Ce fagotage de tant de diverses pieces se faict en cette condition, que je n'y mets la main que lors qu'une trop lasche oisiveté me presse, et non ailleurs que chez moy. Ainsin il s'est basty à diverses poses et intervalles, comme les occasions me detiennent ailleurs par fois plusieurs moys. Au demeurant, je ne corrige point mes premieres imaginations par les secondes: ouy à l'aventure quelque mot, mais pour diversifier, non pour oster. Je veux representer le progrez de mes humeurs, et qu'on voye chaque piece en sa naissance."

142. Barante, *Histoire des Ducs de Bourgogne,* I, ii, ix–x, xiv–xix.

143. Ibid., pp. vi–vii, xv.

144. Ibid., pp. vi, xxvi.

145. "We demand that peoples and individuals be called up and represented living before our very eyes: each one of us will then deduce the lesson he wants, or may even not think of extracting a precise opinion . . . This is the plan I myself have tried to follow in writing the history of the Dukes of Burgundy and of the House of Valois" (ibid., pp. xxxvi, xxxvii). Barante's "modernity" in 1824 emerges clearly from a comparison of his Preface with the preface Sismondi wrote for his *Histoire des Français* (begun in 1818). Like Barante, Sismondi is anxious to reconcile two proper historical concerns, that for detail and that for structure or general order. Whereas Barante requires that they be reconciled in a single continuous narrative, however, Sismondi still envisages two types of historical writing—detailed histories and *résumés* (a term reminiscent of d'Alembert and his suggestion that every hundred years a bonfire be made of all superfluous historical information and that the rest be consigned to résumés). Sismondi requires only that authors of the second type should also be authors of the first type. In sum, Barante requires that the two perspectives be reconciled or fused *in the text* and through the historian's art, while Sismondi proposes that they be adopted *alternatively* by the same spectator.

146. Barante, *Histoire des Ducs de Bourgogne,* I, lxxxii.

147. Ibid.

148. Ibid., pp. lxxvii–lxxxiii, xcii.

149. Just as the narrative historian employs everyday notions of cause-and-effect relations, rather than carefully meditated scientific laws (so-called "covering laws"), everyday cause-and-effect explanations tend to take the form of narratives; on this question, much discussed by Anglo-American philosophers of history, see the recent book by Paul Veyne, *Comment on écrit l'histoire* (Paris, 1971), pp. 115–117, 193–209.

150. Barante, *Histoire des Ducs de Bourgogne,* I, xli.

151. "I removed the scaffolding completely . . . "(ibid., xlv).

152. Cf. Teuteberg, *Prosper de Barante,* p. 119.

153. Barante, *Histoire des Ducs de Bourgogne,* I, v, xlvii. More than sixty years later, Gabriel Monod would praise Green's *History of the English People* for having

"dans toutes ses parties, la fraîcheur de coloris, la chaleur communicative des récits d'un témoin oculaire" (*Histoire du peuple anglais* [Paris, 1888], Introduction, p. x).

154. See the excellent pages in Teuteberg, *Prosper de Barante*, pp. 121 ff.

155. Barante's transitions are often as conventional as those of the chroniclers: "It was at this very time that . . . ," "at the same time . . . ," and so forth. On the use of such devices, even by highly regarded modern historians, to achieve a rhetor   ˈ ï ˈˑk where no logical or causal relation can be established, see the lively pages in S. ˈgfried Kracauer, *History: The Last Things before the Last* (New York, 1969), chap. 7.

156. The difference between the two is clearly demonstrated in a remarkable article by Stephen Bann, "A Cycle in Historical Discourse: Barante, Thierry, Michelet," *20th Century Studies* 3 (1970): 110–130.

157. Thus his first major work was an "editing" of the oral and written memoirs of Madame de la Rochejaquelain. Barante's role in the preparation of this text has been constantly debated; the issue seems presently to be settled rather in favor of Madame de la Rochejaquelain.

158. Anatole France, "La Jeunesse de M. de Barante," in *Oeuvres complètes* (Paris, 1926), VII, 418.

159. Barante, *Histoire des Ducs de Bourgogne*, I, li. A similar justification of his work was given by Macaulay, who also owed his success to his talent as a narrative and portrait artist: "In fiction, the principles are given, to find the facts: in history, the facts are given, to find the principles; and the writer who does not explain the phenomena as well as state them performs only one half of his office. Facts are the mere dross of history. It is from the abstract truth which interpenetrates them, and lies latent among them like gold in the ore, that the mass derives its whole value. . . . The perfect historian is he in whose work the character and spirit of an age is exhibited in miniature . . . By judicious selection, rejection, and arrangement, he gives truth to those attractions that have been usurped by fiction. In his narrative a due subordination is observed: some transactions are prominent; others retire. But the scale on which he represents them is increased or diminished, not according to the dignity of the persons concerned in them, but according to the degree in which they elucidate the condition of society and the nature of man" ("History" [*Edinburgh Review*, 1828], reprinted in *Varieties of History*, ed. Stern, pp. 78, 86). In a thoughtful essay on Macaulay, however, William A. Madden convincingly argues that the historian's "histrionic powers" and his desire not to pursue truth and reality, but to escape from them into the imagined world of the past, were essential elements in Macaulay's historiographical activity ("Macaulay's Style," in *The Art of Victorian Prose*, ed. George Levine and William Madden [New York, 1968], pp. 127-153). In general, synecdoche appears to mediate between Jakobson's two categories of metonymy (association by contiguity) and metaphor (association by similarity). As the part in a synecdoche is contiguous with other parts, it implies succession (and narrative), but as it is contained in the whole, and the image of the whole writ small, it is also constantly being reabsorbed by the unifying entity it represents or is like.

160. Thierry, *Dix Ans d'études*, p. 17.

161. Alexander Herzen, *Sobranie sochinenii*, 30 vols. (Moscow, 1954), II, 7–8. See also Thierry, *Lettres sur l'histoire de France*, pp. 55–57.

162. Thierry does indeed endeavor to locate his characterizations at dramatic points in the narrative and to associate them with specific events. The principal portrait of Edward the Confessor, for instance, occurs not after his death in the conventional place for the obituary portrait, but just before it, when he is over-whelmed by adverse fortune (*Conquête*, I, 255–257). More often the portrait is progressive, rather than all of a piece, and is made up of many different comments and analyses occasioned by different acts or events. Even brief, apparently classical characterizations, such as "Le Saxon, brave et plein de confiance" or "Edouard, homme d'une nature débile et devenu plus sensible à la destinée de son pays" (ibid., I, 247, 255) are in fact related to particular moments and are not intended to be as general and universal as, for instance, the lapidary identifying character-izations common in Voltaire's historical work.

163. Thierry, *Lettres sur l'histoire de France,* Preface, pp. x–xi. Thierry's adoption of the custom of settting down dates in the margins of his text of the *Conquête* was doubtless intended to emphasize the sequential aspect of the narrative, and to make it appear as the unaltered image of an objective temporal sequence rather than as a construct of the historian.

164. Thierry, *Dix Ans d'études,* pp. 20–21.

165. Thierry, *Considérations,* p. 119.

166. Augustin Thierry, *Récits des temps mérovingiens,* Avant-propos par Gilbert Lély (Paris, 1965), p. 224. All references are to this popular edition unless otherwise specified.

167. From a strictly linguistic point of view, the impossibility of translating from phonology to graphology is demonstrated by J. C. Catford, *A Linguistic Theory of Translation* (London, 1965). Translation equivalents suppose common substances, according to Catford; even the translation of phonological items in the source language (SL) into phonological items in the target language (TL), or of graphological items into graphological items, in what we usually refer to as translations, is in fact translation of SL grammatical and lexical items into TL grammatical and lexical items, the specific exponents of these items (phonological or graphological) being basically irrelevant. The *voice,* in short, with all its con-notations of immediacy and authenticity, is irrelevant to the act of translation.

168. Thierry, *Dix Ans d'études,* p. 17.

169. Jules Michelet, *L'Oiseau* (1856; Paris, 1936), pp. 79–80.

170. Review in the *Guardian* of Carrel's *History of the Counterrevolution from the Reestablishment of Popery in England under Charles II and James II,* quoted in publisher's advertising material in Hazlitt's translation of Thierry's *Conquest* (Lon-don, 1847).

171. See Stephen Bann's original and enterprising essay ("A Cycle in Historical Discourse," *20th Century Studies* 3 [1970]: 110–130). I am indebted to Bann for many of the points made in the following two or three pages.

172. Barante, *Histoire des Ducs de Bourgogne,* I, xlv.

173. Teuteberg considers Barante virtually untouched by the critical movement in historiography.

174. Cf., for instance, Thierry's reference to G. B. Depping's *Histoire des ex-péditions maritimes des Normands* (1826), in the *Avertissement* to the third edition of the *Conquête:* "This excellent book is one of three that I recommend to those

studious readers who would like to acquaint themselves exhaustively with all the facts, from which I was obliged to make a selection."

175. The succession of events is likewise maintained across the divisions of reigns. The first sentence of *Jean-sans-Peur* takes up the events recounted in the previous section on *Philippe-le-Hardi,* as though there had been no break in the narrative: "*Tandis que* le convoi du duc Philippe cheminait lentement . . ." (italics added).

176. Augustin Thierry, *Histoire de la Conquête de l'Angleterre par les Normands* (4-vol. ed., Paris, 1867), I, 10.

177. The epigraph at the beginning of the *Conquête,* some lines from the Chronicle of Gloucester, indicates clearly the theme that—at least as much as sequence in time—unites all the elements in the work. Later, in the Preface to *Dix Ans d'études* (1834), Thierry again referred to "the great problem, to the resolution of which all my research was directed, the problem of conquest in the Middle Ages and its social consequences" (p. 8). In the Preface to the still later *Récits des temps mérovingiens,* he describes his plan as "to select the critical point of the first period of the mingling of manners between the two races [that is, Gallo-Roman and Frankish]; and there, in a limited space, to gather the most characteristic facts and arrange them in groups, so as to form a series of tableaux following one after the other in a cumulative manner" (p. 18).

178. Thierry, *Conquête,* I, iv–v.

179. Thierry, *Dix Ans d'études,* p. 9. Engels, who, like Marx, knew Thierry's work well, also described the history of Ireland in terms of conquest and racial struggle—Saxons versus Celts—and also saw Irish history as exemplary (letter to Marx, 23 May 1856, in *Briefwechsel,* II, 171–173).

180. Thierry, *Conquête,* I, 429. See likewise I, 240–242, where a number of exemplary incidents are recounted in order to illustrate the conflict between England and Rome.

181. Thierry, *Dix Ans d'études,* pp. 108, 120, 127, and passim; *Tiers Etat,* pp. 69–71, 72–73, 92–94; *Lettres sur l'histoire de France,* p. 312. See also *Tiers Etat,* pp. 116–117, 238–239, 248–249, 290, 297–298, for associations between the states general of 1484 and those of 1789, the *cahiers* of 1560, 1615, and 1789, the Fronde and the Revolution, and so forth. The use of such devices to order the welter of historical particulars into a few essential categories (tyrant, victim, triumph, conquest, outburst of popular passion) is common throughout both neoclassical and nineteenth-century historiography. Macaulay, for instance, at the end of his essay on Warren Hastings, identifies his hero by comparing him with Richelieu and with Cosmo de Medici ("the capacity of Richelieu," "the judicious liberality of Cosmo"; *Macaulay: Prose and Poetry,* ed. G. M. Young [Cambridge, Mass., 1967], p. 468). The essay on Clive is likewise liberally sprinkled with historical analogies and comparisons. On this aspect of Macaulay see Jane Millgate, *Macaulay* (London, 1973), pp. 20, 45–46, 132–133, 161–189.

182. Thierry, *Conquête,* II, 63. The earliest example given by Robert of the usage of *guerillas* in French is dated 1834. Bloch and Wartburg trace the use of the term to 1820 but quote no text (Oscar Bloch and W. von Wartburg, *Dictionnaire étymologique de la langue française,* 3rd ed. [Paris, 1960]). Thierry's is clearly a very early literary use of the term. Later editions of the *Conquête* substitute the somewhat

less striking and provocative *partisans* in the modern sense this term had acquired in Chateaubriand's usage.

183. Thierry, *Récits,* p. 17.

184. Ibid., p. 277 (end of 6th *récit*).

185. Similar sets of antitheses structure the *Conquête.* In Book IV, for instance, the portraits of William and Hildebrand, Harold and Edward, the description of the continental hordes of robbers and adventurers descending upon the ill-defended island, the contrast between intriguing Rome and Normandy and simple, peace-loving England, at once point to and manifest an essential opposition of victims and victors, rooted and rootless, laborers and predators, exemplified in turn by the entire history of England and Normandy.

186. See for instance, Thierry, *Conquête,* end of Books I, IV, V, VII, VIII; *Tiers Etat,* p. 210; *Dix Ans d'études,* p. 127 (end of the essay on the Revolution of 1688); *Récits,* end of 6th *récit.*

187. Thierry, *Récits,* pp. 222–224.

188. Ibid., pp. 207–208.

189. Trenard, *Salvandy en son temps, 1795–1856,* p. 886. Cf. Thierry himself at the end of Book I of *Conquête:* "the good cause, the cause of the suffering and oppressed."

190. Thierry, *Conquête* (4-vol. ed., Paris, 1867), I, 11.

191. End of Book VIII.

192. Thierry, *Dix Ans d'études,* p. 133. Thierry may have known Moore personally, since the latter was well received in liberal circles during his stay in Paris in 1820–1822. (See Moore's Diary, in *Moore's Life, Journal and Correspondence,* ed. Lord John Russell [New York, 1857], I, 355 and passim.) Many of the *Irish Melodies* were written during the Paris visit, and the poet presented a specially bound copy to Mademoiselle, the daughter of the future Louis-Philippe (ibid., I, 364). Moore kept himself informed, moreover, of French politics and letters, and wrote with admiration in the *Edinburgh Review* of French liberals and of the *Courrier Français,* with which Thierry was associated. Thierry's article was in many ways a tribute from one prominent liberal writer to another: in J. B. Priestley's words, Moore was "after Scott and Byron the most successful man of letters of his time" and "a Troubadour to the Whig society of the Regency" (introduction to *Tom Moore's Diary* [Cambridge, 1925]).

193. Charles Augustin de Sainte-Beuve, *Causeries du lundi,* 3rd ed. [Paris, 1857–1872], VII, 212.

194. See, for instance, a passage, with a telling quotation from Michelet, on the ordinance of May 25th, 1413, that followed popular disturbances in Paris: "Under that anarchical domination of the municipality, itself domineered over by a faction of brutal and violent persons, sober thoughts of the common weal, till then suppressed, now found their way through the midst of the disorder and were, perhaps, produced by it. According to a remark applicable to other periods of revolution, 'the violent have demanded and dictated, the moderate have written' " (Thierry, *Tiers Etat,* p. 100). As early as the essay on the English revolutions of 1817, Thierry had written of "les violences nécessaires" (*Dix Ans d'études,* p. 75).

195. Thierry, *Conquête,* I, 430 (end of Book IV).

196. The theater metaphor occurs in Thierry, "Des Nations" (1817), p. 67. It

recurs in the Introduction to the *Conquête*, where the reader is advised that "the theater of this great drama is the island of Britain, Ireland, and France." See also *Tiers Etat*, pp. 302–303. Rulon Smithson gives several examples of Thierry's use of the language of painting (*Augustin Thierry*, pp. 296–297). A fondness for set pieces and colorful tableaux was shared by all Romantic historians. Describing the trial of Hastings in Westminster Hall, Macaulay lists the many dignitaries in the audience, among them Siddons "in the prime of her majestic beauty" looking "with emotion on a scene surpassing all the imitations of the stage" (*Macaulay: Prose and Poetry*, p. 455). A distinction should probably be made, however, between two uses of the metaphor of the theater. In one, the scene of history is the locus of a vast dramatic action in which all men are actors. The metaphor here indicates a way of experiencing historical existence that appears to have been particularly common during the Revolution, which often staged itself, before being staged by later writers such as Büchner, Michelet, or, in our own day, Peter Weiss. The categories of "tragedy" and "comedy" in historical action, found in Marx and Engels, seem to be related to this first use of the theatrical metaphor. In the second use, history is a spectacle for a viewer who stands outside it and can embrace it in a single glance. This is most often the sense in which history is theatrical in Voltaire. Likewise, Marmontel's article on history in his *Elements de littérature* is conceived entirely in terms of pictorial perspective, terms that are still being used by Macaulay in the 1828 essay on history (Stern, *Varieties*, pp. 75–77). Macaulay characteristically admired "portraits which condense into one point of time, and exhibit at a single glance the whole history of turbid and eventful lives" (ibid., p. 75). In strikingly similar terms, Sainte-Beuve admired Mignet for "le regard sommaire dont il embrassait et resserrait une longue suite d'événements" (*Portraits contemporains*, new ed. [Paris, 1870–1871], V, 229). Michelet dreamed of "le bonheur immense d'embrasser d'un regard l'infinité des choses qu'hier il voyait une à une" (*L'Oiseau* [Paris, 1936], p. 14

197. The nineteenth-century historian insists that his writing embraces the real. Thus Thierry: "We must find a way across the distance of the centuries to men: we must represent them before us living and acting" (*Conquête*, I, 430); Carlyle: "Bygone ages of the world were actually filled by living men, not by protocols, state-papers, controversies and abstractions of men. Not abstractions were they, not diagrams or theorems; but men, in buff or other coats and breeches, with colour in their cheeks, with passions in their stomach" ("Sir Walter Scott," in *Critical and Miscellaneous Essays* [London, 1888], III, 214–215); Edward Everett in 1834 on vol. 1 of Bancroft's *History of the United States:* "You give us not wretched pasteboard men; not a sort of chronological table . . . but you give us real, individual, living men and women, with their passions, interests, and peculiarities" (quoted in David Levin, *History as Romantic Art: Bancroft, Prescott, Motley, and Parkman* [Stanford, Calif., 1959], p. 235). In Michelet's ideal comprehensive vision, it is not a model of the real that is grasped, but the real itself: this vision "permet, non de rétrécir, comme une carte géographique, mais de voir en complet détail cette grande variété d'objets, de posséder et percevoir presque à l'égal de Dieu" (*L'Oiseau* [Paris, 1936], p. 48). For Herzen, the great merit of Thierry was his ability to recall the past to life. In his "great and wide-ranging epics . . . events and individuals stand out in a sort of artistic relief, and ages long past emerge

from the tomb, shake off the dust and the dirt, take on flesh, and live again before your very eyes." Herzen contrasted Thierry's work with that of Capefigue. The latter never achieves the smooth, unbroken, continuous surface of Thierry's narrative; the breaks are always visible where the different pieces that compose it have been placed alongside each other. As a result, "the whole work is dead . . . a dried up compilation." Thierry, however, "fuses all the materials into a sort of organic whole. . . .The deepest lesson of his work, the life in it, imparts animation and authenticity to his narrative" (*Sobranie sochinenii*, II, 7–9). Even at the end of the nineteenth century, in his introduction to a French translation of Green's celebrated *History of the English People* (Paris, 1888), Gabriel Monod expressed admiration for "des descriptions de nature d'un coloris merveilleux, des narrations entraînantes, des portraits d'une fine psychologie et d'un étonnant relief. . . . partout le mouvement, la chaleur et la vie." On the general question of the "effet de réel" in nineteenth-century historiography, see Roland Barthes, "Le Discours de l'histoire," *Information sur les Sciences Sociales* 6:4 (1967): 65–75.

198. Sainte-Beuve, *Causeries du lundi*, VI, 125.

199. It was, of course, difficult to maintain honestly and in good faith the belief that the liberal state was nonviolent. An early critic of Constant's *De l'Esprit de conquête* pointed out that trade and commerce, far from ensuring peace and harmony, would set nation against nation in conflicts of unparalleled ferocity (François-Guillaume Coëssin, *De l'Esprit de conquête et de l'usurpation dans le système mercantile en réponse à l'ouvrage de M. B. de Constant Rebecque* [Paris, 1814]; on Coëssin, see Henri Gouhier, *La Jeunesse d'Auguste Comte et la formation du positivisme*, II [Paris, 1936]). Sismondi was appalled by the sufferings and the degradation of human life that seemed to accompany the free development of industry in a liberal society (see notably "On the Condition of the Work People in Manufactories" [1834], in *Political Economy and the Philosophy of Government* [London, 1847], pp. 196–223). An echo of Sismondi's special interest in the Highland clearances ("On Landed Property," ibid., pp. 159–160, 179–193; *Economie politique* [Paris, 1837], I, 203–238) is heard in the closing lines of Thierry's comments on the Scots in the Conclusion of the *Conquête*. For a moment the liberal consciousness is disturbed by doubt: "Civilization, which makes rapid progress among all the branches of the Scottish population, has now penetrated beyond the Lowland towns into the Highlands. Perhaps, however, in seeking to propagate it there, the means adopted of late years have been too violent . . . Converting their patriarchal supremacy into seigneurial rights of property over all the land occupied by their clans, the heirs of the ancient chiefs, the English law in their hands, have expelled from their habitations hundreds of families to whom this law was absolutely unknown. In place of the dispossessed clans, they have established immense flocks of sheep and a few agriculturalists from other parts, enlightened, industrious persons, capable of carrying into execution the most judicious plans of cultivation. The great agricultural progress of Ross-shire and Sutherlandshire is greatly vaunted, but if such an example be followed, the race of the most ancient inhabitants of Britain, after having preserved itself for so many centuries and among so many enemies, will disappear without leaving any other trace than a vicious English pronunciation in the places where its language used to be spoken."

200. Many looked to receive posts and pensions after the 1830 Revolution, and

some, including Thierry, were bitter because they received less than they expected. The practical involvement of intellectuals and professors in the bourgeois monarchy, as again later in the Third Republic, should not be underestimated, but the appeal of the liberal ideology is by no means fully accounted for by this single consideration.

201. The legend of the gentle Galeswinthe, for instance, is treasured by the historian as "the living and poetic expression of popular faith and feelings" (Thierry, *Récits*, p. 55).

202. Review of "Manuel électoral," *Censeur Européen* 2 (1817): 119.

203. Thierry, *Récits*, pp. 44, 53.

204. Ibid., pp. 212–214.

205. Ibid., p. 227.

206. Ibid., pp. 222, 224.

207. Thierry, *Conquête*, II, 374–375. Cf. II, 156, on the degradation of the Saxon tongue. On the struggle of the Welsh to maintain their tongue, and on the disappearance of Cornish, see *Conquête*, end of Book I and Conclusion, section II; on the desperate struggle of the Irish to sustain their failing tongue against the onslaughts of English, see *Dix Ans d'études*, p. 129.

208. Herzen, "Lettre à Garibaldi," *Sobranie sochinenii*, XXX, 529. On the ambivalence of the liberal view of the people, see note 100 above.

209. Thierry, *Récits*, p. 117.

210. For example, Thierry, *Récits*, pp. 102–103, on Brunehilde and Merowig (3rd *récit*), and pp. 182–183, on Leudaste and Markowefe (5th *récit*).

211. The father is defined as the possessor of the woman, the son as the usurper. Galeswinthe and Radegonde are both prizes wrested from the father after his defeat in battle. In the *Conquête* (Book II), the beautiful Popa, daughter of Count Béranger, falls "in the division of the spoils" to the conqueror and slayer of her father, the Norman Roll. In the essay "Sur l'Histoire de la constitution anglaise," the possession of England, achieved at the cost of so much bloodshed, fills the ailing William with such remorse and such dread of punishment by the heavenly Father that he longs to return his prize. "The possession that caused him so much remorse seemed cursed in the hands of his family. His sons fought each other over it . . . For several generations two families of brothers slaughtered each other" (Thierry, *Dix Ans d'études*, p. 179).

212. Thierry, *Récits*, p. 136, Frédégonde as murderess of her (step-) son Merowig (3rd *récit*); p. 170, Frédégonde as murderess of Bishop Praetextus (4th *récit*); pp. 297–300, Frédégonde as murderess of her (step-)son Chlodowig (7th *récit*); p. 182, Leudaste mutilated by Haribert becomes the lover of Haribert's wife, Markowefe (5th *récit*).

213. Thierry, *Récits*, p. 219.

214. Ibid., pp. 222, 224.

215. Ibid., p. 225.

216. See likewise Sainte-Beuve on the July Revolution as not the work of factions, but of the entire nation: "régulière, pour ainsi dire, et légale," having "un sens général et unanime" (*Causeries du lundi*, VI, 123).

217. Thierry, *Dix Ans d'études*, p. 130.

218. Thierry, *Récits*, p. 224.

219. Ibid., p. 225.

220. In addition to Galeswinthe, Radegonde, and Popa, the daughter of Count Béranger, the list of victims includes Eleanor of Aquitaine, whom Henry II of England weds in defiance of the prohibition to marry without the consent of Louis VII, his suzerain lord (Thierry, *Conquête,* Book VIII).

221. Thierry, *Conquête,* Book X (4-vol. ed., Paris, 1867), III, 293–294.

222. Thierry, *Récits,* p. 178.

223. Ibid., p. 102.

224. See Louis Chevalier, *Classes laborieuses, et classes dangereuses à Paris pendant la première moitié du XIXe siècle (Paris,* 1969).

225. 7th *récit.* In the 3rd *récit,* Frédégonde's hatred of her husband's sons, it is said, "might have become proverbial" (Thierry, *Récits,* p. 100).

226. Though I am concerned here with the bourgeoisie of the Restoration, it seems likely that certain literary themes and practices and a certain philosophy of history are associated in varying forms with the bourgeoisie over a much longer period of time.

227. The reader of Constant's Journal cannot fail to be struck by the author's habit of recalling on specific dates the persons and events of the same date in earlier years. On Constant's preoccupation with time and death, see Georges Poulet, *Constant par lui-même* (Paris, 1968), pp. 28, 29.

228. *De la Religion* (1826), I, 46, in Poulet, *Constant par lui-même,* p. 30.

229. Benjamin Constant, *Journal intime,* ed. D. Melegari (Paris, 1895), p. 32.

230. Quoted in Poulet, *Constant par lui-même,* pp. 37, 41. The image of the devouring sea and the frail barque occurs again and again; see Poulet, pp. 41, 108.

231. Chapter 10.

232. Quoted in Poulet, *Constant par lui-même,* p. 23.

233. See, for example, in chapter 8: "Je savais seul qu'en l'abandonnant je l'entraînerais sur mes pas . . ." "Mais ne savais-je pas que cette conduite était mon ouvrage?"

234. Letter to Madame Récamier, quoted in Poulet, *Constant par lui-même,* p. 37.

235. Constant, *Journal intime,* pp. 47–48.

236. Letter to Madame de Nassau, quoted in Poulet, *Constant par lui-même,* p. 135. Cf. Constant, *Journal intime,* p. 86: "As one grows older, one finds pleasure in seeing again people that one once knew; even when one has little fondness for them, they are like a kind of bond between us and the past which is constantly slipping from us and which we long to recapture."

237. Letter to Madame de Nassau, quoted in Poulet, *Constant par lui-même,* p. 135.

238. Letter to Rosalie de Constant, ibid., p. 105.

239. Constant, *Journal intime,* p. 24. Cf. *Adolphe,* chapter 7: "Oh! let me renounce these useless efforts, let me enjoy the spectacle of time's flow, of my days rushing by one after the other; let me remain motionless, the indifferent spectator of an existence already half spent."

240. *Adolphe,* chapter 1. Cf. Madame de Staël's portrait of Lord Nevil in *Corinne,* chapter 1: "Misfortune and remorse had made him fearful of Destiny; he thought she might be assuaged by his asking nothing of her."

241. "Fragment sur la France," originally published in *Mélanges de littérature et de politique* (1829), in *Oeuvres de Benjamin Constant*, ed. Alfred Roulin (Paris, 1957), p. 817.

242. Critics of bourgeois liberalism on the radical Right have sometimes denounced what they see as a deluded attempt on the part of the bourgeoisie to deny the fundamental condition and reality of politics, namely the distinction between friend and enemy, by substituting words for action, debate and "rational" discussion for struggle. Already for Donoso Cortés, in the aftermath of 1848, the bourgeoisie was "la clasa discutidora." In more recent times, the point has been made with special force by Carl Schmitt: "The essence of the bourgeois is negotiation, indecisiveness and the willingness to wait things out, in the hope that the definitive settling of accounts, the bloody and decisive battle, can be turned into a parliamentary debate and thus endlessly suspended in endless discussion" (*Politische Theologie: vier Kapitel zur Lehre von der Souveranität*, 2nd ed. [Munich and Leipzig: Duncker and Humblot, 1934], p. 80. See also his *The Concept of the Political*, trans. George Schwab [New Brunswick, N.J.: Rutgers University Press, 1976], pp. 57, 78–79). The starkness and abstractness of Schmitt's distinction between friend and enemy is itself, of course, by no means ideologically innocent.

243. "Manuel électoral," pp. 117, 128.

5. Jules Michelet

1. Jules Michelet, *Le Peuple*, ed. L. Refort (Paris, 1946), p. 19.

2. Gabriel Monod, *La Vie et la pensée de Jules Michelet, 1792–1852* (Paris, 1923), II, 10–26.

3. Jules Michelet, *Journal*, ed. Paul Viallaneix and Claude Digeon (Paris, 1959–1976), I, 290 (February 1839). In describing himself as a citizen of the faubourg Saint-Denis, Michelet was defining himself socially. The rue du faubourg Saint-Denis was a busy commercial street, a street of small shopkeepers, in contrast to the rue du faubourg Saint-Antoine, the main street of Paris's working-class East End.

4. "Mémorial," in *Ecrits de jeunesse*, ed. Paul Viallaneix (Paris, 1959), p. 184.

5. Ibid., pp. 184–185.

6. Ibid., p. 215.

7. Jules Michelet, *Le Prêtre, la femme et la famille. Les Jésuites* (Paris, 1900), pp. xxii–xxiii (Preface, dated 1845).

8. On the one hand, woman at the tiller of the great Dutch barge (*Journal*, I, 239, [11 July 1837]); on the other, woman as suffering and sickly, bedridden, "tota morbus," "une blessée" (Jules Michelet, *L'Amour* [Paris, 1899], pp. 57, 345, and passim).

9. Among many pertinent passages, see Preface, *Mémoires de Luther, écrits par lui-même (1835)*, in *Oeuvres complètes de Jules Michelet*, ed. Paul Viallaneix (Paris, 1971–), III, 239–240. (Hereafter cited as *O.C.*)

10. Michelet, *Le Peuple*, p. 20.

11. *Introduction à l'histoire universelle*, in *O.C.*, II, 257; "De la méthode et de l'esprit de ce livre," *Histoire de la Révolution française*, ed. Gérard Walter (Paris, 1952), I, 287; *Le Banquet* (Paris, 1879), p. 207. See also Michelet, *Journal*, I, 378 (30

January 1842): "We must lend a voice to history's silences"; *Le Peuple*, p. 201: "What could I, a poor solitary dreamer, give to this great dumb people? The one thing I possessed—a voice"; *O.C.*, IV, 8: "We want to write the history of that poor dumb creature that no one has bothered with, the history of those who have had no history, who have suffered, toiled, languished, and reached their end without ever being able to speak their suffering" (lecture of 21 April 1842, at Collège de France). Athénaïs's contributions to the natural history works are placed, without acknowledgment, in quotation marks.

12. Edgar Quinet, *De l'Origine des dieux*, in *Oeuvres complètes* (Paris, 1857), III, 415.

13. Michelet, *Le Peuple*, pp. 3–4, 24, 119, and passim; *Journal*, I, 597 (1 April 1845).

14. Michelet, *Ecrits de jeunesse*, p. 212.

15. Ibid., p. 410.

16. See Monod, *La Vie et la pensée*, I, 27–29. Michelet himself recounts an episode that illustrates his bad faith in *Ecrits de jeunesse*, p. 88.

17. Michelet, *Journal*, II, 323 (3 May 1857).

18. Quoted in Stephen A. Kippur, *Jules Michelet: A Study of Mind and Sensibility* (Albany, N.Y., 1981), p. 22.

19. Michelet, *Journal*, I, 330 (23 June 1840): "Even if marriage were possible, is it compatible with the great work that is my life's destiny? Such a work permits of no sharing of time or strength. One has to live and die as a book, not as a man"; *Journal*, I, 385 (27 March 1842): "My ideas are the events in my life"; *Journal*, I, 502 (6 April 1843): "I have thrown all of my life into my book, my entire private life into my course"; *Journal*, I, 677 (12 November 1847): "My book has made me completely forget my life." On *writing* as Michelet's way of *living*, see also *Journal*, II, 439 (5 November 1858); *Journal*, II, 544 (2 August 1860); "Préface de 1869," *Histoire de France*, in *O.C.*, IV, 14. Monod claims that Michelet was a devoted husband and father (*La Vie et la pensée*, I, 179–180, 357–358), but later wavers in his opinion (I, 358).

20. J. M. Carré, *Michelet et son temps* (Paris, 1926), p. 31.

21. Michelet, *Journal*, I, 307 (4 July 1839), 330 (23 June 1840).

22. "Woman should be fed by man" (*Le Prêtre, la femme et la famille*, p. xviii).

23. See Michelet, *Introduction à l'histoire universelle* (1830). See also *L'Amour*, p. 38: "Happy he who rescues a woman!" Similarly for Hegel, universal history is the "Durchdringung des weltlichen Zustandes" by the principle of freedom (*Werke*, Jubiläumsausgabe, XI, 46).

24. Quinet, *Oeuvres complètes*, X, 35.

25. Michelet, *Journal*, I, 673 (14 July 1867). For Louis Blanc also Paris has the right, as the head of the nation, to determine its destiny (*Histoire de la Révolution de 1848* [Paris, 1870], I, 83). In 1848 Blanc was opposed to holding immediate national elections, while Michelet was in favor; but their disagreement seems to have been tactical. Michelet feared delay would give the Right time to organize the uneducated peasants; Blanc felt the Left needed time to organize and educate them.

26. Michelet, *Journal*, I, 358 (11 March 1848): "I have tried to do justice to the things that time has condemned"; *Journal*, I, 378 (30 January 1842): "A voice must be given to history's silences . . . Only then will the dead resign themselves to their tombs"; *Journal*, I, 392 (4 April 1842): "Let not the present kill its father; let it

respect in him, as the law says, its author . . . the beginning of its own being."

27. Michelet, *Histoire de la Révolution française*, I, 125. On *forgetting* as the ideal, see *Journal*, I, 386 (28 March 1842) and *Bible de l'humanité* (Paris, 1864), p. 483.

28. Michelet, *Journal*, II, 87–88 (2 February 1850). In the same passage: "This perfect woman does not have the passions of woman."

29. Athénaïs's ambitions were contradictory. She wanted to learn from the man she revered as teacher, husband, and father, and to resemble him as much as possible. But she also resented his paternalist attitude toward her: "I ought to have remained more myself, I ought not to have been so self-effacing before your tastes, your wishes, your ways" (quoted in Michelet, *Journal*, IV, 398 [October 1868], note). In a gesture universally condemned by scholars, yet surely understandable, the pupil finally succeeded in turning the tables on her charismatic master and in wresting the pen from his hand. After Michelet's death Athénaïs made significant revisions to his manuscripts before having them published.

30. Michelet, *Journal*, I, 387 (28 March 1842). See also *Histoire de la Révolution française*, I, 416.

31. Whatever has power of concentration, creation, centralization, whatever is a source of energy in history (the King of France; Paris, France) or in art (the poet, the historian) is represented as partly feminine, lacking strong definition, and thus capable of receiving and assimilating material brought by others. See also the sympathetic portrait of John Law, the Scottish financier at the time of the Orleans Regency, as *homo duplex* (Michelet, *Histoire de France* [Paris, 1898–1899], XVII, 141–143 and passim) and the repeated affirmation that every artist is his mother's son (*Journal*, I, 442 [7 July 1862], on Rubens; *Le Prêtre*, p. 297).

32. Michelet, *Journal*, I, 626–627 (23 September 1845).

33. See Monod, *La Vie et la pensée*, I, 30, 31.

34. Ibid., II, 2.

35. August Böckh, *Encyklopädie und Methodologie der philologischen Wissenschaften* (lectures at the University of Berlin from the 1820s through the 1850s), ed. Ernst Bratuscheck (Leipzig, 1877), p. 14.

36. Michelet, *Journal*, I, 381 (18 March 1842). See also "Héroisme de l'esprit," in *O.C.*, IV, 38; "Préface de la Régence," in *Histoire de France*, XVII, 10; letter to Alfred Dumesnil, 2 November 1841, in *Lettres inédites (1841–1871)*, ed. Paul Sirven (Paris, 1924), pp. 43–44.

37. "Discours sur Vico," in *O.C.*, I, 288.

38. Quoted by Franz Schnabel, "Die Geschichtswissenschaft und der Staat," in his *Abhandlungen und Vorträge 1914–1965*, ed. H. Lutz (Freiburg, Basle, and Vienna, 1970), pp. 335–336.

39. Böckh, *Encyklopädie*, p. 17.

40. Michelet, *Ecrits de jeunesse*, p. 409.

41. Michelet, *Histoire de France*, XVII, 93.

42. Monod, *La Vie et la pensée*, II, 4.

43. Ibid., II, 118–138.

44. Ibid., I, 139.

45. *"L'Histoire de la Révolution* jugée par George Sand," in Louis Blanc, *Histoire de la Révolution française,* 2nd ed. (Paris, 1869), I, xi.

46. "Premier avis au lecteur," in Blanc, *Histoire de la Révolution française,* I, xxxviii.

47. Quoted in Leo A. Loubère, *Louis Blanc: His Life and His Contribution to the Rise of French Jacobin Socialism* (Evanston, Ill., 1961), p. 168. Similarly, Michelet's teacher Abel Villemain said: "I ask of the historian that he love humanity and liberty. His justice should be impartial but not impassive" (*Cours de littérature française,* 1828, cited by D. F. Sarmiento in *Facundo,* Introduction, ed. Alberto Palcos [Buenos Aires, 1961], p. 9).

48. "I want you . . . to tell me in the morning the forgotten dream of the night," France commands her historians (Michelet, *Histoire de la Révolution française,* I, 287).

49. See Kippur, *Jules Michelet,* pp. 120–121, for many pertinent quotations.

50. On the Parsifal-figure as typical of Germany and the French historian as the translator and transmitter of the powerful, original German spirit, see both the text and the lengthy notes of *Introduction à l'histoire universelle.* On the historian as innocent, see also "Héroisme de l'esprit," in *O.C.,* IV, 31, 33–35; *Journal,* I, 622 (23 August 1845); *Le Peuple,* pp. 118–119.

51. Michelet, *L'Etudiant* (Paris, 1970), p. 65 (2nd lecture, 23 December 1847). See also *Le Peuple,* p. 118: "I do not know what may still be hoped for, in the creation of a broad, open-minded, generous association, from the rich and the middle class. They are very sick; perhaps too far gone. But I still place my hopes, I confess, in their sons. These young men, as I see them in our schools, from my rostrum, have better tendencies. They have always opened their hearts to every good word I have said about the people."

52. Michelet, *L'Etudiant,* p. 63 (1st lecture, 16 December 1847). On the child as mediator, see also *Le Prêtre,* pp. 280, 306.

53. Michelet, *Journal,* I, 546 (25 January 1844).

54. Michelet, *Le Peuple,* p. 103.

55. Monod, *La Vie et la pensée,* II, 2–4.

56. Michelet, *Ecrits de jeunesse,* p. 410 (letter of 14 June 1824).

57. "Discours sur Vico," in *O.C.,* I, 288.

58. "The social world is the creation of men themselves" ("Discours sur Vico," in *O.C.,* I, 299); "Man is his own Prometheus" ("Préface de 1869," *Histoire de France,* in *O.C.,* IV, 13).

59. "Avant-propos," *Histoire romaine,* in *O.C.,* II, 342.

60. "Préface de 1869," *Histoire de France,* in *O.C.,* IV, 14; "Discours sur Vico," in *O.C.,* I, 275.

61. Quoted by Viallaneix in *O.C.,* II, 217.

62. "Préface de 1869," *Histoire de France,* in *O.C.,* IV, 15.

63. Preface to 1866 ed., *Histoire romaine,* in *O.C.,* II, 336.

64. Quoted in Kippur, *Jules Michelet,* p. 43.

65. Ibid., p. 42.

66. "Préface de 1869," *Histoire de France,* in *O.C.,* IV, 12.

67. Blanc, *Histoire de la Révolution de 1848,* I, 4–9, 21–22.

68. "Préface de 1869," *Histoire de France,* in *O.C.,* IV, 15.

69. Michelet, *Journal*, I, 296–302 (29 March–4 April 1839).

70. Michelet, *Journal*, II, 281 (21 September 1854); II, 379 (27 November 1857); II, 705 (6 May 1851), note; Preface (1868) to 1869 ed., *Histoire de la Révolution française*, II, 1000–1004.

71. "Refuted Proudhon" (Michelet, *Journal*, I, 594 [1 March 1845]); "against Leroux, Proudhon (ibid., I, 701 [16 October 1848]).

72. Michelet, *Journal*, IV, 293 (May 1871).

73. Michelet, *Le Peuple*, p. 110.

74. Quinet, *Oeuvres complètes*, X, 35.

75. Michelet, *Journal*, I, 469 (11 August 1842).

76. Michelet, *Lettres inédites*, ed. Sirven, p. 40 (letter of 13 October 1842).

77. Michelet, *Journal*, I, 329 (12 June 1840). See also ibid., I, 354 (22 September 1840). Until the end of his life Michelet wavered between a vision of nature as good, orderly, and unified behind the apparent disorder of its many masks, and a vision of nature as cruel, indifferent, irrational, nothing but meaningless change. On the one hand, "cette mère aimée, la Nature," "rendez-vous de l'amour et de la paix," "harmonie du monde," "magnifique économie du globe, le balancement majestueux des courants alternatifs qui sont la vie de l'océan" (*L'Oiseau* [Paris, 1898], pp. 52, 57, 73, 74); on the other, "l'atroce et méchante mer," "l'odieuse et féconde mer qui menace d'engloutir" [the swift and powerful man-o'-war bird] (ibid., pp. 108, 111).

78. Michelet, *Journal*, I, 360 (4 April 1841).

79. Jacob Burckhardt, *Historische Fragmente*, ed. Emil Dürr (Stuttgart, 1957), p. 270. Burckhardt's reports in the *Basler Zeitung* at the time testify to his strong sympathy with Michelet's stand. What Burckhardt admired was what he took to be the disinterested, ethical position of Michelet and Quinet, their refusal of facile compromises, their readiness to be abrasive at the very moment when art and literature, in Burckhardt's view, were capitulating to the blandishments of the marketplace. (See Werner Kaegi, *Jacob Burckhardt: Eine Biographie* [Basle, 1947–1982], II, 432–435.)

80. Michelet, *Journal*, I, 674 (14 July 1847).

81. Ibid, I, 623 (23 June 1845). Shortly afterwards he noted that whereas he once thought the world would advance "en traduisant le christianisme," he now believes progress requires the destruction of Christianity (ibid., I, 656 [21 November 1846]). Toward the end of his life he returned to this theme in order to deny that his account of the Middle Ages had been influenced by Catholic writers like Ballanche and Lamennais. He had simply viewed the Middle Ages as a time of "haute harmonie"—a vision he subsequently considered a grotesque illusion (ibid., IV, 106–107 [28 March 1869]).

82. Ibid., I, 655 (20 November 1846).

83. Ibid., I, 674 (14 July 1846). As early as 10 March 1841, Michelet noted that Augustin Thierry, whom he revered as one of the founders of the modern French school of historiography, had for a long time been too much influenced by literary sources and had not paid enough attention to documents (*Journal*, I, 358).

84. Lucien Refort, *L'Art de Michelet dans son oeuvre historique (jusqu'en 1867)* (Paris, 1923), p. iv and passim; Kippur, *Jules Michelet*, pp. 184–185, 212.

85. "Préface de la Régence," in Michelet, *Histoire de France,* XVII, 12. See also the disavowal of the dramatically satisfying rather than historically accurate portrait of Caesar in the *Histoire romaine* in the Preface to the later, 1866 edition. "One becomes a historian (which is a virtue) only gradually. At the time, I was still a writer" (*O.C.,* II, 336).

86. Michelet, *Journal,* I, 516–517 (5 August 1843).

87. "*L'Histoire de la Révolution* jugée par George Sand," in Blanc, *Histoire de la Révolution française,* I, x.

88. Michelet, *Journal,* I, 662 (11 March 1847).

89. Kippur, *Jules Michelet,* p. 124.

90. Michelet, *Histoire de la Révolution française,* I, 416.

91. On the two nations, see Introduction to "La Renaissance," in Michelet, *Histoire de France, O.C.,* VII, 76; *Le Peuple,* p. 29, and passim. On his own unifying goal, see *Le Banquet,* pp. 205–212 and passim; *Le Peuple,* pp. 28–29. On Balzac, see *Journal,* I, 592 (20 February 1845); *Le Peuple,* p. 12.

92. On the Federations, see "De la Religion nouvelle," in Michelet, *Histoire de la Révolution française,* I, 414–424. On the unity of the Revolution in popular tradition, see "De la Méthode et de l'esprit de ce livre," ibid., I, 283–284; "Préface de 1847," ibid., I, 3–4; "Préface de 1868," ibid., I, 11–12.

93. Blanc, *Histoire de la Révolution française,* I, 117.

94. Michelet, *Le Peuple,* p. 110.

95. "De la Méthode et de l'esprit de ce livre," in Michelet, *Histoire de la Révolution française,* I, 291–293. See also the comments of Viallaneix in *Journal,* I, 886 (15 February 1845), note 2.

96. Michelet, *Journal,* I, 594 (1 March 1845), 887 (1 March 1845), note 2, on Michelet's critique of Proudhon in his lecture of 10 April 1845 at the Collège de France).

97. Ibid., I, 556, 557 (20 May 1844).

98. Ibid, IV, 418–419 (14 April 1869, note 1).

99. Ibid., I, 467 (1 August 1842), 471 (23 August 1842); Michelet, *Le Peuple,* pp. 56, note 1, 58–61, 66, and passim.

100. Michelet, *Le Peuple,* p. 63.

101. Ibid., p. 92.

102. "Historians who subscribe to economic theories, several of whom have a certain facile talent, seem clear at first, but on closer inspection much remains obscure. They imagine the economic can be isolated and studied separately . . . that it is not necessary to know day by day the moral facts, the social facts, the details of the political crisis which determined this or that financial measure. But everything hangs together" ("Héroisme de l'esprit," in *O.C.,* IV, 38). See also "Préface de 1868," in Michelet, *Histoire de la Révolution française,* I, 10.

103. See my article "The Go-Between: Jules Michelet 1798–1874," *MLN* 89 (1974): 503–541.

104. Michelet, *Journal,* I, 680 (3 December 1847).

105. Ibid., I, 662 (11 February 1847). See also the condemnation of colonial wars, ibid., I, 417 (14 June 1842).

106. Michelet, *Le Peuple,* pp. 107, 263.

107. Michelet, *Journal,* I, 656–657 (21 November 1846).

108. Michelet, *Histoire de France,* Book IV, chap. 5, in *O.C.,* IV, 462: *Introduction à l'histoire universelle,* in *O.C.,* II, 252–253; *Le Peuple,* p. 33; *Journal,* I, 121–161 ("Voyage d'Angleterre").

109. Michelet, *Journal,* I, 627 (28 September 1845); *Histoire de France,* Book IV, chap. 5, in *O.C.,* IV, 464; *Introduction à l'histoire universelle,* in *O.C.,* II, 247–248.

110. "Felt the urgency of educating the people," he noted immediately after the June Days (*Journal,* I, 693 [27 June 1848]). See also ibid., I, 693–694 (19, 21, 28, June 1848).

111. Kippur, *Jules Michelet,* pp. 131, 218.

112. Michelet, *Journal,* I, 662 (11 February 1847); 687 (15 May 1848); 688 (18 May 1848); 689 (28 May 1848).

113. Ibid., I, 662 (11 February 1847).

114. Ibid., I, 683–684 (23 February 1848).

115. Michelet, *Le Banquet,* p. 212. See also *Nos Fils* (Paris, n.d. [1903]), p. 299.

116. Michelet, *Journal,* I, 519 (11 August 1843); letter to E. Noel (13 February 1847), ibid., I, 912.

117. Ibid., I, 691 (13 June 1848).

118. Michelet, *Nos Fils,* p. 300. See also Kippur, *Jules Michelet,* p. 127.

119. Michelet, *Journal,* I, 627 (23 September 1845); Michelet, *Le Peuple,* p. 209.

120. Quoted in Kippur, *Jules Michelet,* p. 226.

121. Michelet, *Le Peuple,* p. 267. Daumier's *La République* of 1848 (Paris, Louvre) is a fine pictorial representation of the idea of the *mère patrie* as nourishing mother and protective father, love and law, in one.

122. Michelet, *Journal,* I, 692 (16 June 1848), 694 (28 June 1848); Michelet, *Le Banquet,* pp. 208–212, 227–234. See also Kippur, *Jules Michelet,* pp. 130–131, quoting a letter to George Sand of 2 April 1856, in which Michelet advocates village theaters to propagate the "true national spirit."

123. Michelet, *Journal,* I, 119 (13 July 1834); Michelet, *La Sorcière,* introduction by Robert Mandrou (Paris, 1964), p. 153; Gossman, "The Go-Between," pp. 515–517.

124. Michelet, *Journal,* II, 120 (25 August 1850).

125. Michelet, *La Mer* (Paris, 1898), p. 5.

126. Ibid., pp. 85–86, 225–226.

127. Quoted in Kippur, *Jules Michelet,* p. 128.

128. "I was born into the people. I had the people in my heart. The monuments of its early ages were my delight . . . But its language, its language remained inaccessible to me and I never succeeded in letting it speak" (*Nos Fils,* p. 300). See also the reference in *Journal,* I, 597 (11 August 1842) to "the two great popular groups both of which are closed to me: the religious Christians and the workers."

129. Michelet, *Journal,* I, 678–679 (20 November 1847). See also note 19 above.

130. Ibid., I, 661 (11 February 1847).

131. Ernest Renan, *Vie de Jésus* (Paris, 1974), Introduction, pp. 106–107.

132. Michelet, *Journal,* IV, 125 (20 June 1869).

133. See Kippur, *Jules Michelet,* p. 132. Michelet's suspension from the Collège de France in March 1851 was the occasion of a scathing cartoon by Daumier in the *Charivari* (28 March 1851; Delteil, no. 2091).

134. "Extinction of political life and the spirit of adventure . . . petty profit and petty minds" (Michelet, *Journal*, II, 213 [11 February 1853]).

135. "Préface de 1868," in Michelet, *Histoire de la Révolution française*, I, 9.

136. Michelet, *Journal*, II, 259 (31 May 1854). In *Le Banquet* Italy is "la grande mère" or "la pauvre nourrice" (pp. 8, 140–141).

137. Michelet, *Journal*, II, 23 (27 February 1849).

138. Michelet, *L'Oiseau*, pp. 4–5.

139. Michelet, *Les Femmes de la Révolution* (Paris, 1898), p. 264.

140. Michelet, *L'Oiseau*, pp. 96–97, 127–134.

141. Michelet, *The Mountain*, trans. W. H. Davenport Adams (London, 1872), p. 213.

142. Kippur, *Jules Michelet*, pp. 192–193. Though I disagree with Kippur on this point, I find his study of Michelet the most informed, judicious, and intelligent general introduction to the historian's work presently available.

143. Michelet, *Journal*, II, 215 (31 May 1853).

144. In Werner Kaegi's biography of Burckhardt, the biographer and his subject join forces to pronounce a common condemnation of the "historical rhapsodies, blown up personal intuitions and reminiscences . . . caricatures, erotic gossip, deformations" of the last volumes of the *Histoire de France* (Kaegi, *Jacob Burckhardt*, V, 300).

145. Quoted by Viallaneix, in Michelet, *Journal*, I, 836 (4 September 1842), note 1.

146. The Englishman is "homme rouge, gros ventre" (*Histoire de France*, in *O.C.*, IV, 462), the English as a whole are a "race de bouchers" (*Journal*, I, 131 [14 August 1834]). On the rapprochement of England and France, see *Histoire du dix-neuvième siècle*, vol. 2, Preface, in *O.C.*, XXI, 272. On the change in English and French eating habits, see ibid., vol. 3, Preface, in *O.C.*, XXI, 462–463.

147. Michelet, *Journal*, I, 121 (6 August 1834).

6. Michelet's Gospel of Revolution

1. Jules Michelet, *Histoire de la Révolution française*, ed. G. Walter (Paris, 1952), 2 vols. Quotations from this work in the text are cited using the abbreviation *HR*, followed by the volume and page number.

2. Cf. *HR*, I, 1021.

3. Jules Michelet, *Introduction à l'histoire universelle. Tableau de la France. Préface à l'Histoire de France*, ed. Charles Morazé (Paris, 1962), pp. 75–76.

4. See Michelet, *Introduction à l'histoire universelle, Tableau de la France*.

5. See Michel Serres, "Michelet—The Soup," *Clio* 6 (1977): 181–191.

6. "Nous voulons faire l'histoire de cette pauvre créature muette, dont personne ne s'est soucié, l'histoire de ceux qui n'ont pas d'histoire" (Jules Michelet, *Oeuvres complètes*, ed. Paul Viallaneix [Paris, 1971–], IV, 8).

7. Jules Michelet, *Histoire de France*, Book 5, chap. 8, "Eclaircissements," in Michelet, *Oeuvres complètes*, IV, 593. See also my "History as Decipherment: Romantic Historiography and the Discovery of the Other," reprinted as Chapter 8 of the present volume.

8. See, toward the beginning of Book 1, chap. 2 of the *History of the Revolution*,

the report a nobleman gives of the enthusiastic feelings that the opening of the Estates General inspired in him: "My God, my fatherland, my fellow-citizens had become myself" (*HR*, I, 89).

9. According to Michelet himself: "Dans l'*Histoire de la Révolution française* la Révolution a été une création, quoi qu'en dise Saint-Simon, une religion du droit opposée à la religion de la grâce, un banquet pour tous, non pour les élus" (Jules Michelet, *Journal*, 4 vols., ed. P. Viallaneix and C. Digeon [Paris, 1959–76], II, 243).

10. "Tellement Dieu était en la France! telle la vertu miraculeuse qu'elle avait alors! L'épée dont elle frappait, au lieu de blesser, guérissait les peuples. Touchés du fer, ils s'éveillaient, remerciaient le coup salutaire qui rompait leur fatal sommeil, brisait l'enchantement déplorable où, pendant plus de mille années, ils languirent à l'état de bêtes à brouter l'herbe des champs" (*HR*, I, 1225—after the victory of Jemappes).

11. Quoted in Oscar Haac, "La Révolution comme Religion," *Romantisme* 50 (1985): 79.

12. See also *HR*, I, 414, on the Revolution as "un prodigieux rêve."

13. See also *HR*, I, 429n.

14. Alphonse Esquiros, *Histoire des Montagnards* (Paris, 1847), I, 4–5. Like Michelet, Esquiros probably had in mind the popular *Histoire parlementaire de la Révolution française* (Paris, 1834) of P.-J.-B. Buchez and P.-C. Roux.

15. *Histoire de France*, "Préface de 1869," in *Oeuvres complètes*, ed Viallaneix, IV, 15.

16. "Une religion nous vient, deux s'en vont (qu'y faire?): L'Eglise et la Royauté" (*HR*, I, 219).

17. On the Revolution as the religion of *all*, see Michelet, *Journal*, II, 243 (13 April 1854). See note 9 above.

18. Cf. *HR*, I, 327: "*la province est abjurée* . . . Tous ensemble ils répètent le serment sacré . . . 'Plus de province! la patrie!' "

19. Georges Poulet in his *Mesure de l'instant* (Paris, 1968), p. 272. Cf. Frank Bowman, "Michelet et les métamorphoses du Christ," *Revue d'histoire littéraire de la France* 74 (1974): 824–844.

20. *HR*, I, 466 (criticism of the Jacobin model of the "cité antique" or the "petite cité monastique du moyen âge"); II, 914 (criticism of Robespierre's utopianism); II, 203 (criticism of the Jacobin belief that unity can be realized by decree).

21. Jules Michelet, *Histoire de France*, 17 vols. (Paris: Hachette, 1833–1867), VII, lx.

22. "Un tel état dure-t-il?" (ibid.).

23. "La Révolution ne peut, sous peine de périr, rester dans l'âge d'innocence."

24. Cf. *HR*, II, 173: "La Révolution, entrant dans le jacobinisme . . . y trouvait une force, mais elle y trouvait une ruine."

25. Letter of 6 April 1867, in *Selected Letters of Friedrich Nietzsche*, ed. and trans. Christopher Middleton (Chicago and London, 1969), p. 23.

26. Michelet was fully aware, however, that history is concerned precisely with the alienated world that is the very opposite of the ideal of unity and unanimity. "Qu'est-ce que l'histoire? La spécification. Plus elle spécifie, précise, caractérise, plus elle est historique, plus elle est elle-même" (*HR*, II, 995).

27. Poulet, "Michelet," in *Mesure de l'instant,* p. 272; Roland Barthes, *Michelet par lui-même* (Paris, 1954), p. 21.

28. At the end of the account of the death of Robespierre, Michelet speculates on the possibility that the great leader foresaw the collapse of the Revolution, the coming reaction, and "l'éternal roc de Sisyphe que roule la France" (*HR,* II, 986). Earlier (*HR,* I, 428), he had already wondered how the enthusiasm and spontaneous unity of the Federations could ever be repeated: "Heure choisie, divine! . . . Et qui dira comment une autre peut revenir?"

29. See Franz Overbeck, *Christentum und Kultur,* ed. C. A. Bernoulli (Basle, 1919).

30. Michelet, *Tableau de la France,* in *Introduction à l'Histoire universelle,* p. 130.

31. Jules Michelet, *La Mer* (Paris, 1900; orig. 1861), p. 5.

32. Ibid., p. 291. On Romme, Reid, etc., see pp. 289–302.

33. Ibid., pp. 85–86.

34. Michelet, *Journal,* II, 584.

35. Jules Michelet, *Histoire romaine,* 2nd ed., 2 vols. (Paris, 1833) I, 71.

36. Jules Michelet, *L'Insecte,* Book 2, chap. 12 (Paris, n.d.; orig. 1857), pp. 159–160.

37. Jules Michelet, *L'Oiseau* (Paris, n.d.; orig. 1858), p. 143.

38. Jules Michelet, *Le Peuple,* ed. L. Refort (Paris, 1946), pp. 134–135.

39. Michelet, *L'Oiseau,* pp. 163–164.

40. On this feature of Michelet's historical writing, see Paul Viallaneix's Introduction to his edition of *Jeanne d'Arc et autres textes* (Paris, 1974) and his contribution to the special Michelet issue of *Clio* 6 (1977): 196–198.

41. *Histoire de France,* "Préface de 1869," in *Oeuvres complètes,* ed. Viallaneix, IV, 15.

42. Frank Bowman, "Michelet et les métamorphoses du Christ," *Revue d'histoire littérature de la France* 74 (1974): 843–844.

43. Roland Barthes, "Modernité de Michelet," *Revue d'histoire littéraire de la France* 74 (1974): 804–805.

44. See note 51 below.

45. The people's knowledge, in contrast, is not analytical but synthetic, not criticism ("cutting") but construction. "Ils rapprochent et lient volontiers, divisent, analysent peu . . . Ils n'aiment pas à scinder la vie" (Michelet, *Le Peuple,* ed. Refort, p. 183).

46. Michelet accepts what he calls the "Revolutionary catechism"—that is, "what all Frenchmen, thirty-four million of them, believe," with the exception of a few small groups of "écrivains systématiques" and some educated workers who, under their spell, forsook the common tradition. He summarizes it as follows: "Who brought on the Revolution? Voltaire and Rousseau.—Who caused the ruin of the King? The Queen.—Who began the Revolution? Mirabeau.—Who were the enemies of the Revolution? Pitt and Coburg, the Chouans and Coblence.—And who else? The English and the priests ('les Goddem et les Calotins').—Who spoiled the Revolution? Marat and Robespierre" (*HR,* I, 283).

47. He knows the sense of rupture felt by the participants in the Revolution, he says, because he himself experienced it: "While I was happily engaged in recovering the true tradition of France, my own link with the past was broken for

good. I lost the being who would so often tell me the story of the Revolution . . . my father with whom I have spent my entire life—forty-eight years. When that blow struck me, I was looking elsewhere; I was elsewhere, as I busily wrote this work which I had been dreaming of for so long. I was at the foot of the Bastille, I was about to take the fortress, to plant our immortal flag on its towers . . . That blow hit me unforeseen, like a shot from the Bastille" (Preface of 1847, *HR*, I, 8). Later, when it came time to recount the falling away from the great days of the Revolution during the Terror, he too was living in wretched exile in Nantes, "in a leaky house that let in the great rains, in January 1853." It was there, and then, that he wrote "about the corresponding month of the Terror": "I plunge with my subject into darkness and winter. The relentless storm winds that have been battering my windows on those hills of Nantes for two months are the constant accompaniment, sometimes heavy, sometimes piercing, of my Dies Irae of '93" (Préface of 1868, *HR*, I, 9). Sometimes the historian's identification with his subject is less explicit. "Et si cette plaine est aride, et si cette herbe est séchée, elle reverdira un jour," Michelet wrote of the Champ de Mars, the site of the great Fête de la Fédération (*HR*, I, 2). "Ma montagne est chauve, mais elle refleurira," he wrote in his Journal on 2 April 1854 from his exile in Italy, referring both to the dashing of his political hopes and to his own feelings of physical, moral, and intellectual exhaustion and impotence (*Journal*, II, 240).

48. Michelet, *Journal*, I, 330 (23 June 1840). See also I, 385 (27 March 1842); I, 502 (6 April 1843); I, 677 (12 November 1847); II, 544 (12 August 1860).

49. The contemporary political significance of the distinction between a problem-oriented historiography and a historiography designed to sustain or even create a sense of national identity is made abundantly clear by the current debate over historiography in the Federal Republic of Germany.

50. Though working in the same narrative tradition as Michelet, Louis Blanc already reproached his rival with this failure to encourage a critical response in his readers. It is important, Blanc noted in his rival *Histoire de la Révolution française,* that the historian cite all his authorities and discuss and compare their testimonies before the reader, who must in the end judge them. It is not enough, according to Blanc, just to add another narrative of events to those that already exist; sources must be recorded and difficult points discussed candidly. ("Premier avis au lecteur," in *Histoire de la Révolution française,* 2nd ed. [Paris, 1869], I, xxxviii.)

51. Though I am arguing that Michelet's way of writing history leaves little room for the discussion and debate we usually associate equally with science and scholarship and with democratic processes but seems, on the contrary, intended rather to promote the unity formed around myth, there is no doubt of his deep-seated hatred of tyranny and oppression. In Michelet's view, the leaders of *all* the parties, the Jacobins as well as the Girondists, were bourgeois who never doubted their superiority to the common people, the "dumb cattle" they were called upon to "save," in spite of themselves if necessary (*HR*, I, 301). "Voilà une bien terrible aristocratie, dans ces démocrates," he noted. The leadership of any fanatical elite, obsessed with its own theories and principles, cut off from the people, and so committed to the future that it loses sight of the present, ends only too easily in cruelty and tyranny. (See *HR*, II, 855, 995.) Again and again Michelet warned, as Trotsky was to do once more later, that Jacobinism prepares the way for military

dictatorship. (See, for instance, *HR,* II, 1004.) The Revolution's need to defend itself against internal and external enemies, which led to the emergence of outstanding leaders like Robespierre and Napoleon, has had a disastrous consequence, he asserted: it has produced in the French people a "grave and deep-seated evil, which will be hard to eradicate"—the worship of strong men, "l'adoration de la force" (*HR,* I, 2). Michelet's own position concerning this cult of power was abundantly clear: Anacharsis Clootz's admonition, "France, guéris des individus," was placed both at the beginning and at the end of the special preface written for the section of the *History of the Revolution* devoted to the Terror.

52. Michelet, *Introduction à l'histoire universelle,* p. 72.

53. "La morale a besoin du temps" (Benjamin Constant, *De l'Esprit de conquête et de l'usurpation,* I, v, in *Oeuvres,* ed. Alfred Roulin [Paris, 1957], p. 999).

54. Oscar Haac observes coolly that although the authorities worried lest Michelet's audiences of eight hundred to a thousand students at the Collège de France "become a center of revolt and revolution . . . the historian never called on them to rise" ("The Nationalism of a Humanist," *Gradiva* 5 [1987]: 36.

55. Franco Moretti, "The Moment of Truth," *New Left Review* 159 (September-October 1986): 39–48. Cf. a debate in the journal *Telos,* in the form of a series of articles by Ferenc Feher, Joel Whitebrook, Richard Wolin, and others, on the propriety and usefulness of the so-called "politics of redemption," which has marked a good deal of left-wing thinking since the early nineteenth century (*Telos* 63 [1985]: 147–168; 65 [1985]: 152–170; 69 [1986]: 46–57).

7. History and Literature

1. Quintilian, *Institutio oratoria* X, 1, 31.

2. Cicero, *De oratore* II, 51–64.

3. Rudolf Unger, "Zur Entwicklung des Problems der historischen Objektivität bis Hegel," in *Aufsätze zur Prinzipienlehre der Literaturgeschichte* (Berlin, 1929), trans. as "The Problem of Historical Objectivity: A Sketch of Its Development to the Time of Hegel," in *Enlightenment Historiography: Three German Studies* (*History and Theory: Studies in the Philosophy of History,* Beiheft 11 [Middletown, Conn., 1971]), p. 63.

4. Jean-Paul Sartre, *Qu'est-ce que la littérature?* (1948; rpt. ed. Paris, 1964), pp. 112–113.

5. See Hugh Blair, *Lectures on Rhetoric and Belles Lettres* (London, 1783), II, 274 (lecture 36): "But an Historian may possess these qualities of being perspicuous, distinct, and grave, and may notwithstanding be a dull Writer; in which case, we shall reap little benefit from his labours. We will read him without pleasure; or, most probably, we shall soon give over to read him at all. He must therefore study to render his narration interesting; which is the quality that chiefly distinguishes a Writer of genius and eloquence."

6. Edward Gibbon, "Remarques sur les ouvrages et sur le caractère de Salluste, Jules César, Cornelius Nepos, et Tite-Live," in *Miscellaneous Works* (London, 1814), IV, 430–431. See similar comments by Voltaire in a "Discours sur l'Histoire de Charles XII" appended to the early editions of this work.

7. Unger, "Problem of Historical Objectivity," p. 73. Cf. Prosper de Barante's judgment of seventeenth-century historiography: "L'art historique doit maintenant

être considéré comme une branche de la littérature" ("De l'histoire," in *Mélanges historiques et littéraires* [Brussels, 1835], II, 34).

8. Barante, "De l'histoire," p. 8.

9. Johann Martin Chladenius, *Allgemeine Geschichtswissenschaft worinnen der Grund zu einer neuen Einsicht in allen Arten der Gelehrtheit gelegt wird* (Leipzig, 1752), pp. 150–152; quoted in Unger, "Problem of Historical Objectivity," p. 71.

10. Quoted from the translation by Gerald F. Else (Ann Arbor, Mich., 1967). Hegel's distinction between history and poetry in *The Philosophy of Fine Art* (pt. 3, subsec. 3, chap. 3, subsec. 2) marks a considerable modification of Aristotle's distinction between history and epic, but the framework in which it is made remains strikingly similar: "The historian . . . has no right to expunge these prosaic characteristics of his content, or to convert them into others more *poetical;* his narrative must embrace what lies actually before him and in the shape he finds it without amplification, or at least poetical transformation. However much, therefore, it may become a part of his labours to make the ideal significance and spirit of an epoch, a people, or the particular event depicted, the ideal focus and bond which holds all together in one coherent whole, he is not entitled to make either the conditions presented him, the characters or events, wholly subordinate to such a purpose, though he may doubtless remove from his survey what is wholly contingent and without serious significance: he must, in short, permit them to appear in all their objective contingency, dependence and mysterious caprice. . . . And, finally, if the historian adds to his survey his private reflections as a philosopher, attempting thereby to grasp the absolute grounds for such events, rising to the sphere of that divine being, before which all that is contingent vanishes and a loftier mode of necessity is unveiled, he is nonetheless debarred, in reference to the actual conformation of events, from that exclusive right of poetry, namely to accept this substantive resolution as the fact of most importance. To poetry alone is the liberty permitted to dispose without restriction of the material submitted in such a way that it becomes, even regarded on the side of external condition, conformable with ideal truth" (quoted from the translation by F. P. B. Osmaston [London, 1920], IV, 41–42).

11. Aristotle, *Poetics,* ed. D. W. Lucas (Oxford, 1968), p. 119.

12. Georg Simmel's interesting essay on "the adventure" (*Gesammelte Essays* [1911: 2nd enl. ed. Leipzig, 1919]) illuminates Aristotle's idea of the action. Simmel argues that the adventure constitutes a unity in itself, an episode that is discontinuous with the normal flow of our lives, yet "somehow connected with the center. . . . It is because the work of art and adventure stand over against life . . . that both are analogous to the totality of life itself. . . . In contrast to those aspects of life which are related only peripherally—by mere fate—the adventure is defined by its capacity, in spite of its being isolated and accidental, to have necessity and meaning" (trans. David Rettler, in *Georg Simmel 1858–1918,* ed. Kurt H. Wolff [Columbus, Ohio, 1959], pp. 243–258).

13. Translated from Voltaire's French version of the *Essay* (1733), in *Oeuvres complètes,* ed. Louis Moland, 52 vols. (Paris, 1877–1885), VIII, 322. Cf. Addison, *Spectator* 2:520: "The Reader may find an abridgement of the whole Story as collected out of the ancient Historians, and as it was received among the Romans, in *Dionysius Halicarnassus.*" The original English text of Voltaire's *Essay* says only:

"Part of the Events included in the *Aeneid* are to be found in *Dionysius Halicarnassus*" (Voltaire's *Essay on Epic Poetry: A Study and an Edition,* ed. Florence D. White [Albany, N.Y., 1915], p. 94).

14. Voltaire, "Idée de la Henriade," in *Oeuvres,* VIII, 39.

15. Letter to Voltaire, 17 March 1757, in *Voltaire's Correspondence,* ed. T. Besterman, 107 vols. (Geneva, 1956–1965), no. 6507.

16. Ibid., letter of 1 August 1752 (no. 4163). These comments on the later prose history were anticipated by an earlier comment on the *Henriade:* "All nations are agreed that a simple unified action, developed gradually and without being forced . . . is more pleasing than a chaotic pile of monstrous adventures. In general, there is a desire that this reasonable unity be ornamented by a variety of episodes which will be like the limbs of a robust and well-proportioned body" (*Oeuvres,* VIII, 308–309).

17. For example, chap. 11: "We might distribute into three acts this remarkable tragedy"; chap. 34: "I am not desirous to prolong or repeat this narration"; chap. 43: "Should I persevere in the same course, should I observe the same measure, a prolix and slender thread would be spun through many a volume, nor would the patient reader find an adequate reward of instruction or amusement." In general, Gibbon holds, the "scope of narrative, the riches and variety of . . . materials" should not "be incompatible with the unity of design and composition" (chap. 48).

18. Fénelon, *Oeuvres* (Versailles and Paris, 1820–1830), XXI, 230.

19. Blair, *Lectures,* II, 261 (lecture 35).

20. Montesquieu, "Quelques réflexions sur les Lettres persanes" (1754), in Montesquieu, *Oeuvres complètes* (Paris, 1964), p. 62; Blair, *Lectures,* II, 262; Fénelon, *Lettre,* in *Oeuvres,* XXI, 230.

21. Philippe Ariès, *Le Temps de l'histoire* (Monaco, 1954), p. 194.

22. J. J. Garnier, ed., *Histoire de France, par M. L'abbé Velly* (Paris, 1770), I, xxii–xxv (editor's Foreword).

23. Fontenelle, "Essai sur l'histoire" (ca. 1690), in *Histoire des Oracles, Du Bonheur, Essai sur l'histoire, Dialogues des Morts* (Paris, 1966), p. 160.

24. An essential text on this subject, in my view, is the delightful fable of the cuckoo and the nightingale recounted at Holbach's by Abbé Galiani and reported by Diderot in a letter to Sophie Volland of 20 October 1760 (*Lettres à Sophie Volland,* ed. André Babelon [Paris, 1938], I, 151–153).

25. Friedrich Schiller, *Letters on the Aesthetic Education of Man,* letter 13, quoted from the translation by Reginald Snell (London, 1954), p. 69. The two poles defined by Diderot and Schiller—the empirical and the rational, the chaotic fullness of reality and the skinny order of the mind—have continued to figure prominently in reflection on history, with preference going now to one, now to the other. In an early essay Kierkegaard expresses the opposition in terms of history and philosophy and expects the latter to include and master the former, though without doing violence to it: "The observer should be an eroticist, no feature, no moment should be indifferent to him; on the other hand, he should also feel his own preponderance, but only use it to assist the phenomenon to its complete manifestation. Even though the observer brings the concept with him, therefore, it is essential that the phenomenon remain inviolate and that the concept be seen

coming into existence through the phenomenon. . . . Philosophy relates to history as a confessor to the penitent, and, . . . as the penitent individual is able to rattle off the fateful events of his life chronologically, even recite them entertainingly, but cannot himself see through them, so history is able to proclaim with pathos the rich full life of the race, but must leave its explanation to the elder [philosophy]" (*The Concept of Irony,* trans. Lee M. Capel [London, 1966], pp. 47–48). More recently, the other view was taken by Albert Guérard in an essay in which he argues that the literary models of the historian prevent him from ever encountering the real: "History, as presented by historians, is a well-made play: not a pageantry of detached episodes, but a situation, with exposition, growth, crisis. . . . History is legend, symbol, and myth. Its rules are not those of political economy but of epic drama. Between history and fiction . . . there is a profound identity which sets them apart from statistical science, social or physical, and from the pure logic of mathematics." Guérard acknowledges that there are differences, "but the boundaries are hard to trace" ("Millennia," in *Generalization in Historical Writing,* ed. A. Riazonovsky and B. Riznik [Philadelphia, 1963], pp. 167–206).

26. Friedrich Schiller, "Was heisst und zu welchem Ende studiert man Universalgeschichte?" in *Werke* (Nationalausgabe, Weimar, 1970), XVII, 372–374.

27. Emile Benveniste, "La Relation de temps dans le verbe français" (1959), in *Problèmes de linguistique générale* (Paris, 1966), pp. 237–250. "[Facts] are characterized as past," Benveniste writes, "by the mere fact of being registered and enunciated in temporal expressions of past time." And "We shall define historical narrative as that mode of enunciation which excludes every 'autobiographical' linguistic form. The historian will never say *I* or *you, here,* or *now,* because he will never make use of the formal devices of discourse, which consist, in the first place, in the relation of the first and second persons—*I: you.*"

28. Voltaire, article "Histoire," in *Encyclopédie,* vol. VIII (1765), in *Oeuvres,* XIX, 346. Cf. Benveniste, "La Relation," p. 240n.1: "The historical enunciation of events is, of course, independent of the 'objective' truth. All that counts is the 'historical' intention of the writer."

29. See Leo Braudy, *Narrative Form in History and Fiction: Hume, Fielding, and Gibbon* (Princeton, N.J., 1970). The historians of the Restoration were already aware of this characteristic of their predecessors' works. According to Barante ("De l'histoire," p. 48), the unity of the eighteenth-century historical narrative "results from the concerns of the author. . . . The past is decomposed, torn to pieces, rendered lifeless: only the author's idea remains alive and animated, and it is that idea that pulls us along."

30. D'Alembert, "Réflexions sur l'histoire," in *Oeuvres* (Paris, 1805), IV, 195.

31. Voltaire, *Siècle de Louis XIV,* supplement, part 1 (Paris, 1966), II, 320.

32. Siegfried Kracauer, *History: The Last Things before the Last* (New York, 1969). The relevant chapter in this volume first appeared as "General History and the Aesthetic Approach," in *Die nicht mehr schönen Künste,* ed. H. R. Jauss (Munich, 1968), pp. 109–127, notably pp. 120–121. Blair (*Lectures,* II, 273) had already noted that "much . . . will depend on the proper management of transitions, which forms one of the chief ornaments of this kind of writing." Cf. H. Stuart Hughes, in *History as Art and as Science* (New York, 1964), pp. 70–71: "Historians have de-

veloped a myriad of literary devices for gliding over what they do not adequately know or understand. With more schematic history, the gaps yawn embarrassingly wide: in narrative prose they can be artfully concealed."

The power of narrative order, and at the same time its distance from "reality," is graphically conveyed by the narrator of Claude Simon's novel *Le Vent* (Paris, 1957). In a passage (pp. 9–10) whose anxious tone and pessimistic emphasis are in striking contrast to the calm optimism of Schiller's essay on universal history of a century and a half before, the narrator describes at length his difficulty in interpreting a story that is being told to him and concludes: "And now, now that it's all over, the effort to report, to reconstruct what happened is a little like trying to glue the scattered, incomplete bits and pieces of a broken mirror back together again, making clumsy efforts to fit them together, and coming up with an incoherent, derisive, idiotic result, in which only our mind perhaps, or rather our pride, enjoins us, on pain of madness and against all evidence, to find at all costs a logical sequence of causes and effects where all that reason can discern is a straying, ourselves being heaved about from all sides, like a cork adrift on the water, aimless, sightless, endeavoring only to stay afloat, and suffering, and dying in the end."

33. See Lucien Febvre, *La Terre et l'évolution humaine* (Paris, 1922).

34. See also Kracauer, "General History," p. 122: "All these devices and techniques [for establishing transitions] follow a harmonizing tendency—which is to say that their underlying intentions flagrantly conflict with those of contemporary art. Joyce, Proust, and Virginia Woolf, the pioneers of the modern novel, no longer care to render biographical developments and chronological sequences after the manner of the older novel; on the contrary, they resolutely decompose (fictitious) continuity over time. . . . Modern art radically challenges the artistic ideals from which the general historian draws his inspiration—from which he must draw it to establish his genre." In an earlier text, "Biography as a Neobourgeois Art Form," originally published in 1930, Kracauer had already argued that the popularity of history, and especially of historical biography in the interwar years, needed to be interpreted in the context of the collapse, after World War I, of the bourgeois ideas of world order and of the autonomous, coherent self. In this context "history emerges as a solid land mass out of the ocean of the formless and the unformable." The meaning of biography in particular is "that in the chaos of contemporary artistic experiments, it represents the only apparently necessary prose form" ("Die Biographie als neubürgerliche Kunstform," in *Das Ornament der Masse* [Frankfurt am Main, 1963], pp. 75–80).

35. Lucien Febvre, *Combats pour l'histoire* (Paris, 1953), pp. 30–31.

36. Murray G. Murphey, *Our Knowledge of the Historical Past* (Indianapolis, Ind., 1973), pp. 16, 63–64. A similar argument, more closely related to historical practice at the present time, is developed by Michel de Certeau in an article roughly contemporary with Murphey's book: "The transformation of 'archivistics' has been the departure point and the condition of a new kind of history. . . . I shall take only one example: the advent of the computer. François Furet has shown some of the effects produced by 'the constitution of new archives stored on punchcards'; signification is a function of a series here, and not of a relation

to a given 'reality'; only those problems that have been formally set up prior to being programmed can be objects of historical research, and so on. Yet this is but one particular element, a symptom in a way, of a vaster scientific institution. Contemporary analysis has overwhemed the procedures associated with the type of 'symbolic analysis' which has prevailed since Romanticism and which sought to *recognize* a sense that was at once *given* and *concealed:* . . . The practice of modern historical analysis consists of constructing 'models,' 'substituting for the study of concrete phenomena the study of objects constituted by their definition,' judging the scientific value of those objects by the 'field of questions' to which they permit us to look for answers and by the answers they provide, and, finally, 'determining the limits within which a given model can provide meanings' " ("L'Opération historique," in *Faire de l'histoire: nouveaux problèmes,* ed. Jacques le Goff and Pierre Nora [Paris, 1974], p. 23). De Certeau's essay brings out the radical character of contemporary historical "science" with respect to the earlier German idealist critique of naive realism. The German idealists still aimed at the perception of a (God-) given reality; they wished to recognize and accommodate the role of subjectivity in the process of perception, but they did not question that "reality" was what was to be perceived.

37. "From the Logic of History to an Ethic for the Historian," in *Cross-Currents* (1961), quoted by Hayden White in "The Politics of Contemporary Philosophy of History," *Clio* 3 (1973): 35–54.

38. Miguel de Unamuno, "Comment on écrit un roman" (French trans. by Jean Cassou), *Mercure de France* 15 (1926): 15.

39. Alain Besançon, "Vers une histoire psychanalytique" (orig. pub. in *Annales,* 1969), in *Histoire et expérience du moi* (Paris, 1971), pp. 66, 68, 70, 85.

40. Roland Barthes, "Le Discours de l'histoire," *Information sur les sciences sociales* 6, no. 4 (1967): 74.

41. R. G. Collingwood, *The Idea of History* (Oxford, 1946; rpt. ed. New York, 1956), p. 246.

42. See Michel Butor: "All writings that claim to be true have a common feature: they are always in principle verifiable. I must be able to cross-check what one source has told me with information obtained from another source, and so on indefinitely; otherwise I am in the presence of an error or a fiction. . . . Whereas the story that claims to be true is always supported by, or can appeal to some external evidence, the novel must be able to call into being on its own the subject matter of its discourse with us" ("Le Roman comme recherche," in *Essais sur le roman* [Paris, 1969; 1st ed. 1960], pp. 8–9).

43. "The whole perceptible world . . . is potentially and in principle evidence to the historian. It becomes actual evidence in so far as he can use it. And he cannot use it unless he comes to it with the right kind of historical knowledge. The more historical knowledge we have, the more we can learn from any given piece of evidence; if we had none, we could learn nothing. Evidence is evidence only when some one contemplates it historically. Otherwise it is merely perceived fact, historically dumb. It follows that historical knowledge can only grow out of historical knowledge; in other words, that historical thinking is an original and fundamental activity of the human mind, or, as Descartes might have said, that the idea of the past is an 'innate' idea" (Collingwood, *Idea of History,* p. 247).

44. In a recent study of autobiography, Philippe Lejeune bases his discrimination of fiction and autobiography on the "pact" contracted between author and reader at the outset of the work. Textual analysis alone, he claims, yields no means of distinguishing the two. "The novelist can imitate and has imitated all the devices which the autobiographer uses to convince us of the authenticity of his narrative." But if we include as part of the "text" the title page and the name of the author, a clear signal is given which establishes the specificity of autobiography. Lejeune insists, however, that the question of *fact*—whether or not or to what extent the narrative is a true account of the life it purports to recount—must not be confused with the question of *right*—that is, the type of contract entered into by author and reader (*Le Pacte autobiographique* [Paris, 1975], p. 26). It seems likely that a similar pact binds the author and the reader of historical works: the reader is advised that the narrative is to be regarded as true and is invited to verify it by comparing it with other narratives or with other evidence.

45. See J. Snyder and N. W. Allen, "Photography, Vision, and Representation," *Critical Inquiry* 2 (1975): 143–169. "What is truly significant about a photograph of a horse is not really that the horse himself printed his image, or that the photograph shows us the horse as we ourselves would (or wouldn't) have seen him, or that it establishes something in the way of scientific truth about this horse. What is significant (it seems to be alleged) is that *this* horse wasn't invented by some artist: this is a picture of a *real* horse" (p. 163). Similarly, Hilton Kramer in a *New York Times* article, "Celebrating Formalism in Photography" (12 December 1976), states that it is "the omnivorous appetite for the 'real' that is the primary basis for the increased popularity that photography has lately won for itself with the art public." The relation between historiography and photography or film is discussed in the opening pages of Kracauer, *History*.

46. Roland Barthes, "Le Mythe, aujourd'hui," in *Mythologies* (Paris, 1957), pp. 213–268.

47. Ibid., pp. 241–242. Barthes has maintained this position with great consistency: see *Le Degré zéro de l'écriture* (Paris, 1953) and the review of Philippe Sollers's novel *Drame* in 1965 (reprinted in *Théorie d'ensemble* [Paris, 1968], pp. 25–40, esp. pp. 35–36 and n. 4).

48. Barante, "De l'histoire," p. 50.

49. Ibid., p. 37.

50. On Jan Mukařovský's categories of normative or structured and functional or unstructured, see the essay "The Esthetics of Language" (orig. pub. in *Slovo a Slovesnost* 6 [1940]: 1–27), in *A Prague School Reader on Esthetics, Literary Structure, and Style*, selected and trans. by Paul N. Garvin (Washington, D.C., 1964), pp. 31–69.

51. It is important to emphasize that Barthes's argument does not rest on a radical opposition between "natural" meaning (authenticity) and the signs of culture (inauthenticity). Barthes makes it clear that both poetry and history are semiological systems. There is no nature, no outside of signs and the act of signifying. The question is whether the signifying system attempts to cover up its tracks so as to appear natural, or whether, on the contrary, in the forlorn yet utopian hope of breaking out of its own constraints, it tests itself to the very limit; whether, in other terms, it is integrationist and thus fundamentally conservative, or disruptive

and revolutionary. Although he shares many common positions with Sartrian existentialism in this essay, Barthes's interpretation of the essentialist aspirations of poetry is quite different from Sartre's.

52. In his introduction to a recent edition of *La Sorcière* (Paris, 1964), Robert Mandrou, for instance, manages to say nothing of the text itself, passing instead immediately through it, as it were, to what in his view it represents—a Weberian ideal type of the witch. *La Sorcière* is thus reappropriated for history by placing in parentheses those aspects of it which, to the literary scholar, are most striking and specific.

53. Roland Barthes, "Drame, poème, roman," in *Théorie d'ensemble*, p. 37n.7.

54. Ibid., p. 36.

55. G. R. Elton, *The Practice of History* (Sydney, 1967), pp. 109, 115, 116.

8. History as Decipherment

1. Quoted in Leonard Krieger, *Ranke: The Meaning of History* (Chicago, 1977), p. 361. Krieger notes Ranke's fondness for terms such as "brings to light" and "unriddle" (p. 10).

2. Charles Baudelaire, "Elévation," in *Les Fleurs du Mal.*

3. See, for example, Jules Michelet, *Histoire romaine*, vol. 2 of *Oeuvres complètes*, ed. Paul Viallaneix (Paris, 1972), p. 365: "What was this Etruscan people? . . . [Historical scholarship] has successively [interrogated] Etruria [as to] whether she was Greek, Phenician, German, Celtic, Iberian[.] The silent genius has made no reply. Let us in our turn examine the monuments of Etruscan art. Let us contemplate those massive blocks of the walls of Volterra; let us disinter those elegant vases of Tarquinii, or Clusium: let us penetrate those hypogea, more mysterious than the Necropoles of Egypt." Quoted from the translation by William Hazlitt, *History of the Roman Republic* (London, 1847), pp. 38–39.

4. See my article, "The Go-Between: Jules Michelet 1798–1874," *Modern Language Notes* 89 (1974): 503–541.

5. Michelet, "L'Héroisme de l'esprit," in *Oeuvres complètes*, IV, 32, 38.

6. Michelet, "Preface," *Vie de Luther*, in *Oeuvres complètes*, III, 239: "pauvre vieille mère du monde moderne, reniée, battue par son fils, certes, ce n'est pas nous qui voudrions la blesser encore." See likewise the historian's farewell to the Middle Ages at the end of bk. 4 of the *Histoire de France*, in *Oeuvres complètes*, IV, 610. These gestures of filial piety are to be contrasted with many vivid accounts of man's cruelty to woman or animals (Nature)—for instance, the savagery of the hunting of the whale in *La Mer* (Paris, 1898), pp. 328–329.

7. Michelet, *Histoire romaine*, in *Oeuvres complètes*, II, 382: "Horace tue sa soeur; Rome tue Albe, sa soeur ou sa mère, ce qui est peut-être la même chose individualisée par la poésie; un nom de femme pour un nom de cité. Mais il fallait justifier ce meurtre de la métropole par la colonie. Les Romains ne pouvant faire que des guerres justes, il faut qu'Albe ait mérité son sort." See also Michelet's review of the French translation of Niebuhr's *Roman History* (*Le Temps*, 15 June 1830) reproduced in *Oeuvres complètes*, II, 680, and *Le Peuple*, ed. Paul Viallaneix (Paris, 1974), pt. 2, chap. 6: "That proud antiquity [Greece and Rome] which refused whatever was not noble succeeded only too well in suppressing everything

else" (p. 177). For Michelet's friend, the Fourierist Alphonse Toussenel, the myth of the Fall was designed to cover up and justify the earliest form of social and economic exploitation, which he identified as man's subjection of woman (*L'Esprit des Bêtes: Zoologie passionnée* [Paris, 1858], p. 57). See also Augustin Thierry, *Dix Ans d'études historiques* (Paris, 1868), pp. 285–287 passim, and his *Lettres sur l'histoire de France* (Paris, 1827), letter 8.

8. Edgar Quinet, *Philosophie de l'histoire de France*, vol. 3 of *Oeuvres complètes* (Paris, 1857), pp. 385–386. The same awareness of "hidden history" underlies the widespread nineteenth-century belief that the truth of the past is to be found in the writings of poets and novelists rather than in official histories. "The bards and minstrels of Erin," according to Augustin Thierry, are "the archivists of their land," and Scott is a better historian of the "true" history of Scotland—the history of its people—than Robertson (*Dix Ans d'études historiques*, pp. 124, 145–146, 148). See likewise Balzac's statement in the Preface to the *Comédie humaine* (1842) that he proposes to write "l'histoire oubliée par tant d'historiens," and Alessandro Manzoni's similar claim for *I Promessi Sposi* in *Opere varie*, ed. Michele Barbi and Fausto Ghisalberti (Milan and Florence, 1943), pp. 625–626.

9. Michelet describes the past as "ce mauvais songe" (*Histoire de la Révolution française*, ed. Gérard Walter [Paris, 1952], I, 125). On forgetting, see Michelet, *Journal*, ed. Paul Viallaneix (Paris, 1959), I, 386 (28 March 1842) and Michelet, *Bible de l'Humanité* (Paris, 1864), p. 483. See Edgar Quinet on the burden of the past in *Le Christianisme et la Révolution*, in his *Oeuvres complètes*, III, 59.

10. See Stephen Bann, "The Historian as Taxidermist: Ranke, Barante, Waterton," *Comparative Criticism: A Yearbook* 3 (1981): 21–41. On the experience of rupture, see the famous conclusion of Chateaubriand's *Mémoires d'Outretombe*, ed. Maurice Levaillant (Paris, 1969), IV, 637: "If I compare the two terrestrial globes, the one I knew at the beginning of my life and the one I now behold at the end of it, I no longer recognize the one in the other."

11. Barante gives a lucid account of his aims in the Introduction to the *Histoire des Ducs de Bourgogne de la maison de Valois*, 12 vols. (Paris, 1824–1826). On Barante, see the important article by Stephen Bann, "A Cycle in Historical Discourse: Barante, Thierry, Michelet," *Twentieth Century Studies* 3 (1970): 110–130. In another essay Bann draws an instructive contrast between Du Sommerard's cabinet of medieval and Renaissance antiquities at the Hotel de Cluny in the 1830s and Alexandre Lenoir's *Musée des Monuments français*. In Du Sommerard's cabinet it was essential that the exhibits be authentic, themselves part of the past they were to represent; in Lenoir's museum the emphasis was on the idea of the sequence, which it was possible to convey equally well by modern replicas as by authentic originals (Stephen Bann, "Poetics of the Museum: Lenoir and Du Sommerard," in *The Clothing of Clio: A Study of the Representation of History in Nineteenth Century Britain and France* [Cambridge, 1984], pp. 77–92). Lenoir's principle of organization seems also to have guided the designers of Louis Philippe's *Musée historique*, which opened at Versailles in 1837.

12. Jules Michelet, *Introduction à l'histoire universelle, Tableau de la France, Préface à l'histoire de France*, ed. Charles Morazé (Paris, 1962), p. 77.

13. Michelet, "Eclaircissements," chap. 8 of *Histoire de France* in *Oeuvres complètes*, IV, 593. On the question of the historical Jesus and the kerygmatic Christ,

see *Der historische Jesus und der kerygmatische Christus,* ed. Helmut Ristow and Karl Matthiae (Berlin, 1961) and Rudolf Bultmann, "Das Verhältnis der Christlichen Christusbotschaft zum historischen Jesus," in his *Exegetica,* ed. Erich Dinkler (Tübingen, 1967).

14. Michelet, "L'Hérosime de l'esprit," in *Oeuvres complètes,* IV, 31, 34–35.

15. Tocqueville's tone was moderate. Others, further to the Right, were more outspoken in their eagerness to overthrow "le fétichisme révolutionnaire ... la seule religion de la plupart des libres penseurs ... réduire l'idole en poussière ... mettre enfin l'histoire de la Révolution à la place de la légende révolutionnaire" (Marius Sepet, in *Revue des questions historiques* 15 [1874]: 276, quoted in Charles Olivier Carbonnel, *Histoire et historiens: une mutation idéologique des historiens français 1865–1885* [Toulouse, 1976], p. 377).

16. See Fustel de Coulanges, Introduction to *La Cité antique: étude sur le culte, le droit, les institutions de la Grece et de Rome* (1864; published in English as *The Ancient City* [Garden City, N.Y., n.d], pp. 11–12) and his Inaugural Lecture at the University of Strasbourg (1862), trans. Fritz Stern, in *The Varieties of History,* ed. Fritz Stern (Cleveland and New York, 1956), pp. 179–188.

17. Jules Michelet, *La Montagne* (Paris, 1899), pp. 112–114, and *La Mer,* bk. 3, "The Conquest of the Sea."

18. Michelet, *Histoire romaine,* in *Oeuvres complètes,* II, 382, and *Introduction à l'histoire universelle,* p. 75.

19. Michelet, *Introduction à l'histoire universelle,* p. 51. The idea was fairly common at the time. According to August-Wilhelm Schlegel in 1804, "Germany must be considered the Orient of Europe" (quoted in René Gérard, *L'Orient et la pensée romantique allemande* [Paris, 1963], p. 132).

20. See, for instance, Michelet, "Tableau de la France," in *Introduction à l'histoire universelle,* p. 130: "The Germanic world is dangerous for me. There is a powerful lotus flower there that makes one forget one's own country." See also *Introduction à l'histoire universelle,* p. 51 and pp. 220–221n., on Germany's capacity for universal sympathy, the affinity of her poets and philosophers for every form of pantheistic mysticism and nature philosophy. Michelet fears that he may "allow his personality to yield to the avid nature which draws him to her and seems to wish to absorb him. The siren's voice is so beguiling." The danger and fascination of indeterminacy characterizes everything that Michelet associates with the Other or the Origin: poetry (as opposed to prose), nature (as opposed to law); see Gossman, "The Go-Between," pp. 515–519.

21. Michelet, *Introduction à l'histoire universelle,* pp. 75–76. See also "Tableau de la France," *Introduction à l'histoire universelle,* p. 156.

22. Michelet, *Introduction à l'histoire universelle,* p. 65.

23. Joachim du Bellay, *Deffence et illustration de la langue françoyse,* ed. Henri Chamard (Paris, 1904), pp. 237–238.

24. Louis-Pierre Anquetil, "Préface," *Histoire de France* (Paris, 1839), I, ii.

25. P.N. Lenglet du Fresnoy, *De l'usage des romans* (Amsterdam, 1734), I, 110.

26. Donald Kelly, *Foundations of Modern Historical Scholarship: Language, Law, and History in the French Renaissance* (New York, 1970), pp. 61, 132.

27. See, for example, Bayle's dry comment in the Preface to his *Dictionnaire*

historique et critique that a historically false narrative may be just as meaningful and rhetorically effective as a true one (*The Dictionary Historical and Critical of Mr. Peter Bayle*, 2nd ed., trans. Pierre Des Maizeaux [London, 1734], I, 1). Montesquieu is also suspicious of narrative history. The author of *The Persian Letters* (1721) and several entertaining tales seems to have deliberately eschewed every opportunity for narrative development in the classical manner in his *Considerations on the Greatness and Decadence of the Romans* (1734). As the title indicates, this work is composed of fragmentary reflections which the reader is invited to put together in the form of an explanatory hypothesis.

28. Quoted in Kelley, *Foundations*, p. 135. On the scholars' suspicion of narrative and rhetoric, see Kelley, pp. 95, 116, 119, 228, 237, 272.

29. Philippe Ariès, *Le Temps de l'histoire* (Monaco, 1954), pp. 194, 209–210.

30. A significant shift in the use and meaning of the word *history* which occurred around the mid-eighteenth century has been noted independently by François Furet ("L'ensemble 'Histoire,' " in *Livre et société dans la France du XVIII siècle* [Paris and The Hague, 1970], II, 101–120) and by Reinhardt Koselleck in "Geschichte" in his *Geschichtliche Grundbegriffe* [Stuttgart, 1975], II, 593–717). Before the middle of the eighteenth century, they point out, the term *history* was almost invariably defined in some way; it was "ancient history" or "the history of Denmark" or "the history of Charles XII." That is to say, it referred to a specific narrative of events. By the end of the century, however, the term *history* was coming to be usable in an absolute way, without definition, in the sense of a regulative concept applicable to all past and future experience.

31. Jacob Burckhardt, *Briefe* (Basle, 1949–1980), I, 201, letter of 13 June 1842; Benjamin Constant, *De la Religion* (1826), quoted in Georges Poulet, *Constant par lui-même* (Paris, 1968), p. 30; Constant, *Adolphe,* chap. 10. On the effect of the Revolution on the consciousness of history, see Koselleck, "Geschichte," pp. 702–704.

32. Michelet, "Discours d'ouverture à la Faculté des Lettres" (9 January 1834), in *Oeuvres complètes,* III, 217–218. See also Michelet, *Le Peuple:* The French people "contains all those early ages, carries and feels them obscurely moving in itself, and does not recognize them. No one tells what that great deep voice is that it often hears within itself, like the dull reverberation of organ notes in a cathedral" (p. 62n.).

33. Friedrich Welcker, *Zoegas Leben* (Halle [Saale], 1912), II, 210, 212.

34. Cf. Welcker's criticism of Voss's neoclassical translation of Homer: "The tree, for Voss, begins above the ground" ["Der Baum fängt ihm über der Erde an"]; quoted by Alfred Baeumler, "Bachofen der Mythologe der Romantik," in *Der Mythus von Orient und Occident: Eine Metaphysik der Alten Welt, aus den Werken von J. J. Bachofen* (Munich, 1956), p. xxxiii.

35. On Champollion, see Hermine Hartleben, *Champollion: sein Leben und sein Werk,* 2 vols. (Berlin, 1906). Hartleben notes that in his opening lecture at the *Lycée* in 1810, Champollion warned against the tendency of historians to provide justifications for what fate has crowned with success. The historian's task, he claimed, is to defend the losers, to act as an arbiter between the past and the future, to right the balance (I, 143).

36. Michelet, *Histoire de France,* bk. 4, chap. 8, in *Oeuvres complètes,* IV, 613. Cf.

Lettres de Champollion le jeune, ed. Hermine Hartleben (Paris, 1909), I, 83–89 (letter to his brother Champollion-Figeac, 6 November 1824).

37. Michelet, *Journal,* I, 378 (30 January 1842). Cf. *Le Peuple,* ed. Lucien Refort (Paris, 1946), pp. 200–201.

38. Quoted in Renate Vonessen, "Der Symbolbegriff in der Romantik," in *Bibliographie zur Symbolik: Ikonographie und Mythologie,* ed. Manfred Lurker (Baden-Baden, 1982), "Ergänzungsband," I, 192.

39. See Johann Joachim Winckelmann, *History of Ancient Art,* trans. G. Henry Lodge (Boston, 1880), I, 173–209.

40. On the need to study Egypt in her own words and not in those spoken about her, see *Lettres de Champollion le jeune,* I, 124 (editorial note); on the superiority of Egyptian art, see ibid., I, 30–32; and II, 103–104, 133, 173, 217.

41. Michelet, *Introduction à l'histoire universelle,* p. 219 (note to p. 50).

42. Jules Michelet, *L'Oiseau* (Paris, 1898), pp. 131–132.

43. Jules Michelet, *Nos Fils* (Paris, 1903), p. 300.

44. Jules Michelet, *La Mer* (Paris, 1983), p. 238.

45. Quoted from the English translation, *History of Ten years, 1830–1840* (London, 1845), II, 520.

46. Throughout his life, Michelet entertained a double view of nature as good, orderly, and intelligible, and at the same time cruel, indifferent, irrational, capricious (see Chapter 5, n. 77 above). "My children gathered flowers, made them into posies, and then discarded them," he noted in 1840 in his Journal (*Journal,* I, 329). "I am afraid that is how nature is too. She entertains herself by making vital compositions, harmonies of existences. Then she discards them by the wayside. But first she snaps the stems and tears the blooms apart." A striking passage at the end of Book 4 of the *Histoire de France* evokes the terrors of an inscrutable nature and man's efforts to overcome them: "In the face of this all powerful nature which delights in teasing us with the delusive fantasmagoria of its productions, we construct a nature designed for ourselves. Against that eternal comedy that distracts but also teases and mocks man, we set our Melpomene" (bk. 4, chap. 8 [1833 version]. *Oeuvres complètes,* IV, 713). But the question how man's art and science are related to nature is not resolved. As "nature" and "history," though sometimes opposed, are also closely related for Michelet, metaphors of each other, the problem of the relation of man's science to nature is also the problem of the relation of historiography to the past. Discontinuity and "meaninglessness" in nature are the mirror of discontinuity and meaninglessness in history. Thus Michelet objects, in *Le Peuple,* that in their writings on the people the new social scientists have taken "the exceptions for the rule and monstrosities for nature." The people is not the shifting, lawless industrial proletariat they focus on, but what it has always been: "I connect it without difficulty with its past" (*Le Peuple,* p. 157). Nevertheless, the fear remains, and to the two-faced, "mère"-"marâtre" in the natural history writings corresponds the two-faced "peuple"-"populace" of the political writings. On the importance of continuity in Romantic historiography, see my *Augustin Thierry and Liberal Historiography,* reprinted as Chapter 4 of the present volume.

47. Michelet, *Le Peuple,* p. 222.

48. Augustin Thierry, *Récits des temps mérovingiens, précédés de Considérations*

sur l'histoire de France (Paris, n.d.), I, 163. Likewise Guizot claimed that the experience of the French Revolution has enabled Frenchmen, such as Villemain or himself, to understand the English Civil War better than Englishmen could (M. [François] Guizot, *Histoire de la révolution d'Angleterre* [Paris, 1841], I, xxii–xxviii).

49. Michelet, *Journal,* I, 380 (1 March 1842); Michelet, *Le Prêtre* (Paris, 1861), p. 297.

50. Michelet, *Le Peuple,* p. 189: "Every one is astonished at the way the inert masses vibrate in reponse to the least word he utters . . . Why so? That voice of his is the voice of the people. Mute in itself, the people speaks in that man."

51. Michelet, *L'Oiseau,* p. 192.

52. Jules Michelet, *La Sorcière* (Paris, 1964), p. 98.

53. Michelet, *Introduction à l'histoire universelle,* pp. 75–76: Michelet, *Histoire de la Révolution française,* I, 287: "De la méthode et de l'esprit de ce livre." See also Michelet, *Le Banquet* (Paris, 1879), p. 207; Michelet, *Le Peuple,* p. 195; a lecture of 21 April 1842 at the Collège de France (Michelet, *Oeuvres complètes,* IV, 8); Michelet, *La Mer,* pp. 27–28: "The silent creatures of the sea leave it to their sublime father, the Ocean, to speak in their stead. They explain themselves through his great voice."

54. Athénaïs's contributions to the natural history works are placed, without specific acknowledgment, in quotation marks.

55. Michelet, "Préface de 1869," in *Introduction à l'histoire universelle,* p. 179.

56. The museum is not, for Michelet, a mere repository of isolated historical or natural curiosities; it is the place where order and continuity are demonstrated and gaps and lacunae shown to be only the result of our ignorance. It thus has an essential ideological function. See Michelet, *L'Oiseau,* pp. 98–99.

57. August Boeckh, "Idee der Philologie," in *Encyklopädie und Methodologie der philosophen Wissenschaften,* ed. E. Bratuschek (Leipzig, 1877), pp. 8–20.

58. Ibid., pp. 10–11.

59. Quoted in Kelley, *Foundations,* p. 61.

60. See Walther Rehm, "Interpretatio christiana," in *Griechentum und Goethezeit* (Leipzig, 1936), pp. 285–334 (chap. 9).

61. Johann Wolfgang von Goethe, *Italienische Reise* [Verona, 16 September 1786], in *Poetische Werke* (Berlin, 1961), XIV, 195.

62. On Winckelmann and Creuzer, the aesthetic and the symbolic interpretation of classical art, see Georg Wilhelm Friedrich Hegel, *Philosophy of Fine Art,* trans. F. P. B. Osmaston (London, 1920), II, 15–19.

63. Michelet, *Histoire de France,* in *Oeuvres complètes,* IV, 714.

64. On their crucial historical and cultural significance, see Leon Poliakov, *The Aryan Myth: A Study of Racist and Nationalist Ideas in Europe,* trans. Edmund Howard (New York, 1974), chap. 9, "The Quest for a New Adam," esp. pp. 183–214.

65. See Johannes Hoffmeister, "Hegel und Creuzer," *Deutsche Vierteljahrsschrift für Literaturwissenschaft und Geistesgeschichte* 8 (1930): 260–282.

66. On Creuzer's influence in France, see Werner Paul Sohnle, *Georg Friedrich Creuzer's "Symbolik und Mythologie" in Frankreich: Eine Untersuchung ihres Einflusses auf Victor Cousin, Edgar Quinet, Jules Michelet und Gustave Flaubert* (Goppingen, 1972).

67. Philippe Buchez, *Introduction à la science de l'histoire, ou Science du développement de l'humanité* (Paris, 1833), pp. 56, 568. See also Edgar Quinet, *Le Christianisme et la Révolution française* (Paris, 1845), pp. 6–7, 65–66, 120, 327–328; and, on the tendency of even some orthodox Christians to view the 1848 Revolution as a fulfillment of the Christian promise, Maurice Agulhon, *Les Quarante-Huitards* (Paris, 1975), pp. 213, 217. After the failure of the Revolution and the coup d'état of Napoleon III, Quinet was critical of this interpretation of the Revolution and of this way of interpreting history in general (see Quinet, *Philosophie de l'histoire de France*, in *Oeuvres complètes*, I, 360–366).

68. Michelet, *Oeuvres complètes*, III, 217–218. Cf. Emerson: "If the whole of history is in one man, it is all to be explained from individual experience. There is a relation between the hours of our life and the centuries of time" ("History," in *The Portable Emerson* [Harmondsworth, 1977], p. 140), and J. D. Guigniaut's summary of Creuzer's view of myth in his eulogy of the latter: "To achieve the aims of mythological exegesis . . . the idea was to put oneself back, by an effort of intuition, into that instinctive and spontaneous state of the intelligence which corresponds to the very nature of myth and which was characteristic of primitive ages, but which can also be rediscovered, in all ages, in the depths of man's consciousness" (*Mémoires de l'Institut National de France: Académie des Inscriptions*, 25, no. 1 [1877], 342).

69. Michelet, *Introduction à l'histoire universelle*, p. 75.

70. Michelet, *Journal*, I, 382.

71. Michelet, "Héroisme de l'esprit," in *Oeuvres complètes*, IV, 40; cf. Michelet, *La Sorcière*, pp. 85, 89, 152.

72. Henri Martin, *Histoire de France* (Paris, 1865), I, vii.

73. Ibid., I, viii.

74. See Poliakov, *The Aryan Myth*, pp. 199–209.

75. See for instance, Toussenel, *L'Esprit des Bêtes*, pp. 116–118, on the Englishman as "un juif roux qui a déclaré, comme celui de Juda, la guerre à tous les peuples du monde, et dont la fortune ne peut se faire que de la ruine de tous les autres peuples." Similar identifications of Jews, Englishmen, and exploiters occur in Michelet.

76. Paul d'Ivot, *Le Sergent Simplet à travers les colonies françaises* (1895), quoted in *Le Nationalisme français 1871–1914*, ed. Raoul Girardet (Paris, 1966), p. 118; see also Clémentel, quoted on pp. 119–120, and Michelet, *Introduction à l'histoire universelle*, p. 64. The idea of France's civilizing mission is one that was common to neo-imperialists like Clémentel and d'Ivot and to neo-Jacobin critics of the Second Empire, such as Blanqui and Delescluze (see Jean Pierre Azéma and M. Winock, *La IIIe République* [Paris, 1970], pp. 31–41).

77. On the relation of anthropology to imperialism, see Felix M. Keesing, "Applied Anthropology in Colonial Administration," in *The Science of Man in the World Crisis*, ed. Ralph Linton (New York, 1945), pp. 373–398, and the more sweeping critique by William J. Willis, Jr., "Skeletons in the Anthropological Closet," in *Reinventing Anthropology*, ed. Dell Hymes (New York, 1972), pp. 121–152.

9. The Rationality of History

1. See the essays "Literature and Education" and "History and Literature: Reproduction or Signification," reprinted as Chapters 2 and 7 of the present volume.

2. Hayden White, "The Historical Text as Literary Artifact" in *The Writing of History: Literary Form and Historical Understanding,* ed. Robert H. Canary and Henry Kozicki (Madison, 1978), pp. 42–43. White has maintained this position with absolute consistency. See his article "The Question of Narrative in Contemporary Historical Theory," *History and Theory* 23 (1984): 19–21.

3. Jack Hexter, *The History Primer* (New York, 1971), pp. 207–208.

4. Reported in Jérôme and Jean Tharaud, *Mes Années chez Barrès* (Paris, 1928), pp. 204–205.

5. "Unpredictability" (1944), in Paul Valéry, *History and Politics,* trans. Denise Folliot and Jackson Mathews (New York, 1962), p. 69 [*Collected Works of Paul Valéry,* vol. 10]. See likewise "Historical Fact" (1932): "The past is an entirely mental thing. It is nothing but images and beliefs. Notice that we use a kind of contradictory procedure for evoking the various figures of the different epochs. On the one hand, we need the free use of our ability to pretend, to live other lives than our own; on the other, we must restrain that freedom in order to take account of documents" (ibid., pp. 122–123).

6. See Jürgen Kempski, "Aspekte der Wahrheit," esp. sec. 2: "Die Welt als Text," in his *Brechungen: Kritische Versuche zur Philosophie der Gegenwart* (Reinbek b. Hamburg, 1964), pp. 278–294; see also my "History as Decipherment: Romantic Historiography and the Discovery of the Other," reprinted as Chapter 8 of the present volume.

7. See Johan Goudsblom, *Nihilism and Culture* (Oxford, 1980). Goudsblom emphasizes the pervasiveness of what he calls "nihilism" in our culture. A hundred years ago, he claims, the "nothing is true" theory was the prerogative of an elite. Today it is so pervasive that "the problematic can no longer be called a personal acquisition; it is a platitudinous clincher, casually adopted and indiscriminately used. In many of the forms in which nihilism is avowedly manifest, one would have to go a long way to find the truth imperative [which, for Goudsblom, is what underlies nihilism], for quite different influences are here at work" (p. 190).

8. Jörn Rüsen, "Historische Erinnerung und Menschliche Identität—praktische Wirkungen der Historiographie," *Universitas* 39 (1984): 393–395, 400. On the contemporary criticism of reason, see also A. Gargani, ed., *La Crisi della ragione* (Turin, 1980), and F. Ferraresi, "Julius Evola: Tradition, Reaction and the Radical Right," *Archives Européennes de Sociologie* 28 (1987): 107–151.

9. Michel de Certeau, the author of *L'Ecriture de l'histoire,* argues that the critical position of the late seventeenth-century scholarly historians is the essential determination of modern history. The distinction of "fiction" and "history," in other words, is the condition of the existence of what we understand by history (*La Philosophie de l'histoire et la pratique historienne aujourd'hui,* [Ottawa, 1982], p. 19).

10. Even the story of Uriel Da Costa (article "Acosta"), which could be read

as one of the earliest narratives of the *philosophe* as hero and martyr, is put in question, since it is taken from Da Costa's own account of his life, and that, Bayle observes in his notes, was inevitably not disinterested; in addition, some of the most elementary facts about it, such as the date of Da Costa's suicide, are unresolved matters of scholarly dispute. If there is disagreement and uncertainty about an event that occurred within living memory, Bayle implies, if there is a space between the logic of narrative and the succession of events in such a case, what confidence can one have in accounts of events that are supposed to have occurred centuries, even millennia ago? Luc Weibel makes a similar point in his discussion of the article "Abelard": "L'insertion de la remarque dans le fil de la narration produit . . . deux effets; elle rompt la continuité, le 'nappé' du récit référentiel; elle fait vaciller son rapport avec la 'réalité' en renvoyant à un autre discours dont le sens est incertain, et en rompant la connivance de la logique du récit avec la succession temporelle des événements" (*Le Savoir et le corps: Essai sur le Dictionnaire de Pierre Bayle* [Lausanne, 1975], p. 59).

11. Quoted from the 2nd English ed. (London, 1734). As Weibel puts it: "Ce discours parfaitement cohérent, parfaitement 'coulé', contient des énoncés dont les référents sont incompatibles, mais ces référents, extérieurs au discours, n'en entravent pas le fonctionnement" (*Le Savoir et le corps*, p. 31). In part, Weibel contends, it was Bayle's publisher Leers who asked him, for the sake of sales, to "tempérer un peu son mépris pour les histoires qu'il a lues, et de faire que son Dictionnaire ne soit pas complètement un anti-dictionnaire, qu'il contienne également des récits et des fables comme le public les aime" (p. 40).

12. Bayle liked to compare reason and philosophy to "une véritable Pénélope, qui pendant la nuit défait la toile qu'elle avait faite le jour" (*Dictionnaire historique et critique,* article "Bunel, Pierre," note E; in another passage, which I have been unable to retrace, reason is "une coureuse qui ne sait où s'arrêter, qui, comme une autre Pénélope, détruit elle-même son propre ouvrage: *diruit, aedificat, mutat quadrata rotundis*"). The same could be said of Bayle's idea of the work of history.

13. William Playfair, *The Commercial and Political Atlas, Representing by Means of Stained Copper-Plate Charts, the Progress of the Commerce, Revenues, Expenditure, and Debts of England, during the Whole of the Eighteenth Century* (3rd ed. London, 1801 [1st ed., 1786], Preface, p. v).

14. Edward R. Tufte, *The Visual Display of Quantitative Information* (Cheshire, Conn., 1983), p. 40.

15. Letter to Thieriot, November 1734 (no. D803), in *Voltaire's Correspondence,* ed. T. Besterman (Geneva and Toronto, 1968–1977).

16. On the whole, I think Hayden White would agree with my judgment of the *Annales* school's criticism of narrative history; see his article "The Question of Narrative in Contemporary Historical Theory," *History and Theory* 23 (1984): 8–10.

17. Leon J. Goldstein, *Historical Knowing* (Austin, Tex., and London, 1976), p. 201.

18. Jörn Rüsen, "Erklärung und Theorie in der Geschichtswissenschaft," *Storia della Storiografia* 4 (1983): 3–29, Jörn Rüsen and Hans Baumgartner in *Erzählforschung: ein Symposium,* ed. Eberhard Lammert (Stuttgart, 1982), p. 697 ("Erträge

der Diskussion" of day 4 of the symposium, devoted to "Erzählung und Geschichte").

19. Chaim Perelman, "Objectivité et intelligibilité dans la connaissance historique" (1963), in his *Le Champ de l'argumentation* (Brussels, 1970), pp. 361–371.

20. Peter Munz, *The Shapes of Time* (Middletown, Conn., 1978), p. 221. See also pp. 16–17: "Whereas we can translate a photograph into a painting and a painting, taking its life into our hands, into a verbal statement and an English text into a Russian text, we cannot translate what actually happened into anything. We can translate what somebody *thought* happened into another language and seek to establish equivalences between different media—at least up to a point. But we cannot translate reality; for to do that we would have to have a picture of or a text about it in the first place . . . But the ineluctable truth is that there is no face behind the mask and that the belief that there is is an unsupportable allegation. For any record we could have of the face would be, precisely, another mask." Similarly Sande Cohen, "Structuralism and the Writing of an Intellectual History," *History and Theory* 17 (1978): 175–206: "Historians 'touch' the object of their discourse only by recourse to the already-meant; hence every shred of historical meaning belongs to the discourse and not to the objects . . . There is no direct communciation possible between the referents of historical discourse and the discourse about a referent."

21. W. B. Gallie, *Philosophy and the Human Understanding* (London, 1964), p. 124.

22. With modifications, Gallie's view does seem to have won fairly wide acceptance; see, for instance, a recent study by the Dutch scholar F. R. Ankersmit: *Narrative Logic: A Semantic Analysis of the Historian's Language* (The Hague, Boston, London, 1983).

23. The experience of 1848 appears to have made Sainte-Beuve sensitive to the element of chance in history and to have encouraged him to criticize the Romantic providentialist view, in which everything seems in retrospect to have been inevitable. Guizot's philosophy of history, in particular, is "trop logique pour être vraie. Je n'y puis voir qu'une méthode artificielle et commode pour régler les comptes du passé" (review of Guizot's *Discours sur l'Histoire de la Révolution d'Angleterre,* added to the 1850 edition, in *Sainte-Beuve, Causeries du lundi* [Paris, 1857], I, 311–331). Whatever does not fit the historian's prearranged plot is discarded, Sainte-Beuve complains: "Toutes les causes perdues . . . sont considérées impossibles, nées caduques, et de tout temps vouées à la défaite. Et souvent à combien peu il a tenu qu'elles ne triomphassent." In the end, the historian acts as a kind of Providence, imposing order on the chaos of historical reality: "L'histoire . . . vue à distance, subit une singulière métamorphose, et produit une illusion, la pire de toutes, celle qu'on la croie raisonnable. Dans cet arrangement . . . qu'on lui prête, les déviations, les folies, les ambitions personnelles, les mille accidents bizarres qui la composent et dont ceux qui ont observé leur propre temps savent qu'elle est faite, tout cela disparaît . . . On ne juge plus que de haut. On se met insensiblement en lieu et place de la Providence. On trouve à tout accident particulier des enchaînements inévitables, des nécessités, comme on dit." The historian, ultimately, is an artist: "L'homme, il faut bien se le dire, n'atteint en rien la réalité, le fond même des choses, pas plus en histoire que dans le reste; il n'arrive à concevoir et à reproduire

que moyennant des méthodes et des points de vue qu'il se donne. L'histoire est donc un art; il y met du sien, de son esprit, il y imprime son cachet, et c'est même à ce prix qu'elle est possible" (essay on Mignet, in *Portraits contemporains* [Paris, 1871], V, 240). Or again: "L'histoire n'est pas un miroir complet ni un fac-simile des faits; c'est un art. L'histoire, quand on parvient à la construire, est un pont de bateaux qu'on substitue et qu'on superpose à cet océan dans lequel . . . on se noierait sans arriver" (review of Saint-Priest, *Histoire de la Royauté*, ibid., IV, 3). So it happens that two histories of the "same" event may well appear to the reader as descriptions of quite different events. Reading Guizot's account of the English Revolution, Sainte-Beuve relates, "je me suis donné le plaisir de lire en même temps des pages correspondantes de Hume: on ne croirait pas qu'il s'agisse de la même histoire!" (review of Guizot, p. 321). Sainte-Beuve's preference for Hume is a signal of the retreat, after 1848, from Romantic historiography to what White would call the "ironical" mode characteristic of Burckhardt: "Ce que je remarque, surtout, c'est qu'il m'est possible, en lisant Hume, de le contrôler, de le contredire quelquefois: il m'en procure les moyens, par les détails mêmes qu'il donne . . . En lisant M. Guizot, c'est presque impossible, tant le tissu est serré et tant le tout s'enchaîne. Il vous tient, et vous mène jusqu'au bout, combinant avec force le fait, la réflexion et le but." As the social conflicts of his time came to appear more and more intractable and as the hollowness of the July Revolution became increasingly obvious, even Michelet, the arch-Romantic, began to fear that the imposing and orderly edifices of science and historical knowledge might be only fragile, man-made constructions built over a terrifying chaos of cruel realities.

24. The summary of White's position is by Suzanne Gearhart, *The Open Boundary of History and Fiction* (Princeton, N.J., 1984), p. 7.

25. Hayden White, *Metahistory: The Historical Imagination in Nineteenth Century Europe* (Baltimore, 1973), p. 6n.5. The proposition that the historian confronts a "chaos" of events—not very different in the end from Sainte-Beuve's view (see note 23 above)—seems to me quite questionable in fact. The historian does not normally confront such a chaos of events; the latter are almost always encountered in more or less intelligible patterns and relations (narratives), which the historian may wish to challenge, reject, or alter. He does not work alone, without predecessors.

26. White: "Historians *constitute* their subjects as possible objects of representation by the very language they use to *describe* them" ("The Historical Text as Literary Artifact," in Canary and Kozicki, *The Writing of History*, p. 57).

27. Louis Mink, "Philosophy and Theory of History," in *International Handbook of Historical Studies* (Westport, Conn., 1979), p. 25.

28. Louis Mink, "Is Speculative Philosophy of History Possible?" in *Substance and Form in History: Festschrift for W. H. Walsh*, ed. L. Pompa and W. H. Dray (Edinburgh, 1981), pp. 107–119. White himself makes his position perfectly clear: The works of the great historians "cannot be 'refuted,' or their generalizations 'disconfirmed,' either by appeal to new data that might be turned up in subsequent research or by the elaboration of a new theory for interpreting the sets of events that comprise their objects of representation and analysis" (*Metahistory*, p. 4); "This is not to say that we cannot distinguish between good and bad historiography, since we can always fall back [sic] on such criteria as responsibility to the

rules of evidence, the relative fullness of narrative detail, logical consistency, and the like to determine this issue. But it is to say that the effort to distinguish between good and bad interpretations of a historical event . . . is not as easy as it might at first appear, when it is a matter of dealing with alternative interpretations produced by historians of relatively equal learning and conceptual sophistication. After all, a great historical classic cannot be disconfirmed or nullified either by the discovery of some new datum . . . or by the generation of new methods of analysis" ("The Historical Text as Literary Artifact," p. 59). It is worth observing that the terms of valuation here ("good" and "bad" rather than "true" and "false" or "valid" and "invalid") themselves direct the reader toward ethical and aesthetic, rather than intellectual, judgment.

29. Adrian Kuzminski, "Defending Historical Realism," *History and Theory* 17 (1979): 316–349.

30. Leon J. Goldstein, *Historical Knowing* (Austin, Tex., and London, 1976), pp. xix–xxi. See also p. 136: "Nothing appears in the practice of history that corresponds to the object of witnesses. The past—real or historical—certainly does not. The witness confronts the object; his account is the result of his encounter with it from his own perspectives. The historian in no way confronts the *real* past. And rather than confront it, he constructs the *historical* past."

31. Ibid., p. 127. The argument developed by Goldstein is similar to that put forward by Murray G. Murphey in *Our Knowledge of the Historical Past* (Indianapolis, 1973).

32. Goldstein, *Historical Knowing,* p. 144.

33. Ibid., p. 147. Goldstein's own authority here is Collingwood. See also pp. 156–157.

34. See, for instance, Goldwin Smith on the great history teacher in "The Gates of Excellence," in *The Professor and the Public: The Role of the Scholar in the Modern World,* ed. Goldwin Smith (Detroit, 1972), pp. 13–42: "When Professor Bossenbrook talked about the trade routes to the East you could almost see the sails of the great spice ships and hear the camels grunt by the wells of Trebizond" (p. 27). "Many of us have read accurate but boring books by authors who have never lifted their eyes from the documents, have never wondered if George Washington liked kidney pie" (pp. 36–37). Not surprisingly, the historian is characterized by Smith as "the high priest of continuity" (p. 40).

35. See Jacob Burckhardt, *Judgments on History and Historians,* trans. Harry Zohn (Boston, 1958), p. 242 (pt. 5, The Age of Revolution; sec. 122, "German and French intellectual development in the eighteenth century").

36. Leopold von Ranke, *Geschichte der romanischen und germanischen Völker,* Preface to 1824 edition, in Ranke, *Fürsten und Völker,* ed. Willy Andreas (Wiesbaden, 1957), p. 4. On the politically conservative significance of the opposition to Enlightenment historiography characteristic of Ranke and of the German historicist tradition as a whole, see Fritz Fischer, "Aufgaben und Methoden der Geschichtswissenschaft," in *Geschichtsschreibung,* ed. Jürgen Scheschkewitz (Düsseldorf, 1968), pp. 7–28. On the deeply anti-Enlightenment tradition in German theories of knowledge, especially in the social sciences, see also Wolf Lepenies, *Die Drei Kulturen: Soziologie zwischen Literatur und Wissenschaft* (Munich and Vienna, 1985), pp. 245–266 and passim.

37. White, *Metahistory*, p. 4.

38. Goldstein, *Historical Knowing*, p. 141.

39. Ibid., p. 141.

40. Ibid., pp. 141–142.

41. Marc Bloch, *The Historian's Craft*, trans. Peter Putnam (Manchester, 1954), pp. 13, 66–69, 21.

42. For Pierre Chaunu, for instance, "no need to insist: quantification, the very condition of the coupling of history with the social sciences, is the condition *sine qua non* of any expansion of knowledge." Ultimately, Chaunu claims, it will be possible to extend quantitative methods to the realm of behaviors and "mentalités" and to extract a society's attitudes to life and death from computerized studies of language and vocabulary, so that our knowledge of these things will finally cease to be subjective and impressionistic. See "Conjoncture, structures, systèmes de civilisations," in *Conjoncture économique, structures sociales: Hommage à Ernest Labrousse* (Paris and The Hague, 1974), p. 30.

43. Goldstein, *Historical Knowing*, p. 99, quoting Gallie, *Philosophy and the Human Understanding*, p. 124.

44. Goldstein, *Historical Knowing*, p. 95.

45. Ibid., p. 137.

46. Ibid., p. 132.

47. Ibid., p. 132. In the case discussed by Goldstein, the point at issue, which it is hoped scholarly analysis and debate will settle, is the time and place at which the Dead Sea scrolls were produced. Without some agreement among historians about "matters of fact" the discipline as a whole would be impossible, as the narrativists themselves would be the first to acknowledge. Significantly, however, changes occur concerning what is agreed upon, as sources and the techniques of investigating them are expanded and refined. Thus in his otherwise severely critical study of Fogel and Engerman, *Time on the Cross*, Herbert Gutman concedes that the old, ultimately racist view of slavery—that the slaves remained obstinately African, that they could not be transformed into diligent workers, and that the planters went broke trying to achieve this impossible transformation, so that slavery was fundamentally unprofitable—has been completely undermined by modern research. "It has been known for nearly half a century that slavery was profitable, and [Fogel and Engerman] deserve credit for reopening that question and focussing on the reason for its profitability" (*Slavery and the Numbers Game: A Critique of Time on the Cross* [Urbana, Ill., Chicago, and London, 1975], p. 169).

48. White, *Metahistory*, p. 13.

49. Goldstein, *Historical Knowing*, pp. 197–200.

50. Goldstein himself sums up his position as follows: if we want to understand the character of historical thinking, "our attention must be riveted to the infrastructure of history and not to the superstructure. Before we can explain historical events, or weave them into the fabric of a narrative, we have to determine what they are . . . Historical thinking is that way of dealing with historical evidence so as to emerge with historical facts." (ibid., p. 201).

51. Ibid., p. 95.

52. Hans Albert, *Treatise on Critical Reason*, trans. Mary Varney Rorty (Princeton, 1985), pp. 75–77.

53. On the changing range of meanings of the term *history*, see the detailed study of Joachim Knape, *"Historie" im Mittelalter und früher Neuzeit: Begriffs- und gattungsgeschichtliche Untersuchungen im interdisziplinären Kontext* (Baden-Baden, 1984), and the important entry by Reinhart Koselleck on "Geschichte, Historie" in *Geschichtliche Grundbegriffe: Historisches Lexikon der politisch-sozialen Sprache in Deutschland,* ed. Otto Bruner, Werner Conze, and Reinhart Koselleck (Stuttgart, 1975), II, 593–717.

54. *Voltaire's Correspondence,* ed. T. Besterman, no. D7203, letter of 17 March 1757.

55. Edward Gibbon, *Essai sur l'étude de la littérature* (London, 1761), p. 105.

56. See Sainte-Beuve's objections to early nineteenth-century historians in note 23 above.

57. F. R. Ankersmit, *Narrative Logic: A Semantic Analysis of the Historian's Language* (The Hague, Boston, London, 1983), p. 8.

58. I make this point myself in "History and Literature: Reproduction or Signification" (Chapter 7 of the present volume).

59. "There are many historians who have an exclusive interest in historical research: they are concerned with establishing how cities or convents acquired legal or feudal rights, how historical monuments came to be erected, how diplomatic treaties came into being, they study changes in the price of bread or the growth and decline in the population of different areas . . . On the other hand, there are the historians with a more synthetic turn of mind . . . They try to integrate the facts found by historical research into large overall views of (parts of) the past. They are concerned not so much with the facts themselves . . . as with what might be the most acceptable representation or synopsis of parts of the past. Their problem is how the history of the past should be narratively written or which narration proposes the best interpretation of (parts of) the past" (Ankersmit, *Narrative Logic,* pp. 8–9).

60. Ibid., p. 11.

61. See, for instance, the recent issue of *New Literary History,* vol. 17, fall 1985, devoted to "Philosophy of Science and Literary Theory."

62. Gearhart, *The Open Boundary,* p. 64. See also David Carroll, *The Subject in Question* (Chicago and London, 1982), chap. 5, and his review of White, "On Tropology: The Forms of History," in *Diacritics* 6 (1976): 58–64. The argument that genre categories are not universal but rather are language- and culture-specific has been made forcefully by Michael Glowinski, "Die literarische Gattung ünd die Probleme der historischen Poetik" (1969), in *Formalismus, Strukturalismus und Geschichte: Zur Literaturtheorie und Methodologie in der Sowjetunion, ČCCR, Polen und Jugoslawien,* ed. Aleksandr Flaker and Viktor Zmegač (Kronburg/Taunus, 1974), pp. 155–185.

63. Wilda Anderson, "Dispensing with the Fixed Point," *History and Theory* 22 (1983): 276. For another critique of White's rhetoricism, from a totally different standpoint, see Leon Pompa, "Narrative Form, Significance and Historical Knowledge," *La Philosphie de l'histoire et la pratique historienne d'aujourd'hui,* ed. David Carr (Ottawa, 182), pp. 143–157.

64. According to Ranke, God "dwells, lives, and can be known in all of history. Every deed attests to him, every moment preaches his name, and most of all the

connectedness of all history. This connectedness stands before us like a holy hieroglyph." To decipher the hieroglyph is to serve God as priest and teacher. (Quoted in Leonard Krieger, *Ranke: The Meaning of History* [Chicago, 1977], p. 361).

65. Hayden White, "The Historical Text as Literary Artifact," in Canary and Kozicki, *The Writing of History,* p. 59; White, *Metahistory,* p. 4.

66. It hardly seems accidental that Pierre Bayle, though he helped to lay the foundations of modern historiography, rarely figures in the elite company of the "great classics." Bayle's doggedly critical stance, his seemingly deliberate refusal of the whole idea of the "great" or "authoritative" work, and his calculated choice of a kind of parasitical strategy of response and commentary (later adopted again by Diderot in many of his best writings) have resulted in his being almost totally neglected by those whose standard is the monument, the self-enclosed classic text. See Weibel's perceptive comment on Bayle's enterprise: "il faut déchirer ce corps qu'on a cru parfait et de ses dépouilles méconnaissables construire un objet sans modèle. Le moment du Dictionnaire des fautes est celui de la pure négativité. Après le moment de la séduction—la lecture—, celui de la lacération: et l'on évitera de tomber dans les errements qu'on dénonce, en s'interdisant d'y donner prise, en refusant d'écrire ce corps de mensonge qu'est le livre de savoir" (Weibel, *Le Savoir et le corps,* p. 34).

67. After writing this essay, I came upon Martin Rudwick's stimulating study of a nineteenth-century controversy in geology, *The Great Devonian Controversy: The Shaping of Scientific Knowledge among Gentlemanly Specialists* (Chicago, 1985). Rudwick makes about science itself—interestingly, about the most historical of the sciences—the point I have been trying to make about history. See also Hans Albert, *Treatise on Critical Reason,* p. 49: "Today's theory of science . . . still displays traits that appear intelligible only within the framework of classical foundationalism. Among them are . . . theoretical monism; . . . the emphasis on the axiomatic method, by which one can develop and justify a privileged theory; and in general an emphasis on the static, the structural, and formal aspects of knowledge, at the expense of its dynamic aspects, which means ignoring developments, conflicts, and the need to choose between alternatives."

68. Robert Fogel and Stanley Engerman, *Time on the Cross: The Economics of American Slavery* (Boston, 1974), 2 vols.

69. The *findings* of the cliometricians, they claim, should always be distinguished from their attempts, as historians, to interpret them, for these attempts "do not stand on the same level of uncertainty." Social science is incapable of producing the "seamless web" that historians desire and that is woven from all the strands of human behavior studied separately by social scientists—"economic, political, psychological, and cultural." Instead it provides "particular bodies of knowledge," which it is extremely difficult, perhaps impossible, to totalize into a unified theory. Above all, the links by which restricted areas of relative certainty are joined together to create interpretative configurations are extremely subject to ideological interference. In a passage that seems not incompatible with the seemingly quite opposite position of Hayden White, Fogel and Engerman explain that "comprehensive ideologies . . . are . . . tempting, because they offer an easy solution to problems of interpretation: they provide the substance needed to cover over the broad and irregular seams of an imperfect historiography and give the impression of a neat

seamless web." Though Fogel and Engerman have tried to resist such temptations, they do not claim to have expunged all ideological influences from their book, since in fact "in the main text we attempted to weave these new findings into a fairly comprehensive reinterpretation of the nature of the slave economy" (Fogel and Engerman, *Time on the Cross,* I, 8, 10; II, 4; Appendix A, p. 34).

70. See, for instance, William J. Wilson and Immanuel Wallerstein in their respective reviews, both in *American Journal of Sociology* 81 (1976): 1192 and 1201.

71. See W. Letwin in *Journal of Economic Literature* 13 (1975): 60.

72. Quoted in Herbert Gutman, *Slavery and the Numbers Game* (Urbana, Ill., 1975), Preface. According to Fogel and Engerman themselves, "The typical slave field hand was not lazy, inert, and unproductive. On average, he was harder-working and more efficient than his white counterpart" (I, 5).

73. Immanuel Wallerstein in *American Journal of Sociology* 81 (1976): 1206.

74. Gutman, *Slavery and the Numbers Game,* Preface and p. 1; see also p. 16.

75. "To have been a hard-working, responsible slave is to have been part of the 'positive' development of black culture, to have contributed to the saga of black 'achievement.' [Fogel and Engerman] berate Stampp and Elkins for having portrayed slaves who lied, stole, feigned illness, acted childishly, shirked their duties—as if these traits necessarily reflect badly on black personality and culture. But they do so only in the context of a Calvinist work ethic and the Boy Scout pledge to loyalty and cheerfulness . . . Themselves equating 'efficiency' with 'achievement' and eager to award blacks their credentials in middle-class white culture, [Fogel and Engerman] reject any suggestion that a slave's refusal to become an effective cog in the plantation machine can itself be seen as an achievement, a testimony to black ingenuity, resistance, pride" (Martin Duberman, quoted in Gutman, *Slavery and the Numbers Game,* p. 165n.299).

76. Gutman, *Slavery and the Numbers Game,* pp. 11–12.

77. Fogel and Engerman, *Time on the Cross,* I, 147.

78. Gutman, *Slavery and the Numbers Game,* pp. 19–20.

79. Ibid., p. 167.

80. Gutman refers to criticism by David Fischer and Harold Woodman, both of whom denounce as a "reductive fallacy" the confusion of "a causal component, without which an event will not occur, with all other causal components which are all required in order to make it occur"—a confusion often found "in causal explanations which are constructed like a single chain and stretched taut across a vast chasm of complexity" (ibid., p. 167). This criticism seems to imply acceptance of some version of Hempel's "covering law" theory.

81. Ibid., p. 170.

82. See Frederick Morton Eden, *The State of the Poor, or An History of the Labouring Classes in England from the Conquest to the Present Period, in which are particularly considered their Domestic Economy with respect to Dress, Fuel and Habitation . . . with a Large Appendix containing a comparative and chronological table of the prices of Labour, of Provisions, and of other Commodities, an account of the poor in Scotland, and many original documents on subjects of National Importance* (London, 1797); William Playfair, *The Commercial and Political Atlas* (London, 1786); the same author's *Inquiry into the Permanent Causes of the Decline and Fall of Powerful*

and Wealthy Nations (London, 1805); and Thomas Robert Malthus, *An Essay on Population* (London, 1798). Malthus's text is worth quoting. The reason why certain underlying regularities in human history have not been noted, he claims, is that "the histories of mankind which we possess are, in general, histories only of the higher classes. We have not many accounts that can be depended on of the manners and customs of that part of mankind where these retrograde and progressive movements [of population] chiefly take place. A satisfactory history of this kind, of one people and of one period, would require the constant and minute attention of many observing minds in local and general remarks on the state of the lower classes of society, and the causes that influenced it; and to draw accurate inferences upon this subject, a succession of such historians for some centuries would be necessary. This branch of statistical knowledge has, of late years, been attended to in some countries, and we may promise ourselves a clearer insight into the internal structure of human society from the progress of these inquiries" (Everyman Library ed., London, 1914, I, 16–17).

83. See Adolf Trendelenburg, *Der Musenchor: Relief einer Marmorbasis aus Halikarnass* (Berlin, 1876 [Winckelmannfest der Archäologischen Gesellschaft, Program 36]), p. 13; Max Wegner, *Die Musensarkophage* (Berlin, 1966), pp. 98–99, 108. Also Elisabeth Schröter, *Die Ikonographie des Themas Parnassus vor Raphael* (Hildesheim and New York, 1977), pp. 176–177.

84. Stanley Fish, "Anti-Professionalism," in *New Literary History* 17 (1985): 89–108.

85. Louis Mink himself emphasized the crucial importance of these distinctions; see the conclusion of his essay in Canary and Kozicki, *The Writing of History*, pp. 148–149.

86. Hayden White, in Canary and Kozicki, *The Writing of History*, p. 59.

87. See, for instance, Peter Paret's review of Nigel Nicolson's *Napoleon 1812* (New York Times, 26 January 1986). Paret distinguishes here between "academic" or professional and "nonacademic" or popular history: "A professional historian writing a new book on 1812 would need to justify his project by presenting new documentation or revising accepted interpretations. Mr. Nicolson, who is not an academic, neither needs nor wants to add to our knowledge of the invasion. He is content to give a coherent, well-informed account of an episode that clearly has long fascinated him and that he has studied seriously. The value of such nonacademic history is not to be underestimated."

88. Rudwick, *The Great Devonian Controversy*, pp. 6, 456.

89. Ian Hacking, review of Kuhn, *The Essential Tension*, in *History and Theory* 18 (1979): 229.

90. Hacking points to a tension between Kuhn the philosopher, who writes of "incommensurable conceptual schemes," and Kuhn the historian, "who provides an internal history of problems and their solutions" (ibid., p. 236). On this see also Toulmin, *Human Understanding* p. 105 and passim. In his article "Anti-Professionalism" Stanley Fish characterizes as ultimately contradictory Toulmin's attempt to mark out a sphere of "reasons" as well as a sphere of "causes" and a set of "disciplinary" criteria distinct from purely "professional" criteria. Essentially, Toulmin's aim is to determine a place in history, if not for reason, then at least for

reasoning. It is obviously simpler and more consistent to deny that it has any and to subordinate one category to another: either history is ultimately rational, or reason is ultimately itself historical.

91. Toulmin, *Human Understanding,* pp. 51, 157, 84, 165. Cf. Hans Albert, *Treatise on Critical Reason,* p. 62: "Science progresses neither by the derivation of certain truths from self-evident intuitions with the aid of deductive processes [i.e., classical rationalism], nor through the derivation of such truths from self-evident perceptions using inductive processes [i.e., classical empiricism]: it advances, rather through speculation and rational argumentation, through construction and criticism."

92. Toulmin, *Human Understanding,* p. 486. See also the epigraph to the book: "A man demonstrates his rationality, not by a commitment to fixed ideas, stereotyped procedures, or immutable concepts, but by the manner in which, and the occasions on which, he changes those ideas, procedures, and concepts." In an interesting application of Toulmin and others to the problems of literary scholarship, Jürgen Klein argues that defining scientific and scholarly rationality— as he himself proposes—"nicht als kognitiver Prozess, sondern als intellektueller Prozedur" will spell the end of the reign of hermeneutic. (Jürgen Klein, *Theoriengeschichte als Wissenschaftskritik: Zur Genesis der literaturwissenschaftlichen Grundlagenkrise in Deutschland* [Haustein, 1980], pp. 86–89). On the long-standing conservative political implications of hermeneutical thinking and the "dubiousness of ontologizing the textual model in hermeneutic philosophy" (an operation unquestioningly accepted by many humanists these days), see Hans Albert, *Treatise on Critical Reason,* pp. 165–198.

93. "Diffuse" or "would-be disciplines" are defined by Toulmin as those in which "the fundamental explanatory task has not been clearly defined," so that "neither an agreed set of disciplinary methods nor a common forum of disciplinary debate [has been] able to establish its authority" (Toulmin, *Human Understanding,* p. 389).

94. Wolfgang Mommsen, "Social Conditioning and Social Relevance of Historical Judgments," in *History and Theory,* Beiheft 17, 1978, p. 33. See also the more cautious and nuanced view of Chaim Perelman, "Objectivité et intelligibilité dans la connaissance historique" (1963), in his *Le Champ de l'argumentation* (Brussels, 1970): "La connaissance historique, produit de notre culture—elle-même produit de notre passé—doit assumer, tout comme la philosophie, la perte de confiance, qui caractérise notre époque, dans des critères absolus et infaillibles, en matière d'intelligibilité . . . S'il est légitime de rechercher, en histoire, des critères sur lesquels tous les historiens s'accorderaient, il est vain de limiter l'histoire, sous prétexte d'objectivité, à ce qui peut être connu grâce à de pareils critères. Mais dans la mesure même où l'historien reconnaît l'imperfection de son oeuvre, il ne peut se refuser au dialogue avec d'autres historiens, en espérant que ce dialogue lui permettra de présenter un récit moins arbitraire, c'est-a-dire plus complet, plus intelligible et plus impartial du passé" (p. 371).

95. Imre Lakatos, *Methodology of Scientific Research Programmes* (Cambridge, 1978), p. 92. On the value of "sticking to a theory as long as possible," see pp. 89, 92, 118. According to Lakatos, "Purely negative, destructive criticism, like 'refu-

tation' or demonstration of an inconsistency, does not eliminate a programme. Criticism of a programme is a long and often frustrating process and one must treat budding programmes leniently" (p. 92).

96. Hans Albert, *Treatise of Critical Reason*, p. 77.

97. Ibid., p. 100.

98. Mommsen, "Social Conditioning and Social Relevance of Historical Judgments," p. 34.

99. Ibid., p. 35. See also Jörn Rüsen, "Historische Erinnerung und menschliche Identität," on history as "das friedliche Mittel des vernünftigen Argumentierens" (p. 400).

100. Weibel, *Le Savoir et le corps*, p. 21.

101. Timothy Garton Ash, "The Life of Death" (review of the films *Heimat* and *Shoah*), in *New York Review of Books*, 19 December 1985, p. 39. I should add that, though I agree with the substance of Ash's reflections on history and memory, I do not altogether agree with his reading of *Shoah*. It seems to me that, faced with the enormity of his subject matter, Lanzmann avoided equally the explanatory patterns of science and the unifying patterns of art. To this is due, in all likelihood, the film's oppressive, one might almost say sublime quality.

102. I am indebted for advice, criticism, or simply the opportunity to exchange ideas on questions of history, to friends and colleagues in the history department at Princeton, notably Natalie Z. Davis, Dan Rodgers, Jerry Siegel, and Lawrence Stone. To the last two, who took the trouble to read this essay and comment on it in some detail, as well as to Robert Palmer, Fritz Stern, and Richard Vann, who were equally generous with their time and counsel, I wish to express special thanks. Finally, I would like to acknowledge the debt that all of us who are interested in historiography owe to Hayden White. The criticism of my essay that has most worried me is that, while there may be some point in making the argument I make in the context of current literary criticism, it does not make sense in the context of historical studies, where the danger is not—it is objected—an overemphasis on the linguistic and literary dimension of historical writing, leading to a crisis of faith in the nature of historical knowledge, but a continued, obstinate indifference to the work of White, Mink, and others who have tried to make historians more aware of what they are doing when they write history. I hope it is clear that without White's work, my own makes no sense. My object has not been to excuse or justify self-satisfaction, and my best interlocutor is the historian who has followed White and the whole inquiry into history writing that his work has stimulated. White was in fact one of the first to read this essay, in an earlier version that I submitted to the organizers of a conference on History and Literature that we both attended at Dartmouth College in the spring of 1985 (under the auspices of the School of Criticism and Theory). I doubt that he accepted my argument, but he recognized the spirit in which it was made, and judged it with his usual sympathy and generosity. My essay is not directed against him, as some may have thought, but to him. I would like it to be seen as a token of almost thirty years of friendship.

Acknowledgments

I would like to thank Lindsay Waters, Executive Editor of Harvard University Press, for encouragement and advice, especially in the preparation of the preface; Mary Ellen Geer for her thoughtful and sensible editing of the manuscript; Denise Wydra for cleaning up an unusually messy set of proofs; and Irena Datchev for painstakingly putting together the index. The book is dedicated to my wife, Eva Reinitz.

The essays in this book originally appeared in the following publications:

Chapter 1: reprinted from *Modern Language Notes* 86 (December 1971): 761–789.

Chapter 2: originally delivered as a lecture at Princeton University in February 1981; published in revised form in *New Literary History* 13 (1982): 341–371.

Chapter 3: originally delivered as a public lecture at Princeton University on October 27, 1988.

Chapter 4: originally published in *History and Theory,* Beiheft 15 (Middletown, Conn.: Wesleyan University Press, 1976).

Chapter 5: originally published (in a shortened version) in *European Writers,* ed. George Stade (New York: Charles Scribner's Sons, 1985), vol. 5, pp. 571–606. Copyright © 1985 Charles Scribner's Sons.

Chapter 6: revised version of "Michelet and the French Revolution," to be published by Pergamon Press in a collective volume of papers from a colloquium on the French Revolution and Modern Political Culture held in Paris, September 1988, under the auspices of the Institut Raymond Aron (Ecole des Hautes Etudes en Sciences Sociales).

Chapter 7: originally published in *The Writing of History: Literary Form and Historical Understanding,* ed. Robert Canary and Henry Kozicki (Madison: University of Wisconsin Press, 1978).

Chapter 8: reprinted from *New Literary History* 18 (1987): 23–57.

Chapter 9: abbreviated version of an essay originally published as "Toward a Rational Historiography" in *Transactions of the American Philosophical Society* 79, pt. 3 (1989).

Index

Abraham, David, 320
Académie des Inscriptions, 280. *See also* Institut Impérial de France
Académie des Sciences Morales et Politiques, 112
Addison, Joseph, 335
Adorno, Theodor, 4, 50, 53–54
Albert, Hans, 303, 321, 399
Alcibiades, 232
Alembert, Jean Le Rond d', 243, 304, 355
Allegory, 62. *See also* Interpretation, allegorical
Althusser, Louis, 4
Anderson, Wilda, 307
Ankersmit, F. R., 305–307, 395
Annales, 292, 390
Anquetil-Duperron, Abraham Hyacinthe, 93
Anthropology, 284, 388
Archives Nationales, 172, 173, 195
Ariès, Philippe, 237, 266
Aristotle, 122, 157, 162, 164, 231–232, 235; *Poetics*, 231–232, 233, 234, 236, 237, 253, 376
Arlès-Dufour, François Barthélemy, 174
Arnim, Achim von, 163, 273
Arnold, Matthew, 6, 9, 26, 32, 42, 43, 46–47, 48, 51, 69–71, 73, 334, 335, 337, 338, 341, 342
Artaud, Antonin, 344
Ash, Timothy Garton, 323, 400
Ast, Friedrich, 67, 71, 73
Auerbach, Erich, 330
Augustine, Saint, 164
Author and authorship, 14–17
Azadowski, Mark, 331

Bachofen, Johann Jacob, 36, 39, 40, 83, 275, 303, 308
Bacon, Francis, 164
Ballanche, Pierre Simon, 38, 368
Balzac, Honoré de, 141, 180, 182, 255, 383
Bann, Stephen, 357, 383
Barante, Prosper de, 84, 86, 117–123, 124, 125, 126, 127, 128, 129, 131, 133, 153, 154, 163, 166, 229, 241, 252–253, 260–261, 276, 351, 354, 355, 356, 375, 378, 383
Barrès, Maurice, 287
Barthélemy, abbé Jean-Jacques, 134
Barthes, Roland, 2, 5, 6, 13, 14, 23, 29, 31, 45, 57, 73, 75–77, 213, 218, 223, 248, 250, 251, 252, 253, 254, 256, 343, 381
Basle, University of, 56, 71
Baudelaire, Charles, 183, 189, 258
Baudouin, François, 266
Baumgartner, Hans, 292
Bayle, Pierre, 230, 290–291, 313, 322, 384, 390, 396
Beethoven, Ludwig van, 11, 206
Belinski, Vissarion Grigoryevich, 84
Bellay, Joachim du, 264
Belleforest, François de, 92
Benedictines, 94, 96, 276, 346
Benjamin, Walter, 64
Benserade, Isaac de, 32
Benveniste, Emile, 242, 378
Béranger, Jean-Pierre de, 147, 188, 204
Berlin, University of, 45, 263, 277
Bernheim, Ernst, 298
Berthelot, Marcelin, 245
Besançon, Alain, 247
Bien, Peter, 58, 60

Blair, Hugh, 231, 236, 294, 375, 378
Blanc, Jean-Joseph Louis, 166, 167, 169, 173, 175, 178, 180, 181, 200, 275, 365, 374
Blanqui, Louis-Auguste, 388
Bloch, Marc, 247, 292, 299
Bloch, Oscar, 358
Blumenberg, Hans, 15
Boeckh, August, 40, 45, 164, 165, 277–279
Bogatyrev, Pyotr, 9–11, 23, 328, 332
Bonald, Louis de, 354
Bossuet, Jacques Bénigne, 32, 36, 162, 335, 352
Boulainviller, Henri de, 102
Bourdieu, Pierre, 27
Bourgeoisie, 364; liberal, 131–132; and people, 104–109, 131–132, 175, 180, 181, 186, 336–337, 351; role in history, 238–239, 265; and violence, 136–137
Bowman, Frank, 217
Braudel, Fernand, 200, 245, 253
Brentano, Clemens, 163, 273
Bronson, Bertrand, 328
Buchez, Philippe, 280
Büchner, Georg, 360
Budé, Guillaume, 265, 279
Buffon, Georges Louis Leclerc, comte de, 35
Burckhardt, Jacob, 3, 48, 176, 198, 268, 292, 293, 297, 308, 368, 371
Buret, Eugène, 174, 216
Burke, Edmund, 351
Burns, Robert, 329
Butor, Michel, 380
Byron, George Gordon Noel, Lord, 359

Cabet, Etienne, 174, 181
Caesar, Gaius Julius, 177, 184, 262
Capefigue, Jean-Baptiste, 361
Carlyle, Thomas, 360
Carrel, Armand, 83, 84, 127, 136
Casimir-Périer, 84
Catford, J. C., 357
Censeur européen, 84, 85, 86, 87, 100, 110
Centre National de la Recherche Scientifique, 75
Certeau, Michel de, 379, 389
Chabot, François, 216
Chadwick, H. Munro, 331
Chadwick, Nora K., 331
Champollion, Jean-François, 37, 271, 272, 273, 277, 336, 385
Chaptal, Jean-Antoine, 84
Charas, Moïse, 32
Charbonnier, Georges, 227

Charlemagne, 90, 96, 347
Chateaubriand, François-René, vicomte de, 163, 166, 177, 359, 383
Chaulieu, Guillaume Amfrye, abbé de, 32
Chaunu, Pierre, 394
Chladenius, Johann Martin, 230
Christianity: and education, 34, 65–68; and historiography of the French Revolution, 202–218, 282–283; and interpretation of history, 266, 270–271, 279–281, 388; Matthew Arnold's view of, 71, 342; Jules Michelet's view of, 176, 184–185, 203, 208, 209, 214, 368; Franz Overbeck's view of, 56, 60, 75, 213–214. See also Socialism, Christian
Chronicles and chroniclers, 90, 118, 120, 238, 264, 276
Church, 178, 180, 212, 283
Cicero, Marcus Tullius, 36, 162, 227–228
Cideville, Pierre Robert Le Cornier de, 235, 304
Clark, Tim, 5
Classicism and neoclassicism, 14, 62, 228, 233, 270–273, 279; in aesthetics, 15, 33, 270; in art, 4, 53, 270; French, 4, 14; in literature, 13, 14, 17, 24–25, 45, 48–49, 163, 228, 338; in rhetoric, 153–154, 177; tradition of, 24. See also Education, classical; Enlightenment and neoclassical historiography; Literary education in the neoclassical age; Narrative, classical
Clémentel, Etienne, 283, 388
Clootz, Anacharsis, 375
Cobden, Richard, 353
Cohen, Sande, 391
Colbert, Jean-Baptiste, 111–112, 114, 351
Colet, Louise, 30
Collège Charlemagne, 158
Collège de France, 39, 75, 152, 155, 157, 165, 166, 167, 168, 172, 174, 178, 186, 194, 195, 201, 204, 237, 281, 282
College of New Jersey, 32, 33. See also Princeton University
Collège Sainte-Barbe, 158
Collingwood, R. G., 248–250, 292, 305, 318, 380
Collins, J. C., 49
Commynes, Philippe de, 261, 354
Condorcet, Marie Jean Antoine Nicolas de Caritat, marquis de, 207
Considérant, Victor, 174
Constant, Benjamin, 100, 102, 108–109, 113, 115, 116, 117, 128, 146–149, 162, 209, 222, 242, 268, 269, 361, 363

Corneille, Pierre, 17, 32, 163, 286
Cortès, Donoso, 364
Courrier français, 84
Cousin, Victor, 163, 170, 202
Creuzer, Friedrich, 153, 163, 172, 230, 280, 281, 348, 388
Cromwell, Oliver, 89, 90, 129
Culture: bureaucratic, 45–48, 52–53; professionalization of, 47–48

Da Costa, Uriel, 389–399
Dacier, Anne Lefebvre, Mme, 59
Daniel, Father Gabriel, 93, 264
Dante Alighieri, 163, 164, 192
Danto, Arthur, 289
Danton, Georges Jacques, 129, 196, 202
David, Paul, 310
Delescluze, Louis Charles, 388
Delessert, Etienne, 84
Denon, Vivant, 272
Derrida, Jacques, 1, 2
Descartes, René, 32, 33, 286
Decazes, Elie, duc, 86
Dialects, 35–36
Dictionnaire de l'Académie française, 286
Diderot, Denis, 11, 16, 239–240, 242, 263, 267, 270, 377, 396
Diogenes, 240
Dionysius Halicarnassiensis, 233
Disraeli, Benjamin, 41
Dostoyevsky, Fyodor Mikhaylovich, 247
Droysen, Johann Gustav, 164, 277
Du Haillan, Bernard de Girard, 90, 91
Du Tillet, Jean, 92
Duberman, Martin, 310, 397
Dullin, Charles, 17
Dumesnil, Alfred, 159, 175, 191, 198
Dundes, Alan, 328
Dunoyer, Charles, 346, 351, 352
Dupleix, Scipion, 92, 264

Eckermann, Johann Peter, 16
Eco, Umberto, 28
Ecole Normale. *See* Ecole Préparatoire
Ecole Pratique des Hautes Etudes, 75
Ecole Préparatoire, 162, 165, 170, 172, 280
Eden, Sir Frederck Morton, 291, 314
Edinburgh Review, 359
Edinburgh University, 33, 42, 236
Education, 178, 186; in the ancien régime, 64–65; classical, 33–35, 40–41, 45, 46,
65–68, 164, 189. *See also* Literary education; Historiography and education
Eichhorn, Johann Gottfried, 32
Eichtal, Gustav d', 174
Eliot, Thomas Stearns, 19, 20
Elkins, Stanley, 312
Emerson, Ralph Waldo, 38, 40, 44, 45, 55, 269, 388
Encyclopédie, 16
Engels, Friedrich, 42, 43, 174
Engerman, Stanley, 309–314, 394, 396, 397
Enlightenment, 6, 25, 61, 67, 78, 106–107, 153, 186, 262–263, 266–267, 279; and neoclassical historiography, 93, 94, 96–97, 121, 152, 228, 230, 233–244, 258, 260, 261, 266–269, 289–291, 297, 304–305, 352, 393. *See also* Literary criticism in the Age of Enlightenment
Epic, 238; history and epic, 227, 234–236, 252–253
Esquiros, Alphonse, 208, 372
Everett, Edward, 360

Falconet, Etienne, 16
Fauchet, Claude, 92
Fauriel, Claude, 39, 84, 95, 98
Febvre, Lucien, 200, 245
Female figure and male figure, 137–145, 159–160, 161, 185, 196, 215–216, 259, 274–275, 336–337. *See also* Mother figure
Fénelon, François de Salignac de la Mothe, 236, 237
Ferguson, Adam, 62, 65, 162, 329, 340
Feuerbach, Ludwig, 209
Feyerabend, Paul, 317
Fichte, Johann Gottlieb, 165
Fiction. *See* Historical narrative and fictional narrative
Fielding, Henry, 163, 255
Fischer, David, 397
Fish, Stanley, 314
Flaubert, Gustave, 30, 330
Fogel, Robert, 309–313, 394, 396, 397
Folklore and folklorists, 9–11, 17, 23, 164, 328, 331; folk culture, 9, 14; folk literature and classical literature, 4, 14; oral culture and literate culture, 39–40; oral literature and written literature, 9–26, 33, 333
Fontane, Theodor, 46
Fontenelle, Bernard Le Bovier de, 239
Fortunatus, Venantius, 126, 131, 138, 140

Foucault, Michel, 2
Fourier, Charles, 174, 182
Fowler, Roger, 329
France, Anatole, 122
Frederick the Great, 78–9, 340
Frege, Gottlob, 318
Frégier, Casimir, 174
French Revolution, 35, 38, 105, 114, 129, 178, 180–182, **201–224**, 257, 262, 282–283, 373, 375, 387
Friedländer, Saul, 60
Froissart, Jean, 91, 122, 127, 261, 354
Frost, Robert, 55
Furet, François, 205, 219, 379, 385
Fustel de Coulanges, Numa Denis, 221, 247, 262, 280, 292, 293
Fuzelier, Louis, 16

Gadamer, Hans Georg, 344
Galiani, abbé Ferdinando, 11, 377
Gallie, W. B., 289, 294, 295, 299–300, 391
Garnier, Jean-Jacques, 237, 238
Gaskell, Elizabeth, 41
Gassendi, Pierre, 32
Gearheart, Suzanne, 306–307
Geneva, University of, 343
Gersdorff, Carl, 212
Gervinus, Georg Gottfried, 230
Gibbon, Edward, 3, 35, 162, 212, 228, 231, 236, 243, 255, 286, 294, 305, 377
Girard, René, 2
Glasgow University, 1, 2, 33, 42, 339
Globe, Le, 84
Goethe, Johann Wolfgang von, 2, 16, 42, 60, 62, 66, 70, 279, 341
Goldmann, Lucien, 2, 57, 308
Goldstein, Leon, 292, 296–303, 393, 394
Görres, J. J., 353
Grafton, Anthony, 59
Gregory of Tours, 131
Grimm, Jakob, 16, 36–37, 92, 153, 269
Grimm, Wilhelm, 153
Guerard, Albert, 378
Guigniaut, Joseph Daniel, 280, 388
Guizot, François Pierre Guillaume, 84, 86, 94, 102, 116, 153, 163, 166, 178, 345, 349, 351, 387, 391, 392
Gutman, Herbert, 310–314, 394, 397
Gymnasium, 40, 46, 68

Haac, Oscar, 375
Hacking, Ian, 317, 398

Hallam, Henry, 32, 163
Hancher, Michael, 28
Harvard University, 33, 334
Hegel, Georg Wilhelm Friedrich, 62, 153, 230, 257, 258, 263, 270, 277, 278, 280, 365, 376
Heidelberg, University of, 280
Hempel, Carl, 397
Hénault, Charles Jean-François, 235
Herder, Johann Gottfried, 33, 34, 163, 170, 329
Hermeneutic, 67, 258, 399
Herodotus, 162, 229, 231
Herzen, Alexander, 84, 124, 130, 139, 150, 336, 354, 360, 361
Hexter, Jack, 287
Hieroglyphs and decipherment, 270–272
Hilferding, Rudolf, 331
Hill, Christopher, 349
Histoire and discours, 242–243
Historical criticism: in historiography, 78–79, 234–235, 267, 290–293; in literature, 20, 64, 69–71, 286–288
Historical fact, 246, 249, 292–293, 296, 304–306. See also Historiography, positivist
Historical knowledge, 288, 294, 304; and scientific knowledge, 230, 245, 262, 296, 298–301, 315, 321
Historical narrative, 96–98, 102–103, 110–112, 118–119, 124–131, 153, 193, 212, 221, 231–256, 260, 290–317; and fictional narrative, 231–256, 289, 294–295, 303–304, 356; incommensurability of historical narratives, 293–295, 299–300, 306, 317, 323; metonymic and metaphorical relations in, 128–129, 192, 199; narrator in, 96–98, 120–121, 126–132, 135, 238, 243, 244; point of view in, 117–118, 230, 237–239; reader in, 96–98, 135, 200, 204, 221, 235–236, 238–239, 243, 260; space in, 245, 248–249; syntagmatic and paradigmatic order in, 98, 127–131, 192, 241–242; as tableau, 134–135, 238, 243, 360; time in, 217–218, 242, 245, 248–249. See also Histoire and discours; Narrative; Novel and history
Historiography: categories and terminology of, 91–93; commentary in, 94, 96–97, 243; critical method in, 78–79, 234–235, 267, 290–293; and education, 86, 87, 166–168, 186–189; and evidence, 248, 249, 296–301, 320, 380–381; and the historian's experience, 83, 95–96, 220–223, 282;

and ideology, 5–6, 88–91, 113, 121–123, 154, 186, 190, 222–223, 244, 250, 265, 268–269, 290, 297, 300–301, 310, 323; and imagination, 94–95, 97, 134, 198, 200, 248, 297; and liberalism, 83–151, 153, 158, 218, 292, 316, 351; as a literary genre, 3, 227–228; metaphors and metaphorical interpretation in, 129, 134–135, 164–165, 183, 198–199, 259; objectivity in, 121, 126, 135–136, 229–230, 244–250; orthography in, 92–93; and political activism, 83–86, 154, 166, 222–223, 283; positivist, 155, 169, 192–193, 230, 296–307, 309; and public opinion, 86; rationality of, 97–98, 109–114, 132, 134, 144, 257, 289–290, 303, 305, 317–324, 398–399; relativism in, 96, 112–113, 303; and representation, 123, 150; and rhetoric, 152, 153–154, 177, 192, 227–228, 231, 256, 264, 288–289, 294–295, 298; signification in, 248, 251, 253, 260; use of sources in, 93–94, 97, 127–128; and testimony, 117–120; and truth, 134, 233–234, 235, 243–244, 304, 318. *See also* Enlightenment and neoclassical historiography; Interpretation in history; Novel and history; Popular culture; Renaissance historiography

History: analytical philosophy of, 288–289; continuity in, 98–99, 210, 258–261, 274; as cycle, 170–172; and evil, 109–110, 212; and nature, 102–103, 196–197, 215, 216, 386; order in, 97, 119–123, 241; providence in, 114, 119, 353, 391; racial conflict in, 100–102, 349; as spiral, 170, 210. *See also* Epic and history; Myth and history; National history; the Sacred; Time and history; Violence in history

Hohendahl, Peter, 5, 63
Holbach, Paul Henri Thiry, baron d', 377
Hollander, John, 333
Homer, 60, 162, 164, 232, 342
Hrushovski, Benjamin, 328
Hudson, Henry, 33, 45, 335
Hugo, Victor, 22, 183, 222, 255
Huizinga, Johan, 305
Humboldt, Wilhelm von, 39, 40, 42, 46, 49, 65, 66, 69, 230, 245, 261, 270
Hume, David, 89, 91, 97, 100, 162, 243, 255
Hutton, James, 267

Ideology. *See* Historiography and ideology; Liberalism

Iggers, George, 295
Indiana University, 332
Ingarden, Roman, 332
Institut Impérial de France, 37
Institution. *See* Literary education; Literature
Interpretation, 19–20, 28, 57–79; allegorical method of, 58–59; in history, 164–165, 245, 261, 271, 305–307; philological method of, 58–59; symbolic, 245. *See also* Hermeneutic; Hieroglyphs and decipherment; Historical criticism; Historiography; Philology
Ivory, James, 30
Ivot, Paul d', 283, 388

Jacobins, 179, 182, 210, 212, 374, 388
Jakobson, Roman, 9–11, 12, 23, 128, 192, 199, 328, 332, 356
Jansenists, 57, 65, 213
Jena, University of, 240
Jenkyns, Richard, 68
Jesuits, 57, 65, 178, 179, 180, 208, 213
Joan of Arc, 161, 184, 196, 262
Johns Hopkins University, 2
Johnson, Samuel, 62, 63, 70, 340, 344
Joinville, Jean, sire de, 91
Joyce, James, 255, 379
Judaism, 209
July monarchy, 141, 180; July days and July Revolution, 171–177, 205, 217, 222, 273, 362, 392

Kaegi, Werner, 371
Kafka, Franz, 255
Kant, Immanuel, 206
Kazantzakis, Nikos, 58
Kelly, Donald, 265, 266
Kennedy, Paul, 220
Kernan, Alvin, 63, 340
Kernodle, George Riley, 12
Kierkegaard, Sören, 377
King's College, Cambridge, 41, 42, 49
King's College, London, 337
Kingsley, Charles, 42, 44
Kinkel, Gottfried, 268
Kippur, Stephen, 186
Kircher, Athanasius, 280
Klopstock, Friedrich Gottlieb, 206
Knapp, Steven, 60
Kosciuszko, Tadeusz, 206
Koselleck, Reinhardt, 385

Kracauer, Siegfried, 244, 379
Kramer, Hilton, 381
Krieger, Leonard, 382
Kuhn, Thomas S., 317, 318, 398

La Bruyère, Jean de, 15
La Calprenède, Gautier de Costes de, 32
La Fayette, Marie-Joseph, marquis de, 84
La Fontaine, Jean de, 78, 163
La Motte, Houdar de, 60
La Rochefoucauld, François, duc de, 20,
   163
Lafitte, Jacques, 84
Lakatos, Imre, 285, 317, 320, 321, 399
Lamartine, Alphonse de, 38, 166
Lamennais, Félicité Robert de, 368
Langue and *parole*, 9, 10
Lanzmann, Claude, 323, 400
Laplace, François de, 74
Laslett, Peter, 293
Lasteyrie, Charles Philibert, comte de, 84
Le Bossu, René, 233
Le Roy Ladurie, Emmanuel, 313
Leavis, Queenie, 40, 51
Leibniz, Gottfried Wilhelm von, 230
Lejeune, Philippe, 381
Lenoir, Alexandre, 383
Lesage, Alain René, 16
Lessing, Gotthold Ephraïm, 163, 238
Lessing, Theodor, 290
Lévi-Strauss, Claude, 227
Liberalism, 55, 324, 346, 353, 364. *See also*
   Historiography and liberalism
Literary criticism, 50, 51, 52–53, 61–79; in
   the Age of Enlightenment, 62–63; de-
   construction, 289; Frankfurt school, 2,
   49–50, 51, 53; French structuralism, 2;
   Geneva school, 2; Leavis school, 50–51,
   52; New Criticism, 1, 50, 51; phenomenological criticism, 2; positivist criticism, 9,
   50, 339; Romantic criticism, 64; reception aesthetics, 6; Russian formalism,
   294–295. *See also* Historical criticism in
   literature; Interpretation; Philology
Literary education, 26–29, **31–54**, 64–73,
   341; democratic, 29, 47; and German
   neohumanism, 40–41, 42, 65–68; institutional aspects of, 45–48, 70–71, 77; in
   the neoclassical age, 33–36; and Romanticism, 36–40, 48, 51, 52; and social division, 27–28, 38–43, 69, 71; in Victorian
   England, 41–43, 68–71

Literature: and history, 3–6, passim; as an
   institution, 288, 344; and language, 254–
   255; negativity of, 3–5, 76; and rhetoric,
   228, 229, 231; and social division, 24–26,
   38–43, 258; as a term, 31–33, 44–45, 166,
   228–229. *See also* Myth and literature; the
   Sacred
Livy, 162, 231, 264, 314
Locke, John, 158, 162
Lord, Albert, 11, 17
Lotman, Iurii, 14, 18, 19, 20, 328–329, 330,
   332
Louis Napoleon. *See* Napoleon III
Louis Philippe, 154, 157, 165, 173, 208, 359,
   383
Louis XIV, 66, 90, 111, 112, 114, 293, 352
Louise, Princess (granddaughter of Charles
   X of France), 157
Lucan, 234
Lucas, D. W., 232
Lucian, 228
Lukács, Georgy, 2, 55
L'Univers, 178
Luther, Martin, 6, 59, 163
Lyotard, François, 2

Mabillon, Jean, 32
Macaulay, Thomas Babington, 41, 231, 255,
   291, 347, 356, 358, 360
Madden, William A., 356
Malthus, Thomas Robert, 257, 291, 297,
   314, 398
Manchester, Victoria University of, 49
Manchester Working Men's College, 41
Mandrou, Robert, 382
Mann, Thomas, 308
Manzoni, Alessandro, 84, 255, 383
Marat, Jean-Paul, 373
Marcel, Etienne, 114, 129
Marivaux, Pierre Carlet de Chamblain de,
   35, 62
Marmontel, Jean-François, 163, 238, 360
Marrou, Henri I., 247
Martin, Henri, 153, 166, 282–283
Marx, Karl, 34, 83, 102, 104, 105, 150, 180,
   182, 189, 350
Mathiez, Albert, 189
Maurice, F. D., 41, 42, 44
Mayakovski, Vladimir, 19, 331
Mazarin, Jules, 90, 114
McIntosh, Angus, 333
Medici, Cosimo di, 358

Metaphor. *See* Historical narrative; Historiography

Mézeray, François Eudes de, 88, 92, 93, 237, 264

Mialaret, Athénaïs (second wife of Jules Michelet), 157, 160, 161, 195, 196, 198, 365, 366, 387

Michaels, Walter Benn, 60

Michelet, Jean-François Furcy (father of Jules Michelet), 155

Michelet, Jules, 3, 36, 38, 39, 40, 41, 42, 48, 84, 85, 87, 94, 102, 114, 121, 125, 127, 131, 143, **152–224**, 231, 253–254, 255, 257, 258, 259, 260, 261, 262, 263, 266, 268, 269, 271, 273, 274, 275, 276, 277, 280, 281–2, 283, 286, 297, 336, 348, 349, 351, 359, 360, 368, 382–387. *See also* Mialaret, Athénaïs; Millet, Angélique Constance; Rousseau, Pauline

Mickiewicz, Adam, 166, 169, 195

Mignet, Auguste, 83, 84, 85, 86, 112, 125, 126, 360

Mill, John Stuart, 136

Millar, John, 297

Miller, George, 332

Millet, Angélique Constance (mother of Jules Michelet), 155, 156

Milton, John, 40, 163

Minard, Charles Joseph, 291

Mink, Louis, 289, 295, 398, 400

Modern Language Association, 31, 52

Moland, Louis, 235

Molière, Jean-Baptiste Poquelin, 17, 32, 78, 163, 214

Mommsen, Theodor, 341

Mommsen, Wolfgang, 319, 321–2

Moniteur universel, 335

Monod, Gabriel, 48, 262, 314, 355, 361, 365

Monstrelet, Enguerrand de, 127, 261

Montaigne, Michel Eyquem de, 355

Montesquieu, Charles de Secondat, baron de La Brède et de, 162, 236, 257, 292, 304–305, 314, 352, 385

Montlosier, François Dominique de Reynard, 101, 102

Moore, Thomas, 133, 359

Moreau, Gustave, 275

Moretti, Franco, 223

Mother figure, 35–39, 156, 158–160, 167–168, 175, 177, 190, 216, 336

Mukařovský, Jan, 4, 5, 13, 14, 253, 329

Müller, Carl Otfried, 40, 134, 153

Munz, Peter, 293–4, 391

Myth, 250–253, 388; and history, 154, 207, 217, 250–251, 283, 381; and literature, 253, 381

Nadeau, Maurice, 344

Napoleon I, 37, 65, 66, 85, 90, 129, 272, 375

Napoleon III, 172, 194, 195, 388

Narrative, 233; classical, 193, 221, 242, 248, 251, 307. *See also* Historical narrative

Nation, 92, 93, 100–101, 115–116, 179, 221, 347; national history, 98–99, 153, 387

National, Le, 84

Natural history, 195–198

Neoclassicism. *See* Classicism and neoclassicism

Neohumanism, 164; relation to history, 67–68, 164, 279. *See also* Literary education and German neohumanism

Newton, Sir Isaac, 32, 257

Niebuhr, Carsten, 134, 153, 163, 261

Nietzsche, Friedrich, 5, 6, 48, 56, 61, 67, 68, 73–74, 209, 212, 213, 218, 289, 308

Nodier, Charles, 92, 93

Noël, François Joseph, 74

Novalis (Friedrich von Hardenberg), 62, 269, 272

Novel and history, 239–243, 260, 267, 294–295

Olsen, Stein, 344

d'Orneval, 16

Ortega y Gasset, José, 292

Overbeck, Franz, 55–56, 59, 60, 61, 62, 66, 68, 71, 74, 75, 77, 78, 209, 213, 308, 342, 343

Owens College, Manchester, 49

Oxford University, 31, 55, 285

Ozanam, Jacques, 32

Pädagogium (Basle), 71, 72

Paine, Tom, 206

Palmer, D. J., 44

Parent-Duchâtelet, Alexandre Jean Baptiste, 174, 216

Paret, Peter, 398

Paris, University of, 33

Parker, Harold, 295

Pascal, Blaise, 17, 18, 122, 163, 266

Patois. *See* Dialects

Pecqueur, Constantin, 174

Pennsylvania, University of, 217

People: Jules Michelet's view of, 139, 157–158, 186–191, 216–217, 219–220, 275–276, 373, 385; role in history, 90; Romantic view of, 258. *See also* Bourgeoisie and people

Perelman, Chaïm, 293, 399

Perrault, Charles, 16

Phillips, U. B., 312

Philology, 45, 66–67, 164, 265, 277–279. *See also* Interpretation

Pirenne, Henri, 244

Piscator, Erwin, 18

Plato, 20, 162

Playfair, William, 291, 314

Plekhanov, George Valentinovich, 350

Plutarch, 158, 228, 231, 264

Polybius, 228

Popper, Sir Karl, 317

Popular culture, 87, 190; books for the people, 166–168, 184, 187, 196; popular historiography, 87, 192–193, 398. *See also* Folklore and folklorists

Porter, Noah, 44

Poulet, Georges, 210, 213

Princeton University, 31, 44, 48, 49, 60, 334, 343. *See also* College of New Jersey

Professionalism (in historiography), 169, 314–324, 398. *See also* Culture, professionalization of

Proudhon, Pierre Joseph, 174, 181

Proust, Marcel, 292, 379

Proverbs, 21–22, 328

Public, 22–26; public sphere, 6, 62–64. *See also* Historiography and public opinion

Pushkin, Alexander Sergeyevich, 11

Querelle des Anciens et des Modernes, 15, 25, 57

Quinet, Edgar, 157, 166, 169, 170, 172, 175, 176, 178, 179, 183, 195, 198, 260, 262, 263, 271, 280, 283, 368, 388

Quintilian, 227

Quintus Curtius, 264

Rabelais, François, 39, 163

Racine, Jean, 20, 32, 36, 56, 57, 73, 163

Radin, Paul, 24

Raleigh, Walter, 49

Ranke, Leopold von, 45, 83, 153, 164, 230, 258, 261, 266, 297, 382, 393, 395

Rapin-Thoyras, Paul de, 97

Rawlinson, Henry, 301–302

Raynal, abbé Guillaume, 16

Raynaud, Jean, 174

Reader, the, 19–20, 23–24, 228, 250–251. *See also* Historical narrative

Realism (historical), 244, 245, 247–248, 260–261, 302, 380. *See also* Historiography, objectivity in

Reitz, Edgar, 323

Renaissance, 15, 24, 25, 26, 29, 59, 152, 157, 330; historiography in, 28, 265

Renan, Ernest, 183, 193, 194, 262, 283

Republic of Letters, 230

Restoration, 96, 169, 177, 257, 354

Revolution of 1848, 100, 113, 154, 191, 194–195, 222, 388, 391

Revue de Paris, 92

Revue Historique, 262, 314

Rhetoric, 227–228. *See also* Classicism and neoclassicism; Historiography and rhetoric; Literature and rhetoric

Richards, I. A., 26

Richelieu, Armand Jean du Plessis, cardinal de, 114, 286, 358

Riehl, Wilhelm, 68

Riffaterre, Michael, 329

Robertson, William, 99, 162, 383

Robespierre, Maximilien Marie Isidore de, 129, 179, 201, 202, 372, 373, 375

Rollin, Charles, 33, 34, 35, 36, 335

Romanticism, 9, 10, passim

Ronsard, Pierre de, 39, 285

Rousseau, Jean-Jacques, 16, 103, 155, 162, 163, 172, 185, 263, 267, 269, 304, 329, 373

Rousseau, Pauline (first wife of Jules Michelet), 158, 159, 160, 175

Royer-Collard, Pierre Paul, 84, 86, 118, 354

Rubens, Peter Paul, 276

Rudolph, Frederick, 334

Rudwick, Martin, 315, 396

Rüsen, Jörn, 289, 292

Ruskin, John, 70

Sacred, the, 204, 229, 305

Sade, Donatien Alphonse François, marquis de, 216

Saint-Just, Louis Antoine de, 202

Saint-Simon, Claude Henri de Rouvroy, comte de, 84, 86, 92, 93, 102, 106, 107, 115, 163, 182

Sainte-Beuve, Charles Augustin, 134, 136, 294, 360, 363, 391–392

Sallust, 231, 264

Sand, George, 85, 166, 178, 182

Sartre, Jean-Paul, 2, 4, 6, 20, 24, 27, 55, 228
Saussure, Ferdinand de, 9, 10
Savigny, Friedrich Karl von, 230, 258
Say, Jean-Baptiste, 84, 100, 102
Schelling, Friedrich Wilhelm Joseph von, 62, 153, 165
Schenkendorf, Max von, 37
Schiller, Friedrich von, 1, 2, 16, 18, 20, 40, 41, 42, 63, 64, 68, 69, 70, 117, 162, 197, 240–241, 329, 342, 377, 379
Schlegel, August Wilhelm von, 62, 384
Schlegel, Friedrich von, 163, 165
Schleiermacher, Friedrich, 64, 153, 230
Schmitt, Carl, 223, 364
Schopenhauer, Arthur, 30
Schorske, Carl, 308–309
Scorsese, Martin, 58, 60
Scott, Sir Walter, 91, 95, 99, 100, 163, 255, 328, 359, 383
Scudéry, Georges de, 32
Self and other, 147–149, 184–185, 192, 197, 200, 270–284
Seznec, Jean, 285
Shaftesbury, Anthony Ashley Cooper, 1st earl, 16, 162
Shakespeare, William, 22, 23, 163
Sharp, Cecil, 328
Shelley, Percy Bysshe, 41
Sidney, Algernon, 90
Siéyès, Emmanuel Joseph, abbé, 100
Signification, 250–253. *See also* Historiography
Simmel, Georg, 376
Simon, Claude, 379
Sismondi, Jean Charles Léonard Simonde de, 103, 112, 163, 166, 174, 351, 355, 361
Smith, Adam, 314
Smith, Barbara H., 12
Smith, Goldwin, 393
Smithson, Rulon, 348, 360
Snyders, George, 64
Socialism, 174, 181, 182, 283; Christian socialists, 181–182, 185, 208
Sollers, Philippe, 254
Somerville, Alexander, 38
Sommerard, Alexandre du, 383
Sontag, Susan, 75
Sorbonne, 158, 268
Sorel, Albert, 237, 264
Spencer, Herbert, 334
Staël, Madame de, 147, 263, 338
Stampp, Kenneth M., 313

Stankiewicz, Edward, 332
State, 116, 141, 145; *mère-patrie,* 189–190, 194, 199
Strauss, David, 56, 280
Stubbs, William, 31
Sue, Eugène, 247
Süssmilch, Johann Peter, 297
Süvern, Johann, 65, 66
Sybel, Heinrich Karl Ludolf von, 83, 164
Synecdoche, 123, 356

Tacitus, 162, 228, 243, 247, 314
Taine, Hyppolite, 262
Tasso, Torquato, 163, 234
Temin, Peter, 310
Thibaudet, Albert, 233
Thierry, Amédée, 84, 104, 153, 154, 166, 349
Thierry, Augustin, 36, **83–151**, 153, 154, 163, 166, 169, 172, 241, 242, 255, 276, 286, 345, 347, 368, 383
Thiers, Louis Adolphe, 84, 86, 166
Thomas à Kempis, 178, 202
Thompson, Denys, 51
Thucydides, 162, 264
Tiers état, 100, 104–108, 113, 150
Time and history, 134, 146, 206, 254–255, 267. *See also* Historical narrative
Tocqueville, Charles Alexis Clérel de, 174, 205, 207–208, 221, 262, 293, 384
Toulmin, Stephen, 318–319, 398, 399
Toussenel, Alphonse, 283, 383, 388
Translation, 59–60, 70, 263, 273, 274, 338, 357, 385
Trilling, Lionel, 51
Trivulzio, Cristina, Princess Belgiojoso, 85
Turner, F. M., 69

Unamuno, Miguel de, 247
Unger, Rudolf, 228
University College, London, 42, 337

Valéry, Paul, 23, 288, 389
Velly, abbé Paul François, 88, 93, 237, 264
Vergniaud, Pierre Victurnien, 196
Veuillot, Louis, 178
Vico, Giambattista, 96, 162, 163, 170, 171, 172, 177, 202, 217
Villehardouin, Geoffroi de, 91
Villemain, Abel, 89, 335, 345, 349, 367, 387
Villeneuve-Bargemont, Jean-Paul Alban, vicomte de, 174

Villermé, Louis René, 174, 216
Vinet, Alexandre, 71–73
Vinokurova (Russian *bylini* singer), 331
Violence in history, 132–147, 184–185, 186
Virgil, 36, 162, 184, 233
Volland, Sophie, 16
Voltaire, François Marie Arouet de, 3, 32, 63, 89, 93, 98, 163, 185, 231, 233–236, 237, 238, 242, 243, 255, 267, 269, 286, 291, 292, 304, 340, 351, 352, 357, 360, 373
Vossius, Gerardus Johannis, 280

Wackernagel, Philipp, 45
Walpole, Horace, 3
Wartburg, W. von, 358
Weber, Max, 52, 55, 201, 223–224, 323
Weibel, Luc, 390, 396
Weiss, Peter, 360
Welcker, Friedrich, 270
Wellek, René, 329

White, Hayden, 247, 287, 289, 294, 295, 298, 301, 306–307, 319–320, 321, 389, 390, 392–393, 396, 400
White, Morton, 289
Whitman, Walt, 9
William and Mary, College of, 33
Williams, Raymond, 2, 26, 28, 55
Wilson, Alexander, 197, 273
Wilson, Woodrow, 48–49
Wimsatt, W. K., 329
Winckelmann, Johann Joachim, 6, 65, 66, 263, 269–270, 271, 272, 279
Woodman, Harold, 397
Woolf, Virginia, 379
Wordsworth, William, 19, 38, 328
Wyatt, Sir Thomas, 12

Yale University, 33, 320

Zoega, Georg, 270, 271, 272, 280